1940 - 1941

BOOKS BY RICHARD COLLIER

FICTION

Beautiful Friend
Pay-off in Calcutta
The Lovely and the Damned

NON-FICTION

Captain of the Queens
(*with* CAPT. HARRY GRATTIDGE)
Ten Thousand Eyes
The City That Wouldn't Die
The Sands of Dunkirk
The Sound of Fury
The General Next to God
Eagle Day
The River that God Forgot
Duce!
The Plague of the Spanish Lady
The War in the Desert
(TIME-LIFE WORLD WAR II SERIES)
Bridge Across the Sky
1940: The World in Flames
1941: Armageddon
The Years of Victory: 1944 – 1945
(FORMERLY PUBLISHED AS *The War That Stalin Won*)

AUTOBIOGRAPHY

A House Called Memory

THE YEARS OF
ATTRITION
1940 – 1941

RICHARD COLLIER

a&b

This omnibus edition first published
in Great Britain in 1995 by
Allison & Busby
an imprint of Wilson & Day Ltd
179 King's Cross Road
London WC1X 9BZ

Both books first published in Great Britain
separately in hardback by
Hamish Hamilton Ltd in 1979 as
1940: The World in Flames
and in 1981 as *1941: Armageddon*

A catalogue record for this book is available from the British Library

ISBN 0 74900 236 0

Printed and bound in Great Britain by
Redwood Books, Trowbridge, Wiltshire

THE AUTHOR

Richard Collier is a highly acclaimed writer and journalist. His works on the second world war combine an historian's accuracy with a war correspondent's flair for telling a good story. Collier is the author of several works of fiction and non-fiction culled from his varied experiences world-wide.

FOR PAT
my wife
with love

Alas, yes! a whole world to remake . . . For all is wrong, and gone out of joint; the inward spiritual and the outward economical; head or heart, there is no soundness in it. As indeed, evils of all sorts are more or less of kin and do usually go together: especially it is an old truth that wherever huge physical evil is there, as the parent and origin of it, has moral evil to a proportionate extent been.

THOMAS CARLYLE, *The French Revolution*

1940

THE WORLD IN FLAMES

CONTENTS

ILLUSTRATIONS

Between pages 118 *and* 119

11 (a) The killing of a German Messerschmitt 110
   (b) R.A.F. pilots 'scramble' into action

12 (a) L.D.V. (Local Defence Volunteers), later the Home Guard, enrolled at Westminster. Dr Jocelin Perkins, Sacrist to the Abbey, being taught rifle drill
   (b) Assistant Divisional Officer Geoffrey Blackstone, London Fire Brigade

13   London burning

14 (a) The King and Queen visiting bombed South London
   (b) The morning after, near Marble Arch

15 (a) Magda Lupescu
   (b) Hitler meets Franco at Hendaye
   (c) King Christian of Denmark, despite the occupation, he rides out among his people

16   Coventry Cathedral

Sources of Illustrations
1 (a) Radio Times Hulton Picture Library   (b) Keystone
2 (a) Paul Popper   (b) Keystone
3 (a) Paul Popper   (b) Keystone
4 (a) Erik Seidenfaden   (b) Keystone
5 (a) Mrs Drysdale   (b) Theodor Broch   (c) Keystone
6 Central Press
7 Keystone
8 (a) Camera Press   (b) Radio Times Hulton
9 (a) Radio Times Hulton   (b) Central Press
10 (a) and (b) Imperial War Museum
11 (a) Imperial War Museum   (b) Press Association
12 (a) Radio Times Hulton   (b) London Fire Brigade
13 Mirrorpic
14 (a) Radio Times Hulton   (b) Central Press
15 (a) Mirrorpic   (b) and (c) Keystone
16 Keystone

1

'A Shabby And Dangerous Place...'

1 January–16 February, 1940

THE OVAL OFFICE of the White House was silent. The President was writing intently; only the scratch of his pen broke the stillness. Smoke from a forgotten cigarette spiralled upwards in the desk light; the flags hung limp on the mahogany standards. In a bold vertical hand, the President was drafting his eighth State of the Union message. 'It becomes clearer and clearer,' he wrote, 'that the future world will be a shabby and dangerous place to live in – yes, even for Americans to live in – if it is ruled by force in the hands of a few . . .'

Thus, on 1 January, 1940, in Washington, D.C., the thirty-second President of the United States, Franklin Delano Roosevelt, prepared himself for the arduous months stretching ahead: the burden of operating a vast peaceable democracy in a war-gripped world, the problem of holding together his 'New Deal', the now-sagging social welfare programme which he had inaugurated back in 1933, the vexed question of whether he should become the first President in American history to seek election for a Third Term.

They were challenges which Roosevelt would face as squarely as he had faced the polio attack which for the past nineteen years had confined him to a wheelchair. Already, on 23 December, 1939, with World War II 120 days old and Germany's twenty-six day conquest of Poland an established fact, the President had written to Pope Pius XII in Rome to explore the prospects for world peace. Prompted by the Book of Isaiah, he had spoken of a time like the present, when 'nations walked dangerously in the light of the fires they had themselves kindled'.

For the first time since 1868, a personal presidential representative had been appointed to the Vatican: Myron Charles Taylor, 65-year-old retired head of the United States Steel Corporation. Along with him as Roosevelt's envoy extraordinary, would journey U.S. Under Secretary of State Sumner Welles, on a fact-finding mission to sound out the statesmen of Europe. 'If Welles' visit delays an offensive by the Germans or even prevents it,' Roosevelt summed up to the State Department's Breckinridge Long, 'that will help Britain and France buy time.'

Time was now of the essence. On 3 January, Roosevelt was to warn a joint

1

session of Congress of 'the vicious, ruthless, destructive' forces that were abroad in the world – and demand of them a mountainous $2,309,445,246 to maintain the greatest peacetime military force America had ever known. Not for the first time he made his stance crystal-clear: 'There is a vast difference between keeping out of war and pretending war is none of our business.'

It was an issue on which Roosevelt and countless million American isolationists were deeply at odds. Many shared the view of their idol, the aviator Colonel Charles A. Lindbergh: 'The wars in Europe are not wars in which our civilisation is defending itself against some Asiatic intruder. There is no Genghis Khan or Xerxes marching against our Western nations.' Few of them had ever forgiven Britain and France, their one-time allies, for reneging on their debts after World War I, while even committed New Dealers feared that any preparations for war would forfeit the social gains made by labour since Roosevelt took office. Others were deeply disillusioned with all things European. All through the 1930s Britain and France had shown little more than a rare talent for appeasement, standing tamely on the sidelines while Germany swallowed up Austria and Czechoslovakia and Italy ravaged first Ethiopia then Albania. How staunch would such faint-hearts prove as allies when the chips were down?

'U.S. citizens', noted the financier Bernard Baruch in his diary, 'seem to have washed their hands of all concern in Europe', a phenomenon confirmed by the British Ambassador in Washington, Lord Lothian. 'Their moral preparedness is about that of England in the Baldwin* period,' he wrote to the Minister for the Co-ordination of Defence, Lord Chatfield. Responded Chatfield cynically: 'They will . . . fight the battle for freedom and democracy to the last Briton . . . Can we blame them?'

But for millions of Americans, fighting was the last thing they had in mind. Eight hundred miles south of Washington, Miami Beach, Florida, was in hothouse bloom, the giddiest, gaudiest season since the Wall Street crash of 1929. Lots on Lincoln Road, the plush shopping street, were fetching $50,000 apiece; the yachts and cruisers in harbour included the *Virago*, lately chartered by the millionaire J. P. Morgan. The actress Nancy Carroll was in town, along with fashionable hatter Lilly Daché and the couturier Hattie Carnegie. Columnists noted that a new arrival was Alfred Ilko Barton, a Philadelphia socialite who taught the new-rich how to be lavish with their money.

For the moment at least, Franklin Roosevelt, bound and gagged by laggard public opinion, must bide his time. Still unresolved was the question: if the 'vicious, ruthless destructive forces' were to triumph, what would the United States be called upon to do?

* Stanley Baldwin (1st Earl Baldwin of Bewdley, 1867–1947), three times British Premier between 1923 and 1937, had been an arch-exponent of appeasement.

More than 3,000 miles closer to the war front, the same indifference to war prevailed. 'The French nation', one Frenchman wrote, 'has gone to war looking over its shoulder, its eyes searching for peace.' Opinion polls placed the Premier, Edouard Daladier, as more popular than either Joan of Arc or Napoleon: despite shortages, he still made gasoline available for spins in the Bois de Boulogne or to the racecourse at Longchamps. The phrase of the day was *Il faut en finir* (We've got to stop it), a resolute motto, embroidered on chiffon handkerchiefs or inscribed on gold charm bracelets, but the reality was a staggering unconcern. In this *drôle de guerre*, bored boulevardiers checked their watches by the air-raid sirens, tested punctually each Thursday at noon, and the most chic gift of the day reduced all war to mockery: terracotta dogs lifting their legs over terracotta copies of *Mein Kampf.*

In Berlin, the author of *Mein Kampf*, Adolf Hitler, Führer and Chancellor of the Third Reich, seemed the one man still determined to prosecute the war to the utmost. If Germany secured Holland and Belgium, he maintained, their airfields could be used to deal Great Britain a lethal blow – a projected offensive against the west which his generals had opposed strenuously and in vain for three months now. But although the coldest European winter in forty-six years had mired down both tanks and aircraft, Hitler would not be deflected. After 9 October, when the British had rejected his first peace offer, he declared angrily, 'They will be ready to talk only after a beating.'

Few Germans shared his enthusiasm. After twenty years in the economic wringer, including seven of building the world's most streamlined military machine, few civilians had reaped much personal benefit. The seventy million Germans outside the armed forces saw meat and butter no more than twice a week. Because of fuel shortages, they enjoyed hot water only at week-ends, and subsisted on a poorhouse diet of stuffed cabbage or boiled potatoes with onion sauce. Even diners-out were beset by loudspeakers barking '*Achtung!* This is the kitchen speaking. There is no more veal.'

Reflecting this disillusion, New Year's Day, 1940, had seen more drunks on Berlin's fashionable Kurfürstendamm than at any time in living memory. Even Dr Josef Göbbels, Hitler's club-footed Minister for Propaganda and Enlightenment, confided in an American newsman: 'The average German feels [about the war] like a man with chronic toothache – the sooner it is out the better.'

In blacked-out England, where the cost of the conflict was running at $24 million a day, the American naval attaché in London noted the same 'undercurrent of distaste and apathy for the whole war'. Three million Londoners, among them 1,500,000 evacuee children and their mothers, had left the capital, but though the British would be rationed, from 8 January, to four ounces of bacon weekly, four of butter and twelve of sugar, they still chose to make light of it. Things, they joked, were 'so quiet you could hear a Ribbentrop'.* Forty-three theatres were open and doing land-office business, among them The Globe with the young John Gielgud in *The Importance of Being Earnest*, for above all Londoners sought to banish the war with a laugh. The lament of a Cockney evacuee in the revue *Lights Up!* caught the mood of the day:

I didn't really never ought 'ave went;
In London I was really quite content.
I wouldn't have been windy with the planes up overhead,
Talk of blinkin' aeroplanes, you should have heard what Father said
They couldn't hit the Forth Bridge, let alone small boys in bed.
No, I didn't really never ought 'ave went.

Most Britons were hoping, like their Tory Premier, Neville Chamberlain, not for a military victory but for 'a collapse of the German home front', though a surprising number went further than that. On 8 January, a memorandum to Chamberlain, drawn up by ten members of the House of Lords urged the Premier: 'It is now widely felt that, on a long view, the weakening or dismemberment of Germany would destroy the natural barrier against the Western march of Bolshevism. We would suggest to you that this is a strong reason in favour of an early peace.' The same feeling was rife in less august circles: Ministry of Information poll-takers estimated that four million Britons would settle for peace at any price.

Did Chamberlain and the First Lord of the Admiralty, Winston Churchill, really own shares in the German armaments firm of Krupp, as the American columnist Drew Pearson alleged? Few Britons showed concern either way.

To be sure, the British had taken precautions – 'just in case'. The National Gallery's director, Kenneth (later Lord) Clark, had seen almost 3,000 pictures off to Penrhyn Castle, near Bangor, North Wales. (Later for greater safety they were transferred to a disused slate quarry at Manod, thirty-five miles north.) Most of the British Museum's treasures were also in Wales, in an underground air-conditioned tunnel in Aberystwyth. At London's Regent's Park Zoo, all poisonous snakes had been humanely killed off, to prevent them getting loose in air raids – but would air raids ever come to pass?

Above all, the British felt an acute sense of anti-climax. For four long months they had been geared for Armageddon. Now, in a winter that had brought twenty-five degrees of frost, they faced only burst water pipes, a chronic coal shortage and a black-out that had plunged the United Kingdom into the pitch darkness of the seventeenth century. As January dawned, the black-out, with its thirty-three deaths a day, was taking more toll than the war, and Britons wanted it to stay that way.

*Joachim von Ribbentrop, Germany's Foreign Minister, and Ambassador to Britain from 1936–38 had aroused ridicule for greeting King George VI with the Nazi salute.

4

The Secretary of State for Air, Sir Kingsley Wood, mirrored perfectly the mood of a war in which as yet neither ally was minded to strike a mortal blow. Urged to bomb the Black Forest and ravage Germany's timber supplies, the little man replied, outraged: 'Are you aware it is private property? Why, you will be asking me to bomb Essen next!'

*

On 24 August, 1939, one week before the German panzer divisions lanced into Poland, the 90/20 Horse Company of the 2nd French North African Division took up stations in a suburb of Toul on the Moselle River, 300 miles from Paris. On that day, the unit's Captain Denis Barlone summed up in his diary what most men felt: 'We know that our land is safe from invasion, thanks to the Maginot Line; none of us has the least desire to fight for Czechoslovakia or Poland, of which ninety-five Frenchmen out of every hundred are completely ignorant.'

From French general to private, this belief in the Maginot Line's impregnability was central to Army thinking. Most men were mesmerised by the sheer statistics of a project that in the twelve years of its construction had come to rival the Great Wall of China. Running 400 miles from the Alps to the Belgian frontier at Sedan, the Line, named after its creator, former War Minister André Maginot, was a veritable honeycomb of fortresses and casemates, 'like row upon row of sunken earthbound battleships', some of them housing formidable 75-mm guns. Of the 1,800,000 *poilus*, who manned its ramparts, at least 200,000 were men living underground in perpetual artificial light.

The Line was the solid embodiment of the play-for-safety strategy of the ageing Commander-in-Chief, General Maurice Gustave Gamelin: 'Whoever is the first to leave his shell in this war is going to get badly hurt.' A future Minister of Propaganda, Louis Frossard, put it in terms that thrifty Frenchmen could understand: 'The gold stays in the bank—each Army in its fortress of ferro-concrete.'

Few of France's 6,500,000 *poilus* realised it, but this was a terrifying fallacy. Both to the north and to the south, France lay naked to her enemies. As far back as 1935, the then Minister for War, 78-year-old Marshal Henri-Philippe Pétain had stubbornly resisted extending the southern end of the Maginot Line. The wooded heights of the Ardennes Forest, Pétain maintained, which girdled either side of the Meuse River, were 'equal to the best fortifications'. Moreover, no man had ever propounded extending the Line northwards, to the sea. To do so would have meant transforming a rich area of mines and furnaces, yielding two-thirds of France's coal, into a potential battlefield.

In truth, the Line was a costly symbol of the arrogance, stupidity and

5

inept leadership which had characterised the Third French Republic for almost seventy years – a Republic which both Right and Left, for diverse reasons, had long yearned to dissolve. As recently as 1934, Communists, Royalists (intent on restoring a monarchy) and Fascists had made common cause in storming the Chamber of Deputies, intent on bringing down the government. For all factions, self-interest, not patriotism, had been the guiding star; despite the need for sizeable new credits to strengthen the armed forces, French financiers had invested 40 per cent of the country's capital in profitable loans abroad. An unbridgeable gulf yawned between businessmen, often dependent on state concessions and corrupt politicians to feather their nests, and a workforce, stubbornly opposed to democracy, which saw the general strike as its ultimate weapon. Since 1875, such bitterly irreconcilable differences had seen the overthrow of 107 Cabinets.

The keynote of Republican feeling had all along been hatred of Germany. The bitterness engendered by the Franco–Prussian war of 1870, when France had been crushed in forty-two days, had, by 1918, hardened into an implacable resolve that 'the Boche will pay'; the harsh provisions of the Treaty of Versailles had been dominated by the memory that Paris, four times within a century, had been within range of German guns. Intent on securing a Germany permanently disarmed and paying war reparations to the hilt, the French had, in fact, achieved neither aim and had sown the seeds of World War II.

Given such dissent, all classes of society prized security above all. The bourgeoisie, six million strong, resisted social change as steadfastly as they resisted taxes; in 1937 they had rejoiced wholeheartedly when Léon Blum's Popular Front government, in an attempt to provide a Roosevelt-style New Deal for millions below the poverty line – including a 40-hour week and paid holidays – had fallen after a year in office. The spectre of Bolshevism, they felt, was now receding. The Army General Staff feared change equally. Composed of what one editor termed 'an odd assortment of Methusalehs', they clung to the time-worn methods of the past; even in 1937 they had urged the purchase of 50,000 saddle horses rather than invest their armament credits in tanks. Thus, by 1940, the Army – and all France – had come full circle; the Maginot Line was, in effect, the fortress cities of 1870 adapted to the twentieth century.

A few more prescient Frenchmen had doubts. At Bachy, in Lorraine, the headquarters of the 3rd British Infantry Brigade, only eight miles from the Line, Lieutenant René de Chambrun was wondering. Though currently serving as a liaison officer with the British, de Chambrun, a 34-year-old Parisian lawyer, had spent three months in the Maginot Line, time enough to qualify as what his fellow-officers termed a *gars-du béton* (concrete guy). Enduring the clammy twilight, the aching claustrophobia, the eternal throbbing of the Diesels pumping in air and light, de Chambrun had felt from the

6

first that this was a strange way to fight a war. And he alone had an advantage over his fellows: as a great-great-grandson of the Marquis de Lafayette, the French soldier and statesman who had embraced the cause of the colonists in the War of Independence, de Chambrun was an honorary American citizen and thus a veteran of Pullman upper berths. It had fallen to him to instruct his men how to pull their trousers off without getting out of their hammocks.

There had been other disquieting factors. Prominent among the orders issued to Maginot personnel was one with a disconcerting ring of peacetime: 'Officers must adhere approximately to the 40-hour week and must not order work at night, or on Saturdays and on Sundays.' At a later stage, de Chambrun had taken the C-in-C of the British Expeditionary Force, General Viscount Gort, on a tour of the line, and Gort had been staggered. How much, he asked, had all this cost? The answer was an unheard of £58 million —which perhaps explained why French assembly lines had turned out 30,000 tourist cars since war began but not one tank.

Now, at Bachy, de Chambrun was pondering a New Year letter from an old friend in New York. It echoed a phrase coined by the isolationist Senator William Borah, of Idaho: 'Dear René, It looks like a phoney war to a lot of us over here.' Momentarily, de Chambrun wondered again, then shrugged his doubts aside. How, after all, could a certified civilian like himself presume to doubt the wisdom of veterans like Gamelin and Pétain?

But de Chambrun could hardly deny that the morale of many *poilus* was at rock-bottom. To them this was a futile and unsought war, and it was plain even to the rawest recruit that their equipment was pitiable. One reserve artillery regiment had only tractors unrepaired for twenty years to tow its guns into battle. The 21st Foreign Volunteers were outfitted both with 1891 rifles and iron rations date-stamped 1920. At Metz, a quarter of the 42nd Active Division's infantrymen, whose socks had rotted away, were reported to be marching barefoot.

The backlash, all too often, was sullen apathy—and blatant disobedience. At Merlebach in the Maginot Line, the dismayed Lieutenant Phillipe de Bosmelet found that no man in his unit would advance into a wood unless an officer went fifty yards ahead to prove that there was no danger. Drunkenness was so rife that large railway terminals now set up drying-out rooms— *salles de déséthylisation*—to sober up stupefied *poilus*.

These unpalatable truths had long been known to Daladier, though Neville Chamberlain remained blissfully unaware of them. The sole British war correspondent to report them to the Foreign Office, Kenneth de Courcy, got short shrift. The Ministry of Information's Ivone Kirkpatrick, had dismissed his warnings summarily: 'Mr de Courcy is a calamitous man.'

Lack of morale was nowhere apparent among the 390,000 men of Lord Gort's British Expeditionary Force, who following the tradition of World

War I, were again subordinate to the French High Command. In this long lull of the 'phoney war', most of them were having the time of their lives. By night, merry on ten francs' worth of white wine, they sang the songs their fathers had sung: *Pack Up Your Troubles In Your Old Kitbag, It's A Long Way to Tipperary*, and a new one which had pride of place, *We're Gonna Hang Out The Washing On The Siegfried Line*. By day they proposed to fight 'Jerry', if he came, in the same way that their fathers had fought him: from trenches dug on the World War I order, six foot deep and four foot six inches wide.

In Tourcoing, Northern France, the lot of Private Bill Hersey of the 1st Battalion East Surreys somehow embodied the British Tommies' cloud-cuckoo land. Within weeks he was to be the only private granted a permanent sleeping-out pass. Hersey, a handsome devil-may-care regular who had soldiered all over India and spent many a night in the guardhouse, had always secretly yearned for a wife and home. Now he was about to get married.

The wildly improbable romance had started when Bill entered the Café l'Épi d'Or one quiet day during the 'phoney war'. He had burned his hand on a camp petrol stove, and when Papa Six, the proprietor, saw the wound he insisted that his daughter attend to it. Was not Augusta learning first aid and in need of practice?

Augusta's methods had seemed a shade primitive, for the alcohol she splashed on the burn sent Hersey leaping for the ceiling. Yet somehow, after that first meeting, Bill found his wound needed dressing at least once a day. There was no better excuse for holding hands.

Augusta spoke no word of English, but Bill launched into a whirlwind courtship with the aid of a pocket dictionary. Soon he and Augusta were deeply in love. One night Bill went to Augusta's father, pointed to the word *mariage* in the dictionary and said simply, 'Your daughter.' Papa exploded. 'He is no good that fellow,' he roared at Augusta. 'He spends too much on cognac!' 'He'll change,' Augusta said confidently. The local clergy, too, had disapproved, but at length the Roman Catholic padre from Bill's brigade had successfully interceded for the young lovers.

The wedding date was now set for 17 April. Neither Bill nor Augusta had any premonition.

*

At 10 am on 10 January, one German officer unwittingly won the Allies a four-month reprieve from Hitler's long-delayed onslaught on the west.

At this hour, Major Helmut Reinberger of the Luftwaffe was crossing the tarmac at Loddenheide airfield, near Münster, Westphalia, along with the airfield's commander, his old friend Major Erich Hönmanns. The two men were bound for Cologne in Hönmanns' new plane, a Messerschmitt 108, on what for Reinberger was a strictly illicit flight.

8

The orders of the Luftwaffe's C.-in-C., *Feldmarschall* Hermann Göring expressly forbade couriers like Reinberger to carry secret papers by air. The prospect of bad rail connections and the promise of a quick flight had persuaded Reinberger to ignore this injunction.

It was a rash impulse. Inside the yellow pigskin briefcase that rested on Reinberger's knees were the top-secret plans of a daring German offensive against Holland and Belgium. The strike, a paratroop drop by men of General Kurt Student's 7th Air Division, to which Reinberger was attached as commandant of the Paratroop School at Stendal, was timed for one week hence: 17 January.

Minutes after Hönmanns' ME 108 was airborne from Loddenheide, Reinberger was already regretting his decision. Abruptly the plane had flown into a bank of fog – 'flying blind as though in a Turkish bath'. Soon Hönmanns, too, became anxious; it was his first-ever flight in a ME 108 and he was uncertain of the controls. In an effort to navigate by the landmark of the Rhine River he took the plane down to 600 feet. Peering through the murk he at length spotted a river, but now his uncertainty increased. 'This is not the Rhine,' he told Reinberger, perplexed. 'It isn't wide enough.'

Now flying in an ever-widening circle, next fumbling with the instrument panel, Hönmanns somehow contrived to cut off his fuel. The engine coughed and spluttered, then abruptly gave out. The ME was going down fast now, racing virtually out of control towards the frozen ground. Next instant, in a terrifying swoop between two trees, both wings were torn bodily from the plane; the fuselage pitched clear to land in a high hedge. As the two men clambered shakily out, Reinberger's first thought was for his still-intact briefcase. 'If it ever comes out that I flew with what's in there, I shall be court-martialled,' he told Hönmanns.

As both men debated, an old peasant came lumbering up to them. Yet strangely he spoke no word of German, and Hönmanns knew a growing disquiet. 'Where are we?' he asked tentatively in French. 'The Maas,' the old man replied. 'My God,' said Reinberger, appalled. 'We've crashed in Holland or Belgium.'

Intent on destroying those incriminating documents, he began groping frantically for matches, but like Hönmanns, he was a non-smoker. It took time to convey their need to the old man, who grudgingly parted with a box. Snatching them, Reinberger quickly ducked behind a hedge, but not quickly enough.

At 11.30 am the sound of the crash had alerted the Belgian guards at the Mechelen-sur-Meuse control point, and soldiers hastening towards the wreckage took in the scene at a glance. An officer in a long coat – Hönmanns – raised his hands at the first sight of their rifles. Behind the hedge Reinberger now had the first batch of papers well alight. The soldiers resourcefully stamped them out, disarmed both men, then brought them before the control-point chief, Captain Rodrique.

Sensing that an interrogation would prove fatal, Hönmanns tried to stage a diversion. He asked to visit the lavatory. As Rodrique stepped back to let him pass, Reinberger, huddled silently in a corner of the guard-house, sprang forward. Seizing the papers he tried to bundle them into the guard-room stove, but Rodrique was quicker. Burning his hand badly, he tore the papers from the stove and once more stamped out the flames.

Now Reinberger vainly tried to snatch the Belgian's pistol from its holster, but Rodrique manhandled him roughly into a chair. 'Sit there and don't move again,' he ordered furiously. Reinberger buried his face in his hands. 'I wanted your pistol to use on myself, not you,' he explained wretchedly. 'There will be no pardon for me.'

By 7 pm the papers had been passed to the Belgian General Staff in Brussels but now a doubt arose. Were they genuine – or were they an elaborate ruse? Despite Reinberger's haste, the fragments from three documents, approximating ten pages of typescript, remained intact. These detailed Dutch and Belgian targets assigned to the Stuka divebombers of General the Baron von Richtofen's 8th Flying Corps, operating along the line of the Maas in conjunction with the German VIth Army. One document, signed by General Student, detailed five dropping areas for the paratroops of the 7th Division.

Despite Belgium's neutrality, King Leopold II, using the French military attaché as intermediary, did pass on this information to the Allies. But as Allied C.-in-C., Gamelin, timid and indecisive as always, shrank from any resolute action. Praying that this was a German trick, he at length persuaded himself that it was no more than that. Apart from placing the French First Army in a state of immediate preparedness, he did nothing.

'The Führer rebuked me frightfully as the C.-in-C. of the unfortunate courier,' Göring lamented to his intimates. 'What a ghastly burden on my nerves.' Later he relaxed, when word arrived from General Wenninger, the German air attaché in Brussels, that he had secured an *in camera* interview with the officers, who claimed to have burned the documents. But Göring was still not certain. At his wife's suggestion he first consulted a clairvoyant, who confirmed Wenninger's story, then, with inconclusive results, tried to burn a similar bundle in his own fireplace.

In any event, as the Luftwaffe's Inspector-General, General Erhard Milch, noted in his diary the 'big event had been postponed for some days because of the weather (thaw)'. Three days later Hitler went further still: the offensive was deferred until the spring. Europe relapsed into its twilight sleep, poised on the threshold between life and death.

*

Despite the threat that hung like a thunderhead over Europe, many nations stayed obstinately neutral. To all intents and purposes, they made common cause with America's isolationists: the Allies' quarrel with Hitler's Third Reich was no concern of theirs.

Some had little to fear. In Spain, the *Caudillo*, General Francisco Franco pronounced a policy of *hábil prudencia* (skilful prudence) and with good reason: after thirty-two months of civil war between Franco's Nationalists and Communist-supported Loyalists, Madrid's ruined suburbs were a silent testimony to the suffering the country had endured. Switzerland held two trump cards: the mighty Simplon and Gothard railroad tunnels, vital links for a Germany dependent not only on transit traffic through Switzerland but on Swiss engineering skills. To some citizens, the whole vexed question of neutrality was a puzzle in itself. In Ireland, when the ailing leader, Eamon de Valera, forbade the use of Irish territorial waters and Irish air-space to any belligerent nation, one man's reaction was truly Irish: 'Who are we neutral against?'

Some nations, to keep the peace they had come to hold so dear, performed near-acrobatic feats of neutrality – particularly the five Balkan nations of Hungary, Yugoslavia, Bulgaria, Roumania and Greece. Most strove for 'faithful collaboration' with Germany and 'greater friendship' with Italy, at the same time keeping the wires open to Paris and London.

Others were patently at risk, but still stayed aloof, disillusioned all through the 1930s by the League of Nations' failure to impose curbs both on Hitler and Benito Mussolini. Despite his timely warning to the Allies, Belgium's King Leopold had imposed a neutrality so strict that Britain had no knowledge whatsoever of Belgium's military dispositions or road system, indispensable in event of war. To all British queries as to their intentions if Holland was invaded, the Belgians maintained a stubborn silence.

In Denmark, the 11-year-old Socialist Government had virtually reduced the Army to sentry duty. 'A Nordic defence alliance,' scoffed the Premier Thorvald Stauning, 'belongs to Utopia' – echoing the cry of the shaky old Dutch Prime Minister Dirk Jan De Geer: 'This totally-wrong war was a self-born evil . . . no good can come of it.' And in Stockholm, former Foreign Minister Rickard Sandler spoke for both Norway and Sweden, which had basked in 126 years of peace: 'No power should count us, or any one of us among its allies. No power should count us, or any one of us, among its enemies. The North must be struck out of the calculations of General Staffs – for or against.'

Then, on 20 January, ten days after the Reinberger briefcase incident, Britain's First Lord of the Admiralty, Winston Churchill, took the neutrals soundly to task. From a studio in London's Broadcasting House, speaking with a back-throat lisp caused by a badly fitting upper plate, Churchill voiced thoughts that hitherto Great Britain had only uttered under her breath. What would happen, he speculated, if the neutral nations 'were with one spontaneous impulse to do their duty in accordance with the covenant of the League [of Nations] and were to stand together with the British and French Empires against aggression and wrong?'

Failing such a stand Churchill offered them scant comfort. 'At present their plight is lamentable and it will become worse. They bow humbly and in fear to German threats of violence, comforting themselves meanwhile with the thoughts that the Allies will win . . . Each one hopes that if he feeds the crocodile enough, the crocodile will eat him last. All of them hope that the storm will pass before their turn comes to be devoured.'

To one nation only did Churchill offer unstinting praise – a nation that ironically had clung to its neutrality to the last, only to suffer the ravages of Josef Stalin's Red Army: 'Only Finland, superb, nay, sublime, in the jaws of peril, Finland shows what free men can do . . .'

*

In Finland at that time of year, the trek from the towns began early. From Tammisaari and Hanko, from Viipuri and Turku, the old men, the mothers and the children, all those useless for fighting, moved out to the spruce and birch glades, a mile beyond the suburbs. There, in the four brief hours of daylight, they held picnics, gossiped, played games. When they heard the roar of bombers in the dead grey sky, they cowered until the droning had died away.

From Tammisaari alone, 3,000 out of 3,800 had gone to fight the Red invader. Meanwhile the people reverted to the Middle Ages, when peasants hid in the forests while armies marched.

Few of the forest dwellers knew precisely why the armies were marching. As yet scant details had been released of a top-secret two-day conference which had been convened in Moscow on 12 October, 1939. To the dismay of the Finnish delegates, Josef Stalin and his Foreign Minister, Vyacheslav Molotov, had been quietly implacable in their demands for territory and base facilities. They sought not only a 30-year lease of the port of Hanko, at the mouth of the Gulf of Finland, with garrison facilities for 5,000 men, but the cession of all islands in the Gulf of Finland. This 'mutual assistance pact', as Molotov styled it, further demanded the shifting of the land frontier on the Karelian Isthmus, on the Russo–Finnish border, seventy kilometres further away from the nearest Russian city, Leningrad.

To the astonishment of Juho Kusti Paasikivi, Finland's Minister in Stockholm and the leader of the delegation, Stalin, who had only concluded a non-aggression pact with Germany in August 1939, made his reasons plain: 'We want to be able to shut off access to the Gulf of Finland . . . if once a hostile fleet gets into the Gulf of Finland, it cannot be defended any longer.

You ask what power would attack us? Britain or Germany. We have good relations with Germany now, but in this world anything can change . . .'

Paasikivi's reply spoke for all those still clinging to neutrality: 'We wish to remain at peace and outside all conflicts.' Stalin's last word was on behalf of all aggressors: 'I understand that, but I assure you that it is impossible. The Great Powers will not permit it.'

On 30 November, 1939, with Finland still stubbornly refusing all pacts, Russian bombs were showering on Finnish soil.

For 105 days thereafter, the Finns were to astonish the world. Their army, only nine divisions strong, lacked almost everything that an army could: not one anti-tank gun, little more than 2,000 Suomi machine pistols. To defend her main cities, Helsinki and Viipuri, from air attack, Finland had barely 100 anti-aircraft guns. Her land defences were primitive. Across the 485-mile waist of the country the much-vaunted Mannerheim Line, named after Finland's C.-in-C., Field Marshal Carl Gustav Mannerheim, covered only eighty-eight miles. No impregnable Maginot, the Line was scarcely more than an ordinary trench system, dug by volunteers in the summer of 1939. At intervals, sixty-six concrete nests, two-thirds of them obsolete, stood in as tank barriers.

To smash it, the Russians claimed, would be 'a deed without parallel in the history of war'—but this was a comfortable fiction to hearten their troops. What held the line was what the Finns called *sisu* (guts), for in Finland, Mannerheim claimed with reason, 'a Thermopylae is fought out each day'.

In the strange false twilight of the forests, where temperatures dropped to minus forty-six degrees Centigrade, *sisu* took many forms. In-fighting with Russian tanks armed only with the wrily-christened 'Molotov Cocktails', bottles packed with potassium chloride, coal oil and sulphuric acid, took *sisu*. To man one of Finland's forty-eight fighter planes, when the Russians were deploying 3,000 planes called for *sisu* and perhaps more. Each time Captain Eino Luukkanen and the pilots of Fighter Squadron 24 took off from Utti Airfield, 200 miles north-west of Helsinki, they drank an unvarying toast before boarding their Fokker DXXI single-seaters: *Tolkku Pois* (Goodbye to reason).

In Finland lay the shape of the war to come, for women were in the front line, too: 100,000 auxiliaries called Lottas, who worked as nurses, fire-wardens and cooks. Some, spotting for Russian planes, lay for hours astride water towers, then, too numb with cold to climb to safety, crashed to their deaths. It took *sisu* for a Finnish bride to put a torch to her new home with its hope chest and hand-embroidered linen rather than yield it to the Russians.

The Finns' stubborn resistance was prompted, in part, by bitter memories; until 1917, Finland had been an autonomous grand duchy of the Russian

Empire for more than a hundred years, and the word *perivihollinen* (heredi-tary enemy) had always been synonymous with 'Russian'. Following the Bolshevik Revolution, a private army – the White Guards, under Manner-heim – had sprung up to eject the 40,000 Russian troops still on Finnish soil, an army savagely opposed by the socialist Red Guards, who supported the Russian presence. In the four months of civil war that followed, more than 1,500 Finns had died, a struggle that had prefigured the merciless combat of 1940.

Few men admired the Finnish stand more than Troop Commander Mikhail Soloviev of the Red Army. As the special emissary of Leo Zakharo-vich Mekhlis, Stalin's Finnish plenipotentiary, and *de facto* head of the Soviet Political Administration, Soloviev travelled everywhere along the front, and what he saw shocked him profoundly. Already, through no fault of its own, the Red Army was taking a beating that would go down to history. Few among them were competent ski-ers, and thus most were road-bound when the thick snows began. All lacked white camouflage clothing, and frost-proof weapons and equipment. Near Viborg, Soloviev chanced on one troop train where the soldiers had five times burnt their bunks in order to keep warm.

Their courage was never in doubt, but initiative was sorely lacking. No man thought to deploy through forest territory; they moved in dense masses, easy prey for keen-eyed snipers. Their fatalism was a byword with the Finns; as they advanced across the minefields, they came on hand in hand and singing, indifferent to the explosions that tore their ranks apart.

Their leaders had told them it would be a four-day campaign at most; after that, they would be 'eating Finnish cream and cuddling the Finnish girls'. Soloviev saw the reality. 'We were suffering from self-confidence passed on to us by our fathers,' he confessed later. 'We believed that Finland could not last for one more day of war, but day followed day . . .'

All through January, touring the front, Soloviev found his disillusions growing. The cold was unbelievable, and many men could not survive it. In one unit, the 45th Mountain Cavalry Division, posted from the burning wastes of Turkestan, 100 men had already frozen to death, despite three sets of warm underwear. The ice-cold metal of the gun-barrels seared the flesh; in the field-kitchens, soup had literally to be hacked from the cauldrons with axes. Often at night, the Russian artillery would open up without aim or direction, baffling the Finns. Soloviev knew why. When the guns had fired long enough the gunners huddled together, warming their hands on the barrels.

Many feared the Finnish snipers more than the cold; eerie white-clad figures, flitting like will o' the wisps, flexible, fast-moving, striking always at the flank and the rear. No matter how hard a man looked, the *Bielaja Smert* (The White Death) was always there, invisible in the silence of the forests.

Unversed in forest warfare, the Red Army used the *motti* (hedgehog) position, digging in behind rings of tanks, and the snipers were ingenious at chopping them into sectors and destroying them piece by piece. At Field-Marshal Mannerheim's headquarters at Mikkeli, in eastern Finland, the *motti* were shown as green circles on a large-scale map covered with mica shields. Each day a duster wiped more circles from the map. At other times the Finns concentrated their fire on the Russian field-kitchens, picking them off one by one. 'A hungry human,' wrote a Russian of the badly-mauled 18th Division, 'is an animal.'

To Troop Commander Soloviev it was the conduct of the 11th Perm Regiment, made up of homespun villagers from the foothills of the Urals, which somehow symbolised all that was wrong with the Finnish campaign. The men were mature by army standards, reservists in their thirties; at home their families were finding life hard on the collective farms and all of them were bitterly discontented. The day that Soloviev visited them, morale was low in any event, and on this day the *Bielaja Smert* caught up with them.

Three men had ventured into the forest to dig a primitive pit for a Russian bath, lighting a brushwood fire to heat pitchers of melted snow. At dawn the snipers found them, and there now began a game of cat-and-mouse. Each time a man raised his head from the pit, a bullet spurted a fountain of snow behind him. After two hours, one man's nerve broke. Crawling forth, he ran naked through the snow towards regimental headquarters, bullets spattering at his head. Hundreds saw him running so that now his panic infected those who had seen nothing at all. In the staff dug-out Soloviev heard shouting and the padding of hundreds of feet; dashing out he saw a floodtide of men pouring to the rear, some of them lashing madly at the flanks of sturdy transport horses. A man with frenzied eyes stumbled past, shouting, 'They're killing us off to the last man.'

For more than five kilometres, Soloviev and the regimental company commanders pursued the fugitives until at last they ran them to earth in a forest glade. Their rifles were flung down in a heap; they had been disarmed by a Red Army Military Police Force armed with sub-machine pistols, and now they huddled in a tight ring, grumbling and defiant. 'How can you behave like that, comrades?' a divisional commissar rebuked them. 'Here's the country in peril and you run away from your posts.' Unabashed, the men roared back: 'Half of us have been wiped out, that's a fact!'

Soloviev, watching them, thought that only narrowly had mutiny been averted.

Back at Viborg, he reported on this and similar incidents to Leo Zakharovich Mekhlis. Stalin's man heard him out in cynical silence before commenting: 'Another two or three Russian victories and nothing will remain of us.'

In the last week of January, Mannerheim reaffirmed the Finns' determination to the world. They were brave and bitter words, soon to hold a terrible significance for all nations still at peace. 'We shall fight to the last old man and child. We shall burn our forests and homes, destroy our cities and industries – and what we yield will be cursed by the scourge of God.'

*

Early in January, two widely disparate men reached the same conclusion: Adolf Hitler had picked the wrong adversary.

From Doorn, in the Netherlands, where he had completed twenty-one years in exile, ex-Kaiser Wilhelm II of Germany pondering the front-line despatches from Finland, set down his thoughts in a letter to his old friend, Poultney Bigelow, of Malden-on-Hudson, N.Y. The son of a former U.S. Minister to France, Bigelow, the Kaiser thought, might prove a sure pipeline to channel those thoughts to President Roosevelt.

'The magnificent stand of the Finns has smashed the nimbus of Bolshevism,' the Kaiser opined, '. . . with the result that the wish for peace is gaining ground. The belligerents should stop fighting and join their forces to help the Finns. They should fight in one line to rid the world and civilisation of Bolshevism.'

On 3 January, Benito Mussolini, who had thus far begged out of the war on the grounds of unpreparedness, despite the Axis Pact he had signed with Germany seven months earlier, plucked up courage to deliver an almost identical warning to his fellow dictator. From his lofty office on Rome's Piazza Venezia, a room as wide and empty as an abandoned temple, Mussolini had despatched a letter urging the Führer to abandon all ideas of an offensive in the West. 'Military successes are possible,' he conceded, 'but all the greater then the danger that the war may spread to involve the U.S.A.'

The German–Russian Pact of 1939, he held, was a disaster of the first magnitude – 'you cannot abandon the anti-Semitic and anti-Bolshevist banner which you have been flying for twenty years, and for which so many of your comrades have died; you cannot renounce your gospel, in which the German people have so blindly believed. It is my definite duty to add that a further step in your relations with Moscow would have catastrophic repercussions in Italy . . .'

'Until four months ago,' the *Duce* wound up, 'Russia was World Enemy No. 1. She cannot become, and is not, Friend No. 1 . . . the solution of your *Lebensraum* problem is in Russia and nowhere else.'

The time when Hitler would share this conviction was not yet come. His sole response to the Italian's plea was an icy two-months' silence.

*

Saturday, 10 February, dawned raw and drizzly in Washington, D.C., but the weather was not bleak enough to damp the spirits of 4,446 cockily defiant members of the American Youth Congress as they surged up Constitution Avenue to seek a confrontation with the President of the United States. One day earlier the delegates, assembled in the capital for a four-day Citizenship Institute, had made their isolationist sympathies abundantly plain. Against a backdrop of banners reading 'SCHOLARSHIPS NOT BATTLESHIPS', the A.Y.C.s New York chapter had condemned any prospect of U.S. aid to Finland as 'an attempt to force America into an imperialistic war'.

As they marched they chanted a rebellious song:

No, Major no Major, we will not go,
We'll wager, we'll wager, this ain't our show,
Remember that we're not so green
As the boys in seventeen.

The youngsters were due for a surprise. By mischance they had arrived an hour too early: the President was scheduled to broadcast to the United States at 12.30 pm and until that time the delegates huddled, miserable under the driving rain, on the White House lawn. More daunting yet, the President who was wheeled out onto the South Portico to address both them and the nation was no benign paternal figure but an angry tight-lipped man, blunt to the point of brutality.

He warned them sharply against passing resolutions on subjects 'which you have not thought through and on which you cannot possibly have complete knowledge'. In a scathing comment on their reference to 'an imperialistic war', he sneered, 'My friends, that reason was unadulterated twaddle.' If Roosevelt heard the resentful chorus of booing that now arose, he affected to ignore it. American sympathy, he told them, was 98 per cent with the Finns in their effort to stave off invasion. 'That the Soviet Union would, because of this, declare war on the United States is about the silliest thing that I have ever heard advanced in the fifty-eight years of my life.'

On this chill Saturday, it was not only a horde of deluded youngsters who had aroused Roosevelt's ire. If the future of civilisation was involved, as he indeed believed it was, the United States was still determined to debate it by committee. Faced with the President's proposal for a modest loan to Finland, the Senate pondered the protocol: should the matter be referred to the Committee on Banking and Currency or the Committee on Foreign Relations? No matter that Secretary of the Treasury Henry Morgenthau urged, 'One battleship to Finland would be the best investment we could make.' The Senate needed time to deliberate – and finally played safe by sending the letter to both committees.

Angrily Roosevelt castigated the Senators as 'a bunch of Uriah Heeps'.

The Finns enjoyed no good friend in Cordell Hull, a courtly Tennessean

17

and Roosevelt's Secretary of State; in this election year Hull feared that any hint of aid to Finland would spark off isolationist charges of projected aid to Britain and France. On 22 January – and again on 8 February – Hull told the Finnish Minister bluntly that there was no chance of a direct loan to enable the Finns to purchase arms.

The outcome was much as Roosevelt had feared. On 13 February, by a vote of 49 to 27, the Senate approved a loan in principle, but two more weeks elapsed before Congress, by 168 to 51, passed the measure on 28 February. In accordance with the Neutrality Act of 1939, the Finns were belatedly granted $20 million – none of it to be used for 'arms, ammunition, or implements of war'.

'The sympathy of the United States,' commented Eljas Erkko, the Finnish chargé in Stockholm, later, 'was so great that it nearly suffocated us.'

The irony was fitting. On the day that the Senate had belatedly given Finland its blessing, the Red Army, now numbering more than one million men, broke through the Mannerheim Line.

*

At 5 pm on Friday, 16 February, Winston Churchill saw his chance. Pacing the floor of the dingy basement that served as the Admiralty's War Room in London, tugging at his coat-tails, chewing on an unlit cigar, the First Lord was as preoccupied as his staff had ever seen him.

Churchill's stern broadcast warning to the neutrals had been no random impulse. As far back as September 1939, he had urged the War Cabinet to mine Norwegian territorial waters; only thus, he argued, could the flow of Swedish iron ore shipped to Germany each year via the Norwegian ore port of Narvik be successfully checked. At the time, Britain's Dominions – South Africa, Australia, New Zealand – had strongly opposed this, fearing that a violation of neutrality would outrage public opinion, but in January, Churchill, undaunted, had raised the issue again. By now, both Dominions and Cabinet were reconciled – until a personal appeal from Norway's King Haakon VII to King George VI saw the project shelved once more.

Now, on 16 February, Scandinavia's 'absolute neutrality' was again at stake, and the decision facing Churchill threatened the onset of a major international incident.

All reports from the British Embassy in Oslo, Norway's capital, indicated that the 12,000 ton tanker *Altmark*, former supply ship of the German pocket battleship *Admiral Graf Spee*, was on the last lap of her homeward journey to Wilhelmshaven. Moreover, rumour suggested that 300 British seamen – the crews of nine merchantmen sunk in the South Atlantic by the *Graf Spee* – were held prisoner below *Altmark*'s decks, en route to P.o.W camps.

Both report and rumour were true. On 19 December, 1939, the *Graf Spee*, dogged hungrily by British cruisers, had scuttled herself in the River Plate estuary, outside Montevideo. Promptly, *Altmark's* Captain Heinrich Dau, a 65-year-old goatee-bearded martinet, had set course for home. All had seemed set fair. At the height of a blizzard, *Altmark* — known always as 'Mother' to *Graf Spee*'s crew — had passed undetected between Iceland and the Faeroe Islands. By 14 February, she had reached Trondheim, on Norway's west coast.

Some 300 miles down that coast, beyond the seaport of Bergen, lay the Skagerrak, the 80-mile wide strait dividing Norway and Denmark — and 200 miles further on, Germany.

Below *Altmark*'s decks, in holds no more than ten feet high, 299 British merchant seamen had almost abandoned hope. Some had endured the dripping fetid darkness for four months now — sustained mostly by black bread and watery goulash, dragging on tealeaf cigarettes, their only latrines the brimming 40-gallon oil drums which were almost never emptied. Few shared the heady optimism of Able Seaman Thomas Foley, of the *Doric Star*, who had offered a £400 to £1 bet on a naval rescue. So many more had reached breaking point that one bearded barefoot seaman confided to *Trevanion*'s second officer, Ronald Cudbertson: 'I wish I was a woman, and then I could have a good cry.'

Though few men suspected it, fortune was to favour them. Overtly a grey-painted merchantman, her 6-inch guns concealed, *Altmark*'s passage through neutral waters was closely watched by the Norwegians — alerted perhaps by her unmercantile custom of posting eleven look-outs. Thus, as she inched at eight knots along the coastline, barely twenty yards from the shore, the bearded Dau, whom the prisoners called 'Knitty Whiskers', was subjected to polite but nonstop harassment. First to board *Altmark* was an officer from the torpedo-boat *Trygg*. In stolid silence, he heard out Dau's protest: *Altmark* was a tanker, unarmed, carrying no prisoners.

In the warm stinking darkness below decks, 299 men, sensing the Norwegian presence, now screamed and caterwauled like madmen, beating on the latrine drums with girders and wooden wedges — but the squealing of the ship's winches, which Dau had ordered must be kept turning, drowned out all sound.

Still the Norwegians kept up their gentle pressure. North of Bergen, the torpedo boat *Snoegg* moved in — the same boarding procedure, the same inquisition — and following her the destroyer *Garm*. For the fuming Dau these delays were crucial, for the waters of the Skagerrak lay barely 100 miles ahead.

Meanwhile, the Admiralty's first instructions had passed to Captain Philip Vian, commander of the 4th Flotilla Group, aboard the destroyer *Cossack*. Ordered to sail from Rosyth, Scotland, on 14 February, along with the cruiser *Arethusa* and four Fleet destroyers, Vian had at first engaged on an abortive sweep of the Skagerrak for German iron-ore ships. Then, at ten minutes past midnight on 16 February, the Commander-in-Chief, Home Fleet, Admiral Sir Charles Forbes, signalled a change of plan: 'ALTMARK YOUR OBJECTIVE. ACT ACCORDINGLY.'

At first Vian was at a loss, for the one picture of the *Altmark* available, in that week's wardroom copy of *The Illustrated London News*, identified her, incorrectly, as a 4-masted freighter. Not until almost 1 pm on 16 February, did a Hudson from R.A.F. Coastal Command signal an 'enemy first sighting': *Altmark* was now at 58° 17′ N, 06° 05′ E, steaming at eight knots. At once Vian ordered the flotilla to intercept at full speed.

It was now, in the Admiralty War Room, that the full implications of the dilemma came home to Churchill. If no prisoners were aboard *Altmark*, to authorise the use of force was a grave violation of neutrality while she remained within Norwegian territorial waters. Yet if *Altmark* was a prison ship, she, too, was in breach of neutrality, and to let her go was unthinkable.

At 5.20 p.m. Churchill's patience snapped. To Albert Victor Alexander, soon to succeed him as First Lord, he ground out: 'I can't wait any longer. Get me Halifax.' Hunched in a green leather armchair, it took him less than a minute to expound his problem to Edward, Lord Halifax, the Foreign Secretary.

Imperturbable as always, Halifax promised him: 'Give me ten minutes and I'll call you back.'

Within the time span, Churchill was dictating to the Duty Signal Officer a message embodying Halifax's verdict. In part it read: UNLESS NORWEGIAN TORPEDO BOAT (the *Kjell*, which had halted *Cossack*) UNDERTAKES TO CONVOY ALTMARK TO BERGEN WITH A JOINT ANGLO–NORWEGIAN GUARD ON BOARD AND A JOINT ESCORT YOU SHOULD BOARD ALTMARK, LIBERATE THE PRISONERS, AND TAKE POSSESSION OF SHIP . . . IF NORWEGIAN TORPEDO-BOAT INTERFERES, YOU SHOULD WARN HER TO STAND OFF . . . SUGGEST TO NORWEGIAN DESTROYER THAT HONOUR IS SERVED BY SUBMITTING TO SUPERIOR FORCE.

As the Signal Officer hastened away, Britain's First Lord was moved to pay spontaneous tribute: 'That was *big* of Halifax.'

Eight hundred miles north-west, Captain Dau was now in desperate straits. Almost three hours before Churchill's signal he had sighted the menacing silhouettes of Vian's flotilla on his starboard, to the south-south-west. Now he ordered First Officer Paulsen: 'Signal to the Norwegians. The English warships are sailing in Norwegian territorial waters. It is their duty to stop them.'

It was too late. As the first destroyer, H.M.S. *Intrepid*, bore down on *Altmark*, the gunboat *Skarv* made a half-hearted attempt to check her, but with the destroyers to starboard Dau's escape to the open sea was cut off. Now he took the only evasive action left to him—ramming the *Altmark* through the splintering pack ice of Jossing Fjord, a 1½ mile-long arm of the sea hemmed in by mountains.

It was a self-defeating gambit for Vian's flotilla could now seal off all hopes of escape as effectively as cats grouped round a mousehole. Dau had just one hope; the Norwegians would resist the British incursion so resolutely that Vian would back down.

But Churchill's fighting message had spurred Vian to action, though at 10 pm he made one last attempt to persuade the Norwegians to see reason. Hailing the gunboat *Kjell* through his megaphone, Vian urged: 'My orders are to ask you to join us and take the *Altmark* to Bergen for inspection. Come on in with me.' But again the Norwegians refused.

'Half-speed ahead,' Vian ordered then. 'We're boarding.'

As *Cossack* ground painfully into the ice of the fjord, men noted a scene of strange and eerie beauty: the destroyer's searchlight gliding among the fir trees and the snow-capped mountains, toy houses perched precariously above the dark-green water. On *Altmark*'s bridge, Dau alerted by a danger signal on his cabin's telephone, was peering ahead of him, almost blinded by the brilliant light. Abruptly, *Cossack*'s searchlight cut out.

'What ship?' the *Altmark*'s Morse lamp blinked again and again. 'What ship?' But no answer came: only the steady inexorable approach of a stranger through darkness.

Aboard *Cossack* Lieutenant-Commander Bradwell Turner, heading the 25-strong boarding party, checked over last-minute details: already the destroyer's rails had been let down, the hazelwood 'fenders' secured with wire to blunt the impact of the collision. Now a message flashed from *Cossack* to *Altmark*: 'Heave-to or we open fire.'

It was 11.12 pm. Alarmed, Dau directed his searchlight onto *Cossack*'s bows. '*Es ist ein Engländer,*' he shouted, and in this moment *Altmark* swung astern towards *Cossack*. 'She's going to ram us,' an officer warned Vian.

Vian had anticipated the move. As *Altmark* closed in, he swung *Cossack* round, as lightly as a yacht, warding off the force of the blow. Now *Altmark* swung in again, to ram at a 30-degree angle, and Turner ordered the boarding party to double from starboard to port. *Cossack*'s port bow was now grinding alongside the tanker's starboard poop at little more than walking pace.

Then, in a manoeuvre which Churchill, to the delight of the waiters, would re-enact with crusts and cutlery in London's smart Mirabelle Restaurant, Turner sprang outwards over five clear feet, to grasp the tanker's rail. 'Come on,' he yelled, 'what the hell are you waiting for?' The others were swift to follow, rifles thudding on the deck.

At a porthole on *Altmark*'s 'E' Deck, Fourth Officer John Bammant, of *Doric Star*, kept up a blow-by-blow account like a sports commentator at a racetrack: 'An officer's jumping across, revolver in hand . . . now a sailor . . . Another! Good! Another . . .'

Pandemonium broke loose. Gunfire crackled, ricocheting from the high mountains. All over the catwalks and the foc'sle, groups of Britons and

21

Germans lunged and gouged and grappled. Suddenly there was a sharp impact, and the combatants staggered, cursing, caught off balance. *Altmark* had run aground on rocks at the far end of the fjord.

Plainly Vian could no longer follow his instructions to take *Altmark* in prize: what mattered now was the captives below. On *Altmark*'s bridge, Turner, revolver levelled, ordered Sub-Lieutenant Geoffrey Craven, whose German was fautless, 'Tell them to take us to the prisoners.'

By now the hatchway above the flats had been lifted; in the humid half-light the captives had listened enthralled to the shouting and the spatter of gunfire. Suddenly from far above a voice hailed them: 'Any Englishmen down there?'

The voices were a thunderous chorus from the darkness: 'We're *all* English down here.'

Turner recalls his own salutation as, 'We've come to rescue you', but at another hatchway an anonymous bluejacket coined a phrase for history, 'Come up – the Navy's here.'

The words were to echo throughout the world for this unrepentant act of piracy struck a chord among the free nations. Whooping and cheering, their faces radiant, 299 grimy bearded men stumbled up the trunkway, to pump the hands of their rescuers, to gulp in the icy air. Most were too euphoric even to bear a grudge against their captors; Second Engineer George King, of *Doric Star*, found himself shaking hands with Captain Dau. Able Seaman Thomas Foley, by contrast, besought a rifle from a *Cossack* sailor; he wanted to shoot 'Knitty Whiskers'. Patiently the bluejacket chided him, 'Don't be silly, old man, this is not for private use.'

At five minutes to midnight on 16 February, a petty officer shouting through cupped hands to Captain Vian marked the end of the *Altmark* affair: 'All prisoners and boarding party aboard, sir.' (Adjudging the situation 'already complex enough', Vian had decided to leave the Germans behind.) The gangplank went up, and a phalanx of wildly cheering men lined the decks as *Cossack* moved slowly out of Jossing Fjord.

The world was swift to react. In the *Storting*, the Norwegian Parliament, Foreign Minister Halvdan Koht protested bitterly at 'this grave violation of Norwegian neutrality', though from the sidelines the United States press comments more resembled rave reviews following a triumphant first night. 'Daringly conceived and brilliantly carried out', was the verdict of *The New York Sun*. 'A boldness reminiscent . . . of the seventeenth century', enthused *The Baltimore Sun*. In Berlin, Dr Josef Göbbels was beside himself. 'All propaganda must be focused on this single incident,' he instructed editors at his press conference. 'Tonight the sea should boil.'

In the space of a night, by violating Norwegian neutrality, Churchill had ended 'the phoney war. Already the first subterranean rumblings of a world-wide avalanche could be heard in the chancelleries of Europe.

2

'The Position of Small Nations ... is Clarified'

17 February–25 April, 1940

AT UTTI AIRFIELD, 200 miles north-west of Helsinki, Captain Eino Luukkanen and the pilots of Fighter Squadron 24, were puzzled and angry. None of them could understand the bewildering reversal of fortune. For weeks, Luukkanen's men had been so sure of ultimate victory that Finnish bombers had even carried out a leaflet raid on Leningrad, offering deserting Russian soldiers specific prices for their arms: 150 roubles for a rifle, up to 1,500 for a machine-gun, 10,000 for a tank.

Then, inexplicably, everything had begun to go wrong. More and heavier Russian artillery was being moved up to the Mannerheim Line, including the formidable 'Little Berthas', with a 25-mile range. In their wake came fresh troops from Siberia and the Caucasus, trained for bitter-weather fighting. In the eighteen days since the Mannerheim Line had been breached, these men seemed irresistible. The thrust of their attack was in the Summa sector, aiming for Viipuri, Finland's Gulf port and second city, and often their advance was backed by 500 aircraft at a time. A new sophistication was apparent: infantrymen were brought into action in armoured sleds towed by tanks, while flame-thrower vehicles sprayed the Finns with burning naphtha. The phrase 'total war' was taking on a new and – up to now unthinkable – dimension.

By 3 March, the Red Army was closing on Viipuri, ten miles behind the Mannerheim Line. A great and ominous quiet lay over the capital, Helsinki, but the blood-soaked snow south of Viipuri had become Finland's Verdun. Block by burning block, the port was yielding, the Russian troops urged on by commissars bellowing through loud-hailers: 'Comrades, destroy the white Finnish snakes.' Their cries jarred incongruously with the voice of Radio Moscow, crooning through the gutted suburbs: 'The Red Army sends affectionate greetings to the people of Finland ... workers in every country love the Red Army.'

By now it was evident that no help would be coming in time from any foreign power. The reason was plain: a mooted Anglo–Finnish expeditionary force could only reach Finland by passing through neutral Norway and Sweden, uncomfortably close to the Swedish iron ore fields at Gallivare, on the Gulf of Bothnia. Fearing an allied plan to 'guard' and 'protect' both Gallivare and the Norwegian iron ore port of Narvik, Norway and Sweden, insistent on their neutrality, would permit no access to Finland.

Meanwhile, by 4 March, Finland's Fighter Squadron 24 had moved closer to the battle zone. Now, oppressed by the news of Viipuri's plight, they were shuttling between Lemi airfield, south-west of Ruokolahti, and the solid ice of Lake Kivijärvi. On this overcast Monday, with ten-tenths cloud cover, and a ceiling nearing 600 feet, there seemed little chance of action: Luukkanen and his men, huddled in the alert shack, had settled to a game of cards. Then, soon after noon, the phone bell jangled. A coastal artillery battery reported an attempted Russian landing in force across the frozen gulf at Virolahti. The squadron was to strafe the advancing columns.

Luukkanen and his men exchanged glances. Their experience of ground strafing was almost nil – and close to the gulf was the Russian fighter base at Suursaari.

Assigning four pilots to act as top cover, Luukkanen took the squadron off in sections through broken cloud. As they flew the weather deteriorated still further. Over Luumäki, wet spattering drifts of snow assailed them. At Miehikkälä, black snow-laden clouds forced them to treetop level. Mercifully, as they reached the Gulf, the ceiling lifted. The squadron climbed to an altitude of 1,000 feet.

As Luukkanen first sighted the Russian column, he sucked in his breath. As yet it was six miles away – but where, he thought, is Stalin finding these reinforcements? From the air the column was an unending line of men and horses, more than 500 strong, a long black snake seeming motionless on the ice. And Suursaari airfield was blanketed by fog; not a Russian fighter was in sight. Luukkanen signalled: 'Single file strafing run.'

The column was a perfect target. Not one among the Russians was wearing white camouflage clothing; they were black ant-men, sharply defined against the glittering ice. Strangely, as Luukkanen eased forward on the control column they made no attempt to break formation, even as the snarl of the Mercury engines ruptured the silence. At thirty feet Luukkanen levelled off; a bright stream of bullets from his four Browning M-36 machine guns sliced into the trudging men.

Panic seized the Russians. In fleeting seconds Luukkanen saw some men drop dead in their tracks; others were grabbing at the bridles of rearing plunging horses. Scores were scattering in all directions, slithering as ludicrously on the ice as drunken men. As Luukkanen began his pull-up, he was so low that his Fokker's undercarriage came close to scraping their heads.

Now the squadron's ace, Flight Master 'Illu' Juutlainen, took up the strafing, and the others were close behind him. Luukkanen had already reefed round, picking out a four-barrel organ gun mounted on a cart as target. At thirty feet, Fighter Squadron 24 moved up and down the column like tractors ploughing a field; eight planes, thirty-two machine guns, pumping 8,000 rounds into the squirming diving Russians. Luukkanen was surprised to feel a fierce atavistic joy, such as he had never felt when aerial combat was involved. Here was one Russian formation that would never attack Virolahti.

By early afternoon, the fighters were once again touching down on the ice of Lake Kivijärvi. Already the coastal artillery had signalled its congratulations. More than 200 Russians lay dead or dying in the snow. The rest were in full retreat, forced-marching painfully back across the ice.

*

On the evening of 10 March, Erik Seidenfaden, political editor of the Copenhagen daily *Politiken*, boarded the Copenhagen–Stockholm ferry, on his way to cover the Finnish war, along with United Press correspondent Webb Miller. From the saloon-deck the two men could hear the lusty singsong of a dozen young Danish volunteers, en route to offer their services to Mannerheim. 'That's a pity,' Seidenfaden commented casually. 'There'll be peace long before they get there.'

Miller was curious. Did Seidenfaden have inside information? The Dane confessed that he hadn't. He had spoken unthinkingly, prompted by some inner hunch.

At thirty, Seidenfaden was already a veteran of the turmoil besetting Europe. In Germany, in 1932, he had so accurately charted Hitler's rise to power that the Nazis had warned him to stop filing stories or face arrest. Seidenfaden, a tall relaxed man who smiled a lot, had taken the hint – but he had gone on to cover Franco's civil war in Spain, and, later, in 1939, he watched the German columns roll into Prague as Hitler breached the Munich Agreement and annexed Czechoslovakia. In all this time Seidenfaden had seen himself as an anti-Nazi crusader, striving desperately to awake the apathetic Danes to the menace that Hitler posed.

Eight years' reporting had given Seidenfaden a profound faith in inner hunches. In Stockholm, he took pains to contact a Foreign Office source close to the Minister, Christian Günther. His man was unreserved. The first Finnish peace-feeler to Moscow had gone out on 6 March. An armistice would take effect from 12 March.

Seidenfaden knew some anxious moments. By 6 pm on 11 March he had cabled the story to Copenhagen, and Editor Nils Hasagdr, scenting a scoop, had ordered an emergency run of stop press leaflets rushed onto the streets. Only at midnight, when the news became official, did Seidenfaden relax.

The world at large was less concerned with the when than the why. What indeed had induced the Finns to give up after 105 days of titanic struggle? In truth, the decision had rested with Mannerheim alone. As early as 2

25

March, he had asked himself: How long could his exhausted army hold Viipuri? By now the front had become dangerously extended, and the ice so thick and strong that it bore the weight of Russian tanks across Viipuri Bay. Trained manpower was now so short that even convicts serving light sentences were being rushed into uniform. To save his soldiers from annihilation, Mannerheim reluctantly opted for peace.

It was Stalin, as the U.S. ambassador to Moscow, Lawrence A. Steinhardt, reported to the State Department, who in this last hour, overruled the Red Army's leaders and the Politburo, both of whom had favoured a war to the death. But Stalin was adamant. If the war continued his troops might become embroiled with that Anglo–French Expeditionary Force – which had never ever taken physical shape.

The average Finn was stunned. Towards noon on 13 March, scores of them crowded into Helsinki's large co-operative restaurants, to listen in numb proud solitude to the broadcast voice of Foreign Minister Väinö Tanner, enumerating the conditions of surrender. A band played Luther's hymn, 'Ein feste Burg', and slowly in the too-bright sun, the white and blue flags slipped to half mast.

The Russians were exacting a harsh price: 25,000 square miles of land, including all the islands in the Gulf of Finland, the ports of Viipuri and Hanko, most of the Karelian Isthmus. Captain Eino Luukkanen saw it, above all, in terms of people. Over 500,000 people in the areas ceded to the Soviet must now quit their homes; along the roads of Karelia, he watched 1940's first refugees, men young and old, trudging beside their cattle, women, young children, the aged and sick, riding atop piled carts.

Some Russians had mixed feelings. Troop Commander Mikhail Soloviev heard the news in a field hospital, following a pile-up on a motor cycle and found himself thinking long and deeply about the Finns. 'Had they weakly laid down their arms,' he thought, 'all of us would have despised them. We wanted simply to maintain our self-respect as a people.' The Finns' bravery, he thought, had helped the Russians to do that.

'Did we defeat them?' Soloviev wondered. But that was a harder question to answer. 'Our victory seemed very much like a defeat – and their defeat like a victory.'

*

North of Viipuri, now, the land lay littered with the aftermath of battle. For mile upon mile, the snow was polka-dotted with black and yellow craters, trees gashed by shells and machine-gun fire. The surreal debris of war was everywhere: empty vodka bottles, torn copies of *Pravda*, mounds of frozen dung, gutted tanks, the grinning heads of horses with wide-open frozen eyes, festoons of field telephone wire.

In the forests, snow was falling very fast upon the dead.

26

The bitter inquests began within the week – the first of many such to be held throughout 1940. Finland blamed Sweden for not permitting Allied aid. Sweden accused Britain and France of spoiling to turn Scandinavia into a battlefield. The French blamed the British for not pressing aid to Finland. The British blamed the Swedes.

In Sweden, the sense of shame went deep. The Premier, pudgy little Per Albin Hansson excused his stubborn stand by saying: 'I have to deal with a nation that is selfish about peace.' Yet the majority of the Swedish General Staff had favoured armed intervention before Russia reached Sweden's borders and many Swedes were bitter that in the last resort, Sweden had saved her own skin by leaving Finland to perish. 'Sweden . . . failed democracy's case', a Göteborg newspaper charged roundly. 'She failed a brother in the hour of distress. She failed her historic obligations and failed her future.'

There was soul-searching in Britain, too: only thirty field-guns had been sent out of 166 promised, no more than twenty-five howitzers out of 150 pledged. Even these, like the United States loan, the 11,500 foreign volunteers spoiling to fight for Finland, had arrived too late, for the Chamberlain Government's heart had never resolutely embraced the Finnish cause. All along their intention had been to improve relations with the Soviets and wean Russia away from her unholy German alliance. No one had seriously encouraged Finland to resist Russian demands for bases and military facilities.

'The position of small nations in the world as it is at present is clarified,' summed up the columnist Dorothy Thompson, in *The New York Herald Tribune*, 'They have no position.'

But what rankled most bitterly, for the free world was that a dream had died. After a decade in which brute force had ruled, it had seemed, for 105 days, that right could triumph over might against insuperable odds. Now this illusion had perished.

Davids could in no way worst the Goliaths. The gods of war marched with the big battalions.

*

In his office at 10, Downing Street, London, overlooking the Horse Guards Parade, Neville Chamberlain had visitors in the late afternoon of 11 March. Watched by his Foreign Secretary, Lord Halifax, and Joseph P. Kennedy, the isolationist American ambassador, Chamberlain was studying a sheet of blue notepaper, die-stamped in red, 'The White House', handed to him by a tall aloof man in full morning dress.

'My dear Chamberlain,' the Prime Minister read, 'Sumner Welles, my

Under Secretary of State and old boyhood friend, will give you this. What you tell him will be maintained in the strictest confidence – and will be told solely to myself and to Cordell Hull. At this grave moment, I deeply hope this exchange of views may be of real value towards a peace which is neither "inconclusive nor precarious" – Enough said. My warm regards, Faithfully, Franklin D. Roosevelt.'

Welles was unaware that Chamberlain, inherently anti-American, had dubbed his fact-finding mission, 'a sensational intervention', certain that it would 'cause embarrassment to the democracies from which Germany, still unconvinced of the failure of the policy of force, will reap advantage'. Most of the Prime Minister's talk, Welles noted, was of German treachery: how Hitler had lied to him, how Hitler had deceived him. His dark eyes piercing, his voice low and incisive, Chamberlain made no effort to contain his 'white-hot anger'.

Welles did not attempt to stem the flow. In any event, as Roosevelt had told the State Department's Breckinridge Long, Welles' visit to Chamberlain and to the French Premier, Daladier, was no more than 'window-dressing'. The real purpose of his European mission, Roosevelt explained, was 'to get the low-down on Hitler and get Mussolini's point of view . . .'

As he left No. 10, Welles was unaware that Chamberlain had just cause for agitation. Pressed by the forceful Churchill, the Premier was now unwillingly involved in a military manoeuvre of which he had grave moral doubts: an unprovoked invasion of both Norway and Sweden.

At next day's War Cabinet Meeting, on 12 May, all Chamberlain's revulsion against war, which had prompted his long appeasement of the dictators, was readily apparent. The burly Chief of the Imperial General Staff, General Sir Edmund Ironside, faced a Premier who at first appeared 'tired and lugubrious', then 'more and more horrified' as he grappled with the implications of the coup. Peering at a chart of Narvik, he first asked Ironside what scale it represented, then pondered what effect an 8-inch shell would have on shipping. Told that it could be devastating, Chamberlain promptly opted for 4-inch shells. Faced with such vacillation, the Chief of the Air Staff, Air Chief Marshal Sir Cyril Newall, pronounced the whole scheme as 'hare-brained'. 'I came away disgusted with them all,' Ironside noted in his diary.

The essence of Churchill's project, Operation Wilfred, was the mining of Norwegian territorial waters, regardless of whether Norway agreed or not. But this operation, if need be, was to be supplemented by Plan R.4 – a countermeasure designed to thwart any German violation of Norwegian neutrality which might follow on the mining.

In this event, a force under General Pierse Mackesy, 20,000 strong, was to seize Narvik in three-division strength, with simultaneous landings along the Norwegian coastline at Trondheim, Bergen and Stavanger. Trekking on to

28

Sweden, this force was then to seize and destroy the contested Gallivare ore-fields at the mouth of the Gulf of Bothnia.

The crucial obstacle to this plan was the Swedes themselves, for no road connected Narvik with the Swedish frontier – hence Narvik's key-role as a port when the Gulf of Bothnia was frozen. The Swedes had only to cut off the railway's electric current to bring Mackesy's force to a standstill.

Pressed as to his views, Mackesy conceived the idea of somehow reaching the Swedish frontier then courteously demanding passage across. 'And if the way was barred?' Chamberlain asked. 'If he could not get through without fighting,' Mackesy assured him, 'he would call it off.' Lord Halifax agreed. 'If we can't get in except at the cost of Norwegian lives, I am not for it,' he decided, 'ore or no ore.'

On this same day, the news of the Finnish surrender robbed the British of all pretext for the foray, but in the weeks following Sumner Welles' visit, Churchill kept up the pressure. Even so, his Cabinet colleagues remained uncertain. The *Altmark* incident had had 'a good press' in the United States, Lord Lothian reported from Washington, D.C., 'but action such as we now proposed might be less well received. Anything which would be regarded as bullying a small neutral would be resented . . .' Chamberlain, too, added his warning: 'We entered the war on moral grounds and we must be careful not to undermine our position.' Now Halifax seemed to veer in Churchill's favour: could Britain feel bound to keep the rules of war 'and thereby allow the enemy the double advantage of disregarding those rules which suited him'? Churchill had no doubts at all. Such action was more than a naval foray; it might prove to be one of the turning points of the entire war.

But many still had misgivings – among them Premier Edouard Daladier, of France, who wanted no part in the operation. It was, in his words, 'a dangerous toy', and one which might well bring serious German reprisals against French aircraft factories. Others, fighting men among them, had doubts on moral grounds. On 5 April, Captain Ralph Edwards, R.N., Director of Operations (Home) on duty in the Admiralty War Room, noted in his diary: 'We deliberately infringe international waters and therefore the law – I thought we were fighting for international law and order.'

At this hour, however, there was no turning back. With or without the French, the British were going ahead, and Mackesy's final operational order left wide scope to provoke an international incident: 'Subsequently (to the seizure of the Norwegian ports) an opportunity may arise to go on to Gallivare, and the role of the force would then become the denial of the Gallivare ore fields to Germany . . . In this event you are to obtain instructions from the War Office before entering Sweden.'

Now the die was cast, Chamberlain seemed more confident. 'Hitler,' he told a meeting of the Conservative Central Association on 5 April, 'has missed the bus.'

29

Six weeks earlier, in Berlin's Reich Chancellery, Adolf Hitler, unusually for him, had yielded to rational argument.

Until mid-February Hitler had genuinely had no territorial plans for the Baltic. What the Führer wanted, in event of war, was to keep Norway, Sweden and Finland neutral, for, in this way, the Baltic would remain an open sea for Germany, with the area's resources and raw materials available for the German war economy.

As early as October 1939, *Grossadmiral* Erich Raeder had proposed the seizing of Norway's bases to increase Germany's power of attack against British sea-routes. His reasoning was impeccable. In November 1937, Hitler had alerted his Chiefs of Staff to prepare for 'Case I', a period between 1943 and 1945, at which time his 'unalterable resolve to solve Germany's problem of space' might bring him into conflict with the British. Accordingly, Raeder had formulated Plan 'Z', which provided for the completion, by 1945, of a modern high-seas fleet built around eight huge battleships, five battle cruisers and two aircraft carriers.

Thus, in September 1939, the news of war with Britain and France had come to Raeder like a thunderclap. Moreover, Hitler had scrapped Plan 'Z', so that Germany's naval potential was less than half the size of the French and Italian fleets and was altogether eclipsed by the British. The two large battleships, *Bismarck* and *Tirpitz*, the aircraft carrier *Graf Zeppelin*, and the heavy cruisers *Prinz Eugen*, *Seydlitz* and *Lutzow* had been launched but not yet completed. Only the 32,000-ton battle cruisers *Gneisenau* and *Scharn-horst* were in commission. Thus the German Navy could never at any time venture into the Atlantic as a fleet, while the U-Boat arm had less than half the strength required to cripple Britain's supply line.

At first Hitler, preoccupied with his western offensive, had shown scant interest in Raeder's Norwegian proposition; as much as any German war-lord, he suffered from the historical sense of inferiority that saw Britain as invincible at sea. Then the onset of the Finnish war gave him pause to think. If the Allies gained access to Norway, Germany's Swedish ore supply was threatened – and that supply totalled eleven and a half million out of Germany's total annual consumption of fifteen million tons.

Two factors now combined to galvanise Hitler into action. The incident of Major Reinberger's briefcase, which had temporarily stalled the western offensive, had for the time being freed his hands, and Churchill's impulsive *Altmark* signal to Captain Vian set the seal on it. Exercise *Weser*, which called for the invasion of Norway and a simultaneous seizure of Denmark to secure her air bases, was on with a vengeance.

On 20 February, General Nikolaus von Falkenhorst, 55-year-old com-mander of the XXIst Corps, stationed at Coblenz, was summarily hailed to

Berlin and given command of the Norwegian invasion forces. Von Falkenhorst was bewildered, and with reason: although he had served in Finland in 1918, and thus had practical experience of northern warfare, his meeting with Hitler was no more than a matter of minutes before the Führer's midday conference. Since no one thought to provide him with a map, von Falkenhorst had to move fast; Hitler had given him five brief hours to finalise his plans. Hastening to the city centre, the General bought a Baedeker guide to Norway and returned to his hotel room. By 5 pm the invasion was charted, and von Falkenhorst returned to the Reich Chancellery. Allotted only five divisions, his choice seemed logical: one division apiece would be launched against the five large harbours of Oslo, Bergen, Stavanger, Trondheim and Narvik.

The target date, set for 5 April, marked Hitler's biggest gamble yet, for Raeder was staking virtually the whole German fleet to achieve success. And on 8 April, five cruisers and six destroyers of the British Navy would move out on their 'hare-brained' Operation Wilfred – with a sporting chance of occupying precisely those ports earmarked by the Germans.

*

It had been an exhausting trip, and he was glad to be done with it, but in forty-one days he had become the best-informed man on World War II. By special train, aeroplane and steamer he had covered 14,000 miles. He had conferred with one Pope, two Kings – Britain's George VI and Vittorio Emmanuele III of Italy – one Führer, one Duce and three Premiers (Neville Chamberlain, Daladier and the fiery little Paul Reynaud, who had succeeded Daladier on 20 March). Finally on 28 March, Sumner Welles returned to Washington.

No one, aside from Franklin Roosevelt, had ever had the slightest faith in his mission. Assistant Secretary of State Adolf A. Berle, had viewed it as 'one of the most difficult and unhappy trips a man ever started on'. Secretary of State Hull had been less charitable; the mission was 'calculated to hold out false hopes'. Both the British and the Germans had been at one in distrusting Welles' motives. 'He can say what he wants to,' was Ribbentrop's lofty comment. 'I have nothing to say to him.' Sir Alexander Cadogan, Permanent Under-Secretary to the Foreign Office, stigmatised the trip as 'an awful half-baked idea'.

Chamberlain, who could never raise his eyes above the squalid level of party politics, went further. 'President Roosevelt is ready to play a dirty trick on the world and risk the ultimate destruction of the Western Democracies in order to secure the re-election of a Democratic candidate in the United States,' was his considered verdict. 'I feel strongly that we should exert the greatest and most immediate pressure on (him) to prevent him

31

selling the world for his own particular mess of pottage." His cynical appraisal mirrored that of General Franz Halder, Chief of Staff of the German High Command: 'Elections! Angel of Peace!'

Even so, in his search for peace, Welles had endured much. Aside from Chamberlain's querulous self-justification, he had heard Count Ciano, Mussolini's son-in-law and Foreign Minister, denounce Germany's perfidy for concluding her Soviet alliance without even informing Italy. He had twice met an 'elephantine' Mussolini, 'his close-cropped hair snow-white', predicting lugubriously: 'The minute hand is pointing to one minute before midnight.' He had been harangued for two hours non-stop by von Ribbentrop, who sat with eyes almost continually closed as he delivered a hissing monologue denouncing England's 'craft and guile'. 'The man,' Welles noted later, 'is saturated with hate for England.'

From Hitler he had received a raucous tirade: 'I did not want this war. It has been forced upon me against my will . . . My life should have been spent in constructing not destroying.' From Deputy Führer Rudolf Hess he had learned of the necessity for 'a total and crushing German military victory'. Hermann Göring, garbed in a white tunic, his diamond-studded hands 'like the digging paws of a badger', had told Welles that the German Luftwaffe was supreme 'and would remain supreme'.

In Paris, the President of the French Republic, Albert Lebrun, had contributed a potted history of his own life and a conducted tour of the portraits in the Elysée Palace. Premier Edouard Daladier saw no hope for Europe without an airborne international police force to maintain peace. His successor, Paul Reynaud, proudly proclaimed himself 'the hardest man in the French Government with regard to our relations with Germany'.

Out of all these parleys, Welles himself saw one probably vain hope – that some promise of economic assistance, conceivably coal, might yet induce Mussolini to stay out of the conflict.

On 29 March, at a White House press conference, Roosevelt digested these tortuous deliberations into a bleak sentence: 'There may be scant immediate prospects' – a phrase he twice read and emphasised – 'for the establishment of any just, stable and lasting peace in Europe.'

A sense that Western civilisation was now irrevocably at risk prompted *The New York Times* to headline with involuntary humour:

WAR SEEN ENTERING
PHASE OF VIOLENCE

*

As Britain courted trouble in Scandinavia, her enemies in other parts of the world were alerted to step up the pressure. Millions of Indians, Burmans and Malays now looked to Hitler as their liberator from the hated yoke of

32

imperialism, for the Axis looked set to create the new world order which was the Far East's dream.

On 19 March, at Ramgarh, India, one such body-blow to British prestige was narrowly averted. At this, the fifty-third session of the All-Indian National Congress, held in the jungles of Bihar, the party leadership of the tiny ascetic Mahatma Gandhi, whose white cotton loin-cloth was almost a trade-mark was being challenged by a six-foot lawyer and *bon viveur* who had sedulously courted the axis powers all through the 1930s: Subhas Chandra Bose.

From the moment that Hitler secured power in 1933, Bose had been a familiar figure in Berlin's Reich Chancellery. Although he hated the Nazis and all that they stood for, he hated the British who had enslaved his country for three centuries even more. 'It must be done, even if it means the collapse of Europe,' he told all who looked askance at the company he kept. 'British Imperialism in India is as intolerable as Nazi-ism is in Berlin.'

To Bose's chagrin, Gandhi, in September 1939, when India stood at 'the crossroads of history' had approached the Viceroy, Lord Linlithgow, to pledge the Congress Party's unconditional help in prosecuting the war. As Bose saw it, 'an unique opportunity for winning freedom', had been cast away.

Bose promptly seized his own opportunity. He founded the Forward Bloc of the Congress Party, a splinter group pressing for a campaign of civil disobedience – both sit-down strikes and mass demonstrations designed to paralyse British India's shaky economy. By March 1940, he had harangued a thousand meetings, overt subversion which the British tolerated, lest repression led to a nation-wide passive resistance campaign.

To outsiders, it seemed likely that Bose would carry the day. On 28 February, the American Consul-General in Calcutta, J. C. White, reported the air 'thick with rumours of anti-Gandhi demonstrations at Ramgarh'. At railway terminals, Bose supporters had lately greeted the Mahatma with a silent phalanx of black flags – an Indian symbol of rebuke for his devious dalliance with the British Raj. The demand for instant Home Rule was now so clamorous that on 5 March, White reported further: 'The principal danger of these subversive activities at present is sabotage in industrial plants...' Bose declared, '... that if the Government did not retrace its steps, he and his friends would again consider that British gaols were places of pilgrimage for them.'

Gandhi, a master of political timing, adjudged that the moment was not yet ripe. Civil disobedience at the height of a war which the British were waging for their lives, would be 'suicidal', the Mahatma argued. It could lead only to 'anarchy and red ruin', and he would not unleash it.

Thus, on 19 March, as 100,000 Congress Party delegates met in a specially constructed city of bamboo huts at Ramgarh village, the battle for leadership was joined. From the outset, though, the British were in luck, for it was Gandhi who made the running. He urged the Congress guiding committee to pass a resolution in favour of delaying civil disobedience, while yet pressing for independence by negotiation. The Mahatma – whom Consul-General White summed up as 'very shrewd and quite unscrupulous . . . loves the limelight' – next flattered and won his supporters anew by a speech bristling with humility. 'I am called Mahatma (one with supernatural powers) but I am an ordinary man,' he told them. 'I am perhaps the poorest general any army ever had.'

As a result, the Punjab leader Gopal Singh Himh's attack on the Mahatma's behind-the-scenes tactics – 'Everyone is ready for action except Gandhi' – was swiftly rebutted by other top Punjabis. 'Gandhi and Congress,' asserted Sardar Kartar Singh, 'are identical.'

The next day, under blazing sunlight, Bose staged his counter-challenge. In a field across the Damodar River, within shouting distance of the Gandhi camp, he harangued 5,000 of his followers. Damning Gandhi's dilatory tactics, he cited Mussolini's exemplary march on Rome in 1922, when the Fascists stormed the capital and seized power. Then, mounting a farmer's cart drawn by two white bullocks, Bose rode in noisy triumph through the Gandhi lines.

Gandhi's final supporter clinched his victory, for now the Congress President Abul Kalam Azad rose on the dais. Although Gandhi was a Hindu, Azad, himself a Moslem, still hailed the Mahatma as the Congress Party's natural leader – a man who sought Indian's independence as purposefully as Bose but who would attain it more shrewdly.

The next day, 21 March, the delegates, hit by a sudden cloudburst, stood bedraggled and up to their shins in water, and hastily and unanimously voted that their confidence still reposed in the Mahatma. It was, reported Consul-General White one week later, 'an overwhelming triumph' for Gandhi – and, he might have added, for the beleaguered British, too.

*

Restless spring had come to Europe, and with it, a chill wind of fear. Not since Napoleon Bonaparte's nineteenth-century rampage had the small nations, caught up by the relentless pressures of *Realpolitik*, felt so helpless.

There were small signs, but few were yet so sophisticated in war to interpret them correctly. On 6 April, as the Swedish liner *Drottningholm* edged into harbour at Bergen, Norway, the passengers abruptly learned of an unforeseen delay. Word had come that the liner must anchor in mid-harbour for two hours before the quays could be cleared for docking. At this moment, a German depot-ship the *Karl Peters*, was alongside, and, inexplicably, twenty German ore freighters, riding at anchor, with no sign of life aboard.

From mid-harbour, they seemed like ghost ships, their bridges deserted, only faint wisps of blue smoke curling from their funnels.

No one aboard the *Drottningholm* viewed them more curiously than Polly Peabody, a 22-year-old socialite from New York. The grand-daughter of George Peabody, the Massachusetts shipping magnate and philanthropist, Polly was one American of whom Franklin Roosevelt would have whole-heartedly approved; nine-tenths of her childhood had been passed in France and Germany and Polly felt passionately that Europe was her concern. Determined to give all the help she could, Polly had enlisted the aid of Baron Bror Blixen-Finecke, the King of Denmark's cousin, to raise $100,000 through charity appeals and found the American Scandinavian Field Hos-pital, a 28-strong team of doctors and nurses, equipped to furnish post-battle medication to the Finns. Now Polly's smart flat on East Fifty-Fourth Street, the fashionable life of first nights, hectic parties at the Stork Club and weekends with the Vanderbilts on Long Island, were behind her. Ahead stretched the war's front line.

Stepping ashore in Bergen, en route for Oslo with forty-five tons of medical equipment, neither Polly nor any of her team suspected that the front line was even closer at hand. Crouching in the darkened holds of those freighters, German soldiers were awaiting H-Hour.

Two days later on 8 April, strange reports were coming out of Esjberg, Denmark. Truck drivers heading for Hamburg with loads of North Sea fish reported an awesome column of German troops thirty-five miles long marching for the Danish frontier. Even now neutrality died hard; the Prime Minister, 66-year-old Thorvald Stauning, rejected all suggestions that he should mobilise the Army. To do so would be 'a hostile act which would entail consequences'.

Here, too, in four German colliers moored near Copenhagen's Langelinie, the favourite summer promenade dominated by the statue of Hans Ander-sen's 'Little Mermaid', 2,000 German troops lay in readiness.

On the afternoon of 8 April, Erik Seidenfaden, the Danish newsman, who a month before had scooped the world's press on the Finnish armistice, boarded the afternoon flight from Copenhagen to Oslo, a 16-seater Junkers JU 52. This time Seidenfaden thought himself fully briefed on the story he was to cover; the British had announced to the world their intention of mining Norwegian waters and Seidenfaden aimed to see them in action.

He was due for a surprise. Among the passengers was a man he knew well, Captain Riiser-Larsen, Chief of Staff of the Norwegian Air Force. Suddenly a white-jacketed steward came hastening down the aisle: Larsen was wanted in the cockpit.

Curious as to why, Seidenfaden craned from the window and beheld an astounding sight. Six thousand feet below, the grey waters of the Kattegat separating Denmark from Sweden, were black with German warships: the

35

battle-cruisers *Scharnhorst* and *Gneisenau*, the cruisers *Blücher* and *Emden*, along with many torpedo boats, destroyers, E-boats and other craft. By pure chance, Seidenfaden had netted another scoop — yet such was the mental climate of 1940 that he failed to recognise it.

His first instinct was to rationalise the scene: the German Navy was reacting swiftly to Britain's defiant pronouncement. Thus there seemed every chance that the two Navies would do battle to the death in the Atlantic Ocean off the Norwegian coastline. The realisation that he was witnessing a full-dress invasion of Norway never even occurred to him.

Thus when the plane touched down at Oslo's Fornebu airport, Seidenfaden hastened not to a phone booth but to the Press Gallery of the *Storting*, the rotunda-shaped Parliament building on Karl Johansgaten. The day's big story, he thought, would certainly be the formal protest that Foreign Minister Halvdan Koht would deliver to the British. But the debate dragged on so long and inconclusively that it was too late to file a cable for *Politiken*'s morning edition. By midnight, Seidenfaden was in bed and asleep at Oslo's Grand Hotel.

Soon after 4 am on 9 April, a phone call brought him very wide awake. It was his colleague Sten Gudme, calling from Copenhagen. German troops had crossed the Danish frontier.

It was an invasion with bizarre undertones. At 4.30 am the German Minister, Count Cecil von Renthe-Fink, who had all along believed Ribbentrop's assurance that Denmark's neutrality would be honoured, tearfully awoke the Foreign Minister, Dr Peter Munch, to announce that they were now at war. Munch's first thought was to arouse King Christian X, but despite his efforts the phone at Amalienborg Palace rang on unanswered. In desperation Munch at last despatched a taxi-driver to wake up the Court for the most fateful Cabinet meeting in Denmark's 1,000-year history.

As the lights of Copenhagen burned brightly in the night, Admiral Rechnitzer, the Naval C.-in-C. stubbornly refused to order his ships to open fire; one year earlier, Admiral Raeder had solemnly assured him that Germany would never attack Denmark. Few among the country's four million citizens ever realised that within a two-and-a-half hour time span, a bloodless occupation was taking place; as German troops poured ashore unopposed along the Langelinie, night shift workers cycling home thought that a movie was being shot. Sporadic rifle fire spattered through the streets but no one, least of all the Danish Cabinet, knew for certain what was going on. At Amalienborg Palace, King Christian X, aware that his army was in no shape to fight, ordered an immediate cease-fire, but the C.-in-C., General W. W. Pryor, indignantly refused to pass on the order. At 6.25 am, the King's Adjutant did it for him, and all fighting ceased.

In the *Politiken* newsroom, near the City Hall, Seidenfaden's colleagues were bemused as the teletypes of the Ritzaus Bureau, the national news agency, clattered out its messages: 'Korsør, 9th April, R.B. – German troops landed here at 5 am.' Even as they debated, an aerial blizzard of green surrender leaflets, couched in a gibberish mixture of German, Danish and Norwegian was descending on the city. Nearby, in the Palace Hotel, the German Commandant, General Leonhard Kaupisch, who had checked in as a tourist one day earlier, was placidly changing into uniform.

Despite the humiliation that had befallen his country, King Christian received the German Chief of Staff, General Kurt Himer, in sporting spirit: 'General, may I tell you something? As soldier to soldier? You Germans have done the incredible again!'

Three hundred miles north, in Oslo, the Germans had achieved a surprise as total. At 11.30 pm on 8 April, the Prime Minister, Johan Nygaardsvold, was abruptly awoken by a call from his Minister of Defence, Colonel Birger Ljungberg. The ships that Erik Seidenfaden had sighted earlier were now entering Oslo Fjord.

'Have mines been laid?' Nygaardsvold asked, but Ljungberg's answer was negative.

'Why not?' the Premier wanted to know. 'It was too late,' Ljungberg replied lamely. 'They can't be laid in the dark.'

For the last time, the tired old man who controlled Scandinavia's destinies had hesitated too long.

Inexplicably, the lights in the city centre had been extinguished by a master switch; the 11-man Norwegian Cabinet, unable to find a taxi between them, had to grope their way in total darkness to the Foreign Office on Vika Terrassen. Inexplicably, too, for no aircraft were as yet overhead, the air-raid sirens kept up an eerie non-stop wail – 'like a bunch of trucks with their horns jammed', one man was to recall. In the Foreign Minister's office, the Cabinet could confer only by the wavering light of candles; when the German Minister to Norway, Dr Curt Bräuer, arrived to deliver his ultimatum, Foreign Minister Koht had to hold a candle above the text to enable the German to read it.

The news grew worse hourly. At intervals the telephone, a direct link with the Ministry of Defence, rang shrilly in the darkness. At 2 am the Germans were pouring ashore in Bergen, from the freighters which Polly Peabody had noticed, then at Kristiansand, at Trondheim and at Narvik. At length, the Cabinet decided on mobilisation, though incredibly no man among them thought of using the radio. Towards dawn on 9 April, mobilisation notices were sent out by post.

But on one point the Cabinet was unanimous: neither they nor King Haakon VII and his Court or the 150 Members of Parliament must fall into German hands. Promptly they issued an Order in Council transferring their seat to Hamar, seventy miles north, along with twenty truck-loads of gold reserves. It was a decision taken so hastily that many citizens of Oslo still

37

had not realised that the Germans were on their way. When the President of the *Storting*, Carl Hambro, told the Chief of Police, the man just stared at him sceptically.

'Surely you have the date wrong, Mr President?' he ventured. 'This is not the 1st of April, this is the 9th.'

*

In the iron-ore port of Narvik, 700 miles up the coast from Oslo, the Mayor, 36-year-old Theodor Broch, was asleep in his house on the Framnes Peninsula, fifteen minutes' walk from the main square. A dark dedicated man, and a lifelong Socialist, Broch had hung up his lawyer's shingle in Narvik ten years earlier and for six of those years had officiated as Mayor. Although he and his wife Ellen were natives of Oslo, both found Narvik's smalltown ambience curiously beguiling; the roast beef and tinned pineapple dinners that every family of substance took turns to give, the sedate 8 pm promenades along Street One each evening after supper, when a man might raise his hat fully thirty times in ceremonial greeting. 'Could anything ever happen in such a sleepy little town?' Broch had asked Ellen once.

At 4.45 am on 9 April, Broch, belatedly, had his answer. The little yellow house with the green window frames was rocking as violently as if an earthquake had struck. As explosion followed explosion, Broch and Ellen tumbled from bed. 'It's probably dynamiting on the iron company's grounds,' was Broch's first explanation, but as he parted the window curtains he knew that he was wrong. The thick mist that blanketed the harbour was shot through with tongues of flame. 'That's not from the company, that's from the sea!' Ellen cried distraught.

Above the thunder of the bombardment, the Brochs now heard the patter of small bare feet. The noise had awakened their 3-year-old daugher, Siri, mindful of her father's promise that all ships in harbour would stage a firework display on Christmas Eve. 'Is it Christmas?' Siri asked anxiously.

Dressing hastily, Broch ran for Narvik's town centre. There he stopped short, stupefied. Huge flags with black swastikas were flying above the City Hall and the Telegraph Building. German soldiers loaded with hand grenades 'as though they were walking Christmas trees', swarmed everywhere in the cobbled square. Broch acted fast. In his City Hall offices, he buttonholed the first clerks arriving, speeding them to contact all members of the City Council and the railway and hospital authorities. Within the hour, as the first arrivals gathered round the green baize table, disquieting news was filtering through. Two Norwegian men-of-war, the *Eidsvold* and the *Norge*, had been torpedoed in the harbour, with appalling loss of life. Few among the council members could find words to express what they felt;

all of them, as neutral Norwegians, were still groping in the dark. 'We understood, and yet could not understand,' Broch said later.

At dawn, an escort of German soldiers stomped into City Hall. Broch and the Chief of Police were summoned to the Grand Hotel to meet the commanding general, *Generalleutnant* Edouard 'The Bull' Dietl, a pre-war ski-ing champion. To Broch's astonishment, Dietl, a tall stooping man, was crimson with mortification; he lacked the necessary Norwegian kröner to pay off the cab which had brought him from the harbour. 'Only an oversight, Herr Mayor,' he apologised profusely.

Then, crisp and businesslike, Dietl made the German position clear. 'We have come as friends to protect your country against any further British breaches of your neutrality. Norway is now occupied peacefully in the name of *Der Führer.* 'Meanwhile,' Dietl added, 'the civil administration must continue as usual.'

Still bewildered, Broch and the Police Chiefs returned to the City Council. A long day stretched ahead, and with it many decisions. Their first was to evacuate as many civilians as possible, and within this time-span as many as 1,500 civilians left by boat for neighbouring islands. The Germans had fixed the currency rate at one *kröne* sixty *öre* to the *reichmark* and this fact had to be explained to countless shopkeepers. Ration cards must be printed; to avoid incipient trouble, liquor stores must close. The whole day was a nightmare of activity, and Broch, a devout man, thanked God for it. For the moment, at least, there was no time to think about what had gone wrong.

It was late when Broch arrived home. Soon, drugged with exhaustion, he and Ellen had retired to bed. Next morning, Siri woke them early.

'Isn't it Christmas today either?'

'No, it is war,' her father told her.

'Is war nice?' Siri asked.

*

On this same eventful day, at 7.32 pm a legend was born. A tall fair-haired blue-eyed man, untidily dressed, with bulging eyes, accompanied by three henchmen, bluffed his way into Oslo's radio station and seized a microphone to tell almost three million Norwegians: 'The Nygaardsvold Government has withdrawn. The national government has assumed power with Vidkun Quisling as its head.'

In this way Vidkun Quisling passed into history as one of Dr Göbbels' greatest propaganda triumphs. Embodying as he did the myth of the Fifth Column, Quisling unwittingly helped to spread the clever innuendo that the Germans had previously recruited a large army of secret agents, 'the patriotic traitors' in every country they took over.

The truth was more prosaic. A stubborn opinionated man, Quisling was an ineffectual dreamer, patterned on the lines of Ibsen's Pee Gynt. A one-time Minister of Defence, and founder of the ultra-right Nasjonal Samling (National Unity) Party, he had been for years in the political wilderness — never at any time polling more than 30,000 votes. Even so he saw himself as a political messiah, believing with many of his European ilk that Bolshevism was the 'unspeakably dangerous enemy' which Germany alone could quell.

To be sure, in December 1939, Quisling had had two meetings with Hitler in Berlin, an encounter stage-managed by Admiral Raeder, who was exploring the chances of a Norwegian coup from within. 'What were the chances?' Hitler asked them, but Quisling had thought very few. He had barely 80,000 supporters in all Norway.

Despite subsequent legend, there was little evidence that Quisling had any coup in mind. Although a Nasjonal Samling congress had assembled in Oslo days earlier, Quisling had dispersed the party caucus on the final day. The sudden arrival of the Germans had surprised him as much as anyone — and General von Falkenhorst had received no instructions to seek his co-operation. It was not treachery but the total passivity of the departed Government that abetted his take-over; Quisling saw the vacuum and moved swiftly to fill it.

The result was as vexed a chapter of misunderstandings as any in Norwegian history. 'When the German arrived,' Quisling was to complain bitterly, 'they did not even pay their respects.' The reason was simple: few of them even knew he existed. In his extempore broadcast, Quisling had grandiloquently named an 8-man Cabinet — but most of them were not Party members and had never met Quisling.

Thus, on 11 April, a stinging rebuke for Quisling came in a phone call from von Ribbentrop. Germany could not possibly recognise his pretensions, Ribbentrop raged, since Ambassador Bräuer was still trying to find the king and reach a settlement with him. As Quisling listened to this savage tongue-lashing, his secretary, Harald Franklin Knudsen, watched his face turn ashen.

Now, as so often, Hitler stepped in to complicate the situation anew. Over-ruling Ribbentrop's objections that Quisling had little value and that the King was the constitutional monarch, the Führer insisted that Germany must stand by Quisling. Heartened by this backing, Quisling, as *de facto* Premier, sent an emissary, Captain Kjeld Irgens, Commodore of the Norwegian–American line, to persuade King Haakon to return to the capital. He suggested that an arrangement could be reached similar to that of Denmark, where Haakon's brother, King Christian, continued to rule.

When the King, predictably, refused, Ribbentrop once again went to work on Hitler. Far from winning friends for Germany, he urged, Quisling's presence was making matters worse for the occupation forces. Hitler, reluctantly, then yielded to persuasion. At noon on 15 April, six days after appointing himself Premier, Quisling was forced to resign. The logic was inescapable: since none of his 'Cabinet' had answered the call, there was no Government for him to head. On 24 April, Josef Terboven, the *Gauleiter* of Essen, became Hitler's *Reichskommissar* for Norway.

Four months later, Hitler's further intercession put Quisling back into politics, despite the vehement opposition of von Ribbentrop, Terboven and General von Falkenhorst. But since the Government was now subservient to Terboven, Quisling refused to serve in it; as leader of the Nasjonal Samling Party, he merely exercised indirect influence on the eight Party members in the 13-strong Cabinet. Even so, his ultimate fate would be to take the blame for every error that they perpetrated thereafter.

Unwittingly, though, Quisling served Germany better than he knew. In the weeks and months that followed, his name, symbolising treachery from within, was to cast a pall of fear and suspicion over all Europe.*

*

For thousands of Norwegians, Quisling's impulsive broadcast had just one effect: it stiffened their will to resist. At first, stunned by the impact, Oslo's 258,000 citizens had watched with awe as 1,500 goose-stepping troops of General von Falkenhorst's advance guard took over the capital unopposed. Dazzled by the bandoliers of bronzed bullets gleaming in the sunlight, they stared, as one man put it, 'like children seeing a new kind of animal'. Many flocked to hear the 12-piece German band playing 'Roll out the Barrel' in the park beside the *Storting*, and The Grand Hotel's doorman was quick to cultivate the Nazi salute. But with Quisling's broadcast, much of the passivity was changed. 'If the choice is between Quisling and war,' one man summed up, 'we'll take war.'

By 10 April, the greatest migration in modern Norwegian history was under way. The southern half of the country came quietly alive with moving men: young men in sports coats, toting rucksacks, armed with nothing more than sheath knives, trekking across Oslo's Nordmarka Park and slipping northwards into the forests. Some were college students, others were labourers and taxi-drivers, and few had ever fired a gun, but all of them were intent on fighting a desperate delaying action from village to village and farm to farm. To one American observer, recalling the War of Independence, these were Norway's Minute Men, militia who had pledged to enter the fray at a moment's notice, and for them each township would be as bitterly contested as Lexington, Massachusetts.

* On 19 April, the London *Times*, pondering Quisling's name had an alliterative field-day: 'Visually [the word Quisling] has the supreme merit of beginning with a Q, which has long seemed to the British mind to be a crooked, uncertain and slightly disreputable letter, suggestive of the questionable, the querulous, the quavering of quaking quagmires, and quivering quicksands, of quibbles and quarrels, of queasiness, quackery, qualms and quilp'.

Even the 'regulars' like the men of the Alta Battalion, north of Narvik, who rallied to the Norwegian C.-in-C., General Otto Ruge, were fishermen and crofters, some with no more than forty-eight days military training, who went into battle wearing ski-ing outfits made from old table- cloths.

The lot of a youngster like Eiliv Hauge, a clerk living in Asker, a small suburb of Oslo, was typical. Reaching the city by street-car around 9 am on 9 April, Hauge found his office deserted. At the Norsk Telegrambyra (Norwegian News Agency) Bureau, nearby, he heard that mobilisation had been cancelled. But back in Asker, other rumours were current: mobilisation day was Thursday, 11 April, and the mobilisation point was at Hönefoss, thirty miles away. Promptly Hauge and a friend hitched a ride there but not a soldier was to be seen. Another group of youngsters, chatting on a street corner, said they had been told to wait; the Army was not yet ready to take on recruits.

Soon a fresh rumour was current; the nearest military H.Q. was at nearby Helgelandsmoen, and recruits should report there. Hitching another ride, Hauge finally hit on a barracks, where soldiers were loading up trucks, preparatory to pulling out. A passing officer protested that he was too busy to talk; what did Hauge want? 'We thought of joining up to fight the Germans,' Hauge explained. The man brushed him aside: 'Then simply go into the depot and find a uniform that fits.' Almost before he realised it, Hauge was an infantryman.

Later that day, the unit, now 250 strong, moved out, crammed into trucks and buses, moving steadily northwards. Hauge thought he was part of the 6th Regiment, but nobody knew for certain. As they went, cheering storekeepers made up their deficiencies, pressing free sleeping bags on them, skis, even sets of plus fours. By night they bedded down in barns and sheds and farm women cooked for them, feeding them on smoked lamb and potato cakes. By day, Hauge grappled for the first time with the mysteries of a Krag-Jörgensen service rifle.

Two days later, crouched in a mountain pass, Hauge and all of them got their first taste of action. A long column of German buses was stalled by the tree-trunk barrier the Norwegians had erected and as the Germans descended, puzzled and angry, the unit opened fire. The surprise was complete: rifle and mortar-gun fire tore into the scattering Germans. Within minutes, four buses were blazing; the dead and wounded lay in heaps, groaning and crying aloud. White flags of truce were waved in vain; coming shamefully of age, Hauge and his comrades fired on these, too, until 200 Germans lay silent in the snow.

'Earlier wars were like boxing,' summed up the Columbia Broadcasting System's Ed Murrow, at this time, 'hitting only with the fists and above the belt. This one is rapidly reaching the point where nothing is barred – teeth, feet, heads, toes and fingers will be used by all belligerents; anything to get at a vulnerable part of the opponent's anatomy.'

Erik Seidenfaden, still in search of a story, was meanwhile dogging the Norwegian Cabinet on their journey north. Plans were formulated, then changed overnight: no sooner had they reached Hamar, seventy miles from Oslo, than it was decided to split the party in two. The Cabinet and 150 members of Parliament moved on to Elverum, thirty miles north-east. King Haakon VII with Crown Prince Olav and their entourage went to Nyberg-sund, forty-five miles farther on and barely twenty miles from the Swedish frontier.

Seidenfaden was fascinated by his first-ever glimpse of government-on-the-run. When officials needed petty cash, Finance Minister Oscar Torp, had to dig deep into the rucksack that he kept beneath his bed. Other Ministers toured the village, buying up its entire stock of paper and pencils to transact Cabinet business. Already Elverum was filled to bursting point as more and more refugees poured in, and even staid Ministers were living a gipsy life. In one guest-house kitchen, twenty-seven people were attempting to boil eggs on one stove. Others clustered at the pump in the yard, breaking icicles to clean their teeth.

By sheer mischance, Seidenfaden had arrived one day too late for the most sensational aspect of the flight thus far. Angered that King Haakon had spurned entreaties to return to the capital from both the German Minister, Dr Bräuer and Quisling's emissary, Captain Irgens, the German High Command made an illiberal attempt to wipe out the Royal party.

At 5.20 pm on 11 April, as the King was conferring with his Cabinet in the inn at Nybergsund, an urgent tooting of car horns from the road signalled enemy aircraft were approaching. Minutes later, as the King, still struggling with his topcoat, hastened towards the edge of the forest, followed by his Ministers, seven German bombers swooped low over the rooftops. As the King dived head first for a spruce grove, crawling on hands and knees, a whistling rain of high explosive bombs bracketed the forest. Machine-gun bullets whipped the snow into frantic flurries, and barns and outhouses took fire, the flames bright red against the white dead land. In a panic-stricken effort to make themselves invisible, some Ministers took off their dark topcoats, then, shivering and numb with cold, hastily put them on again. For more than one hour the bombers raked the forest, swooping low more than a dozen times: tall firs snapped like matchsticks and earth and snow cascaded skywards until every man's face and hair was plastered black with dirt.

At long last the bombers gave up, droning away in a straight line towards the west, and an eerie hush descended. The sun had gone down below the edge of the forest, leaving the sky a livid red. Stiff and frozen, the Government Party picked their way back towards the burning village. At their head marched the gaunt 68-year-old King Haakon, still clutching a spent machine-gun bullet.

'This is a personal present,' he proclaimed dryly, 'from Hitler to me.'

*

For Theodor Broch, in Narvik, there could be no thought of flight. As Mayor, it was his duty, for the time being, at least, to stay put.

News from the outside world filtered through with difficulty. All the townsfolk were shattered by the news of the bombing attack on their King, although they took fresh heart as they heard of the gallant resistance of the Minute Men. On 13 April, crouched in a cellar out of earshot of the Germans, Broch and his Council heard a secret broadcast by the King urging them all to stand fast. By now, the fury of the naval battle raging between the Germans and the Allies in Narvik Fjord decided Broch to move Ellen and Siri away from the house on the Framnes Peninsula. At night, all three bedded down on the floors of friends' houses in the city centre. In daylight hours, Broch worked from the City Hall basement, cohering the rationing system, regulating wages according to each man's family burden, planning the conversion of cellars into air raid shelters with the City Engineer.

On Sunday, 14 April, Broch, sitting sombrely outside the office of General Edouard Dietl in Narvik's Royal Hotel, saw the end of all he had striven for. Under Section 36 of German Military Law the General had just condemned him to death for sabotage.

Broch reflected wryly that the sentence was just. Towards 4 pm on 13 April, the British naval bombardment had become so awe inspiring that many German troops had withdrawn from the town. Fully nine destroyers — among them the flotilla leader, *Heidkamp*, *Roeder* and *Schmitt*, and the ammunition ship, *Ravenfels* — had been sunk or crippled in the harbour.

With only a few Germans remaining in Narvik, Broch saw this as the moment when the Allies had to land. Along with three of the town's volunteer firemen he hastened to the telephone exchange. Only one non-com remained on duty, but though Broch and his men were unarmed, the Mayor bluffed the German that the game was up. The British were already disembarking, and Narvik was once more Norwegian. The corporal, bowing to the inevitable, surrendered his pistol, but Broch's triumph was short-lived. As they prepared to leave the exchange, a squad of fifty Germans came marching down the street. Abandoning their prisoner, Broch and his volunteers fled precipitately, bullets whining in their wake. That evening he had been arrested and now, on the early morning of 14 April, he sat awaiting the firing squad.

Two hours later, the situation had changed again. An uncomprehending Broch heard from the German Army prosecutor that an urgent plea from

44

the City Council, stressing that Broch spoke German and was indispensable to the civil administration, had decided General Dietl to pardon him. He must report to German Military H.Q. twice a day, but was otherwise free to go. 'They wanted to win the Norwegian war without fighting the Norwegians as well,' was Broch's later appraisal.

Nonetheless, in the Narvik area, the Norwegians alone were contesting Dietl's troops. Word had come through, on 17 April, of Anglo–French landings, but where, Broch and the townsfolk asked one another, and when?

As Broch stared out across the shell-torn piers and blackened wreckage of the harbour, a German lieutenant seemed to read his thoughts. 'I can assure you of one thing,' he told Broch scornfully. 'Your friends the British will never come.'

*

On Monday, 15 April, some 20,000 British troops, aboard warships at anchor along the Norwegian coast, were indeed preparing to go ashore. Their task, in Churchill's words, was to 'purge and cleanse the soil of the Vikings . . . from the filthy pollution of Nazi tyranny'.

In the course of the next seventy-two hours they would find tentative toe-holds on Harstad island, forty miles from Narvik, at Bödo and Mo, towns below Narvik, at Namsos, 100 miles north of the vital port of Trondheim, at Molde and Andalsnes, 125 miles south-west of Trondheim and at Laerdal, 130 miles from Norway's biggest (and German-held) airbase, Stavanger.

Though their commander, General Mackesy, did not yet realise it, their chances of establishing any permanent bases were minimal. Mackesy, in any case, was at his wits' end: between 5 April and 12 April, when he sailed from Scapa Flow, he had received three separate sets of orders from the War Office, each cancelling the other. One instruction, however, remained finite: Mackesy was not to attempt any landing if the Norwegians opposed him. Yet the operation's naval commander, Admiral of the Fleet the Earl of Cork and Orrery, had been briefed by the Admiralty to prepare for a no-holds-barred assault.

Most of Mackesy's other instructions had been concerned with minutiae — 'There should be considerable numbers of ponies [in Narvik] . . . let no question of paying trouble you . . . don't allow any haggling over prices.' But what troops were at his disposal, where they were located, and how they were armed, as yet remained a mystery.

The answers to these questions finally appalled him. At Andalsnes, the total strength of the so-called 148 Brigade, added up to two battalions — two companies of Sherwood Foresters, and one of Leicesters — raw conscripts, lacking entrenching tools, all of them armed with rifles but some of them lacking topcoats. These men, equipped with mortars but with only smoke

45

bombs as ammunition, were expected to stand fast against the Germans in the freezing slush of Tretten Gorge, inland from Andalsnes.

At Harstad, the 1/4th Kings Own Yorkshire Light Infantry, having landed on the island, found no boats to transport them ashore. They, too, lacked artillery and field-pieces, yet were so weighed down with kit they could scarcely walk; their lambskin Arctic coats alone weighed 15 lb. They had been victualled with just two days supplies and since ponies were nowhere to be seen, the sole communication between companies was a runner on a bicycle.

These troops were as ill-equipped to fight a campaign in barren mountainous land as the Russians had been in Finland, but with this difference: no irresistible flood-tide of men existed to reinforce them if they failed.

Predictably, within four days, the front had fallen apart.

At Steinkjer, north of Trondheim, on 20 April, the two British battalions comprising 146 Brigade, the King's Own Yorkshire Light Infantry, and the Hallamshires, lacking both anti-aircraft guns and air cover, were soon punch-drunk and reeling as the Luftwaffe enjoyed a field-day of strafing along the Namsos–Steinkjer road. 'It was just bloody slaughter,' one K.O.Y.L.I. officer raged impotently.

By 21 April, 146 were withdrawing by night, linking hands to maintain contact in the darkness, discarding their steel helmets to avoid recognition from the air when daylight came. After four days in Norway, they were in headlong retreat, a 58-mile flight, that lasted forty-two hours. 148 Brigade, pulling out from Tretten, were down to 300 men and nine officers. With no more concrete orders than, 'Make for Andalsnes', they too, had ceased to exist as a fighting unit.

Even as General Otto Ruge rallied his Norsemen, 'The time for retreating is past,' that time for the British, had only just begun and the first of many bitter recriminations they would incur from their Allies were about to be voiced. On 30 April, as the Navy re-embarked the battered battalions from Andalsnes, a Norwegian, who had covered the withdrawal of 146 Brigade from Steinkjer commented: 'It looks as if the British are going to fight to the last Norwegian.'

Within two weeks, the remnant of these bruised bemused men would come under a new Commander, who on his own initiative supplanted Mackesy: Major-General Claude Auchinleck, a veteran of the Indian Army. His assessment of their calibre as soldiers was unremittingly stern, and presaged trouble for other British commanders if and when Hitler launched his offensive in the West.

'By comparison with the French, or the Germans for that matter,' Auchinleck growled, 'our men for the most part seemed distressingly young, not so much in years as in self-reliance and manliness generally.

'They give an impression of being callow and undeveloped, which is not reassuring for the future . . .'

46

3

'This War Is Sheer Madness'

25 April–25 May, 1940

IN LONDON, on Tuesday, 7 May, the atmosphere in the fine panelled Chamber of the House of Commons was electric with suspense. By 3 pm the Peers' Gallery was crowded, the Distinguished Strangers' Gallery packed out with the massed ambassadors and ministers of two dozen nations. One of the gravest debates in the history of Parliament, whose outcome might decide the fate of the British Empire, was about to begin. Its central issue was the ignominious flight of the British Expeditionary Force from Namsos, Norway.

As Neville Chamberlain rose from the Government Front Bench at 3.48 pm a volley of boos and catcalls from the Labour Opposition greeted him. 'He missed the bus! He missed the bus! Resign! Resign!' At first the Premier rocked slightly, as if receiving a physical blow, but there was otherwise no sign that he was affected. Although he had been challenged to address the House on the mounting disaster in Norway, Chamberlain's faith in his own judgement was still unwavering. 'I'm quite confident we shall get away with it,' he had told an aide earlier, as he left 10, Downing Street. On his own briefing he had noted in longhand: 'Extenuate nothing, but exaggerate nothing. Not a Gallipoli.'

But even a Chamberlain supporter as devout as Henry 'Chips' Channon, the Tory M.P. for Southend-on-Sea, was forced to admit that the Premier 'did not make a good case'. In the face of defeat, he could do little but praise the courage of the soldiers, sailors and airmen as they retreated from position to position. He angered the Labour Opposition by reminding them haughtily that the debate was a concession at most. Now the baying cries of 'He missed the bus!' echoed from Tory dissidents, too, but still, for fifty-seven minutes, Chamberlain rambled on, a querulous spate of self-exculpation such as Sumner Welles would have recognised. It was a speech so devoid of substance that the Egyptian Ambassador dropped off to sleep.

Try as Chamberlain might to juggle the book-keeping, the balance on Norway showed deep red. Even as the debate wore on, Hitler was in the process of snatching a neutral state from under the muzzles of British naval guns, and this was only one ironic aspect. At one moment on 9 April, the rumour that 800 British bombers were approaching Oslo had emptied the streets of the capital, yet all told, the British only possessed 200 bombers and none of them was then approaching Norway. In the vital forty-eight hours when the Germans were taking over Oslo, no Allied bombers had struck at Fornebu Airport. 'If the British had struck then,' a German colonel told the *Christian Science Monitor*'s Edmund Stevens, 'our whole expedition would have ended in disaster. Fortunately, one can always count on the British to arrive too late.'

There were other disquieting factors – among them, Churchill's irrational obsession with Narvik. It was true that whoever controlled central and southern Norway would ultimately gain Narvik as a prize – but to single out Narvik as an operational base for the entire Norwegian campaign was never remotely on the cards. Yet even now, on 7 May, as the first contingent of raw and routed troops returned to Britain, 25,000 men were still involved in a vain attempt to capture the port. The prestige factor of Narvik now outweighed all other considerations.

The true prize of war, as Norway's General Ruge had urged Chamberlain, had been Trondheim, for whoever held Oslo and Trondheim would ultimately hold Norway, once the linking valleys had been secured. 'We are coming in great strength,' had been Chamberlain's reply to Ruge, meaning the diversion of three battalions of conscripts, all of whom had been badly mauled and then shipped out from Namsos.

Still convinced from his weekly postbag that Britons saw him as their saviour, the man whose 1938 Munich agreement had averted the onset of war by ceding much of Czechoslovakia to Germany, Chamberlain's obstinacy and vanity permitted him no self-doubts. Burdened by 'a mind considered enlightened and advanced at the end of the nineteenth century', he barely recognised that not only the Opposition but the rebels of his own Tory Party, men whose phones he had not hesitated to tap, were out to topple him.

Few among the latter were more determined than tubby little Leo Amery, a former Secretary of State for the Colonies. But Amery, noted as a turgid orator, had emptied the Chamber more than once in the past; at 8.3 pm, when he rose to speak, all but twelve among 500 M.P.s had left the House. It was the Liberal Party's Clement Davies, sensing Amery's wrath, who took it upon himself to act as an unofficial Whip, hustling through lobbies, the smoking room and the dining room, urging Members to return. And many, as they drifted back, sensed like Major-General Edward Spears, Tory M.P. for Carlisle, that Amery's 'small squat figure' was 'hurling stones as large as himself'.

Amery himself, though bitterly incensed against the Chamberlain regime, was uncertain as to how far he could decently go. The immortal words of Oliver Cromwell dismissing the Long Parliament in 1653, had earlier crossed his mind, but he at first shrank from using them. Then suddenly, catching the admiring glance of David Lloyd George, the Liberals' elder statesman and himself a former Prime Minister, Amery summoned up courage. 'You have sat here too long for any good you have been doing', was his savage finale, 'Depart, I say – let us have done with you. In the name of God, go!'

'I hope the matter will not end with fine speeches in the Commons,' the South African Premier, Jan Smuts, noted in his diary, but his concern was premature. The next day, 8 May, saw fine speeches in plenty, but much more besides. At first light, Captain Martin Lindsay, the first Namsos staff officer to reach London, alighted from the night train from Scotland and called Clement Attlee, Leader of the Labour Opposition, at the House of Commons. Although a pre-war Tory candidate, Lindsay saw plainly where his duty lay. Over lunch at the Athenaeum, he gave Attlee a chapter-and-verse briefing on the scandal of the territorial battalions at Steinkjer and Tretten, evidence which Attlee was quick to pass on to Labour's Herbert Morrison, the pugnacious one-eyed leader of the London County Council. Morrison was opening that afternoon's debate for the Opposition.

Although Morrison, no military man, blithely confused 'divisions' with 'battalions', the case he presented was overwhelming. He concluded it with a flat ultimatum: not only Chamberlain but his old cronies from the appeasement era, Secretary for Air Sir Samuel Hoare and Chancellor of the Exchequer Sir John Simon must also resign.

It was then, with three sentences, that Chamberlain destroyed himself. Although he had yawned all through Morrison's speech, he was on his feet in an instant – 'showing his teeth like a rat in a corner', as Labour's Hugh Dalton pictured him. 'I accept the challenge,' he cried petulantly, 'I welcome it, indeed! At least we shall see who is with and who is against us, and I will call on my friends to support me in the lobby tonight.'

Those words were a fatal blunder. By reducing so grave a debate to the level of personal loyalties, Chamberlain gave his opponents a club which they now wielded mercilessly. On the evening of this day, Churchill, who bore as much blame for Norway as anyone, did his best to support his leader, but Lloyd George, in one sharp sentence, demolished much of his effectiveness. 'The right honourable gentleman,' he countered, 'must not allow himself to be converted into an air-raid shelter to keep the splinters from hitting his colleagues!'

Churchill's speech, though no great oration, was at least an honest exposition of the Norwegian failure and an earnest plea for national unity. Moreover, in the fifty minutes that he spoke, he demonstrated that he was the one man present commanding the respect of a vast majority of the House. As Big Ben's chimes sounded 11 pm, it was Churchill who called for a vote of confidence on the question of adjournment or further debate.

'Don't speak too convincingly,' the Tory M.P. for Stockton-on-Tees,

Harold Macmillan, had warned him earlier in the smoking room. 'We must have a new Prime Minister and it must be you.'

Now an astonishing sight was seen. Despite the implacable resentment on the face of the Tory Chief Whip, Captain David Margesson, almost every Tory in uniform was streaming into the Opposition lobby to vote against the Government. At least one officer had tears streaming down his face. One dissident was Captain Quintin Hogg (later Lord Hailsham), protesting 'the total failure of the War Office to provide for his battalion's equipment or training'. Another was the Tory M.P. for Smethwick, Captain Roy Wise, a Namsos veteran, who explained simply: 'I voted on behalf of my men.'

Ten minutes after the division, Margesson announced the result: for adjournment, 281 votes, against, 200. A split second later, Labourites, Liberals and dissident Tories reverted to the same steady barracking that had marked much of the debate: 'Resign! Go! Go!' In vain, Margesson signalled to the faithful to cheer their Leader; the scene of what Chamberlain's Minister of Information, Sir John (later Lord) Reith, termed 'disgusting jubilee', continued unabated. As Harold Macmillan struck up a tuneless chant of 'Rule Britannia', Chamberlain's loyal Transport Minister, Captain Euan Wallace, barely restrained himself from striking Macmillan across the face.

Pale and angry, smiling wanly, Chamberlain left then, picking his way with difficulty over the outstretched legs of his followers. The time was 11.10 pm on Wednesday, 8 May.

*

Few Prime Ministers, aside from Neville Chamberlain, would have tried to cling to office with a majority of 81, in a House traditionally Tory by a lead of 210. Even so, for two days thereafter, Chamberlain worked stubbornly to maintain himself in power. One Churchill crony, Brendan Bracken, commented disgustedly. 'It's as hard getting rid of him as getting a leech off a corpse.'

The accommodation that Chamberlain now sought was one that he had rejected in the past: a National Government, with seats in the Cabinet for Labourites Attlee and Arthur Greenwood, along with the Liberal leader, Sir Archibald Sinclair. But even initial parleys between intermediaries revealed this as a hollow hope. Labour would be prepared to discuss entering the Government, Hugh Dalton told the Tory Under Secretary of State for Foreign Affairs, R. A. Butler, provided that Chamberlain, Sir John Simon and Sir Samuel Hoare resigned. Although Butler objected – 'there is great loyalty to Neville among the Tories' – Dalton was inflexible. 'In our view, Chamberlain and Simon have failed so often, both in peace and war, and have such long crime sheets that they must go.'

Ironically, the last man that Labour sought as Prime Minister was Winston Churchill, whom they viewed as a die-hard reactionary. Their unanimous choice was Lord Halifax, known to some for his air of pious sincerity as 'Lord Holy Fox '. But Halifax all along demurred; he could not sit in the House of Lords and at the same time serve as Prime Minister. On the morning of 10 May, Chamberlain, who had once stigmatised Attlee as 'a cowardly cur' made one last effort to wheedle the Labour Party to accept seats in his Cabinet. Attlee's reply left little room for doubt: 'Mr Prime Minister . . . our party won't have you, and I think I am right in saying that the country won't have you either.'

King George VI had as little enthusiasm for Churchill, but Halifax's refusal to assume power left him little choice. It was left only for Attlee and Greenwood to hasten to Bournemouth and obtain approval for their negotiations from the Labour Party Congress. 'Not very impressive,' commented the Labour pundit, Harold Laski. 'I feel as though the cook and the kitchen-maid were telling us how they sacked the butler.'

The next day, one silent confrontation said it all. Back in 1937, Chamberlain had installed his *éminence grise*, Sir Horace Wilson, in an office adjoining his Cabinet Room, overlooking the Horse Guards Parade. As Permanent Head of the Civil Service, seconded to the Treasury for service with the Prime Minister, Wilson somehow symbolised the whole shabby process of appeasing the dictators that had brought Britain low.

On 11 May, Sir Horace opened his office door and received a shock. There on his sofa sat Randolph Churchill, Winston's son, together with Brendan Bracken. In hostile silence they stared at him, not smiling, not speaking. Sir Horace hesitated, then withdrew. A door closed softly. An era died.

*

After forty years of political frustration and vacillation, Winston Churchill had come into his own. Known primarily to a generation of parliamentarians as a brilliant but somewhat untrustworthy political chameleon, who had been by turns, Tory Democrat, Liberal, Anti-Socialist, Constitutionalist and Conservative, he now faced the task of welding a people that had never wanted war into a nation of willing warriors. Despite his outward buoyancy, Churchill had few illusions as to the task ahead. To Chamberlain, whom he loyally retained as his Lord President of the Council, he wrote on 10 May of 'the long dangerous defile through which we must march for many months'. When his bodyguard Detective-Inspector Walter Thompson, congratulated him on taking office, Churchill answered with tears in his eyes, 'I only pray it is not too late.' He told his new Minister for Economic Warfare, Hugh Dalton, soberly: 'The public will stand every-thing except optimism.'

This was the Churchill seen by his intimates. The public Churchill, by contrast, was a dynamic hustler, moving so fast to transform the laggard war economy that he left secretaries and Civil Servants gasping.

51

Chamberlain's Secretary for War, Oliver Stanley, received a cryptic telephone message from Buckingham Palace: would Sunday be a convenient day to deliver up his seals of office? In this way Stanley learned that he formed no part of Churchill's Cabinet. The Minister of Information, Sir John Reith, more accustomed to dispense news than to receive it, heard by chance from the Assistant Editor of the London *Times* that his shoes were now filled by Alfred Duff Cooper. 'Filthy treatment,' Reith raged in his diary, 'and what a *rotten* government.'

From Admiralty House, where he continued to work for the time being, Churchill daily poured forth up to fifty pink-tagged 'Action This Day' memos, probing into every aspect of the war effort. Bells rang continuously and staid civil servants were seen to run; his Chiefs of Staff, summoned to Churchill's presence at 9.30 pm often staggered wearily forth at 2 am, protracted sessions which staffers soon dubbed 'The Midnight Follies'. Intolerant of opposition, Churchill told one official who found his methods cavalier: 'I am indeed honoured to sit at the same table with a man who so closely resembles Jesus Christ, but I want to win the war.'

His 15-hour working day, which he began in bed, dictating from 8 am onwards in a resplendent dragon-patterned dressing-gown, was as much a part of his life as his Cuban cigars, his 4 pm catnap, his nightly black-tie dinner parties. Outwardly an Edwardian figure, from his gold-knobbed cane to his 1900 taste in hats, his speed was still mid-twentieth century. He was almost never punctual, and his chauffeur Joseph Bullock soon learned to clip the time schedule on journeys by shooting red lights and steering the wrong side of traffic islands. Often, at journey's end, swooning secretaries who had been taking dictation had to be revived with brandy.

'The war', wrote his Director of Military Operations, Brigadier John Kennedy, 'would certainly have been much duller without him.'

It would have been duller, too, without the hard-bitten single-minded toe-tramplers whom Churchill brought in to aid him, men who cared for little but Britain's survival – what the Father of the House of Commons, Earl Winterton, termed 'a Government of all the toughs and all the talents'. 'Labour', exulted Harold Laski, with some truth, 'dominates the economic organisation of the war.' Not only was Attlee serving as Deputy Premier and Greenwood as Minister without Portfolio; Herbert Morrison had already left the London County Council to become Minister of Supply and Ernest Bevin, former boss of the mammoth Transport and General Workers' union, became the new Minister of Labour, coining at the same time a new slogan: 'GIVE 'ITLER 'ELL'. But to unsnarl what Churchill called 'the muddle and scandal of the aircraft production branch', the Premier had appointed an unrepentant capitalist: bustling ruthless little William Maxwell Aitken, 1st Baron Beaverbrook.

From the first 'The Beaver', nicknamed 'Tornado' by the former King

Edward VIII, seemed to vie with Churchill as to how many toes he could trample on. If Beaverbrook sought storage space he snatched it from the Air Ministry without any prior consultation, then padlocked it. To make aircraft factory workers feel 'important' he flashed messages on to cinema screens, recalling them to duty. Working from Stornoway House, St James's Park, his London home, Beaverbrook soon refused to conform to any appointment schedule. All took pot-luck, first come, first served.

Often, in an office plastered with slogans – 'Organisation is the Enemy of Improvisation' – 'It is a long way from Knowing to Doing' – six officials were lined up before his desk at one time with memos to present.

When he decided to merge the industrial complex of Lord Nuffield, the 'British Ford', with the old-guard firm of Vickers-Armstrong, Beaverbrook despatched a secretary to haul Nuffield out of bed at midnight to break the news. Nuffield's subsequent impassioned plea to Churchill fell on deaf ears. 'I cannot interfere with the manufacture of aircraft,' was Churchill's firm rejoinder.

Beaverbrook's credo was aptly expressed in a letter to Sir Samuel Hoare, soon en route as Ambassador Extraordinary to Franco's Spain: 'I don't care if the middle classes lie sleepless in their beds, so long as the workers stay active at their benches.' For what Beaverbrook was out to do, fearing the massed might of Luftwaffe bombers, was deliberately to disrupt bomber production at the expense of fighters. Out of 4,576 planes produced between May and August, 875 were new fighters and 1872 fighter repairs.

It was not a programme achieved without the 'blood, toil, tears and sweat' which were all that Churchill had offered the British. One man, who looked in on a midnight meeting of Beaverbrook and his department chiefs at Stornoway House, never forgot it. The exchanges were as staccato as Browning machine-gun fire.

'How many planes are you producing this week? Double it!'

'I'm short of mechanics.'

'How many do you need?'

'Thirty or forty.'

'Which figure do you mean?'

'Thirty.'

'You'll have them Monday. Double your figures.'

The urgency was in keeping. At 5 pm on 10 May, the air raid sirens screamed from Lyons to Newcastle-on-Tyne. Hitler had struck in the west.

＊

The telephone wires were whispering in the night – 'René, René, René' – as the code word passed from Army post to Army post along the Belgian frontier. Yet a curious air of unreality prevailed. In these first hours, there was nothing to indicate that this was the onset of a human event darker than any night: a day, that, as Hitler had said, would 'decide the fate of the German nation for the next 1,000 years'.

At his Supreme Headquarters in the sombre casemates of the Château of Vincennes, which one officer likened to 'a submarine without a periscope', General Maurice Gamelin, the Allied C.-in-C., was conferring on the telephone with General Claudel Georges, Commander-in-Chief, North East. All reports confirmed that Hitler had just launched a concerted 136-division assault from the North Sea, to the Moselle, striking simultaneously against Holland, North-East Belgium and Luxembourg. Promptly at 6.30 am, Georges called General Gaston Billotte, commanding the Allied First Army Group. He ordered: 'Holland – Belgium, manoeuvre Dyle.' The Allies would move up to occupy a line based on Belgium's easterly Dyle river.

The fateful decision – to place their two strongest armies, the Seventh and the First, north of Namur, and their weakest the Ninth, to the south, in the wooded hilly region of the Ardennes – had now been taken.

Already, in olive and black 3-ton trucks, labelled 'Snow White', 'Doc' and 'Sneezy', Gort's British Expeditionary Force was on the move. Among them was the 1st Battalion, The East Surreys, whose ranks included the newly-wed Private Bill Hersey. For Hersey, who had married Augusta Six only twenty-four days back, the sudden parting had come as a wrench; the marriage seemed right from the very first. In the long twilight of the phoney war, he and Augusta had shared many warm moments; quiet games of pontoon, sing-songs, spirited evenings at the Café L'Épi d'Or's rifle range with Augusta, whose father had taught her to shoot, handling her .22 as well as any. Now, with a sprig of lilac in his steel helmet, Bill was off to fight the Germans – but he went as a conqueror, Augusta noted, perfectly confident.

At G.H.Q. Vincennes, the same air of confidence prevailed. At 6.30 am Captain André Beaufre, of the General Staff, found Gamelin striding up and down the fort, humming with 'a pleased and martial air'. Gamelin had valid reasons; from this day on, by courtesy of the British 'Enigma' machine,* his High Command was to be provided with the Germans' entire order of battle, situation reports and operational orders, intelligence as perfect as any commander could desire. Even so, Gamelin's total misconception of the nature of modern warfare would result in the heaviest defeat ever inflicted on a French Army in the field.

Even at Gamelin's level, the full implications had scarcely been grasped:

* The much-discussed 'Enigma' dated from August 1939, when a model of the German cipher-machine (code-named 'Enigma'), reconstructed by the Intelligence Department of the Polish General Staff, reached London via a courier from the British Embassy in Paris, who brought it in the diplomatic bag. This model, code-named 'Ultra', was sited at Bletchley Park, a Victorian mansion forty miles north of London. Its first real contribution was to warn the Allies of Hitler's attack in the west.

following the incident of Major Reinberger's briefcase, Germany's strategy had changed. The original plan of attack had never found real favour with Hitler. 'This is just the old Schlieffen plan,' he objected to *Generaloberst* Wilhelm Keitel, his Chief of the Armed Forces, meaning the World War I plan of attack through Northern France and Belgium to the Channel ports, named after Alfred (Graf) Von Schlieffen, a former Chief of the General Staff. But as late as 17 February, no one had produced a viable alternative until *Generalleutnant* Fritz Erich von Manstein, Chief of Staff of *Generaloberst* Gerd von Runstedt's Army Group 'A', had come up with a plan of his own. Manstein's plan envisaged first a daring thrust to the south through the 'impenetrable' Ardennes with a sudden armoured breakthrough at Sedan and a sweep to the Channel. Then, reversing the Schlieffen Plan, the main force would swing north, boring into the rear of the Anglo–French Army.

Thus Hitler's much cherished surprise element would be fully gratified, for Manstein's plan called not for eliminating France at a stroke, but for a swift advance to the Channel coast that would cut the Allies in half.

The imminence of Armageddon was hard for most men to grasp. At Metz, on the Moselle River, General Georges Boris, Inspector General of Artillery, hearing the ominous rumble of guns, enquired of an aide: 'Where are they holding the manoeuvres?' 'That, *mon Général*,' the officer replied, 'is the start of the German offensive.' The Belgians were equally at a loss. In the small holiday town of Bouillon, across the frontier, the French Second Army's General Charles Huntziger, seeking to requisition a hotel, met with a blank refusal. 'Bouillon is a summer resort,' the Mayor protested. 'Our hotels are reserved for tourists!'

The sluggish incomprehension of those in command infuriated the men on the spot. On the night of 11 May, Captain René Gavoille, a reconnaisance pilot of Group II/33, took off in his twin-engined Potez 63 from Laon, some seventy miles west of Sedan, to survey the Ardennes sector. He returned agog with excitement: the forest was alive with motorised convoys. He had seen dim blue ribbons of light winding for miles through the woods. The French High Command shrugged this off as 'nocturnal illusions', so next day the incensed Gavoille took off in broad daylight. This time his Potez limped home riddled with flak holes but now Gavoille had not only seen for himself endless trucks and vehicles and a formidable array of tanks: he had photographed them. Yet even the sharp prints that emerged were rejected out of hand by Ninth Army, whose sector this was: the Ardennes were impassable to armour. On 13 May, Gavoille, airborne to gather yet more evidence, was shot down in flames; he escaped with his life but the film was lost.

In Holland, the men at the top had also had prior warning, though scarcely putting it to great advantage. Soon after 9.30 pm on 9 May, Colonel Hans Oster, Chief of Staff of the *Abwehr* (German Military Intelligence) and a bitter opponent of Hitler, was dining in Berlin with his friend, Major J. G.

Sas, the Dutch Military Attaché. 'The swine has gone off to the Western Front,' Oster warned Sas. 'Now it is definitely all over.' Sas promptly phoned a cryptic message to the Dutch Intelligence Service in The Hague: 'Tomorrow at dawn; hold tight.' But dawn found the Foreign Minister, Eelco van Kleffens and his colleagues still debating what was to be done, with few conclusions reached. His wife had thoughtfully closed the window shutters tight; late passers-by must not be alarmed by the Minister's lights burning late.

Among those debating was Van Kleffens' Permanent Secretary-General, Snouck Hurgronje, who a few nights back, had bragged at a dinner party that he had known of the Norwegian invasion five days in advance but had warned neither the British nor the French. 'They're not *our* Allies,' was his complacent rationalisation. Now, rather too late, Hurgronje realised that the bells tolled for Holland, too.

Even as they talked a new kind of fighting man was descending on the darkened tulip fields: the parachutist, neither flier nor foot-soldier but an amalgam of both, a Russian concept of five years earlier to which the Germans now gave new scope and validity. It was a phenomenon so novel that many Dutch citizens failed to react at all; as the parachutists hit the deck, milk and bread were still being delivered from door to door and many housewives were on their way to market. In the fields near Haarlem, farm workers were making an early start sowing the beet. In the Amsterdam office of the newspaper *De Groene Amsterdammer*, Editor Louis de Jong was chuckling over a rough proof of that day's cartoon; it pictured Chamberlain dressed as the dude in the Johnny Walker whisky advertisement with the caption, 'England Still Going Wrong'. Suddenly, to his alarm, De Jong realised that planes were swooping as low as 150 feet over the steep pitched roofs of the city.

It was a war so sporadic that many families hardly realised it was taking place. At her home in the fashionable Benoordenhout quarter of Holland's capital, The Hague, 13-year-old Ida van de Criendt was conscious of little more than an undefinable tension; people were crowding into the streets, craning upwards, while others peered from attic windows, shading their eyes against the brilliant sunshine. To Ida, her mother's injunction that she and her three brothers, Girrit, Jan and Hans must pass the rest of the day beneath the stairs, seemed a cruel waste of a sunlit day, but all too soon Eitje van de Criendt had blotted the sunlight out. Sheets of black paper were spread across every window; the corridors glowed with an eerie blue light from the shaded bulbs her mother had hoarded for just this purpose.

Above all, Ida envied the soldiers. Were they involved in some kind of manoeuvre, she wondered. Until today soldiers had never been seen in Benoordenhout, but by early morning they were everywhere in the street. In their green uniforms they seemed to be playing a macabre game of hide-and-seek, crouching behind bus shelters, wriggling noiselessly through bushes. Were they hiding – or were they seeking? Ida didn't know.

*

Everyone was agreed on one thing: the speed and ferocity of the German advance was devastating. Soon after dawn on 10 May, Belgian's much vaunted Fort Eben Emael, guarding the important city of Liège, and the Albert Canal, was captured by another weapon new to war: nine gliders weighing no more than 34 hundredweight apiece, towed from Cologne by JU52 transports, to crashland twenty yards away. Due to a foul-up in timing, thirty-two out of the forty-one gliders that set out never made the target, yet once eighty-five trained engineers had placed hollow charges on the fort's cupolas, blasting holes in them to immobilise the guns, the garrison gave up with scarcely a fight.

By 11 May, the war was on with a vengeance in the Sedan sector. For the first time, Panzers were seen for what they were, armoured cavalry forging ahead; out of the window went decades of military theory as the motor columns cut through the Allied lines. By the late afternoon of this day, General Heinz Guderian of the XIXth Armoured Corps, whom his men called 'Hurrying Heinz', had crossed the French frontier north of Sedan, and became the first 'tourist' to reach Bouillon – where the Second Army's Huntziger had demanded 10,000 land-mines and received 200. Less than two days later, at 3 am on 13 May, Hitler's directive No. 11 – an all-out assault across the Meuse – was in full swing. In boats, rubber canoes, straw rafts and even by swimming across, the Germans were gaining the west bank of the river. Joyfully *Oberstleutnant* Hermann Balck of the 1st Rifle Regiment, greeted Guderian: 'Joy riding in canoes on the Meuse is forbidden!' – the echo of a rebuke Guderian had let fall during training exercises in the Moselle.

Men who recalled an older war realised that unlike Verdun the terrors of combat were now vertical as much as horizontal. At Sedan, fifty miles up-river from Verdun, on the banks of the Meuse, the *drôle de guerre* for the French defenders ended promptly at 7 am on Monday, 13 May. Endless waves of Dornier 17 and Heinkel 111 bombers pounded the crouching troops until the telegraph wires hung in useless loops and the roads were cratered and useless. Then the bombing began in earnest. While groups of Stuka dive dombers screamed like banshees towards the bunkers and the gun emplacements, their 500-pounders ripping through solid concrete, up-ending French artillery pieces, spreading a curtain of acrid choking fumes. Until three that afternoon, the dive bombing of the French positions on the south bank continued without cessation. 'Five hours of this nightmare was enough to shatter their nerves,' wrote their commander, General Edouard Ruby, 'They became incapable of reacting.'

At midnight on this day, one staff officer at G.H.Q. Vincennes recalled many of his colleagues were 'quite openly sobbing at having to admit the shame they felt': demoralised beyond recall, the stunned smoke-blinded defenders of Sedan had walked out of their positions and given up.

No man was more shattered by the turn of events than René de Chambrun, the former Maginot Line officer, now seconded for liaison with the British. Promoted captain one week earlier, de Chambrun was at Dibeck, a village near Brussels, when news of the débâcle reached him. His first intimation of trouble came when he glanced from the window of a small café: a captain wearing the Maginor Line badge was dismounting from an army truck, along with a group of weary helmet-less men. De Chambrun was puzzled: surely the Maginot Line was being held? He hastened out to greet the man.

At the sight of an officer wearing the same badge, the captain poured out his heart. 'The day before yesterday we received the signal to send many of our men on leave,' he expostulated. 'I had to abandon my fort without firing a shot, without seeing a German.' 'But why?' de Chambrun wanted to know. Growing more excited by the minute, the captain told of the sorry muddle: 'Orders had come to abandon the Line even before dawn on 10 May. The bridges over the Albert Canal had not been blown up. The Panzers, rumbling over them, had outflanked the Maginot Line. There had been nothing for it but to abandon their posts and retreat.'

'*C'est formidable, c'est formidable*,' the captain repeated despairingly. 'That line cost millions to build. It could have saved Belgium. I wanted to live and die in my fort. Now what can we do here without a gun?'

On 14 May, the day following Sedan's collapse, de Chambrun, at nearby Ogy, heard worse news yet from a Belgian major of the *Chasseurs Ardennais*, the unit told off to defend the Belgian sector of the Ardennes Forest. A ludicrous attempt to stall the German armoured advance by stacking mines in small dumps had literally backfired: the Germans had merely fired on them from a distance and forged ahead. 'It's too late now,' the major lamented. 'An enormous number of tanks and armoured cars are breaking through the front of your Ninth Army.'

Not surprisingly, the Ninth Army War Diary for 15 May made bleak reading: 'No information – communications cut – liaison unworkable – back areas blocked with convoys and wrecked columns – petrol trains in flames – wholesale chaos.' Already individual groups of men were cracking under the strain. 'Look, men,' one artillery colonel rallied a group of gunners. 'Here are some guns! There's plenty of ammunition. Carry on fighting!' But his answer was a disillusioned chorus: 'Colonel, we want to get home and carry on with our jobs. There's nothing to be done. We're finished, betrayed!'

On this same day, General Henri Honoré Giraud, with whom Gamelin had replaced General André-Georges Corap as head of the Ninth Army, sent to his Assistant Chief-of-Staff, one of the most incredible requests ever made by a commander in the field: 'Send me some chaps who won't bolt – I mean, who'll get killed where they stand.'

*

In Holland, Ida van de Criendt, the 13-year-old schoolgirl who had watched the soldiers playing what looked like hide-and-seek in the green gardens of The Hague, realised that after four days' fighting her countrymen had given up.

Her mother, Eitje, had not been the only Dutch housewife to be profoundly shocked on learning that Queen Wilhelmina and the Royal family, including Princess Juliana and Prince Bernhard, had fled to London on a British destroyer. The Government had departed, too – some of them so precipitously that Foreign Minister Eelco van Kleffens, speeding for England in a private seaplane, had made a belly-landing in the sea off Brighton, Sussex, when his fuel-tanks ran dry. To Ida, a teenage realist, the Queen's eleventh-hour departure made sense. 'Surely it's the best solution when she's a symbol,' she argued. 'How can our Queen be taken prisoner?'

In fact, Queen Wilhelmina had done her unavailing best. At 5 am on 14 May, she had put through a phone call to a notably unresponsive King George VI at Buckingham Palace, to plead for planes. The King had duly informed his Chiefs of Staff, then gone back to sleep. 'It is not often one is rung up at that hour, and especially by a Queen,' he noted in his diary, 'but in these days anything may happen.' The King's reaction was predictable; at 6.30 am on 10 May, the day of the invasion, a distraught Dutch Ambassador had arrived at the Air Ministry, off Whitehall, to plead for squadrons of fighters. When the Deputy Chief of the Air Staff, Air Vice Marshal Sholto Douglas, assured him that this was impossible, the diplomat dissolved in tears on Douglas' desk.

Yet, weeks earlier, when the British had proposed setting up a skeleton organisation for fighter operations in Holland, the Dutch Government had refused to discuss it. Now Holland's eight million citizens were to pay the price of this neutrality.

Ida van de Criendt saw the end of everything while scarcely realising what she saw. At 3 pm on 14 May, Eitje, greatly daring, had ventured to the roof, and lingered there aghast: fifteen miles away tall inky pillars of smoke were rising above the city-port of Rotterdam. 'Mother, come down, you'll be shot,' Ida was dissuading her, but despite herself she stayed on to watch. Never in her life had she seen a fire so all-consuming.

All later post-mortems suggested that the bombing was a tragedy of errors. An attack on Rotterdam had indeed been scheduled for 3 pm, embracing a strictly military target: the powerful Dutch defence force to the north of the city's two main bridges. But by 2 pm a parley was already under way between *Oberstleutnant* Dietrich von Choltitz, commanding III Battalion /IR 16, and Colonel Scharroo, troop commander for Rotterdam. Shortly before take-off from Delmenhorst, Germany, *Oberst* Lackner, O.C. of Bomber Group 54, had been warned that Rotterdam was verging on surrender. Thus he was alerted that if a shower of red Very lights clustered above the target, the city had given in, and the raid was off.

At 2.15 pm the Airborne Corps' Signals Section at Rotterdam's Waalhaven Airport, passed on a vital message: 'Attack postponed owing to parley.' But at this same hour, the 100 Heinkel 111s of Bomber Group 54 were already over the German–Dutch frontier. To reach their target by 3 pm, an early take-off had been essential.

Now Air Fleet Two's H.Q., at Münster, stepped into the picture. They, too, were bent on recalling the raid, but Bomber Group 54's own operations room, at Delmenhorst, was the only headquarters on the same radio frequency as the speeding Heinkels. In a vain attempt to head them off, the Air Fleet's Operations Officer, *Oberstleutnant* Hans-Jürgen Rieckhoff, leapt into an ME 109 and took off from Münster.

Even this endeavour came too late. As Bomber Group 54 approached Rotterdam, the planes slid apart, as planned, into two columns: the 1st Wing's Commander, *Oberstleutnant* Otto Höhne, turned to approach from the south-west while Lackner's planes bored on. From an island in the Maas, Choltitz' men were now sending an imploring display of red Very lights soaring skywards, but in the mist and swirling smoke that blanketed the city, they were invisible. Only one man among 100 pilots – Höhne himself – spotted 'two paltry little Very lights' and shouted the order to turn back, although even he was too late to check his own automatic bomb-release.

Forty-three bombers in Höhne's wing now swung away to the south-west, but Lackner's fifty-seven Heinkels, seeing nothing, moved on to straddle the old city with ninety-seven tons of high explosive. Fanned by a gentle wind, the old timbered houses took fire like a forest, a conflagration which the obsolete two-wheeled pumps of Rotterdam's citizen's fire brigade were powerless to handle. In some sections of the city, the fires were to smoulder sullenly on until the third week of August, and many legends arose from their ashes. Thus, although 814 citizens died in the ruins, legend claimed that 25,000 had been incinerated. Even by the yardstick of 1940, the raid had been pitifully bungled – yet the legend now was that no city could resist the Luftwaffe after Rotterdam.

At 11 pm on this same day, all fighting in Holland ceased. To spare the people further suffering, the C.-in-C., General Henri Winkelmann, had accepted the German surrender terms. Ida van de Criendt saw it happen as she and countless million Dutch had seen it from the first: from the vantage point of her own street in Benoordenhout.

On 15 May, an olive-green *Wehrmacht* truck drove in from the southern end. A *Gefreiter* shouted a command, and from the bushes and the little walled shelters emerged the same Dutch troops that Ida had first seen five days earlier – 'just sweet farm boys putting on a big stage act as soldiers'. Orders rapped out, and one by one the soldiers came forward, throwing their rifles over the truck's tailgate. Most of them, weeping, stood ludicrously proud at attention.

To Ida van de Criendt, on 14 May, this cameo summed up Holland's surrender: the thud-thud of the rifles hitting the truck floor, the tears running down the young unlined faces.

*

It was a week for wake-up calls. One day after Queen Wilhelmina's call to King George VI, Churchill, in Admiralty House, was roused from sleep at 7.30 am by a near-hysterical Paul Reynaud. 'We are beaten,' Reynaud hailed him dramatically. 'We have lost the battle.' Churchill was both somnolent and sceptical, but Reynaud persisted: 'A torrent of tanks is bursting through.'

Reynaud was right; the Allied cause in France was already lost beyond redemption. On this day, 15 May, with a 40-mile gap south and west of Sedan, the Meuse front was crumbling. The last chance to plug the German penetration of the Sedan bridgehead was vanishing even as the Premiers conferred.

Yet the myth of German invincibility was as much a triumph of propaganda as of military hardware. Against 156 Allied divisions, Hitler had committed no more than 136; his 2,800 strong Panzer force faced up to 4,000 Allied tanks. The Führer's secret was one as yet unplumbed by the Allies – extreme mobility backed by close air-support – and those in the Allied camp who had long advocated such tactics had spent lonely years in the wilderness. Only now was Colonel Charles de Gaulle, a 50-year-old veteran who had campaigned tirelessly for a French armoured force, given charge of a newly cobbled-up 4th Armoured Division. 'There, de Gaulle,' observed General Georges, Commander-in-Chief, North East, ironically. 'For you who have so long held the ideas which the enemy is putting into practice, here is the chance to act.'

An ardent Francophile, Churchill was loath to believe the worst, but at 4 pm on 16 May, intent on obtaining a clearer picture, he landed at Le Bourget airfield, Paris. But in Reynaud's office on the Quai d'Orsay, the air of gloom was palpable; from the long office windows, the bonfires of Foreign Office files, burning in the courtyard below, were clearly visible. As Gamelin, the Supreme Commander, demonstrated the Allied plight on a large-scale map, it dawned on Churchill that the French High Command were already contemplating defeat. '*Où est la masse de manoeuvre*? (Where is the strategic reserve?)', he asked, but Gamelin's reply was a terse shake of the head: '*Aucune*. (There is none.)'

Back at the British Embassy, Churchill was now more than aware that a crisis loomed. At 9 pm General Sir Hastings Ismay, Assistant Secretary to the War Cabinet, had despatched a telegram – worded, for topmost security, in Hindustani – asking the War Cabinet to authorise the transfer of six more R.A.F. squadrons to back up the French. But the appeal fell on hostile ears. Though the Cabinet was at first inclined to agree, Air Chief Marshal Sir Cyril Newall, Chief of the Air Staff, took an obdurate stand. France, Newall pointed out, had neither the airfields nor the facilities to accommodate six extra squadrons; support for the French, if it was forthcoming, could be given by fighters operating from British south coast bases.

Just as in Norway, the shape of things to come was emerging. The British, with one eye cast across the Channel, were already looking to their own moat.

*

Franklin Roosevelt was always a man alert to danger signs. As far back as October 1937, he had deliberately chosen the isolationist city of Chicago to deliver a considered warning: 'Let no one imagine that America will escape, that America may expect mercy, that this Western Hemisphere will not be attacked.' Now, as the Panzers lanced through France, Roosevelt wondered increasingly: could America ever hope to stand aside from this conflict? To his entourage, his own sentiments were plain. Each night, as he relaxed over his stamp collection, the President would confide to his personal physician, Admiral Ross T. McIntire, 'England *has* to be saved.'

The problem was: what should the United States do? Holland had gone, and France was fast going; if Britain, too, succumbed, what would become of their empires? Should America seize such colonial outposts as Greenland, Barbados, Curaçao and French Guiana while there was still time? Should she try to establish a new relationship with an independent Canada? If Britain surrendered her Fleet to Germany, how would the United States face the resultant threat in the Atlantic coupled with the Japanese Fleet in the Pacific? Already, with each German conquest, America's export trade was shrinking – so what of her own economic future?

As things stood, America was in no immediate position to venture any gesture beyond moral wrist-slapping. Ironically, the most mechanically-minded people on earth, the builders of 65 per cent of the world's automobiles, had neither the aeroplanes to fight a Hitler-style war nor the trained men to build plants to create them. In the knowledge that America had only 178 Flying Fortress bombers to defend her own hemisphere, Secretary of State Cordell Hull had stressed to Roosevelt, on 13 May, that the United

States should aim for a production of 50,000 planes a year. The President was speechless, and with reason: the figure was ten times that of current annual production.

On 16 May, Roosevelt met this challenge squarely. For defence purposes he demanded – and got – from the U.S. Senate $3,297,000,000 for the Army and Navy alone. In addition, the planes that he sought would cost $3,500,000,000 to buy, plus an additional $70,000 dollars per plane for annual maintenance. Even the Republicans, noted Secretary of the Interior Harold Ickes, 'will have to go along with this programme, because the country is for it and they dare not do otherwise'.

Slowly America was stirring, like a man trying not to wake from a pleasant dream. The old ideal of 'three thousand miles of good green water' on each coast no longer seemed a total guarantee of security. For the first time, American citizens were divining what Europeans had known since Munich: that life in a fear-dominated world could become less tolerable than war itself.

The realisation was bringing Roosevelt unlikely allies. Colonel Charles A. Lindbergh might dismiss the risks of war as 'hysterical chatter', while author Clarence Budington Kelland charged that Roosevelt headed America's Fifth Column, but many isolationists were themselves beginning to feel isolated, consorting with such ultra-rightist bedfellows as William Dudley Pelley's Silver Shirts of America, Fritz Kuhn's German–American Bund, and the rabidly anti-Semitic radio priest, Father Charles E. Coughlin, weekly spewing forth his venom against 'Franklin Double-Crossing Roosevelt'.

Meanwhile, other voices, many of them Republican, were speaking loud and clear in Roosevelt's support. 'Neutrality has no meaning when such a merciless military machine is in full operation,' averred *The Washington Post*, 'nor can it be said realistically the U.S. is any longer neutral.' Rebutting Minnesota's isolationist Governor, Harold Stassen, the year's Republican candidate for the Presidency, Wendell L. Willkie, snapped back 'If he . . . attempts to put the Republican Party on record as saying what is going on in Europe is none of our business, we might as well fold up.' *The New York Herald Tribune* was blunter still: 'The least costly solution in both life and welfare would be to declare war on Germany at once.'

In the mid-western town of Emporia, Kansas, the renowned editor of the *Emporia Gazette*, 72-year-old William Allen White, made a move which would have been impossible before Rotterdam: the drumhead organisation of a Committee to Defend America by Aiding the Allies. No utopian sentimentalist, White saw the British clear-sightedly: 'The old . . . lion looks mangy, sore-eyed. He needs worming and should have a lot of dental work. He can't even roar.' Nonetheless, he felt that the risk of giving her all legal aid short of armed force must be taken.

Churchill, however, was seeking a more positive commitment, and Roosevelt was worried. As long ago as September 1939, the President as a former Assistant Secretary of the Navy, had congratulated Churchill on his appointment as First Lord – an occasion which Churchill had exploited as a chance of plugging in a highly unorthodox private line to the White House. Now, following Reynaud's call, he had put in his first plea for the loan of forty or fifty old U.S. destroyers, following up his appeal, on 20 May, with a polite hint of blackmail. 'Putting this nightmare bluntly,' Churchill hinted that if his government fell, his successors might regard the British Fleet as 'the sole remaining bargaining counter with Germany'.

It was not a request which met with sympathy from American Ambassador Joseph P. Kennedy. 'It seems to me that if we had to fight to protect our lives we would do better fighting in our own backyard', was his assessment to Hull. The opinion, however, was unlikely to sway Roosevelt, who thought of Kennedy as 'an appeaser . . . a pain in the neck' – a verdict expressed more tartly still in Foreign Office circles: 'I thought my daffodils were yellow until I met Joe Kennedy.'

Even so, Roosevelt felt the need to bide his time. On 16 May, he replied to Churchill that only Congress could authorise a transfer of destroyers, and he was uncertain as to whether this was the time to put such a request. As Roosevelt explained to Harold Ickes, 'We cannot tell the turn the war will take, and there is no use endangering ourselves unless we can achieve some results for the Allies.'

Was Roosevelt playing his hand too cautiously? William Allen White thought so, for one; on 15 May, he warned the President, 'You will not be able to lead the American people unless you catch up with them.' But Roosevelt was less certain: as the head of the last great democracy still at peace, with only twenty-four weeks remaining of his second term, there were so many factors to be weighed. Still unresolved was the question of whether he should run for a third term at all, for what happened in Europe would be vital to that decision.

'The question of whether Mr Roosevelt will run for a third term,' noted the Assistant Secretary of State, Adolf A. Berle, on 15 May, 'is being settled somewhere on the banks of the Meuse River.'

*

At Madrid's Pardo Palace, a Frenchman, who in sixty-four years of military service had known three world wars on French soil, counted World War II as already lost for France. It was not an opinion he sought to hide. As early as 19 March, he had stated openly that 'France's greatest mistake has been to enter this war' – a remark which the German Embassy had noted and taken pains to pass on to von Ribbentrop in the Reich Chancellery. Now, on 17 May, Marshal Henri-Philippe Pétain, 84, was paying his last call as French Ambassador on General Francisco Franco, *Caudillo* of Spain.

Days earlier a desperate Reynaud had summoned him to return to France and serve as Minister of State and Vice-President of the Council. As the hero of Verdun, Reynaud felt that Pétain would be a father-figure who would inspire confidence and bolster flagging French morale. But this was not the role Pétain saw for himself. The war, he believed, was already lost. He was returning to conclude an honourable peace.

To the last Franco did his utmost to dissuade him. 'Don't go, Marshal,' he begged. 'Shelter behind your age . . . You are the victorious soldier of Verdun. Don't allow your name to be linked with what other people have lost.'

'My country is calling me,' the old man replied, 'and it is my duty to go. It will perhaps be the last service I can render.'

'He embraced me, very moved,' Franco remembered later, 'and left for the sacrifice.'

*

The tempo of the German advance was alarming even Adolf Hitler. 'A most unfortunate day,' General Franz Halder, Chief of Staff of the German High Command, noted in his diary on 17 May, 'the Führer is terribly nervous. He is frightened by his own success, is unwilling to take any risks, and is trying to hold us back.'

Certainly the German success was unprecedented. Within seven days, they had annihilated two French armies, gained a massive foothold in France, and nullified the Allied strategic plan. Already the French First Army and the British Expeditionary Force were making a fighting retreat to the line of the Escaut River; Brussels, Louvain and Malines were to fall before the day was out. 'We were through the Maginot Line!' exulted *Generalmajor* Erwin Rommel, commanding the 7th Panzer Division, 'It was not just a beautiful dream. It was reality.'

At the Quai d'Orsay, Paris, Reynaud was making desperate attempts to stop the rot. On assuming the Premiership, he had appointed Edouard Daladier, his predecessor, as War Minister; now, in the space of a day, he took over this role himself, replacing Gamelin as Commander-in-Chief with General Maxime Weygand, a bow-legged 73-year-old Cavalryman. On the surface, Weygand seemed spry enough; at G.H.Q., now transferred to Montry, he amazed Captain André Beaufre and other General Staff officers by sprinting 100 yards across the grass by way of relaxation, then taking the stairs to his first conference four at a time.

But by 6.30 pm on Sunday, 19 May, his mood was graver. At a War Ministry meeting with Reynaud and the newly-arrived Marshal Pétain, he warned them: 'You will not be surprised if I cannot answer for victory.' A chance remark to General Wladyslaw Sikorski disturbed the Polish Commander-in-Chief profoundly. France, Weygand thought, was doomed to endure a period of suffering as punishment for twenty years of laxity. 'As a Catholic you may talk like that,' replied Sikorski, shocked, 'but not as a Commander-in-Chief.'

For time was running out. On 20 May, General Heinz Guderian first took Amiens and then reached Abbeville at the mouth of the Somme, moving with such speed that his XIXth Armoured Corps caught French troops still drilling on the parade ground and captured a British battery with all its guns intact in the market place at Albert. Now, by gaining the Channel coast, the *Wehrmacht* had severed all connection between the French, British and Belgians in the North – one million strong – from the French in the south.

On 21 May, euphoric once more, Hitler bounced out of his headquarters, the *Felsennest* in the Eifel Rhineland country, twenty miles west of Remagen Bridge, and hailed Raeder's aide, *Korvettenkapitän* Kurt Freiwald: 'Isn't everything just great? This morning for the first time in ages I heard nightingales singing.'

In keeping with the Führer's mood, the German radio this day proclaimed: 'People of France, cease thinking the world is with you. It is overwhelmingly ours.'

Despite all evidence to the contrary, Churchill still believed that French muscle would prevail. By noon on 22 May, he was once more back in France, this time at the former G.H.Q., Vincennes, to meet Reynaud and Weygand, whom he found 'brisk, buoyant and incisive'. To the scepticism of Captain André Beaufre, standing by, the three men, along with Dill and Ismay, began to improvise plans. How could they extricate the French First Army Group from the disaster of encirclement? On paper, the plan they formulated seemed promising: the Belgian Army must withdraw to the line of the Yser River and stand fast. The French First Army and the B.E.F. must by tomorrow attack south-west towards Bapaume and Cambrai. Meanwhile, a new French Army Group, the Seventh, should strike northwards to link up with the British. To cohere Franco–British liaison, faulty until now, Churchill was appointing Major-General Edward Spears, who had headed Britain's Military Mission to France in World War I, as his personal liaison officer to Reynaud.

Captain Beaufre listened in cynical silence. Men are made of flesh and blood, he thought; the troops in whom Weygand and Churchill pinned such faith had been harassed and divebombed for twelve days now. In his heart, Beaufre knew it was all too late. The French were finished – and most likely, he thought, the British, too.

*

Soon after noon on Saturday, 25 May, Major-General Spears, after presenting

66

his credentials to Reynaud, sat in on his first meeting with the French War Committee in the Premier's Quai d'Orsay office. Along with him at the polished Louis XV table sat Reynaud, Weygand, Pétain, Paul Baudouin, the War Committee's tall handsome secretary, and Admiral Jean François Darlan, the Naval C.-in-C.

The atmosphere of defeat and distrust appalled Spears. Unknown to him, Churchill had telephoned Reynaud to question whether 'it would not be better if the British Army fought in retreat towards the coast'. At once Weygand had called General Ironside in London to insist that any suggestion of a British evacuation would be disastrous. By 24 May, however, Weygand had grown suspicious. All evidence suggested that the British were still falling back towards the Channel ports.

To Spears, an unexpected visitor was a staff officer from General Blanchard's First Army Group, who, 'in the voice of a seasick passenger asking a passing steward for a basin', told the meeting: 'I believe in a very early capitulation.'

Suddenly, turning towards Reynaud, Weygand burst out uncontrollably: 'This war is sheer madness. We have gone to war with a 1918 army against a German Army of 1939. It is sheer madness.'

Spears was badly shaken, and a meeting later that day with his old friend the Minister of the Interior, Georges Mandel, gave him no crumb of comfort. 'The men want to get out of it at any cost,' Mandel told him. 'That's what's the matter with the Army.' Almost as an afterthought, he added: 'I suppose you realise that Weygand is already thinking in terms of a surrender?'

By painful degrees, Spears was coming to accept this fact. Weygand was calculating that by mid-June the French would be fighting against odds of three to one. Pétain in turn was thinking bitterly in terms of unequal sacrifice: against France's eighty divisions, Britain had fielded no more than ten. All through that meeting, the issue of a separate peace, as yet unvoiced, had still been in the air.

It was Pétain who had worried Spears most. His defeatism seemed to communicate itself to the others. When the meeting ended, he had not risen along with the rest but sat there, head bent, staring intently at the carpet. Had he heard half of what had been said? Had he even been listening?

Or was he, Spears wondered, 'following some memory or notion of his own'?

*

When the deal was first broached, only five men were present. The time was 2 pm on Sunday, 26 May, the meeting place the Cabinet Office at 10, Downing Street, and the air of conspiracy among those seated round the green baize table palpable.

Farther along Whitehall, in an ante-room at Admiralty House, Paul Reynaud, who had flown from Paris to pose one of the year's more moment-ous questions, awaited on their deliberations. The point at issue was crucial: what could be offered to Benito Mussolini to keep Italy out of the war?

If Mussolini held back from declaring war on France in her hour of crisis, Reynaud had professed himself ready to offer *Il Duce* territorial gains from France's North African Empire – Djibouti, in French Somaliland, facilities in Tunisia – at the same time hinting that Germany's juggernaut progress threatened Italy's independence.

All this had originated in the fertile brain of André François-Poncet, the French Ambassador to Italy, who had initially suggested Pope Pius XII as an intermediary. The British Foreign Office, however, preferred Roosevelt in this role, and had authorised Lord Lothian to approach him. Now, on Sunday, 26 May, Churchill, after lunching Reynaud at Admiralty House, was putting the French Premier's proposals to four senior Ministers: Attlee, Chamberlain, Greenwood and Halifax.

If such an approach was made, Churchill invited his colleagues to consider what terms Italy would demand of Britain. Probably, he thought, the neutralisation of Gibraltar and the Suez Canal, the demilitarisation of Malta, and the limitation of British naval forces in the Mediterranean.

At first, it was plain that some were tempted. The last thing Mussolini wanted, Halifax suggested, was a Hitler-dominated Europe. *Il Duce* would be the first man to persuade Hitler to take a more reasonable attitude. If Britain could obtain terms which would not postulate the destruction of her independence, 'we should be foolish if we did not accept them'. Labour's Arthur Greenwood saw 'no objection to this kind of approach being tried'. Chamberlain, a fervent appeaser to the last, noted in his diary: 'If we could get out of this jam by giving up Malta and Gibraltar and some African territories, we would jump at it.'

Churchill himself was sceptical. He thought that little would come of an approach, but this was a matter for the War Cabinet.

At Admiralty House, where the Ministers now adjourned to meet him, Reynaud did little more than reiterate the proposals Churchill had outlined. But once he had departed to take the plane back to Paris, Churchill spoke more frankly. He thought it best to decide nothing until it was seen how many of Gort's B.E.F., now fighting towards the coast, could be re-embarked from France. But, in the long run, 'if France could not defend herself, it is better that she should get out of the war rather than she should drag us into a settlement which involved intolerable terms'.

From the first, the Foreign Office had wanted any proposals to Mussolini couched in the vaguest possible phrasing. Roosevelt, it was suggested, might offer *Il Duce* a settlement of 'reasonable Italian claims' at the war's end, and 'participation at the peace conference with a status equal to that of the belligerents', provided always that she stayed on the sidelines. But at 4.30 pm on Monday, 27 May, as the debate continued, Halifax reported a stumbling-block. The French Ambassador, René Corbin, had visited him that morning to press Reynaud's point still further. Any approach to Mussolini, he stressed, must be one that gave specific 'geographical precision'.

With this, the War Cabinet, now in full session, shied as guiltily as men caught with their fingers in the till. The shameful aura of Munich hung over the conference table. 'The suggestion that we were prepared to barter away pieces of British territory would have a deplorable effect', was Sir Archibald Sinclair's outraged reaction. Labour's Greenwood, more forthright still, spoke as a true politician: the worst crime, he implied, was to be found out. If Mussolini held out for Malta, Gibraltar and Suez, Hitler would certainly get to know. And 'if it got out that we had sued for terms at the cost of ceding British territory, the consequences would be terrible'.

It was at this point that Mussolini, who had already told the American Ambassador in Rome, William Phillips, that all such overtures were 'too late', lost all hope of pickings in the Mediterranean and France was abandoned to her fate.

The only way that Britain could recover her prestige in Europe, Churchill maintained, was 'by showing the world that Germany had not beaten us'. 'Let us therefore avoid,' he urged his Ministers, 'being dragged down the slippery slope with France.'

*

That Sunday evening was a gloomy one at the White House. Roosevelt sat with a small group of intimates in his study, mixing old fashioneds, talking abstractedly. It was no time for laughter or cocktail party chatter. The dispatches came in – from Ambassador Bullitt in Paris, from John Cudahy in Brussels – and Roosevelt studied them minutely. 'All bad, all bad,' he muttered, handing them to Eleanor.

Late that evening, facing the microphones for one of his renowned 'Fireside Chats', he delivered a clarion call. In a sense it was a message all too stirring, for it held out hope that Roosevelt was at that moment powerless to give. It was no time, he said, for fear or panic, even though the last two weeks had shattered many illusions of American isolation.

'On this Sabbath evening, in our homes in the midst of our American families, let us calmly consider what we have done and what we must do . . . We defend and we build a way of life, not for America alone, but for all mankind. Ours is a high duty, a noble task.'

4

'Are We Building Golden Bridges for the British?'

25 May–2 June, 1940

ON THIS SAME Sunday night, as Roosevelt spoke of the task that faced America, all Major-General Spears' earlier forebodings were justified. A vast military disaster was in the making. Along the canals of Northern France, from Nieuport to Seclin, from Carvin to Gravelines, the 390,000 men of Lord Gort's British Expeditionary Force, the Belgians and the French First Army gripped tight on their rifles and waited.

Retreat was now inevitable. That very morning, Secretary for War Anthony Eden had authorised a complete British withdrawal to the coast. But was a successful retreat now even possible? At G.H.Q., Premesques, a small stone château south-east of the Ypres–Comines Canal, General Lord Gort, now had his doubts. 'I must not conceal from you that a great part of the B.E.F. and its equipment will inevitably be lost in the best of circumstances,' he had cabled Eden. Then because his whole life was the army, he turned to his aide, Captain the Earl of Munster, and in a rare moment of self-revelation confided: 'You know, the day I joined up I never thought I'd lead the British army to its biggest defeat in history!'

For Gort, the prospect of defeat had come with terrifying suddenness. On 10 May, when his troops had moved up like conquering heroes to cross the Belgian frontier, the C.-in-C. had expected great things of his men. Yet within twelve days the British had abandoned riverline after riverline—the Dyle, the Dendre, the Escaut—without a fight.

The tragedy was that Gort's Army, like the French, was magnificently equipped—to refight World War I. Against the Germans' 2800 Mark IIs and Mark IVs, Gort could marshal only such lumbering, heavily-armoured tanks as the 'Matilda', with its frail two-pounder gun. Even the French tanks, 2,400 strong, moved cumbrously, geared to infantry support, often running short of fuel during a battle.

The result had been disaster from the first. The only real armament against the tanks of von Runstedt's Army Group 'A', were 25-pounder guns detached in an anti-tank role to fire solid shot against the Panzers. Infantry used the .55 rifle, the Boys, whose bullets bounced back from the tanks' hide like peas from a window-pane. The artillery was as bad. Not one gun which Gort possessed had much more than half the range of the latest German

70

models – and many, due to an absence of firing locks, had never been fired before 10 May.

Thus by 26 May, Gort faced a bitter decision. King Leopold's Belgian Army, 700,000 strong but equipped only with rusty rifles and horse-drawn cannon, had begun to crack. Boulogne had fallen; Calais was under siege. Gort's sole remaining hope was to deny the French High Command who were his masters and to fight back down a corridor fifty miles long and fifteen miles wide to the thousand-year-old port of Dunkirk. But he could not overlook the grim likelihood: that 300,000 men would be prisoners by week's end.

Few suspected this yet, and British units posting their sentries in a hundred vehicle parks and market towns and châteaux could only hope the top brass knew what they were about. 'This is Mons all over again,' a veteran assured Lance-Corporal Thomas Nicholls, a young anti-tank gunner defending Wormhoudt. 'We're forming a thin red line to throw them out.' But increasingly a note of cynicism crept in. At Ypres, when Major Cyril Huddlestone of the 4th East Yorks opened a War Office telegram routed to all units and read, 'We are holding a National Day of Prayer for you', he snorted and crumpled it into his pocket. 'Why the hell don't they send us some 25-pounders?' he asked angrily.

Late this Sunday night Captain Harry Smith, stationed on the outskirts of Roncq, abruptly roused his East Surreys from sleep; word of the disaster was spreading now. 'We are making a general retreat to the coast,' he announced when they had shuffled into an uneasy company parade. 'The idea is to get back to England so we can return to France later.'

To Private Bill Hersey, the news was frightening. The instant the company was dismissed he approached Captain Smith and snapped to attention. 'Sir,' he asked, 'is there anything you can do for my wife?' The answer was succinct. 'Go and get her.'

Grabbing a bicycle, Hersey pedalled furiously for the Café L'Épi d'Or at Tourcoing. For the past two weeks he and Augusta had been separated by the sudden stunning war, and in the last ten days he had fought through an exhausting retreat from Brussels. Tonight his one thought was to get Augusta safely away to England. At 11.30 pm he reached the café and knocked thunderously.

When Augusta opened the door and saw her husband's face, she knew immediately why he had come. 'Get your things,' he greeted her. 'You're leaving.'

Augusta swiftly dressed and packed a suitcase. Her father had already gone south to find safer quarters for his family, and her mother was too distressed to speak when Augusta awakened her to say good-bye. But when Bill Hersey urged, 'Augusta is British now; only this way can she be safe,' she seemed to understand.

71

'Dépêchez, dépêchez (Hurry, hurry),' Bill kept imploring as Augusta wheeled out her bicycle. It seemed a night for speed. Machine guns hammered faintly in the east, and sappers were laying mines by the roadside as they pedalled to Roncq. Transport was already moving off there, and Captain Smith made a quick decision. 'Your wife can go with the driver in my truck,' he told Hersey. 'But first you had better get her kitted out.'

Bill, a company storeman, soon outfitted Augusta as a British Tommy — rifle, steel helmet, khaki greatcoat. Then she climbed into the truck, and the captain impatiently signalled 'Off'. For Hersey, who would be marching, the strangeness of it all almost numbed the pang of parting.

*

Across the Channel, in an office carved into the chalk cliffs 500 feet above the sea, Admiral Sir Bertram Home Ramsay, Flag Officer Commanding Dover, studied a nightmare assignment. Operation Dynamo, the evacuation of British troops from France, seemed to the aloof silver-haired admiral to offer little chance of success. Dunkirk, the one remaining bolthole in British hands, had already been bombed for a week by the Luftwaffe, and the fine harbour that had made it France's third port was now out. The twenty-five miles of tortuous, shoal-ridden coast, known as 'the graveyard of ships', was unapproachable with heavy craft; the evacuation would have to be a small-ship affair.

Quietly, clinically, Ramsay chewed it over with Captain William Tennant, newly appointed Senior Naval Officer, Dunkirk, who had been sent post-haste to help him. Only forty destroyers were immediately available from the 202 with which the Navy had began the war; moreover, these slim, whippet-like vessels, crammed with guns and depth-charge racks, were not built to carry men. Thus the bulk of the lifting would have to fall on lightly armed merchant ships — coasters, cross-Channel ferries, flat-bottom Dutch barges. But only 129 such vessels were available on this warm May morning, though more were on the way from a score of ports.

To conduct the evacuation — which would continue as long as Gort's men could hold off the Germans — Tennant would be assisted by twelve naval officers and 150 ratings. Few on the ships knew about the project, but all through the Navy there was a pleasant tingle of expectancy. If something strange was afoot, the Navy was ready.

Some learned the news in devious ways. Chief Petty Officer Wilfred Walters, summoned from a pub in North Shields on the Tyne and now en route for Harwich in the old coalburning minesweeper *Ross*, had the romantic notion they were speeding to the rescue of the Dutch royal family, who had reached England fourteen days back. Lieutenant Victor de Mauny, skipper of the contraband-control vessel *Ocean Breeze*, thought his mission

72

was concerned with Belgian refugees – until, at breakfast in the shore Naval base at Ramsgate, a Scots Guards officer put him right with a withering: 'Refugees? Good God, it isn't refugees – it's the B.E.F.!'

Few had it as straight from the shoulder as the officers of the minesweeper *Leda*. Finger stabbing at a map of the coast, Commander Harold Unwin told them: 'The situation is bad, almost as bad as it could be . . . we are going over tonight to bring off the B.E.F. . . . and now we are for it, boys, good and hearty.'

The way things looked, 'night' was the operative word. As Tennant left Ramsay's office, the admiral almost casually added one last word: at the most, Tennant and his staff could expect to bring off 45,000 men.

*

The steady retreat of the British towards the north had not gone unremarked by Weygand. As early as 25 May, following the meeting with Spears, he signalled to the B.E.F.'s commander: 'In view of the gravity of the circumstances, General Weygand appeals personally to Lord Gort. The British Army should participate vigorously in the necessary general counter-attacks. The situation demands hard hitting.'

Now, at Reynaud's midday conference on 27 May, Weygand confessed to the Premier that he had just dispatched a message as strongly-worded to King Leopold. 'There will probably be reactions to these rigorous telegrams on the part of the two Governments,' he warned Reynaud. 'Tell them that you can do nothing and that I am a swine. Not only do the English not attack, but they retreat, and the Belgians are giving way.'

Reynaud appeared the soul of conciliation. 'But I think your telegrams are very moderate,' he replied gently.

*

That the B.E.F. had any chance of reaching the coast was itself amazing, for the British held Dunkirk only because of an almost inexplicable switch in German strategy. At 6.10 pm on 23 May, Rundstedt had confirmed a request that was later to set the entire German High Command by the ears. In response to a phone call from *Generaloberst* Günther Hans von Kluge, commanding the German Fourth Army, who reported that 'the troops would welcome an opportunity to close up tomorrow', Rundstedt assented freely. Promptly, Kluge telephoned the chiefs of staff of Panzer Groups Kleist and Hoth to notify that neither their tanks nor the men of Fourth Army should advance on the morrow. All should hold their positions until rearward troops had closed up.

Although Rundstedt had not initiated the halt, it was in keeping with his

73

psychology. Unlike such dashing Panzer leaders as Guderian, Army Group 'A's commander, a cautious 65-year-old patrician, distrusted this new concept of independent tank warfare. More than once, as the Panzers speared through the Ardennes, he had clamped down brief halt orders: the tanks were advancing too far and too fast for the infantry to catch up, leaving a long exposed flank.

Now the Army's Supreme Commander, *Generaloberst* Walter von Brauchitsch, stepped in. The tanks, he felt, were wasted in the west, since the British were no longer a force to be reckoned with. The entire Panzer contingent, von Brauchitsch ordered, along with the German Fourth Army, were to transfer from Rundstedt to *Generaloberst* Fedor von Bock, whose Army Group 'B', attacking from the east, lacked any armour at all.

Then, at 11 am on 24 May, Hitler, trim in snuff-brown jacket and breeches, paid a surprise visit to Rundstedt's headquarters at Charleville, in the Ardennes – so unexpectedly that an orderly barely had time to humour the ascetic Führer and fling wide Rundstedt's window, wafting out the heavy tobacco fumes of a chain-smoker. But that day, *Oberst* Günther Blumentritt, Rundstedt's Operations Officer always recalled, Hitler was quiet, almost docile. Flicking a pointer at the big operations map, he asked finally what Rundstedt intended to do with the armour now that it was halted.

Rundstedt was puzzled. The armour, he explained was no longer his to command. Von Brauchitsch had transferred it to Army Group 'B' twenty-four hours back.

Now every man sensed that something was wrong. Though Hitler's only comment was a quiet 'That order will be cancelled', plainly he had known nothing of the switch.

Hitler pursued his theme. The tanks, now halted, should stay halted. The marshy Flanders plain was not tank country. There was also 'Plan Red' to consider, Hitler's already blue-printed armoured thrust across the Somme River, against the heart of France. Supposing the French attacked from the south in force while the Panzers were bogged down in the marshes encircling Dunkirk?

'I hope and I believe we will come to an agreement with Britain,' he had told Rundstedt a week earlier in this very room. '*She* should rule the globe and the seas. I should rule Europe.' The meeting over, Rundstedt had commented drily to Blumentritt: 'Well, if he doesn't want anything else from England, we'll have peace in about six weeks.'

This story, quickly circulated among the generals, led General Hans Jeschonnek, Chief of Staff to the Luftwaffe, to remark: 'Hitler has withdrawn the tanks from Dunkirk to save the British from a shameful defeat.' Then, as the top brass grasped the full implications of this decision, there came a mighty yell of protest.

At Hitler's headquarters, near Munstereifel, General Hans von Greiffen-

74

berg, of the Operation Staff, burst out: 'What is the meaning of this insane order? Are we building golden bridges for the British?' From Brussels, General von Bock protested angrily to von Brauchitsch: 'It's essential the tanks attack at once! If Dunkirk isn't taken, the British can move their army wherever they want.'

As *Kapitän* Jesko von Puttkamer, the Führer's naval adjutant, was later to reveal, this was a truth that Hitler had signally failed to grasp. In common with General Weygand, he had always believed that the British in Flanders would stand to the last man; the concept of a pull-back by sea had barely crossed his mind. If he could contain the B.E.F. without pushing it to annihilation, he would at one and the same time render it harmless and gain a powerful political club.

Others were early in the fray, and none more eagerly than *Feldmarschall* Hermann Göring. On 23 May, hearing that the Panzers had almost reached Dunkirk, Göring had pounded the table and cried: 'I must call the Führer. This is a special job for the Luftwaffe.' 'Within minutes,' *Generalleutnant* Josef Schmid, Chief of Staff to the Air High Command, recalled, Hitler had agreed without demur – a day before he had even consulted with Rundstedt. Dunkirk should be left to the Luftwaffe.

In fact, only Göring had such faith, and General Albert Kesselring, Chief of Air Fleet Two, telephoned him from Brussels to protest. Surely Göring realised that three weeks' air war had reduced some Luftwaffe units by 50 per cent? That most available bombers were still based at airfields 300 miles from Dunkirk? At last, convinced that Göring's desire for vainglory overrode all other factors, Kesselring, with a curt *'Nicht lösbar'* (It won't work), slammed down the phone.

Thus, for three days while the argument raged, the British and the French had breathing space to reorganise, to re-group their forces to defend the shattered port. And though by Monday, 27 May, Hitler had agreed to a limited use of tanks within thirteen miles of Dunkirk, they were still to by-pass the port. On this point, the Führer remained adamant: Dunkirk remained the Luftwaffe's job.

*

Late on the Monday afternoon, Captain William Tennant and his party set out from Dunkirk aboard the old destroyer *Wolfhound*. Soon enough their task became a chill reality; scarcely had the ship cleared Dover than German dive-bombers came snarling from the hazy sky. For the next two hours, with the ship swerving from port to starboard to dodge the rain of bombs, Tennant's men crouched on deck beneath the 'X' gun, straining their ears to catch their captain's briefing.

But the salient points were clear: Commander Jack Clouston was to meet incoming ships, Commander Renfrew Gotto would handle troops from the harbour end, Commander Harold Conway would reconnoitre the beaches, each officer to be assisted by a dozen ratings.

Yet as Dunkirk came in view, Tennant's heart sank. Never in his wildest dreams had he imagined such havoc. Black smoke from the burning oil refineries at St Pol enveloped the harbour. The miles of warehouses and quays seemed on fire from end to end. In the sky above, dive bombers wheeled and turned and bombs screamed down incessantly. Even as they watched, a stick of bombs fell beside the nearest quay with hammer-blow precision, to send concrete and white water founting. 'A nice welcome to Dunkirk,' Commander Gotto murmured.

It was just 6 pm when Tennant landed and took swift stock of the appalling situation. For four days there had been no water supply in Dunkirk. Only one telephone line remained open to London. Through an error in interpreting orders, 100-odd heavy anti-aircraft guns had been destroyed, leaving almost no defence against planes. And on that Monday alone 30,000 incendiaries and 15,000 high-explosive bombs had been dropped. The 115 acres of docks and five miles of quays were reduced to rubble, and in the ruins of the town 1,000 men, women and children lay dead.

Defeat and shame had bred a savage anarchy, and whole groups of men, deserted by panic-stricken officers, prowled through Dunkirk in an ugly mood of violence. As Tennant's party marched through the blazing town they saw sights to turn them cold: soldiers smeared with lipstick, howling and screeching, a sergeant, blind drunk, sporting a woman's feather boa, a litter of pigskin brandy flasks and toilet cases dropped by hastily departing officers.

Suddenly there was a crack, and a bullet whined past Tennant's head. A snarling, trigger-tense mob of British soldiers, rifles at the ready, was advancing toward them through the dusk. To Commander Harold Henderson, it seemed high time to turn back. But Tennant, confidently approaching the ringleader, quietly but firmly disarmed him.

'Here, old chap,' he invited, producing a hip flask. 'Have a drink. You'll feel better.'

For one electric moment, Henderson thought the troops might open fire. But the ice was broken. Convinced the Navy was there to help them, the men became pathetically docile, forming readily into queues.

Now Tennant gave crisp orders to his staff. The troops were to line up on the dunes and advance to the water's edge in groups of fifty. No man was to embark without arms. The Admiralty's last order had been: 'Mind you bring back the guns.' If Britain itself was to be the last line of defence, even rifles might soon be at a premium.

Aside from the beaches, which lay open to the roaring northern winds, the sole remaining embarkation facilities were the east and west moles — long wooden gangways, merging into concrete substructure that thrust 1,400 yards into the roadstead. These had been erected to protect the harbour, and were not designed for berthing ships. At this season, a surging three-knot tide raced between the concrete piles and made it extremely difficult to bring craft alongside.

Later that evening Tennant saw that at low tide Channel waters had receded a full half mile. Medical corps men, stretchers lifted head high, were struggling toward two solitary lifeboats that had been rowed within 100 yards of the shore. The parent ships were merely dark specks a mile offshore, and every lifeboat that rowed in would face a back-breaking 20-minute pull, and could load, at most, twenty-five men.

With two of his staff, Tennant thoughtfully tramped to the east mole. 'This would certainly be quicker,' he said, 'if only we could get a ship alongside.'

For a grim moment he considered the alternatives. 'We'll try it,' he announced. 'Signal the nearest ship to come in.'

As the *Queen of the Channel* responded, cutting a path toward them, the minutes seemed to crawl. First the bow had to be nosed in gingerly. Next a head rope was made fast. Then, as Tennant watched tensely, the ship's stern swung around and against the pier. Minutes later she was secure fore and aft, and men were filing aboard.

Tennant breathed a sigh of relief. At least it *could* be done – with luck.

During the first experimental day, 7,669 men were safely transported to England.

*

At 11 pm on that Monday night, Gort arrived for a conference at Bastion 32, the vast underground headquarters of Admiral Jean Abrial, French commander at Dunkirk. Their main task now was to finalise the Dunkirk bridgehead – though for political reasons no mention was made to Abrial of a total British withdrawal. (Even the French Naval Liaison Officer in London, Admiral Odend'hal, only learned through a chance visit to Dover; the Admiralty had not seen fit to tell him.) But suddenly General Koeltz, Weygand's personal emissary, asked nonchalantly: 'Is Lord Gort perhaps aware that the King of the Belgians has asked for an armistice from midnight?'

For a moment Gort sat quite still, palms outspread on the table, staring into space. Now for twenty miles the whole left flank of the British Army lay open to the sea.

But Gort's poker face was born of foreknowledge. Three days earlier Leopold had warned him that such a surrender was forthcoming, an intimation that Gort had shrunk from sharing with Churchill or Eden. 'My God, Geordie, they're shits!' he had burst out to Captain George Gordon-Lennox, one of his staff officers, but in more sober moments he knew this was unfair.

77

Twenty-four hours before the Belgian surrender, Gort had begun the slow withdrawal of *his* Army, without informing Leopold – and the King, like Finland's Field-marshal Mannerheim, had a duty to his troops. 'Do the Belgians think us awful dirty dogs?' Gort had asked Admiral Sir Roger Keyes, Britain's representative in Belgium, shamefacedly.

No news of the Belgian surrender reached Augusta Hersey that night, yet somehow she had known. A French liaison officer had sought shelter for her in a farmhouse east of Dixmude, but all his pleadings had not softened the Belgian farmer's heart; he had no beds for the British and their kind. Augusta had settled for a heap of dry straw in the farmyard. Next morning when she and Captain Smith's driver sought to quench their thirst, they found that the farmer had locked the well.

Augusta understood this hostility. As a Frenchwoman, she knew better than most the anguish that had befallen the land. Two weeks earlier the Belgians had pressed wine and flowers on the British, and priests had blessed the army as it streamed past. But now the liberators were pulling out. Belgium had surrendered, and for the second time in their lives these people were to be overrun by the Germans.

Sudden despairing signs of defeat were everywhere: white flags flapping from soldiers' bayonets; white sheets hanging from the windows of houses until it resembled washday; a Belgian general in a car, hastily changing into civilian clothes. And every village gave the British the same bitter, hostile glances.

'Why have they turned against us?' one puzzled sergeant asked, unaware that the British troops were going back to England. 'Search me,' a sergeant-major replied. 'But you never know who's going to win this flaming war!'

René de Chambrun, now far from the Maginot Line, was fast reaching one conclusion. Whoever won the war, it could scarcely be the French. Weygand's army was cracking, and de Chambrun knew it.

On Tuesday, 28 May, de Chambrun reached Dunkirk for a near-implausible reason: vital papers from the First Army's General Blanchard must be delivered to Weygand in Paris. But with the Allies surrounded, there was now only one way to reach the French capital: by hitching a speedboat ride from Dunkirk to Dover, then crossing the Channel once more in a plane from London to Le Bourget airfield.

'You'll have to take a chance if you really want to go this morning,' a naval officer told de Chambrun when he reported at Bastion 32. 'Our defences at sea will only be well organised tomorrow.'

As de Chambrun's car raced for the harbour, he saw what the officer had meant. Already eight bombers were over the port, and gutted ships leaned on their keels in the oily muddy water. Taking cover in a bomb crater, with a group of British officers, de Chambrun listened intently to a naval petty officer's instructions: when his whistle blew they were to form two groups and dash for the incoming speedboats.

Piling aboard the second boat, de Chambrun could see the bombers still circling the harbour. 'What are they doing?' he asked the pilot, as the craft slipped away from the ruined pier. 'Dropping mines for us. They've been doing that for days,' was the laconic answer.

But the crossing was uneventful, and four hours later, de Chambrun was thankful to reach London's Victoria Station. Almost at once he sensed that something was wrong. Small groups of people were clustered silently round the news-stands. The first poster he saw contained just two words:

CALAIS

FALLS

*

In London there was now no escaping the facts. At 2.45 pm, packed tensely on the green leather-padded benches of the House of Commons, the Members heard out Churchill in shocked silence: following a brave unequal struggle, the Belgians had thrown in their hand. 'Meanwhile,' Churchill warned, 'the House should prepare itself for hard and heavy tidings . . .' In just four minutes he had given them the worst.

Later, in the Cabinet Room at 10, Downing Street, he called in a score of Ministers outside the War Cabinet and told them plainly how bitter the future might be. Almost casually, he concluded: 'Of course, whatever happens at Dunkirk, we shall fight on.'

There was a split second's silence. Then, to Churchill's astonishment, there were cheers. Twenty-three sober politicians were cheering as one . . . the First Lord, A. V. Alexander . . . the Minister of Food, Lord Woolton . . . some pounding the table with their fists, others leaping up to slap Churchill on the back. The room rang with their loyalty.

Although dozens of ships had now brought more than 25,000 survivors from Dunkirk, the process was still too slow. The east mole could berth only sixteen vessels at top high water, and Tennant sent word to Ramsay that the crying need was for small ships – motor boats, whalers, lifeboats, any craft capable of inshore ferrying.

Ramsay called Rear Admiral Tom Phillips, Vice Chief of Naval Staff, then handed the phone to Tennant's emissary, Captain Eric Bush. 'Here,' he said, 'you tell him.'

Phillips listened to Bush for a time, and then asked, 'Well, how many small boats *do* you want. A hundred?'

To Bush it didn't seem that anyone as yet appreciated the full gravity of the situation. His voice tight with emotion, he answered, 'Look, sir, not a *hundred* boats – every boat that can be found in the country should be sent if we're even to stand a chance!'

*

All that day, thirty miles to the south, the perimeter of the escape route was held open only by the grim determination of some 3,500 men, the crack battalions of the B.E.F. Along the line of the Ypres–Comines Canal, units like the 3rd Grenadier Guards, Lord Gort's old battalion, the North Staffordshires, and the famous Highland regiment, the Black Watch, stemmed the German advance. Farther south, on La Bassée Canal, the line held, too, though with appalling losses: the whole of General Noel Irwin's 2nd Division, 13,000 strong was reduced to brigade strength, 2,500 men.

Towards noon, the 3rd Grenadiers faced a situation as desperate as any. Armed with 100 rounds per man at the outset of the battle they were now, after sixteen hours, running short. When Captain Stanton Starkey, commanding one of the forward companies, opened the last ammo boxes available, an eerie chill settled over his men. A hard pressed ordnance officer had slipped up; the boxes contained Very signal lights.

But Starkey had noted one salient fact: the Germans were attacking by a rigid pattern. To keep the Grenadiers pinned down they first called for a withering mortar barrage, signalled by a red-white-red Very light. Then another Very cartridge – white-red-white – signalled the barrage to stop so the infantry could advance.

As the day wore on, Starkey resolved on a last fling of the dice. As the German infantry again surged forward, he raised his pistol and sent a red-white-red pattern into the evening sky. On all sides the Germans doubled in confusion as molten mortar fragments showered among them like an up-ended brazier.

From the German forward positions an urgent 'stop' signal went soaring: within seconds the barrage died. Recovering the infantry once more moved forward. Again Starkey fired, signalling a mortar barrage.

Now, as the Germans strove to countermand the order, red and white signals spangled the sky like a millionaire's firework display. But as Starkey kept firing, the Germans gave up. Abruptly the mortaring ceased.

At a cost of more than 1,000 lives along the eight-mile front, the Ypres–Comines Canal had been held. On that Tuesday, the second day of the evacuation, 17,804 troops were lifted from Dunkirk.

*

In the pre-dawn darkness of Wednesday morning, Captain Eric Bush, having made his plea for small ships, returned to the evacuation area on the

80

minesweeper *Hebe*. One fact now consoled him: the Admiralty, which had begun a register of privately owned craft two weeks earlier, had agreed to call on every available small boat in England.

But in the waters off La Panne – where Gort had established his headquarters, nine miles up the coast from Dunkirk – Bush sensed something strange about the beaches. 'What do you make of those dark shadows over there?' he asked Lieutenant Commander John Temple, for the dawn mists made it hard to see.

'I can't think, sir,' Temple replied, 'unless it's shadows thrown by the clouds.'

But the sky was perfectly clear. Then as the mists parted, the appalling truth dawned and the two men caught their breaths in awe. 'Soldiers,' Captain Bush exclaimed. 'Yes, by God it is . . . ten thousand of them!'

In huge dense squads they blocked the beaches, long queues of them winding like black serpents from the sandhills. Every few yards of the nine-mile stretch from La Panne to Dunkirk, the piers seemed to jut a long way into the sea – human piers, the front ranks up to their necks in chill grey water, patiently waiting for boats.

And more were coming, as Bush soon discovered – thousands more, streaming across the countryside toward Dunkirk, in the strangest retreat a modern army ever made. Some came on scooters and children's bicycles; some pushed their wounded in wheelbarrows. Sergeant Bob Copeman rode on a white hunter twenty hands high. A bombardier drove a tractor, towing a gun. Trooper Paddy Kennedy and his mates journeyed in a Brussels garbage truck; others came astride dairy cattle. Some Lancashire Fusiliers rode in a truck; when the radiator ran dry, they solemnly passed a watering can to relieve the needs of nature, filled the radiator, then drove on. 'Make for the black smoke,' they were told for the fiery destruction that was Dunkirk was visible almost thirty miles away.

It was a tragic cavalcade. Not since Corunna, more than 100 years back, had a British Army fallen back like this – leaving ruin behind it, shocked and in defeat. At dusk, fevered with mosquito bites and nettle rash, they slumped thankfully on to the dry straw of barns or into ditches lined with boughs. They were always hungry – so hungry that Driver Percy Case, of the Service Corps, remembers 29 May, his nineteenth wedding anniversary, as the day he washed down mouthfuls of cattle cake with gulps of stagnant ditch water. They were harassed by leaflets, which read, 'Your generals have gone home', and often they were in pain; their feet misshapen with huge blisters, they marched with their insteps bound in sacking or with the blood seeping through the soles of their boots.

Despite themselves, they absorbed shameful skills that the years cannot blot out, for a man had to eat. Gunner Hugh Fisher still recalls: 'God help me, I learned to pick dead men's pockets – but someone had always been there first.'

Only one thought sustained them all: if they made Dunkirk the Navy would see them through.

But Tennant and his staff had no such confidence: the pace of the evacuation was still maddeningly slow. At the east mole a 15-foot tide made it difficult to board ships at top speed, and a heavy surf thwarted loading on the beach. By Wednesday afternoon eleven ships lay at the east mole's seaward end, and the inshore waters swarmed with destroyers, ferryboats and other craft. Worse, after days of overcast, the skies had cleared – an open invitation to General the Baron von Richthofen, who commanded a force of 180 Stukas from the farmhouse headquarters of VIII Flying Corps near St Pol, fifty miles away.

Close to 4 pm the skies to the west of Dunkirk seemed to darken. Within minutes the first wave of Stukas swelled into an inky cloud sliding beneath the sea and the sun. Richthofen had rigged both planes and bombs with toy whistles, and as the bombers came lower and lower their unearthly screaming chilled the blood. Now, in a long plummeting dive they fanned out over the harbour, over the nine miles of water between Dunkirk and La Panne.

It was worst for the ships at the east mole; tight packed like pleasure-steamers at a jetty, they did not stand a chance. But as long as a boat remained afloat, the troops continued to file defiantly aboard. From the personnel ship *Canterbury*, Captain Bernard Lockey watched them neatly closing their three-abreast ranks, while man after man was blown to smithereens.

Close by, the Stukas screeched for the destroyer *Grenade*, three bombs plunging home, one going plumb down her funnel, to leave the sailors floundering in a slippery film of blood and oil. Then, blazing like a pine brand from stem to stern, the *Grenade* swung slowly into the fairway out of control. For seconds it seemed certain the destroyer would sink, blocking the entrance to the harbour, to bring the entire evacuation to a standstill. Captain Tennant's party saved the day. Commander Jack Clouston shouted for a trawler to take the destroyer in tow, and slowly the stricken ship was pulled clear of the fairway. The next instant her magazine ignited, and with a violence few men have witnessed, 1,000 rounds of ammunition went sky-high.

As the sand quaked with the force of the bombing, smothering those whose foxholes were too deep, some men went as completely to pieces as Major-General Auchinleck had foreseen at Narvik. Stripped to a loin cloth, one man raved in circles, proclaiming himself Mahatma Gandhi; others roamed distractedly, clutching children's teddy bears and weeping hysterically. Now as an inferno of flame engulfed the harbour, molten metal dripped from the buckled cranes; waving an axe atop a truck's bonnet, a sergeant yelled, 'Come down and fight fair, you bloody bastards'. Through the dunes a man ran wildly, crying like a lost soul, 'Lord have mercy on us, Christ have mercy on us.'

Vast columns of water geysered 100 feet high, and in the sunlight men were screaming.

Yet, faced with unimagined horror, others summoned up matchless courage. On the coaster *Bullfinch*, a high-hearted Tommy whipped a bugle from his lips, knocked a hysterical mate cold and resumed playing 'Land of Hope and Glory' without missing a note. On shore *Chef de Peloton* Jean Demoy, finding the blind fury of the raid unbearable, suggested to a British major that they take shelter. But the major, blandly manicuring his nails, refused; he must guard some mortars. Later, Demoy returned to find his friend mutilated beyond recognition. Turning to his men, he burst out: 'The British are brave. This officer died with his hands well-groomed but now, look—even his finger nails are blown to pieces.'

*

Unknown to the men who survived this hell on earth, an incredible armada of small craft had for two days been assembling along Britain's south coast. They came from Margate and Dover, Portsmouth and Sheerness, and from down the tidal rivers, a fleet almost a thousand strong—salt-stained trawlers, motor launches, sleek cabin cruisers, barges, tugs and lifeboats. On Thursday, 30 May, knowing nothing of the devastating raid that had put twelve ships out of action, their skippers were given their final briefing at the small fishing port of Ramsgate, near Dover.

'Off you go and good luck to you,' Commander Eric Wharton of the Small Boats Pool, told them, 'and steer for the sound of the guns!' Then to the distant thunder of the Dunkirk guns, reverberating over the water, the little boats moved out.

There had never been an armada like it. Manned by the rich and famous, the poor and unknown, the old and young, it was an international mercy fleet: a true United Nations of boats and men. A Dominican monk in a reefer jersey skippered the yacht *Gulzar*. Bank of England clerk Wilfred Pym Trotter reported for duty on a lifeboat with an umbrella, bowler hat and pinstripe pants. Chinese steward Ah Fong brewed tea aboard the *Bideford*, the Earl of Craven served as third engineer on the rescue tug *St Olave*. California-born John Fernald commanded one of the twelve lifeboats towed by the tug *Racia*; an Irish crew worked with its own Gaelic interpreter on the minesweeper *Fitzroy*.

Some had talked their way into it despite official qualms. Stewardess Amy Goodrich, the only woman to rate a Dunkirk decoration, had sworn that as long as nurses were sailing on the hospital ship *Dinard*, she would sail, too. When the Navy tried to commandeer the 70-ton motor vessel *Bee* without

83

also taking her crew, Engineer Fred Reynard objected so violently that he was hustled before Admiral Sir William James, Commander-in-Chief, Portsmouth.

'Beg pardon, sir, what do your young Navy gentlemen know about Swedish engines?' Fred asked obstinately. 'I've been looking after them since 1912.'

'We've no guarantee you'll get back,' the admiral said dubiously. 'Ever been under shellfire?'

A World War I soldier, Fred had the answer to that one: 'Ever heard of Gallipoli?'

The Admiral knew when to surrender, and Fred Reynard and his crew set off for Dunkirk – though they had never before sailed wider waters than the 4-mile channel of the Solent between Portsmouth and the Isle of Wight.

Hundreds of boats, built for short-run river work, had never before put out to sea. Few had protection against mines and almost all lacked adequate weapons or provisions. One crew set out with no more food than a bottle of malted-milk tablets. Aboard the tug *Sun IV*, Charles Jackson's ambulance team discovered a shortage of surgical dressings; without further ado they stripped off their underclothes and began slicing them into bandages. Not to be outdone, the skipper soon had men shearing through towels, pillowcases, even his shirts.

And still they streamed across the water: the *Count Dracula*, former launch of a German admiral, scuttled at Scapa Flow in 1919 but salvaged years later; the fishing trawler *Jacinta*, reeking of cod; Tom Sopwith's famous racing yacht, *Endeavour*; the Yangtze gunboat *Mosquito*, bristling with armament to ward off Chinese river pirates; the beach boat *Dumpling*, built in Napoleon's time, carrying a 70-year-old skipper.

As the cockleshell armada fanned out towards Dunkirk even seasoned naval officers felt a lump rise in their throats; absurd yet magnificent, it was without all precedent in the world's naval history. On the bridge of the destroyer *Malcolm*, Lieutenant Ian Cox was moved almost to tears to see the boats led by the *Wootton*, the old Isle of Wight car ferry, wallowing like a sawn-off landing-stage through the water. His voice shaking with emotion, Cox burst out with the classic lines from Shakespeare's *Henry V*, which spoke of another battle in France:

And gentlemen in England, now abed,
Shall think themselves accurs'd they were not here:
And hold their manhoods cheap, whiles any speaks
That fought with us upon St Crispin's Day.

They sailed into an inferno which was now almost beyond description. Two million tons of oil from the port's bomb-shattered tanks roared in a vast conflagration, 11,000 feet high and a mile wide. The air reeked with an unholy compound of smoke, putrid horseflesh, rank tobacco, cordite, garlic and rancid oil. Unearthly sounds smote the ears; the frenzied braying of a jammed klaxon in an abandoned ambulance; the screams of French cavalry horses, wheeling and plunging in panic; and incongruously, the far keening of bagpipes from the dunes.

Along twenty miles of beaches, which for two days were now mercifully shrouded by fog, endless lines of men still stretched across the sands. Sometimes the seeming nearness of the waiting ships caused scores to throw aside all caution and rush into the waters, often to their deaths. From the deck of the destroyer *Impulsive*, Stoker Walter Perrior watched a slow-motion horror: men in full kit, rifles raised above their heads, were wading out toward his ship. On and on they struggled, apparently completely bemused, until the sea engulfed them for ever.

By now, thousands of troops were near starvation. With its railhead bombed out, Dunkirk had been cut off from almost all supplies for days, and desperate men scavenged anything their jaws could chew. Lance-Corporal Syd Garner and his mates fell on a 14-lb chunk of corned beef soaked in diesel oil and carved it up with their bayonets. Private James Wilson, serving up sausage and tomato from a field cooker, piled it on the hands of senior officers who gobbled like hungry dogs.

It was now that Major-General Harold Alexander, the imperturbable commander of the 1st Division, hit on an inspiration. Gort had ordered all but essential transport destroyed so that nothing left behind would be useful to the Germans — 'Burn, smash everything that belongs to Britain!' And on all sides men had been wielding sledge hammers and blowtorches with the fierce energy of vandals. Truck after truck was shunted into appointed fields and burned in great funeral pyres.

Now Alexander reasoned: why not wreck the vehicles and make good use of them at one and the same time? If the Navy had a dire need for piers, why not drive a pier of trucks as far as possible into the sea?

Within hours the plan was under way. At Braye Dunes, Sapper Bill Searle was one of scores sitting grimly at the wheel of a 30-cwt truck, careering down the beach and far into the sea until the water had almost reached the windshield level, while a jolting groaning line of trucks followed behind. Other sappers took up the task, sawing planks and lashing them to the truck roofs until jetties 20 trucks in length had taken shape. By Friday, 31 May, troops were marching three abreast along these gangways out to lifeboats and whalers they might otherwise never have reached.

It was none too soon. Every hour now, the traffic snarl along the retreat lines was getting worse; the rattletrap laundry vans and milk carts which had served the men as emergency transport were breaking down. Everywhere vital roads were blocked.

One private was so baffled by the chaos that he stormed up to General

Alexander and snapped, 'You look like a big brass hat – perhaps *you* can tell me where we get a boat for England?' Though his staff officers bristled with anger, Alexander was unperturbed: 'Follow that lot there, son.' In tribute, the private flashed back: 'Thanks a lot – you're the best pal I've had in 100 kilometres.'

The disrespect was typical. For many officers – and troops too – a bitter truth was dawning: the true qualities of leadership rather than the rank and birth that had dominated the Army hierarchy hitherto, would see this war through. For thousands of Britons, Dunkirk would mark a sombre milestone in military history; as the rank-and-file realised that officers could equally show the yellow streak the old idols were tumbling, and forever.

In a foxhole close to Private Sidney Grainger, a senior officer, paralysed with dread, was explaining to all who would listen that he couldn't venture out to comfort his men: he must guard a basket of eggs. Approaching, Grainger saw no eggs – only the man's hands hovering protectively over nothingness. Not far from Private James Wilson, a major cracked up, too – thrashing wildly through the water, bypassing the queue, and almost capsizing a ship's whaler. Without hesitation, the naval officer in charge drilled him between the eyes.

At La Panne, Private Bill Hersey, at last reunited with Augusta, felt a flash of the same rebellious spirit. In the clammy heat, Augusta had discarded her army greatcoat and her blue topcoat was plainly visible. Now an army beachmaster stepped forward: 'No women allowed on the beach.'

'She's my wife,' Hersey explained. But the officer's voice was curt, final: 'I said no women on the beach.'

As the officer rapped out his veto, Hersey, eyes blazing jerked his rifle to the ready, snicking back the bolt: 'I said she's my wife!' After an ugly pause, the officer turned and walked away.

The Herseys were just in time. At midnight on 31 May, time was running out for Gort's Army. Of the last 5,000 souls to be lifted from La Panne beach, Bill and Augusta numbered two. Yet against almost impossible odds, 68,014 troops were ferried to England that Friday, against 53,823 men on the Thursday: the evacuation's highest 24-hour total.

But the cost was horrifying. By Friday, the Dover waterfront had become a vast shipyard in which carpenters, engineers and divers worked frantically to repair crippled vessels; and every approach to Dunkirk was a navigator's nightmare, a forest of sunken masts and superstructures. A high wind blew up that morning, and as the surf rose in the shallow waters, dozens of small craft beached and grounded. Moreover, the defence lines had contracted to the point where German guns were finding the range of the harbour. All morning the docking berths rocked under artillery fire; at La Panne shells were falling along the water's edge for three-quarters of a mile.

Rarely had ships or troops taken such a beating. To Ramsay and Tennant it seemed that only a miracle could save these men – more than 100,000 of them – still waiting for boats.

But Britain was in the mood for miracles. The crews of the little ships worked dazedly on; and more and more small craft joined them until *Capitaine de Corvette* Toulouse-Lautrec, on the French ship *Sirocco*, was reminded of the Champs Elysées in the rush hour. All through the day they kept coming – river barges with massive oars and russet-coloured sails, an R.A.F. seaplane tender, the naval pinnace *Minotaur*, manned by teen-age Sea Scouts, even the fire float *Massey Shaw* from the London Fire Brigade.

Few of the crews had steel helmets to protect them against the hail of shell; the men on the oyster-dredger *Vanguard* shielded their heads with enamel bowls and zinc buckets as they ferried troops to a yacht. But even under shellfire many boats returned to the shore time and again.

At 5 am, Saturday, 1 June, Lord Gort, expressly 'ordered home' by Churchill to avoid capture, reluctantly stepped ashore at Dover from a motor anti-submarine boat. A Whitehall official met him with a government limousine and bustled forward to express relief that the commander-in-chief was safely back.

'That I've come back safe?' Gort flashed angrily. 'That isn't what matters – it's that my army gets back!'

Much of it *was* back. Most of the B.E.F. (as well as thousands of French troops who Churchill had wholeheartedly agreed were to be evacuated, too) were now in England. But more than 65,000 British soldiers, including the best rear-guard defence troops, were still at Dunkirk, as were 50,000 French soldiers. Gort feared that the Germans would reach the beaches, and thus end the evacuation.

An impressive number – 64,429 – were lifted to England that day, despite another all-out attack by the Luftwaffe. But by 6 pm it seemed to Captain Tennant that now the fog had lifted the Navy was paying too dear a price for daylight evacuation. Only nine destroyers were left now, and shipping losses were mounting out of all proportion to the number of men still to be saved.

Even as he watched, six Stukas attacked the old destroyer *Worcester*, pounding her every five minutes without mercy, sending her staggering from the harbour with a casualty list of 350 dead, 400 wounded. Leaping to his feet, Tennant told Gort's successor, General Alexander, flatly: 'I'm sorry, but that finishes it. I'm signalling Ramsay to stop any more stuff coming in by day.'

Ironically, the Luftwaffe men ended the day with a sense of bitter disappointment and frustration. For when the last of the Stukas limped home in the dusk, Baron von Richthofen knew that the bombing of Dunkirk was all but over. Hitler had ordered a change of target: from Monday on, all planes must be in readiness to bomb the airfields around Paris. If the Führer had indeed laid plans to spare Gort's Army, his wish had been fulfilled to the letter. In his diary, Richthofen penned his bitter epitaph on the whole campaign: 'The Luftwaffe can't halt the Dunkirk embarkation at this last moment . . . a victory over England has been thrown away.'

*

As the minesweeper *Speedwell* inched into Dover late Saturday afternoon, an embarkation officer hailed her captain from the quayside: 'How many aboard?' By megaphone the reply boomed back: 'Five hundred and ninety-nine men – and one woman!' As a shock-wave of laughter travelled through the ship, Augusta and Bill Hersey knew they were safely home at last.

They had come back to an England bursting with welcome. As tens of thousands of troops continued to stream ashore, it was obvious that most of the British Army had been saved, and a joyous, carnival atmosphere filled the port.

All day Sunday, huge crowds lined every street and embankment along the forty miles from Dover to London, cheering the troop trains. Everywhere there were signs of tribute; the gay bunting and flags saved from King George VI's 1937 Coronation, the slogan 'Well Done B.E.F.' daubed on garden walls, bands playing 'See the Conquering Heroes Come'. The *Daily Mirror* summed up popular feeling with one jubilant headline: 'BLOODY MARVELLOUS!'

Aboard a tug fussing into Ramsgate Harbour, one French liaison officer voiced an outsider's query: 'If this is how the British celebrate a defeat, how do they celebrate a victory?'

The query was apposite. True, the vainglorious British Expeditionary Force was home – but with its tail between its legs. Only a handful of men – above all, Major-General Bernard Montgomery's 3rd Division – remained mobile to repel Hitler's next onslaught.

Already, for 68,000 fighting men, the war had ended. Of those, 40,000 faced only the cruel monotony of five years behind bars. Incredibly, the evacuation, now conducted by night, continued until the early hours of Tuesday, 4 June – to bring the final total to an amazing 338,226 men. But to rescue them, Britain had paid a staggering price.

To many Germans, not least the Führer the combat was now numbered in weeks. When General Ewald von Kleist demurred at the halting of the Panzers, Hitler gave him an airy assurance: 'We will not hear much more of the British in this war.' But a few far-sighted men had doubts. On Saturday, 2 June, *Generalleutnant* Hans von Salmuth, Chief of Staff to Army Group 'B', in Brussels, took time out to make up his diary. 'In the discussions between the Führer and von Rundstedt on the 24th,' he noted carefully, 'were born those decisions which cost us an assured victory in Flanders.'

88

The corollary seemed evident, even then: '. . . and which perhaps have lost us the whole war.'

*

In London, Winston Churchill had business to do. Two days from now he must render his report to the nation. In the long room at Admiralty House pacing slowly, he marshalled thought. On the far side of the room, poised at the noiseless Remington typewriter, only Mary Shearburn, his secretary, stood vigil. To sit closer – within earshot – would never do. The Old Man liked freedom to pace.

Almost thoughtfully, Churchill began: 'We must be very careful not to assign to this deliverance the attributes of a victory. Wars are not won by evacuation.' Swiftly Mary Shearburn's fingers flew over the keyboard, each paragraph in the triple spacing that was the Premier's whim.

By the unlit fireplace, Churchill marched: from fireplace to velvet draped french windows and back. Often he rumbled, 'How many?' and the answer must come pat: the total of words dictated already. Sometimes he growled, 'Gimme!' ratcheting paper from machine to scan a phrase.

Still he marched. Once he took thought on history: 'When Napoleon lay at Boulogne for a year with his flat-bottomed boats . . . he was told by someone "there are bitter weeds in England"!' He mused on a parallel: there were certainly a great many more since the B.E.F. returned.

Past midnight now. The room was colder. As yet Miss Shearburn had no sense of a disciple's role. She was tired and now, as often, Churchill was gripped by the pain of gestation. His voice had grown faint. She could barely hear.

Moving myopically, head bowed, he struggled with tears.

Loving him because his feelings were naked to the bone, Mary Shearburn yet invoked a silent curse on his mumbling. Now sobs shook the firm foundation of his voice.

'. . . we shall not flag or fail. We shall go on to the end. We shall fight in France, we shall fight in the seas and oceans . . . we shall defend our Island whatever the cost may be. We shall fight on the beaches, we shall fight on the landing-grounds, we shall fight in the fields and in the streets, we shall fight in the hills . . .'

It came home to Mary Shearburn then as the most painful of all dictations. Racked by grief for his stricken land, he could not go on.

A full minute passed. Almost trumpeted, the next sentence hit her like a fist: 'We shall NEVER surrender.'

It was the turning-point. 'All the tears,' Mary Shearburn recalls in wonder, 'had gone from his voice.' Her fingers had flown to the keyboard. Churchill was marching again.

'. . . and even if, which I do not for a moment believe, this Island or a large

89

part of it were subjugated or starving, then our Empire beyond the seas . . .
would carry on the struggle . . .'

On and on Churchill marched, faster and faster, his voice a drumbeat,
charged with faith, thundering to a finale.

'. . . until, in God's good time, the New World, with all its power and
might . . .'

5

'Thank God We're Now Alone'

2 June–27 June, 1940

'. . . STEP FORTH TO the liberation and rescue of the Old . . .'

In a dimly lit studio at London's Broadcasting House, Churchill was concluding a broadcast of his fighting speech to the United States, via the Columbia Broadcasting System. Then the speech delivered, he grinned mischievously, clapped his hands over the live microphone and told the commentator, Ed Murrow: 'And if they do come we shall hit them on the head with beer bottles, for that is all we shall have to fight them with . . .'

Despite his brave words to rally the nation, Churchill's sally was not far from the truth. Against Germany's 200 divisions, Britain could now muster but a score – without equipment for a tenth of that number. To repel a German assault on England, Britain had just 500 18-pounder guns and howitzers, many of them stripped from museums. The equipment of ten divisions was gutted or strewn across the fields of Flanders.

Worse, of 200 destroyers, only 74 were out of dockyard hands – and the R.A.F. had fared no better. Of their first line bomber strength, 40 per cent had been lost in the battle of France.

At Seaford, Sussex, Second Lieutenant John Watney, of 19th Holding Battalion, was one of many officers seeking arms, ammunition and billeting accommodation for men returning with little more than the uniforms on their backs. When Area H.Q. hopefully requested rifles for 10,000 men, Watney was incredulous: 'All we've got here is thousands and thousands of men with hardly a rifle between them.'

The position was as grave across the almost thirteen million square miles that made up the British Empire. From Scapa Flow to Singapore, from Alexandria to New Delhi, men, ships and aircraft were scattered in small vulnerable units across one-fifth of the globe's surface. East of Malaya, only one British infantry brigade, plus an Indian battalion, defended the Crown Colony of Hong Kong. No R.A.F. fighter squadrons were based in India, or in the entire Far East. Only twenty-three naval destroyers were available to patrol the Western Approaches; the security of Scapa Flow depended on the presence of nine destroyers and three cruisers. 'We must have eight battalions from Palestine home at the earliest possible moment,' Churchill had minuted Ismay on 29 May, but such far-flung elements could scarcely buy time for the British if the crunch came.

True, the Dominions were rallying to the flag, but time was of the essence. Australia had undertaken to raise 20,000 men for active service, and New Zealand had promised one infantry division. South Africa had agreed to expand her special service battalions to two brigades, but it became plainer daily how hopelessly over-extended Britain's overseas commitments had become. On 10 May, the Government in Ottawa had agreed to hasten the 2nd Canadian Division to Britain to join the 1st, already encamped, but here, too, shortage of supplies was a crucial factor. As late as January, Canada had been unable to mobilise 100,000 men; shoes, uniforms and guns to equip them simply did not exist.

For once, the gloomy prognostication of the American Ambassador, Joseph P. Kennedy, that 'to suppose the Allies have much to fight with except courage is fallacious' accurately summed up the situation.

At War Cabinet level, even the courage was in doubt. Stressing the need 'to take a leaf out of the Germans' book and to organise special squadrons of Storm Troopers', Secretary of War Eden had to admit that 'many of the Territorial officers who joined in peace-time were not really suitable men'. From now on leaders lacking in drive 'had to be ruthlessly eliminated'. Over lunch with the Vice Chief of the Imperial General Staff, General Sir John Dill, Chamberlain heard his estimation that the troops were 'demoralised ... and may not be steady when the time comes'. At a top-secret conference of senior officers at the Royal Station Hotel, York, Eden heard much the same verdict. Regular officers and non-coms might dutifully soldier on, even continuing the fight from Canada, if need be, but wartime inductees would take their chance with their families or not at all. The conscript army would desert en masse rather than fight on from Canada.

In truth, they were unlikely to have the chance. This far-fetched suggestion was originally mooted by the isolationist Key Pittman, Chairman of the United States Senate's Foreign Relations Committee, in the hope of appeasing Hitler, but on 25 May, Roosevelt and Cordell Hull, discussing the proposal with the Canadian Premier, Mackenzie King, had advised against it. If King George VI arrived in Canada, with Roosevelt's backing, the President might be accused of 'establishing monarchy on the North American continent'. Nor did the Canadian opposition party want any truck with Churchill, whom they deemed a Victorian imperialist. The one non-controversial refuge for King George and his subjects was thought to be the Bahamas — where the King's brother, the former King Edward VIII, now Duke of Windsor, was soon to take over as Governor and Commander-in-Chief.

But more than the British Army's morale was faltering after Dunkirk. The 300 scrutators of the Mass Observation Organisation, who reported on current topics to the Ministry of Information adjudged morale in many areas as zero. Only 50 per cent of the population expected Britain to fight on alone – 'everyone is going around looking as if they want to put their heads in a gas oven', ran one report. Ten million citizens were so apathetic they had not yet applied for their ration books.

In an era when it took a munitions worker eleven hours to earn £1 sterling as against a Cabinet Minister's twenty-four minutes, the feelings of thousands were summed up by one determinedly articulate man-in-the-street: 'This is not our war – this is a war of the high-up people who use long words and have different feelings.'

Most felt, perhaps with reason, that some of their leaders were as out of touch as the denizens of another planet. The radio sneer of the Minister of Information, Alfred Duff Cooper, that Hitler was not a gentleman because he did not drink wine and ate grapefruit jarred oddly with workers hard put to it to find the coppers for carrots at 6d a lb. Instead, perversely, the admiration was all for Hitler, like an astrologer whose predictions persistently came true. 'He's done everything he said he would – he really is a wonderful bad man.'

'Hitler,' urged one Ministry of Information memorandum, with what sounded like desperation, 'must be reduced in status to the level of a man who eats and drinks and cleans his teeth.'

*

A handful of British scientists had farther-reaching ambitions. Their aim was to reduce Hitler to a loser's level in the technological war that already loomed on the horizon.

On Thursday, 12 June, Dr R. V. Jones, a 28-year-old adviser to A.I. 1(c), the Air Component of M.I.6, the British Secret Intelligence, called by invitation on Group Captain L. F. Blandy, chief of the R.A.F.'s 'Y' Service, which intercepted German radio signals, in his Whitehall office. Even as Jones was seating himself, Blandy, pulling a scrap of paper from his desk drawer, asked, 'Does this mean anything to you? It doesn't seem to mean much to anybody here.'

The message read: KNICKEBEIN, KLEVE, IST AUF PUNKT 53 GRAD 24 MINUTEN NORD UND EIN GRAD WEST EINGERICHTET. (Cleves Knickebein is confirmed (or established) at position 52°24′ north and 1° west.)

Jones was elated. 'Yes, it means a lot!' he told Blandy, simply.

For Jones, the details of three months' patient scientific investigation were now slotting into place. Back in February, studying a transcript of a bugged conversation between two German prisoners of war, Jones had chanced on a casual mention of something called the 'X-Gerät' or X-Apparatus. Over tea at the Bath Club with Squadron Leader Denys Felkin, head of the

R.A.F.'s P.o.W. Interrogation Centre, Jones had learned more. The conversation had suggested that the X-Gerät was an apparatus used in a bomber and involving radio pulses.

March had seen further progress. A page Felkin had salvaged from a shot-down Heinkel 111 of Bomber Group 26 translated as follows:

NAVIGATIONAL AID: RADIO BEACONS WORKING ON BEACON PLAN A. ADDITIONALLY FROM 0600 HOURS BEACON DÜHNEN. LIGHT BEACON AFTER DARK. RADIO BEACON KNICKEBEIN FROM 0600 HOURS ON 315.

This had been the first hint of Knickebein. From the context Jones adjudged it to be a beamed beacon, set to transmit in a north-westerly direction, from which a bomber's navigator might take rough bearings. Now, on 12 June, Knickebein had surfaced once more.

Jones' interpretation was shrewd. The geographical position pinpointed was in the rough vicinity of the Great North Road, a mile or two south of Retford, Nottinghamshire. Thus Jones deduced that a radio beam transmitter code-named Knickebein (Crooked Leg), set up at Cleves, in North Rhine-Westphalia, provided for a crudely-effective system of intersecting beams for bombing England – 'a blunt instrument', as Jones was later to put it, 'rather than a finely-honed tool'.

Were Knickebein and the X-Gerät one and the same – or variations on a theme? As yet, Jones did not know, but the circle was narrowing daily. At his headquarters at Cockfosters, Middlesex, Felkin questioned sundry German bomber pilots but drew a blank. Then a further fragment of bugged conversation put Jones on the right scent; no matter how hard the British tried, one P.o.W. told another, they would never find the equipment. The challenge seemed implicit. The evidence was there for the British to see, but they would never have the mother-wit to find it.

In his office at 54, Broadway, by St James's Park Underground Station, Jones fell to studying the technical report on a Heinkel 111 shot down in an early raid on the Firth of Forth. It struck him that the one possible item was the receiver installed for a normal blind landing on the Lorenz beacon system, by then standard on many aerodromes. On the off-chance, Jones phoned the technician who had evaluated the radio equipment at the Royal Aircraft Establishment, Farnborough, Hampshire.

'Is there anything unusual about the blind landing receiver?' Jones asked.

'Now you mention it,' the technician replied thoughtfully, 'it is much more sensitive than they would need for blind landing.'

Jones was within sight of success. Knowing the receiver, and the frequencies to which it could be tuned, he thus knew those on which the Knickebein beam must operate.

On the afternoon of Sunday, 16 June, Jones reported to Air Marshal Sir Philip Joubert, who had just now taken charge of Air Ministry work on the beams. Also present was Air Chief Marshal Sir Hugh Dowding, the remote taciturn Commander-in-Chief of Fighter Command. Both men listened in silence as Jones presented his evidence.

'Well, C.-in-C.,' Joubert asked finally. 'what should we do?' Dowding answered with just one word: 'Jam!'

Jones was in complete agreement, but one formidable problem still remained. First he must find the beams.

*

By now, the French had ceased to hope for much from the British. On 1 June, Roland de Margerie of the French Foreign Office approached General Spears with a bizarre request: could not all the British troops saved from Dunkirk be sent back to France, armed only with rifles, to dig strong positions behind the Somme front? Three days later, on 4 June, Weygand asked for the despatch of no less than twenty British fighter squadrons. Neither request was to be granted, and as a result Captain René de Chambrun became involved in one of this year's most fraught missions.

It was the American Ambassador, William C. Bullitt, who first set events in motion. A longtime friend and an ardent Francophile, Bullitt no sooner heard that de Chambrun had successfully returned from London and completed his mission as a courier than he summoned him to the Embassy beyond the Place de la Concorde. To Bullitt's astonishment, de Chambrun gave him a novel assessment: 'We have lost – but England will never be attacked.'

Bullitt was incredulous. What prompted such a certain judgement, he wanted to know.

De Chambrun elaborated. He had seen British fighters in action over the Channel, and he believed they were second to none. Moreover, the British had committed little more than twenty squadrons to the Battle of France; they were husbanding them for their own defence. And despite Germany's sweeping victories, de Chambrun seriously doubted whether she had enough reserves to assault and conquer England.

Bullitt was impressed. 'Would you be prepared to see Franklin Roosevelt and tell him that?' he asked. De Chambrun, assuming this to be a joke, burst out laughing. 'Bill,' he protested, 'I'm just a captain in the French Army.' but Bullitt was in deadly earnest. 'I'm going to see Reynaud and General Weygand tomorrow,' he promised.

Thus, at 7 pm on 1 June, de Chambrun found himself in the bare dungeon-like office at Weygand's Vincennes headquarters. Weygand, 'as alert as a company commander', at first questioned him intently as to all he had seen and heard in the field, then ordered him to write a report. Next day, he instructed, de Chambrun must also wait on Marshal Pétain. Then he added:

'I've decided to appoint you Assistant Military Attaché to our Embassy in the United States. I wish you to leave by the first Clipper from Lisbon.'

He wound up sombrely: 'Please explain in the United States to what extent the odds are against us. We have neither the men nor the needed equipment.'

At the Quai d'Orsay, Reynaud, a darting five feet three inches, harrying secretaries with his '*Vite! Vite! Vite!*', was now trying every expedient. On 5 June, impatient for action, he called Roosevelt long-distance and was immediately buoyant again: the President saw a possibility of sending 150 planes. At once as sanguine as Weygand and Pétain were dejected, Reynaud was now pinning all his hopes on another long-shot: a Breton Redoubt, entailing the withdrawal of all French forces to Brittany, with the Government transferring to Quimper, south of Brest.

But by 6 June, the French had abandoned five river-lines: the Bresle, the Aire, the Oise, the Seine, the Ourcq. The concept of stand-and-take-it warfare was dying beneath the treads of German tanks, blasted into extinction by Stukas.

Before catching the Clipper that left Lisbon on 9 June, René de Chambrun submitted his report. All told, it was a lamentable tale: he skimped nothing of what he had seen. The sheer negligence of the *Chasseurs Ardennais*, who had neglected both to fell trees and place mines, had enabled the Germans to cross the forest in less than forty-eight hours. Anti-aircraft and service corps units had fallen back without orders: the appearance and conduct of many troops had been 'deplorable', their morale bad. Nor were the civilians by any means blameless. Almost all the Mayors of Northern France had fled their towns, adding to the panic.

This much de Chambrun conveyed to Marshal Pétain, an old friend of his father, in his office at the Hôtel des Invalides. As always, the Marshal seemed calm and serene, but now somehow remote from the anguish that was besetting France – as if he had 'just left a world of agitation and chaos to penetrate into a refuge of quiet and peace'.

As de Chambrun left, Pétain's faithful aide in the outer office asked him reverently: 'What would we do if we did not have him?' De Chambrun didn't know – but before long he was to divine the answer to that question.

*

Given the tools of war, the French could still fight to the death, as *Hauptmann* Werner Mölders, of the Luftwaffe, acknowledged in grudging admiration on 6 June.

It was no idle tribute, for at twenty-seven, Mölders, the leader of Fighter Group 53's 1st Wing, was known as the Luftwaffe's deadliest ace. Two years earlier, in the Spanish Civil War, Mölders, as commander of the German-staffed Condor Legion, had notched up fourteen confirmed 'kills', at the same time evolving fighter techniques which were as yet a closed book to the British and the French: the 'Finger Four' formation, which saw pilots flying in pairs, one man swooping for the primary attack while a wingman protected his tail, the staggering of altitudes to eliminate the distraction of flying in precise formation.

A lean dark youngster with piercing eyes, his solicitude for the squadron's new boys had already earned him the nickname 'Daddy Mölders'. Few divined that his calm confident manner was a facade concealing many doubts. In the Spanish Civil War, Mölders, giving air support to Franco's Nationalists, had seen it as a straight anti-Communist combat, but World War II found him less certain. A devout Catholic, the Nazi Party's attacks on his religion disturbed him profoundly, and he was worried, too, by Hitler's inexorable advance. 'If only he won't talk himself into the role of Ghengis Khan,' Mölders confided in his intimates.

There was no time for such introspection at 5.15 am on 6 June. Only this morning, Mölders had shot down his twenty-fifth fighter plane, but suddenly, over Amiens, he was involved in a whirlwind combat with six French Moranes who fought back as tenaciously as furies. As fast as he lined up one Morane in his sights, it jinked mischievously to port, then re-appeared to starboard; soon his Messerschmitt 109 was a hawk-shadow swooping only 2,400 feet above the Somme valley. Suddenly his cockpit seethed with sparks; the throttle lever shattered into jagged fragments and the control column tilted uselessly. As the ME went into an uncontrollable power dive Mölders baled out.

Grimly he realised that he was over enemy territory, at least forty-five miles behind the French lines, to the west of Compiègne. As he hit the brown baked earth, releasing the parachute harness, shots from French sporting rifles were detonating close to his ear-drums.

Throwing off his fur-lined flying jacket, Mölders doubled forward, diving head-first into a field of lupins. Inch by inch, using his knees and elbows, he began to crawl forward, but the shots and the shouting had redoubled. The bright flower spikes quivered in the evening light; the farmers were systematically working over the field like beaters at a shoot. Rising reluctantly to his feet, Mölders found himself hemmed in by a tight ring of fifty men. As a French officer led him to a car, the German ran a painful gauntlet of kicks, punches and accurately-swung rifle butts.

Towards 10 pm, Mölders was undergoing the makeshift lot of all P.o.W.s as the French front crumbled; bedded down on straw in a goat shed and guarded by two sentries, he had at least enjoyed a scratch meal of tinned sardines, bread and wine. Next day he and nine German infantry officers were shunted by truck to Chantilly, and from there, on 9 June, through Paris, Versailles and Chartres to a prison barracks at Alençon.

Mölders took all of it phlegmatically; in the days to come, he thought, he would need calm nerves. Rooting round the barracks he found spare wood, and at once began methodically to carve himself a chess set. Like all the Germans, he knew that now it was only a question of time.

*

Time was at a premium in Norway, too. The tragi-comedy of Narvik was reaching its last act.

Now the indecent haste of the Flanders campaign decreed that the whole venture was to be abandoned as capriciously as it had been launched. Yet although the War Cabinet had finalised this decision on 24 May, prestige demanded that Narvik must still be taken, on 28 May, and destroyed before the final evacuation. 'Norwegian Government have not repeat NOT yet been informed', ran the Cabinet's orders to the Earl of Cork and Orrery; they, like the French, were to be kept in the dark until the last.

Even a man unaccustomed to question orders, like Lieut.-Colonel Magrin-Vernerey, commanding the French Foreign Legion's 13th Demi-Brigade, was moved to bitter comment. On 28 May, his troops had stormed ashore to win the Legion's first victory in World War II; now on 6 June, they were pulling out. 'Well,' he asked his officers, 'what do you think of the Norwegian campaign? Not even a little bit of glory. We take Narvik, and then we clear out like a lot of blasted idiots.'

More senior commanders, privy to the deception, felt an acute sense of shame. 'Why?' the Norwegian C.-in-C., General Otto Ruge, had earlier asked Major-General Bernard Paget, commanding 15 Brigade, 'when your troops are undefeated?', and Paget could find no words to answer him. 'One feels a most despicable creature in pretending that we are going on fighting,' Major-General Claude Auchinleck wrote to Dill, newly-appointed C.I.G.S., 'when we are going to quit.at once.'

No bystander who watched the Allies depart was more shocked than Polly Peabody, the New York socialite who had brought her American Scandinavian Field Hospital ashore at Bergen on 6 April, unaware that the German ore freighters in the harbour had been crammed with hidden troops. No sooner had Polly's team reached Stockholm than news of the Norwegian invasion reached them; at once they had decided they must return to give succour. Within days, their 18-truck convoy adorned with the Red Cross emblem and the Stars and Stripes, led by Polly's white Ford, 'Leaping Lina', had set off on its long journey north.

They had equipment enough to support a 200-bed Field Hospital for six months, including three mobile surgeries, but at Namsos, the first port they struck, the war had passed them by. For the first time, Polly saw a devastation that would soon become commonplace: bombs and shells had reduced a trim white-painted Norwegian town to a waste of black and dripping ruins. To her horror – for, like all her team she had believed that Namsos and the North could be held – she heard that the port was to be abandoned.

By the light of a blazing ammunition dump, Polly Peabody witnessed 'one of the most poignant scenes of my life'; Tommies and *poilus* embarking by night, shuffling silently through the gutted wreckage of the port, the warships' heliographs blinking and flashing offshore. At this moment she reached a snap decision: if the State Department forbade her unit to operate in hostile territory, she would make for France on a one-woman mission, signing up with the International Red Cross at Geneva on her way in.

More troops were pouring along the dockside as she watched, cursing monotonously as stretcher bearers shouldered them aside, their words lost in the strident blast of ships' whistles, the long black files standing out in silhouette against a red, unearthly glow. Behind them they were leaving three million Norwegians to their fate – among them, Theodor Broch, the Mayor of Narvik, now, for the second time, awaiting sentence of death.

*

His friends the British *had* come, Theodor Broch thought wryly, confounding the prophecy a German lieutenant had made him as far back as 17 April, but only to depart as swiftly.

Once more under armed guard, this time in the dining room of the Nobel Hotel, Harstad, forty miles from Narvik, Broch thought the events of the past two months had taken on a near-surreal aspect. On 26 May, when a combined task force of British, French and Poles streamed ashore at Narvik the National flag was the first to fly above any Norwegian City Hall since the Germans came. Alongside it streamed the Union Jack, which city wives under Ellen Broch has stitched with their own hands while sheltering from air raids. Food had been scarce and beer non-existent, but at least the liberators had been made welcome with an impromptu feast of anchovies, bread and bilberry jam.

But the elation was short-lived. On 2 June, acting on a hunch, Broch sent Ellen and Siri north to Tromso, a wise precaution, for the Luftwaffe were returning in strength. As the bombs hailed down, Broch sensed with pain that his life in Narvik now lay in the past. Danielsen's Building, where he had first set up as a young lawyer, had vanished in a corona of flame. The harbour which had formed the hard core of Narvik's prosperity was now the graveyard of more than thirty ships.

Most townsfolk heard the news that the Allies were leaving with anger as much as incredulity. Broch tried to damp down passions which were close to flashpoint. 'They have to go back to their own country and fight there,' he excused the British. Already it had crossed his mind to wonder: could the

99

Germans be aware that in the days before the Allies came ashore the unerring accuracy of the naval broadsides had been aided by harbour plans which Broch had smuggled out to them by rowboat?

The Germans were well aware. On 6 June, as the British left Narvik, Broch, hitching a ride in a friend's car, went north to Tromso to find Ellen and Siri. King Haakon and his government were just then leaving for England in a British cruiser, but now the quixotic streak which had been the mainspring of his municipal life betrayed Broch. Word reached Tromso that refugees in sorry shape were arriving on Harstad Island. Broch, determined to help, took his family back south by ferry.

On 15 June, he was crossing Harstad's main square when a squad of German soldiers halted him. By chance, General Dietl's adjutant, *Korvettenkapitän* Reichmann, had spotted him from the hotel window. 'We have some very interesting information about you, Mr Mayor,' he greeted Broch ominously. 'You are under arrest.'

In the Nobel Hotel's dining room, guarded by two sentries, Broch thought fast. Once Narvik's City Council had interceded to spare him from death under Section 36 of German Military Law, but the Council no longer existed, and even disarming a German non-com paled beside the crime of overt espionage, passing maps to the British. Acknowledging that he was on his own, he strolled casually across the dining room, reconnoitring prospects. The room lay on the first floor, its windows overlooking the street, although one, already open, gave onto a back yard piled with barrels. Behind the bar, in one corner, a staircase led directly to the cellar. Still strolling, Broch glanced through the back window into the yard. A young boy prising open a cask looked up and caught his eye. Nodding confidentially, Broch whispered: 'For God's sake, get me a taxi. Tell it to wait in the second cross street to the north.'

Turning back, he saw the sentries eye him thoughtfully, Broch lit a cigarette, perching nonchalantly on a high stool, as if awaiting a bartender. Presently the sentries turned away. Outside, trucks were groaning up the street from the dockside and they grew curious. Flinging wide the windows, they craned out. Now or never, Broch thought.

Dropping lightly from the stool he ducked behind the bar, taking the cellar stairs three at a time. Now he was in the yard, doubling between the barrels, sprinting into the street at the rear. Mercifully, his sense of direction held good, taking him due north. Just as he had prayed, a taxi was parked, ticking over. Broch flung himself flat on its floor, blurting out garbled directions. From the lodgings where Ellen and Siri were billeted, the taxi sped them on across the island, one already-packed knapsack crammed with everything they possessed.

Luck was with them; in the island's tiny port of Hindö, white wraiths of mist were drifting in from the sea. On the dockside, Broch did a quick deal with a fisherman to row them to any offshore island with a sizeable fishing harbour. From there, he knew, another bargain could be cemented: a passage for all three on any fishing vessel voyaging further north.

Soon the rowboat was drifting out across the grey waste of the Atlantic. The fog was still thickening; from a few hundred yards out, Hindö was no longer visible. But where they were going, and when they would at last find refuge, Broch did not know.

*

At dusk on Monday, 10 June, Paris was a melancholy sight to all who loved her. Out through the Porte de Châtillon, in the fading light, groaned an endless line of trucks and private cars – Citroens, Mercedes – heading southwest by day and by night for Tours, 145 miles distant. After much heart-searching, Paul Reynaud's administrative machine was abandoning the capital as an open city – leaving only the Préfect, Roger Langeron, and 25,000 gendarmes to represent the French Government in Paris.

To the very end, there had been bitter argument for and against. Weygand himself was anxious to stay, convinced that if he fell into German hands, he would be cleared of all blame. On 8 June, De Gaulle, the new Under-Secretary for War, saw signs that Weygand was throwing in the towel. 'When I'm beaten here,' he prophesied, 'England won't wait a week before negotiating with the Reich.' One of the few opposing voices had been Reynaud's, convinced that any armistice could bring only dishonourable terms. Pétain all along veered between pessimism – 'It is our duty to get out of it' – and sentiments devoid of reality. 'We don't seem to be making much use of carrier pigeons,' he interrupted one Cabinet meeting. 'There should be a dove cote in the rear which is permanently linked up with Supreme Headquarters.'

Now, as the Government quit Paris, hope in France vanished, as a dam gives way before an inexorable flood. On this hectic Monday night, all the city – and soon all France – became obsessed by one single thought: to get away.

By dawn on Tuesday, an endless cavalcade jammed the highways leading south. Like animals fleeing before a forest fire, a bizarre array of vehicles was streaming from the city: fire engines bearing firemen and their families, tricycles, furniture vans, coal and ice-cream carts, street sweepers with rotating brushes, even eight funeral hearses crammed with living freight. Whole stud farms had taken to the roads, headed by grooms riding stallions, along with manure carts and little trailers for the stud books.

In their desperate effort to get away, people surprised even themselves. A lecturer, Peter Fontaine, realised that he had not mounted a bicycle for twenty-five years, but he clocked up 400 miles on one now, daily drying his underwear on the handle-bars as he headed south for Bordeaux.

101

Black smoke from burning fuel dumps cast a sooty pall over the city – at times so dense that no man could see across the Place de la Concorde, where lowing cattle now wandered untended. Soon every railway terminus was closed save the Gare de Lyon, where a frantic trampling horde of would-be refugees clawed at the iron railings. By now more than a million had gone, and Paris was dying by inches. Newspapers closed down, Maxims put up its shutters and rare taxis were stormed on sight. The sight of expensive Vuitton luggage piled outside the Ritz showed that the rich had been among the first to go.

On the roads leading south it was worse. No man or woman who made the journey would ever forget the stripped and silent villages, where not a crumb of bread or a thimbleful of milk remained as sustenance. The main café at Le Mans, more resembled a stage set for a poorhouse, littered with orange peel, and refugees bedding down on the banquettes. In this chaos, where petrol was priced at fifty francs a litre, and ten sous charged for a glass of water, profiteers were having a field day. One woman was even mulcted £50 for a racing bicycle.

The panic was spreading from town to town, to the very foothills of the Pyrenees. Whole communities, like Evreux in Normandy, evaporated as swiftly as morning mist, reduced from 20,000 to 172 overnight. At Alois, a fear-stricken woman in a heavy fur coat, afraid that engineers would blow the bridges, swam the breadth of the river, looking like a 'drowning bear'.

In this week, the French writer, Paul Valéry, wrote what might have been the epigraph for 1940: 'Nothing that we could fear is impossible; we can fear and imagine absolutely everything.'

By now, almost ten million were on the roads, mindless of a destination, coursing blindly on, like lemmings, although to travel 200 yards an hour was now a rare achievement. In one column, the inane cries of a wheel-of-fortune man, shouting to keep himself awake, jarred the nerves: 'No blanks, ladies and gentlemen, no blanks! Every number wins.' In other columns, some men, numb with fatigue, just gave up. Bone-weary *poilus*, clinging to the tailgates of trucks, fell insensible, and the rearmost trucks rolled on over them.

'The Middle Ages,' wrote the deeply-shocked General Guderian to his wife, Gretel, 'were humane compared to the present.'

The deep disgust of defeat gripped civilian and military alike. On the Boulevard Sebastopol, Paris, the writer Arthur Koestler greeted a waiter from his favourite bistro, mobilised in March but no longer in uniform: 'I thought you were at the front?' The man merely grimaced: 'The front is where the Lieutenant is, and the Lieutenant has beaten it in his car.' As disillusioned with their officers as many of the English, some *poilus* made their feelings even plainer. On the outskirts of Nantes, one young soldier flung a fistful of mud through a limousine's window, splattering an officer's cheek. The officer's lips tightened, but he drove on without comment.

The tired old slogan *Il faut en finir* had abruptly become *Il fallait en finir* (It had to be stopped). In this mood Breton housewives mobbed retreating troops to tear the rifles from their hands, putting an end to all resistance. At Vierzon, near Bourges, a tank commander preparing to defend the town was seized by citizens anxious to avoid German reprisals and battered to death.

To one 6-year-old boy, Pascal Jardin, at Trouville, that week, in retrospect, would always be associated with 'a revolting noise in my memory — forty million Frenchmen were shitting their pants at the same time.'

*

In his office on Rome's sixteenth-century Piazza Venezia, a room so lofty (seventy feet long by thirty-nine feet wide) that he had to communicate with his orderlies by hand-signals, Benito Mussolini had reached a decision destined to change the face of the war in Europe — and ultimately to topple his own Fascist régime. On 26 May, standing hands on hips, behind his writing desk he broke the news defiantly to two key officials: Marshal Pietro Badoglio, the cunning 68-year-old Chief of the Supreme Staff, and Marshal Italo Balbo, Governor of Libya.

'I wish to tell you,' Mussolini announced abruptly, 'that yesterday I sent a messenger to Hitler with my written declaration that I don't intend to stand idly by with my hands in my pockets. After 5 June, I am ready to declare war on England and France.'

To both men, the decision came like a thunderclap. As Badoglio, the first to speak, was quick to point out: 'Your Excellency, you know perfectly well that we are absolutely unprepared — you have received complete reports every week.' The gist of those reports, Badoglio hammered home, had made one thing plain: Italy's military involvement throughout the thirties — in Ethiopia, the Spanish Civil War, and Albania — had left her a spent force. With twenty Army divisions possessing only 70 per cent of their equipment, another twenty only 50 per cent, she could wage no war worth the name.

'We haven't even sufficient shirts for the Army,' Badoglio expostulated. 'How is it possible to declare war? It is suicide.'

The crippling shortages were everywhere apparent. Italy's annual imports totalled twenty-five million tons of food — none of which might be available in the event of conflict. The Air Force had fuel for just forty sorties. Italian colonies such as Tripolitania reported weapons better suited to a war surplus dump: rusting water-cooled machine-guns, tanks so frail that trucks were needed to transport them into battle. In Libya, Balbo had only cannon dating from Garibaldi's wars of the 1870s, precariously mounted on garbage trucks. Only the Fleet, numerically powerful and including six battleships, nineteen modern cruisers and 120 destroyers, offered a challenge which Churchill was to sum up as 'formidable'.

The Minister for War Production, General Carlo Favagrossa, had most aptly summed it up: if industrial plants worked non-stop shifts, Italy might conceivably enter the war in 1949. Failing this, he would set the date at 1959.

But ever since 1922, when his Fascists seized power with their much-publicised March on Rome, *Il Duce* had been obsessed with dreams of Italy's military destiny. Thus, the concept of non-involvement was ultimately unthinkable, for Mussolini, all his life veering between abject self-abasement and overweening confidence, could only equate his country's inadequacy with his own. 'We should be like Swizerland multiplied by ten,' was his shamefaced definition of total neutrality.

Yet for days before the meeting with Badoglio and Balbo, Mussolini had been tugged by the winds. His Minister of Justice, Count Dino Grandi, a man so bitterly opposed to the Axis alliance that three years later he would mastermind a conspiracy deposing Mussolini, never forgot his 17 May visit to Palazzo Venezia, only nine days earlier. Standing before a beflagged wall-map of France, studying troop dispositions, Mussolini had declared that despite the Germans' belief in victory, they would never reach Paris.

'There will be a new Battle of the Marne,' he told Grandi with characteristic lack of prescience. 'The hated Boches will break their heads for a second time and all Europe will be liberated from them.'

This curiously wishful thinking had been known to the British War Cabinet as long ago as 7 April, through a cable summarising a private conversation between Amadeo, Duke of Aosta, nephew of King Vittorio Emmanuele III, and the British Ambassador's wife, Lady Loraine. Mussolini, the Duke had stressed, felt threatened on all sides – by the prospect of an Allied flank attack on Germany through Italy, by a sudden German invasion of Italy from the North. Although Mussolini 'was aware of, and shared, the hatred of the whole country for Germany, he feared Germany's military strength'.

The lessons of Hitler's sneak attacks on Norway, Denmark and Belgium, which the Führer had never deigned to reveal to his junior partner, had been far from lost on Mussolini. 'Even if Italy were to change her attitude and go over bag and baggage to the Anglo–French side, she would not avoid an immediate war with Germany,' he had argued in a top-secret memorandum of 31 March, 'a war which Italy would have to carry alone.' Following reports that the war scare had brought booming business to furriers and jewellers in the north, a hedge against the collapse of the lira, Mussolini rapped out 'The Milanese should know that it's better to negotiate than have the Germans in Milan.'

Racked as always by his own inferiority complex, he would admit no fears of Hitler to Badoglio or Balbo. 'You are not calm enough to judge the situation, Marshal,' he told Badoglio condescendingly. 'I can tell you everything will be over by September, and that I need only a few thousand dead to sit at the conference table as a belligerent.'

But at the Palazzo Chigi, Italy's Foreign Ministry, the diplomats knew that any warning word from Germany swiftly brought Mussolini into line. On 27 May, the day following Mussolini's meeting with Badoglio, one official, Count Luca Pietromarchi, received a swingeing rebuke from the Palazzo Venezia. After months of negotiations, Pietromarchi had worked out a *modus vivendi* which had that day been announced in London; although the British fought shy of the territorial concessions that Reynaud had urged, they had still agreed to relax their contraband controls in the Mediterranean. But the news, simultaneously relayed to Berlin, had brought a sharp reprimand from Hermann Göring.

'You're to cancel every agreement you've made with the British and the French,' Pietromarchi was instructed. 'The Duce says that he's not a brigand, doing business with a gun in one hand and a Bible in the other.'

From this moment on, Mussolini was to see life as in a splintered mirror – the reality that he was shrewd enough to perceive, the distorted image that he urged himself was the truth.

For Italy the ultimate tragedy was that no lack of sycophants existed to assure him that all was well. Despite his token protest, Badoglio stayed on in his post – loath to resign and forego emoluments of two million lire a year. The Under Secretary for War, General Ubaldo Soddu, obligingly put on a show of martial might – upping the Army's on-paper strength from forty to seventy-three divisions, stripping every division of one regiment to swell the totals. At military reviews, Mussolini never spotted that fourteenth-century brass cannons stood in for more lethal hardware – or that the armoured cars were loaned by the police, painted khaki for that day's parade.

A 6 pm on Monday, 10 June, for the first time following his nine months of indecision, the glass doors swung open onto the Palazzo Venezia's balcony, and Mussolini – who twelve days earlier had appointed himself Supreme Commander of the Armed Forces – stepped forward. His voice strangely high-pitched, he told the well-drilled crowd mustered by the Party Secretary the fate that awaited Italy – at the moment that the code-word announcing his decision, 'Duplicity' flashed to all British Ministries.

Among those listening in the tight-packed square was Erik Seidenfaden, the Danish reporter whose thirst for news had thus far netted him notable scoops in both Stockholm and Oslo. But as *Politiken's* newly-appointed Rome correspondent, Seidenfaden felt no professional pride in the story he was about to file – merely 'a terrible feeling that I'd seen all this before'. There had been just such a scene, he recalled, in Hamburg, in 1932, the year before Hitler attained power, yet still, eight years later, Seidenfaden could ask himself, how is it possible that all these teenagers are wild for war?

In truth, the bulk were party hacks, a handful of them fanatics but more

105

of whom had sworn allegiance to a meal ticket. Most Italians felt only a true sense of horror as Mussolini's voice crackled out through amplifiers all over Italy; in Genoa and Turin, the crowds massed in ominous silence, without a cheer, without a handclap. And in Milan's cathedral square, men were seen crying that day, under the clear and windy sky.

'A declaration of war has been handed to the ambassadors of Great Britain and France,' Mussolini trumpeted vaingloriously. 'Italian people, rush to arms and show your tenacity, your courage, your valour!'

Yet, at 5 pm in the Villa Camilluccia, on Rome's Monte Mario, Myriam, the 20-year-old sister of Mussolini's mistress, Claretta Petacci, had answered the phone to hear the Duce sounding palpably shaken. 'In one hour's time,' he told her, 'I shall declare war. I'm forced to declare it.'

Like most Italians, Myriam was thinking only of a token *coup-de-grace* against France. 'But it will be short, Duce,' she reassured him.

'No,' Mussolini disillusioned her, 'it will be long – not less than five years.' His final prophecy made Myriam shiver: 'Hitler's tree reaches as high as the sky – but it grows only towards ruin.'

*

The Presidential train was racing through the red and green Virginia foothills. Aboard it, Franklin Roosevelt was making the final changes in the speech of a day that would become history. One hour before leaving Washington, the President had heard of Mussolini's decision. Now he was angry.

A light rain was falling as the train reached Charlottesville, but Roosevelt, pale and strained when he embarked on the journey, now seemed relaxed. Whatever decision he had reached had seemed to strengthen him. His mind was made up as he drove to the Memorial Gymnasium of the University of Virginia, there to don his cap and gown, and address the graduating class.

It was a fighting speech that the world heard, powerful and more determined than any since the war began – specific in its promise of aid, bitter in its condemnation of the dictators. When Roosevelt spoke of Italy's preserving its 'freedom of action', it was plain he meant freedom to murder.

Now came the crunch; the phrase that the cautious Sumner Welles had already excised from the speech but which had lodged all day like an obstinate burr in Roosevelt's brain. 'The old red blood said "Use it",' he was to recall later, and now he did: 'On this tenth day of June, 1940, the hand that held the dagger has stuck it in the back of its neighbour.'

With that one sentence, America had taken sides, and many myths were ended. The myth of U.S. neutrality, for one – 'Let us not hesitate – all of us – to proclaim that victory for the gods of force and hate will endanger the institutions of democracy in the Western World . . .' The utopian hope that

America could remain an island of democracy in a totalitarian world was ended, too – 'Such an island represents to me . . . a helpless nightmare of a people without freedom, a people lodged in prison . . .' The vacillating talk of the value of aiding the Allies was dead. One thing now remained: to get on with the job.

To be sure, there were still cautious voices, sensing in Roosevelt's non-belligerent intervention a pull towards war. 'Whoa, Mr President,' cried the *Detroit News*, in alarm. Hundreds of citizens approved, by eight to one, the *St Louis Post-Dispatch*'s round declaration that the President, unless checked, would take the U.S. to the brink of war. But there were contrary mani-festations, closer to the core of current fears and feelings. On this same day, in New York's Century Club, thirty private citizens combined to voice the unspeakable in a nation-wide newspaper advertisement that both *The Los Angeles Times* and the *Boston Globe* refused to run: 'Let us declare war on Germany.' Among the signatories: Henry W. Hobson, Episcopal Bishop of Cincinatti, Admiral William H. Standley, retired Chief of Naval Opera-tions, the urban planner Lewis Mumford, and Harvard's President, James Bryant Conant.

'Only a tightrope walker could keep his balance here,' lamented the German Chargé d'Affaires in Washington, Hans Thomsen, 'They want Britain to win.' Belatedly America was taking to heart the warning that Ambassador Lothian had delivered to the alumni of Columbia University. 'Let our Navy disappear and Hitler will be thundering on your doorstep.'

In the *New York Times*, the plea of the poetess Edna St Vincent Millay seemed to say it all:

Oh build, assemble, transport, give,
That England, France and we may live . . .
Lest . . . we be left to fight alone . . .

*

In France, the fruitless Anglo–French sessions, where no meeting of minds seemed possible, dragged on for three more days. On 11 June, the day after Roosevelt's speech, Churchill returned yet again, supported by Eden, Dill and Ismay, for a meeting at Weygand's new headquarters, the Château du Muguet, near Briare. But the talk, in Spears' view, was little more than a recital of familiar recriminations. When would more British squadrons be forthcoming? Where were Britain's divisions? De Gaulle, watching Pétain closely all through, sourly diagnoscd him as 'suffering from senility, pessi-mism and ambition, a fatal combination'.

Next morning, Churchill, who had remained as an overnight guest, raised a gnawing preoccupation with Admiral Jean François Darlan. Whatever the outcome of the battle, he urged, Germany must never lay hands on the

107

French Fleet. Darlan emphatically shared his concern. Rather than that, he would give the Fleet sailing orders for Canada.

A constant spectre at this feast was Reynaud's mistress, Madame Hélène des Portes, whose harsh importunate voice was heard offstage all through the conference. As defeatist as Reynaud was staunch, surrender was the one thought on her mind. Once, as Reynaud and De Gaulle conferred privately, debating the last-ditch Breton Redoubt, Madame des Portes burst in unannounced to berate her lover: 'What is this ridiculous talk about going to Quimper? I certainly don't propose to go and sleep in Breton four-poster beds.'

On 13 June, when Churchill, along with Beaverbrook and Halifax, arrived for a last melancholy meeting with Reynaud at the Prefecture in Tours, Madame des Portes was again in evidence. Twice, using Baudouin as her emissary, she sent strident messages to Reynaud: 'Tell Paul we must give up, we must make an end of it. There must be an armistice.' From an ante-room came the angry voice of Weygand, shouting like a barrack-room lawyer 'They sit there with their arses on their chairs and don't give a damn that all this time the French Army is being massacred.'

As Churchill left the building, Madame des Portes attempted to accost him, crying imperiously 'Monsieur Churchill! Monsieur Churchill! My country is bleeding to death.' Pink with annoyance, pretending that he had not heard, Churchill bored on, butting head first into his Citroen.

It was 5.50 pm on Thursday, 13 June, just thirty-seven days after Hitler had launched his blitzkrieg, and only one thing had been settled. 'America is our only hope,' Reynaud had put it to them, 'without her we are powerless.'

Beaverbrook, a man to whom time had always been money, agreed wholeheartedly. 'Telegraph to Roosevelt,' he advised Churchill, 'and await the answer.' Suddenly irritated, he rattled his loose change. 'We're doing no good here,' he said tersely. 'Let's get along home.'

*

At first, there was only one man to be seen: a solitary German motor cyclist in field grey with a coal-scuttle helmet tut-tutting across the lonely expanse of the Place Voltaire, in Paris. It was 3.40 am Friday, 14 June.

But by 8 am they were coming in their hundreds, a solid goose-stepping phalanx moving across the heart of Paris, past the posters that since February had proudly proclaimed, *Nous vainquerons parce que nous sommes les plus forts.*' (We shall win because we are the strongest.) Simultaneously, braking their landing speed to 25 mph, two Fieseler 'Storch' spotter planes set down on the Place de la Concorde, to disgorge, among other officers, *Oberst* Walter Warlimont of Hitler's Operations Department. Within the hour, the Swastika was floating from the Arc de Triomphe and from the

985-feet Eiffel Tower, where, since the elevators were not working, the flag-bearers had to climb 1671 steps.

To bewildered Parisians, now undergoing what Finns, Danes, Norwegians, Dutch and Belgians had already undergone – the humiliation of surrender – the first Germans they encountered seemed ebullient to a degree but reassuringly human. Outside the Hôtel de Ville, a beaming officer hailed a woman in the crowd: 'Madame, without doubt you eagerly await your husband's return?'

'Yes!'

'Well, so's my wife looking forward to seeing me again. Once we've signed the peace with you we'll settle the whole thing with the British in fifteen days.'

They came, it seemed, less as conquerors than as hungry tourists. In the bistros that night, men who had lived on Army tack for two years were demanding one kilo steaks and 12-egg omelettes, even buying chocolate bars and smearing them thickly with butter. Every man seemed to have a camera and was busy focussing on the Arc de Triomphe, Nôtre Dame and Les Invalides. With a nice sense of what was due to them, senior officers took over the Crillon, the Meurice and the Plaza Athénée Hotels. At Rundstedt's H.Q. at St Germain, orderly officers set up a new type of ops map that promised pleasures to come: blue dots for the best gourmet eating, red dots for the apartments of compliant Parisiennes.

In those regions of France still nominally free, there was no such rejoicing. At Brest, in Brittany, on the evening of 14 June, Second Lieutenant Zygmunt Litynski, of the Polish Highland Brigade, who had shared in the fiasco of Narvik, never forgot the pitiful appearance of the French soldiers on the quayside – 'useless pathetic wrecks', innocent of weapons, cap peaks pulled down, tunics unbuttoned.

Suddenly, from the open doorway of a garage, a woman's voice was heard over the radio – a soft melodious voice, but unmistakably an English accent.

'I, who have always loved France deeply,' the woman was saying. 'I now share with you your sufferings. France is now defending with heroism and courage not only her own land but the lands and liberty of the whole world . . .'

Queen Elizabeth of England was speaking to the people of France. As Litynski watched, first one soldier, then a second and third, got slowly and heavily to his feet, drifting towards the door of the garage. Soon there was a crowd, listening intently, 'the strange weaponless remnants of an army'.

The Queen's tribute continued. '. . . A nation defended by such men, loved by such women, sooner or later is bound to conquer. Such a nation is the mainstay and hope of the whole world . . .'

Suddenly the irony became unbearable. A murmur rippled through the men, and one, raising his empty hands towards his face, cried out: 'Oh God, oh God!' Still the Queen went quietly on, recalling her visit to a hospital of wounded French soldiers. When she had asked them how they were, 'all of them, even the most gravely wounded, replied with one voice "*Ça va*".'

'I do believe with all my heart that when these dark days are gone the time will come when our two nations will be able to say with one voice once more: "*Ça va*".'

*

All through the afternoon of Friday, 14 June, aboard the Presidential yacht, *Potomac*, René de Chambrun was conscious, as men rarely are, of living through history. In the three days since he had arrived in the United States to carry out Weygand's mission, he had realised the magnitude of his task. Both in New York and Washington, D.C., the polite consensus was that France and Britain were finished.

The young Captain sensed no personal hostility. At the White House, Roosevelt had welcomed him warmly as one of the family, which de Chambrun indeed was; as the nephew of the redoubtable Alice Longworth, Theodore Roosevelt's daughter, he and the President had blood ties. It had been 'Dear René' from the first, and de Chambrun was relieved to learn that the only week-end guests aboard the yacht would be 'family' too: Harry L. Hopkins, Roosevelt's Secretary of Commerce and most intimate adviser, Marguerite 'Missy' Le Hand, the President's secretary, Averell Harriman and his wife.

At 4 pm, as the *Potomac* slipped away downstream from the Navy Yard, the heat was torrid. Sipping tea on the quarter-deck, de Chambrun watched Roosevelt and Hopkins intently. These men were symbols of the free world — but how would they react to a chain of events in which total war looked more and more like world revolution?

The answer, it seemed, was with despair. Towards 5 pm a bluejacket handed the President a radiogram and Roosevelt silently passed it over: the Germans had entered Paris, and were marching towards the Loire. In that moment, de Chambrun saw only defeat in Roosevelt's face; his arms had dropped helplessly to his wheel chair. 'René,' he said, 'the show is over. I don't think that Great Britain can hold out.'

De Chambrun's answer was identical to his response to Ambassador Bullitt back in Paris. 'Mr President, unfortunately you're right so far as France is concerned. But I think you're completely wrong as far as Great Britain is concerned.'

For almost an hour thereafter, de Chambrun held the stage. Conscious that both Roosevelt and Hopkins were weighing every pro and con, he advanced the same argument he had given Bullitt: if France kept her Fleet and America supplied Britain with food and bombers, the day would come when air attacks could hit Germany's most vulnerable region, the Ruhr.

110

Unexpectedly, Roosevelt cut in: 'René, you have convinced me.' Then, after a moment, 'I am going to ask you to fulfill an important mission – convince this country.'

De Chambrun smiled uncertainly. 'Mr President, there are 130 million Americans and they all seem to believe in Germany's victory.' But Roosevelt, smiling in return, merely countered, 'What I have just asked you to do is less difficult than that which you have already done. Isn't that right, Harry?'

Taking de Chambrun's silence for assent, Roosevelt got down to cases. Even before dinner was announced, he had scribbled out, on one of the *Potomac*'s telegraph forms, a list of twenty-two influential people whom he wanted de Chambrun to see. Some, Cabinet Ministers or intimate friends were already more than halfway convinced – Hull, Ickes, Eleanor Roosevelt, the financier Bernard Baruch – but others, like Senator Key Pittman and Republican Minority Leader Joe Martin, were hard-core isolationists. De Chambrun would begin on Monday by addressing the Senate's Foreign Relations Committee.

Still de Chambrun wondered: what hope lay ahead for France? In an appeal which likened his country to 'a drowning man', Reynaud had besought Roosevelt to send 'clouds of planes', but America, as Roosevelt gently explained, had no clouds of planes to give. The provisions of the Neutrality Laws decreed that even those he might dredge up – ninety Navy bombers, 173 Army attack planes – must first be flown to tiny Houlton, Maine, towed across the border into Canada, then sold to private manufacturers who in turn would sell them to the Allies.

On Saturday, 15 June, as the yacht once again neared the Navy Yard, de Chambrun drafted a hasty cable for Paul Reynaud. In part it read: (THE PRESIDENT) IS CONVINCED THAT HIS COUNTRY, THE BRITISH EMPIRE AND ALL THAT REMAINS OF THE FRENCH FLEET AND COLONIES CONSTITUTE THE ONLY RAMPART AGAINST WORLD DOMINATION BY GERMANY STOP AS THE CHAMPION OF A CAUSE HE HAS AN ALMOST MYSTICAL BELIEF THAT THE EVENTS OF TODAY MAKE HIM THE ONLY MAN WHO CAN STOP HITLER STOP THE PEOPLE WILL FOLLOW HIM EVEN TO WAR ON TWO CONDITIONS . . . THAT ENGLAND . . . AFFIRM THAT SHE WILL WIN IN SPITE OF THE SETBACKS . . . THAT FRANCE KEEP HER FLEET AND HER EMPIRE.

Thinking back on all he had seen over nine months, de Chambrun had only one reservation. To him it was less than puzzling that France was losing the war. The puzzle was: How could anyone have ever expected her to win it?

*

In Bordeaux, 360 miles south of Paris, where his government had now transferred yet again, Reynaud, on Sunday, 16 June, was anticipating far more than the cautious measure of comfort offered by de Chambrun's cable. Buoyant to the last, he still nourished hopes that Roosevelt, with the classic timing of a Seventh Cavalry squadron, would come to France's aid by declaring war on Germany.

On this day, too, Reynaud was pinning his faith in another last-ditch project: a mooted Franco–British Union, reviving an earlier abortive union effected by Henry V through the Treaty of Troyes in 1420. The brainchild of René Pleven, of the French Economic Mission in London, who had discussed it with both Chamberlain and Churchill, it looked to a joint Franco–British War Cabinet to carry on the struggle, the subjects of both nations to enjoy a common citizenship and a common flag. Even more to Churchill's taste, it called for a mass evacuation of French troops across the Channel, 'to make the island stiff with soldiers'.

Over lunch at the Carlton Club, de Gaulle, on a brief visit to London, had discussed it further with Churchill, who was cautious but impressed. A two-hour Cabinet session at Downing Street had followed, but at last Churchill emerged to tell de Gaulle that the plan was agreed. Promptly de Gaulle had telephoned the details to Reynaud in Bordeaux. At 5 pm Reynaud met with his Council of Ministers, determined 'to die defending these proposals'.

But to a French Cabinet half of whose members were bent on capitulation, the Franco–British Union was stillborn at birth. 'France would be nothing more than a dominion,' one Minister protested. 'It would be fusion with a corpse,' Pétain shrugged. Reynaud had at length reached stalemate, for although no votes were taken, his supporters numbered thirteen, while those in favour of an armistice totalled eleven.

The day held another painful shock for Reynaud. A message whose contents de Chambrun had already discerned arrived from Roosevelt. Its gist was plain; although war matériel would be forthcoming, 'you will understand that these declarations imply no military commitments. Congress alone can undertake such engagements.'

As he read it, Spears noted that Reynaud's face grew paler and contracted, 'his eyes became just slits'. 'Our appeal has failed,' he said, in a small toneless voice, 'the Americans will not declare war.'

*

Late that night, a small false hope flared through Bordeaux like a fading comet. For four unavailing hours Reynaud had pleaded with his Cabinet to go with him to North Africa and carry on the fight from there. In a forlorn hope that he would prevail, he had asked U.S. Envoy-Extraordinary Anthony Drexel Biddle to return at midnight, at which time he could give him news.

112

Somehow word had spread through the port that America *had* declared war – and as Biddle's car nosed through the darkened streets it was greeted by a storm of cheering: '*Vive Les Etats-Unis*' – '*Vive Les Etats-Unis!*'

'I sat there in that car,' Biddle recalled later, 'and I had a lump in my throat, because I knew we weren't going to do a damn thing.'

*

By 10 pm in a 'sarcastic disparaging voice', Reynaud had resigned, and Pétain was confirmed as France's new Premier. It was to this end that the old Marshal had worked all along, for promptly he pulled from his briefcase the list of Cabinet members he had selected. Foreseeing this, Churchill had released France from her obligations as an ally and given her freedom to negotiate an armistice – but only provided that the French Fleet now sailed for British harbours.

At noon on Monday, 17 June, Pétain, through the Spanish Ambassador, set his armistice negotiations in train. Half an hour later, the nation first heard of his intention through a studio broadcast from Bordeaux, where Pétain, in a fine fury, deliberately kicked an errant radio technician on the shin. But the calculated pathos was there as the quavering voice, broken by a dry cough, began hesitantly: 'With a broken heart I tell you that fighting must cease.' One man remembered with shame: 'An old man with the voice of an old woman told us he had asked for peace.'

All over France, on Town Hall steps, in bistros and tenements, people listened as if turned to stone, uncomprehending. Exactly ninety-six days after the Finns had acknowledged defeat, France, the last of the prosperous complacent democracies, had succumbed.

At Ligny-en-Barrois, in the department of the Meuse, the heart of the champagne country, the face of France in defeat showed plain that sunlit Monday afternoon. Marooned in the station was an entire train, twenty waggons long, loaded with champagne and liqueurs. Soon after noon, whole columns of infantrymen, debouching on the station, chanced upon it.

By mid-afternoon, a man approaching the platform had to wade through a sea of broken glass. Hundreds of bottles had been emptied and smashed on the spot; a sticky light brown syrup of cognac and champagne oozed from the looted cars. An old drunken woman who had fallen from a champagne crate lay bleeding face downwards in a glittering mosaic of glass.

The whole station reeked of drink. Soldiers lay recumbent between the rails, snoring or humming in their sleep. Along the tracks, a horde of soldiers, joined by an officer and two non-coms, had set up champagne bottles like ten-pins, bowling at them with other bottles. Each time glass splintered against glass, the players joined hands, yelling and capering and

113

kissing one another. A Bedouin in a bright-coloured turban leaned out of the station-master's office and vomited on the platform.

Only one man seemed to care, a middle-aged captain slumped on a crate, his head buried in his hands. '*La ligne Daladier,*' he moaned repeatedly. '*La ligne Daladier!*' But nobody heeded him, or even understood what he meant. The Maginot Line had already passed into history.

*

It might have been one of Churchill's most historic wartime broadcasts – yet for reasons of state he was never to deliver it.

Its aim was to demonstrate yet again to the Americans that Britain, if down, was not out, whatever poison Ambassador Joseph P. Kennedy might drop in the collective ear of the State Department – and its delivery was timed for the evening of 18 June. Among its enthusiastic proponents was A. V. Alexander, the new First Lord of the Admiralty, who encouraged Churchill: 'The U.S.A. must be on tiptoe for an authoritative voice from this country.'

It was as American-oriented as Churchill, the son of an American mother, could make it. Hitler, he declared, was 'using men's souls and bodies as poker chips'. True, on the basis of territory gained, 'the German supreme gambler has met with success; and success flushes a gambler like bad liquor'. But the end was not yet. 'An army much greater than the entire standing army of the United States today,' had been ferried across the Channel to fight again. 'I say to you,' ended the Premier's peroration, 'what your John Paul Jones said: "*Surrender?* We're only just *beginnin'* to fight."'

But at the last moment Churchill decided against it, unwilling to give ammunition to the American isolationists with whom Roosevelt must contend. Instead he wisely preferred to rely on his private link with 'Potus', as Churchill called the President of the United States, and he didn't hesitate to pressure Roosevelt unmercifully with every passing day. On 11 June, his cry was 'The only counter is destroyers... Not a day should be lost.' On 14 June, he urged the President to publish his message to Reynaud – a plea which Roosevelt and Hull flatly refused to countenance. On 15 June: 'Events are moving at a pace where they will pass beyond the control of American public opinion.' Later on the same day: 'If your reply does not contain the assurance asked for (the entry of the U.S. into war) the French will very quickly ask for an armistice.'

Presumably, Roosevelt's silence on this last one gave Churchill cause to feel he was pressing too hard. As he was later to tell Herbert Morrison, who was unaware of this intimate White House link: 'Only events will serve to turn public opinion in America.'

This was sound thinking. Roosevelt was moving gingerly, a step at a time,

1a Franklin D. Roosevelt

1b The embodiment of France's play-safe strategy – the Maginot Line

2a   Count René de Chambrun

2b   General de Gaulle in London with Major-General Edward Spears

3a   Finnish ski patrol attacking Russian troops dug in on the Salla front

3b   Rescued from the German prison ship *Altmark*

4a Erik Seidenfaden – skilled observer of Europe's turmoil

4b Sumner Welles, U.S. Under Secretary of State (*left*) i London with Winston Churchi and the American Ambassado Joseph P. Kenned

5a Polly Peabody

5b Theodor Broch, mayor of Narvik

5c Vidkun Quisling

6   Oil tanks ablaze at

7 Dunkirk: troops in background wading out from the beaches to embark

8a   Werner Mölders on the eastern front

8b   Fleeing before the Nazi invader: refugees in northern France

9a German troops in Paris

9b Oran

10a   Sheltering in the tube, Piccadilly

10b   Battle of Britain –
newsvendor's view

11a   The killing of a German Messerschmitt 110

11b   R.A.F. pilots 'scramble' into action

12a L.D.V. (Local Defence Volunteers), later the Home Guard, enrolled at Westminster. Dr Jocelin Perkins, Sacrist to the Abbey, being taught rifle drill

12b Assistant Divisional Officer Geoffrey Blackstone, London Fire Brigade

13   London burning

14a The King and Queen visiting
bombed South London

14b The morning after
near Marble Arch

15a Magda Lupescu

15b Hitler meets Franco at Hendaye

15c King Christian of Denmark, despite the occupation, rides out
among his people

16   Coventry Cathedral

like a man testing thin ice, though on 19 June he took a giant one. Out of his Cabinet went the isolationist Secretary of War Harry Woodring, in came the stalwart Republicans, Frank L. Knox and Henry G. Stimson as Secretaries for Navy and War. It was Roosevelt's first step towards a coalition government, prompting outraged cries of 'Dirty politics!' from those Republicans still wedded to isolationism.

But France's fall had clinched one resolution in Roosevelt's mind. With the spectre of Britain alone standing between America and the Axis conquerors, to run for a third term had become imperative. Until now he had kept the options open – 'his decision had been to reserve a decision' as one biographer put it – but by early July his mind was made up. He told the Democrats' Party Chief, James A. Farley: 'Jim, if I'm nominated and elected I could not in these times refuse to take the inaugural oath.'

In Knox, for one, the President had picked a doughty ally. 'Frank,' wrote Harold Ickes, '. . . knows that we must prepare and lose no time about it. He believes that as soon as Germany has consolidated its gains in Europe . . . it will proceed to penetrate South America – and then we will have our work cut out for us in this country.'

*

Secretary Knox's prediction was premature. In this week, Adolf Hitler's thoughts were occupied solely with France's fall and the avenging of the Treaty of Versailles. From the first, the armistice proceedings were to be as carefully stage-managed as a Nazi Party rally. To be sure, the peace terms would not be so harsh as to drive France closer to Britain; the Führer looked as unfavourably on the prospect of a potential French Government in North Africa as on the Free Frenchmen now rallying to General de Gaulle in London. Thus, while Germany would occupy three-fifths of France, including the rich industrial areas north of the Loire, the remaining two-fifths would come under Pétain's aegis. From the first, Hitler was as intent on recognising the Marshal's Cabinet as the official French Government as he was to disavow interest in her Fleet. 'If need be,' Hitler snapped, 'let them sink it.'

But for the rest, the subtle undercurrents of humiliation would be there. The French delegates under General Huntziger, arriving on 21 June, were to meet in the Forest of Compiègne, where Marshal Foch had confronted the Germans who came to sue for peace at the end of World War I. Moreover, the French would hear Hitler's terms in the very same coach, Dining Car 2419 D, which for twenty-two years had been preserved in a nearby museum, complete with printed cards indicating the former seating arrangements.

The frenzied preparations gave rise to some bizarre sights. Under Dr Paul Schmidt, the official interpreter, teams of translators worked all night in a candle-lit church to ensure the terms of surrender were made plain. In a forest glade nearby, so quiet that a woodpecker could be heard tapping against a beech tree, one German diplomat, Erich Tuch, chanced on Hitler quite alone – pirouetting, rehearsing salutes and gracious smiles, the entire act performed in dumb show like a pantomimist at rehearsal.

This was truly the Führer's hour, and once the French delegates had arrived at 3.15 pm on 21 June, he lingered no more than fifteen minutes for the ceremony round the green baize table. The mundane details of surrender were left to *Generaloberst* Wilhelm Keitel, nominal Chief of the German Armed Forces, for Hitler, like his soldiers before him, was in a mood to play tourist in Paris. The Battle of France had cost him barely 150,000 casualties, 111,000 of them wounded men, who would most likely fight again, while his troops now patrolled the Atlantic coast from the North Cape to the Pyrenees. It was the hour wherein a conqueror might relax.

For the most part, Hitler was in rare high spirits. He revelled, like any globe-trotter, in the glory of the Paris Opera and the Panthéon. At the Dôme des Invalides, he launched into a soliloquy beside Napoleon's sunken tomb: 'They have made a big mistake . . . you should look up at Napoleon, feeling small by the very size of the monument.' Three days later, touring Alsace, he rallied one mass parade: 'Do you like this beautiful country?' When the troops chorused, 'Yes, *mein Führer*,' Hitler promised, 'Well, we shall hold on to it forever then.'

It was at this stage that Hitler's architect, Albert Speer, was given the charge of reconstructing Berlin, Nuremberg, Munich, Linz and twenty-seven other cities by way of celebration – most of them to be recast in Swedish granite which had been ordered as long ago as February.

In Berlin, Göbbels, too, was formulating grandiose victory plans: whole oxen were to be roasted at street corners, with free cuts and cold beer for all comers, plus a brand new production of Hitler's favourite operetta, Lehár's *The Merry Widow*. But even Göbbels was careful to keep from the press the alcoholic victory fantasy of Minister of Labour Robert Ley: the construction of five million new apartments and ten 20,000-bed hotels.

In the lower echelons, too, there was an implicit belief in a total and speedy victory. Werner Mölders, transferred from Alençon to a prison camp near Toulouse, recalled a long-standing vow with his fellow fliers: the first drinks on reaching London would be in the R.A.F. Club, Piccadilly. A non-com billeted on the Van Duren household in Breda, Holland, told them nonchalantly: 'Any day now I'm off to Downing Street.' In an Antwerp jewellers, a *Hauptmann* haggling for a bargain in diamond rings, finally pushed the tray aside – 'Probably I'll do better in London.'

At the Staff H.Q. of Schützenregiment 11, 9th Armoured Division, *Gefreiter* Wilhelm Prüller was as fiercely confident as any. 'Give us the right to live of our own free will, Mr Churchill,' he wrote in his diary, 'and . . . you will spare the English nation useless mountains of corpses.' He ended on a note of challenge: 'Choose, Mr Churchill!'

*

In London, Winston Churchill had chosen – to fight tyranny with tyranny.

On 22 May, the mild-mannered Clement Attlee had risen in the House of Commons to ask Parliament to approve the Emergency Powers Defence Bill – technically an extension of one passed in August 1939, giving the King wide powers to govern by decree in wartime, following his Privy Council's advice. In effect it gave Churchill and his Ministers wider powers than had been vested in any caucus since the death of absolute monarchy.

It had been sparked off only twenty-four hours back by a memorandum from General Sir Hastings Ismay, Assistant Secretary to the War Cabinet – a thesis which credited Hitler with plans he had never remotely formulated. 'It can be taken for granted,' Ismay posited, 'that the Germans have the plan for an invasion of this country worked out to the last details . . . We can be sure that Hitler would be prepared to sacrifice 90 per cent of the whole expedition if he could gain a firm bridgehead on British soil with the remaining 10 per cent . . .'

'The counter to such forces,' Ismay maintained, 'is a scheme of well-planned demolitions covered by resolute troops.' But he warned, 'no real progress can be made unless the powers over persons and property, which it is intended the Government should assume in a grave emergency, are taken at once.'

Next day, within two hours forty-three minutes, and opposed by only two dissenting voices, the Bill became law – as momentous a step as any in British history. To resist Hitler, Britons had surrendered the rights over persons and property which they had wrested from King John at Runnymede 725 years earlier. From this day on, for example, an Englishman's home was no longer his castle: any man with a uniform or badge could enter his house, search it, turn out his lights, send him to bed or take him to gaol.

Not only his house, but his factory, his 'car, and his bank account were now the intimate concerns of the State. Supply Minister Herbert Morrison not only assumed powers to control factories needed to produce munitions and equipment but to prescribe the hours of work, the labour employed, the price of the goods. By a strange anomaly, Minister of Labour Ernie Bevin, who had battled all his life for a 40-hour week, now commanded workers to ban strikes, work a 7-day week, and toil uncomplainingly alongside unskilled non-union labour.

Although Bevin at first used his powers sparingly, the Act empowered him to march into any Pall Mall club, demand details of a member's war effort, and if need be, direct him forthwith to the nearest Labour Exchange.

Overnight, after nine months' stagnation, Britain was on a total war footing. As early as 14 May, Eden, as Secretary of State for War, had made a radio appeal for what he privately called 'a broomstick Army', known to the public as the Local Defence Volunteers. Soon to be re-christened the 'Home Guard' by Churchill – and dubbed by a later generation 'Dad's Army' – the force consisted of any man not in uniform, aged between sixteen and sixty-five, who was committed to a minimum ten hours' duty a week scouting for paratroops.

The response was overwhelming. The first volunteers were besieging police stations within four minutes of Eden's appeal – although only one in three of the 500,000 strong force could be equipped with rifles.

Even in this hour of crisis, the London *Times* felt moved to make a nice distinction: 'It would not be correct for country gentlemen to carry their guns with them on their walks and take flying or running shots as opportunity is offered . . . Such action would put them into the position of *franc-tireurs . . .*'

From 28 May on, as the Dunkirk evacuation gathered momentum, Britain was honeycombed with ghost towns. To the bafflement of 117,000 London school children evacuated to remote villages by the Great Western Railway, all signposts, milestones, village signs and street names now came down – an idea to fox potential invaders thought up by the thriller writer Dennis Wheatley in a strategic plan submitted to the War Cabinet. Already pill-boxes, three and a half feet of solid concrete, bulked as tank traps in thousands of village streets. In South Wales, the miners made plans to blow up the pits and take to the hills armed with picks and shovels.

But what gravely preoccupied Churchill and his Ministers was not only the vulnerability of the south and east coasts, but the potential threat to their own back door through the green republic of Eire. On 4 June, the First Sea Lord, Admiral Sir Dudley Pound, had urged his chief, A. V. Alexander: 'Would it not be worth while trying to get de Valera to agree to British forces being sent to Eire, on the understanding that at the end of the war our troops would be immediately removed?'

The bones of contention were the Irish treaty ports of Queenstown (now Cobh), Berehaven and Lough Swilly, Royal Naval bases in World War I, which Chamberlain, to Churchill's fury, had handed back to Eire in 1938. 'A more feckless act can hardly be imagined,' Churchill had fulminated then, and now, fearing their seizure by Germany, he debated the idea of seizing them first, as bases against U-boat operations in the North Atlantic.

But even as France fell, Eire's leader, 58-year-old Eamon de Valera, was still bent on a neutrality as unswerving as Sweden or Switzerland. On 18 June, he made his position abundantly clear to the German Ambassador, Dr Eduard Hempel: if England invaded Eire, the Irish would fight them shoulder to shoulder with the Germans. But if Germany invaded, the Irish would make common cause with the English.

One day earlier, a 'tired and frightened de Valera', afflicted by near-blindness, had put this same viewpoint to the British Minister of Health, Malcolm MacDonald, an old friend and son of a former Labour Prime Minister, who had journeyed to Dublin as Churchill's secret emissary. His every action was being studied and analysed, de Valera complained bitterly, lest he strayed from the path of strict neutrality.

What maddened the ailing *Taoiseach* past all patience was that the British refused to take no for an answer. Almost as if the first interview, lasting three-and-a-half hours, had never taken place, MacDonald was sent back on 25 June to propose the unthinkable: a joint union of Eire and Northern Ireland, with Eire not only affording sanctuary to British troops and offering the use of her ports but entering the war as Britain's ally.

'An invasion of your country would embarrass us but it would be disastrous for you,' MacDonald had hinted. But de Valera was unyielding. The presence of any foreign troops on Irish soil would destroy Eire's national unity, he maintained. Thus he would resist either belligerent to the utmost limit of his power. The situation was so frustrating that even the law-abiding Chamberlain was tempted to consider entering the ports by force – though he counselled caution 'in view . . . of the possible unfavourable reaction which would be caused in the United States'.

In the last resort, the War Cabinet placed infinite faith in MacDonald's powers of persuasion. On 27 June, the weary Minister returned to Dublin, to continue, in Halifax's words, 'the process of educating Mr de Valera as to the dangers of invasion'.

*

At Miss Coffey's boarding-house in the genteel Dublin suburb of Dun Laoghaire, a morose stranger whom the other guests knew as a commercial traveller named Mr Robinson was debating his dubious future.

Since early May, when a Heinkel 111 airborne from Kassel, Germany, had dropped him near Ballivor, County Meath, seventy miles wide of his target, *Hauptmann* Dr Hermann Goertz, a 50-year-old agent of the *Abwehr* (German Military Intelligence) had seen everything go as wrong as it feasibly could.

Briefed by the *Abwehr* to explore chances of stirring up 'a partisan war in Ulster', Goertz had had all the strikes against him from the first. At the moment that he baled out and hit Irish soil, his second parachute containing not only his radio set but the spade to bury the chute by which he descended, had drifted far from sight. When he was forced to swim the Boyne River, because the footbridge was guarded by police, the invisible ink pad concealed in his shoulder padding had been ruined, staining his underwear a sickly yellow.

Goertz' intention of travelling in full uniform to establish his 'international status' had thus been doomed to failure. Discarding his sodden flying suit and service dress jacket, he soldiered on in a pullover, breeches and riding boots, a black beret perched on his head. Four days later, keeping scrupulously to by-roads, he reached Laragh, in County Wicklow, the home of his one and only Irish contact, Professor Francis Stuart. Stuart, a lecturer in Anglo–Irish literature at Berlin University, was a patriot of the de Valera stripe, but he had no links with the *Abwehr* and few with the Irish Republican Army, the paramilitary force whose goal was a united Ireland.

Stuart's wife, Iseult, given no warning of Goertz' arrival, was at first highly suspicious. Finally she agreed to travel to Dublin and buy him a civilian suit, at the same time tipping off Jim O'Donovan, a one-time I.R.A. agent, who obligingly took Goertz off her hands. Hidden up in O'Donovan's garage in the Dublin suburb of Shankill, Goertz next became the concern of I.R.A. activists. Willy-nilly, he found himself shunted to another 'safe' house – the home of Stephen Carroll Held, who had once visited Berlin to urge the Germans to invade Ulster.

Only when a police raid turned over Held's house, narrowly missing Goertz, as he took off over the garden wall, did the German realise that de Valera's Eire and the I.R.A. were not as one, as the *Abwehr* had always believed. Then as now, the I.R.A. were proscribed terrorists and as such, hunted men. But the raid was to cost Goertz more than a loss of faith. In Held's safe, the police had found $20,000 in American currency, the bulk of Goertz' travelling expenses, which he had entrusted to the Irishman.

Thus by the first week in June Goertz was a fugitive who had lost his money, his transmitter, his secret ink, his uniform and all faith in the I.R.A.; he alone could have told both Churchill and de Valera that the Germans had absolutely no plans for Ireland at all. In fact, on 25 May, having had no radio contact, the *Abwehr* had written him off – at roughly the same time as Goertz wrote off the I.R.A.

'The organisation,' he went on record bitterly, 'was rotten at its roots.'

*

On the night of 21 June, Dr R. V. Jones, the ebullient young scientist who sought the elusive German detector beams called Knickebein, was a preoccupied man. In the flat which he and his wife Vera rented at Richmond Hill Court, South London, Jones twisted uneasily in bed, counting the hours. In spirit, he was far from Richmond; he was a passenger in a twin-seater Anson trainer plane, airborne from Wynton airfield, Huntingdonshire, flying steadily north.

The Anson's pilot, Flight Lieutenant Hal Bufton, had reason to view the flight more phlegmatically. Knowing nothing of the Knickebein story, he had been told only to scout for Lorenz-type transmissions – but this was the third night that he and his wireless operator, Corporal Mackie, had searched without success.

Earlier that day, Jones had been startled to find himself in the Cabinet Room at 10, Downing Street, expounding the story of his Knickebein investigations to Winston Churchill. Conscious that most men present – Professor Lindemann, Sir Archibald Sinclair, Dowding, Sir Cyril Newall – were some thirty years his senior, Jones had left the meeting elated by the reception of his far-flung theory.

For Churchill had shown a lively interest. If the beams did exist, he had asked, what could be done? Jones had ready answers. Once found, they could be jammed, as Dowding had earlier suggested. Or false cross-beams could be introduced, to fool the Germans into dropping their bombs too early. The question arose: where should an aircraft search for the beams? Jones, remembering the Germans had pinpointed a location near Retford, Nottinghamshire, played a hunch. Supposing the director beam was laid on Derby, where the Rolls-Royce works were turning out Merlin engines for Beaverbrook's Hurricanes and Spitfires?

The hunch paid off. Around 10 pm, as Jones was retiring uneasily to bed, Bufton and Mackie struck lucky. A series of dots, sixty to the minute, were suddenly mosquito-shrill in Mackie's headphones. As the Anson flew on, the dots merged into a steady monotone, then abruptly broke up. At the same steady rate of sixty to the minute, the dots had been supplanted by dashes.

What the two-man crew had chanced upon was a narrow beam, not more than 500 yards wide, passing just south of Spalding, Lincolnshire, with dots to the south and dashes to the north. A second beam, intersecting with the first, was passing over Beeston, Nottinghamshire – but this time with dots to the north and dashes to the south.

Although Knickebein could be roughly traversed over any sector of eastern England on a line between London and Edinburgh, Bufton and Mackie had struck it where Jones and predicted – trained on Rolls Royce, Derby.

Next day, 22 June, saw such exultation at the Air Ministry that one elderly Air Commodore actually skipped like a faun across his office. Now counter measures could be brought into play against Knickebein. A special anti-beam organisation, No. 80 Wing, R.A.F. was set up at Radlett, north of London, under Wing-Commander Edward Addison. At Swanage, Dorset, the Telecommunications Research Establishment, under Dr Robert Cockburn, got even higher priority. Their first jammers were electro-diathermy sets hastily snatched from hospital wards, to set up a 'mush' of noise on the Knickebein frequencies, but soon high-powered custom-built jammers, nicknamed 'Aspirins' were superimposing powerful morse dashes on the German beam wavelengths. Thus the steady monotone the bomber pilot needed to guide him to the target was now lacking, he heard only a nonstop sequence of dashes. If he swung to the dot zone by way of correction, he met up with a mind-boggling confusion of both dashes and dots.

The beams were never 'bent', as legend claimed, merely confused enough to ensure that many bombs aimed at provincial industrial targets went wide of their mark. Such technical details were too trifling for Churchill; for him, thereafter, Jones was always 'the man who broke the Bloody Beam'.

*

In the air, the British were thus far holding their own. On the ground their chances looked slimmer.

In the quiet south-coast resort of Bognor Regis, Sussex, 11-year-old Sonia Bech watched the landscape transformed with each passing day. The daughter of a Danish porcelain dealer, who had stayed on in London, Sonia, her mother, 14-year-old Barbara and 9-year-old Derek, had remained at the family's summer home, for fear the capital was bombed. But now even Bognor, beloved of King George V, where the Royal Norfolk Hotel had always insisted on black ties at dinner, had become a cat's cradle of mines and barbed wire. Sentries were posted everywhere, manning pill boxes and even bathing machines filled with pebbles. Bognor had become the front line.

Sonia wondered how long the Bechs would stay put; her mother, Marguerite, was becoming uneasy over Britain's future. Her memories of bombing in World War I were all too vivid, and the sight of the beaten men from Dunkirk beaches, unshaven, swathed in bloody bandages, reeking like polecats and prone to sudden bursts of hysteria, did nothing to reassure her. The idea of the whole family seeking refuge with a relative in Montreal was already in her mind.

The sights that Sonia saw on her way to school were being re-enacted in scores of coastal towns. By early July, the voluntary evacuation of the 185-mile coastal area between Sheringham, Norfolk, and Folkestone, Kent, had been extended 180 miles further, as far south-west as Portland, Dorset. The hardships were manifold — one town, Lowestoft, Suffolk, was already in the hands of a bank — and many houses blocking a field of fire were flattened out of hand. On hand to supervise their demolition was one of the new fire-eating commanders whom Eden had sought, Major-General Bernard Montgomery, zestfully gesticulating with his swagger stick: 'Have them out. Blow up the house. Defence must come first.'

The ground defences were pitiful. If only one Home Guardsman in three had a rifle, the Army was in poor shape too. To defend 2,000 miles of coastline, of which 800 were assailable, the new C.-in-C., Home Forces, General Ironside, had in theory twenty-six divisions — fourteen badly mauled from France and Norway, twelve totally unequipped raw training divisions.

From Dover to Southampton, there was one machine gun to defend each 1,500 yards of beach. At Deal, Kent, the men of the 5th Battalion, Shropshire Light Infantry, had one Bren gun between 750 men.

All along the coast, the weird barricades showed the shape of the war to come, a guerilla war with the people caught up in its midst. At Chilham, Kent, Home Guardsmen manhandled tree trunks from the sawmills; at Tonbridge, nearby, it was tar barrels from the distillery. At Goring-by-Sea, in Sussex, the locals made do with a flimsy latticework of old iron bedsteads. Inland, at Sidcup crossroads, the police had dumped 100 tons of broken glass, as if for a medieval siege.

Spy scares abounded. At Winchester, a clergyman's daughter even denounced as a spy a British officer billeted at her father's rectory; he had shown 'un-English' behaviour by visiting the lavatory and failing to pull the chain afterwards. But other authorities, who should have known better, over-reacted too, none more so than the Home Secretary, Sir John Anderson, 'Pompous John', a one-time Governor of Bengal. From June onwards, 'alarm and despondency' fines ranging from £50 to £100, and wholesale incarcerations in gaol were visited on all who spoke their minds too freely. 'It'll be a good thing when the British Empire is finished,' was one man's opinion: it netted him a year in gaol. 'You're bloody fools to wear those uniforms,' a woman told a group of soldiers: her reward was three months' gaol and a £20 fine.

'Begging your pardon, Sir John,' scolded the London *News Chronicle*, 'we would remind you that you are no longer in Bengal . . ' After seventy such prosecutions, Churchill, who had never relished the idea, vetoed all further proceedings.

More at risk in this climate of fear and suspicion were Britain's 100,000 aliens, of whom the heavy-handed Sir John gaoled fully 30,000 in sub-human conditions — so many that Churchill chided the Cabinet that it was 'unjust to treat our friends as foes.' Why not, he asked, consider forming a Foreign Legion?

But for many months yet, thousands were to suffer like the 4,000 interned at Huyton, Lancashire, housed under appalling conditions, without hot water; two-thirds of them were sleeping in tents on rain-sodden ground, in a camp where rations were so scarce that the rueful commandant could do no more than console them: 'I can only prevent you from starving.' Hemmed in by the very sentries and barbed wire that many of them had fled Hitler's Europe to escape and faced with the prospect of deportation to Canada, at least one each day committed suicide.

'I can't believe,' wrote one shocked observer to the Deputy Director General of the Ministry of Information, Sir Walter Monckton, 'that English people would allow it to go on.'

Unhappily, the English would. The humiliations of France, Belgium and

Norway had nourished a fierce irrational xenophobia, a hard and unforgiving core, which the Ministry's Mass Observers were swift to perceive. 'There ought to be an earthquake in France and swallow the whole bloody lot up.' . . . 'They might be spies – they're a dirty lot' were two typical comments. Noted one observer in despair: 'It is becoming the socially done thing to be anti-refugee.'

In the week that France fell, Air Chief Marshal Sir Hugh Dowding, C.-in-C. of Fighter Command summed up the way most Englishmen felt as Britain awaited the worst. Staring across the rose garden from his office window at Stanmore, Middlesex, Dowding turned back abruptly to his guest, Lord Halifax.

'Thank God we're now alone,' he said.

6

'I Am ... The Victor Speaking In The Name Of Reason'

27 June–7 August 1940

THE FATE OF the French Fleet a major prize for any warring nation was causing Britain grave concern. Until now, the British and the French had between them dominated the Mediterranean but without France, the British faced an Italian challenge. Although marginally superior in battleships – seven against Italy's six – plus the added might of two aircraft carriers, the British Mediterranean Fleet was still outnumbered in cruisers and destroyers. Italy, by contrast, boasted the world's largest submarine fleet, and ten land-based aircraft for every plane that the R.A.F. could spare. If France joined the war on the Axis side, the British could be swept from the Mediterranean.

Ironically, the seeds of distrust were first sown in the British by a Frenchman, René Cambon, of the London Embassy. On 17 June, Orme Sargent, the Foreign Office's Deputy Under Secretary of State, minuted Sir Alexander Cadogan: 'Cambon remarked to me this morning that the new French Govt would behave worse than King Leopold, and that we should not put too much trust in Ad. Darlan.'

This led the First Sea Lord, Sir Dudley Pound, to speculate that the French would sink their Fleet rather than undergo the humiliation of surrender – adding 'if the French would not sink their Fleet we could perhaps do it for them'.

The idea did Darlan, Pétain's new Minister of Marine, less than justice, both as a patriot and as a politician. France's intention was to keep firm hold on her Fleet as a prime bargaining card – a card she was in no way disposed to yield to Britain despite Churchill's insistence. Already, on 18 June, Darlan had ordered the unfinished battleship *Richelieu* to leave Brest for Dakar, Senegal, at full speed. One day later, although also incomplete, the battleship *Jean Bart* left St Nazaire for Casablanca.

The stumbling-block Darlan sought to overcome was Article 8 of the Franco–German Armistice treaty, which laid down that warships were to be returned to their peacetime stations and disarmed under Axis supervision. Under these conditions, two-thirds of the Fleet would lie at anchor in German-occupied ports.

Thus, Darlan took no chances. By 29 June, the bulk of his Fleet was

125

assembled at Oran and Mers-el-Kebir, harbours in the Bay of Oran, Algeria, 200 miles east of Gibraltar. From his flagship, the *Dunkerque*, Admiral Marcel Henri Gensoul, C.-in-C. of the Atlantic Fleet, held a watching brief over the great battle-cruiser *Strasbourg*, as well as two battleships, seven light cruisers, four submarines and a torpedo boat.

Three days later, unknown to the French, the British War Cabinet had evolved four courses of action for their Fleet to follow: to sail with the British Fleet to fight the Axis, to sail under supervision to British ports, to sail with reduced crews to the West Indies, or to scuttle their ships within six hours. Failing this, the British would use 'whatever force may be necessary'.

This last alternative appalled Churchill. On the night of 2 July, Beaverbrook was summoned to the Cabinet Room to find a highly agitated Premier closeted with Pound and Alexander. If the French did not comply with one of the first three alternatives, Pound favoured an all-out bombardment, and Churchill could not stomach it. He saw an alliance between France and Britain, born thirty-six years ago and twice sealed with blood in Flanders, rushing towards a nightmare end.

Beaverbrook did not hesitate: there was no choice but to attack. He foresaw that the Germans would force the French Fleet to join the Italians, thus taking command of the Mediterranean. 'The Germans will force this,' Beaverbrook prophesied, 'by threatening to burn Bordeaux the first day the French refuse, the next day Marseilles, and the third day Paris'.

Suddenly, overcome, Churchill seized Beaverbrook's arm and ran almost headlong into the garden of No. 10. 'I had trouble keeping up with him,' Beaverbrook was to recall, 'and I began to have an attack of asthma.' He remembered, too, Churchill's words: 'There is no other decision possible.' A high wind had blown up through the garden, and Churchill was crying.

*

Soon after 4 pm on Wednesday, 3 July, five men met in the stifling cabin of Admiral Marcel Henri Gensoul aboard the flagship *Dunkerque*. It was a meeting which Gensoul and his aides had been seeking to avoid since 9.30 that morning, so that until now all the efforts of Captain Cedric Holland, R.N., the former Naval Attaché in Paris, to come aboard, had been unavailing. Since Gensoul had refused point-blank to receive him, Holland had been forced to negotiate aboard a barge in the broiling heat of mid-harbour with the Admiral's Flag Lieutenant, *Lieutenant de Vaisseau* Bernard Dufay.

At their first 10 am meeting, Dufay had warned that Gensoul was mortally offended by Britain's threats of force — and by the ships of Force 'H', under Vice-Admiral Sir James Somerville, making steady legs to seaward in the Bay of Oran. It was to Dufay that Holland had been forced to entrust Somerville's ultimatum to Gensoul.

Gensoul, when he scanned it, was in no way mollified. Not only was he angered that Britain suspected Darlan of operating under Axis duress; he felt slighted that the British by implication, doubted his capability to scuttle his own ships if the need arose.

As early as 9.45 am Gensoul had signalled a précis of the situation to Darlan's temporary headquarters near Bordeaux, though strangely he made no mention of the West Indies option. But Darlan, at this hour, was absent from the office, and his Chief of Staff, Rear Admiral Le Luc, was momentarily at a loss. At 1.30 am, however, unable to reach Darlan, Le Luc, on his own initiative, sent fifty French warships full steam ahead for Oran to back Gensoul's resistance.

Meanwhile, in London, the last chance to avert imminent tragedy had been thrown away on this same morning. Although Pound had drafted a signal authorising Somerville to accept the de-militarisation of the French ships where they lay, the War Cabinet rejected it, 'since this would look like weakening'.

'The deadly stroke', as Churchill was to call it, was coming nearer by the hour.

By 1.30 pm, the mining of the outer harbour entrances had been carried out by planes from the aircraft carrier *Ark Royal*. Gensoul was all but trapped and he knew it. However, stalling for time and planning to make a break after nightfall, he finally agreed to see Captain Holland and his party. By this hour, 4 pm, the mining of the inner harbours had effectively sealed off his Fleet inside Oran and Mers-el-Kebir.

The atmosphere was hostile from the start. 'The first shot fired . . . will be tantamount to a declaration of war between France and Great Britain,' Gensoul told Holland, stiffly. 'Is this what you want?'

'Of course not.'

'Do you not trust my word of honour?' asked Gensoul coldly.

'I am quite sure you will do everything possible to prevent your ships falling into enemy hands,' Holland conceded. 'However, we do not trust the Germans or Italians.'

Holland, like Somerville, who called the whole venture 'A filthy job', was sickened by the role he had to play. By accepting any one of the alternatives, he urged Gensoul, he would be yielding to *force majeure* and the blame would fall on the British. Gensoul, stubborn and correct, rejected this: 'I have my code of honour.'

Then, to Holland's total dismay, Gensoul unbent sufficiently to hand him a copy of Darlan's top-secret instructions, dated 24 June. Rather than have them fall into Axis hands, Gensoul was authorised either to scuttle his ships or to head for the United States. 'It's so nearly what we are asking you to do now – to sail for America,' Holland pleaded. But Gensoul's pride was also involved. 'Yes, but not under the threat of your guns,' he answered.

But already two signals had decided the fate of the French Fleet. At the same time as Gensoul learned from Admiral Le Luc's Message 3309 that 'all French forces in the Mediterranean will rally to you immediately', the Admiralty on receipt of an 'Enigma' intercept, cautioned Somerville with their own Message 1614/3: 'Settle matters quickly or you will have reinforcements to deal with.'

From his own flagship, H.M.S. *Hood*, Somerville at once issued his final ultimatum: if the French had not complied with one or other alternative by 5.30 pm, he would open fire. Sick at heart, Holland left *Dunkerque* for the last time.

In fact, not until 5.54 pm, to enable Holland to get clear, did Somerville's battle squadron open fire, but the timing was immaterial. In this first Franco–British sea battle for over a century, fought between the sworn allies of two weeks' back, the French never stood a chance. As the 15-inch shells came screaming through a drifting smokescreen over a 7-mile range, only *Dunkerque* and the battleship *Provence* were even close enough to hit back.

As columns of water and oil spouted 300 feet high, there was little for the other ships to do but die bravely. Aboard the blazing battleship *Bretagne*, orders were given to abandon the crow's nest, but the ladder descending to the deck was red-hot; as the burning ropes frayed and parted, the look-outs plummeted to their death. The duty officer, *Lieutenant de Vaisseau* Etienne Sicard, grasping a handrail, found himself hurtling into space along with the bridge; as he sank forty feet below the water he thought quizzically of a ski-jump. Fighting slowly back to the surface, he witnessed astonishing sights.

With a tortured howl of escaping steam, *Dunkerque*, caught by a shell in a starboard boiler room, was drifting slowly aground like a killer whale beached in the shallows. *Provence*, hit in the stern by a salvo, split apart and capsized with a loss of 900 lives. In the thick 2-inch film of fuel which covered the harbour, dotted with bobbing red matelots' pom-poms, exhausted men choked on the oil then died

At the moment the destroyer *Mogador* was hit, blown up by her own depth charges, Sicard and his fellow survivors took comfort from a sight which moved them to tears: the battle-cruiser *Strasbourg*, escaping for Toulon amid the confusion, speeding full ahead past the pier, all guns firing, her guard presenting arms, a band playing full blast on her stern.

After ten minutes all firing ceased. The massacre was over. Within hours on this day, which had also witnessed bloodless French surrenders at Alexandria and Plymouth, the world's fourth fleet had been knocked out of action to an astonishing extent: 84 per cent of its battleship strength, 48 per cent of its cruiser strength, all its aircraft carriers, 16 per cent of its destroyers, 14 per cent of its submarines, 50 per cent of its sub-chasers.

Yet this was a battle, unusually for 1940, where the aggressors felt only guilt. 'It was an absolutely bloody business to shoot up those Frenchmen who showed the greatest gallantry,' Somerville wrote to his wife. 'We all feel thoroughly dirty and ashamed.' Most British naval officers echoed wholeheartedly the bleak words of Admiral Gensoul at the mass funeral of 1,297 Frenchmen in the cemetery at Oran: 'If there is a stain on the flag it is certainly not on ours.'

Only one man, it seemed, approved unreservedly, for to him it demonstrated a truth which Ambassador Joseph P. Kennedy had long been at pains to deny: that the British were mean fighters when roused. On the bottom of the daily military report submitted to Franklin Roosevelt, Lord Lothian noted in longhand: 'You will see that Winston Churchill has taken the action in regard to the French Fleet which we discussed and you approved.'

*

On the day that news of Mers-el-Kebir hit the world's headlines, René de Chambrun had almost talked himself hoarse. For eighteen days, with missionary fervour, de Chambrun had travelled non-stop across the United States, as Roosevelt had urged him, clarifying, persuading, arguing. The President's first list of twenty-two contacts had long since been ticked off. From there de Chambrun had gone on to talk with Lord Lothian at the British Embassy, with influential publishers like Henry Luce and Roy Howard, and with pollster George Gallup. In the mid-west he had conferred with farmers, bankers and civic leaders. He had dined with men as loyal to Roosevelt as William Allen White and with Roosevelt-haters like Governor Harold Stassen of Minnesota. Wherever he had journeyed, his theme had been the same: Great Britain needed arms and planes to survive, southern France, where Pétain held sway, needed food and medicine.

To de Chambrun's surprise, his own father-in-law, Pierre Laval, had been called upon to serve as Pétain's Vice-President. A canny businessman from Auvergne, whose drooping moustaches and white piqué ties were the delight of cartoonists, Laval was no stranger to politics: twice Premier of France and Foreign Minister from 1934–36, he had openly opposed all involvement in a war he knew that France would lose. Now, by letters and cables, de Chambrun learned from his wife, Josée, that her father had taken office with rueful resignation, comparing himself to the receiver of a firm in bankruptcy. On one count, de Chambrun had no doubts: France's role as combatant had now ceased. When Pétain, bristling with rage, proposed bombing Gibraltar to square accounts for Mers-el-Kebir, Laval replied wearily: 'We have just lost one war. Are we about to start and lose another?'

Some American politicians foresaw another stumbling block: the inevitable clash of interests between Laval, who must seek accommodation with the Germans, and the first cadre of 2,000 Free Frenchmen who had rallied to de Gaulle in London. In reply, de Chambrun quoted Laval's words to Josée: 'There are two policies, that of resistance abroad and that of mine in France. Both must be carried out.'

In all these weeks, de Chambrun had been sure of one thing: he had put the case for Great Britain as forcefully as any native son. Even as early as 17 June, Secretary of the Treasury Henry Morgenthau had assured him: 'You have galvanised the President.' One day later, Senator Robert Taft, until now an isolationist to his fingertips, had conceded: 'I am ready to envisage going to war if I were absolutely certain that by doing so it would save England.' On 27 June, Cordell Hull told de Chambrun: 'You have given our President courage. He and we need it.'

The most heartfelt tribute came later, in a personal letter dated 9 August, from a man who was more involved than most, Lord Lothian: 'Practically single-handed you were able to sway official opinion over here in favour of my country . . . Great Britain will never forget what you did for her in her days of plight and distress.'

The climate of opinion, de Chambrun saw, had swung overwhelmingly towards Britain. But how would his own country fare?

It was Roosevelt himself who raised this issue, in a White House meeting on 1 August. The young Captain had done everything that had been asked of him. 'Now,' the President queried, 'what can *I* do for France?'

'There is only one policy to embrace,' de Chambrun answered incisively, 'feed her.'

Roosevelt seemed reluctant. 'I would like to – but if I send supplies there the Nazis will grab them.'

De Chambrun was sceptical. 'Mr President, do you think the Nazis would dare cross the demarcation line to take from French mouths condensed milk that Americans may have sent over? It is true that they have made many mistakes, but I doubt that they would make this one.'

Already, he explained, he had worked out a formula with Lothian and Harry Hopkins. There would be successive deliveries, three or four weeks apart, to limit the risk of cargo confiscation. From these cargoes, America would derive major political and moral benefits, which would help arouse French public opinion against Germany.

Roosevelt thought hard, then finally came up with a plan. De Chambrun must return to see France and see Pétain. The Marshal must call a press conference and make a pro-American statement in favour of the democratic ideal. At the same time Pétain must silence the floodtide of press vituperation that had followed Mers-el-Kebir. If those conditions were met, 'I shall see to it that the free zone receives regular food shipments . . . for the duration of hostilities.'

'Bring me back a good letter from the old Marshal,' Roosevelt rallied him. 'I shall release it during one of my press conferences.'

Only one query was still unanswered: the reaction of Churchill and the War Cabinet. But at 6 pm on this same day, de Chambrun called at the British Embassy to receive Lothian's assurance. 'My government agrees,' Lothian told him, 'on the condition that the quantities shipped are reasonable and that the ships have a rather low tonnage.'

De Chambrun was ecstatic. For almost two months he had worked with everything he knew to ensure two prime essentials: arms for free Britain, food for impoverished France. His last call before returning home was at the White House to tender his thanks.

Roosevelt, he always remembered, winked at him hugely as they said good-bye. 'René,' were his parting words, 'it's a deal.'

*

True to her vow, Polly Peabody arrived in Unoccupied France, still convinced that she could in some way help the French. It seemed logical to head for the spa town of Vichy, once just a name on a bottle of mineral water, where the Pétain Government was now established, and where Polly was to witness 'some of the saddest and most amazing pages of French history'

What struck her most forcibly, six days after Mers-el-Kebir, was the pervasive hatred of England. Pétain had at once broken off diplomatic relations with Great Britain, but the timely warning Roosevelt had voiced to de Chambrun was still some weeks away; the columnists of the Vichy press had traded in ink for vitriol. 'To those who recall the clarion calls of . . . a fortnight ago for sacrifice,' cabled Ambassador Bullitt to the State Department, 'it is revolting to watch the complete about-face of the French Press.'

In part due to Bullitt and the U.S. Chargé d'Affaires, Robert Murphy, Americans were still accepted in Unoccupied France. But Polly sensed that feelings ran high. 'Hell, we'll be just as well off under German rule,' a French soldier sneered aboard the crowded train bound for Vichy, but when Polly rebuked him, the entire compartment flew at her as one. 'An American! If you're as patriotic about France as all that, why didn't you send us some guns instead of cotton wool and pills?'

In defeat, Polly felt, the people of Vichy France were determined that all should share in the blame. In a mass-wave of self-recrimination, they saw their débâcle as Weygand had done, the price of laxity: paid holidays for workers and the 40-hour week, changes which the leftist Léon Blum's Popular Front government had wrought in the 'thirties, were now blamed along with such strange concomitants as adultery and aniseed aperitifs. 'Better Hitler than Blum,' many had said then, and now they reaffirmed this view. The messiah of this new asceticism was Pétain himself, who was soon to

131

ban both Pernod as decadent and nail varnish for women as 'a demoralising Jewish–Oriental habit'. On 10 July, winding up the Third French Republic with a new and inward-looking slogan, '*Travail, Famille, Patrie*', Pétain told Bullitt morosely, 'It's all been the fault of Socialist schoolteachers.'

Polly Peabody was appalled by the 'snake's nest' that was Vichy, though she was willing to stay on if her help was needed. Through the intercession of Gaston Henri-Haye, an old family friend and Vichy's Ambassador-designate in Washington, she counted herself lucky to get a fourth share in a hotel room for five francs a week. Already the little spa was bursting at the seams with refugees from the German-occupied zone; hundreds were sleeping in armchairs, bath tubs and even parked cars.

All over France, as the world crumbled, refugees were on the run. The Baron and Baroness Robert de Rothschild had fled to England on a tramp steamer, along with former French Air Minister Pierre Cot, Eve Curie and the political commentator Geneviève Tabouis. The Grand Duchess Charlotte of Luxembourg and the jeweller Pierre Cartier were among thousands seeking refuge in Spain; former Premier Edouard Daladier was en route to Lisbon, soon to be followed by ex-King Edward VIII. Homeward bound from Genoa on the U.S.S. *Manhattan* went 2,000 American expatriates, along with artificial tree trunks for forty dogs.

In this strange new world of topsy-turvy values, the most anachronistic refugee was perhaps Archduke Otto – 'Otto the Last' – returning to Lisbon with his mother, the Empress Zita, to plot the restoration of the Habsburg Empire.

As a socialite, Polly Peabody had known many of them, but now she was impatient of that old life. She wanted to help, but the problem was how. Her American Scandinavian Field Hospital was still stranded in Sweden, forbidden transit through Germany to France, yet nursing skills were needed here as everywhere. Through an introduction from Ambassador Henri-Haye, Polly often met Marshal Pétain in the lounge of the Hotel Parc et Majestic, and Pétain, rising gallantly to the occasion, offered her coffee and *petit-fours*, listened drowsily to her adventures and praised American women as *débrouillardes* (resourceful). But even he had no helpful suggestions; his main concern was to quit Vichy for Paris, to assert an authority he did not possess. 'I am going to Versailles in two weeks,' he told Polly sharply, 'I have quite made up my mind. I have sent word to the Germans to evacuate the premises.'

Polly had no more luck with Vice-President Pierre Laval, de Chambrun's father-in-law – a convenient post-war scapegoat but one whose moves accurately reflected contemporary opinion. Bidden to lunch, Polly found Laval good company and a witty raconteur, but the excesses of the sycophantic women who dogged his table at mealtimes nauseated her. No sooner had one pressed a little gold saint's medal on him than another snatched away his glass of Vichy water, replacing it with her own — '*Monsieur le Président*, do me the honour of dipping your lips in my glass.'

One belief that Laval shared, in common with many Vichyites, was that a Franco–German entente now formed the only possible basis for world equilibrium, and that all things could be subtly arranged to France's advantage. *C'est enfantin* (child's play) was a phrase much in vogue.

Polly Peabody wondered. Although no student of politics, the lessons of Poland, Austria and Czechoslovakia suggested otherwise. In the meantime, while awaiting transit to Paris to work for the American Red Cross, she toyed with the concept of a one-woman Relief Plan for refugees from the north, spending her afternoons as a hospital visitor.

Every afternoon, for two hours, she sat at the bedside of the red-haired Private Auguste Gringer, a 26-year-old hairdresser from Paris. On many days, crossing the hospital's threshold, she could hear his screams from as far away as the second floor. For two months he had been in constant unendurable pain from a bullet in his bladder, which had nicked the base of his spine. Clutching her wrist until she thought it would snap he would time and again ask Polly the question all France seemed to be asking: '*Mademoiselle*, why must I suffer so? Surely it can't be right?'

*

As July dawned, the fear that René de Chambrun would express to Roosevelt was already being realised. Vichy France, the two-fifths of the country that Hitler had assigned to the Pétain government, was suffering. To support Germany's army in the Occupied Zone she was mulcted of 400 million francs a day, while her own armed forces, on Hitler's *diktat*, were reduced to 100,000. To his French counterpart, Huntziger, General von Stülpnagel of the German Armistice Commission expressed himself in terms reminiscent of a riding school: 'If France rears, we will tighten the curb. We will loosen it to the extent that France is amenable.'

It was worse in the Occupied Zone. No French citizen there had a right to a radio, a telephone, to send cables or to leave town without permission. At 7 pm a curfew was clamped down. In the long silent evenings, the citizens were forbidden to read authors as diverse as Thomas Mann, Vicki Baum, Sigmund Freud, Erich Maria Remarque and André Maurois. In Alsace, a German domain from 1871 to 1919, the rules were harshest. Gallic symbols such as berets were forbidden, French Christian names were Germanised (Yvonne became Irmgard), and even thermometers, with their blue casing, white background and red alcohol were banned as reminiscent of the Tricolor.

The clampdown affected all occupied Europe. In The Hague, Holland, 13-year-old Ida van de Criendt noted that prayers for the Queen in church

133

were now forbidden, and no cleric could preach a sermon based on Psalm 130: 'Out of the depths have I cried unto Thee, O Lord.' The word 'Royal' was erased from streets and parks. Here, as elsewhere, Jews were early forced to register, then excluded from public office.

Under newly-appointed *Gauleiters*, *Reichsleiters* and *Reichskommissars*, arbitrary decrees multiplied. In Norway, where the inhabitants faced a bill of 360 million kroner for the costs of occupation, Quisling's successor, *Reichskommissar* Josef Terboven, lost no time in tampering with the economy. Wages were reduced by 7 per cent and peasants were summarily set to work ploughing 80,000 hectares of land to create new farms. Though dairy cattle and pigs were cut down to conserve fodder, sheep were upped to a four million high. No forester, fisherman, farm worker, seaman or any member of his family could change jobs or place of residence.

To the badgered inhabitants, some decrees had a ring of Alice-in-Wonderland. Hitler's man in Belgium, General von Falkenhausen, abruptly forbade the supply of soap to any save manual workers, women pregnant at home, the habitually-incontinent or colostomy patients.

By contrast, the Third Reich was thriving. Into a Germany depleted by years of sacrifice flowed a tide of Danish butter, Dutch vegetables, Polish coal and Norwegian timber: at least 200 tons of prime-quality Norwegian fish were shipped to the German Army daily. In Belgium, whose levy was 8,000 tons of industrial coal a day and 100 dairy cattle a week, one Brussels doctor, Paul Duner, beheld an astonishing sight: a convoy of trucks, forty strong, heading for the German border loaded solely with pots of jam.

In Paris alone, machinery from the Simca, Blériot and Hispano-Suiza factories was stripped and transported to Germany, but what the U.S. Chargé d'Affaires in Vichy, Robert Murphy, described as 'scientific looting' was going on all through the Occupied Zone.

In Germany it was confidently expected now that peace was just round the corner. Brand-new 'Visit Heidelberg and the Rhineland' posters blossomed in the tourist agencies on Berlin's Kurfürstendamm. Mileage tickets were in the course of preparation by German Railways, enabling citizens to gratify their long-harboured desires to visit Paris and the Riviera. Most enquiries though, centred round a monument in Occupied France, which was soon to become the world's most expensive and elaborate tourist attraction: the Maginot Line.

*

Suddenly the world was talking peace. There were rumours of it everywhere, although with what degree of reliability nobody knew. In Washington, D.C., there was talk of a peace personally negotiated by Roosevelt. In New York, it was reported that Germany was offering Britain peace with 95 per cent of her Empire intact.

134

Any unguarded utterance nourished fresh rumours. In Madrid, the Duke of Windsor, the former Edward VIII, remarked incautiously to an American diplomat: 'The most important thing now is to end the war before thousands more are killed or maimed to save the faces of a few politicians.' By noon next day, Ambassador Alexander Weddell had put it on the wire to Cordell Hull. The Swedish Minister in London, Bjorn Prytz, heard from the Under Secretary of Foreign Affairs, R. A. Butler, that Halifax thought 'commonsense and not bravado' would prevail. From this remark, Prytz drew his own pacifist conclusions.

In Berne, Switzerland, the British Minister, David (later Sir David) Kelly talked several times that summer with Prince Max of Hohenlohe-Langenburg, who repeatedly passed on an offer said to come from the German Foreign Ministry: guarantees for the British Empire in return for giving Germany a free hand in Europe. Each time, affecting keen interest, Kelly passed on the information without comment to the Foreign Office. If it served no other purpose, Kelly thought, he was buying time.

There was no lack of self-appointed and self-important doves. The founder of the Royal Dutch airline, K.L.M., Dr Alfred Plesman, flew into Berlin from The Hague to propose a 3-fold carve-up to Hermann Göring, just then appointed *Reichsmarschall*: Britain should have her Empire, Germany the Continent, the United States, Latin-America. But after ten days the talks fell down – at the same time as Malcolm R. Lovell, an American Quaker, made an abortive attempt to bring the British Ambassador, Lord Lothian, and the German Chargé, Hans Thomsen, together for peace talks in Washington.

On 19 July, Hitler himself, although he cavilled at the idea of 'crawling up English backsides' decided, in a rabble-rousing Reichstag speech, to 'appeal once more to reason and commonsense in Britain . . . I consider myself in a position to make this appeal since I am not a vanquished foe begging favours, but the victor, speaking in the name of reason . . .'

But the British, it seemed, were too short-sighted to realise they were beaten. 'The Germans,' Halifax noted in his diary, 'have got to be more knocked about.'

*

As Hitler's victories were recognised as inescapable, restive voices were heard once more far to the east of the Suez Canal. In India, following the fall of France. Subhas Chandra Bose had once more urged Mahatma Gandhi to launch a passive resistance campaign: it was clear now that the British Empire would be overthrown. But the canny little Mahatma was still sitting on the fence. 'We do not seek our independence out of Britain's ruin,' he reiterated in his reedy high-pitched voice. 'That is not the way of non-violence.' He ended ambiguously: if Bose's efforts to win India's freedom succeeded, Gandhi's telegram of congratulations would be the first through Bose's letter-box.

Bose bearded other Indian leaders with equal lack of success. Mohammed Ali Jinnah, the monocled elegant leader of the Muslim League, was cool; the British, he thought, might one day help realise his dream of Pakistan and a divided India. Vinayak Damodar Savarkar, the President of the *Mahasabha*, a right-wing nation-wing Hindu political party, saw other uses for the British. By entering Britain's army in India, members of his Fascist paramilitary arm might receive valuable training in weaponry.

On 2 July, khaki-clad police officers calling at 38/2, Elgin Road, Bose's Calcutta villa, temporarily put an end to his career as a freedom-fighter. For the eleventh time in his forty-three years, Bose was clapped into gaol.*

In Burma, other voices had taken up the cry. The former Premier Ba Maw had united three parties into a Freedom Bloc akin to Bose's, but the one concession they wrested from the British was a promise of full self-government after Britain's victory. 'Not even a world in flames could teach these people anything new,' Ba Maw flared to his confederate Aung San, a student who had attended Gandhi's Ramgarh congress as an observer and been sorely disappointed by the Mahatma's pacific stand. Both men resented bitterly the assumption that Burma must fight alongside Britain to free enslaved nations of whom they had never heard. 'What must be, must be,' Ba Maw decided, 'and this revolution of ours must be.'

As August dawned, Ba Maw's plans met the same setback as Bose's. For contravention of the Defence of Burma rules he was gaoled for one year in Mandalay.

But in more than one region of the Far East, the British writ did not run, and the voices that hailed Hitler's triumphs sounded loud and clear throughout the Empire of Japan. 'Japan,' warned the U.S. Ambassador, Joseph C. Grew in a despatch to the State Department, 'is in a state of political turmoil of unusual intensity.' 'The German victories,' Grew noted, 'have gone to their heads like strong wine.'

Already Grew anticipated that the 'present (Yonai) Cabinet may fall, with the result that a pro-German Cabinet will take over – with disastrous results for Japan'. Such a Cabinet, he thought, would likely be headed up by 49-year-old Fumimaro Konoye, an insomniac who doped himself with ten different kinds of sleeping pills, a certified hypochondriac who sterilised his food with boiling water and alcohol and used an antiseptic mask as a germ-trap in crowded meetings.

* Bose's rejoinder, in November 1940, was to notify the Governor of Bengal that he intended to fast himself to death. Six days later the authorities released him. At the end of January 1941, Bose slipped away from Calcutta, finally reaching Berlin, via Afghanistan and Moscow, at the end of March. In 1943, he took over the Indian National Army, a force of 10,000 dissident officers and men made up from former Japanese P.o.W.s, to fight against the British in Burma. He was killed in an air crash in 1945.

Konoye himself saw nothing but catastrophe looming ahead – but by now it was too late for Japan to turn back.

The reasons were inescapable: the Japanese were prisoners of history. Unable to support a population increasing by millions annually, Japan had been expanding compulsively for years – into Korea in 1910, into Manchuria in 1931, into China in 1937. By 1939, when Admiral Isoroku Yamamoto became Commander-in-Chief of the Japanese Combined Fleet, this obsession with a southern Eldorado had become a grandiose project.

The fall of France and the Low Countries now made the expansion feasible. But to counter this came hints from Washington's Japanese Embassy of a massive U.S. naval building programme. Action, if it came, must come before the U.S. tipped the naval balance against Japan in the Pacific.

Japan's needs were now paramount: to obtain metals and raw materials solely within their own sphere of control – for a victorious Germany might equally hamper Japan's expansionist programme. Thus, April 1940, had already seen the move of the Japanese Fourth Fleet to the Palau Islands, in the Western Pacific, to move against the Dutch East Indies if any other power tried to seize them. By 20 June, operational research on the Southern advance – against British Malaya, the Dutch East Indies, even the Phillipines – had begun, even though it was plain that this would mean war with the United States, Britain and Holland. By mid-July, Japan had accepted this: if need be they would meet any American challenge with war.

At the prospect of this head-on encounter, the Yonai Cabinet vacillated, so that, as Grew had predicted, a Konoye headed Cabinet replaced them by mid-July. Ironically, Konoye had been pressured into acceptance of the programme by the military before even being considered for office, though the last thing he sought was an Axis alliance.

Yamamoto, equally, was categorically opposed to war with the United States. As Naval Attaché in Washington, D.C. between 1925 and 1927, he had seen their industrial might at first hand. In the event of a Jap attack, Yamamoto saw the U.S. fleet in Hawaii no longer as a potential threat to Japan proper but as an actual danger to the flank of the Japanese southern expansion force.

To his trusted friend, Admiral Ryunosuke Kusoka, Yamamoto mused: 'If we are ordered to fight the United States we might be able to score a runaway victory and hold our own for six months or a year.' But in the second year, he thought, America would increase its strength.

The logic seemed inescapable: the only way to secure Japan's threatened flank was to destroy the United States Fleet before it ever left its Hawaian base of Pearl Harbor.

*

Meanwhile, with Britain and France in no position to resist, the Japanese were stepping up the squeeze play. On 17 June, France was instructed to close the road from Hanoi, French Indo-China (later Vietnam) to China. The British were ordered to close both the Hong Kong border and the Burma Road.

This was a body-blow for the Chinese, for the Burma Road, literally clawed by coolies' hands out of the 715 miles of mountain and ravine between Lashio, Burma and Chungking, China, was China's lifeline in her three-year old war with Japan, carrying 3,000 tons of supplies a month.

Promptly, through a lower-level Lothian-Hull meeting, Churchill appealed to Roosevelt: would the United States back up Britain in resisting this? But Hull saw no way to oblige. America could not leave the Pacific wide open to aggressors to send warships to Singapore; moreover they were so weak in military hardware that at that summer's manoeuvres trucks marked 'This Is A Tank' had stood in for the real thing. Nor could Roosevelt risk involving America in a war to rescue British Imperial possessions.

All Halifax's instincts, as he told Hoare on 8 July, had been 'to tell the Japanese to go to the devil', but Churchill was more cautious. At this stage in history, Britain could not risk war on another front, nor did Churchill believe the Japanese were bluffing. The Japanese Director of Military Intelligence in Tokyo had been quite blunt with the British Military Attaché: 'If you do not close the Burma Road, we shall seize Hong Kong.'

Rationalising it, the British took the easy way out. For the next three months the rainy season would make the Burma Road near-impassable in any case. From 12 July, the Burma Road would be closed to 'military supplies, arms, munitions, trucks and gasoline'.

*

In Chungking, the foggy walled city above the Yangtse River that was China's wartime capital, one man heard of the Burma Road's closure with a burst of uncharacteristic rage.

'*Nimen ta suan pan!* (You people are counting beads on the counting board!),' he railed at the British Ambassador, Sir Archibald Clark-Kerr, for to 53-year-old Generalissimo Chiang K'ai-Shek, President of China, the British preoccupation with trivial detail – rounds of ammunition and gallons of gasoline – was a truly galling factor. A man of far-reaching historical perspective, Chiang looked back not on the three years of the China Incident, as the war with Japan was known – years in which the Japanese had captured 465,000 square miles of Chinese territory, including Shanghai and Canton – but on the larger picture, the seventeen years in which he had marched north, beaten the war lords, province by province, and united China.

'Let the Japanese come,' Chiang threatened. 'If they drive me back to Tibet, in five years I will be back and will conquer all China again.'

It was appropriately fighting talk. Five months back, on Chinese New Year's Eve, the Year of the Rabbit had been succeeded in the Chinese zodiac cycle by the Year of the Dragon, the nation's patron beast – sharp of claw, smoky of breath. On the stroke of midnight, an auspiciously fierce dragon, fashioned from tinsel and crepe, borne aloft by six men, had led a stamping snaking conga-style dragon dance of cabinet ministers, generals and lovely ladies across the ballroom of Chungking's Visitors' Hostel.

Now, for three long months, Chiang's troops would be denied the crucial supplies which would have enabled them to wage a dragon-war against the Japanese invader. In those three months, Chiang would face another problem: a group of Chinese, ostensibly loyal, but waging war against the Japanese in their own territory, on their own terms, with their 400,000 strong Eighth Route Army under General Chu Teh. Chiang tolerated these Chinese Communists solely because he had to; without them, there would have been no trickle of Russian supplies to sustain him. It was Chiang's uneasy espousal of Mao Tse-Tung and Chou-en-Lai that had transformed him, in *Pravda*'s eyes, from a 'Fascist reactionary' to a 'national leader and hero'.

'The Japanese are a disease of the skin,' Chiang would observe shrewdly. 'The Communists are a disease of the heart. They say they wish to support me but secretly all they want is to overthrow me.'

But the 'Gissimo', as his followers called him, was giving hostages to fortune. In his fine walled villa at Hoangshan, across the Yangtse, his strategy, like the British and French during the phoney war, was one of masterly inactivity. He had no plan for victory: only for survival. Like the British and French before him, he believed that sooner or later, America would enter the war – and when that time came he would be rewarded for tying up a million-odd Japanese soldiers. So why fritter away strength – when the real confrontation, with the Communists, was still to come?

Meanwhile, the Communists sedulously fostered two myths which the world came to believe in earnest: that Mao's men alone bore the brunt of the Japanese war and that none among them were true Communists, merely mild agrarian reformers. Passive in his Chungking eyrie, Chiang was little by little relinquishing the prize for which he had striven all his life: China.

The Communists were getting their message across. Some months would elapse before one of Roosevelt's administrative assistants, Lauchlin Currie, reached Chungking for meetings with Chiang, bearing an oral message from the President. The 'Gissimo' found its tenor profoundly disturbing. For the first time but not the last, Roosevelt, so canny in keeping his finger on the pulse of the United States' feeling, was to minimise the Communist danger. 'Your Communists,' his message ran, 'seem more like Socialists to us. Surely you should be able to work together?'

*

Now was the time when all nations who could took up a minatory stance. Even tiny Switzerland made brave noises. On 25 July, 65-year-old General Henri Guisan, Swiss Commander-in-Chief, though handicapped by a pro-Nazi President and 1,200 miles of frontier to defend, took a decisive step. Along with his staff, his senior and junior commanders, Guisan repaired to the Rütli, a meadow on the shore of Lake Lucerne, symbolic in Swiss history as the meeting place which in 1291 saw the birth of the Swiss Confederation. 'We are at the turning point of our history,' Guisan told his officers. 'The existence of Switzerland is at stake.'

Who threatened Switzerland's independence? This was a question to which Guisan prudently gave no answer, but the will to resist was made plain. From this time on, the Swiss Army was to press forward with the concept of a National Redoubt, an Alpine stronghold covered by Switzerland's three principal forts, Sagans in the east, St Maurice in the west, the Gotthard in the south. In this mountain fortress, 400,000 militiamen would have adequate supplies to hold out against attacks from all sides, ready in the last resort to blow up the Gotthard and Simplon Tunnels and all roads over the Alps.

*

As always, Josef Stalin had moved faster than any. Now apprehensive that Britain and France might sue for peace, leaving Hitler free to turn eastward, Stalin consolidated an earlier gain. In September 1939, the Baltic states of Lithuania, Latvia and Estonia had capitulated where Finland held out — agreeing to provide Russia with bases, and if need be to support 20,000 Russian troops apiece. On 15 June, Red Army troops moved in. Russia was now virtually on a war footing — and as separate entities Lithuania, Latvia and Estonia ceased to exist.

One hapless group of nations could take no stance at all: the Balkans. Despite ethnic differences, Yugoslavia, Hungary and Rumania had three things in common: they depended on Germany, feared Russia, and looked vainly to Italy for police protection. Hungary's Premier, Count Paul Teleki, like Yugoslavia's Regent Prince Paul, balanced all the time on a tightrope of evasion. 'Why should Hungarians be slaughtered if Britain and France are ill-prepared?' Teleki would demand rhetorically, for he knew that his country's officer-caste dreaded Communism more than Nazi-ism. Many saw Hungary's true future as a German model dictatorship supplying raw materials to the Third Reich, with Parliament, trade unions and political parties abolished.

In Bucharest, the tawdry capital of Rumania, a city where, legend had it, 'the flowers had no scent, the men no honour and the women no shame', King Carol II, a flabby green-eyed descendant of Queen Victoria, also emulated Bunyan's Mr Facing-Both-Ways. Britain and France, the King prophesied to his Secretary-General for Foreign Affairs, Alexandre Cret-zianu, would ultimately triumph – 'but we must avoid the destruction of our country in the meantime'. For this reason, seeking to be all things to all men, Carol had been privy, on 6 April, to an amateurish British attempt to block the Danube at Giurgiu with ninety-four barges crammed with cement and dynamite, towed by six British tugs and crewed by 100 British agents. This clandestine manoeuvre, to which the Rumanian authorities were prepared to turn a blind eye, was designed to check the flow of oil from Rumania, the world's fifth oil-producing country, into Germany.

But the agents dallied too long at Giurgiu, drinking and flirting with the local girls, and the port authorities, tipped off by *Abwehr* agents, searched the barges to uncover both cement and dynamite. The mission ended in a fiasco, as the British agents were hastily spirited back to London

Hitler, incensed, stepped up the pressure on Carol. Even though the bitter winter of 1939 had played havoc with the crops, he demanded $10 million worth of wheat, more even than Rumania had exported to the Reich in 1939. When Carol expostulated, Germany's Trade Negotiator, Dr Karl Clodius, proposed a simple solution. If Rumania delivered the wheat, Germany would relax her demands for oil which had now risen to 1,820,000 tons a year – up to 300 tank cars a day. To sow the wheat, Clodius suggested, Carol could demobilise 500,000 peasants from his army – and Germany would send 6,000 agricultural experts to show them how to do it.

The last thing Carol wanted on Rumanian soil was 6,000 German experts of any kind. To stay their coming, the four million boys and girls of Rumania's National Youth movement were given staggered two-week leave periods from school, bundled into overalls and put behind ploughs.

As France crumbled, the Balkan nations reacted like dogs, fawning round Hitler's table for scraps, and it was now that Carol began to hand Rumania to Hitler lock stock and barrel. He actively sought a German military mission in Bucharest. He restored freedom to the pro-Nazi Jew-baiting Iron Guard, replacing his pro-Ally Foreign Minister Grigore Gafencu with the pro-Axis Ion Gigurtu. Finally on 21 June, with one decree, Carol made Rumania totalitarian with a single new Party of the Nation.

As sophisticates of *Realpolitik* had guessed, it was now Stalin's turn to apply the screws. On 26 June, Premier Molotov brusquely demanded from Carol the 17,000 square miles of Bessarabia, eastern Rumania, formerly a Russian domain. The Red Army, Molotov announced, would be marching in at 2 pm that day. The Rumanian Army had four days to vacate the territory.

King Carol flew into a most unregal panic. All that night, his cheeks smudged with tears, he paced his study, chain-smoking until every ashtray was overflowing with butts, downing tumblers of neat Scotch. At first, in desperation, he sought help from Hitler, but the Führer was unresponsive:

above all he wanted peace in the Balkans, to ensure his oil supplies. He advised Carol to yield to the Russians.

Carol might have called Hitler's bluff by threatening to destroy the oil-wells, but fearing for his personal fortune he did not dare. Even before his Cabinet met to debate the matter he had surrendered.

Personal fortune was an intimate concern of both Carol and his red-haired mistress Magda Lupescu. To finance a palace larger than Buckingham Palace with a 100-seater theatre and portraits of Carol looming twenty feet high, they had for nine years treated the country as a cash register to be milked at will – with regal rake-offs from both the State railroad and the State textile mills. Not surprisingly, Carol listed 'designing uniforms' as his principal hobby. In nine years he had even changed the uniforms of the Boy Scouts three times to keep the State looms humming.

But Carol's climb-down, after boasting early in January that no foot of Rumanian territory would ever be yielded, lost him face with his people. On 1 July, he let drop the mask, denouncing all the British guarantees offered him in 1939. In future his orientation was with the Axis.

Germany, however, would offer no military alliance, or any other crumb of comfort. If clarification had been needed, the position of small nations in the world had been clarified afresh.

*

Theodor Broch, no longer Mayor of Narvik, saw that truth as plainly as any man. As long as Hitler's armies held sway, a small nation such as Norway was no more than a geographical location on the map of Europe – and there was no longer any place in Norway for Theodor Broch.

On 15 June, following his breakneck flight from the Germans on Harstad island, Broch had had no clear idea where he and his family would find sanctuary as the hired rowboat pulled out across the foggy Atlantic. From a nearby harbour, together with Ellen and Siri, he had journeyed north on a two-man fishing vessel, still uncertain as to their destination. But by degrees it dawned on Broch that over the years he had forged an endless chain of goodwill throughout the Lofoten Islands. On a score of farmsteads he had drawn up wills and wrestled with tax complaints for crofters and farmers often enough, when times were hard for them, deliberately waiving his fee.

At Tysfjord, near the island of Torghatten, Broch located just such good friends, a retired doctor and his wife. But the couple warned Broch that he was already a hunted man: the radio had broadcast his name. For the time being, it was safer for Ellen and Siri to hide up here. Later Broch could send for them; now he must journey on alone.

Broch decided to head for Sweden. With Leif, an 18-year-old Laplander, as his guide he set out on the long mountain trek towards the border. Bowed

142

beneath his knapsack, pausing only for catnaps beside birchwood fires, he toiled on for ten hours until the cairn that marked the border of neutral Sweden came in sight.

In Stockholm, a tranquil brightly-lit enclave in a blacked-out Europe, Broch sought out an old friend from Oslo days, Erling Falk, a Socialist professor whose teachings had inspired a generation of students. Now Falk was in the Royal General Hospital, dying of a brain tumour, but as Broch sat miserably at his bedside, his mind seemed diamond-clear. For twenty years, Broch knew, he had lived and taught in America, and now his thoughts reverted to those times. 'This is a revolutionary era,' Falk told him, 'and the United States will become the deciding power. Go there.'

Broch was in luck. Hearing that Mrs Florence Harriman, American Minister in Norway, had just arrived in Sweden, after accompanying King Haakon on much of his journey north, Broch, who had met her in the past, sought her out at Stockholm's Grand Hotel. Over dinner, Mrs Harriman proved solicitous: what were his future plans? 'I'd like to go to America,' Broch confessed, 'to make propaganda for Norway. But perhaps a visa would be difficult?'

Florence Harriman saw no difficulty. Once Broch had secured a loan from the Norwegian Embassy to cover his passage money, a debt he contracted to pay off by instalments, his visa was granted. Like all who travelled in 1940, he embarked on a cramped and snail-paced journey: by air from Stockholm to Moscow, thence by slow train to Vladivostok, Siberia, finally on a battered Norwegian freighter via Tokyo and Yokohama. On 18 August, still bearing only the knapsack he had toted across the Swedish border, he reached his final port of destination, a world away from Narvik and the cold high mountains: the noisy sprawling sun-drenched city of Los Angeles.

*

The auditorium of the Renacimento Theatre in downtown Buenos Aires was jammed, and the mood was ugly. Across the screen flickered a German propaganda film of Hitler's triumphs in the west, *The Siegfried Line*, a heady brew for the 200 young Nazi Party supporters, who had come to pay homage to their Führer. As the Panzers rolled victoriously forward, staccato cries of '*Heil Hitler*' resounded through the stalls.

It was too much for 100 young Argentine hot-bloods, mostly athletes and amateur boxers, who had also chosen that night to see *The Siegfried Line*. As counterpoint they set up an angry barrage of '*Abajo* (Down with) Hitler'. Suddenly a fusillade of jumbo fireworks was lobbed through the darkness towards the hostile Nazis. As the lights came up, the air was blue with spent gunpowder and women were screaming. With a massed yell, the Argentines went to work on the Hitlerites, pounding, kneeing, gouging. Police flooding

143

in to break up the mêlée had the clubs torn from their hands and used mercilessly on the Germans. Two score Argentines were arrested, only to be released next day. Further showings of *The Siegfried Line* were banned by President Roberto M. Ortiz.

All over Latin America, the twenty-one republics which, like the United States, had won their freedom from Europe by revolution, were reacting in the same way. Unlike the United States, they were already wide-awake to the dangers posed by the Axis presence. In La Paz, Bolivia and Montevideo, Uruguay, students stoned Italian commercial establishments, and staged monster rallies outside the German and Italian Legations. Other countries acted more coolly but no less decisively. Colombia's Government-owned airline, Avianca, fired all its German employees. Ecuador gave marching orders to its Italian Military Mission. Hitler's man in Mexico City, Arthur Dietrich, heard sourly that he was no longer *persona grata*.

Late in June, as the U.S.S. *Quincy* steamed slowly up to the quay in Montevideo Harbour, the only show-the-flag gesture that America, vigilant in the Pacific, could afford to make, her reception was rapturous – '*Viva Roosevelt! Viva Los Estados Unidos!*' The reason was plain: the *Quincy* was berthing in the wake of a Trojan-horse scare prompted by the arrest of Hitler's man, Julius Dalldorf and twelve other agents operating under German Minister Otto Langmann.

Shocked Uruguayans now learned that they had unwittingly been the headquarters of a movement to fuse all Latin-America into a German-dominated economy. Nor was there any doubt that Germany had a powerful lever, for fully 55 per cent of South American exports went to Europe – Brazilian coffee, Peruvian tin, Argentine beef. Those exports must be sold, even to a Europe dominated by Hitler, or Latin-America faced an imminent crisis.

Cordell Hull, the courtly Tennessean, had as much to fear, for if Latin-America became an Axis bloc this threatened the security of the entire United States. Every country, Hull warned in his habitual log-cabin language, 'could be swallowed as a boa constrictor swallows a squirrel'.

All this was grist to the mill of Getulic Vargas, the affable smiling dictator of Brazil's Estado Nôvo who four years earlier had consolidated his ten-year reign with Nazi support then proceeded to declare the party illegal. Now the canny Vargas – the man they said could be silent in ten languages and remove his socks without taking off his shoes – saw a way of extracting some long-sought concessions from the United States.

On 7 June, Brazil's Foreign Minister, Oswaldo Aranha, dubbed by the Nazis 'a hireling of North America' gave a gentle nudge to the U.S. Ambassador, Jefferson Caffery: 'You hold conversations with us, and the Germans give us arms.' On 14 June, he was blunter: 'If (the United States) are interested in stopping this country from going Nazi . . . good will and speeches will no

144

long satisfy our people. We need a few results.' On 16 July, he was quite specific as to the results he had in mind: United States credit to finance a monster Brazilian steel plant, thereby saving foreign exchange.

On 21 July, delegates from twenty-one republics, in neat white suits that would soon wilt in the sticky heat, met at the Capitolio, Havana, Cuba, for a Pan-American Conference hastily convened by Cordell Hull. Prominent on the agenda were four crucial items: to secure some form of mandate over European colonies in the Western Hemisphere, to control Fifth Column activities, the defence of the hemisphere, and the disposal of surplus exports.

It was a conference that some attended with misgivings. Costa Rica, Guatemala, Honduras, El Salvador and Bolivia had had veiled threats to stay away – but all realised that ultimately, delay could be fatal. Proof was daily forthcoming that General Wilhelm Faupel, President of Berlin's Ibero-American Institute, had planted Axis eyes and ears all over Latin-America: Alfred Muller, an able henchman, in Buenos Aires, H. H. von Cossel, Press Attaché at the Rio de Janeiro Embassy, even a von Ribbentrop – Erich, the Foreign Minister's nephew – in Bogota, Colombia.

Five days later, on 26 June, when Cordell Hull was the first to scrawl his name on the Act of Havana, he was tired but satisfied. If a piece of paper would keep the Americas free from the Axis, he had that paper. Above all, he had wanted Pan-American support for the Monroe Doctrine – and this he had got in the Convention of Havana, which set up the machinery to seize and administer any European possession in the Western Hemisphere threatened with transfer of sovereignty. But he also needed Pan-American sanction, in case the United States found it necessary to seize a colony before the Convention went into effect. An emergency resolution had granted him this, too.

But in exchange for the execution of the Monroe Doctrine, Hull had pledged the United States to mammoth responsibilities – virtually to guarantee a military protection to the entire Western Hemisphere. And many of the signatures that crowded after Hull's on the Act were prompted by the hope, soon realised, that Congress would authorise half a billion dollars in aid to Western Hemisphere countries. 'It was', exulted *El Mercurio* of Santiago, Chile, 'the most important and significant agreement ever reached in the American hemisphere, and perhaps in the world.'

The happiest delegate after Hull was perhaps Getulio Vargas' Secretary-General to the Ministry of Foreign Affairs, Mauricio de Nabuco. Like Hull, he, too, was bound for Washington, to collect a few favours for Brazil in return for his staunch pro-American stand in Havana. Brazil, deprived of her European coffee and cotton markets, was soon to be amply compensated in her struggle for economic recovery. A hefty $20 million loan from the United States Export-Import Bank would help establish Brazil's first steel plant at

Volta Redonda, ninety miles from Rio, with the help of United States equipment and United States technicians.

'When I go back to my country,' mused Foreign Minister Aranha in Washington, D.C., 'I shall propose that we erect a statue to Herr Hitler. It is (he) who at last succeeded in drawing the attention of the United States to Brazil.'

*

Afterwards, Werner Mölders looked back to those July days on the French Channel coast as no more than an illusory calm. He sensed that a bitter battle lay ahead, for if Churchill had promised the British only 'blood, toil, tears and sweat' the same would be true for Germany. The Luftwaffe had an awesome task ahead of them: first to destroy the R.A.F. and with them the Royal Navy before the *Wehrmacht* could cross the English Channel.

Mölders knew that Göring was supremely confident – perhaps too confident. Following his release from the prison camp near Toulouse, Mölders had been flown as guest of honour to Karinhall, Göring's mighty mansion outside Berlin, and *Der Dicke* (The Fat One), as the pilots called him, had scarcely mentioned the combat to come. Instead he had delighted, like any new-rich host, in showing off Karinhall's glories: the private cinema, his elaborate model railway, silver tapestries and gold-plated baths, even canary cages shaped like dive-bombers. Once, in an ebullient moment, he had commented, 'We'll beat up the Tommies', but that had been all.

Mölders' only hint of misgiving had been when Göring, half way through dinner, had clapped an empty water glass over the gleaming white cloth and hailed his wife, 'Look, Emmy! Look what I've got! A flea! A present from Mölders from captivity!' As he shook with crazy laughter, the first faint doubt crossed the embarrassed Mölders' mind.

Other Luftwaffe officers shared Mölders' conviction that the fight would be long and hard. On 19 July, now promoted Major, Mölders took command of Fighter Group 51, at Wissant, near Calais, where the regional fighter commander for Air Fleet Two, *Oberst* 'Uncle Theo' Osterkamp, took pains to dispel any complacency. An Anglophile, to whom the British were always 'The Lords', 'Uncle Theo' warned: 'Now we're going to fight "the Lords", and that's something else again. They're hard fighters and they're good fighters – even though our machines are better.'

On this score, Mölders fully agreed. As Group Commander, he had been privileged to carry out test flights on two captured British fighters: the Vickers-Supermarine Spitfire and the Hawker Hurricane. Neither plane, in his view measured up to the Luftwaffe's ace machine, the Messerschmitt 109. Easy to handle and fauntless in a curve, the Spitfire was as fast as the ME109, but its Merlin engines sometimes cut out for a split second, reducing its manoeuvrability. The Hurricane, though a tougher plane, was a slower performer, sluggish in the ailerons.

Nine days later, on 29 July, Mölders knew what 'Uncle Theo' had meant about the British pilots. North of Dover, he and Fighter Group 51 chanced on a swarm of Spitfires above the Straits. True, he scored a hit on one Spitfire, but instantly the others were on him like a swarm of hornets, so eager to close that they blocked each other's field of fire. Their flight discipline, Mölders thought, was lamentable, but their courage and determination were awe-inspiring. His radiator and starboard tank shot up, Mölders broke hard for France, belly-landing at Wissant, his landing-gear jammed like a concertina.

In the flaring excitement of battle, he had felt nothing; only now did he notice that his flying overalls were thickly daubed with blood. The Tommies had peppered him with everything they had; shell splinters had punctured his knee-joint, his thigh, the calf of his left leg. Mölders felt no pain, only intense chagrin. Until further notice he was transferred as a patient to the Luftwaffe Hospital, Berlin, and the battle hadn't even started.

*

For one élite arm of the German war machine, the battle was already on — and the fortunes of war were with them all the way.

In less than a year, *Kapitänleutenant* Otto Kretschmer, 28-year-old commander of U-Boat 99, and the fifty-six other skippers operating under the submarine chief, *Konteradmiral* Karl Dönitz, had seen their war transformed from a kid-glove affair to a no-holds-barred combat. At first, still hopeful of Anglo–French acquiescence, Hitler had insisted that all U-Boats must surface when sighting merchant vessels, ensuring the safety of both passengers and crew before sinking the ship. Those days were long past. Now the U-Boat war had become a threat that was, in Churchill's words, 'the only thing that ever frightened me'.

The logistics were simple. The very survival of Great Britain depended on 3,000 ocean-going merchantmen importing fifty-five million tons of supplies annually: every gallon of oil, half of the food consumed, most raw materials. Yet such was Britain's plight that only fifty-six special escort vessels were available to protect them.

Otto Kretschmer knew early on that the Royal Navy were as yet no match for the U-Boats. The reason was strategic ignorance. The Admiralty's policy favoured the random tracking of individual submarines instead of the staid but effective policy of escorting convoys en bloc. Moreover, their faith in the Asdic submarine detector device was misplaced; Asdic could operate only at a fixed angle, for a range of rather less than a mile, and was of little use when U-Boats were travelling faster than eight knots. No more than 180 warships had been equipped with Asdic in 1939, and of these 150 were destroyers, which were needed to protect the fleet. And since Admiralty Plans refused even to accept that submarines could operate by night, Britain, as early as January 1940, had lost 150 merchant ships, half a million tons of shipping. As the year dawned, even bread rationing had been a possibility.

At the same time, the war had taken a ruthless turn which Kretschmer, like his fellow commanders, accepted but did not relish. Hitler had now forbidden the rescue of survivors and the care of ships' boats, although Kretschmer, like most others, blandly ignored these orders.

June alone had seen 300,000 tons of shipping lost to Dönitz's torpedoes – a fact reflected on every British breakfast table, where sugar was now limited to half a pound per week, butter was reduced, the bacon ration in jeopardy, and tea limited to two ounces a week for every citizen. Now was the beginning of what the U-Boat skippers would always remember as *Die-Glückliche Zeit*, The Happy Time, for with the Admiralty concentrating their destroyer flotillas on anti-invasion patrols, the U-Boats, heading for the Western Approaches, were to enjoy a field-day.

On 5 July, Kretschmer set out from Wilhelmshaven, on Heligoland Bay, for the first of his Atlantic adventures. Until now, like the other commanders, he had operated in the Fair Isle Passage, between the Orkneys and the Shetlands. As always, when the 500-ton U-99 put out to sea, her conning tower marked with the insignia of two golden horseshoes, her 44-strong crew knew that things would be done the Kretschmer way. Despite leavening qualities of humour and compassion, Kretschmer ran a tight ship, intolerant of weakness or slovenly demeanour. A school teacher's son from Lower Silesia, 'Silent Otto's' only betrayal of inner tension was the non-stop chain of black cheroots he smoked when U-99 was surfaced.

At 4.15 that day, Kretschmer spotted his first Atlantic prey: the 2,000-ton Canadian steamer *Magog*, approaching on a zig-zag course. Almost by rote, Kretschmer gave the order: 'Engineer, prepare to fire one torpedo. Keep the bows steady at trim.' All this was routine, and so, too, was the sight of the steamer breaking in two like a riven plank, her crew scrambling to launch the lifeboats clear of her rear section. But far from routine, to newcomers aboard U-99, was Kertschmer's flaring anger as a young petty officer rushed to the conning tower, sub-machine gun at the ready, anticipating trouble. Furiously ordering the man below, Kretschmer, part-educated in Devonshire, hailed the bobbing lifeboats in fluent English: 'Sorry about that gun. We don't intend to harm you.'

By way of farewell, Kretschmer first gave the Canadians bearings to reach the Irish coast, then passed down a full bottle of brandy. Baffled by a U-Boat commander who had first sunk him and then stood him drinks on the Third Reich, the skipper could only mumble a bewildered thanks.

At midnight that day, U-99's look-out reported a convoy heading out from

148

the Western Approaches. Tossing his cheroot from the conning tower, Kretschmer ordered action stations. His manoeuvre was already decided: to steam at full speed on the surface and attack the convoy's port bow before dawn. Only one thing perturbed him: against all the law of averages, the convoy seemed to be screened by a strong destroyer escort. Soon after dawn on 6 July, caution prompted him to submerge ahead of the convoy, dropping back at periscope depth.

One freighter, the *Humber Arm*, broke up in a yellow-white flash as the first torpedo struck, but it was enough to alert the escorts to Kretschmer's presence. Soon after 8 am, he noted in his War Diary: 'Propeller noises heard approaching to starboard. I believe my crew are going to get their baptism of depth charging.' Four minutes later: 'Escort picking up speed. This is the attack.'

Within seconds, it came. In fact, Kretschmer's pursuer was not a destroyer but a corvette, one of the first to join the Atlantic escort groups, but to the crew of U-99, fast submerging to 350 feet, the distinction was academic. With the first pattern of ten depth-charges, the submarine rocked like a truck hitting a brick wall; there was a noise 'like the grating of a thousand chisels on steel'. At once Kretschmer ordered emergency precautions: all electrical equipment, save hydrophones and gyro compass, to be shut down, speed was reduced to the point where only the propellers were turning over, enabling U-99 to maintain depth. But after two hours of these concussion-like blows, the oxygen supply cut out. The crew donned breathing masks, connected by tubes to cases of alkali.

Stealthily, maintaining listening speed, U-99 was creeping away from the path of the convoy. But the corvette, implacably, was keeping pace, and now Kretschmer's crew strove to remember the training school's text-book rules for survival: to conserve precious air for breathing, each man lay prone at his action station. Unable to use the lavatory, in case the tell-tale discharge rose to the surface, all of them in turn shame-facedly fouled their overalls. Often, for twenty minutes at a time, they drifted into a deep trance-like sleep. The shuddering impact of the depth charges continued, and as the carbon dioxide content mounted, the men began to pant like dogs behind their masks. Their heads ached abominably; a cold dew of sweat bathed their bodies. Soon the batteries would run dry; without power, U-99 would sink like waterlogged jetsam to the sea-bed.

Twelve hours passed . . . fourteen . . . then nineteen. In the War Diary, Navigator Petersen now marked up the 127th depth charge. Yet to the puzzlement of Radio Operator Jupp Kassel, Kretschmer, sitting placidly on the control deck, seemed absorbed by a paperback whodunnit. Only later, peering over his commander's shoulder, did Kassel realise that Kretschmer was calling on all his iron reserves of will to stiffen his crew's morale. Not only had he neglected to turn the pages; the book was held upside down.

But the depth charge that Petersen had noted was the last. Around 12 July, U-99 limped into harbour at Lorient, France, the new headquarters of Dönitz's submarine arm. All her movable parts had been put out of action; everything breakable had been smashed to smithereens. On the quayside, Dönitz, no man to betray his emotions, felt a twinge of anxiety as the crew came ashore: their sea-overalls caked with excrement, leather jackets stained with salt and oil, their faces strained and emaciated, bristling with untended beards.

The hell of their first depth-charging would stay with them a long time yet, but Kretschmer was undeterred. 'Now we have received all the presents the enemy can give us,' was his last entry on that voyage. 'We all have a fresh confidence in our ship.'

Kretschmer's confidence was not misplaced. On 24 July, U-99 was ordered to sea once more. Caught up in a convoy of twenty merchant ships, Kretschmer sent three freighters to the bottom, then, down to his last four torpedoes, sank three tankers and a freighter. On 8 August, U-99 steamed triumphantly back into Lorient. Seven victory pennants, each bearing the golden horseshoe insignia, flew from her raised periscope. For Otto Kretschmer, it was still The Happy Time.

*

If the successes of Otto Kretschmer and his fellow aces were costing Winston Churchill sleep, his Cabinet were unaware of it. Immersed in minutiae, he often failed to see the wood for the trees, driving his Ministers to distraction in the process. Many would have endorsed the verdict of Lord Halifax: 'I have seldom met anybody with stranger gaps of knowledge or whose mind worked in greater jerks.'

A titanic leader, though by no means a great strategist, Churchill was by turns ardent, inspiring, impetuous, voluble, stubborn and determined to poke his finger into every pie, often spurred on by the sometimes erratic advice of his scientific adviser, Professor Sir Frederick Lindemann (later Lord Cherwell). The newly-appointed Commander-in-Chief, Southern Command, Lieutenant-General Alan Brooke, summed it up: 'The more you tell that man about the war, the more you hinder the winning of it.'

Ideas – not always welcomed by his colleagues – poured from Churchill in a spate. Long before the war he had been urging on the then Minister of Air, Kingsley Wood, an idea of Lindemann's to beat the night bomber which he thought surpassed the tank: a million air mines a week to 'create a lethal drizzle very unpleasant for aeroplanes to fly through'. Since the idea involved suspending the mines on parachutes at the end of 2,000 feet of piano wire, defending R.A.F. fighters were equally prone to tangle with them, but it took

150

one R.A.F. squadron a year of experiment to convince Churchill they were useless.

The R.A.F.'s shortage of pilots puzzled Churchill, too – even when Air Minister Sir Archibald Sinclair pointed out that R.A.F. squadron strength had been upped from thirty-nine to sixty, preparing for the air battle to come. The Premier was unconvinced: why then were only three pilots out of every ten with wings operational?

The horrified Sinclair had to explain that a pilot was awarded his wings after eighty to ninety hours' flying-training – 'but he was in no circumstances operationally qualified at this stage'. To attain this pitch, at least 200 hours were needed.

This led Professor Lindemann, on the strength of his stint as a World War I test pilot, to interpose: 'Are not our training standards too high? The final polish should be given in the squadrons.'

As a result, the training period was reduced from three months to one. At a fearful cost to the R.A.F. that 'final polish' would be given them by aces like Werner Mölders and others.

The Minister of Food, Lord Woolton, felt the same sense of frustration when dealing with Churchill. Despite mounting shipping losses, Churchill took him severely to task for rationing diners-out to one main course. A resolute trencherman, Churchill grumbled: 'Is it worse for the country for a man to eat a little of three or four courses of food, daintily cooked out of scraps, or a good solid plate of roast beef?'... Is it wrong to eat up the luxury foods already in the country, or ought they to be wasted?'

Woolton was unrepentant. A spot check had revealed no less than eighty items on the menu at London's smart Grosvenor House Hotel – too large a choice by far in a Britain at war. Moreover, he reminded Churchill shrewdly, 'it is important from a political point of view. My mail shows that the working class is concerned that rich and poor should be treated alike, and the reason why I introduced the phrase "luxury feeding" [in a broadcast] was in order to balance the rationing of tea and margarine, which undoubtedly affects the poorer classes the most.'

His whole world centring round No. 10, Chequers, the Prime Minister's country residence, or 'The Hole', a 6-acre honeycomb of offices beneath Whitehall, where one in ten of War Cabinet meetings were held, Churchill did not realise that the England he had known was changing irretrievably. To the naked eye the changes were there for all to see. In Piccadilly Circus, Eros was a shrouded obelisk of sandbags; the railings had gone for scrap metal from the London parks; restaurant entrances had long been heavily sandbagged against possible bomb blast. As host to five governments-in-exile, London was now more cosmopolitan and colourful than at any time in history: the black *képis* of Free Frenchmen who had rallied to Charles de

151

Gaulle, vying with the vivid electric blue of Dominions pilots' uniforms and the black silver-braided uniforms of the Dutch police.

This was a world where shortage was the established norm: a world of newspapers whittled to six pages, where waiters had been replaced by waitresses in clubs, where teashop customers had grown used to one lump of sugar and a thin shaving of butter with their bread.

But these were only surface changes. All over Britain one woman in three now went hatless and wore slacks – 'Horrible!' lamented the couturier Victor Stiebel, 'Women seemed to think that now at last they could forget about fashion and go about as they liked.' On 26 July, one theatre-goer noticed lounge suits in the stalls replacing black ties for the first time. Even at the Ritz Hotel, august dowagers dined with portable radios on their table, keeping up with the war news.

The mood of Britain was changing fast. Clothes, style, wealth, the King's English, suddenly mattered less. 'In the England of the future,' conceded the novelist Somerset Maugham, 'evening dress will be less important than it has been in the past'. Already a Socialist tomorrow was looming. 'Either we turn this war into a war of revolution,' warned the left-wing *New Statesman* in mid-July, 'or we shall be defeated,' Ernest Bevin, on taking office as Minister of Labour, had made his concept of the future abundantly plain: 'When this war is over, the task of rebuilding the world has to be done by the working-class. We are taking none of the promises . . . the plausible stuff of the last war. This time it must be the economic reconstruction of the whole foundation of society.'

In this climate, a friend's assurance to Lady Cunard at a party – 'Don't worry, Emerald, within three weeks of the declaration of peace, all the classes will be back in their proper places' – was less than prophetic.

This vision of an egalitarian future, which by degrees was stiffening the British will to resist, was ironic, for much of the world, the Axis apart, had already written them off. 'The German victories are putting great heart into my Opposition,' noted the South African Premier, Jan Smuts, on 10 July. 'The Allies are finished, they say' – and he predicted that the opposing Nationalists, if returned to power, would plump for secession from the Commonwealth and an alliance with Germany. In Washington, D.C., the isolationist Senator Arthur Vandenberg, infuriated the Australian Minister, Richard Casey, by suggesting that a German victory would be 'unpleasant, but not catastrophic'. The British, Vandenberg thought, could be re-housed in Canada and the U.S.A. and a self-contained democracy built up again in North America.

Few men were more aware of Britain's unpopularity than Ambassador Sir Samuel Hoare in Madrid. 'Whenever I go out, I have to have an army of gunmen, as if I was going to have to fight a battle in the streets,' he complained in a letter to Beaverbrook. On 22 June, having granted Hoare an audience after keeping him waiting for three weeks, General Francisco Franco was bold enough to put into words what the rest of the world was thinking. 'Why do you not end the war now?' he asked Hoare contemptuously. 'You can never win it. All that will happen if the war is allowed to continue will be the destruction of European civilisation.'

*

Five weeks after Franco's prediction, Hitler unwittingly ensured that European civilisation would, however precariously survive.

The first hint of a change in priorities came on 29 July to *Oberst* Walter Warlimont of Hitler's Operations Department (Section L) and his three senior officers. The four men were assembled in the restaurant car of their special train, code-named Atlas, in a siding at Bad Reichenhall station, Bavaria, hard by Hitler's Berchtesgaden retreat. Briefed to wait on a visit from the newly-promoted General Alfred Jodl, all of them had one thought in mind: promotion for their good work in the West was on the cards. But to their astonishment, Jodl, like a spy in a melodrama, prowled through the car checking every door and window tight-shut.

Then, in a quiet dry voice, Jodl let fall his bombshell. The Führer had decided to rid the world 'once for all' of the danger of Bolshevism. A surprise attack on Soviet Russia was scheduled for May 1941.

At first, gripping on to his chair arms for support, Warlimont couldn't speak. Then, just as when Hitler had halted the tanks before Dunkirk, a torrent of objections arose. The struggle against England, the projected invasion, code-named 'Sea Lion' only seventeen days earlier, was not yet accomplished fact. What about the two-front war they had always been careful to avoid? Jodl was emphatic: the victory over Russia, 'the last force on the continent', would be the best possible method of forcing England, shorn of a potential ally, to make peace.

'That's impossible,' objected *Oberst* Bernhard von Lossberg, one of Warlimont's officers. Surely, he protested, England was first priority? Jodl's answer was revealing: 'The Führer is afraid that the mood of the people after a victory over England would hardly permit him to embark on a new war against Russia.'

Warlimont's own objections were clamant. What about the 'pact of friendship and non-aggression' concluded with Moscow only eleven months back? Had not Russia delivered all war material promptly and in full, as promised? Again Jodl had pat answers: the collision with Bolshevism was bound to come, so it was better to fight it out now while Germany was at the height of her military powers. And by the autumn of 1941, the Luftwaffe, tempered by victories in the east, could bring its full brunt to bear against England.

153

Finally, Jodl, who had himself presented similar arguments to Hitler, clamped down on further dissent. 'Gentlemen, it is not a question for discussion but a decision of the Führer.' From this time on, Warlimont and his staff were to concentrate on planning papers under the code-name Build-Up East.

None of the officers privy to this astonishing about-face were even aware that Hitler had been debating this decision as far back as 3 June. On that date he had told *Generalleutnant* Georg von Sodenstern, Chief of Staff of Army Group A: 'Now that things have got to this point, I can begin settling my accounts with Bolshevism.'

There were many factors to account for this resolve. All his life Hitler had dreamed of winning a great Eastern empire. Now he saw urgent reasons to achieve this aim before an unbeatable coalition of enemies united to oppose him. The Soviet forces were bound to modernise; by 1942, the United States might have entered the war. Moreover he was convinced that the Slavs, whom he despised, were 'ripe for dissolution', and since they 'bred like vermin' they would be a fertile source for slave labour.

In the weeks that followed, Hitler's conviction slowly assumed the proportions of an obsession. At first he was bent on an attack in the autumn of this year, until the impassioned arguments of Jodl and Keitel persuaded him to postpone it.

Throughout July, Halder's diary recorded the determined progress of Hitler's thoughts. 3 July posed the problem: 'The main question is how to deal Russia a military blow which will force her to recognise Germany's preponderant role in Europe.' On 13 July: 'England still has some hope of action on the part of Russia.' On 22 July: 'The problem of Russia must be dealt with.'

What hardened Hitler above all was the memory of the Red Army's lamentable showing in the Finnish campaign. Architect Albert Speer, summoned to Hitler's presence, always remembered how the Führer was pacing the gravel drive at Berchtesgaden along with Jodl and Keitel as he approached.

'Now we have shown what we are capable of,' Hitler was saying. 'Believe me, Keitel, a campaign against Russia will be like a child's game in a sandbox by comparison.' He was, Speer noted, in radiant good humour.

*

'The Battle of France is over,' Churchill had warned the nation as long ago as 18 June. 'I expect the Battle of Britain is about to begin.' Now the world held its breath. 'The future of our Western civilisation,' Ismay told General Raymond E. Lee, U.S. Military Attaché in London, 'rests on the shoulders of the Royal Navy and about 5,000 pink-cheeked young pilots.'

154

7

'The Whole Bloody World's On Fire'

8 August–7 September, 1940

ACROSS THE ENGLISH CHANNEL from France, the pilots of whom Ismay had spoken – the crews of twenty-three fighter squadrons, preparing to defend a 250-mile front from thirteen south coast airfields – waited for the worst that would happen.

Although every man was aware that the first Luftwaffe sweeps marking the prelude to the Battle of Britain had been evident from 8 August, none as yet suspected that Göring's plan was to knock out the R.A.F. in four days flat, an air battle that would be the harbinger of a full-scale 13-division invasion of England from Ramsgate, Kent, to the Isle of Wight.

'The British Air Force,' stressed Hitler's Directive No. 16, 'must be eliminated to such an extent that it will be incapable of putting up any substantial opposition to the invading troops.'

Few men gave much for their own chances – an estimate which Fighter Command's C.-in-C., Sir Hugh 'Stuffy' Dowding, accepted as the painful truth. Although a few pilots were natural-born aces – among them 242's Squadron-Leader Douglas Bader, whose tin legs, the result of a pre-war crash, were already legend, and 257's Robert Stanford Tuck, who sported monogrammed silk handkerchiefs and long cigarette holders – they were the exception. As the battled gained momentum, scores of R.A.F. pilots were to be swept brutally from the sky; hundreds more would survive by luck rather than judgement.

Their morale was never in question. On the south coast airfields that were now Britain's front line – Hawkinge, Manston, Tangmere – the legends on their planes testified to their don't-give-a-damn spirit: Leslie Charteris' The Saint, Walt Disney's Figaro, the little cat swatting a swastika as blithely as a mouse, even a sharp-edged scythe, dripping blood, to symbolise death, the grim reaper. But on all these airfields the pilots were as hard-pressed as any men alive. At least 100 would be at readiness – at their dispersal points, life-jackets already adjusted – since dawn. Others, more sorely tried, would be on stand-by – strapped in their cockpits, facing the wind, engines ready to turn over. Only the fortunate few would draw 'available' – in the mess and ready to take off within twenty minutes. Garbed in flying overalls or rolltop sweaters, with silk scarves for comfort, they lolled on the grass or on canvas cots, the thump-thump of the petrol bowsers' delivery pumps dinning in their ears, lucky enough to breakfast off lukewarm baked beans and tepid tea.

For many food, even a bed, was a luxury. At Rochford, Essex, 151 Squadron's pilots bedded down in their cockpits; the airfield's dew-soaked grass was the one alternative. At North Weald, Essex, one squadron, starting lunch soon after noon, were airborne so often they didn't reach dessert until 3.30 pm.

It was a battle the English shared as they would share no other throughout World War II. For five long weeks, the sights they saw did not vary: the cold white contrails scoring the enormous bowl of the sky, the dragonfly glint of silver wings spinning and snarling over Kentish apple orchards and Sussex valleys. On many days the sky became a place of terror, raining blazing planes, shell splinters, parachutes, even flying boots. On the chalk hills, farm workers would find rabbits, bolt upright on their hind legs, paralysed with sheer terror.

These were heart-stopping sights, but everywhere along the southern coast hundreds who had never been under fire now walked taller, as if conscious it was now fashionable to be a frontliner. At Dover's Grand Hotel, one luncheon guest complained of shrapnel in his soup, but headwaiter George Garland coaxed him to rise above it, and greeted newcomers to the dining room: 'Good morning, sir! A nice table here, sir, away from the broken glass . . .'

Whatever the inconvenience, people were careful to shrug it off. At Home-field, Kent, ancestral home of the wealthy Smithers family, William, the butler, did the rounds of the velvety lawn after each dog fight, sweeping up spent machine-gun bullets as deftly as ever he had brushed crumbs from a damask tablecloth. Fifty miles south-west, at Worthing, Sussex, Miss Vera Arlett's maid was equally matter-of-fact: 'Shall we have plums and custard for dessert – oh, and they're machine-gunning the back garden.'

But still the R.A.F.'s losses mounted, for on most days the pilots fought against odds of three to one. By 23 August, Beaverbrook's Ministry of Air-craft Production was to achieve the battle's highest ever total – 440 fighters delivered from the assembly lines – but what Dowding lacked was the trained pilots to man those planes. It was a need so dire that on 16 August – the day the Luftwaffe struck the airfields at Manston, Tangmere and West Malling – Dowding was 209 pilots below strength.

Haggard, scarcely able to snatch more than three hours sleep a night, it was the pilot-shortage that plagued the weary Dowding above all.

It was no idle concern. The casualty rates now made plain that a pilot's expectation of life was no more than eighty-seven flying hours, and many were so near collapse their reactions were a long way off the medical board's touchstone: one-fifth of a second quicker than average. At Hawkinge, pilots taxied in, then slumped in their cockpits dead to the world like men under morphia. After eight daily sorties, Peter Hairs, another Hawkinge Hurricane pilot, would stare at his log book, unable to remember how to write.

Many cushioned their fears with drink; as 32 Squadron's C.O. John Worrall recalled it: 'If you weren't in the air, you were plastered.' But some couldn't drink at all. At Northolt near London, Canadian Roland Dibnah, though no teetotaller, found that one jigger of liquor drove him vomiting to the lavatory.

Despite Churchill's immortal tribute in the House of Commons on 20 August – 'Never in the field of human conflict was so much owed by so many to so few' – no pilot saw himself as a hero. At North Weald airfield, Pilot-Officer Michael Constable-Maxwell, on hearing the Premier's words, grinned, 'He must be thinking of our Mess bills.' Flying Officer Michael Appleby, at Warmwell, Dorset, thought of the fourteen shillings and sixpence a day at which the country valued his services. Irreverently he capped Churchill's speech: '. . . and for so little'.

But the public had taken Churchill's words to heart. The R.A.F.'s crucial losses, the acute shortage of pilots, was still a closely guarded secret; on all sides there seemed cause for jubilation, even complacency. In south coast towns, newspaper sellers chalked up each day's result in terms of a cricket match: 'R.A.F. v. Germans, 61 for 26 – Close of Play Today. 12 for 0.' For now, after many false starts, the English knew why they were fighting. The battle had moved away from distant fjords with unpronounceable names and cobbled streets that smelt of caporal tobacco in the Pas de Calais. Now they were fighting for things that were dear; for His Majesty King George VI, King and Emperor by the Grace of God, for hedgerows and village greens, thatched roofs and sooty chimney-pots, for bewigged judges and horses with heart, for Yorkshire pudding and overcooked cabbage and verbal sniping in the House of Commons. Chamberlainism was dead, the Old School Tie was going fast; a strange radiant calm had invested their world.

Hard as each pilot strove, it was bitter uphill work; many had never flown a fighter sortie before 8 August. One Spitfire pilot, Dudley Williams, of 152 Squadron, airborne over Portland, never forgot opening fire on an Me 110 and seeing the chips of metal showering. A glow of joy was followed by a sober realisation; though he had been once allowed to fire his Browning machine guns into the sea for practice, this was the first time he had ever fired them in anger.

He was no lone example; barely 10 per cent of Dowding's pilots had undergone more stringent gunnery practice Their training had stressed only disciplined pre-war air display flying in rigid V-shaped formations – a copybook procedure which baffled Luftwaffe aces like Mölders. Most, unaccustomed to sighting their guns, opened fire at 600 yards – then, at the surer range of 200 yards, broke from combat. Still doing things by the book, they

157

flew the four standard Fighter Command attacks on bombers – based on the theory that German bombers would fly in straight unwavering lines, without rear gun turrets, and would be unescorted by fighters.

Thus even the newest trainees perfected the No. 1 Fighter Command attack – where every man in the squadron swung into line behind their leader, queuing to deliver a 3-second burst before breaking away, their underbellies a sure target for the German tail gunners.

By 18 August – the day that the Luftwaffe pounded the airfields at Kenley, Biggin Hill, Croydon and West Malling – Dowding was at his wits' end. One day earlier, the Air Ministry had at last acceded to his pleas so that Fighter Command's thinning ranks would now be stiffened by pilots trained on Fairey-Battle day bombers, by Army Co-Operation Command pilots, by allied pilots like No. 1 Royal Canadian Air Force Squadron. But again the training period had been slashed – from one month to two weeks. Many of the pilots who bore the brunt of the battle that lay ahead had never fired their guns, could not use a reflector sight, and had done no more than twenty hours on Spitfires and Hurricanes.

Now the steady induction of novices into the front-line only accelerated the rate of attrition. At Croydon, down to nine pilots, 111 Squadron's Squadron Leader John Thompson greeted two unfledged sergeants: 'I'm sorry, but I'm afraid you'll have to go in today – you see, we're so terribly short.' Outside the mess, he saw their old rattletrap car, jam-packed with luggage. By 5 pm the same day, one of them was dead, the other in hospital – their gear still unpacked.

The man in hospital was Sergeant Raymond Sellers, who had earlier noted twenty minutes' dog fight practice in his logbook. Now he was so deep in shock that despite the medical orderlies' probing he couldn't even remember his name.

By the third week in August it was not surprising that many R.A.F. pilots were growing angry. To them these thin red line tactics, geared to foolhardy sorties from coastal strips like Manston and Hawkinge, made increasingly less sense. If the squadrons withdrew to the airfields north of London – North Weald, Duxford, Debden – they would be beyond the range of the ME 109s – and could steadily gain operational height as they came south. True, the northern airfields would still be within German bomber range – but without the protection of their fighters, who could not range so far north, the bombers would be easy meat. At Manston and Hawkinge, the R.A.F. had always to climb under the surveillance of hovering German fighters, knowing they would be jumped at 18,000 feet.

It was hard for the pilots to grasp, but Dowding and senior commanders like Air Vice Marshal Keith Park, of 11 Group saw the show of front-line strength as paramount. Large-scale air-raids on British cities were still an unknown bogey; gloomy estimates still predicted 200,000 casualties within ten days, and four million mental cases after six months of bombing. Even Churchill believed that up to four million would flee from London once the first bombs fell.

Thus even retaining advanced bases, like Manston, though tactically wrong, was politically expedient. To keep British morale at peak, every one of Dowding's planes must be up there in the sky – fighting against any odds that Göring chose to decree.

*

Across the English Channel, the growing concern of Dowding and his pilots would have puzzled Werner Mölders and his comrades. As each day passed, the clear-sighted among them realised that their onslaught was being slowly but irrevocably repulsed.

The inescapable truth was that the Luftwaffe was as unequal to its task of neutralising the R.A.F. as Gort's British Expeditionary Force had been to stem the onrush of the Panzers in the West.

Designed primarily to support the Army in the field, its main strength lay in short-range fighters, dive bombers like the Stukas that had pounded Sedan, and twin-engined level-flight medium-weight bombers. Though on paper it was the world's largest air force, fielding 4,093 first-line aircraft (of which 3,646 were operational) it totally lacked night bombers, bombs larger than 1,000 lb, air torpedoes, modern mines, modern armaments and bomb sights.

Incredibly, Göring all along was to pin his faith in two planes supremely unfitted for the combat. His special pride was the twin-seater, twin-engined ME 110, christened the Zerstörer (destroyer), a long-range escort fighter, designed to clear the way for mass bomber attacks, with a maximum cruising range of 680 miles. Yet when loaded the 110 outweighed the streamlined ME 109 by almost 10,000 lb. Despite the easy laurels the 110s had won in the French campaign, their lack of manoeuvrability and speed were a byword with every pilot.

In combat their stock tactic was what the R.A.F. called 'the circle of death' – a defensive gambit which had the machines circling, warily, each guarding the other's tailplane, perilous to friend and foe alike. In the first days of the combat, Major Hennig Strümpell of Fighter Group Two had found himself in one such circle dogfighting with a Spitfire – while 110s blasted tracer at both of them impartially.

Yet to all arguments Göring was obdurate: 'If the fighters are the sword of the Luftwaffe, the ME 110 Zerstörer is the point of that sword.'

Göring's unwavering belief in the Stuka troubled his commanders, too. Unrivalled in precision bombing and close infantry support when the Luftwaffe held the sky, they now made up one-third of the Luftwaffe's bomber force. Yet one disastrous Channel attack on a convoy of merchantmen on

8 August had written off thirteen Stukas; the ME 109s, lacking diving brakes found themselves screaming for the sea at 375 miles per hour, while the Stukas' air brakes throttled them back to half this speed. Time and again, as they flattened out unprotected at the end of their dive, the R.A.F. had picked the Stukas off with deadly accuracy.

On 18 August, when 28 Stukas attacked targets around Portsmouth Harbour in an effort to draw up British fighters the losses were appalling: eighteen Stukas lost or severely damaged. Beside himself with fury, Göring had still been forced to withdraw the remaining 280 Stukas from the battle.

Another bitter bone of contention with Mölders and his fellows was the use of the 109. It was a fine plane, to be sure, but playing nursemaid to the lumbering Heinkel and other bombers – 'furniture vans', the fighter-men called them – was not the task for which they had been designed. Often 120 fighters were slated to protect a bomber formation forty miles long, so that the ME 109s, with an operational radius of 125 miles and a tactical flying time of ten minutes, were severely hampered. If the R.A.F. were in the mood for combat, the 109s were left with just eight minutes to fight before breaking away.

Soon, as with the R.A.F., every pilot was feeling the stress. Many a man found himself watching his fuel gauge as anxiously as he scanned the sky; the red warning bulb on the instrument panel that showed fuel running out now prompted a code-cry: 'Trübsal' (Distress). One pilot, *Oberleutnant* Hans von Hahn of the 3rd Fighter Group, reported the plight of all of them in a letter home: 'There aren't many of us who haven't made a forced landing in the Channel in a badly shot-up plane or without a propeller.'

Above all, Göring's tactics puzzled the pilots, for day by day the attacks jumped spotily from target to target, seeming to lose all technical advantage. On 12 August, the crack Luftwaffe unit Test Group 210 had struck at the R.A.F.'s key southern radar stations: Dunkirk, near Canterbury, Pevensey, Rye, Ventnor and Dover. As the R.A.F.'s sole early warning system, these were vital targets, the eyes and ears that alerted Fighter Command's Sector Controllers how many raiders were in cross-Channel flight, and thus how to deploy their defences. By mid-afternoon on 12 August, all these stations, save Ventnor, a write-off for three weeks, were functioning again on stand-by generators – yet never again were they to figure as targets for Luftwaffe bombers.

Were the stations vital or not? Which factories should be attacked to neutralise Beaverbrook's Spitfire and Hurricane production? Which airfields most merited attack, and when attacking them which targets mattered most – the hangars and buildings or the planes on the ground? None of these questions had been adequately studied or thought through by Luftwaffe planners.

At Karinhall, on 16 August, Göring still steadfastly ignored the implications of the battle to date. The losses of the ME 110 Zerstörer were mounting steeply, for inevitably the span of the plane – fifty-three feet as against the 109s thirty-two feet – led the R.A.F. to single it out. Stubbornly insistent that the planes could do the job, Göring could no longer ignore the losses – and now he reached a well-nigh unbelievable decision.

In future, he decreed, every ME 110 unit must be shepherded into battle by an escort of ME 109s – a fighter in the ludicrous position of itself needing fighter protection.

It was then that *Oberst* Werner Junck, regional fighter commander for Air Fleet Three, made a telling point. If extra burdens were to be thrown on the 109, surely serious thought must be given to stepping up fighter production? Aircraft production had been virtually static since war began; in the last four months of 1939, only 1,869 aircraft had been delivered.

Even in July, Junck pointed out, German aircraft factories had produced only 220 ME 109s – less than half Beaverbrook's total output. By the end of August the figures would have slumped again to 173.

Mock-solicitous, Göring stretched out his hand. 'I must take your pulse to see if you are all right physically – it seems you have taken leave of your senses.'

This was not the first time that Göring had heard such an argument from his production experts, and as summarily rejected it. Others had stressed that at the present rate of attrition, the Luftwaffe would need to shoot down four British fighters for every one they lost – yet even so, the ME 109 factories at Regensburg and Augsburg often worked a minimum six-hour day against the ten or twelve needed.

Only recently, when General Thomas, Göring's production co-ordination chief raised the question of non-stop shifts, Göring had crimsoned with rage. Any such move would be fatal to home-front morale.

Thus all German strategy was becoming increasingly subordinate to Göring's inflated estimates of his Luftwaffe's potential, a private war waged with no attempt to co-ordinate with the needs of the Army or the Navy. Dazzled by the public's concept that he himself was leading the battle from the front line, Göring had even been surprised in a Paris hotel suite by his signals officer, clad only in a sky-blue silk dressing gown and describing by telephone to Emmy, his wife, how he was at that moment on the cliffs at Calais, with squadrons of aircraft thundering overhead to England.

And little by little, on every Luftwaffe airfield, from Vannes, in Brittany, to Amsterdam-Schiphol, disillusion was setting in. Though the pilots lacked inside knowledge, many still had the uncanny hunch that Hitler saw the much vaunted 'Operation Sea-Lion' as no more than a study plan. 'If he didn't invade after Dunkirk,' opined *Oberleutnant* Victor Bauer, of the 3rd Fighter Group, 'he can't really mean business.'

Bauer and his fellow pilots were more sceptical still when the only visible signs of invasion planning materialised off the coast at Le Touquet: a fleet of weatherworn apple barges. The men of Major Max Ibel's 27th Fighter Group, near Calais, felt the same: in the one combined operation that they carried out with the Army, thirty pontoons had broken loose from their moorings and been carried away by the tide. Before the exercise could proceed, the Luftwaffe had to lay on rescue launches to tow the drifting engineers back to safety.

It was near Calais, too, that *Hauptmann* Hans-Heinrich Brustellin, one of Mölders' flight commanders, felt a mingled sense of mirth and disgust at the unit's only glimpse of the great invasion armada. Overnight, a fussy flotilla of old Rhine steamers had assembled near the harbour mouth. Somehow it seemed to debase all they had striven for over the Channel: had the blood and the fear and the young lives lost been just for this? '*That* is Sea-Lion?' Brustellin asked Mölders incredulously, 'But it's like a travelling circus.'

*

Six hundred miles from the Channel coast, in the pine-scented air of the Baltic at Peenemunde, a frustrated coterie of German scientists knew that they could succeed where the Luftwaffe was failing. But the one obstacle standing in their way was then insuperable: Adolf Hitler's profound distrust of technological innovation.

Their project had been launched ten years back, when the German Army Weapons Office appointed *Hauptmann* Walter Dornberger, a 35-year-old chemist's son, to explore the chances of developing military rockets on a massive scale. Two years later, Dornberger recruited a scientist to his team who was to achieve world renown: Dr Wernher von Braun, then aged twenty.

From 1937 on, von Braun's team had conducted secret full-scale trials along Peenemunde's 300-mile water-range, fringing the Baltic's southern shores. Test stands, laboratories, workshops, even the world's most powerful supersonic wind-tunnel, capable of developing velocities in excess of Mach 4, mushroomed among the pine forests, all of them geared towards the perfection of one rocket-prototype, the A3. This was a remote-controlled missile powered by the combustion of 75 per cent ethyl alcohol in liquid oxygen, lending its motor a 1½ ton thrust. Still in the drawing-board stage was the A4, a rocket forty-two feet long designed to carry a ton of high-explosive warhead over a 160-mile range.

But Hitler, who had briefly viewed an abortive test of the A1 prototype in 1933, had shown little interest. In November 1939, convinced by his Polish victory that rockets would never be needed, he halved Peenemunde's steel allocation. That the project was still in being as late as August 1940, was due to two secret benefactors: Hitler's architect, Albert Speer, who connived with the Army Ordnance Officer to continue building, and Walter von Brauchitsch, now promoted *Feldmarschall*. Both men were excited by the potential of a missile which von Braun believed might be brought to such a pitch of accuracy it could level Whitehall.

Four years later, the first A4s (now rechristened the V-2s) were to shower on southern England. Von Braun, a belatedly-enthused Hitler now declared, was a young man 'who would change the face of the future'. But in August 1940, he and his team were merely the Cinderellas of the Third Reich, powerless to play any determinant role in Operation Sea-Lion.

*

In the Hotel Terminus, at Lorient, France, six U-Boat commanders were grouped anxiously round the bedside of Admiral Karl Dönitz, who had taken to his bed with a heavy cold and a stomach ache. Despite the pain, Dönitz could not refrain from chuckling wryly at the concern on their faces. 'Don't worry,' he reassured them, clutching a pillow to his midriff, 'I'm only having a child.' Then, conscious of the sensation he was about to cause, he explained the reason for their summons: 'Gentlemen, you are here to receive your orders for Operation Sea-Lion.'

Kapitänleutnant Otto Kretschmer felt an almost palpable tingle of excitement pass through the room. Now every man was craned forward, listening intently.

'The day for invasion has been set,' Dönitz told them, 'September 15. Those of you on patrol in the Atlantic will receive orders directing you to proceed to Cherbourg to refuel and reload with torpedoes. Your task will be to bar entry to the Channel through the western approach. No warship of the British Navy is to get through to interfere with our cross-Channel supply lines.' He paused meaningfully: 'I must stress this point. No British ship must enter the Channel.'

Along with the others, Kretschmer now waited expectantly. Surely further details of the over-all operation would now, on 26 August, be forthcoming? But if Dönitz knew more he did not choose to reveal it – and Flag Lieutenant Hans Meckel now signalled dismissal. Kretschmer and his fellow commanders left the room none the wiser – though with no reason to doubt that Sea-Lion was going according to plan.

If the rank and file of the Navy still had faith, *Kriegsmariners* in the higher echelon were less sanguine. Some, like *Grossadmiral* Raeder, felt that Hitler was not wholeheartedly committed. Sea-Lion was always to be a last resort, he had stressed, against an enemy already broken by blockade and air attacks – but since Sea-Lion was less of a seaborne assault than the transportation of an army to occupy a defeated nation, the British collapse would have to be considerable. Yet Hitler had never once convened any conference with Göring to discuss aerial strategy.

Moreover, even on 31 July, before the Battle of Britain began, the Führer had ordered significant increases in the Army's strength – to 180 divisions – but only sixty were slated to garrison the west. The remaining 120 were earmarked to attack Russia.

In the days that France toppled, Hitler, perhaps playing devil's advocate, had gone out of his way to decry the whole concept of an invasion. 'How can we do an operation of this sort?' he had demanded of his naval aide, Puttkamer, rhetorically, 'It looks completely impossible to me. Losses would be heavy and no guarantee of success. How can we take on such casualties after conquering France with none to speak of?'

Nonetheless, from 16 July, physical preparations of a kind had been ordered – to the great perturbation of the Navy, for the dateline was initially set for 15 August and the prerequisites seemed daunting. A defeated R.A.F. was the first essential, but the use of mine-free routes, the laying of flak mine-barriers, the readiness of the coastal artillery and a completely-neutralised Royal Navy were of equal importance.

Yet, incredibly, Hitler had given no man overall authority for co-ordinating the operation, and Raeder and von Brauchitsch never met until mid-July. Only one man, forgotten by history, General Georg-Hans Reinhardt, director of technical experiments at Putlos, on Kiel Bay, had grasped the need for landing craft, since this was primarily an assault from the sea on a beach position.

By dint of much wire-pulling, Reinhardt rounded up 2,000 river and canal barges, called *prahms*, each capable of carrying 2–4 vehicles and 150 troops, though all needed much modification. But all these craft between them could ferry no more than six divisions, four infantry and two armoured, and Reinhardt thus advised the Army to scale down their requirements.

From 22 July a great air of bustle was apparent. The Todt Labour Organisation was engaged on harbour clearance, and 24,000 troops had been inducted to man the invasion craft, for paradoxically, after Hitler's 29 July Barbarossa bombshell, the estimates for Sea-Lion requirements were stepped up. Now the planning called for at least 1,800 barges but also for 274 tugs, 156 steamboats, 1,586 motor boats, 137 trawlers and 127 motor coasters. Many of the smaller craft, though, could do only 4–5 knots and bow waves were likely to sink them en masse.

But their naval losses off Norway had left the *Kriegsmarine* stripped of formidable ships, and Raeder ultimately refused to guarantee the Army's safety on their ambitious 150-mile Ramsgate–Isle of Wight front. Thus the front was scaled down to encompass the coastline from the Thames Estuary to Brighton, to be assaulted by three waves, in all 700,000 men.

By 12 August, Hitler's thinking more closely resembled the waverings of a psychograph than the reasoned deliberations of a war lord. 'Independent of the eventual decision,' the War Diary of the German Navy noted, 'the Führer wishes the *threat* of invasion to be maintained against England in every way. The preparations must therefore proceed, however the decision may fall.'

'The fiction of an invasion', as the War Diary put it, now became the order of the day. Landing barges were still assembling at the seven main invasion ports: Rotterdam, Antwerp, Calais, Boulogne, Le Havre, Ostend, Dunkirk. The swank Paris Plage at Le Touquet, fifteen miles south of Boulogne, was set up as a propaganda exercise beach for manoeuvres watched by Halder, Admiral Friedrich Ruge and von Brauchitsch, but not by the sceptical old Gerd von Rundstedt, whose opinion was summed up by one explosive, 'Sea-Lion, rubbish!'

In truth, Hitler was in a quandary. By refusing to sue for peace, the British had thrown all his plans awry, but he knew full well that all his senior men — Kesselring, Guderian, Göring, Milch — were lukewarm on Sea-Lion. Only Halder was full of a drive which nobody else shared, and on 6 August he noted their half-heartedness in his diary: 'The Navy is full of misgivings, the Luftwaffe is very reluctant to tackle a mission which at the outset is exclusively its own, and O.K.W., which for once has a real combined-forces operation to direct, just plays dead.'

Two days later, Halder scented further naval obstructionism, when the Navy opined that a broad front invasion could drag on for forty-two days. 'I might as well put the assault troops straight through a sausage machine,' Halder declared furiously.

Other officials, meanwhile were going through the motions. Plans formulated by the Reich Central Security Office for the total occupation of Britain went steadily ahead. All able-bodied men between seventeen and forty-five — approximately eleven million in all — were to be shipped to the continent as slave labour. The rate of exchange was pegged at 9.60 Reichsmarks to the pound sterling. S.S. *Standartenführer* Dr Franz Six, prepared to take up headquarters in London, to implement the rounding up of all persons ranging from Churchill to Nöel Coward on a 2,700-name black list. 'My dear,' Rebecca West, also prominent on the list, commented dryly to Coward, 'the people we would have been seen dead with.'

One British family, however, was singled out for elitist treatment from the first, the special responsibility of S.S. *Haupsturmführer* Otto Begus, who was based near Boulogne. On D-Day Begus, along with twenty-three young officers and a task force of 100 men, was to parachute directly into the grounds of Buckingham Palace to seize King George VI, his Queen and their two daughters, Elizabeth and Margaret, for with them held hostage Hitler foresaw a speedy end to the war.

The only Wehrmacht unit to have pin-ups of the British Royal Family in their billets, for recognition purposes, Begus and his men had firm instructions to give the Army not the Nazi salute when face to face with Royalty. By now they had rehearsed their greeting so often they knew it by heart: 'Good morning, your Majesties. The German High Command presents its respectful compliments. My duty, on the instructions of the Führer, is to inform you that you are under the protection of the German Armed Forces

*

As the British steeled themselves for what Churchill called 'their finest hour', Roosevelt took time out to examine the budding evidence of budding U.S. defence.

At Ogdenburg, New York, on 17 August, along with Secretary of War Stimson and Governor Lehman, the President rode in brilliant sunshine through the rolling green of St Lawrence County to witness a formidable display of manpower. Eight times in six hours his motorcade pulled up before stiffly-assembled divisions of the 94,000 men of the First Army of the United States. Eight times he heard the 21-gun salutes, followed by ruffles and flourishes; eight times he sat at attention for the national anthem, while Old Glory stirred in the breeze above regimental colours dipped in salute.

When it came to war machines, the picture was bleaker. The President saw just five anti-aircraft guns, forty World War I 155-mm howitzers, a large number of 75-mm guns and approaching 100 aircraft. There were no automatic rifles in sight, and no anti-tank guns, with good reason: there were no tanks. How was the equipment of the 44th Division, Roosevelt asked Major General Clifford Powell. 'It's pretty good, what there is of it,' Powell conceded. 'But we are using broomsticks for machine guns and rain pipes for mortars.'

The President laughed ruefully. Everybody, he admitted, seemed to be in the same boat.

In a sense, the nation's growing awareness of its fragile frontiers was working to Roosevelt's advantage. Much had changed since the June day when he had confided his misgivings to Secretary Ickes as to the wisdom of supplying destroyers to Britain. Despite heated isolationist speeches against conscription in Congress, Gallup polls showed that 71 per cent of American citizens now favoured it. The fall of France had influenced more than the President's decision to run for a third term. On 28 June, Congress had passed the Naval Defence Act, which now permitted the sale of naval equipment provided the Chief of Naval Operations, Admiral Harold Raynford Stark, certified it as surplus. Now Roosevelt saw a way of belatedly acceding to Churchill's long-standing plea for destroyers, for the United States had 200 old four-stackers in cold storage.

166

On 13 August, four days before setting out on his defence survey, he had hit on a way to break the log jam. It would be a straight Yankee horse-trade, for if, in return for fifty over-age flush-decker destroyers, Britain gave the United States the right to fortify and defend eight crucial British-held bases in the Atlantic – Newfoundland, Bermuda's reefbound Great Sound, the Bahamas, Jamaica, Antigua, St Lucia, Trinidad and British Guiana – Roosevelt, invoking the Naval Defence Act plus his executive privilege, could successfully bypass Congress, provided that Stark agreed.

Thus Stark could, on 21 August, endorse the transfer with a clear conscience, pencilling at the end of his memo, 'This is the time when a "feller" needs a friend.'

It was, Roosevelt would claim to Congress on 3 September, 'the most important action since the Louisiana Purchase', for the bases offered much-needed protection to the Panama Canal, Canada and Mexico. The gesture won him unexpected allies. As a Republican, Stimson was in frequent touch with William Allen White and his Committee to Aid the Allies, and White could give him assurance that the Republican candidate for the forthcoming election, Wendell Willkie, would in general support the plan, although Willkie later castigated the bypassing of Congress as 'the most dictatorial and arbitrary act of any President in the history of the United States'.

Support came too, from the doughty old General John J. Pershing, Commander of the World War I American Expeditionary Force, who advocated backing the 'destroyer deal' in a broadcast on a nation-wide radio hook-up. 'If the destroyers help save the British Navy,' Pershing reasoned sagely, 'they may save us from the dangers and hardships of another war.'

Even so, it was a colossal political risk for Roosevelt to run, one which he admitted might have cost him the election. 'Congress is going to raise hell over this,' he prophesied to his secretary, Grace Tully, anticipating the storm of protest that was to arise from Capitol Hill, though the Republican press gave him an even rougher ride. 'If we want to get into war,' the *Chicago Tribune* opined, 'the destroyers offer as good a way as any of accomplishing the purpose.' 'The United States', claimed *The New York Daily News*, 'has one foot in the war and one foot on a banana peel.' 'Of all the sucker real-estate deals in history, this is the worst,' sneered *The St Louis Post Dispatch*, 'and the President of the United States is the sucker.'

The Third Reich thought otherwise. On 6 September, the first eight of the old destroyers, looking like absurd little floating factories with their flat decks and four tall funnels steamed into the hill-fringed harbour of Halifax, Nova Scotia, where 2,000 Canadian and British tars were waiting – 'by the long arm of coincidence', as Churchill explained guilelessly – to receive them. 'The deal,' exploded the German Chargé in Washington, Hans Thomsen, 'is evidence of Roosevelt's ruthless determination, devious modes . . . and total disregard of congressional and military advice.'

167

Roosevelt had acted none too soon. Like a running torch applied to tinder, Hitler's New Order was engulfing much that remained of free Europe.

Ever since the Führer began his redemption of minorities in Czecho-slovakia and Poland, Rumania, too, had been ripe for partitioning. The first step had come in June, when Russia, to the anguish of the venal King Carol, had moved into Bessarabia and northern Bucovina. Now Hitler, intent on maintaining absolute peace within the Balkans, became painfully conscious that Rumania was still pockmarked with islands of foreigners whose parent states coveted their return. Two such large and solid islands were the Bulgarian minority in Dobruja and the Hungarian minority in south-east Transylvania, almost at the country's dead centre.

King Carol, who had wooed the Axis too late in life, now realised that Hitler was exacting his price. As the summer of 1940 neared its end, Hungary was preparing to go to war for Transylvania, which Rumania had taken from her following World War I. To Hitler such a war was unthinkable. Not only would it cut off the Reich from its main source of crude oil; it could conceivably prompt the Russians to step in and occupy all Rumania.

Hitler acted fast. On 28 August, he ordered Carol to settle the claims of both Hungary and Bulgaria before 1 September. When the King stalled and vacillated, Foreign Minister von Ribbentrop and Italy's Count Ciano lost patience. Rumania was ordered to submit the dispute to arbitration at an Axis-convened conference held in Vienna's Belvedere Palace on 30 August. When the Rumanian Foreign Minister, Mihail Manolescu, saw the map that the Axis powers had drawn up, ceding not only Dobruja to Bulgaria, but 16,000 square miles of Transylvania to Hungary he fainted dead away across the conference table. Physicians had to revive him with spirits of camphor.

Though the 'Vienna Award' was received sourly by Stalin, who had not been consulted, Hitler, for the time being, had achieved all that he wanted. Both Rumania and Hungary would continue vying for his favours, the one in the hope that she might regain what she had lost, the other in the hope of further bounty.

In Bucharest, Rumania's capital, the smouldering resentment of the people at Carol's sell-outs now exploded into rage. Shocked and sullen crowds milled before the King's Palace and the German and Italian Legations, shouting 'Fight the Hungarians'. Across the muddy Pruth River, dividing Rumania from Bessarabia, the Red Army lay in waiting. Promptly Hitler sent word to the capital, that unless the disorders stopped Germany would occupy all Rumania with troops, ringing down the curtain on the land of Carol.

The King saw the red light. On 5 September, he entrusted the reins of power to General Ion Antonescu, Chief of the Fascist Iron Guard and a friend of Hitler's. Antonescu responded by giving his sovereign marching orders. Rumania wanted no more of its king; if he valued his life he should leave while the going was good.

One day later Carol agreed to abdicate in favour of his son, 18-year-old Prince Michael.

His farewell to the land he had mulcted for so long was suitably Ruritanian. He and his red-haired mistress Magda Lupescu, under the travelling aliases 'Mr and Mrs Carol Caraiman', fled the country by night in a 9-coach train with three bullet-proof automobiles, the Royal stamp collection, four Rembrandts, sixteen poodles, six pet white turkeys, $2,500,000 worth of jewels, a flock of peacocks and a million dollar haul of gold coins.

As the Royal special careened towards the Yugoslavian frontier, armed members of the Iron Guard were lying in wait at the railroad station of Timisoara. Forewarned, Carol had told the engineers to stop for nothing and nobody. Amid a hail of bullets the train pounded through Timisoara, as Carol dived into a bath-tub and his foppish former Lord Chamberlain, Ernest Udarianu, took refuge in a lavatory. Only Madame Lupescu remained superbly unruffled.

The King's fellow dictator, Benito Mussolini, at once sent a pilot train full of Italian police to lead Carol's special from Yugoslavia across Italy to Switzerland. At journey's end, Lugano, the King became belatedly aware that one of the locomotive's firemen in running the gauntlet of bullets, had been wounded in the arm. To mark his gratitude, Carol handed him a two-dollar tip.

The engineer surveyed the coin judicially. Then he flung it in the former monarch's face.

*

The British were soon aware that Herman Göring had switched his aerial priorities yet again. For threefold reasons – reprisals for an R.A.F. raid on Berlin, the hope of flushing up the R.A.F. fighters into free combat, to wield a lethal blow against dockland traffic – the Luftwaffe's target was now London.

Now it would become a war against people, a war that Londoners had not known and would not relish.

One man with cause for concern was Assistant Divisional Officer Geoffrey Vaughan Blackstone of the London Fire Brigade. Aged thirty, a six-foot-plus ex-public schoolboy, Blackstone had been three years with the Brigade and was already noted for his trenchant views. On the afternoon of Saturday, 7 September, Blackstone had no apparent motive for worry; stretched out on the grass at a friend's tennis party in Dulwich, South London, he was enjoying a rare spell off duty from Fire Brigade Headquarters, Lambeth.

But Blackstone was looking to the future. Of the 30,000-strong Brigade, 28,000 were wartime auxiliaries, some conscripts, more of them volunteers,

169

but all with one thing in common: at least 90 per cent of them had never tackled a fire of any kind.

In Blackstone's view, the auxiliaries had had a raw deal from the first. Unlike peacetime firemen, who were fully kitted-out, the newcomers lacked not only topcoats but a change of uniform; any man getting wet in line of duty had to shiver in his underwear until his tunic and trousers had dried out. In the long lull of the phoney war, the public had singled them out as scroungers and parasites, deriding them as 'the darts brigade', a lot so unenviable that many men had quit in protest. By June 1940, alarmed by the exodus, the Home Office had been forced to 'freeze' them in the service, and thus Blackstone wondered how such unwilling volunteers would face up to danger if danger came.

Few others on this warm sunny afternoon gave danger a thought. Couples lay flirting on the grass in St James's Park; others were queuing for theatre matinées — Celia Johnson in *Rebecca* or Robert Donat in *The Devil's Disciple*. Even over many coastal districts, random raiders were now commonplace; as the first London-bound raiders of *Oberst* Johannes Fink's Bomber Group 2 swept over the cattle-market at Canterbury, Kent, a newsboy by the traffic signals hailed them cheerily: 'Hey wait for the lights to turn green!' At Shepperton, on the Thames, spectators at a Saturday afternoon cricket match broke into brisk applause from the pavilion as a batsman's stumps flew: 'Oh, well bowled, sir — a beauty!'

Looking upwards, they saw Heinkels at 15,000 feet sliding towards the blue haze that marked the city's boundary and thought complacently: they'll never get to London.

One man was determined that they should: *Reichsmarschall* Herman Göring, who had already arrived at Cap Blanc Nez, on the Channel, in his private train, code-named Asia, with its ornate mahogany-panelled saloons. For Göring, at this eleventh hour, all the magic and soon-discarded formulas of the past weeks — Stukas, Zerstörers, radar attacks, close fighter escorts — had boiled down to one solution: *he* must infuse the fighter pilots with the bellyfire they so obviously lacked.

To a reporter with a recording van, Göring announced that he personally had taken command of the battle. Watching him, Werner Mölders wondered why he was wearing pink patent-leather boots.

But as the teleprinter chattered out its first reports Göring grew more angry still: of the 247 bombers despatched to the target, forty would not return. The reason, although the *Reichsmarschall* refused to admit it, was plain enough to commanders like Mölders. By insisting that a fighter escort 600 strong accompany the bombers, Göring had created such a mêlée in the sky over London that fighters had been too busy dodging each other to stop the R.A.F. taking toll of the bombers.

On 7 September, Göring was blind and deaf to any such logic. Without

170

further ado, each fighter group and wing commander was ordered to report to his private train for a bitter diatribe. 'Your job is to protect the bombers,' he assailed them, 'and each time you fall down on it.' When one man next to Mölders raised the question of British fighters, Göring swung on him: 'Don't tell *me* the sky is full of enemies – I know they haven't more than seventy fighters left.'

It was in vain that Mölders and the others sought to defend their men. Impatiently, Göring brushed their arguments aside: the pilots were cowards.

In London, where the air raid sirens wailed around 5 pm the realisation that the city was under attack was slow to dawn at first. Armed with little more than a whistle, a white tin hat marked 'W', the knowledge that Lewisite gas smelt of geraniums, and that bomb blast travelled in all directions, 9,000 London air raid wardens and their part-time unpaid volunteers set out to face their first blitz. For others the first intimation of disaster came in observing an apparent freak of nature. Tonight, it seemed, the sun was not setting in the west, over Putney and Wimbledon, but in the east. Above the docks at Poplar and Whitechapel, the whole skyline was a shifting orange glow.

From his office roof by St James's Park, the scientist, Dr R. V. Jones, watched the blaze with a sense that he was beaten before he started. Three months after identifying the Knickebein beams, Jones was on the eve of coming to grips with the mysterious X-Gerät system – a device he believed to be a vastly more sophisticated refinement of Knickebein. Now the gloomy thought struck him; even if the beams were traced and jammed, a fire like this would be a marker beacon in itself.

In Chiswick, West London, a social worker, Nesca Robb, recited to herself, scarcely crediting that it could be true, an old childish jingle: *'London's burning, London's burning, Fire, fire! Fire, fire! Pour on water! Pour on water!'*

It was an apt jingle, but in some areas the fires were already so intense that water was useless. At Surrey Commercial Docks, on the Thames at Rotherhithe, Geoffrey Blackstone, who had hastened from his tennis party to take command, found 250 acres of resinous timber stacked twenty feet high burning with a dry and terrible crackling; from his control car he watched water pumped by fireboats from a river already choked with blazing barges evaporate in hissing clouds as it struck the warehouses. Closer to, even the wooden blocks that formed the dockland roadway burned with a merry glare. From Paget's Wharf Fire Station, in the heart of the conflagration, the hard-pressed Station Officer Plimlett, using the professionals' word for fire-engines, phoned Fire Brigade Headquarters: 'Send every pump you've got. The whole bloody world's on fire.'

It was a night when every man and woman had cause to hold their breath, for as dusk fell it was plain that London's ordeal was far from over. Under cover of darkness, the bombers were still coming, unimpeded now by British

171

fighters, to stoke up the fires that the pathfinders had lit until 4 am on the Sunday. From the Colonnade of St Paul's Cathedral, the Dean, the Very Reverend William Matthews, dressed, like the other volunteers on his watch, in battle-dress and steel helmet, gazed with silent awe on a city whose Fire Brigade had now logged 1,000 separate calls.

Close at hand, someone muttered, 'It's like the end of the world', and another voice replied quietly, 'It's the end of *a* world.'

By 8 pm, on this apocalyptic night, the British saw this as the truth. Nobody viewed it as a raid to preface peace terms, to avenge Berlin, or to draw the R.A.F. into combat. This non-stop air armada could mean one thing only.

The invasion fleet was coming. It was H-Hour.

8

'The Way Across The Channel Will Soon Be Clear'

7 September–27 September, 1940

FROM THE WAR CABINET downwards, this belief was common: Hitler was making good his boast. At 8.7 pm Lieutenant-General Alan Brooke, from his headquarters at St Paul's School, West London, issued the code-word 'Cromwell', signifying Alert No. 1, to the Army's Eastern and Southern commands – 'Invasion imminent and probable within twelve hours.'

At Gosport Army Co-operation Command Station, on Portsmouth Harbour, Pilot Officer 'Nobby' Clarke, R.A.F., in a Skua target-towing plane, had word: 'Get cracking – light all the points, working from east to west.' From Weymouth, 150 miles east along the coast to Beachy Head, Clarke knew that on every available landing beach petrol pipe-lines jutted almost level with the water's surface. Now his task was to dive-bomb each with incendiaries, to transform the inshore waters into a raging cauldron of fire.

Since early July, the newly-formed Petroleum Warfare Department had been working all out to install some 200 'Defile Flame traps', ranging from Dover, Kent, to Fowey, Cornwall. Now their testing time had come. On the main roads leading inland to Canterbury and Maidstone, in Kent, and Horsham, in Sussex, troops stood by beside 600-gallon tanks, sited ten feet above road level, ready to spray a petrol and gas-oil mixture on to the advancing Germans – pumping at a rate of thirty gallons a minute, to burn at a heat of 500 degrees Fahrenheit. Professor Lindemann had grimly assured Churchill: 'Nothing could live in it for two minutes.'

But why had the Germans delayed? Flying east towards Littlehampton, Pilot Officer Clarke could see no invasion barges: only the grey wash of the sea at sundown, white surf creaming on the sand. Then abruptly his radio-telephone crackled. Without explanation he was recalled to Gosport.

Along the south coast confusion multiplied. At Folkestone's Hotel Mecca, panicky officials whipped out Mrs Lillian Ivory's telephone, then remembered that her boarding house was Intelligence Corps Headquarters and hastily brought it back again. Inland, on the Berkshire downs, Land Girl Barbara Hornsey, mounted on her black horse, Nero, was one of a select vigilante patrol, anxiously scanning the sky for descending paratroops. If she spotted them, her instructions were clear: to gallop helter-skelter for the nearest telephone box and use the two-pence provided from Government funds, and returnable after each mission, to call the nearest Home Guard unit.

It was a night of strange alarms. On the drive from Brighton to Worthing, motorists kept their passes at the ready: bayonets glinted eerily at every checkpoint. At Dover, bugles sounded along the white cliffs; in a score of villages from Portsmouth to Swansea, Home Guardsmen, unbidden, rang the church bells, to warn against invasion, a lonely tolling over dark fields. In Reg Cooke's little coastguard cottage at Pett, Sussex, the telephone shrilled and the Home Guard was on the line: 'They've landed at Lydd.'

Peering east through the darkness, Cooke could see nothing – and in any case he had only a duck gun. He and his wife Lydia went to bed.

All that night, the Home Guard stood by, half a million men alerted for the first invasion in more than a century, gripping a weird armoury of weapons – from assegais, the relics of a spectacle, supplied from London's Drury Lane Theatre to boarding pikes from Nelson's *Victory*. At Stubbington, Hampshire, Colonel Barrow told his Home Guard company: 'They may be landing paratroops behind you, but there will be no turning back.' Doggedly his farm-workers and shepherds agreed – though only one among them had a .22 rifle, the rest had stout sticks.

All next day, Sunday, 8 September, strange rumours multiplied in the Channel ports. In Folkestone, the people numbered Dover's fate in hours: the Germans had completed a cross-channel tunnel and were preparing to launch bombs against Dover torpedo-fashion. Dover knew the worst about Folkestone: their ground defences had caved in, and German planes were already operational from nearby Hawkinge Airfield. Station Officer Thomas Goodman, a London fireman on relief at Dover, heard of an attempted landing at Sandwich Bay, fourteen miles north: the inshore waters, it was said, were black with German dead. Taking a staff car, Goodman set off – to find only baking sands and blue sea, not a soul in sight.

In Whitehall, hastily recalled Civil Servants made contingency plans to transfer the Government en bloc to Malvern College, Worcestershire, although one key figure had made it plain that he was staying put to the last. 'I do not think much will be left of Downing Street after a few weeks,' Churchill wrote to Chamberlain's wife, Anne, 'I propose to lead a troglodyte existence with several "trogs".'

Unknown to all save the Cabinet and the General Staff an invisible army now almost 5,000 strong, was preparing for a similar existence. Operating under Major (later Major-General) Colin McVean Gubbins, a veteran of Narvik, the bulk of these Auxiliary Units Groups were concentrated on a southern coastal strip no more than thirty miles deep – men dressed, for security reasons, in the khaki battledress of ordinary Home Guardsmen. But no Home Guardsman, in 1940, ever saw weapons such as theirs.

The inside pockets of their battledress blouses bulged with charges of 'plastic' — a form of cyclonite three times as powerful as TNT. Their underground caches in outbuildings and chicken runs were stacked with weapons unknown to the men of Dunkirk: the first Thompson sub-machine guns imported from the United States, Piat anti-tank weapons, phosphorus handgrenades, tyre-bursting mines disguised as lumps of coal or horse manure. Selected snipers among them carried .22 B.S.A. rifles, fitted with powerful telescopic sights and silencers, capable of picking off German officers and their tracker dogs from a mile away.

Their hide-outs were a triumph of ingenuity. By December, there were more than 300 of them, sited six feet below ground, twenty feet by ten feet wide, designed to house up to seven men for days at a time if need be. At Charing, Kent, Captain Norman Field's 'operational base' was a converted rabbit warren sited beneath a sheep trough — but other men were holing up in one-time badger setts, camouflaged by rotting farm carts, in abandoned Cornish tin-mines, even beneath cucumber frames. On the Bowes-Lyon estate in Berwickshire, Scotland, owned by King George's brother-in-law, resistants had first to scale a cliff overhanging a salmon river then leap for their cave through a waterfall.

Most of this Army were men attuned to move by night — poachers, gamekeepers, fishermen, ghillies — but others were natural-born soldiers of fortune, unable to resist a challenge. At Bilting, Kent, Captain Peter Fleming, Old Etonian, author and jungle explorer had already mined every house in the district likely to attract the Germans, using milk-churns packed with high explosive. North of the Thames at Kelvedon, Essex, Captain Andrew Croft, onetime A.D.C. to the Maharajah of Cooch-Behar, and former secretary of Cambridge's Fitzwilliam Museum, ran his private army from the sanctuary of his father's vicarage. Captain Anthony Quayle, a Shakespearean actor more used to grease-paint than burnt cork, now spent his nights on the moors of Northumberland, dogging imaginary tanks.

All these men had their secret letter-boxes — in garbage heaps or abandoned birds' nests — where messages could be left for collection by 'cut-outs', along with out-station transmitters, sometimes sited in pub cellars or in disused farm privies. For camouflage, their radio aerials were buried half an inch deep in the trunks of trees, the channels filled in with plaster of Paris and painted to match the bark. All of them were geared to one purpose, and would remain so for the foreseeable future: to go under cover if the Germans invaded, to remain there, living rough, by day, to launch hit-and-run raids by night, to fight on as they had been taught to fight — killing until they triumphed or until they themselves were killed.

*

175

Meanwhile on Saturday, 14 September, one week after the dockland blitz, a heated argument was taking place in Berlin between Hitler and his service advisers. The Chief of the Luftwaffe General Staff, General Hans Jeschonnek, was maintaining stubbornly that there had been 'no mass panic (in London) up to now because residential districts have not been attacked or destroyed'. Jeschonnek now sought permission to extend his target area, a plea backed by Admiral Raeder, who felt that without that 'mass panic', Sea-Lion stood little chance of success.

Hitler did not agree. 'Attacks on military objectives,' he ruled, 'are always the most important because they destroy irreplaceable war material.' This was sound reasoning. After three nights of blitz, the Port of London had been closed to ocean-going shipping and vessels were being re-routed to ports all over Britain.

Jeschonnek, Hitler conceded, could extend his area to railroad stations and power supplies but 'bombing with the object of causing a mass panic must be left to the last'.

To some it seemed that the spectre of Franklin Roosevelt hovered over the conference table, for Hitler went further still. 'Terror bombing might invite reprisals against German towns,' he pointed out, 'to say nothing of having an adverse effect on neutral opinion in the United States.' In Rome, the U.S. Ambassador William Phillips had already warned Count Ciano that a bombardment of London with many civilian deaths might yet induce America to intervene.

The alternative – one last massed London raid to induce the R.A.F. to come up and be destroyed – was timed for Sunday, 15 September.

At 11 am on this historic morning, the German formations were soon apparent as V-shaped blips of light on the convex glass screens of the coastal radar stations: wide deep steadily-beating echoes swimming into focus, arising from the mists of the morning.

By 11.03 am, Wing Commander Eric Douglas-Jones, Duty Controller in the Operations Room at H.Q. 11 Group, Fighter Command, could wait no longer. Already every bulb on the panels lining the opposite wall was glowing red – a signal that every squadron throughout Fighter Command's six sectors was standing by. He reached for the first of six telephones, and automatically thirty-five miles away, a bulb lit up on the Sector Controller's desk at Biggin Hill, in Kent. The day's first squadrons were to patrol Canterbury at 20,000 feet.

At 11.25 am, with every 11 Group squadron now committed, a 60-strong wing from 12 Group were speeding from Duxford, Essex, to lend support over London.

To the first pilots airborne, it seemed that this morning, the Luftwaffe, as never before, held the sky – as if a dense black swarm of insects was advancing, trailing ever-lengthening miles of black ribbon. As they drew nearer, a

176

high and watery sun picked out their strange and colourful insignia: the green heart of Major Hannes Trautloft's 54th Fighter Group, the poised black sledgehammer of *Oberst* Johannes Fink's Dorniers, the frowning eagle's head of Werner Mölders.

Of the twenty-one R.A.F. squadrons airborne, twenty-one intercepted the raiders, though not all with equal success. Over Biggin Hill at 18,000 feet Squadron Leader Ernest McNab's No. 1 Canadian Squadron never saw the group of 109s that bounced them from the sun; only two of their Hurricanes even closed with the raiders. Above Gravesend, 41 Squadron, equally baulked, watched yet more bombers sliding towards London.

As Big Ben boomed noon, 148 bombers broke through to the centre of the capital, raining bombs to the south-west and south-east, one Dornier landing an unexploded bomb in King George VI's back garden at Buckingham Palace. For this *lèse-majesté* the pilot paid dearly; Sergeant Ray Holmes, of 504 Squadron, hot on its trail, delivered a burst so lethal that his victim crashed with pile-driving force in the forecourt of Victoria Station. At the same time, Holmes, his Hurricane hit, baled out, landing feet first in a dustbin in nearby Ebury Bridge Road.

By now, Mölders and every German fighter pilot was anxiously watching his fuel gauge, knowing that the moment to break for the Channel must come within seconds. At this psychological moment, the 60-strong 12 Group wing led by the legless Squadron Leader Douglas Bader fell like falcons from above.

The sky over London was suddenly a whirling wheeling arabesque of fighters – in Bader's words 'the finest shambles I'd ever been in'. But for the German bombers, suddenly shorn of protection, these were moments of naked terror. High above the city, crewmen were baling out from a Dornier which broke ludicrously in half, level with the black crosses. Another Dornier fell from the sky before a shot had been fired; to those watching it seemed the pilot must have reached the peak where the strain could be borne no longer.

As Major Hannes Trautloft of Fighter Group 54 noted in his diary: 'Who'd know that it was Sunday if it hadn't been announced on the radio?'

By 2 pm, in this last effort to force the R.A.F. into a fight to extinction, the Luftwaffe had committed every plane they could muster – and every R.A.F. plane still serviceable was airborne to meet the challenge. At H.Q. 11 Group, Winston Churchill, who had arrived to join the Controller on the dais, asked the Air Officer Commanding, Air Vice Marshal Keith Park, 'What other reserves have we?'

Noting that every bulb was glowing red once more, Park admitted soberly: 'There are none.'

At this moment, Sector Controllers all over southern England were marshalling their squadrons as Wing-Commander Douglas-Jones instructed

177

them and the radio-telephones were crackling with the weird call-signs in use between sectors and squadrons. 'Hello, Garter, this is Caribou, your message received and understood.' . . . 'Turkey leader, this is Runic, patrol Maidstone, angels twenty.' . . . 'Laycock Red Leader to Calla Leader . . . watch it, Calla Leader, here the bastards come!'

They were coming in force; Pilot Officer Patrick Barthropp, who after his very first sortie that morning, had noted in his logbook, 'Thousands of them,' now added a mental rider, '*Still* thousands of them.' But the Luftwaffe were destined to pay a bitter price; a 2-hour respite had given the R.A.F. the chance to refuel and rearm, and even though Dowding was 170 pilots below strength, many pilots were gripped, as rarely in the past, by the fierce elation of combat.

The sky was suddenly a clawing, stalling mass of fighters, bent on destruction, fighting within a cube eighty miles long by thirty miles broad, more than five miles high: a battle that within thirty minutes would number above 200 individual dog-fights.

Once more deprived of fighter cover, the bombers were to suffer most. Above Maidstone, Pilot Officer Mike Cooper-Slipper, 605 Squadron, knew that his Hurricane had taken fire, then saw three Dorniers dead ahead of him, closing in. With a sudden snap decision to ram them, Cooper-Slipper bored in on the middle plane, conscious only of 'a swishing and a swooshing' as the shattered Dornier fell steeply to port. At 20,000 feet, ripping three fingernails from his right hand, Cooper-Slipper baled out.

Over Appledore, Kent, seeing two unescorted Dorniers approaching, Pilot Officer Paddy Stephenson, 607 Squadron, came to the same decision. With no time to take aim, Stephenson charged both with a left and right blow from both wings, then baled out above the blazing bombers – probably the only Battle of Britain pilot to bring down two German aircraft without firing a shot.

To more than one bomber pilot, glimpsing no fighter escort above and astern, it seemed fruitless even to attempt the journey. Airborne from Juvaincourt, in a Junkers 88 of the 77th Bomber Group, *Oberleutnant* Dietrich Peltz found the whole sky empty of 109s; without hesitation he sent his entire 4,000 lb bomb load tumbling towards the Channel then turned for home. Even the fighter pilots, who for six weeks had heard Göring's hollow promises that the R.A.F. were a write-off, found their cynicism hard to contain. As yet more glinting cohorts of Spitfires hove into view, *Oberleutnant* Ludwig Franzisket of Fighter Group 27, broke radio silence with a sardonic comment: 'Here come those last fifty Spitfires!'

At 3.50 pm, as the last raiders receded across the Channel, it seemed a day for tributes. At Marden, Kent, a gang of field labourers lifting potatoes rose as one man when a squadron of Spitfires roared overhead, lifting their caps in salute. At Maidstone, nearby, a shot-down German pilot acknowledged his opponent's merit to his captors: 'Well done, Spitfire.' To the surprise of Wing Commander Douglas-Jones, the 11 Group Controller, Churchill suddenly clapped him on the shoulder with a heartfelt, 'Good show, old boy.'

It was hours before Fighter Command knew the extent of their losses — twenty-six planes, thirteen pilots — though the legend of their counter claim was to persist for many years: a total bag of 183 German planes. Within days, Air Ministry crash investigators had arrived at the truth: the German losses totalled no more than fifty-six, of which thirty-four were bombers. Yet another truth was becoming equally apparent: the Luftwaffe's attempts were slackening, and the R.A.F. was still a force to be reckoned with.

One day earlier, in Berlin, Hitler had noted: 'Four to five days' good weather are required to achieve decisive results.' But by 17 September, Raeder had dictated for the War Diary: 'The enemy air force is by no means defeated. On the contrary, it shows increasing activity. The Führer therefore decides to postpone Sea-Lion indefinitely.' From now on, the onslaught on Russia, Operation Barbarossa, would assume full priority.

In a rare moment of honesty, Göring confessed ruefully to General Student: 'We'd forgotten that the English fought best with their backs to the wall.' But within days he had retreated into fantasy, assuring himself that night bombing alone would break British morale. 'After all, man isn't a nocturnal animal,' was his solemn reasoning.

Did the decision rankle with Hitler? No man could be sure. To *Oberst* Martin Harlinghausen, Chief of Staff of 10th Flying Corps, the Führer seemed to take it philosophically: 'I want colonies I can walk to without getting my feet wet.' Werner Mölders, though, was less certain. On 23 September he flew to Berlin to meet Hitler for the first time, and receive the award of the Oak Leaves to the Knight's Cross. At first Hitler seemed 'almost fatherly', taking both his hands, steering him to a settee in the Reich Chancellery, appearing well informed about the Channel battles.

Suddenly Mölders made a random remark: 'The way across the Channel will soon be clear.' Abruptly Hitler's face clouded. Totally disregarding Mölders' remark, he turned away from him. 'It was as though, spiritually, he was enclosed within himself,' Mölders was to recall. 'Like a snail in its shell. No one may enter.'

Again Mölders felt a twinge of doubt. Wasn't Sea-Lion going to come off after all? And if the project had been abandoned, one factor was more perplexing yet: Why were they still fighting?

*

Aboard the S.S. *City of Benares*, three days outward bound from Liverpool, ninety British youngsters, aged between five and fifteen, some accompanied

179

by their parents, along with a sprinkling of adults bound on business, rejoiced that they had left bombs and battles behind.

None of the 408 souls aboard was more content than Sonia Bech, the 11-year-old schoolgirl from Bognor Regis, who in June had watched the war transform her quiet Sussex coastline into a cat's cradle of barbed wire and concrete pillboxes. After Dunkirk, just as Sonia had anticipated, Marguerite, her mother, had finally taken the plunge and written off to an uncle by marriage in Montreal. Could he offer her and her three children a home for the duration?

Since the fall of the Low Countries, 3,000 children – some State-aided, some financed by their families – had gone to start new lives in the United States, Canada and South Africa.

There had been the pang of leaving her Scottie, Mackie, behind with relatives, but Sonia, romantic and impulsive, had revelled in the voyage from the start. The 11,081 ton *City of Benares*, flagship of the Ellerman line and formerly on the India run, was Sonia's idea of a dream ship: the Lascar stewards, with their pale blue and white uniforms and ornate blue sashes, the mountains of American ice-cream on which the youngsters gorged themselves twice daily, seemed part of a vanishing world. After rations that had now scaled down to 8 oz of sugar, 4 oz of butter and tea, 2 oz of bacon and 1s 10d worth of meat weekly; life aboard the *City of Benares* for Sonia, was filled with a glamour known only at secondhand from books and movies.

For three days now the weather had been choppy, but the Bechs didn't let this deter them. Barbara, fourteen, the family bookworm, had found the ship's library. Derek, aged nine, displayed to envious friends the sackful of hardware he had gleaned during the Battle of Britain from the fringe of Tangmere airfield: blackened ME 109 pistons, part of a charred flying helmet. Sonia preened herself over her new camel-hair coat from D. H. Evans' department store and her six pairs of new silk stockings.

At eleven, Sonia was too extrovert to have premonitions, although some adults had been disturbed when the ship sailed on Friday, 13 September. Nor was Sonia aware that the U-Boat menace coupled with the shortage of flotilla craft decreed that the Royal Navy could not provide ocean convoys with anti-submarine escorts more than 300 miles west of Ireland.

If the passengers were ignorant, the crew had no illusions. Fashion designer Digby Morton, on a business promotion trip for the Board of Trade, along with his wife Phyllis, had been chatting on the first day out with the ship's Master, Captain Landles Nicholl. 'Why,' the Mortons asked, 'hadn't Nicoll, a family man, evacuated his own children along with the others?' The Captain met their gaze steadily. 'I'd rather put their hands in the fire,' was all he said.

At 1 am, on 17 September, the escort – a destroyer and two sloops – withdrew. Convoy OB 213, nineteen ships strong and wallowing at eight-and-a-half knots, half the *Benares*' speed, was now adjudged to be in safe waters.

As night fell, a Force 5 gale was raking the Atlantic. Towards 10 pm, the *City of Benares* was 600 miles off the British coast, approaching latitude 56 43 North, longtitude 23 15 West. At this hour, most of the children, Sonia included, were sleeping soundly. None aboard the ship was aware that half a mile to port *Kapitänleutnant* Heinrich Bleichrodt, of U-boat 48, had the merchantman squarely in his periscope. Bleichrodt already knew the ship's name through monitoring her wireless traffic, but not her cargo or her destination. At 10.05 pm, as 500 lb of torpedo streaked through the water, the *City of Benares* to Bleichrodt, was no more than a routine naval target.

For most passengers still awake, the first impact was minimal. Fifteen-year-old Anthony Quinton, sitting with his mother in the first class lounge, noticed a mighty cloud of dust arise from the pile carpet — but the Lascar steward, serving coffee, was still enquiring politely, 'Black or white, sir?' Phyllis Digby Morton, already in her cabin ready for bed, was conscious of a strange smell 'as if a huge wax match was dying out'.

Others came swiftly face to face with disaster. Mary Cornish, a 41-year-old music teacher and volunteer escort for the Children's Overseas Reception Board, was groping through the darkened alleyway towards the children's cabins when she stopped short. Where the cabin class bathrooms had been there was only a black abyss. A vast hole had been blown in the liner amidships.

In fact, the torpedo had exploded in No. 5 Hold on the ship's port side, blasting away the hatches. Water was rushing into the lower hold, and the vessel was settling slowly by the stern, where the State-aided evacuees were quartered.

Now alarm bells were jangling urgently through the darkness — plainly audible to Barbara Bech, still awake and browsing through a library book. Shaking the sleepy Sonia awake, she ran to the next cabin to arouse her mother and Derek.

Dazedly, groping their way through a misty blue curtain of high-explosive fumes, the Bechs followed the instructions they had been given: if the alarm bells ring, muster in the first class lounge for further instructions. But in the brightly-lit lounge a curious calm prevailed. Some passengers were still drinking, others playing bridge, wondering what the 'bang' had portended. Suddenly a ship's officer rushed in: 'My God, what are you all doing here? Don't you realise the ship is sinking? Get to the boats fast!'

At No. 4 boat station, the Bechs found more confusion. A bitter sleet was driving from the sea; distress flares were livid against the night sky. Though the lifeboats should have been slung from the davits for the passengers to climb into, most had already been amateurishly launched and were bobbing far below. The resourceful Barbara Bech shinned down a rope and scrambled aboard one, but all the time the lifeboat was drifting clear across the choppy sea. The last thing Barbara saw was Derek, incongruously wearing his school cap, outlined against the rails, cradled in a seaman's arms.

Now the presence of a B.B.C. technician, Eric Davies, saved the remainder of the Bech family. 'Come quickly,' he called to Sonia, motioning them forward, 'We'll find rafts.' Somehow though the rafts were 6 feet square, three feet deep, and buoyed with canisters, Davies managed to lift them clear of the deck and hurl them in. In the howling darkness of the Atlantic night, the Bechs found themselves scrambling down a rope ladder and jumping into space, Sonia dismally conscious that her new camel-hair coat was slicked with black oil. As they sought to maintain hand-hold on the raft, Davies was all the time swimming beside them, pushing them away from the terrible suction of the dying ship.

Already the sea bobbed with flotsam: potted plants, wicker chairs, life-jackets, the floating bodies of men and women desperately treading water. Not far away the *City of Benares* was listing like a black leviathan heavily to port. At 10.45 pm, as she sank by the stern, Phyllis Morton, waist deep in a water-logged lifeboat, looked up to see a never-to-be-forgotten sight: Captain Nicoll, still leaning over the bridge, as the *Benares* reared as if alive then sank in a column of flame.

At the same moment, Sonia Bech felt a great buoyancy, as the wash lifted their raft high on the water. It was then that she caught Derek's eye, and the same thought occurred to both of them: 'What a rotten waste of good ice-cream!'

Then for most there was only darkness, and thin cries for help, and a deepening silence in which all of them felt small and afraid. Twice Sonia, slipping from the raft, resigned herself to die. 'A rather soothing feeling,' she recalls now, 'a humming in my ears, a whiteness before my eyes . . . all rather calm.' With implicit faith in a world beyond, she pondered: 'I wonder what God's going to be like.' Twice a ship's engineer on the same raft saved her life, hauling her back, spitting and spluttering salt water, from eternity.

Now scores of adults and children who had lived on the sidelines of war acknowledged a painful truth: they would plumb the secrets of survival or they would perish.

One secret was to maintain morale. Escort Mary Cornish was one of forty-six people, among them six boys, huddled into a life-boat thirty feet long. For eight days thereafter, as the boat pitched and yawed, Miss Cornish kept their minds alert and occupied. At first there were sing-songs – 'Roll Out the Barrel', and 'There'll Always Be An England', but later there was story-telling on a Homeric scale. Racking her brains for a nonstop cliff-hanger, Mary Cornish singled out 'Sapper's' hero, Captain Bulldog Drummond, somehow contriving to spin yarns which involved him in an unending battle of wits with slinky sirens and Nazi agents.

182

At noon each day, a steward inched with difficulty along her boat doling out rations: half a ship's biscuit with a fragment of sardine, and, once only, an eighth of a canned peach.

In other boats, the going was harder. Escort Lillian Towns recalled how, as the dawn of 18 September broke over her lifeboat, 'the children started to go into a coma one by one . . . we slapped their hands and faces and then we kept their heads above water until we could tell it was no use'. As the day passed, boat after boat, over the wide waste of water gently committed their dead to the sea.

Overnight, many children came suddenly of age. In the Mortons' lifeboat, 11-year-old Colin Ryder-Richardson spent hours with a dying woman's head cradled in his lap, stroking her hair, assuring her that rescue was at hand. Thirteen-year-old Bessie Walder and her friend Beth Cummings stayed for twenty hours glued precariously to the keel of a capsized boat, their only company two delirious Indian seamen calling on Allah.

Bessie Walder did not know it, but her brother, 10-year-old Louis, in another boat, had struck it luckier. At the outset his friend, Jimmie, the bartender, had pressed on him half a bottle of neat Scotch to ward off the chill. Swigging it down like Coca-cola, and topping it up with four cans of condensed milk, Louis felt no more pain for twenty-eight drowsy hours.

It was the sense of challenge that ultimately saved Sonia Bech. Her mother, far gone, was on the point of giving up. 'Darling,' she murmured, 'I think we'll take off our lifebelts and go to sleep in the water.' But all Sonia's instincts rebelled against this. 'Oh, no, Mummy, don't do that yet – I'm sure we'll be picked up.' For Sonia the worst thing was holding on to the wood of the raft. Her fingers had begun to bleed, for under the buffeting of the waves the canisters were working loose, and she sensed the raft was doomed to disintegration.

At dawn, with swooping gulls, and wreckage 'as big as houses' looming, Sonia sighted a sail. All of them whooped and hollered and soon it was bearing down on them. Their saviour was Skipper Leslie Lewis, of the S.S. *Marina*, another torpedoed merchantman, who had rigged a sail on his ship's lifeboat, sent radio messages to Land's End and was now all set to row to England. At last gasp, with barely one hour of life left to their raft, the Bechs were hauled aboard, along with an elderly Australian woman and the *City of Benares*'s second engineer.

Now, as Sonia and her family gulped down rum – 'which tasted horrible' – and condensed milk, which was better, Lewis circled, picking up survivors, many of them Lascars, near-dead with cold. Around noon, H.M.S. *Hurricane* a destroyer hastily rerouted from the Mediterranean, for rescue operations, sighted them. Cold and drenched, caked with black oil and brine, the Bechs were hauled aboard.

Not until three hours later, when Sonia and the others dried out, fed with bacon, eggs and baked beans and reattired in tropical whites, were resting on the wardroom floor, did *Hurricane* sight Barbara Bech's lifeboat. By this time, Marguerite Bech had alerted the entire crew that she was missing. As Barbara scrambled on to the deck, a sailor greeted her for all the world as if she had been playing truant from school: 'Are you Barbara Bech? Your mother's been very worried about you.'

Then there was a brief period when the bitter battle for survival was succeeded by a strange aura of surreal glamour. At Greenock, the port of Glasgow, where *Hurricane* landed them at noon on 20 September, reporters and cameramen were already waiting. Newly-attired in clothes from a top department store, Sonia now embarked on a marathon press conference, revelling in it all as she had revelled in the luxury of the *City of Benares*. She was still posing for photographs like a new-born Hollywood starlet long after 10 pm – clad now in pyjamas and dressing gown outside her bedroom in Glasgow's Central Hotel.

Later that week the Bechs returned to Bognor Regis. Their house at Aldwick Bay was not yet up for sale; Sonia's grandmother, along with Mackie, the Scottie, was still in residence. For Sonia, the final accolade came as the taxi drew up outside, and Marguerite Bech asked the driver: 'What do I owe you?'

The chauffeur brushed her request magnificently aside. 'Mrs Bech, it's been an honour.'

*

Afterwards, for all the Bechs, the sheer joy of being alive faded like an anaesthetic. Instead there came the pain of knowing from the press reports that few had been so fortunate. Of the ninety children aboard the *City of Benares*, only thirteen – among them Bessie and Louis Walder, Beth Cummings, Anthony Quinton – had been saved. Of the adults, the Digby Mortons, Lillian Towns and Mary Cornish had come through, but 181 others had not. In all, 258 out of the 408 passengers and crew aboard had perished.

From this time on, no more British children were evacuated overseas. They stayed and took their chances with the adults.

Appropriately, it was for those children who would not celebrate New Year's Day, 1941, that the Children's Hour programme of the B.B.C. held its own memorial service. The speaker's closing text, from Revelation XXI, 4, seemed almost a lament for a waning civilisation:

> *... And God shall wipe away all tears from their eyes; and there shall be no more death, neither sorrow, nor crying, neither shall there be any more pain: for the former things are passed away ...*

*

As September dawned, Polly Peabody had quit Vichy. After six weeks in the capital, she had almost given up hope for France. In Vichy, the French seemed prostrated, apathetic, indifferently accepting defeat. Most banks were closed or scattered to the four corners of the land and the collapse of money, with credit unobtainable and cheques refused, seemed to bring out the worst in the Vichy French. Polly was among the lucky ones; her few dollars would still fetch 100 francs each on the black market.

Typical of Vichy's topsy-turvy fortunes was the dapper Frenchman with the rosette of the Legion of Honour in his button-hole whom Polly saw ordering lamb cutlets and champagne in a smart restaurant. A few days later she saw the same man standing in line before a soup kitchen.

Some citizens were burrowing little holes in their gardens hiding jewels, banknotes and gold, but this stifling preoccupation with greed sickened Polly. She resolved to leave for Paris and the Occupied Zone, and join a relief organisation there. She would give her beloved France one more chance to redeem itself.

It was still a shock to enter the Occupied Zone. All through her six-hour drive to the capital in a Red Cross car, past arrows that pointed the way 'Nach Paris', France teemed with Germans. Paris itself seemed one vast garrison. From the Bois de Boulogne to Montparnasse, millions of shining black boots thronged its pavements. A cloud of sadness hung over the city.

Friends had loaned Polly a variety of apartments on the left bank of the Seine, hoping that her presence would exempt them from German occupation. From here, since no taxis, buses or trams were running, Polly set out on foot for the American Hospital at Neuilly, to sign on as an ambulance driver, transporting food and clothing to the prison camps. It was here she heard by chance that her old outfit, the American Scandinavian Field Hospital, were just then on their way back to the States. Good luck to them, Polly thought. She meant to stay where the action was.

By degrees she took heart. Armed with a German pass issued only to relief workers and prostitutes – 'Mademoiselle Polly Peabody is allowed to walk the Paris streets at night for professional reasons indispensable' – she was able to ignore the curfew and go everywhere. What she saw of the native Parisians gave her new faith.

At first, the mood of the people was shown only through surreptitious graffiti. Overnight, as the Metro began to run again, posters on the tiled walls were adorned with slogans: *'Vivent les Anglais!'* *'Vive De Gaulle!'* Propaganda posters designed by Dr Göbbels to cash in on French bitterness at the British assault on the fleet at Oran were wittily defaced. *'N'oubliez pas Oran!'* (Don't forget Oran); ran the original slogans, above a cut of a French sailor drowning in waters reddened with blood. By night, unseen hands changed this to *'N'oubliez pas votre costume de bain'* (Don't forget your

185

bathing costume). The gibe was not lost on German troops awaiting the Channel crossing to England.

To deface posters was punishable by a 10,000 franc fine, but Polly noticed that the mutilations did not cease. At first policemen were kept busy with knives and wet sponges to erase the scribbling. Later they could not keep pace; Göbbels' posters had to be sited higher and higher, beyond human reach.

Imperceptibly, the manifestations grew bolder. As German officers entrained in their first class carriages on the Métro, the train drivers kept up a steady tuneless whistling of the British Tommies' song from World War I, 'It's a Long Long Way to Tipperary'. In those parts of France where Italian soldiers were garrisoned, French girls boldly sported short lengths of macaroni in their buttonholes.

Polly Peabody was encouraged. At the A.B.C. Music Hall, where the reigning queen was suddenly an unknown waif from the slums, Edith Piaf, the nightly running gag was the two clowns who leaped upon the stage in the middle of a Piaf number. When one of them insisted on speaking English, his colleague, in mock embarrassment, pointed out that most of the audience were German and took a poor view. 'You are in *France*!' the stooge expostulated. 'Can't you speak French like us?' To which the clown, provoking a scream of delight from the French, responded solemnly '*Ja wohl!*'

One evening, on the terrace of Fouquet's Restaurant, on the Avenue des Champs-Elysées, Polly was dining surrounded by German officers. Suddenly a drunken old Parisienne, wisps of white hair straggling down her neck, hands planted belligerently on her hips, began abusing them from the street. '*Eh, bien,*' she bawled, '*moi, je vous dis* MERDE!' The waiters began to snigger. Polly and the few French present chuckled discreetly into their napkins. The Germans merely stared ahead of them, saying nothing, betraying nothing.

All is not lost, Polly thought, there is still hope. For the time being she was staying put.

*

Three thousand miles from Paris, in the Ritz Hotel, New York City, Count René de Chambrun felt bitterly disillusioned. He felt that Franklin Roosevelt had betrayed not only him but France besides.

No sooner had de Chambrun returned from Vichy than he had phoned 'Missy' LeHand. When would the President find it convenient to see him? But 'Missy' had seemed patently evasive, explaining that the meeting would be with Harry Hopkins and not in Washington but New York. Indeed, learning of de Chambrun's return, Hopkins was on his way and would be with him before dinner.

'It was then that I was to know a terrible disappointment,' de Chambrun recorded later, for Hopkins, pallid and unemotional, had wasted no time on small talk arriving at the Ritz. Roosevelt, he told de Chambrun bluntly, had renounced his 'project' of supplying France with food and medicine. It was all, Hopkins explained disingenuously, really Churchill's fault. He had insisted that the President apply the blockade integrally.

De Chambrun was appalled. He harked back to his August meeting with Roosevelt, the mission on which he had returned to France, and the President's final words, 'René, it's a deal.'

Now Roosevelt was reneging on that deal and de Chambrun was outraged. The President, he pointed out to Hopkins, had made a treaty with Pétain, and he, de Chambrun, had been the instrument of that treaty. On 19 August, as Roosevelt had requested, Pétain had duly called a press conference in Vichy, laying on champagne and canapés – 'the first time I shall hold a Press conference' – and the American press had run his words in full. 'France will remain firmly attached to the ideal she shares with the great American democracies, an idea founded on the respect for individual rights, the family, the country, and love of justice and humanity.'

Angrily, de Chambrun told Hopkins that he should make sending food to France a condition for continuing to supply arms to Britain.

Hopkins was unyielding. Roosevelt's mind was made up. Only years later did de Chambrun learn from General George Marshall that Churchill's about-face had been occasioned by de Gaulle, who had pressured him to tighten the screws on Vichy, strongly backed by Hugh Dalton's Ministry of Economic Warfare.

De Chambrun was in a quandary. Republicans like Herbert Hoover and Thomas Dewey were campaigning for supplying Europe – but since an election was coming up they were the President's political opponents. Even now, de Chambrun could not bring himself to stoop low and confide in them the details of this double-cross. He must just work on his own to raise funds for sending American Red Cross packages.

In the last resort, there was the letter Roosevelt had requested from Pétain, which de Chambrun had helped the old Marshal to draft. One paragraph in particular had been carefully calculated to appeal to the President's sense of compassion. 'Millions of refugees from the most fertile regions of France are bringing (to Unoccupied France) nothing with them except their retinue of fatigue and misery . . . sharing with Belgian, Austrian and Czechoslovakian refugees . . . the pain and problems of Frenchmen in Free France . . .'

That evening, following Hopkins' departure, de Chambrun took his letter to the lobby and sent it by registered mail to the White House.

Days passed, but there was no reply. He never heard from Roosevelt again.

*

The smouldering resentment that Polly Peabody was noting in Occupied

187

France was no lone example. By degrees a palpable spirit of resistance was arising in all of occupied Europe.

Its slow genesis was only to be expected; history had set no precedents. In past centuries, countries like Belgium had endured occupation under Spanish, French and Dutch rulers with rueful grace. But now there was more than an alien presence in streets and squares to breed opposition. The slow encroachment of Hitler's New Order, with all its ideological implications, was an outrage to many.

That autumn, following a decision that Norwegian schools should devote time to 'introducing children to the New Order', the history teachers went on unanimous strike, and were promptly arrested. Attempts to force them to join a political union resulted in 12,000 out of 14,000 resigning. The schools closed down, but after six months *Reichskommissar* Terboven ordered the puppet government to 'relent'. Like most of Hitler's appointed overlords, Terboven wanted no trouble so early in the war.

On all sides, the occupied peoples sought solidarity. One such occasion was 26 September, the seventieth birthday of King Christian X of Denmark. The fact that for five months the old King had ridden out on horseback each morning, acknowledging the greetings of his humblest subjects, stonily ignoring the punctilious salutes of the Germans he passed en route, was known to every Dane. Now, on his birthday, the square before Amalienborg Palace was jampacked with Danes chanting patriotic songs and hymns. Nor was this loyalty confined to Copenhagen alone. Even in smaller towns like Odense, crowds 3,500 strong packed out every public hall.

Early Danish resistants took their tone from the King, offering the coldest of shoulders to the invader. If a German civilly asked the way in the street, passers-by walked blithely on as if no one had spoken. The same technique caught on early in Oslo, Norway. When German officers sought membership of an exclusive tennis club, the committee ostensibly welcomed them – then held a drumhead meeting to convert the courts to a potato patch in the interests of the national economy.

Emblems and lapel badges conveyed sentiments that it was prudent not to utter. Danish badges stamped DKS (Den Kolde Skulder) showed where a man's sympathies lay. Norwegians sported wire paper-clips, which meant 'Stick together', or advertising slogans cut from milk cartons: '100 per cent Norwegian'. Patriotic dairy farmers even branded their milch cows with the emblem of King Haakon VII.

Gradually, resistance became more overt. Hand-made Danish printing presses began churning out leaflets called strew-slips, crudely printed fragments of brown adhesive paper that could be gummed on walls or lamp posts: 'DON'T BECOME A TRAITOR', 'HELP HITLER LOSE THE WAR'. As the Battle of Britain was joined, Danish students sported red, white and blue woollen caps, the colours of the R.A.F. rondel. As the battle swung in Britain's favour, the wearers, accused of 'provocative conduct', often faced fines or gaol.

Even the smallest gestures assumed significance, for they gave back to the occupied peoples something they had forfeited at the time of Hitler's conquests: self-respect. Alert for trouble, the authorities in Holland early forbade the wearing of flowers in the buttonhole: both the white carnation that was the trademark of Prince Bernhard of the Netherlands and the marigold that symbolised the House of Orange spelt resistance. But as early as 29 June, Bernhard's birthday, many Dutch citizens defied the ban – and the bully-boys of Anton Mussert's pro-Nazi N.S.B., swift to snatch them from lapels, recoiled with bleeding fingers. Behind each innocent flower lurked a sharp-edged razor blade.

The will to resist bred many new routines. In The Hague and other Dutch cities, 13-year-old Ida van de Criendt recalled that no one ever answered a phone call around 7 pm. Like Ida's family, most were tuned in to hear Radio Oranje, broadcasting from London with its message from the exiled Queen Wilhelmina. Already hiding places had been devised for these radios; Ida's family kept theirs under the floorboards of the cupboard that housed the family bicycles.

Sometimes the clandestine broadcasts posed a problem. In Verviers, Belgium, one woman, believing her husband had died in the 18-day campaign, appointed a day for the funeral and sent out invitations. On the eve of the burial, she was in a quandary: Radio London had announced her husband was safe and well in England. Should she cancel the funeral and thereby reveal that she listened to the freedom radio – or go ahead?

Playing safe, she asked the priest to go ahead, but found herself the sole mourner. All her friends had listened in, and felt that condolences were unnecessary.

Underground news-sheets were another way to hit back, though their circulation was limited at first. In Copenhagen, Erik Seidenfaden's newspaper, *Politiken*, printed one solely for distribution to the reporters, to update them on the news the censors kept from the public. In Belgium, 1940 saw the birth of no less than ninety-five resistance journals, though the total print was no more than 20,000 copies. Some sheets were little more than chain-letters, like the one called *Geuzenactie* (The Giants), produced by Bernard Ijzerdraat, a carpet weaver in Haarlem, Holland. Lacking carbon paper, the diligent weaver had to write it out by hand, one copy at a time.

Only one country, the tiny Duchy of Luxembourg – knew the savage satisfaction of publicly registering their distaste for the invader. On 10 October, their Nazi *Gauleiter*, Gustav Simon, a man unafflicted by doubt, ordered a plebiscite in favour of Hitler's occupation. The Luxembourgers, trudging to the polls, recorded a verdict that spoke for all of occupied Europe: a 97 per cent hostile vote.

189

From his Thames-side eyrie atop Fire Brigade Headquarters at Lambeth, Assistant Divisional Officer Geoffrey Vaughan Blackstone, watched eight million Londoners, day by day, waging their own war of resistance.

On these bitter autumn nights, Blackstone's routine, as Deputy Chief of the Southern Division, almost never varied. Jolting in his control car through the high-risk dockland area that was his bailiwick – Southwark, Bermondsey, Rotherhithe – he co-ordinated the battle plan against the scores of warehouse fires threatening London's food supplies. Often it was mid-morning next day before he could return to his quarters for a bath and a change of uniform. At dusk, following office routine and a brief catnap, he was once more alert for the wail of the siren.

Afterwards, looking back, no single fire stood out above the others. The nights merged into one like an enveloping flame: intense heat and nipping cold, the eyes inflamed by smoke and the feet sore from the chafing of rubber boots, hasty snacks of coffee and meat pies from the mobile canteen van.

On one score at least Blackstone had ceased to worry after 7 September: the courage of London's auxiliary firemen, despised until then, had become a byword. Often, as they returned at dawn, smoke-grimed and sodden, early-morning shift workers lined the streets to cheer them; at the sight of them on a newsreel screen the audience broke into applause. One fireman, pointedly ignored for a whole year by the barmaid in his local pub, was now always served first, frequently out of turn.

Other fire-fighting problems were far from resolved. Every firm employing more than thirty workers was obliged to furnish night-time fire-watchers, but few drew up such rosters and the new Minister of Home Security, Herbert Morrison, seemed oddly reluctant to enforce the law to the letter. A bigger headache still was London's water supply. In a large-scale fire-raid, a square mile of the city needed 600,000 gallons of water a minute to keep the flames in check. Yet the cast-iron public mains, sited barely three feet below street level, could be fractured by the impact of a 50-kilo bomb. At low tide, the Thames was almost unapproachable, separated from the shore by fifty feet of black mud.

The answer, Blackstone and his chief, Lieutenant-Commander John Fordham, argued, was on-the-spot emergency reservoirs – a solution condemned as too costly by the Home Office, the Treasury and the London County Council. Their own compromise was a series of 5,000-gallon steel dams scattered at remote intervals. Blackstone's reaction was scathing: a trailer pump delivered 500 gallons a minute, so a 5,000 gallon drum ensured just ten minutes supply. 'It's like pissing against a thunderstorm,' was Blackstone's acid comment.

Although backed by Fordham and Major Frank Jackson, the Fire Brigade chief, his arguments were brushed aside by Sir Arthur Dixon, chief of the Home Office Fire Department. If an all-out fire-raid ever came, London might burn like a prairie in a drought – but Blackstone, for his pains, was dismissed as 'a cheeky young man'.

Despite these drawbacks, Blackstone had no doubts on one score; morale would hold up. Like the Finns before them, Londoners were adapting. From 11 September, when General Frederick Pile's Anti-Aircraft Command loosed off its first box-barrage over 200 square miles of Greater London – firing 13,500 rounds without damaging a single bomber – Londoners had had a buoyant sense of hitting back. Not more than 6 in 100 ever resorted to ear-plugs; the fearful martial music was like a lullaby.

Other sounds became an integral part of this life: the bombers circling, as one woman noted, 'like dogs trying to pick up a scent', the aching empty silence after a bomb fell, broken only by small sounds, the rustle of water from fractured pipes, the little cries of the trapped and wounded, the stealthy shifting of debris. Dawn brought the most welcome sound of all: the notes of the All Clear, like a liner nearing safe haven, crying over the city.

Each night thousands of Londoners burrowed underground like gophers into damp shelters and subways. Many with gardens slept in corrugated-iron outdoor so-called Anderson shelters, buried four feet deep. By September's end, 177,000 of them had taken to the Underground railway, squatting figures throwing forlorn shadows on the tiled walls, bedded down on floors gritty and buff-coloured from leaking sandbags.

Armed with suitcases, blankets, rugs and pillows many queued in the street for places as early as 10.30 am; by 4 pm, the permitted hour of descent, every yard of platform and passage space would be staked out behind the painted line that reserved the front yard of platform for passengers.

Those who could afford twopence bedded down on copies of the London Times, by far the thickest paper. Sanitation was primitive, confined to bucket latrines behind hessian screens. Privacy was non-existent, though at least one marriage was consummated in full public view in a shelter in London's slatternly Tottenham Court Road.

In scores of shelters, from the sandy caves at Chislehurst, Kent, thirteen miles south, which the denizens had equipped with double beds, to Mickey Davis' in Stepney's dockland, kept by a hunchbacked East End optician, Londoners gathered each night from 7 pm to 7 am. At dawn they emerged to what were soon familiar scenes: vast mounds of timber and lath and plaster, torn window curtains, the fine glitter of powdered glass that covered the pavements like hoar frost.

In time, the smells became familiar, too: the harsh acrid smell of cordite from high explosive bombs, leaking gas and blue London clay, charred wood and pulverised plaster.

It was a weird unnatural life, even for the birds, which awoke and sang when the searchlights turned night into day, and no man or woman who took part in it was ever to forget it. International order had given way to universal insanity, and even the laws of nature had become mixed up. In some communities, the blind now offered their services as guides during total blackouts.

London was now a city where strange sights had become the norm. Thus one man would always remember a girl kneeling by night in fashionable Pall Mall, smothering the sizzling thermite of a foot-long incendiary bomb with her evening cloak. Others recalled a man striding down Piccadilly in black coat and striped trousers, shielding himself from falling shrapnel with an open umbrella. On one night waiters and chefs were seen racing a raw sirloin of beef from a club that had been hit into a club whose kitchen still functioned.

Between 7 September and 13 November, 13,651 tons of high explosive and 12,586 incendiary canisters were showered upon the city. Now not only tiny red-brick homes were at risk, but those parts of London charted by that indefatigable German tourist, Karl Baedeker. Names of heroes and works of great memory were trampled. Somerset House, where Shakespeare's will, among others, was filed, lost its superb staircase. John Nash's curving Regent Street was ripped by a delayed-action bomb. So, too, were the National and Tate Galleries, William Hogarth's panelled house in Chiswick, the Gothic House of Lords, Westminster Abbey and that haunt of dandies, Savile Row. St Giles, Cripplegate, where John Milton's remains lay, did not survive the bombings as it had the fire in 1666. Other churches suffered: Christopher Wren's St James's, Piccadilly, and his much-admired St Stephens, Walbrook, St Mary-at-Hill, St Dunstan-in-the-East and the Church of Our Lady of Victory.

'We are as continuously alive to danger as animals in the jungle,' noted a Canadian diplomat, Charles Ritchie. This was true, but by degrees the pattern was changing. At first, Londoners went religiously home each evening to an established routine: blacked-out windows criss-crossed with transparent paper against blast, the shelter with a sixpenny Penguin Book for company, sometimes a bath in five inches of tepid water to conserve fuel, a breakfast egg from a bucket of isinglass. But ultimately the lures of cinemas (open until 9 pm, although theatres were closed) friendly pubs and the opposite sex proved too potent. To socialise, defying bombs and landmines, became part of the pattern, too. 'See you tomorrow,' one warden heard a girl promise her boy briend, 'same time, same sandbag.'

Whatever the hazards, Londoners were determined to keep their cool. Posted on the notice-board of one golf-club outside London was a new emergency rule: 'Players may pick out of any bomb crater, dropping ball not nearer hole without penalty.'

192

To outsiders, it seemed that the security bred by three centuries of immunity from warfare on their own soil had given the English an invincible sense of their own superiority. Few among them could now conceive of being beaten. Pierre Bourdan, chief of the London-based Agence Française Indépendante news agency, never forgot an interview he was granted around this time by Sir Archibald Sinclair, Churchill's Secretary of State for Air.

Studying a huge wall-map of the world, Sinclair told Bourdan seriously: 'We shall probably lose Egypt, Malta, Aden, the Middle East, perhaps the Indies, Singapore, and, I'm very much afraid, dear old Gibraltar, too.'

As he reeled out this formidable list like a geography master, Bourdan gazed at him in awe. Then, shaking his head and frowning, Sinclair confessed: 'Yes, I very much fear it will be five or six years before we win this war.'

'Dead Lucky If We See The Sun Again'

15 October–15 November, 1940

IN THE VAST Hall of the Ambassadors of Berlin's Reich Chancellery, at 1.15 pm on 27 September, a long-awaited pact was in the making. As Adolf Hitler entered with a nervous cat-like tread, three men seated at the long table, a thin document printed in triplicate lying before them, rose to greet him: Ribbentrop, Italy's Count Ciano, and a newcomer to the scene, the slim suave Saburo Kurusu, Japan's man in Germany. A moment's pause, then Ribbentrop swivelled to confront a battery of microphones. In a staccato 419-word preamble he announced to the assembled foreign correspondents that Japan had joined the Axis.

'The pact which has been signed,' Ribbentrop proclaimed, 'is a military alliance between three of the mightiest States on earth . . . It is to help bring peace to the world as quickly as possible . . . Any State, should it harbour the intention of mixing in the final phase of the solution of these problems in Europe or Eastern Asia, or attacking one State signatory to this three-power pact, will have to take on the entire concentrated might of three nations with more than 250 million inhabitants.'

What Ribbentrop was making clearer than crystal was a fact that was crystal-clear already: the treaty was an alliance against the United States.

If America were to join Britain in the European war, its text implied, Japan would attack in the Pacific. If America interfered in the Chinese war, Germany and Italy would attack in the Atlantic. In sum, with the United States scared into isolation, the Rome–Berlin–Tokyo Axis could dismember the British Empire piecemeal.

The treaty was, in fact, no bombshell through the roof of the State Department. Though no man could deny that it was a diplomatic defeat for the United States, which for the first time in its history was now surrounded by enemies, the treaty did no more than confirm the warnings that Ambassador Joseph C. Grew had been routing to the State Department for months past. 'The era of democracy,' predicted Japan's Foreign Minister, Yosuke Matsuoka, in a press interview on 21 July, 'is finished', amply justifying Grew's later report of 5 September, 'The new (Konoye) Cabinet has every earmark of a totalitarian regime.'

The tenor of events had so alarmed Grew that on 12 September he had despatched an uncompromising telegram to Cordell Hull: 'Japan today is one of the predatory powers; she has submerged all moral and ethical sense, and has become frankly and unashamedly opportunist, seeking at every turn to profit by the weakness of others.'

But if the Axis hoped to frighten the United States out of its everything-short-of-war policy to help Great Britain, it had almost certainly failed. Since American security in the Atlantic – hence liberty to maintain her Fleet in the Pacific – depended on the British Fleet, the U.S. could now do no less than help Britain more.

'We should profit by Mr Chamberlain's bitter experience in Europe,' was Grew's considered counsel, 'We know by experience out here that Japan's word of honour can be trusted no further than Hitler's word of honour . . .'

Certainly there was no hint of irresolution in either Washington or London. In the face of a muttered Japanese threat that the gesture could mean war, the British, on 11 October, reopened the Burma Road. At Lashio, Burma, on this cold clear night, 5,000 coolies were busy loading some $20,000,000 worth of China's future into 2,000 U.S.-built trucks – including such vital cargoes as aeroplane wings, high-octaine gasoline, rifle barrels and raw cotton.

The U.S., it seemed, was beginning to meddle in earnest. After France's fall, Roosevelt had stopped the export of aviation fuel and top-grade scrap to Japan. Then, in September, he had cut off scrap iron and steel. Within two years' time, these embargoes, designed to halt Japan's march to exploit Allied difficulties, would have sapped her economic strength. Thus, in the naval race, America would have begun to outstrip Japan.

The message was not lost on Prince Fumimaro Konoye and his Cabinet: Japan must act fast. 'Anglo–Saxonism,' declared Matsuoka's deputy in Tokyo, Chuichi Ohashi, 'is about to become bankrupt and will be effectively wiped out.'

*

Despite the seeming invincibility of the Axis, some commanders were beset by doubts. In mid-October, Major Fritz von Forell of the Wehrmacht visited his old friend Major Werner Mölders at the headquarters of Fighter Group 51, which lay at Pihen, near Calais.

That evening Fighter Group 51 had nothing more martial in mind than an uproarious stag party: Göring had awarded silver cups to three young officers of merit, *Oberleutnants* Joppien, Pape and Fleig, and first, in the elegantly-furnished villa that served as the officers' club, Mölders had to make the formal presentation. 'Let this be a happy day,' he rallied them by way of conclusion, 'Let us forget the struggle for tonight. I will celebrate with you!'

195

As the evening wore on, the champagne flowed faster. Each pilot in turn was hoisted shoulder high and borne in whooping triumph through the brightly-lit salons. But as the party reached fever-pitch, it seemed to Forell that Mölders could not forget the struggle, not even for that night. Though he smiled mechanically and matched toast for toast, his face was drawn and earnest. Forell was troubled. In the past, Mölders had always thrown himself into a party as if there was no tomorrow.

Towards midnight, Mölders abruptly strode from the villa. Forell followed. The night was dark and without stars; a cool wind blew from the sea. For a moment the two walked in aimless silence, towards the dispersal ground where silver Messerschmitts stood camouflaged beneath tall poplars. Suddenly, jerking his head towards them, Mölders broke out: 'I am terribly worried.'

Forell said nothing. 'I am *terribly* worried,' Mölders repeated. 'We're not making any progress. What's happening to Operation Sea-Lion? When are we going over to England? I've spoken to high naval officers. They don't know either. "The Tommies are still flying," they said.'

Deep in thought, Mölders had stopped walking, scuffing at the sand with his toe. 'My boys shoot down one after another,' he complained, 'but it's as though they grow new heads on the other side of the Channel, like a hydra. For every Briton shot down, two new ones seem to rise up!'

'Has the Reich Marshal been told?' Forell asked.

Mölders was sombre. 'Of course. But I have the impression he either doesn't want to believe it – or that he doesn't know what to do about it. But God in Heaven something has to be done!'

Forell was deeply disturbed. Mölders was voicing doubts dangerous to a man when he is fighting an air war: doubts as to the whole meaning of the combat, doubts as to whether it was worth going on.

'Shall we be able to overpower England?' he asked with increasing agitation, 'and will she be the last enemy? And if the worst comes to the worst, and America comes in to help the British, what then?'

Forell was realistic. America was already helping wherever she possibly could. 'Wouldn't it be helpful,' he suggested, 'to talk things over with Göring?'

Mölders ran his fingers through his hair. 'It will turn out all right,' is what he says when told of such things, 'Everything's been all right so far.' He ended gloomily: 'So far! I wonder if Göring really is the general, politician and strategist that we need? It isn't enough to be able to lead a mass of mercenaries . . .'

Forell watched him in silence, miserably, wanting to help. He wished that there was something he could say.

*

In Britain, the War Cabinet's uncertainty as to Hitler's intentions decreed that 'The Happy Time' of *Kapitänleutnant* Otto Kretschmer and his fellow U-Boat aces continued undisturbed. Still intent on countering Operation Sea-Lion, if it came the Chiefs of Staff were insistent that the bulk of the British Fleet was scattered throughout the east and south coast ports, effectively stripping the Atlantic convoys of their escorts.

From September on, what Dönitz termed *Rudeltaktik* (pack attacks) – U-boats hunting in tactical groups – came into being. On his undersea forays, Kretschmer was now supported by other seasoned skippers: Günter Prien, whose U-47 had slipped cunningly into Scapa Flow to sink the battleship *Royal Oak*, Günter Kuhnke, of U-28, Heinrich Bleichrodt, whose U-48 had accounted for the *City of Benares*, Joachim Schepke, commanding U-100.

In October, one date alone – Thursday, 19 October – marked Kretschmer's greatest triumph in the U-Boat war.

At dusk on that day, operating with seven other U-Boats, Kretschmer, in U-99, was edging ever closer to the convoy codenamed SC (for Slow Convoy) 7, outward bound from Sydney, Nova Scotia, for Liverpool. He had counted her escort as strong for these days – three destroyers and several smaller warships – but the fact did not deter him. What Kretschmer now planned was to cause maximum havoc by a new tactic of the Atlantic war – striking from within the convoy itself.

At 10 pm the classic attack began. As seven other U-Boats, including Schepke in U-100 and Prien in U-48, attacked from outside the convoy screen, firing salvo upon salvo, Kretschmer headed for the starboard side covered by the three destroyers – one ahead of the convoy, one on the beam, another on the bow.

Now, as he headed between the beam and the bow destroyers, neither showed any signs of spotting him, gliding one mile distant from each. Three minutes later he was through, fast approaching the convoy's outer column. Closing to 700 yards range U-99 fired at the first ship – and missed by yards. But on this calm clear night, with the targets standing out in vivid silhouette against a hunter's moon, the life of his quarry was destined to be short. Again U-99 fired, her second torpedo striking amidships. Within twenty seconds, the ship had wallowed from sight.

Suddenly, as two more explosions sounded from the other side of the convoy, the long line of ships abruptly altered course, and Kretschmer seized his chance. Sweeping down the outer column, now only 100 yards distant, he spied a gap and slipped through it. Now U-99 made part of the convoy itself.

One large cargo ship spotted her and tried to ram, firing starshell as she came, but Kretschmer dodged prudently back towards the escort screen. By now he was near the convoy's stern, aiming at the end ship of the outer column. Missing, the torpedo went home on another ship in the next column. As she broke in two, her radio signal for help marked her sole claim to identity '*Empire Brigade*'.

At the front of U-99's conning tower, Kretschmer now told Sub-Lieutenants, Elfe and Bargsten, 'We're going to tear this convoy down.'

It was an attack that was to go down in allied naval history as the worst convoy disaster of the war. At midnight, another of U-99's torpedoes struck a large freighter forward. Seconds later, in a huge spurt of red and yellow flame, she tore apart before their eyes, a cloud of smoke mushrooming 500 feet high. In fifty seconds she had vanished from sight. At 1 am another torpedo capsized a fifth merchantman, her red-hot plates hissing and boiling as she sank. Next it was the turn of S.S. *Fiscus*, broken in two near the stern.

In the unholy confusion of this night, the destroyers were dropping depth charges at will, and starshells made frenzied, spangled patterns of light across the water. Unperturbed, Kretschmer turned hard to starboard, conning U-99 to the freighter *Shekatica*. At 300 yards range, he order 'Stern tube, fire.' watching the ship rear in the air like a wounded beast. His next target, the *Sedgepool*, executed as perfect a crash-dive in her death throes as if herself was a submarine, propellers churning the water as she drove towards the sea-bed with a roar of ruptured girders.

Enough was enough, Kretschmer decided then. It was surely only a question of time before the escort guessed where he was, and effectively barred his escape route from inside the convoy. One small straggler lying to the stern, the S.S. *Clintonia*, was U-99's last victim this night. She settled slowly in the water, seemingly unremarked, as the main convoy drove ahead at maximum speed.

On 22 October, U-99 arrived at her cleaning up anchorage in the island bay off the approach to Lorient. Kretschmer was well satisfied. In three hours of one night he had sent nine merchantmen to the bottom, while his fellow U-boat commanders, between them, had accounted for another eight.

The loss of seventeen ships had cost the Allies 80,000 tons of shipping, 100,000 tons of supplies, and this was only the beginning. For all October, the month's total losses would escalate to one third of a million tons. Kretschmer and all of them felt that victory could not be far away.

*

In a suite in the Palace Hotel, Estoril, outside Lisbon, the phone was ringing stridently, and Polly Peabody hastened to answer it. Earlier that day, acting on impulse, she had cancelled a liner passage to the States, deciding that bombed and beleaguered London was where she most wanted to be. After two months, Paris under German occupation had finally palled.

To her surprise, the switchboard operator announced, 'Senhora Peabody, New York is calling you.' It was the evening of 5 November, a date which for

198

Polly held only one significance. Even before she had exchanged greetings with an old friend she was shouting, 'What about Roosevelt?'

'To hell with Roosevelt,' the friend rejoined. 'Tell me about you.'

'I'm going to London,' Polly told him triumphantly, but her friend demurred. 'You'd better come home,' he advised, 'New York is very gay. There are lots of good plays. Your old hang-outs are going strong . . .'

'I want to go to London,' Polly insisted.

'Haven't you had enough?'

Polly was adamant. 'No! Now tell me about Roosevelt!'

'Oh him,' the voice announced, with monumental indifference. 'He's been re-elected.'

That ended the conversation. As Polly saw it, if the election of the one man who could open American eyes and lead them into the fight for freedom was of no importance to her New York set, that clinched it. In future her New York set could get along very well without her – and she without them.

*

It was a night when all the traditions were faithfully observed. Inside the big house at Hyde Park, on the Hudson River, a bevy of family and friends had celebrated with a scrambled egg supper, as the teletype machines in the pantry clattered out the irrefutable returns. The President had sat tensely at the dining room table, coatless, his necktie loosened, studying the final tallies. Towards midnight, the familiar jostling crowd of neighbours thronged the entrance road to the mansion, torches flickering ruddily on the white painted balustrade and the hemlock hedge that bordered the rose garden. A drum-and-bugle corps launched into 'The Old Grey Mare', and Harry Hopkins, standing to the rear of the portico, executed a sudden spontaneous pirouette of triumph, smacking right fist into left palm. More plainly than any words, the gesture spelled out: 'We made it.'

For the first time in history, an American President had been elected to a third term of office – 'SAFE ON THIRD', proclaimed one jubilant banner – with 27,243,460 votes against the Republican Wendell Willkie's 22,304,755. He had opened a door that no other president had ever opened; now he prepared to walk through it.

Ironically, it had been a campaign in which Willkie had seemed to have more in common with his adversary than with his party's hard core. Though he embarked on 560 speeches in fifty days, until his voice died to an inaudible croak, many issues that were a sore point with Republicans were barely raised. Even the passage of the Selective Service Act, which on 16 October saw the registration of all American males between twenty-one and thirty-five for the first peacetime conscription, met with Willkie's favour – as did the earlier 'destroyers for bases' deal. Only as his opponents began to link

199

him with Fascist sympathisers did Willkie belatedly yield to temptation, charging that Roosevelt sought a third term to assume a dictator's mantle and involve America in Europe's war.

It had not been a campaign in which the President had visibly exerted political muscle. All through the fall, jauntily confident, he studiously ignored Willkie's band wagon. Only in the third week of October did he announce that he would make five addresses in the two weeks preceding Election Day to answer 'deliberate falsifications of fact by the Republicans'.

Roosevelt's confidence was by no means shared by other Democrats. From all over America, a steady stream of messages from jittery politicians warned him that the cause was lost unless he guaranteed to American mothers that their boys, though inducted into the armed services, would never be called upon to fight. In vain they even sought to dissuade him from presiding over the drawing of the first draft papers from a mammoth gold-fish bowl in Washington, D.C., while the cameras recorded his presence for history.

On 30 October, in Boston – the same night that Willkie charged stridently, 'You may expect war by April 1941, if he is elected' – Roosevelt finally yielded to party pressures. 'I burn inwardly whenever I think of those words,' his speechwriter, the playwright Robert E. Sherwood, confessed later. 'And while I am talking to you mothers and fathers, I give you one more assurance,' Roosevelt told them roundly, 'I shall say it again and again and again. Your boys are not going to be sent into any foreign wars.'

Always before, he had qualified this statement 'except in case of attack', but at the last when this was raised, he flashed back irritably, 'If somebody attacks us, it isn't a foreign war, is it? Or do they want me to guarantee that our troops will only be sent into battle in the event of another Civil War?' But the statement was to haunt him 'again and again and again' in the months that followed – and so, too, did his pronouncement in Buffalo: 'Your President says this country is not going to war.'

Yet the hysterical demands for reassurance at any price had been there, as none knew better than Theodor Broch, the former Mayor of Narvik.

Ever since arriving in Los Angeles in August, Broch had embraced Roosevelt's cause – 'I felt I had him with me from the start,' he confessed later. For three months, as a lecturer on the books of the Redpath Agency, Chicago, Broch, in an old second-hand Ford, had travelled everywhere in the United States where Norwegian immigrants had settled – to Montana, North and South Dakota, Minnesota, Iowa and Wisconsin. Often speaking in children's schools, Masonic lodges, or neat white prairie churches, he gave three lectures a day, sometimes in hamlets so remote that third-generation Norwegians on the streets still spoke the dialects of Narvik and Trondheim.

Yet the dichotomy of emotions disturbed him. Tough Norwegian farmers who wept unashamedly at the strains of Norway's national anthem played on a church organ recoiled at Broch's message that Hitler posed a threat to all mankind. 'You can't expect us to declare war and send our boys abroad?' they asked incredulously.

Wherever Broch journeyed, a tidal wave of isolationist fear seemed to be sweeping the country. Insurance companies warned their policy-holders that Roosevelt's election would reduce their policies to worthless scraps of paper. Telegrams warned doctors that Roosevelt's return meant the socialisation of medicine. One Chicago bank solemnly advertised: 'In a last stand for democracy, every director and officer of this Bank will vote for Wendell Willkie' —a broad hint to depositors to do likewise or lose their money.

To the people of this land of plenty, Europe seemed very far away, and many counted her cause as lost. 'Do you think you'll ever get back?' the Norwegians would ask Broch, and most were dubious when he affirmed his faith. 'But the Germans are overwhelming,' they would point out. 'They are,' Broch agreed quietly, 'and in the end they'll provoke the whole world against them.'

Scurrilous rumours, designed to damage Roosevelt's reputation, abounded. Some isolationists charged that Crown Princess Martha of Norway, who had sought sanctuary in the United States, had become the President's mistress, and that Eleanor Roosevelt, to spite her husband, had taken a negro for a lover. Even Broch himself, as a man who sought American commitment, was not immune. Some Norwegian businessmen circulated the smear that he had never set foot in Narvik. He was a Roosevelt agent, paid to embroil America in the war.

On 5 November, Broch, in Minneapolis, heard of Roosevelt's triumph with undisguised joy. But still it seemed to him that many hurdles lay ahead. By paring his expenses to around two dollars a day, he was slowly saving the 6,500 Swedish kroner (almost $2,000) that would finance a passage from Stockholm for Ellen, his wife, and daughter Siri. But that was four months away, and America had not yet reached the hour of decision. What turn of events, Broch wondered, could ever involve her in this war?

*

Six days after Roosevelt's re-election, the British quite unwittingly, brought America's involvement in World War II perceptibly closer.

At 10 pm on the bright moonlit night of 11 November, twenty-one Fairey-Swordfish torpedo-bombers of the Fleet Air Arm, operating from the aircraft carrier, H.M.S. *Illustrious*, and escorting cruisers, swooped 170 miles from off the coast of Cephalonia to attack the Italian fleet at Taranto, the major naval base in the Ionian Sea.

'A black day,' noted Count Galeazzo Ciano, Mussolini's Foreign Minister, in his diary, for the planes of what the British styled 'Operation Judgement',

201

venturing as low as 150 feet, had sunk the dreadnought *Cavour* and severely damaged the 35,000 ton battleships *Littorio* and *Duilio*, faster and more up-to-date than any warships the British possessed.

The moral of this operation was not lost on Roosevelt's Secretary of the Navy, Frank Knox. 'The success of the British aerial torpedo attack against ships at anchor,' he wrote to Secretary Stimson in the War Department, 'suggests that precautionary measures be taken immediately to protect Pearl Harbor against surprise attack in the event that war should break out between the United States and Japan.'

Knox could not know it, but Admiral Isoroku Yamamoto, Commander-in-Chief of the Japanese Combined Fleet, had also taken the lesson of Taranto to heart. In a locked drawer of his desk aboard the flagship *Nagato*, there already reposed a 500-page mimeographed book, titled, *The Habits, Strengths and Defenses of the American Fleet in the Hawaiian Area*. Every fact of relevance to Pearl Harbor was in that book — its berthing plans, training areas, defences and zones of reconnaissance.

Already, having scouted the Japanese coastline, Yamamoto had found a place that strikingly resembled Pearl Harbor — south of Kyushu in Kagoshima Bay. This, like Pearl, was accessible only through a single entrance channel, which all ships, coming and going, had to use.

Now had come Taranto — simon-pure proof that an attack on Pearl was as feasible in a shooting war as the aerial exercises carried out over Kagoshima. From 12 November on, 'Operation Z', as Yamamoto called it, was allotted priority above and beyond all other projects.

*

By 3 November, the bombs had rained on London for fifty-seven nights, and Churchill was in his element. 'Let us go on together through the storm,' he rallied his former chief Neville Chamberlain in a letter written as October dawned, 'These are great days.' The sentiment was inopportune, for Chamberlain was to die of intestinal cancer before the year was out, but Churchill was now mindful of little else but the nightly stimulus of danger.

To his anxious bodyguard, Detective-Inspector Walter Thompson, 'The Old Man' often proved a sore trial. When raids were heaviest, Churchill often chose for sheer devilment to sleep on the top floor of 10, Downing Street or duck from doorway to doorway along Whitehall dodging a hail of shell splinters. When Thompson urged him to move to safe quarters, Churchill, irked, replied: 'Thompson, the Prime Minister of this country lives and works in this house — and until Hitler puts it on the ground, *I* work here!'

The sufferings of London's East Enders, the Cockneys, who had most to lose in the raids on East London dockland boroughs like Poplar and Stepney, moved him profoundly. He took pains to visit them after each heavy raid —

always stepping out briskly, Thompson noted, to boost morale – and the Cockneys warmed to his presence in these mean streets. 'We are with you, Winnie,' the cry would go up, 'Give it to them, Winnie.' Turning to Ismay, his eyes filled with tears, Churchill blurted out: 'What fellows they are. Did you hear them? They cheered me as if I had given them a victory, instead of getting their houses bombed to bits.'

King George VI and his Queen were as instrumental as Churchill in boosting Londoners' morale. 'I'm glad we've been bombed,' Queen Elizabeth confessed after 15 September. 'It makes me feel I can look the East End in the face.' After one East End visit, the Queen sent sixty suites of furniture from Windsor Castle, along with linen, carpets and rugs and the gesture was not forgotten. Nor did the Queen lack the common touch, as Minister of Food, Lord Woolton had cause to observe during one Royal tour of communal feeding centres in South London.

At one centre, a grime-smeared baby in its mother's arms grabbed for the Queen's rope of pearls. Minutes later, the Queen moved on – too late for a hapless photographer who was trying to snap a picture. 'Your Majesty,' Woolton murmured under his breath. 'You've just broken a press man's heart.' With no indication that she had heard the Queen moved discreetly back, within the baby's reach. Next day the picture made most front pages – prompting one Cockney housewife's spontaneous tribute: 'Ain't she just *bloody* lovely!'

In all these weeks of Calvary, no Londoner was fighting to win a battle, as at Ypres or Waterloo, but merely to survive, yet this in itself was a kind of victory. And, significantly, anxiety states diminished as the blitz continued; in the first three months of bombing, less than three patients a week reported sick with nervous disorders. Scores of pubs displayed a notice recalling the earlier words of Queen Victoria following a reversal in the South African war: 'We are not interested in the possibilities of defeat because they do not exist.' There was suddenly a new belief in a common purpose, a shifting of ambition from the self towards others, a live-for-today philosophy in which new tolerances were born.

From a passive acceptance of discomfort and disrupted routine, Londoners were swiftly changing to a stubborn refusal to be subjugated. Evening concerts belonged to the past, but lunchtime concerts at the National Gallery, with artistes like the pianist Myra Hess, had become the daily norm. By mid-October, too, the city was witnessing a phenomenon unique in contemporary history: lunchtime Shakespeare.

The concept was the brainchild of a 38-year-old classical actor, Donald (later Sir Donald) Wolfit, who hit upon the idea of renting London's Strand Theatre for a nugatory £10 a week. Assembling a company of twelve stalwarts, who were paid three guineas a week expenses, among them the now veteran actress Cathleen Nesbitt, Wolfit's repertoire was an hour long (1 pm–

2 pm) symposium of Shakespearean excerpts – the sleep-walking scene from *Macbeth*, the casket scene from *The Merchant of Venice* and what Wolfit called 'potted versions' of *Othello* and *Richard III*. Only the theatre's stalls were used, and the audience paid one shilling a head admission.

On the first day – 13 October – they played to an audience of sixty-one. On the next day, following a direct hit by a bomb on the rear of the theatre, they arrived to find the dressing-rooms in ruins and the stage ankle-deep in dust and soot. But as troupers they were not deterred; they changed on the stage before curtain-up and the show went on.

By October's end, Wolfit's company was playing to audiences of 1,000 a week, and the *Daily Express*'s appropriate headline was: SHAKESPEARE BEATS HITLER. Ever ingenious, Wolfit had even been prompted to add the graveyard scene from *Hamlet* to the repertoire; the stage door, which had been blown clean into the street, would make a perfect bier for Ophelia.

The Minister of Food, Lord Woolton, was a seasoned enough politician to record a shrewd insight in his diary as the winter drew on: 'It isn't the Government of this country that's going to win the war – it's the people!'

*

Outside the Axis camp, one man remained resolutely disenchanted with the British: Eire's Eamon de Valera.

On 5 November, speaking in the House of Commons, Churchill had harked back to the vital treaty ports of Queenstown, Berehaven and Lough Swilly, which Chamberlain had handed back to Eire in 1938. Now that the U-Boats had intensified their war on British shipping. Churchill said, the deprivation of those ports was 'a grievous burden'.

Now Roosevelt's Envoy Extraordinary and Minister-Plenipotentiary in Eire, David Gray, entered the picture. Over lunch outside Dublin with de Valera's Permanent Secretary for External Affairs, Joseph P. Walshe, Gray put the U.S. case plainly: many Americans would view Churchill's complaints with sympathy. There was likely to be impatience with de Valera for withholding those bases.

Walshe was equally blunt. If the Irish ever leased those ports to the British, the devious British would never hand them back.

Gray looked further ahead. Supposing at a later stage, America was attacked by Japan, and needed those ports – what then? As far back as April, de Valera had told Gray: 'If you (America) should become involved in the war, of course that would change matters for us overnight.'

Walshe agreed. Whether or not Ireland entered the war, there would be little difficulty in arranging to lease the Americans ports and airfields. But even if the Americans stood in as guarantors, he doubted if the British would be granted such a lease.

'As we see it here,' Gray summed up in his despatch to the State Department, 'any attempt by Churchill to negotiate for the ports would be hopeless. He has the choice between seizing them and paying the price in possible bloodshed and certain hostility, or doing without.

'De Valera's whole power,' he pointed out shrewdly, 'is based on his genius for engendering and utilising anti-British sentiment . . . He is probably the most adroit politician in Europe and he honestly believes all he does is for the good of his country. He has the qualities of martyr, fanatic and Machiavelli. No one can outwit him, frighten or blandish him. Remember that he is not pro-German or personally anti-British but only pro-de Valera . . .'

*

In contrast with Churchill's buoyant demeanour, Adolf Hitler knew only frustration. In the last week of October, his potential allies were one by one proving bent or broken reeds.

As far back as 6 September, alarmed by Roosevelt's destroyer deal, Hitler had set the seal on Operation Felix – the seizure of Gibraltar, designed to give Germany control over the Mediterranean before any further American intervention. In this he counted confidently on Spain's readiness to enter the war. One week later, Ribbentrop, in Berlin, began applying the first pressures to General Francisco Franco's Foreign-Minister-designate, Ramon Serrano Sûner. Sûner temporised. If Spain were to be involved, he pointed out, she would need 38-centimetre guns – which he knew Germany could not supply – to say nothing of up to 700,000 tons of grain to feed her people, food and equipment for her army, aircraft and artillery. Then, too, Spain had territorial rights in Morocco, which she would call on Germany to support.

Thus, on 22 October, as his armoured 9-coach train rolled into the sunny little French town of Hendaye, hard by the Spanish border, Hitler had two objectives in his first-ever meeting with Franco: to bring Spain into the Axis alliance and to gain Franco's assent for the attack on Gibraltar. Franco, by contrast, had but one objective: to avoid precise commitments of any kind.

The *Caudillo*'s motives were unimpeachable. Fifteen days earlier, he had informed Roosevelt that it was now in his power to affect the whole course of the war: if the United States provided Spain with wheat, Spain would stay neutral. The British Cabinet, sounded out by the State Department, had approved, provided always that American agents handled the distribution, and that none was re-exported. Franco was on the point of clinching a better deal than the Führer could hope to offer, one that would fill his country's granaries.

In the panelled saloon of Hitler's train, there now ensued some of the most frustrating hours of the Führer's life – 'rather than go through it again', he told Mussolini later, 'I would prefer to have three or four teeth taken out'.

For the most part, Franco sat huddled impassively on his chair, saying nothing, as Hitler launched into flights of strategic fancy. In the New Year, he urged, Spain could declare war on England, and the crack assault troops who on 10 May had stormed the Belgian fort of Eben Emael would seize Gibraltar. Then it would be restored to Spain.

When Hitler finally subsided, Franco began to speak in a high quiet voice which reminded the interpreter, Paul Schmidt, 'of a muezzin calling the faithful to prayer'. Spain, Franco said, was hungry and needed several thousand tons of wheat immediately. Could Hitler undertake to fill her granaries? Then it was unthinkable to offend Spanish national pride by using foreign troops against Gibraltar. Spanish troops must be used, and they would need modern equipment.

In growing irritation, Hitler began to drum his fingers on the side of his chair, but Franco had by no means finished. It was very premature, he opined, to say, as Hitler had said, that the British had been defeated, for they would fight to the last man on their own soil, and behind them stood the enormous power of the United States.

When Hitler countered this with hints of an anti-British alliance with France, Franco was scornful. This was pure delusion on the Führer's part, for France would never ally herself to fight with Germany.

At one point, Hitler sprang to his feet, exclaiming that there was no point in going on, but although he controlled his temper within minutes, he won no ground from the canny Galician. That evening, after an expansive dinner, Hitler sought to pressure Franco further, but in vain. After nine hours of fruitless parley, he left Hendaye with no more than a protocol providing for Spain's entry into the war, on a date unspecified, subject to prior deliveries of food and arms.

From the frustrations of meeting with 'that Jesuit swine', Hitler journeyed on, for a galling encounter, on 24 October, at Montoire, near Tours, with 'that dirty democratic cheapjack politician', Pierre Laval, Vice-Premier of France, who had persuaded the reluctant Marshal Henri-Phillipe Pétain to accompany him. Once more the Führer was irked by the French statesmen's evident awe of the United States – 'the thought of an American landing on the Continent is militarily speaking a pure illusion', he told Pétain irritably – and by their palpable desire to stay on the sidelines. Pétain was ready to accept the principle of collaboration, he agreed, but he could not define the limits. 'Don't press us to make war on Britain,' Laval interjected; 'it will be necessary to prepare public opinion.' Pétain, he added, could not declare war without a vote from the Chamber of Deputies, which the Chamber would probably refuse.

The one man thirsting for action, Benito Mussolini, had already embarked on the precise commitment from which Hitler had sought to avert him. 'This is downright madness,' the Führer had raged. 'How can he do such a thing?'

for at 9 am on 28 October, passing through Bologna en route to Florence, Hitler and his party had learned from the railway telegraph office that they were two hours too late to halt Mussolini in a reckless invasion of Greece.

'The Italians will never get anywhere against the Greeks in autumn rains and winter snow,' Ribbentrop had explained to his entourage before the blow fell. 'The Führer intends at all cost to hold up this crazy scheme.'

No man among the Germans could divine the real reason for Mussolini's action: the Italian's lifelong persecution-phobia. On 4 October, when the two directors had met on the Brenner Pass, dividing Austria from Italy, Hitler had made no mention of the fact that he was sending troops to occupy oil-rich areas of Rumania. The news of this coup on 12 October, reduced Mussolini to trembling fury.

'Hitler always faces me with a *fait accompli*,' he exploded to Count Ciano. 'This time I am going to pay him back in his own coin. He will find out in the papers that I have occupied Greece. In this way the equilibrium will be re-established.'

Hitler, knowing nothing of this, was not only angry but perplexed besides. 'If he wanted to pick a fight,' he asked *Feldmarschall* Keitel rhetorically, 'why didn't he attack in Malta or Crete? It would at least make some sense in the context of war with Britain in the Mediterranean.'

Nor was his humour improved by Mussolini's greeting as his train reached Florence. As Hitler's face, smiling strainedly, appeared at his compartment window, Mussolini hailed him from the platform in the high-flown style of a Fascist war communiqué: 'Führer, we are on the march! Victorious Italian troops crossed the Greco–Albanian border at dawn today!'

'The whole outcome will be military catastrophe,' were Hitler's first words as the two men entered the privacy of a waiting-room, but neither man could then foresee that with this foolhardy gesture Mussolini had ultimately doomed both the Third Reich and his own Fascist regime.

Within weeks, the Duce's ill-equipped troops were in headlong retreat, surrounded at the ports of Durazzo and Valona, their backs to the sea. To rescue them, and to maintain German supremacy in the Balkans, Hitler had to divert 680,000 troops to strike at Greece through Rumania and Bulgaria. But to achieve this, in April 1941, called for a ruinous change of priorities; Operation Barbarossa, Hitler's long-awaited assault on Russia, had to be delayed four weeks, until 22 June – time enough to bog down the German armies in the sub-zero nightmare of a Russian winter. Nor did the Führer's efforts to redeem his ally save the 20,000 Italians who died on Greek battlefields, the 40,000 wounded, the 26,000 taken prisoner, the 18,000 crippled with frost-bite.

Mirroring the Führer's mood of black futility as October ended, an editorial in that day's *Le Temps* of Paris confessed: 'There are days when it is difficult to write anything at all on any subject whatsoever.'

207

Around 5.30 pm on Thursday, 14 November, Dr R. V. Jones was once again in a quandary. In his London office by St James's Park, the young scientist was listening with growing disquiet to Wing Commander Edward Addison, of No. 80 Signals Wing, which handled the jamming of the German detector beams. A Luftwaffe raid was scheduled for that night, and Addison needed a snap decision.

In the weeks since the dockland raid of 7 September, Jones, with the help of 'Enigma' cryptographers at Bletchley Park, had at last plumbed the long-standing mystery of the X-Gerät. An intricate device involving up to six intersecting beams, codenamed after German rivers – 'Weser', 'Spree', 'Rhein', 'Elbe', 'Isar' and 'Oder' – the X-Gerät ensured the German bomber pilots using it an aiming accuracy of around ten yards at 200 miles. The first aircraft to have been equipped, the Heinkels of *Hauptmann* Friedrich Karol Aschenbrenner's Bomber Group 100, could thus find their target even under blind bombing conditions – and start up fires which the bombers in their wake could not fail to see.

Since 3 pm, Addison now explained to Jones, the beams had been inter-secting over the industrial Midlands. So on what frequency should the hammers be set tonight?

Jones had known for days now that an all-out German air attack, called 'Operation Moonlight Sonata', was imminent. This much 'Enigma' traffic had established, although predicted targets had included Greater or Central London, the Farnborough–Reading area, and the Isle of Sheppey. To con-found confusion, Coventry and Birmingham had been mentioned, too – with the raids timed for any night between 15 November and 20 November.

Thus Jones could offer little more than an inspired guess. The filter of a salvaged Heinkel 111, which had crashed at Bridport, Dorset, on 6 Novem-ber, had been tuned to 2,000 cycles per second – a high-pitched note, corre-spondent to a piano's top 'C'. Feasibly, he told Addison, 2,000 cycles would be the frequency in use that night.

Few men had any inkling that Coventry was the target, and none less so than Winston Churchill. At this hour, the Premier was departing for a working weekend in the country, along with his duty private secretary, John Martin. At the last moment, a top secret message arrived, which he tucked inside the yellow box reserved for 'Enigma' messages. But barely had his car reached Kensington Gardens than Churchill was instructing chauffeur Joseph Bullock: 'Back – back to Downing Street!' The beams, he explained to Martin, indicated a mammoth raid – 'and I am not going to spend a night peaceably in the country while the metropolis is under heavy attack.'

Later the legend was to arise that Churchill, following days of anguish, had abandoned Coventry to its fate rather than compromise the 'Enigma' secret, but the truth was more prosaic. Aside from indicating a large-scale raid on a variety of targets, 'Enigma' had made no more positive contribution, and Churchill's night of anguish was passed on the Air Ministry roof, along with General Ismay, awaiting bombers that never came.

Even the duty cypher watch, at Hut No. 6, Bletchley Park, were sure of only one thing: tonight's target had never yet been attacked in strength. All of them by now knew *Liebe* as Liverpool, and *Mülkasten* (dustbin) was Hull, but tonight's target bore a codename never previously encountered: *Korn.*

Coventry was indeed a prime industrial target. To its 238,000 citizens it was much more than the medieval 'City of Three Spires', with its crooked timbered back streets, and its legend of Lady Godiva and Peeping Tom. Scattered across its thirty square miles were scores of shadow factories given over to vital war production: the Vickers Armstrong and Hawker Siddeley works, turning out engines for Blenheim and Whitley bombers, a Rolls Royce plant, whose Merlin engines powered the Spitfire, the Daimler factory, producing scout cars, Courtauld's, devoted to nylon parachutes, and the Dunlop tyre company.

By now, after seventeen tip-and-run raids, the citizens had grown wary. Trekking – by bus, train or bicycle – to country chalets or 'safe' towns like Kenilworth or Warwick, had become a way of life; up to half the population slept away from the city each night. Hundreds of garden gates bore a laconic chalkmark, 'S.O.' (Sleeps Out), to save rescue parties needless digging if the house was hit.

On 14 November, few had premonitions. At 62, Tennyson Road, Mrs Dorothy Prideaux was baffled by the strange antics of her Aberdeen terrier, Susan, recently the proud mother of seven puppies. As early as 5.30 pm Susan became uneasy – whining and tugging her mistress' skirts, urging her towards the outdoor Anderson shelter. In vain, Dorothy Prideaux protested, 'Go on, you fidgety Phil!'; finally, past patience, she flung open the shelter door. At once the terrier carried all seven pups to their boxes beneath Mrs Prideaux' bunk, then returned to the kitchen door, yelping a warning.

At The Bell Inn, Keresley, the landlord, Harry Ward, was uneasy, too. On an impulse, not knowing why, he phoned his staff of three, bidding them not to come on duty.

Thousands left in the city had no choice; almost every factory was working at full pitch now, a 12-hour seven-day week. At the main Daimler works, on Sandy Lane, due north of the city centre, 400 workers were just then punching the time clock for the night shift. It was the same all over Coventry.

At a score of airfields in Northern France and Holland – Vendeville, near Lille, Castle Roland, by Versailles, Eindhoven – the German bomber pilots had assembled for their pre-flight briefing as early as 5 pm. *Oberfeldwebel* Werner Handorf was one of many who heard the official reason for the

209

sortie: a reprisal raid for an attack on Munich, Hitler's cherished city, on 6 November. The truth would have been less reassuring: the need to stage a knock-out blow before American industrial output gave Britain the edge over Germany. But there seemed every chance of success. Between them, over an 11-hour period, 500 HE 111s and JU 88s were to drop an unprecedented 503 tons of high explosives, including fifty parachute (or land) mines on the city known as Target 53, a city already ablaze with incendiaries dropped by Aschenbrenner's spearhead force.

Nothing was left to chance. At 6.17 pm, local time, as the first HE 111s of Bomber group 100 crossed the English coastline at Lulworth, Dorset, riding the tone zone of the Director beam 'Weser', every man was flying in unwavering Indian file, as if the pilots walked a kind of aerial tightrope, until the main cross signal beam indicated Coventry five kilometres ahead. In the bluish light of the instrument panels, the plane commanders examined their pocket streets maps of the city, the key objectives clearly circled in red: the Hill Street gasholders, the Alvis aero-engine works, the British Piston-Ring Company.

At 7.11 pm, the cold high voice of the siren wavered and cried for one long minute over Coventry's rooftops. Then the first of 30,000 incendiary bombs came whistling from the sky.

To those watching, the scene was indescribable. The bombs were falling on tenement gutters, and on warehouse roofs; lodging in drain-pipes and window ledges; on pavements and in doorways; on the chancel roof of the thirteenth-century St Michael's Cathedral. They burned with a sizzling blue-white glare; above them, chandelier flares came dripping beautifully down, like Chinese lanterns, bathing the streets, the factories, the slate roofs in a purer whiter glow than moonlight.

Even trained observers were aghast, as if they sensed already this was bigger than anything a British city had ever known. At the thirteenth century Church of Holy Trinity, in the city centre, the Reverend G. W. Clitheroe remarked to his curate, Kenneth Thornton: 'Strangely persistent, this raid tonight, Kenneth.' At Gulson Road Hospital, Student Nurse Kathleen Colwill, heading for the Emergency Operating Theatre, clutched a precautionary plate of baked beans on toast; who knew when she would get to eat again?

The unearthly beauty of the fires mesmerised all who saw them. To City Chamberlain John Bayley Shelton, in Little Park Street, the leaping flames seemed to drift 'like the sparks from a blacksmith's forge'. For hairdresser Megan Ryan, watching from her flat, atop a wooden table, 'it was like a transformation scene in a pantomime'. Deputy Chief Fire Officer John Watkin, on duty at the Roote's plant, saw the yellow licking flames as 'like a row of beautiful crocuses in early Spring'.

Now the high explosives followed – a whining shuddering roar like an express train flashing from a tunnel. Between each shockwave of sound, eerie noises became audible: distant bombs, 'as if a truck was unloading a consignment of bricks'; the sinister 'adder-like hissing' of burning incendiaries; very far away, a fire-engine tolling like a passing-bell. Bargee William Prue, sheltering with a crowd under a railway arch at Longford, heard one woman voice the awestruck feeling: 'He means it tonight.'

As the blind fury of the raid struck home, one single thought outraged the citizens: the bombers were having it all their own way. For Dr R. V. Jones, 100 miles south in Richmond, Surrey, his sense of guilt was at first overwhelming: because he had guessed the wrong frequency, hundreds were doomed to die. Yet by tragic irony, Jones had been right: every bomber airborne this night was operating on the carrier frequency that he had forecast.

Later a post-mortem revealed that a careless — or tone-deaf — jamming technician had identified an audible frequency of 1,500 cycles per second — a note equivalent to the 'G' below top 'C'. Thus with the jammers operating on the wrong frequency Aschenbrenner's spearhead force could home in on their targets unopposed — with only twenty-four 3.7 inch anti-aircraft guns and twelve quick-firing 40-mm Bofors guns to defend the stricken city.

By 8 pm, the Central Fire Station had charted 240 fires, many of them out of control — and thirty minutes later, volunteer firemen drafted in from Rugby found the city centre's water mains fractured. By 9.30 pm, the telephones were out; Coventry was cut off from the outside world. Slowly the defenders were acknowledging defeat; at 11 pm Provost Richard Howard and his firewatchers abandoned the battle to save St Michael's Cathedral. From the doorway of St Mary's Police Station they listened, sick at heart to the steady drip-drip of molten lead, until the great steel girders spanning the nave, glowing white-hot, 'tugged the walls and pillars from their foundations like so many Samsons'.

It was a night of horror that none would ever forget. Gunner William Davies, on ten days' leave, stumbled over a prostrate body in Hertford Street and recoiled aghast — then realised it was one of the city's three statues of Peeping Tom. Along with a colleague, Daimler's Labour Manager, Leslie Wale, tussled for minutes on end to free a signalman on the railway embankment nearby; telephone wires had fallen to enmesh the man from head to foot like an escapologist. Ambulance Driver Wilfred Bevan recovered one torso so maimed that only the absence of genitals told him that this had been a woman; bomb blast had concertinaed both stomach and breasts. At Courtauld's, Fire Officer Bert Bucknall and his mate Cecil Heward were buried by blast astride the main steam duct to the nylon factory, the scalding steam playing like a geyser's jet on Bucknall's legs and Heward's head.

Both men were to survive — though Bucknall was to endure twenty-six plastic surgery operations, and Heward, for whom surgeons fashioned a new face, a new ear and new thumbs, double that number.

Everywhere there were alien sights . . . drifting barrage balloons bobbing like giant whales at roof-top level . . . a kitten patting absorbedly at charred scraps of paper floating across the gardens . . . a length of streetcar track sailing twenty clear yards like a monstrous rocket, clean over a 3-storey house. Landlord Harry Ward emerged from his pub cellar, where he had taken shelter, then ran for his life; a knee-high river of boiling butter from a dairy nearby was coursing down the street.

At 167, Beechwood Avenue, William Heynes, a liaison officer with Short's Aircraft, was fascinated by what seemed like a large tree felled across the road – a trunk almost twelve feet long, two feet in diameter. 'Come and see this tree,' he called to Dorothy, his wife, then a second later, 'Get *back* – there's a mine outside!' At that moment, in a thunderclap of sound, 1,560 lb of high explosive went sky-high, bursting Heynes' eardrum, burying him upside down in blue clay, showering Dorothy with broken glass, and killing outright their 4-year-old son, Simon, who was crouched beneath the stairs.

For every civil defence worker, it was the most frustrating night they ever knew. Ambulance Driver Katie Fensom never got within sight of the city's two hospitals – the Coventry and Warwickshire and Gulson Road – all evening; high explosives had cratered the roads like a lunar landscape, cutting off all access. Auxiliary Fireman John Bowles, who brought a fire-engine eighteen miles from Birmingham, was checked by a policeman who counselled, 'You may as well go back, mate; you can't even get in.'

By midnight, many men were as resigned to die as Rescue Worker Albert Fearn. He told himself: 'This is the end – we'll be dead lucky if we see the sun again.'

A few found relief in action. In the sixteenth-century courtyard of Bond's Hospital, a home for aged men, old Edwin Walsh was up all night smothering incendiaries with sand. Told to lie down, he demurred stoutly; he had lain down for no man all his life, and he didn't aim to break the habit at ninety years of age. It was the same with Dr Harry Winter, a young Canadian, at the Coventry and Warwickshire Hospital. Amid carnage which reminded one doctor of 'the wounded in *Gone With The Wind*', Winter carried out fifteen emergency operations this night – most of them by the light of an automobile headlamp rigged to a battery set.

Blitz philosophers had an old adage – 'A bomb never falls in the same place twice' – but tonight even this comforting fiction failed. Soon after midnight, word came to St Mary's Street Police Station: a shelter under Smith's Furnishing Store had been hit and fourteen people were trapped. Police Constable Wilfred Burchett was one of eight men making up a volunteer party to rescue them – but at length, after an hour's digging, he and two others were despatched to enlist more help.

The errand saved their lives. Minutes later, a hurtling bomb wiped out the five men who had remained.

Even miles from the target, Coventry's agony was a terrible and palpable force. At 6,000 feet above the city, in JU 88 'Bruno', *Oberfeldwebel* Werner Handorf felt his nostrils prickle; the smell of burning buildings had penetrated even the bomber's cockpit. Nine miles away, in Leamington Spa, Station Officer John Barnes, of the Auxiliary Fire Service, watched stupefied as shockwaves of blast lifted slates from the rooftops in a prickly mass like a hedgehog's spine.

Six weeks before 1940 ended, a new word had entered the language of war: to lay waste a city by aerial attack was now to *koventrieren*, to 'coventrate'.

An unwilling eyewitness of this 'coventration' was Assistant Divisional Officer Geoffrey Blackstone. On 13 November, following sixty-six consecutive nights on duty, Blackstone was the first London Fire Brigade Officer to be granted a rare privilege: twenty-four hours leave. Even so, Major Frank Jackson had added two provisos: Blackstone must travel in a fire car with a driver and leave a telephone number. Almost too weary for jubilation, Blackstone headed ninety miles north for his sister's home near Stamford, Lincolnshire.

At 4 am on 15 November, Jackson awoke him groaning from sleep: 'There's been a heavy raid on Coventry. Get over there – they want 200 London firemen.' One hour later, after a hasty breakfast, Blackstone set off at top speed. But in a village some miles from the city centre he stopped short. A huntsman in pink coat and black cap had loomed like a ghost rider from the early morning mist, peremptorily signalling him to halt. As Blackstone watched incredulously, a pack of thirty fox-hounds ambled slowly across the road, then vanished from sight. With mingled anger and disbelief, Blackstone thought: Coventry may burn to the ground, but England's still going on.

He drove into a city that had been gutted almost beyond recognition. At 6.16 am as the last wave of bombers receded towards the coast, fully 60,000 out of 75,000 buildings had been destroyed or badly damaged – among them twenty-seven vital war plants, whose production was checked for weeks. At least 568 men, women and children had died, and more than 1,200 had been injured – and of those fatalities 420, never identified, were buried in a communal grave.

Few of the survivors even knew the raid had ended; with the electricity cables torn apart, the sirens stayed silent that day. Only the wardens' shouts of 'It's all over', echoing into basements and Anderson shelters, brought the people forth into drizzling rain to view a terrible devastation.

For more than a square mile, the city's centre lay in ruins – grotesque piles of rubble and masonry, twisted steel girders and looped telegraph wires, wastes of open space pock-marked by gutted shells. 'The streets are

213

plastered with thick red mud,' noted Daimler's Leslie Wale in his diary. 'Everywhere destruction.'

All over Coventry the scene was the same – the silent staring crowds grouped before ruined landmarks, before fires that would smoulder on even until Christmas morning. In hundreds of gardens, dogs and cats waited patiently for their owners to return, outside homes that had vanished forever. Ironically, the smell of the city that morning was the smell of affluence: burning cigars in gutted tobacconists, 300 tons of Sunday joints roasting in the Government Meat Store.

Even a veteran war correspondent, Hilde Marchant of the *Daily Express*, could scarcely take in this year's oft-repeated lesson: nothing and no one was immune. 'It was a familiar sight,' she wrote, as thousands thronged from the city, pushing handcarts and prams piled with belongings, 'one I had seen in Spain and Finland. Yet this was worse . . . These people moved against a background of suburban villas, had English faces, used the English tongue, wore English clothes. They were our own kind . . .'

Many more of them were staying – deeply thankful to be alive, striving to carry on somehow. Gunner William Davies spent his entire ten days' leave at his rented home in Dartmouth Road, cleaning up the mess of plaster dust. Mrs Jessie Pykett set out from Hinckley, thirteen miles away, incongruously clutching a steak-and-kidney pie; the detours, when she reached Coventry's outskirts, took her almost ten miles through cratered streets, and the gravy was running down her skirt, but somehow her fireman-husband was going to be fed. In Cox Street, one shopkeeper seemed to those who saw him a symbol of the will to carry on. Sitting stolidly before his ruined premises, he was trying to boil a kettle on a still-smouldering incendiary bomb.

For weeks yet, most citizens would lack the bare essentials of life – gas, running water, electricity – yet the Englishman's sense of business-as-usual still prevailed. Master confectioner Herbert Moore, finding his twelve shops and his bakery miraculously intact, set his staff to work and produced £1,000 worth of eatables by the Saturday. At one branch of Barclay's Bank, the cashiers paid out money next day standing on bricks, to dodge the water lapping round them. A department store took press space to announce: 'Messrs Marks and Spencer of Smithford Street are playing their part in defying the activities of the Hun by opening up in Whitefriars Street.'

All through this Friday, the hours ticked away, and Blackstone kicked his heels in black frustration. With the water mains fractured, there was nothing he or any fireman could do. Towards 7 pm, however, an emergency telephone link was established with London, and one of the first calls was for Blackstone. It was from Major Jackson: 'The X-beam is on London. Come back at once.'

His twenty-four hours leave was over.

10

'For Me You Shall Always Be Greatheart'

15 November–31 December, 1940

ON TUESDAY, 3 DECEMBER, quite suddenly, Roosevelt dropped from the sight of official Washington. On the face of it, it seemed a curious decision, as if the President, following his electoral triumph, had grown indifferent to Europe's plight. Even so, at Miami, Florida, on this day, he went purposefully aboard the navy cruiser, *Tuscaloosa*, which had been tied up at Pier 3 since dawn. Thousands gathered to cheer him, at 2 pm as Roosevelt, standing on the quarterdeck, lifted his hat at arm's length to wave them goodbye.

There was mystery in the air. Reporters aboard the presidential train which had brought him hither had heard more esoteric talk of fishing tackle than of global strategy. The President 'expected' to be absent from Washington 'for about fifteen days'; rumour – unconfirmed – had it that he would 'combine rest with a tour of inspection of defences in the vicinity of Puerto Rico'. Accompanying him were only his close aide, Harry L. Hopkins, and his personal physician and Navy Surgeon General Admiral Ross T. McIntire. There thus seemed no prospect that earth-moving decisions would be reached aboard *Tuscaloosa*.

The President was thinking. 'I didn't know for quite a while what he was thinking about, if anything,' Hopkins said later. 'But then – I began to get the idea that he was refuelling, the way he so often does when he seems to be resting and carefree. So I didn't ask him any questions.'

There was much for the President to think about. As far south of the Caribbean as Ecuador, hemisphere defence rested largely on U.S. shoulders, since both the Caribbean and the Panama Canal were vital to the defence of the continental United States. True, Argentina, Brazil and Chile were arming fast, promising a strong southern half of the hemisphere to balance the strong northern half that American and Canada were building. What loans could do to shore up the hemisphere, the U.S. was doing: $60,000,000 was slated for Argentina, $7,500,000 to Uruguay. Already the United States was becoming banker to the world, a role she would assume increasingly from this time on.

America was giving its all, but could its all ever be enough? China was

215

begging for old trainer planes, for almost anything that would fly. Concerned citizens were urging whole fleets of planes, to aid the Greeks and knock Italy out of the war.

Meanwhile, the last vestige of British influence had been banished from the continent of Europe. Hungary, Rumania and Czechoslovakia had all joined the Axis. King Boris of Bulgaria, the last of the Balkan monarchs, was manoeuvring for his life. Only Yugoslavia stayed — until March 1941 — outside the Axis enclave.

If the President was inwardly concerned, it was his particular pride not to show it. On the surface, this was no more than a placid tropical cruise to banish post-election traumas. Following a radio signal from that intrepid fisherman Ernest Hemingway, Roosevelt trawled for marlin between the Dominican Republic and Puerto Rico. He used pork rind on a feathered hook, as Hemingway advised, and caught nothing. He gave lunch aboard ship to the Duke of Windsor, now Governor and C.-in-C. of the Bahamas, and his Duchess. In the evening he played poker, watched boxing matches between crew members, and motion pictures: Alice Faye and Betty Grable in *Tin Pan Alley*, Jean Arthur and William Holden in *Arizona*.

But all along the Chief Executive seemed to be waiting.

On the morning of Monday, 9 December, his vigil was rewarded. In the bright sunlight off Antigua, two Navy seaplanes came roaring out of a cobalt sky, gliding to rest beside the *Tuscaloosa*. Harry Hopkins, who watched them come, felt a perceptible quickening of interest. One of the mail pouches aboard those planes, he thought, might contain a long-awaited letter from Churchill, who had signalled its composition back on 16 November. It would be, the Premier had promised, 'a very long letter on the outlook for 1941'.

It was indeed a long report that Roosevelt read and re-read, reclining in his deck-chair: 4,000 words of it, its tenor universally bleak. The year's escalating losses of over one million tons of British merchant shipping were beginning to make themselves felt. Not less than three million tons of additional merchant shipbuilding capacity would be required for 1941 — a need which only the United States could supply.

But, Churchill warned, 'the more rapid and abundant the flow of munitions and ships which you are able to send us, the sooner will our dollar credits be exhausted . . . The moment approaches when we shall no longer be able to pay cash for shipping and other supplies. While we will do our utmost and shrink from no proper sacrifice to make payments across the exchange, I believe that you will agree that it would be wrong in principle and mutually disadvantageous to us if, at the height of this struggle, Great Britain were to be divested of all saleable assets so that after victory was won with our blood, civilisation saved and time gained for the United States to be fully armed against all eventualities, we should stand stripped to the bone.'

The letter bore out much that Roosevelt had gleaned back in late October from Lord Lothian. 'You must let me know when the red light goes up,' the President had impressed on the ambassador, meaning 'when the British cupboard was bare'. Lothian, who harboured a suspicion that America's bill for the sinews of war might entail selling British holdings in South American railways and Malayan rubber, had replied with a covert warning: if Britain lost her foreign investments and the war's end brought a sharp fall in her living standards, this might precipitate a British revolution. Roosevelt had taken due heed of this.

Although Churchill was not specific in terms of hard cash, Britain was nearing rock-bottom. On the economic battlefield, the country's adverse balance had risen from £27,000,000 (then $108,000,000) to £49,000,000 ($196,000,000). On the home front, she was close to the breadline. In three weeks' time, a gloomy Lord Woolton would report to the Cabinet wheat stocks for fifteen weeks, meat supplies for no more than two weeks, eight weeks butter supply, three weeks margarine, twenty-seven weeks bacon. A stringent cut in the meat ration – to one shillingsworth per head per week – was imminent. Due to tonnage losses, imported fruits – grapes, apricots, bananas – were now a thing of the past. For lack of imported feeds, milk, pork and eggs were running short.

The sole crumb of consolation came from Egypt, where a task force of 80,000 Italians who had rashly invaded from Libya in September found themselves hopelessly routed following a surprise attack launched by the Commander-in-Chief, Middle East, General Sir Archibald Wavell. By 12 December, 39,000 Italians had been taken prisoner, but even this triumph was short-lived when Hitler in February 1941 despatched *Generalleutnant* Erwin Rommel, whose 7th Panzer Division had harassed the British all the way to Dunkirk, to succour the Italians.

Roosevelt fell to brooding. He recalled not only the 'destroyers for bases' deal but a more recent proposal to build merchant ships in the United States and then lease them for a stated period to Britain. Then, too, there was the 1892 statute, unearthed in the summer by a Treasury lawyer, Oscar S. Cox, empowering the Secretary of War to lease Army property 'not required for public use' for not more than five years 'when in his discretion it will be for the public good'. So, if ships could be leased, why not guns? Why not other munitions?

'One evening he suddenly came out with it,' Hopkins recalled excitedly later. 'The whole programme. He didn't seem to have any clear idea how it could be done legally. But there wasn't a doubt in his mind that he'd find a way to do it.'

'The whole programme' – the answer to Britain's impasse, the weapon that was ultimately to destroy Hitler – was to be known as Lend-Lease, or, appropriately, House Bill 1776, embodying the notion that the United

217

States could supply Britain with munitions for free, to be repaid not in dollars but in kind once the war was over.

On a chill and drizzly afternoon, Roosevelt returned to Washington to share his 'brand new thought' with the White House press corps. It was Tuesday, 17 December, and observers noted that he was tanned and jovial, deceptively off-hand in his manner. 'Of course,' he began, 'there is no doubt in the minds of a very overwhelming number of Americans that the best immediate defence of the United States is the success of Great Britain in defending itself – and that, therefore . . . we should do everything to help the British Empire defend itself . . .'

Then, for forty-five unbroken minutes, Roosevelt held forth in monologue. 'What I am trying to do,' he explained, by way of preliminary, 'is eliminate the dollar sign . . . get rid of that silly, foolish old dollar sign.'

He amplified. Henceforth, he proposed, the United States Government should place *all* the contracts for munitions manufactured by U.S. factories – using some of the products themselves but leasing or selling others if they could prove of greater use in Britain.

Noting the puzzled frowns, he hit upon a homely aphorism. Supposing, he suggested, his neighbour's house caught fire, and he, the President, had a length of garden hose four or five hundred yards long. By taking that hose and connecting it with his neighbour's hydrant he might help quench the fire.

'Now what do I do?' the President asked, 'I don't say to him before that operation, "Neighbour, my garden hose cost me $15; you have to pay me $15 for it." What is the transaction that goes on? I don't want $15 – I want my garden hose back after the fire is over.'

In the question period that followed, the reporters were pressing, but all through Roosevelt contrived to reassure them. No, convoys would not be involved – nor would the Neutrality Act need to be amended. Yes, the United States would pay for all British arms under a 'gentleman's agreement'; the British could pay in kind after the war. Right now, the British were being told to go ahead and order all they needed, up to $3,000,000,000 worth, regardless of ability to pay. No, such steps would not mean a greater danger of getting into war. Yes, a great speed-up of defence production *was* needed – 'to keep all the machines that will run seven days a week in operation seven days a week.'

Such speed would be necessary to meet a grim short-term deadline: the spring of 1941, when Hitler might invade Britain.

With their own deadlines in mind, the reporters took his point. The conference ended; they scrambled from the room.

Roosevelt had acted in all good faith, but the danger to the British mainland was receding with each passing day. True, the long night of the bombing was to endure for six months more, and now the fury of the Luftwaffe was extended to the provincial ports, as the bombers smote Southampton, Bristol, Liverpool, Plymouth and Hull. But on 17 December, the same day that Roosevelt had taken the press into his confidence, Hitler set the seal on what he saw as his life's mission: the destruction of Bolshevism.

Twelve days earlier, on 5 December, the Führer had conferred with Brauchitsch and Halder on their basic plan of attack against Russia. To their dismay, he took exception to a move that both men saw as of supreme importance: a blitzkrieg drive for Moscow, in line with Napoleon's initiative in 1812. Not only was Moscow the key to the Soviet communications centre, Brauchitsch protested, but an important armaments centre besides. Hitler would have none of it. 'Only completely ossified brains, absorbed in the ideas of past centuries, could see any worthwhile objective in taking the capital,' was his insulting retort. Now Leningrad and Stalingrad – *there* were the seed-beds of Bolshevism. Wipe out these and Bolshevism would be dead.

On 17 December, the revised plan was laid before Hitler. Once more he made amendments: any advance on Moscow must be delayed until the Baltic States were cleared and Leningrad captured. The operation's title became Barbarossa (Red Beard), after Frederick I, the Holy Roman Emperor, whose legions had marched east in 1190 towards the Holy Land. Its final objective became 'to erect a barrier against Asiatic Russia on the general line Volga–Archangel'.

Next day, 18 December, these decisions were codified in Directive No. 21, the most consequential and far-reaching of all Hitler's directives:

The German Armed Forces must be prepared, even before the conclusion of the war against England, *to crush Soviet Russia in a rapid campaign.*

The Army will have to employ all available formations to this end, with the reservations that occupied territories must be insured against surprise attacks.

The Air Force will have to make available for this Eastern campaign supporting forces of such strength that the Army will be able to bring land operations to a speedy conclusion . . .

The main efforts of the navy will continue to be directed against England . . .

The secret was well-kept. Only in the villages of East Prussia, around Lötzen and Rastenburg, were the farmers and field-workers bewildered: an official circular from the local branch offices of the Nazi Party had forbidden them to prepare their fields for spring planting. At the same time every man was told to submit a return of all his available draught horses. By degrees, it seemed, the area was being transformed into a vast military operations zone.

*

This was the year when the Christmas message of peace on earth and goodwill to men could mean everything or nothing at all. For much of occupied Europe, in this second year of war, it meant nothing. Few would have heat, fewer still enough to eat, not one in a thousand could travel where he pleased or hear uncensored news. Comfortable clothing would be a luxury, and the old killer diseases were stalking the land: influenza and pneumonia, typhus, tuberculosis and cholera.

Nor was this bleak outlook confined to the occupied nations. Italians in the hills of Greece passed Christmas chewing on raw mule flesh, and the average German civilian's Christmas fare would have been unacceptable in any American gaol.

Many lessons had been learned, and many of them were negative. Twelve months of anguish had trespassed on human hope. Young men had been struck down, boundaries had been swept aside, loyalties had faltered. The whole world, from the Arctic to the Southern Pacific, had learned to fear, to suspect, and to hate. Everywhere there had been symptoms of insanity. Saxons had fought against Anglo–Saxons and destroyed their monuments; ally had turned against ally; oriental had fought against oriental in China. Nations had made alliances to destroy other nations, preparing to turn on one another when the task was complete.

Many lucky enough to celebrate Christmas at all celebrated in alien surroundings. Count René de Chambrun and his wife Josée, passed Christmas not in their Paris flat, but in a suite in New York's Ritz Hotel. Ex-Mayor Theodor Broch, whose wife and daughter would not arrive until February, saw out Christmas far from Narvik, in Minneapolis, Minnesota.

Werner Mölders, promoted *Oberstleutnant* at twenty-seven, had eleven months to live before a flying accident ended his life in 1941. But already, as 1940 ended, his disillusionment went deep. The R.A.F. had not been beaten, the Royal Navy had not been destroyed; so many brave and good men from Fighter Group 51 had died in vain. At last he acknowledged the truth; from the first Göring had been a crass egotist who had lost all interest in the war. It was out of this anguish that Mölders cried to his friend Fritz von Forell: 'A world is breaking up under my feet.'

Kaptänleutnant Otto Kretschmer was disillusioned, too, for different reasons. Christmas with his crew at Krummheubel, a Silesian ski resort, had been unwarrantably interrupted by a publisher from Berlin, pestering him to write his memoirs and refusing to take no for an answer. 'The answer is still no!' Kretschmer retorted, pale with rage, on the second occasion. It was days before his anger subsided; he and his men were fighting a private war, a combat only they and perhaps those who hunted them could comprehend. On 16 March, 1941, the destoyer H.M.S. *Walker* put an end to that war, sinking U-99 and taking Kretschmer prisoner, but until that time he kept faith. Neither he nor any of his men ever jumped through hoops for Dr Göbbels' three-ring propaganda circus.

Polly Peabody finally got air passage from Lisbon to England on Christmas Eve and passed a subdued Christmas in Bristol's Royal Hotel. A handful of people with paper hats perched on their heads sat in the hotel's dining room, silently eating the traditional plum pudding. Suddenly a poker-faced man alone in a corner picked up a cardboard trumpet lying beside his plate and blew a defiant toot. Fired by the challenge, a middle-aged woman tripped across the floor and blew a whistle in somebody's ear. A mild frenzy took hold; wads of pink cotton wool splashed in Polly's soup and eddying confetti spangled her hair. Just as suddenly, the gaiety petered out; the room relapsed into silence.

The year was dying as it had dawned – 'not with a bang but a whimper'.

*

At the White House, Washington, D.C., it had been a quieter Christmas than usual for the Roosevelts. For the first time the family were scattered; only Franklin Roosevelt III, aged two-and-a-half and Harry Hopkins' small daughter, Diana, were in the right age bracket to hang their stockings on the President's bedroom mantelpiece. One tradition, though, remained unbroken; on Christmas Eve, following the family dinner, Roosevelt, as always with dramatic relish, read from Dickens's *Christmas Carol*, winding up with Christmas dinner at the Cratchits' and the jubilation of Tiny Tim.

This year, too, he had set his speechwriters Sam Rosenman and Robert E. Sherwood a harder task than usual. The last Fireside Chat of 1940 was scheduled for 29 December, and Roosevelt was determined to make an end of the euphemisms that, aside from his famous 'stab in the back' reference, had peppered his speeches all through 1940. For the first time he was going to mention the Nazis by name and lash out against the isolationists. 'We cannot escape danger or the fear of danger,' he would warn them,'by crawling into bed and pulling the covers over our heads.'

As late as the afternoon of 29 December, Hopkins raised a final point. 'Mr President,' he ventured, 'do you feel that you could include in this speech some kind of optimistic statement that will hearten the people who are doing the fighting – the British, the Greeks, the Chinese?' Roosevelt pondered this, tilting his head, puffing his cheeks, until finally he dictated: 'I believe that the Axis powers are not going to win this war. I base this belief on the latest and best information.'

Both Sherwood and Rosenman were intrigued; what, they wondered, could that 'latest and best information' be? Only later did they learn that it was no more than Roosevelt's unquenchable optimism that the Lend-Lease Bill would pass through Congress and make an Axis victory impossible.

That night saw the climax of all that Roosevelt had worked for in the months since he had sat in the silent Oval Office drafting his eighth State of

221

the Union message. Wearing pince-nez and a bow tie, he was wheeled into the stuffy little diplomatic reception room where a plain desk housed a battery of network microphones. A small intensely partisan group surrounded him: his mother, Sara Roosevelt, Cordell Hull and sundry Cabinet members, Clark Gable and his wife, Carole Lombard, both militant New Dealers.

It was a speech to echo like a clarion-call across the free world. Within minutes of its culmination, telegrams from all over America were streaming into the White House, and their keynote was set by a letter from Secretary of the Navy Frank Knox: 'For me you shall always be "Great-Heart" after that speech of last night.'

'Never before since Jamestown and Plymouth Rock,' Roosevelt told his listeners, 'has our American civilisation been in such danger as now . . .The Nazi masters of Germany have made it clear that they intend not only to dominate all life and thought in their own country, but also to enslave the whole of Europe and then to use the resources of Europe to dominate the rest of the world.'

Appeasers in high places, he charged, were in most cases unwittingly aiding foreign agents. 'The experience of the past two years has proven beyond doubt that no nation can appease the Nazis. No man can tame a tiger into a kitten by stroking it . . .'

Renewing his pledge to keep America out of the war, the President still rallied his fellow Americans. 'There is far less chance of the United States getting into war if we do all we can now to support the nations defending themselves against attack . . .'

That support, he made clear, would be unstinted. 'There will be no "bottlenecks" in our determination to aid Great Britain. No dictator, no combination of dictators, will weaken that determination by threats of how they will construe that determination.'

In a phrase that went down to history, Roosevelt charted the course that Americans must follow for all the days ahead: *'We must be the great arsenal of democracy. For us this is an emergency as serious as war itself . . .'*

*

Even as Roosevelt was on the air, democracy was again under fire. Promptly at 6.15 pm, the 'Fire Raisers' of *Hauptmann* Friedrich Karol Aschenbrenner's Bomber Group 100 zeroed in on the vulnerable square mile of the old walled City of London. The recipe for disaster was total: a Sunday night in Christmas holiday week, shops and office blocks closed, churches locked, most fire watchers off duty. Incredibly, after four months, the Minister of Security, Herbert Morrison, had still fought shy of introducing a compulsory firewatching service.

By 8 pm, the situation that Geoffrey Blackstone had all along predicted was reality. A strong westerly wind sprang up to fan the billowing flames; the Thames was at low tide and fifty feet of sticky black mud in which the firemen floundered and struggled, trying to get fireboat hose ashore, lay between the river and the bankside wharves.

Again, emergency water supplies could have proved the answer, and again the Home Office and the London County Council had left it too late.

Huge fires were started, stretching from Moorgate to Aldersgate, from Old Street to Cannon Street. In the wake of 600 incendiary canisters came a hail of high-explosive bombs, to fracture no less than twelve of the City's largest water mains, among them the dirty water main laid to cope with fire-fighting emergencies between the Thames and the Grand Junction Canal by Regent's Park.

It was typical of Polly Peabody to contrive to be in the thick of it. On arriving in London and checking in at a hotel, she had made a beeline for Fire Brigade Headquarters, intent on hitching herself a ride before the raid had even started. Her father, she explained, had been an active Honorary Member of the New York Fire Department, with two sets of fire-alarms in his front hall and boots and raincoat always at the ready. Her plum reward for being good as a child was always to be taken to a fire.

Jackson, Fordham and Blackstone heard out this breathless stranger in open-mouthed amazement, until Lieutenant-Commander Newcome Hoare, Blackstone's opposite number for the Northern Division, saved the day. Convulsed with laughter, he assured Polly, 'Come on, America, you shall ride in my fire-car as a mascot.' Now, helmeted, booted and in outsize trousers, Polly watched the City burn.

Nearby, a bank had taken fire, and cheques and letters of credit were eddying past, performing a frenzied flamenco in hot whirling air. A charred fragment of a cheque fluttered at her feet — 'Pay Bearer, £10,000' — and Polly grabbed for it as a souvenir. Then it spiralled out of reach, caught in the updraft, and was gone.

The firemen's overall reaction was one of total frustration. At Guy's Hospital, south of the river, whose frontage was one wrapping mass of flame, Geoffrey Blackstone realised at length that there was nothing for it; though much of the hospital was ultimately saved, the patients would have to be evacuated. Suddenly Blackstone recalled that in The Ship and Shovel pub, blazing nearby, was a mighty wooden table carved with the names of past generations of medical students. 'There's a table in there,' he yelled to two passing firemen. 'Get it out.' To the hospital's eternal gratitude, they did.

Few other achievements were as positive. Auxiliary Fireman Maurice Richardson, watching other firemen on a turntable ladder vainly seeking to save the City's fifteenth-century Guildhall, the home of the City Corporation, was reminded of 'little boys peeing on an enormous bonfire'. Another fuming fireman, Michael Wassey, found no water units, no control centres – two had already been bombed out and evacuated – and 'not one pennyworth of salvage effected or performed'.

By 9 pm, as the last bombers droned southward, almost 1,500 fires were raging – so intensely that 2,600 pumps mobilised by London Region, and 300 brought in from outside, could achieve almost nothing. Despatched north of the river in the small hours, Blackstone found the same familiar scene – 'lots of pumps, lots of men, no water'. As he watched, St Paul's Cathedral, ringed by fire, seemed on the point of being engulfed.

From the roof of the Air Ministry, west of the City boundary, the Deputy Chief of the Air Staff watched London burn with an emotion that he recalled as akin to anger. Eight Wren churches – among them, St Lawrence Jewry, St Bride's, St Andrews' – were flaring as brightly as birthday candles; the spectacle of the leaping livid light was so extraordinary that he went downstairs to fetch his chief, Air Chief Marshal Sir Charles Portal. 'Well,' he told Portal, as they watched, 'they are sowing the wind.'

The deadly precedent for Dresden and Cologne, for Berlin and Hamburg, had been established. The Deputy Chief of the Air Staff was Air Vice-Marshal Arthur Harris.

Hundreds of feet above the blazing City, on the roof of St Paul's Cathedral, the Dean, the Very Reverend William Matthews and his fire-watchers, saw disaster as imminent. One incendiary bomb had struck the mighty 148-foot dome, and Matthews and all of them realised the danger; between the outer dome, visible from the street, and the inner dome, floating above the nave, was a hollow space packed with old dry beams.

The incendiary that they watched was lodged upright, halfway through the dome's shell; the lead of the roof was melting and no man could reach it. Then, perhaps appropriately on such a night, in such a place, a miracle occurred. The bomb tilted sideways and fell harmlessly on the Stone Gallery, where a rush of fire-watchers extinguished it.

Though the Cathedral emerged from the inferno almost unscratched, the Chapter House, the Dean's Verger's House, and the Organist's House, all hard by, were gutted. 'Six pails of water,' the Dean noted bitterly later, 'could have saved any one of them.'

The bitterness was justified, for the British Government were still painfully slow to learn the lessons of total war. On New Year's Eve, Herbert Morrison, broadcasting over the B.B.C., threw all the blame on the public for 29 December. Over half the fires could have been avoided if compulsory watching had been in force, yet only now did Morrison announce that all males between sixteen and sixty would register for up to forty-eight hours of fire-watching each month. 'Now we are ready,' commented the Labour Mayor of Stepney, Frank Lewey, sardonically, 'after the event.'

Geoffrey Blackstone was too tired to know what to think. It was 11 am, on the Monday before he reached his quarters in Southwark Bridge Road for a bath and a change of uniform. Then it was the same routine as always: office paperwork, an afternoon of drugged and weary sleep, up once more at dusk to dress and await the siren.

It was Major-General Harold Alexander, G.O.C., Southern Command, who on New Year's Eve produced a suitably detached verdict. Over lunch with the Ministry of Information's Harold Nicolson, Alexander summed up the wry equation: 'Archie Wavell mops up 40,000 Italians and we claim a victory. In two hours the Germans destroy five hundred years of our history.'

*

On New Year's night, Hitler was at the Berghof, his white-painted chalet-style retreat perched on the Obersalzberg, high in the Bavarian Alps. Those present never forgot the Führer's air of calm confidence. It was in keeping with the Christmas card he had selected that year, received by a few intimates such as *Il Duce* and the Göbbels family: a photograph of the Winged Victory of Samothrace, which had been taken from the Louvre in Paris to stand in his Berlin office. The card showed a frieze of German bombers and fighters hovering above the statue, with the caption, 'Our Winged Victory'.

Because it was New Year's Eve and all his thoughts were focussed on 1941, Hitler permitted himself a rare glass of champagne. On impulse he approached the huge picture window of the main salon. He signalled to a servant, and the window slid soundlessly from sight. For some time the Führer stood with glass raised, looking out into the night, staring eastward towards invisible sights: the snow-capped Carpathian mountains and the territory of the Ukraine. The most triumphant year of his life was behind him.

Beyond lay the unknown.

ACKNOWLEDGEMENTS

This narrative of 1940 derives in part from the recollections of several hundred eye-witnesses of events, and in part from records and archive repositories in the United States and six European countries. Those participants whose testimonies I have used is hereby gratefully acknowledged; the details of their individual contributions are listed in the appropriate sections of the source apparatus.

I have to thank Victor Gondos, Jr, Elmer O. Parker and John E. Taylor, of the National Archives and Records Services, Washington, D.C., for furnishing valuable microfilms, and most particularly, Mrs Kathie Nicastro, of the Diplomatic Branch, National Archives, for help in tracing the despatches of individual ambassadors and ministers. My thanks is also due to Lieut.-Col. Asbury H. Jackson, Lieut.-Col. Carl W. Ivins, and Major William A. Hintze, of the U.S. Army Historical Division, Karlsruhe, Germany, for the chance to study several unpublished monographs, and for a number of valuable introductions. Equally I owe a special debt to Professor Gordon Prange, of the University of Maryland, and to CWO Katherine V. Dillon for background guidance on the events preceding Pearl Harbour.

In Germany, Professor Dr Jürgen Rohwer, of the Bibliothek für Zeitgeschichte, Stuttgart, was of inestimable help in gaining fresh perspectives on the Battle of the Atlantic. I must also acknowledge the kindness of *Generalleutnant* Panitzki, *Briggade-general* Rudolph Jennett, *Oberstleutnant* Technau and Dr Lupke, for the long-standing loan of Luftwaffe records held by the former Führungsakademie, Hamburg, and of General a.D. Paul Deichmann, Werner Andres, Hans-Joachim Jabs, Robert Kowalewski and Hans Ring in providing both manuscripts and introductions. In France, similar help was most generously accorded by the late Professor Hervé Cras, of the Service Historique de La Marine, and M. Henri Michel, of the Comité d'Histoire de la Deuxième Guerre Mondiale. Poth for the original material that they indicated and for useful interpretations of vexed questions, I am likewise indebted to archivists and officials in the following countries: *Denmark:* Colonel Prince Georg of Denmark, Dr Jørgen H. Barfods, of the Museet fur Danmarks Frihedskamp, Copenhagen, Dr Jørgen Haestrup, of the University of Odense and Bjarne Maurer. *Netherlands:* Dr Louis De Jong, of the Rijksinstituut voor Oorlogsdocumentatie, Amsterdam and Colonel W. Epke. *Norway:* Lieut.-Col. N. Borchgrevink, of Forsvarets Krigshistoriske Avdeling, Oslo and Lieut.-Col. Jørgen Mørtvedt.

British archives for this period proved singularly revealing, and for permission to study, and in some cases to quote from, records in their keeping, I am grateful to the following: Corelli Barnett and Mrs Patricia Bradford, Churchill College, Cambridge; Dr G. M. Bayliss, Keeper, Department of Printed Books, Imperial War Museum and Mr T. C. Charman; Dr B. S. Benedikz, Head of Special Collections, University Library, Birmingham; Maurice Bond, Clerk of the Records, House of Lords and Dr A. J. P. Taylor; Sir Norman Chester, Nuffield College, Oxford; Dr Felix Holt, Kent County Archivist, Maidstone; the National Maritime Museum; the Public Record Office; Angela Raspin, British Library of Political and Economic Science (London School of Economics); Robert Shackleton, Bodley's Librarian, Oxford; the University of Sussex (Mass-Observation Archive), in particular Professor David Pocock and Dorothy Wainwright.

All writers in this field are well aware that the documentation and literature of 1940, have now grown beyond all possibility of total coverage. That I have been able to study even a fraction of it has been largely due to a loyal band of researchers and translators.

Hildegard Anderson once again covered every phase of my American research meticulously, and in England her efforts were matched by the pioneer investigations of Pamela Colman in many university archives, the long hours spent by both Joan St George Saunders and Alexandra Lawrence in the Public Record Office, and by the valuable translations of Elly Beintema, Inga Forgan and Eva Travers. A special debt is here acknowledged to Margaret Duff, who tackled assignments as diverse as interviewing Coventry blitz survivors and synthesising French secondary sources and whose final marathon typing stint enabled the manuscript to be delivered on time.

The whole daunting project was first broached by my American publisher, James O'Shea Wade, in the reassuring setting of the cocktail lounge in the Algonquin Hotel, New York, and I have to thank both him and my English publisher, Christopher Sinclair-Stevenson, for waiting so long and so patiently for the final draft, as well as Roger Machell for his invaluable editorial counsel. During that time, also, my agents in London and New York, Graham Watson and John Cushman, offered moral support and solid counsel; Joe and Christine Garner came up with secretarial help whenever it was needed, and Jill Beck, as always, oversaw an impeccable final typescript. In addition I must thank the staffs of the Library of Congress, the British Library, the London Library and the Wiener Library for their unfailing help and courtesy.

The heaviest burden fell on my wife, who not only researched, typed and collated as devotedly as she has always done in the twenty-five years leading up to our silver wedding, but miraculously contrived to nurse me back to health following a prolonged bout of sickness when the manuscript was almost due. Whatever is of value between these covers is in essence due to her inspiration.

SOURCE APPARATUS

Chapter One: 'A Shabby And Dangerous Place'
Background on Roosevelt's 'State of the Nation' speech and American involvement is from Baruch, Burns, *Lion and the Fox* (hereafter Burns, *Lion*), Kenneth Davis, Langer and Gleason, *The Challenge of Isolation* (hereafter, Langer, *Challenge*), Long and Sherwood. The Miami scene is from *Time*, issues of 15 January and 19 February. Lothian's correspondence with Chatfield is in the Chatfield Papers, CHT/6/1–5.

The number from *Lights Out*, 'I didn't really never ought 'ave went' was written by Jack Warner and sung by Doris Hare.

For France, see Beaufre, Boothe, Fabre-Luce, Fonvielle-Alquier and Worth. For Germany, see Bayles, Shirer's Diary and Kirk's Telegram 1727 to the State Department, 24 January. For Britain, see Busch, Brittain, Calder, Kenneth Clark, Lampe's *Last Ditch* and Laurence Thompson. Britain's peace-wish is in Mass Observation Report No 164, Morale. The peers' memorandum to Chamberlain is in NC 7/11/33/1–26D (Misc. Correspondence). The armaments allegation is File NC 8/29/1–8/31/19 (Armaments Scandal).

The Maginot Line mentality is based on an interview with Count René de Chambrun (who also contributed material to Chapters III, IV, V, VI, VIII and X) and on books by Barlone, Chapman, Cot, de Bosmelet, Draper, Horne and Shirer, *Third Republic*. B.E.F. material (and in Chapters III and IV) is from interviews with Mr and Mrs William J. Hersey. The Reinberger incident is from Bartz, supported by Irving's *Luftwaffe*. For Finland (and in Chapter II), see Auren, Cowles, Langdon-Davies, Luukkanen, Mannerheim, Paasikivi, Soloviev, Stowe, Tanner, Upton and Wuorinen. Mannerheim's declaration is from *Time*, 5 February.

The Kaiser is from *Time*, 12 February. Mussolini's advice is quoted by Payne. Roosevelt's brush with the AYC is in Lash, *Eleanor and Franklin*. U.S. waverings over Finland are from Langer, *Challenge*. *Altmark* material is based on an interview with Cdr. Bradwell Turner, R.N., A. V. Alexander's papers, Dalton's diary entries for 15 April and 2 May, and books by Foley, Jackson and Frischauer and Vian. The Göbbels comment is from Bölcke.

Chapter Two: 'The Position of Small Nations . . . Is Clarified'
The finale of the Finnish war (and further material in Chapter V) is based on an interview with Erik Seidenfaden. Roosevelt's letter to Chamberlain is from the Chamberlain Papers, NC 7/11/33/1–26D, 14 February. For 'Operation Wilfred', see Ash, Ironside and Kennedy. Lothian's reservations are CAB/65/WM 50(40); Daladier's from WM 80(40). The operational plan forms part of Chamberlain's file NC/8–35, Norway Debates. Edwards's objection is quoted by Roskill, *Churchill and the Admirals*.

Gandhi and Bose (and also in Chapter VI) derive from White's Telegrams to the State Department, Nos 1426, 1441, 1459 and 1488, and from books by Ayer, Bose, Kurti, Roy and Toye. Material on the Norwegian scene (and further details in Chapters V, VI, VIII, IX and X) is based on an interview with Mrs Polly (Peabody) Drysdale, and supplemented by her book. Denmark's fall is based on Gudme and Telford Taylor's *Conquest*; the invasion of Norway on accounts by Dik Lehmkuhl and Stowe. Narvik material comes from an interview by Theodor Broch, who further supplied information used in Chapters V, VI, IX and X. For Quisling, see Hewins, Knudsen and Vogt. Hauge's trek is from his account, *Odds Against Norway.* For the British débâcle in Norway, see Ash, Connell, Derry and the appropriate regimental histories.

Chapter Three: 'This War Is Sheer Madness'
The Chamberlain debate (and subsequent attempts to cement a deal between the parties) is based on information supplied to the author by Sir Martin Lindsay of Downhill, on Dalton's diary entries for 8, 9, 12 and 16 May, Euan Wallace's diary for 8 May, and published accounts by Amery, Blythe, Channon, Donoughue, Duff Cooper, Macmillan, Mosley (*Backs To the Wall*), Nicolson, Spear, Tree and Francis Williams. Gilbert and Gott describe the ousting of Sir Horace Wilson.

Churchill's working methods were described in interviews with Det.-Supt. Walter Thompson and Mrs Mary (Shearburn) Thompson (who also supplied material for the conclusion of Chapter IV). Other sources were Dalton's diary entries for 29 August and 3 September, Wallace's diary for 11 May, and accounts by Cadogan, Colville, Kennedy, Mark and Reith. Churchill's letter to Chamberlain is in File NC 7/9/59–93 (Churchill Correspondence). Beaverbrook's methods emerge from the Beaverbrook Papers (File D338, letter of 26 August) and from books by Farrer, Maisky, A. J. P. Taylor and Kenneth Young. Churchill's 'muddle and scandal' comment is from the Sinclair Papers (AIR 19/162/1a). The Beaverbrook midnight meeting is from Lockhart.

Accounts of the French campaign (and in Chapters IV and V) are based on works by Allard, Barber, Bardoux, Baudouin, Beaufre, Bell, Bertrand, Bloch, Bois, Chapman, de Chézal, Gamelin, Gontatut-Biron, Guderian, Horne, Janon, Jardin, Macksey, Reynaud, Ruby, Soubiran, Spears, Waterfield, Weygand and Williams (*Ides*). Gavoille's experiences are from Mason's *Luftwaffe*.

Dutch material, here and in Chapter VI, is in part based on an interview with Mrs Ida (Van de Criendt) Oxenaar, and on accounts in Boothe, *Dagboek*, De Jong, Douglas of Kirtleside, Maass, Strijdbos, Van Kleffens, Van Someren and Wheeler-Bennett's *George VI*. For Rotterdam, see Bekker.

Roosevelt's dilemma is outlined by Baruch, Berle, Blum, Davis and Lindley, Hull, Ickes, Langer, *Challenge*, and Sherwood. Pétain's farewell to Spain is from Crozier's *Franco*. Sikorski's meeting with Weygand is from Dalton's diary entry of 25 December. Hitler's euphoria is from Ansel. The British Cabinet's mooted deal with Mussolini is based on Chamberlain's diary entry for 25 May (NC 2/24a) and on CAB 65/13/WM 40, 142nd Conclusions, Confidential Annex.

Chapter Four: 'Are We Building Golden Bridges for the British?'
Based in part on interviews with Maj.-Gen. Sir Allan Adair, Lt.-Col. Geoffrey Anstee, Thomas Benstead, Herbert C. Bidle, Thomas Blackledge, Gen. Günther Blumentritt, Lord Bridgeman, Field-Marshal Lord Alanbrooke, Capt. Eric Bush, R.N., Percy Case, Cdr. Harold Conway, R.N., Robert Copeman, Lt.-Cdr. Ian Cox, R.N., Gen. Paul Deichmann, Victor de Mauny, M. Jean Demoy, *Oberst* Oscar Dinort, *Oberst* Gerhard Engel, Hugh Fisher, Sidney Garner, Amy Goodrich, Lt.-Gen. Sir George Gordon-Lennox, Capt. Renfrew Gotto, R.N., Sidney Grainger, *Generaloberst* Franz Halder, Capt. Harold Henderson, R.N., Cyril Huddleston, Charles Jackson, Capitaine de Frégate François Kerneis, Bernard Lockey, Lt.-Col. Jack Lotinga, Haydn Mathias, Field-Marshal Lord Montgomery, the late Earl of Munster, Thomas Nicholls, M. Eugene Pauchot, Walter Perrior, Lt.-Gen. Henry Pownall, Fred Reynard, Brig. Eric Rippingille, Gen. Hans von Salmuth, Bill Searle, Gen. Hans Seidemann, Sidney Mason Springgay, Col. Stanton Starkey, Capt. James Stopford, R.N., *Oberst* Gustave Streve, Admiral Sir William Tennant, Admiral de Toulouse-Lautrec, Wilfred Pym Trotter, Lt.-Col. G. F. Turner, Cdr. Harold Unwin, R.N., Wilfred Walters, Capt. Eric Wharton, R.N., Fred Williams and James Wilson.

Hitler's halting of the tanks is discussed at length in Speidel's unpublished monograph. The Admiralty's reticence in respect of the French is from Mengin. Gort's failure to inform the Cabinet of the Belgian crack-up is Dalton's diary entry for 23 July. Gort's enquiry to Keyes is from Keyes's report in the Gort Papers.

229

Chapter Five: 'Thank God We're Now Alone'
Churchill's broadcast is from Agar; Kennedy's estimate is from *Foreign Relations Of the United States* (hereafter FRUS), Vol. III, p. 37. Eden's search for 'Storm Troopers' is in CAB/65/WM 170(40). Chamberlain's meeting with Dill is NC 2/21a, diary entry for 1 July. Eden's York conference is from Hudson's diary. The transfer of Britons to Canada is discussed in Longmate's *Fallen*.

Comments on British morale and incipient Hitler-worship are from the following Mass Observation Reports: Attitudes to Hitler; Science, Morale and Propaganda; Defeatism (dated 19 June); A New Attitude to the Problems of Civilian Morale (dated 12 June), and The New Leadership.

Material on Mölders (and in Chapters VI, VII, VIII, IX and X) is drawn from Forell, and from interviews with Hans-Heinrich Brustellin, Hartmann Grasser, Erich Hohagen, Erich Kircheis, Gunther Matthes and Victor Mölders.

For the end in Norway, see Ash, Connell and Lapie. The flight from Paris follows accounts by Barber, Beaufre, Boothe, Chapman, Dorothy Clarke, de Bosmelet, Fontaine, Habe, Koestler, Mackworth, Paxton, Salesse and Vidalenc. Mussolini's declaration of war is based on interviews with Gen. Giacomo Carboni, Count Dino Grandi, Count Luca Pietromarchi and the Marchesa Myriam Petacci, supplemented by the accounts of Badoglio and Favagrossa. Aosta's meeting with Lady Loraine is in CAB/65/WM 87(40). 'Duplicity' is Dalton's diary entry for 10 June. For growing U.S. involvement, see Burns, *Lion*, Chadwin and Compton. The German occupation of Paris is documented by Barber, Blumentritt, Corday and Langeron. The Queen's speech is from Litynski. The liquor-train incident is from Habe.

The text of Churchill's undelivered broadcast is in the Alexander Papers (AVAR 13/3). His comment to Morrison is from Morrison's Papers, letter of 5 July. Facets of Hitler at Compiègne and in Paris are from Andreas-Friedrich, Bopp and Huss. Ley's fantasy is from Orlow. German euphoria is from Moen, Pruller and Van Duren.

Ismay's invasion countermeasures are in CAB/65/WM 133(40). The inception of the Home Guard is from CAB/65/WM 130(40). The first invasion precautions are from Wallace's diary entry of 6 June, and accounts by Arnold, Horner and Reith. Initial approaches to de Valera are based on Pound's letter of 4 June to Alexander (Alexander Papers); Macdonald's mission is described in CAB/65/WM 168(40) and 173(40), as well as in Chamberlain's diary entries for 18 June and 25 June. The fate of the spy Goertz is in Stephan.

The exploits of Professor R. V. Jones (continued in Chapters VII and IX) are taken from his book and supplemented by an interview which he kindly granted to the author. For British ground defences, see Wallace's diary for 2 July, CAB/65/WM 218(40) and works by Bryant, Connell and Horrocks. The Winchester spy is from Royde-Smith; alarm and despondency fines are from *Time's* 29 June issue. Churchill's plea for a Foreign Legion is in CAB/65/WM 174(40). Conditions at Huyton are in the Monckton Papers (Reports of 13th, 16th and 17th July). British xenophobia features in the following Mass Observation reports: Public Feeling About Aliens; German Bomber Down at Eype (dated 11 June); Refugees (dated 6 June). Dowding's remark is from Robert Wright.

Chapter Six: 'I am . . . the Victor Speaking In The Name Of Reason'
The Cabinet thinking that prompted Mers-el-Kebir is contained in F.O. 371/24311(2), C 7301/65/17 of 17 June and F.O. 371/2438, C 7074/5/18 of 8 June. The best overall analysis is in Bell. The Churchill-Beaverbrook encounter is from A. J. P. Taylor's *Beaverbrook*. Events at Mers-el-Kebir are documented by Sicard and Tute. Lothian's footnote is from Lash's *Roosevelt and Churchill*.

For conditions in occupied Europe, see, for France: Bopp, Corday, Galtier-Boissière, Langer, *Gamble*, Murphy and Warner. For Holland: De Graaff, Engels and Maass. For Norway: see Alan S. Milward, *The Fascist Economy in Norway*, Clarendon Press, 1972. For Belgium: see Delandsheere, Duner and Moen. Peace-feelers are in Ansel, FRUS, III, 41 (the Duke of Windsor) and Laurence Thompson.

Grew's early warnings on Japanese intentions are from his lengthy Telegram No 400 of 3 June to the State Department; further details (as in Chapter IX) are in Farago, Pelz and

230

Prange. Halifax's attitude on the Burma Road is in Hoare's Papers (TEM XIII, 12, of 8 July). For Chiang's reactions, see Crozier/Chou and White/Jacoby. Swiss and Hungarian material derives from Kimche and Listowel respectively. Carol's Rumania (as in Chapter VII) has been treated by Cretzianu, Hollingworth, St John and Waldeck. For Latin-American material, see Fernandez Artucio, Dulles, Hull, and issues of *Time* for 27 May, 24 June, 1 July and 12 August. For Vargas see, also, Caffery to the State Department, Telegram No 14 of 14 June, and FRUS, V, 46, 49.

Material on the Battle of the Atlantic (and in Chapters VII, IX and X) owes much to information from Prof. Dr Jürgen Rohwer, Flotillenadmiral Otto Kretschmer, the definitive study by Robertson and private information from John Costello and Terry Hughes. Churchill's brushes with the Air Ministry begin with his memo to Kingsley Wood (AIR 19/26/1a, dated 27-3-39) and continues with his correspondence with Sinclair (AIR 19/162/1a of 3 June, 6a-6b of 5 June, 12a of 18 July and 18a of 9 August). Lindemann's memo is from the Cherwell Papers, dated 10 July. Churchill's letter to Woolton is from the latter's papers, dated 12 July; Woolton's reply is dated 13 July. For the changing face of London, see the Mass Observation Report on Fashion, and books by Bilainkin, Lee, Panter-Downes and Sansom. Hoare's complaint to Beaverbrook is from the Templewood Papers, dated 6 June. For the inception of Operation Barbarossa, see Ansel, Cecil, Leach, Lossberg, Speer and Warlimont.

Chapter Seven: 'The Whole Bloody World's On Fire'
Battle of Britain material, both British and German (and in Chapter VIII) is based primarily on interviews with Michael Appleby, Vera Arlett, Patrick Barthropp, Victor Bauer, Hans-Ekkehard Bob, Bryan Considine, Michael Constable-Maxwell, Michael Cooper-Slipper, Roland Dibnah, G./Capt. Eric Douglas-Jones, Air Chief Marshal Lord Dowding, Johannes Fink, Ludwig Franzisket, Gen. Adolf Galland, G./Capt. Denys Gillam, Marshal of the R.A.F. Sir John Grandy, Hans "Assi" Hahn, Peter Hairs, Gen. Martin Harlinghausen, Hans-Joachim Helbig, Gen. Max Ibel, Hans-Joachim Jabs, Bryan Kingcome, G./Capt. Thomas Lang, G./Capt. James McComb, Eduard Neumann, Gen. Theo Osterkamp, G./Capt. Robert Oxspring, Air Chief Marshal Sir Keith Park, Dietrich Peltz, G./Capt. Norman Ryder, Raymond Sellers, Eva Smithers, Gen. Johannes Steinhoff, Paddy Stephenson, Henning Strümpell, Mrs Johanna Thompson, Air Cdr. John Thompson, Gen. Hannes Trautloft, W/Cdr. Robert Stanford Tuck, Dudley Williams, Air Vice Marshal John Worrall and W/Cdr. Robert Wright. Peenemunde details are from David Irving's *The Mare's Nest*, William Kimber, 1964. Otto Begus appears in Comer Clarke.

The onset of the London Blitz (and further details in Chapters VIII, IX and X) is based on interviews with Chief Fire Officer Geoffrey Vaughan Blackstone, and accounts by Bryher, Calder, Harrisson, Lambert, Lewey, Matthews, Barbara Nixon, Robb and Sansom,

Chapter Eight: 'The Way Across The Channel Will Soon Be Clear'
Details of Britain's petroleum warfare capability are from the Lindemann Papers. Eyewitness accounts of the night of 7 September came from interviews with Alfred Brind, W/Cdr. D. H. Clarke, Reg Cooke, Mrs Barbara (Hornsey) Cunningham, Chief Fire Officer Thomas Goodman, Mrs Lillian Ivory and Alfred Neill. Churchill's letter to Anne Chamberlain is dated 20 September (File NC 7/9/59–93). Britain's underground fighters are described in Lampe's *Last Ditch*.

City of Benares details are based on information supplied by Derek Bech, Mrs Bess (Walder) Cummings, Phyllis and Digby Morton, Mrs Barbara (Bech) Partridge, Paul Shearing, Mrs Lillian Towns, Louis Walder, Mrs Beth (Cummings) Williams and Mrs Sonia (Bech) Williams. Further valuable documentation was supplied by CPO Arthur Bartle of H.M.S. *Sussex*. Mary Cornish's story is in Huxley.

The birth of resistance in Europe comes from background supplied by Dr Jørgen H. Barfods, Dr Louis De Jong, Dr Jørgen Haestrup, Bjarne Maurer, M. Henri Michel and Mrs Ida Oxenaar and on published works by De Graaff, Delandsheere, Engels, Foot, Gudme, Gunderssen, Hendrikse, Michel, Myklebost and Riess.

231

Chapter Nine: 'Dead Lucky If We See The Sun Again'
Churchill's letter to Chamberlain is in File NC 7/9/59–93, dated 24 September. His comment to Ismay is recorded by Lee. Woolton's diary entries for 11 October and 30 November record his impressions of Queen Elizabeth the Queen Mother and the British will to resist. Gray's interviews with Walshe and de Valera are summarised in his Annexure No 1, Despatch No 96 to the State Department, dated 7 November. Franco's approach to Roosevelt is Dalton's diary entry for 7 October. The section on the Coventry blitz is based mainly on interviews with John Barnes, Wilfred Bevan, Bert Bucknall, Kathleen Burrell, Mrs Emily (Caskie) Fairclough, William H. Davies, Albert Fearn, Mrs Kathleen Fensom, Dr Henry Gregg, Ernest Hazlewood, Evelyn and William Heynes, Alfred Holt, Herbert Moore, John Poole, Mrs Dorothy Prideaux, Mrs Jessie Pykett, Josephine Salond, Leslie Sidwell, Mrs Mollie Simpson, Sydney Taylor, Dr Charles Turner, Leslie Wale and John Watkin. The hitherto anonymous account held by the Imperial War Museum (reference K. 6. 066) was written, vide the *Coventry Evening Telegraph* of 14 November, 1950, by Police-Constable W. G. Lambert. The controversy as to whether Churchill had prior warning of the raid is well summarised in Longmate's *Air Raid*.

Chapter Ten: 'For Me You Shall Always be Greatheart'
Roosevelt's cruise and his speech of 29 December are amply detailed by Burns, *Soldier*, Kenneth Davis, Langer, *Challenge*, and Sherwood. Knox's tribute is from Lash, *Roosevelt and Churchill*. Roosevelt's confidential talk with Lothian is Dalton's diary entry for 24 October. For Britain's parlous food situation, see the Beaverbrook Papers, File D 337, Correspondence with Woolton, letter of 30 December).

Hitler's New Year's Eve is recorded by Schirach. His Christmas card featured in *Time*'s issue of 30 December.

232

BIBLIOGRAPHY

Acart, Captain, *On s'est battu dans le ciel*, Algiers: Arthaud, 1942.
Acevedo, C. de, *A notre corps défendant*, Paris: Dupont, 1945.
Addison, Paul, *The Road to 1945*, London: Jonathan Cape, 1975.
Agar, Herbert, *Britain Alone*, London: The Bodley Head, 1972.
Ailesbury, Marquis of, *I Walked Alone*, London: Routledge & Kegan Paul, 1950.
Albert-Sorel, Jean, *Le Calvaire*, Paris: Juilliard, 1944.
Aleramo, Sibilla, *Dal Mio Diario*, Rome: Tumminelli, 1945.
Alfieri, Dino, *Dictators Face To Face* (trans. David Moore), London: Elek Books, 1954.
Allan, James, *No Citation*, London: Angus & Robertson, 1955.
Allard, Paul, *La Verité sur l'affaire Corap*, Paris: Les Éditions de Frappe, 1941.
Allen, F. L. (with Agnes Rogers), *I Remember Distinctly*, New York: Harper, 1947.
Allingham, Margery, *The Oaken Heart*, London: Michael Joseph, 1941.
Amery, Leopold, *The Unforgiving Years*, London: Hutchinson, 1955.
Amouroux, Henri, *La Vie des Français sous l'Occupation*, Paris: Fayard, 1977.
Andenaes, Johannes, *Svek Och motstånd under Norges ockupationsår*, Stockholm: Bonnier, 1950.
Andersson, Ingvar, *A History of Sweden*, London: Weidenfeld & Nicolson, 1956.
Andreas-Friedrich, Ruth, *Berlin Underground* (trans. Barrows Mussey), London: Latimer House, 1948.
Ansel, Walter, *Hitler Confronts England*, Durham, N.C.: Duke University Press, 1960.
Archer, Laird, *Balkan Journal*, New York: W. W. Norton, 1944.
Arenstam, Arved, *Tapestry of a Debacle*, London: Constable, 1942.
Armstrong, Warren, *The Red Duster at War*, London: Victor Gollancz, 1942.
Arnold, Ralph, *A Very Quiet War*, London: Rupert Hart-Davis, 1962.
Aron, Robert, *Le Piège ou nous a pris l'Histoire*, Paris: Michel, 1950.
Ash, Bernard, *Norway 1940*, London: Cassell, 1964.
Astley, Joan Bright, *The Inner Circle*, London: Hutchinson, 1971.
Auren, Sven, *Signature Tune: Conditions in Europe* (trans. Evelyn Ramsden), London: Hammond & Hammond, 1943.
Ayer, S. A., *Unto Him a Witness: The Subhas Chandra Bose Story*, Bombay: Thacker, 1951.
Badoglio, Marshal Pietro, *Italy in the Second World War* (trans. Muriel Currey), London: O.U.P., 1948.
Baldwin, Hanson W., *The Crucial Years, 1939–41*, London: Weidenfeld, 1977.
Ba Maw, *Break Through in Burma: Memoirs of a Revolution, 1939–46*, New Haven: Yale University Press, 1968.
Banks, Sir Donald, *Flame Over Britain*, London: Sampson Low, 1948.
Barber, Noel, *The Week France Fell*, London: Macmillan, 1976.
Bardoux, Jean, *Journal d'un Témoin de la Troisième . . . 1940*, Paris: Fayard, 1957.
Barlone, D., *A French Officer's Diary*, Cambridge: Cambridge University Press, 1942.
Bartz, Karl, *Swastika in the Air* (trans. Edward Fitzgerald), London: William Kimber, 1956.
Baruch, Bernard, *The Public Years*, London: Odhams Press, 1960.
Baudouin, Paul, *Private Diaries* (trans. Sir Charles Petrie), London: Eyre & Spottiswoode, 1948.
Bauer, Eddy, *Der Panzerkrieg*, Bonn: Bodo Zimmermann, 1965.

Bayles, William, *Postmarked Berlin*, London: Jarrolds, 1942; *Wartime Germany*, in *Life*, New York, 7 January, 1940; *Hitler's Salesman*, in *Life*, New York, 11 March, 1940; *Raeder The Raider*, in *Life*, New York, 29 April, 1940.

Beard, Charles A., *President Roosevelt and the Coming of War*, New Haven: Yale University Press, 1948.

Beaton, Cecil, *The Years Between*, London: Weidenfeld & Nicolson, 1965.

Beaufre, General André, *1940: The Fall of France* (trans. Desmond Flower), London: Cassell, 1967.

Beesly, Patrick, *Very Special Intelligence*, London: Hamish Hamilton, 1977.

Bekker, Caius, *The Luftwaffe War Diaries* (trans. Frank Ziegler), London: Macdonald, 1966.

Bell, P. M. H., *A Certain Eventuality*, London: Saxon House, 1974.

Belloc-Lowndes, Marie, *Diaries and Letters* (ed. Susan Lowndes), London: Chatto & Windus, 1971.

Bénoist-Mechin, J., *Sixty Days That Shook the World* (trans. Peter Wiles), London: Jonathan Cape, 1963.

Bentwich, Norman, *A Wanderer in War*, London: Victor Gollancz, 1946.

Berle, Adolf A., *Navigating the Rapids* (ed. Beatrice Bishop Berle & Travis Beal Jacobs), New York: Harcourt Brace Jovanovich, 1973.

Bernanos, Georges, *Les Enfante Humiliés*, Paris: Gallimard, 1949.

Bertrand, Gustave, *Enigma*, Paris: Plon, 1972.

Bethouart, General Emile, *Cinq années d'espérance*, Paris: Plon, 1968.

Bidou, Henri, *Une Bataille de 45 Jours*, Pointe-à-Pitre: Imprimerie d'Entr'aide, 1941; *La Bataille de France*, Geneva: Éditions du Milieu du Monde, 1941.

Bielenberg, Christabel, *The Past is Myself*, London: Chatto & Windus, 1968.

Bigham, Hon. Clive (Viscount Mersey), *Journal and Memoirs*, London: John Murray, 1952.

Bilainkin, George, *Diary of a Diplomatic Correspondent*, London: Allen & Unwin, 1942.

Billingham, Mrs Anthony, *America's First Two Years*, London: John Murray/The Pilot Press, 1942.

Birkenhead, Earl of, *Halifax: The Life of Lord Halifax*, London: Hamish Hamilton, 1965; *Walter Monckton*, London: Weidenfeld & Nicolson, 1969.

Blackstone, Geoffrey, *A History of the British Fire Service*, London: Routledge & Kegan Paul, 1957.

Bloch, Marc, *The Strange Defeat* (trans. Gerard Hopkins), London: O.U.P., 1949.

Bloch-Michel, Jean, *Les Grandes Circonstances*, Paris: Gallimard, 1949.

Blum, John Morton, *Years of Urgency, 1939–41: From the Morgenthau Diaries*, Boston: Houghton Mifflin, 1965.

Blum, Léon, *Mémoires*, Paris: Michel, 1955.

Blumenstritt, General Günther, *Rundstedt, the Soldier and the Man* (trans. Cuthbert Reavely), London: Odhams Press, 1952.

Blythe, Ronald, *The Age of Illusion*, London: Hamish Hamilton, 1963.

Boas, J. H., *Religious Resistance in Holland*, London: George Allen & Unwin, 1945.

Bodley, Ronald, *Flight into Portugal*, London: Jarrolds, 1941.

Bois, Elie J., *Truth on the Tragedy of France* (trans. W. Scarlyn Wilson), London: Hodder & Stoughton, 1941.

Bölcke, Willi, *The Secret Conferences of Dr Goebbels, 1939–43* (trans. E. Osers), London: Weidenfeld & Nicolson, 1970.

Bolitho, Hector, *War in the Strand*, London: Eyre & Spottiswoode, 1942.

Bond, Brian, *Liddell Hart: A Study of his Military Thought*, London: Cassell, 1977.

Bonnet, Georges, *Dans la Tourmente*, Paris: Fayard, 1971.

Boothe, Clare, *European Spring*, London: Hamish Hamilton, 1941; '*Der Tag*' *in Brussels*, in *Life*, New York, 19 May, 1940; *Europe in the Spring* in *Life*, New York, 29 July, 1940.

Boothby, Lord, *My Yesterday, Your Tomorrow*, London: Hutchinson, 1962.

Bopp, Marie-Joseph, *L'Alsace sous l'Occupation allemande*, Le Puy: Éditions Xavier Mappus, 1945.

Bose, Subhas Chandra, *An Indian Pilgrim*, London: Asia Publishing House, 1965; *The*

Indian Struggle, London: Asia Publishing House, 1964; *Crossroads*, London: Asia Publishing House, 1962.

Bourdan, Pierre, *Carnets des Jour d'Attente*, Paris: Trémois, 1945; *Carnet de Retour avec la Division Leclerc*, Paris: Trémois, 1945.

Bourget, Pierre, *Histoires secrètes de l'Occupation de Paris*, Vol. I, Paris: Hachette, 1970.

Bourne, Richard, *Getulio Vargas of Brazil*, Maidstone, Kent: C. Knight, 1975.

Bouthillier, Yves, *Le Drame de Vichy*, Vol. I, Paris: Plon, 1950.

Brasillach, Robert, *Journal d'un Homme Occupé, 1940–41*, Paris: Au Club de l'Honnête Homme, 1963.

Briggs, Susan, *Keep Smiling Through*, London: Weidenfeld & Nicolson, 1975.

Brittain, Vera, *England's Hour*, London: Macmillan, 1941.

Broch, Theodor, *The Mountains Wait*, London: Michael Joseph, 1943.

Brusselmans, Anna, *Rendezvous 127* (trans. Denis Hornsey), London: Ernest Benn, 1954.

Bryans, John Lonsdale, *Blind Victory*, London: Skeffington, 1951.

Bryant, Sir Arthur, *The Turn of the Tide: the Alanbrooke Diaries*, London: William Collins, 1957.

Bryant, Rear-Admiral Ben, *One Man Band*, London: William Kimber, 1958.

Bryher, Winifred, *The Days of Mars*, London: Calder & Boyars, 1972.

Brzeska, Maria, *Through a Woman's Eyes*, London: Max Love, 1944.

Bullitt, William C., *For the President: Personal and Secret* (ed. Orville H. Bullitt), London: André Deutsch, 1973.

Bullock, Alan, *The Life and Times of Ernest Bevin*, Vol. I, London: Heinemann, 1967; *Hitler*, London: Odhams Books, Edn. of 1965.

Burns, James McGregor, *Roosevelt: The Lion and the Fox*, London: Secker & Warburg, 1957; *Roosevelt: The Soldier of Freedom, 1940–46*, London: Weidenfeld & Nicolson, 1971.

Busch, Noel, *England at War*, in *Life*, New York, 1 January, 1940; *Little Lord Beaverbrook*, in *Life*, New York, 5 August, 1940.

Butler, Ewan, *Amateur Agent*, London: George Harrap, 1962.

Butler, Lord, *The Art of the Possible*, London: Hamish Hamilton, 1962.

Byrnes, James F., *All in One Lifetime*, London: Museum Press, 1958.

Cabanis, José, *Les Profondes Années*, Paris: Gallimard, 1976.

Cadogan, Sir Alexander, *Diaries, 1938–48* (ed. David Dilks), London: Cassell, 1971.

Calder, Angus, *The People's War*, London: Jonathan Cape, 1969.

Calvocoressi, Peter, *The Ultra Secrets of Station X*, in *The Sunday Times Weekly Review*, London: 24 November, 1974;

Calvocoressi, Peter and Wint, Guy, *Total War*, London: Allen Lane, 1972.

Cammaerts, Emile, *The Prisoner at Laeken*, London: The Cresset Press, 1941.

Carcopino, Jerome, *Souvenirs de Sept Ans*, Paris: Flammarion, 1953.

Carroll, Joseph T., *Ireland in the War Years*, New York: Crane Russak, 1975.

Cartwright, Reginald, *Mercy and Murder*, London: Iliffe, 1941.

Casey, Lord, *Personal Experience*, London: Constable, 1962.

Cecil, Robert, *Hitler's Decision to Invade Russia*, London: Davis-Poynter, 1975.

Cervi, Mario, *The Hollow Legions* (trans. Eric Mosbacher), London: Chatto & Windus, 1971.

Chadwin, Mark, *The Hawks of World War II*, Chapel Hill, N.C.: University of North Carolina Press, 1968.

Chamberlin, Eric, *Life in Wartime Britain*, London: Batsford, 1972.

Chambrun, René de, *I Saw France Fall*, London: Jarrolds, 1941.

Chandos, Lord, *Memoirs*, London: The Bodley Head, 1962.

Channon, Sir Henry, *Chips, The Diaries of Sir Henry Channon* (ed. Robert Rhodes James), London: Weidenfeld & Nicolson, 1967.

Channon, Howard, *Mid-Ocean Massacre: The Sinking of the City of Benares*, in *The Liverpool Echo and Evening Express*, 13–21 September, 1965.

Chapman, Guy, *Why France Collapsed*, London: Cassell, 1968.

Charles-Roux, F., *Cinq Mois tragiques*, Paris: Plon, 1949.

Chatterton, E. Keble, *The Royal Navy*, Vol. I, London: Hutchinson, 1941.

Chézal, Guy de, *En Auto-Mitrailleuse à travers les Batailles de Mai, 1940*, Paris: Plon, 1941.
Christophersen, Major-General Bjorn, *Krigen i Norge 1940*, Oslo: Forsvarets krigshistoriske avedling, 1965.
Churchill, Sir Winston S., *The Second World War*, Vol. I, *The Gathering Storm*, Vol. II, *Their Finest Hour*, London: Cassell, 1948-9.
Ciano, Galeazzo, *The Ciano Diaries, 1939-43* (ed. Hugh Gibson), New York: Doubleday, 1946.
Ciano-Mussolini, Edda, *My Truth* (trans. Eileen Finletter), London: Weidenfeld & Nicolson, 1977.
Citrine, Sir Walter, *My American Diary*, London: George Routledge, 1941.
City We Loved, The, Coventry: Three Spires Publications, 1942.
Claire, (pseud.), *Escape From France*, London: Robert Hale, 1941.
Clark, Douglas, *Three Days to Catastrophe*, London: Hammond & Hammond, 1966.
Clark, Kenneth, *The Other Half*, London: John Murray, 1978.
Clarke, Comer, *If The Nazis had Come*, London: World Distributors, 1962.
Clarke, Dorothy, *No Time To Weep*, London: Robert Hale, 1942.
Clegg, Howard, *A Canuck in England*, London: George Harrap, 1942.
Clitheroe, Rev. G. W., *Coventry Under Fire*, Gloucester: British Publishing Co., 1942.
Clonmore, William, (The Earl of Wicklow), *Fireside Fusilier*, London: Hollis & Carter, 1958.
Cole, Hubert, *Laval*, London: Heinemann, 1963.
Cole, J. A., *Lord Haw-Haw – and William Joyce*, London: Faber & Faber, 1964.
Collier, Basil, *The Defence of the United Kingdom*, London: H.M.S.O., 1957.
Collier, Richard, *The Sands of Dunkirk*, London: Collins, 1961; *Eagle Day*, London: Hodder & Stoughton, 1966; *Duce!* London: Collins, 1971.
Collins, Sarah, *The Alien Years*, London: Hodder & Stoughton, 1949.
Colville, Sir John, *Footprints in Time*, London: William Collins, 1976.
Colvin, Ian, *The Chamberlain Cabinet*, London: Victor Gollancz, 1971.
Compton, James V., *The Swastika and the Eagle*, London: The Bodley Head, 1968.
Connell, John, *Auchinleck*, London: Cassell, 1959.
Constable, Trevor and Toliver, Raymond, *Horrido!* London: Arthur Barker, 1968.
Cooper, Alfred Duff, *Old Men Forget*, London: Rupert Hart-Davis, 1953.
Cooper, Diana, *Trumpets from the Steep*, London: Rupert Hart-Davis, 1960.
Corday, Pauline, *J'ai vécu dans Paris occupé*, Montreal: Éditions de l'Arbre, 1943.
Cortvriend, V. V., *Isolated Island*, Guernsey, C.I.: Guernsey Star and Gazette, 1947.
Cosgrave, Patrick, *Churchill At War*, Vol. I, London: Collins, 1974.
Costello, John and Hughes, Terry, *The Battle of the Atlantic*, London: William Collins, 1977.
Cot, Pierre, *Triumph of Treason* (trans. Sybille & Milton Crane), Chicago: Ziff-Davis, 1944.
Cowles, Virginia, *Looking for Trouble*, London: Hamish Hamilton, 1941.
Craigie, Sir Robert, *Behind the Japanese Mask*, London: Hutchinson, 1946.
Crawley, Aidan, *De Gaulle*, London: Collins, 1969.
Cretzianu, Alexandre, *The Lost Opportunity*, London: Jonathan Cape, 1957.
Cross, J. A., *Sir Samuel Hoare: A Political Biography*, London: Jonathan Cape, 1977.
Crozier, Brian, *Franco*, London: Eyre & Spottiswoode, 1967; (with Eric Chou), *The Man Who Lost China*, London: Angus & Robertson, 1977.
Crozier, William, *Off The Record* (ed. A. J. P. Taylor), London: Hutchinson, 1973.
Cruikshank, Charles, *The German Occupation of the Channel Islands*, London: Oxford University Press, 1975.
Cudahy, John, *Belgium's Leopold*, in *Life*, New York, 25 November, 1940.
Curtis, Monica, *Norway and the War*, London: Oxford University Press, 1941.
Dagboek fragmenten, 1940-45, Gravenhage: Martinus Nijhoff, 1954.
Dahl, Colonel Arne, *Med Alta Bataljon mot tyskerne*, Stockholm: Bokförlaget Natur och Kultur, 1945.
Darling, Donald, *Secret Sunday*, London: William Kimber, 1975.
Dawidowicz, Lucy S., *The War Against the Jews, 1939-45*, London: Weidenfeld & Nicolson, 1975.

236

Davis, Forrest and Lindley, Ernest K., *How War came to America*, London: George Allen & Unwin, 1943.

Davis, Kenneth S., *The American Experience of War*, London: Secker & Warburg, 1967.

De Bosmelet, Diana, *In Golden Spurs*, London: Frederick Muller, 1945.

De Graaff, F. A., *Op Leven en Dood*, Rotterdam: Brusse, 1946.

Deighton, Len, *Fighter*, London: Jonathan Cape, 1977.

De Jong, Louis, *Holland Fights the Nazis*, London: Lindsay Drummond, 1941; *The German Fifth Column in The Second World War* (trans. C. M. Geyl), London: Routledge, 1956.

Dekobra, Maurice, *Sept ans chez les Hommes libres*, Paris: Sfelt, 1946.

Delandsheere, Paul and Ooms, Alphonse, *La Belgique sous les Nazis* (4 Vols.), Brussels: L'Edition Universelle, 1946.

De Monchy, Salomon, *Twee Ambtsketens*, Arnhem: Van Loghum Slaterus, 1946; *Bezetting en bevrijding*, Den Helder: Van Stockum & Zoon, 1953.

De Polnay, Peter, *The Germans Came to Paris*, New York: Duell, Sloan & Pearce, 1943.

Derry, Thomas, *The Campaign in Norway*, London: H.M.S.O., 1952.

Deutsch, Harold C., *The Conspiracy against Hitler in the Twilight War*, Minneapolis: University of Minnesota Press, 1968.

Diary of a Staff Officer at Advance HQ, North BAFF, The, London: Methuen, 1941.

Documents on British Foreign Policy, London: H.M.S.O., 1946.

Documents on German Foreign Policy, London: H.M.S.O., 1948.

I Documenti Diplomatici Italiani, Rome: Ministero degli Esteri, 1952.

Dönitz, Admiral Karl, *Memoirs: Ten Years and Twenty Days* (trans. R. H. Stevens and David Woodward), London: Weidenfeld & Nicolson, 1951.

Donoughue, Bernard, *Herbert Morrison: Portrait of a Politician*, London: Weidenfeld & Nicolson, 1973.

Doorman, P. L. G., *Military Operations in the Netherlands*, London: George Allen & Unwin, 1944.

Douglas of Kirtleside, Lord, Marshal of the R.A.F. (with Robert Wright), *Combat and Command*, New York: Simon & Schuster, 1966.

Downing, Rupert, *If I Laugh*, London: George Harrap, 1940.

Draper, Theodore, *The Six Weeks' War*, London: Methuen, 1946.

Drawbell, James Wedgwood, *The Long Year*, London: Allan Wingate, 1958.

Drees, Dr Willem, *Van mei tot mei*, Assen: Van Gorcum, 1958.

Dubois, Edmond, *Paris sans lumière*, Lausanne: Librairie Payot, 1946.

Duhamel, Georges, *Lieu d'asile*, Paris: Mercure de France, 1945; *Chronique des Saisons Amères*, Paris: Hartmann, 1946.

Dulles, John W. F., *Vargas of Brazil*, Austin, Texas: University of Texas Press, 1967.

Duner, Paul, *A Year and a Day*, London: Lindsay Drummond, 1942.

Dunning, George, *Where Bleed the Many*, London: Elek Books, 1955.

Durand, Ralph, *Guernsey under German Rule*, London: The Guernsey Society, 1946.

Dybwad, Ejnar, *I saw the Invader*, London: The Pilot Press, 1940.

Eden, Rt. Hon. Anthony (Lord Avon), *Memoirs, Vol. II: The Reckoning*, London: Cassell, 1965.

Ehrlich, Blake, *The French Resistance*, London: Chapman & Hall, 1966.

Einzig, Paul, *In the Centre of Things*, London: Hutchinson, 1960.

Ekpenyon, E. I., *Experiences of an African Air Raid Warden*, London: The Sheldon Press, 1942.

Eliot, Major George Fielding, *France's Weygand*, in *Life*, New York: 20 May, 1940.

Ellis, Major L. F., *The War in France and Flanders, 1939–40*, London: H.M.S.O., 1953.

Eloy, Victor, *The Fight in the Forest* (trans. N. C. Hunter), London: Robert Hale, 1949.

Engels, Adriani, *Nacht over Nederland*, Utrecht: Privately printed, 1946.

Fabre-Luce, Alfred, *Journal de la France*, (2 Vols.), Geneva: Bourquin, 1946.

Farago, Ladislas, *The Game of the Foxes*, London: Hodder & Stoughton, 1972; *The Broken Seal*, London: Arthur Barker, 1967.

Farrer, David, *The Sky's the Limit*, London: Hutchinson, 1942; *G for God Almighty*, London: Weidenfeld & Nicolson, 1969.

Favagrossa, General Carlo, *Perchè perdemmo la guerra: Mussolini e la produzione bellica*, Milan: Rizzoli, 1946.
Fernandez Artucio, Hugo, *The Nazi Underground in South America*, New York: Farrer & Rinehart, 1942.
Fernet, Vice-Admiral Jean, *Aux Côtés du Maréchal Pétain*, Paris: Plon, 1953.
Fest, Joachim, *Hitler* (trans. Richard & Clara Winston), London: Weidenfeld & Nicolson, 1974.
Feuchtwanger, Lion, *The Devil in France* (trans. Phyllis Blewitt), London: Hutchinson, 1942.
Fitzgibbon, Constantine, *The Blitz*, London: Allan Wingate, 1957.
Flannery, Harry, *Assignment to Berlin*, London: Michael Joseph, 1942.
Fleming, Peter, *Invasion 1940*, London: Rupert Hart-Davis, 1957.
Foley, Thomas, *I was an Altmark Prisoner*, London: Francis Aldor, 1940.
Fontaine, Peter, *Last to Leave Paris*, London: Chaterson, 1941.
Fontes, L. and Carneiro, G., *A Face Final de Vargas*, Rio de Janeiro: O Cruzeiro, 1966.
Fonvieille-Alquier, François, *The French and the Phoney War* (trans. Edward Ashcroft), London: Tom Stacey, 1973.
Foot, M. R. D., *Resistance*, London: Eyre Methuen, 1976.
Ford, Corey, *Donovan of O.S.S.*, London: Robert Hale, 1971.
Foreign Relations of the United States (5 Vols.), Washington, D.C.: U.S. Government Printing Office, 1959–61.
Forell, Fritz von, *Mölders*, Salzburg: Sirius, 1951.
Foster, Reginald, *Dover Front*, London: Secker & Warburg, 1941.
Fourcade, Marie-Madeleine, *Noah's Ark* (trans. Kenneth Morgan), London: George Allen & Unwin, 1973.
François-Poncet, André, *Au Palais Farnese, 1938–40*, Paris: Fayard, 1961.
Frank, Wolfgang, *The Sea Wolves* (trans. Lt.-Cdr. R. D. B. Long), London: Weidenfeld & Nicolson, 1955.
Franzero, C. M., *Cinquantanni a Londra*, Turin: S.E.I., 1975.
Führer Conferences on Naval Affairs, (Vol. II), Admiralty mimeograph, Official Publications Library, British Museum.
Galland, General Adolf, *The First and the Last* (trans. Mervyn Savill), London: Methuen, 1953.
Galtier-Boissière, Jean, *Mon Journal pendant l'Occupation*, Garas: La Jeune Parque, 1944.
Gamelin, General Maurice, *Servir* (3 Vols.), Paris: Plon, 1946–47.
Gaulle, General Charles de, *The Call to Honour, 1940–42* (trans. Jonathan Griffin), London: William Collins, 1955.
Gérard-Libois, J. and Gotovich, J., *L'An 1940*, Brussels,: Crisp, 1971.
Gex Le Verrier, Madeleine, *France in Torment* (trans. Eden & Cedar Paul), London: Hamish Hamilton, 1942.
Gibson, Guy, *Enemy Coast Ahead*, London: Michael Joseph, 1946.
Gide, André, *Journal, Vol. IV* (trans. Justin O'Brien), London: Secker & Warburg, 1951.
Gilbert, Martin and Gott, Richard, *The Appeasers*, London: Weidenfeld & Nicolson, edition of 1967.
Girier, René, *Chienne de Vie*, Paris: André Martel, 1952.
Gladwyn, Cynthia, *The Paris Embassy*, London: William Collins, 1976.
Goffin, Robert, *Was Leopold a Traitor?* (trans. Marjorie Shaw), London: Hamish Hamilton, 1941.
Gontaut-Biron, C. A. de, *Les Dragons de Combat*, Paris: Maillet, 1954.
Gow, Alexander, *Letters from Cambridge*, London: Jonathan Cape, 1945.
Graebner, Walter, *One Year of War in Britain*, in *Life*, New York, 30 September, 1940.
Graves, Charles, *Off the Record*, London: Hutchinson, 1942; *The Home Guard of Great Britain*, London: Hutchinson, 1943.
Grazzi, Emanuele, *Il Principio della Fine*, Rome: Faro, 1945.
Grew, Joseph C., *Turbulent Era* (Vol. II), London: Hammond & Hammond, 1953.
Guastalla, Pierre-André, *Journal, 1940–44*, Paris: Plon, 1951.
Guderian, General Heinz, *Panzer Leader* (trans. Constantine Fitzgibbon), London: Michael Joseph, 1952.

Gudme, Sten, *Denmark: Hitler's Model Protectorate* (trans. Jan Nolle), London: Victor Gollancz, 1942.

Guéhenno, Jean, *Journal des Années noires*, Paris: Gallimard, 1947.

Guerlain, Robert, *A Prisoner in Germany*, London: Macmillan, 1944.

Gunderssen, Karl, *Ordførerens dagbok*, Drammen: privately printed, 1946.

Habe, Hans, *A Thousand Shall Fall* (trans. Norbert Guterdan), London: George Harrap, 1942.

Halder, General Franz, *Hitler as War Lord* (trans. Paul Findlay), London: Putnam, 1950; *War Diaries*, Vols. *III*, *IV*, *V*, Washington, D.C.: Infantry Journal Press, 1950.

Hambro, Carl J., *I Saw it Happen in Norway*, New York: D. Appleton-Century Co., 1940.

Hanselaar, Bert., *De Zwarte Duivels van Rotterdam*, Rotterdam: Wijt, 1954.

Harriman, Florence, *Mission to the North*, London: George Harrap, 1941.

Harrisson, Tom, *Living Through the Blitz*, London: William Collins, 1976; and Madge, Charles, *War Begins at Home*, London: Chatto & Windus, 1940.

Hart, B. H. Liddell, *The Other Side of the Hill*, London: Cassell, 1948.

Harvey, Oliver, *Diplomatic Diaries, 1937-40*, London: William Collins, 1970.

Harwood, Ronald, *Sir Donald Wolfit*, London: Secker & Warburg, 1971.

Hassell, Ulrich von, *The Von Hassell Diaries, 1938-44* (ed. Hugh Gibson), London: Hamish Hamilton, 1948.

Hauge, Eiliv, *Odds Against Norway* (trans. V. Firsoff), London: Lindsay Drummond, 1941; *Salt Water Thief* (trans. Malcolm Munthe), London: Gerald Duckworth, 1958.

Hauser, Ernest, *Konoye of Japan*, in *Life*, New York, 9 December, 1940.

Hautecloque, Françoise de, *La Guerre chez nous en Normandie*, Paris: Colbert, 1945.

Heckstall-Smith, Anthony, *The Fleet that faced both Ways*, London: Anthony Blond, 1963.

Hedin, Sven, *German Diary* (trans. Joan Bulman), Dublin: Euphorion Books, 1951.

Heide, Dik Van Der, *My Sister and I* (trans. Mrs Anton Deventer) London: Faber &, Faber, 1941.

Hendrikse, Dick, *De Dag waarop mijn vader huilde*, Haarlem: Drukkerij de Spaarnestad, 1960.

Herriot, Edouard, *Episodes 1940-44*, Paris: Flammarion, 1950.

Hewins, Ralph, *Quisling: Prophet without Honour*, London: W. H. Allen, 1965.

Higgins, Trumbull, *Winston Churchill and the Second Front*, New York: Oxford University Press, 1957.

Higgs, Dorothy Packard, *Guernsey Diary*, London: Linden Lewis Ltd., 1942.

Hitler e Mussolini: Lettere e documenti, Rome: Rizzoli, 1946.

Hoare, Sir Samuel, *Ambassador on Special Mission*, London: William Collins, 1946.

Hobson, Harold, *The First Three Years of the War*, London: Hutchinson, 1942.

Hodgkinson, George, *Sent to Coventry*, Bletchley: Robert Maxwell, 1970.

Hodgson, Vere, *Few Eggs and No Oranges*, London: Dennis Dobson, 1976.

Hoehling, A. A., *America's Road to War*, London: Abelard-Schuman, 1970.

Hoemberg, Elisabeth, *Thy People, My People*, London: J. M. Dent, 1950.

Hoffmann, Peter, *The History of the German Resistance, 1939-45*, London: Macdonald & Janes, 1977.

Hollingworth, Clare, *There's a German just behind me*, London: The Right Book Club, 1943.

Homa, Corporal, *Onze 80 urige Oorlog*, Amsterdam: De Uil, 1961.

Horne, Alastair, *To Lose a Battle*, London: Macmillan, 1969.

Horner, Arthur, *Incorrigible Rebel*, London: MacGibbon & Kee, 1960.

Horrocks, Lieut.-Gen. Sir Brian, *A Full Life*, London: Collins, 1960.

Horsley, Terence, *Find, Fix and Strike*, London: Eyre & Spottiswoode, 1943.

Howard, Provost Richard, *Ruined and Rebuilt*, Gloucester: British Publishing Co., no date.

Hull, Cordell, *Memoirs, Vol. I*, London: Hodder & Stoughton, 1948.

Humble, Richard, *Hitler's Generals*, London: Arthur Barker, 1973.

Huskinson, Air Commodore Patrick, *Visions Ahead*, London: Werner Laurie, 1949.

Huss, Pierre J., *Heil! And Farewell*, London: Herbert Jenkins, 1943.

Huxley, Elspeth, *Atlantic Ordeal*, London: Chatto & Windus, 1941.

239

Hyde, H. Montgomery, *British Air Policy between the Wars*, London: William Heinemann, 1977; *The Quiet Canadian*, London: Hamish Hamilton, 1962.

Ickes, Harold, *The Secret Diaries, Vol. III: The Lowering Clouds, 1939–41*, London: Weidenfeld & Nicolson, 1955.

Idle, E. Doreen, *War over West Ham*, London: Faber & Faber, 1943.

Ingham, H. S. (Ed.), *Fire and Water: An Anthology of The National Fire Service*, London: Lindsay Drummong, 1942.

Ironside, General Sir Edmund, *Diaries, 1937–40* (ed. R. Macleod and D. Kelly), London: Constable, 1962.

Irving, David, *The Rise and Fall of the Luftwaffe*, London: Weidenfeld & Nicolson, 1973.

Ismay, Hastings Lionel, Baron Ismay, *Memoirs*, London: William Heinemann, 1960.

Jackson, Robert and Frischauer, Willi, *The Navy's Here*, London: Victor Gollancz, 1955.

Jacobsen, Hans-Adolf and Rohwer, Jürgen, *Decisive Battles of World War Two* (trans. Edward Fitzgerald), London: André Deutsch, 1965.

Jakobsen, Max, *The Diplomacy of the Winter War*, Cambridge, Mass.: Harvard University Press, 1961.

James, Admiral William, *The Portsmouth Letters*, London: Macmillan, 1941.

Jamet, Claude, *Carnets de déroute*, Paris: Sorlot, 1942.

Janeway, Eliot, *Struggle for Survival*, New Haven: Yale University Press, 1951.

Janon, René, *J'avais un sabre*, Algiers: Charlot, 1945.

Jardin, Pascal, *Vichy Boyhood* (trans. Jean Stewart), London: Faber & Faber, 1975.

Jasper, Marcel, *Souvenirs sans retouche*, Paris: Fayard, 1968.

Joesten, Joachim, *Stalwart Sweden*, New York: Doubleday, 1943.

Johnen, Wilhelm, *Duel under the Stars* (trans. Mervyn Savill), London: William Kimber, 1957.

Johnson, Brian, *The Secret War*, London: B.B.C. Publications, 1978.

Johnson, Bryan, *The Evacuees*, London: Victor Gollancz, 1968.

Jones, Professor R. V., *Most Secret War*, London: Hamish Hamilton, 1978.

Jones, Thomas, *A Diary with Letters, 1939–50*, London: Oxford University Press, 1954.

Jourdain, Francis, *Jours d'Alarme*, Paris: Correa, 1954.

Jucker, Ninette, *Curfew in Paris*, London: The Hogarth Press, 1960.

Junger, Ernst, *Gärten und Strassen*, Berlin: Mittler, 1942.

Kammerer, Albert, *La verité sur l'Armistice*, Paris: Éditions Médicis, 1944.

Kankrud, Johan, *1940, Krigshendinger i Gausdal-bygdene*, Ostre Gausdal: Mariendals Boktrykkeri, 1956.

Keitel, Field-Marshal Wilhelm, *Memoirs* (trans. David Irving), London: William Kimber, 1965.

Kennan, George, *Memoirs, 1925–50*, London: Hutchinson, 1968.

Kennedy, Major-General Sir John, *The Business of War*, London: Hutchinson, 1957.

Kenney, Rowland, *Northern Tangle*, London: J. M. Dent, 1946.

Kerkmeijer-De Regt, C., *Hoorn in de verdrukking*, Hoorn: West Friesland, 1953.

Kernan, Thomas, *Report on France*, London: John Lane, 1941.

Kesselring, Field-Marshal Albert, *Memoirs* (trans. Lynton Hudson), London: William Kimber, 1953.

Keun, Odette, *And Hell Followed*, London: Constable, 1942.

Kimche, Jon, *Spying for Peace*, London: Weidenfeld & Nicolson, 1961.

King, Cecil, *With Malice Toward None*, London: Sidgwick & Jackson, 1970.

Kleczowski, Stefan, *Poland's First 100,000*, London: Hutchinson, 1945.

Kleffens, Eelco Van, *The Rape of the Netherlands*, London: Hodder & Stoughton, 1940.

Klein, Catherine, *Escape from Berlin* (trans. Livia Laurent), London: Victor Gollancz, 1944.

Knowles, Bernard, *Southampton, The English Gateway*, London: Hutchinson, 1951.

Knudsen, Harald Franklin, *Jeg var Quislings Sekretaer*, Copenhagen: privately printed, 1951.

Koestler, Arthur, *Scum of the Earth*, London: Collins with Hamish Hamilton, 1955.

Koht, Halvdan, *Norway Neutral and Invaded*, London: Hutchinson, 1941; *For fred og fridom i krigstid 1939–40*, Oslo: Tiden, 1957.

240

Kops, Bernard, *The World is a Wedding*, London: MacGibbon & Kee, 1963.
Kramer, G. and Ballintijn, G., *De Meidagen van 1940*, Enschede: M. J. Van Der Loeff, 1945.
Krier, Pierre, *Luxembourg under German Occupation*, New York: Western Newspaper Union, 1941.
Krock, Arthur, *Memoirs*, London: Cassell, 1970.
Kruk, Zofia, *The Taste of Fear*, London: Hutchinson, 1973.
Kurti, Kitty, *Subhas Chandra Bose as I knew him*, Calcutta: Mukhopadhyay, 1965.
Lambert, Derek, *The Sheltered Days*, London: André Deutsch, 1965.
Lampe, David, *The Savage Canary*, London: Cassell, 1957; *The Last Ditch*, London: Cassell, 1968.
Langdon-Davies, John, *Finland: The First Total War*, London: George Routledge, 1940.
Langer, William L., *Our Vichy Gamble*, New York: Knopf, 1947; and Gleason, S. E., *The Challenge to Isolation*, New York: Harper, 1952; *The Undeclared War*, New York: Harper, 1953.
Langeron, Roger, *Paris Juin 1940*, Paris: Flammarion, 1946.
Lapie, Captain Pierre O., *With the Foreign Legion at Narvik* (trans. Anthony Merryn), London: John Murray, 1941.
LaRuche, P., *La Neutralité de la Suède*, Paris: Nouvelles Éditions Latines, 1953.
Lash, Joseph P., *Eleanor and Franklin*, London: André Deutsch, 1972; *Roosevelt and Churchill, 1939–41*, London: André Deutsch, 1977.
Launay, Jacques De, *Secrètes Diplomatiques*, Brussels: Brepols, 1963.
Laval, Pierre, *Unpublished Diary*, London: The Falcon Press, 1948.
Lazareff, Pierre, *The Fall of France*, in *Life*, New York, 26 August, 1940.
Leach, Barry, *German Strategy Against Russia, 1939–41*, Oxford: The Clarendon Press, 1973.
Lean, E. Tangye, *Voices in the Dark*, London: Secker & Warburg, 1943.
Lee, General Raymond E., *The London Observer*, London: Hutchinson, 1972.
Lehmkuhl, Dik, *Journey to London*, London: Hutchinson, 1946.
Lehmkuhl, Herman, *Hitler Attacks Norway*, London: Hodder & Stoughton, 1943.
Leitch, Michael, *Great Songs of World War II*, London: Wise Publications, 1975.
Lemkin, Raphael, *Axis Rule in Occupied Europe*, Washington, D.C.: Carnegie Endowment for International Peace, 1944.
Leske, Gottfried, *I was a Nazi Flier*, New York: The Dial Press, 1941.
Lespes, Henri, *Corps à Corps avec Les Blindés*, Paris: Plon, 1944.
Leuchtenberg, William E., *FDR and the New Deal*, New York: Harper & Row, 1963.
Lewey, Frank, *Cockney Campaign*, London: Stanley Paul, 1947.
Liebling, A. J., *The Road back to Paris*, London: Michael Joseph, 1944.
Lina, H., *Dagboek van een motor-ordonnans*, Amsterdam: Scheltens & Giltay, no date.
Lind, Jakov, *Counting my Steps*, London: Jonathan Cape, 1970.
Listowel, Judith, *This I have Seen*, London: Faber & Faber, 1943.
Littlejohn, David, *The Patriotic Traitors*, London: William Heinemann, 1972.
Litynski, Zygmunt, *I Was One of Them* (trans. Anna Maclaren), London: Jonathan Cape, 1941.
Lloyd, Alan, *Franco*, London: Longman, 1970.
Lochner, Louis P., *Germans Marched into a Dead Paris*, in *Life*, New York, 8 July, 1940.
Lockhart, Robert Bruce, *Comes the Reckoning*, London: Putnam, 1942.
Loewenheim, Francis L., Langley, Harold D. and Jonas, Manfred, *Roosevelt and Churchill: Their Secret Wartime Correspondence*, London: Barrie & Jenkins, 1975.
Lomnitz, Alfred, *Never Mind, Mr. Lom!* London: Macmillan, 1941.
London Children In Wartime Oxford, London: Oxford University Press, 1947.
Long, Breckinridge, *The War Diary* (ed. Fred L. Israel), Lincoln, Neb.: University of Nebraska Press, 1966.
Longmate, Norman, *If Britain Had Fallen*, London: Hutchinson, 1972; *How we Lived Then*, London: Hutchinson, 1971; *Air Raid*, London: Hutchinson, 1976.
Lossberg, Bernhard von, *Im Wehrmachtführungsstab*, Hamburg: H. H. Noelke, 1950.
Lothian, Lord, *The American Speeches of Lord Lothian*, London: Oxford University Press, 1941.

Lu, David J., *From the Marco Polo Bridge to Pearl Harbour*, Washington, D.C.: Public Affairs Press, 1961.
Lukacs, John, *The Last European War, September 1939–December 1941*, London: Routledge, 1977.
Lundin, C. Leonard, *Finland in the Second World War*, Bloomington, Ind.: Indiana University Press, 1957.
Luukkanen, Eino, *Fighter over Finland* (trans. M. A. Salo), London: Macdonald, 1963.
Lyall, Gavin, (ed.), *The War in the Air, 1939–45*, London: Hutchinson, 1968.
Lytton, Neville, *Life in Unoccupied France*, London: Macmillan, 1942.
Maass, Walter, *The Netherlands at War*, New York: Abelard-Schumann, 1970.
Macdonald, Rt. Hon. Malcom, *People and Places: Random Reminiscences*, London: William Collins, 1965.
Macintyre, Donald, *Narvik*, London: Evans Bros., 1952.
Macksey, Kenneth, *Guderian, Panzer Leader*, London: Macdonald & Janes, 1975.
Mackworth, Cecily, *I Came Out of France*, London: Routledge, 1941.
Macleod, Ian, *Neville Chamberlain*, London: Frederick Muller, 1961.
Macmillan, Harold, *The Blast of War*, London: Macmillan, 1967.
Maisky, Ivan, *Memoirs of a Russian Ambassador, 1939–43*, London: Hutchinson, 1967.
Maitland, Patrick, *European Dateline*, London: The Quality Press, 1946.
Makucewicz, Peter, *I Escaped from Germany*, London: Max Love, 1944.
Manchester, William, *The Glory and the Dream*, London: Michael Joseph, 1975.
Mangan, Sherry, *Paris under the Swastika*, in *Life*, New York, 16 September, 1940.
Mannerheim, Marshal Gustav, *The Memoirs* (trans. Count Eric Lewenhardt), London: Cassell, 1953.
Manstein, Field-Marshal Erich von, *Lost Victories*, London: Methuen, 1958.
Marder, Arthur, *Operation Menace*, London: Oxford University Press, 1976.
Mark, Jeffrey, *Mr Churchill runs the War*, in *Life*, New York, 9 December, 1940.
Martienssen, Anthony, *Hitler and his Admirals*, London: Secker & Warburg, 1941.
Martin, Joe (with Robert J. Donovan), *My First 50 Years in Politics*, New York: McGraw-Hill, 1960.
Marwick, Arthur, *The Home Front*, London: Thames & Hudson, 1976.
Mason, Henry C., *The Purge of Dutch Quislings*, The Hague: Martinus Nijhoff, 1952.
Mason, Herbert Molloy, *The Rise of the Luftwaffe, 1918–40*, London: Cassell, 1975.
Mastny, Vojtech, *The Czechs under Nazi Rule*, New York: Columbia University Press, 1971.
Matthews, Very Rev. W. R., *St Paul's Cathedral in Wartime*, London: Hutchinson, 1946.
Maugham, R. C. F., *Jersey under the Jackboot*, London: W. H. Allen, 1946.
Maugham, W. Somerset, *Strictly Personal*, London: William Heinemann, 1942.
McKee, Alexander, *The Coalscuttle Brigade*, London: Souvenir Press, 1957.
Meerloo, Major A. M., *Total War and the Human Mind*, London: Allen & Unwin, 1944.
Mees, Dr H., *Mijn Oorlogsdagboek*, Rotterdam: Van De Rhee, 1945.
Mengin, Robert *No Laurels for De Gaulle* (trans. Jay Allen), London: Michael Joseph, 1960.
Menu, General Charles, *Lumière sur les ruines*, Paris: Plon, 1953.
Mercer, Asja (with Robert Jackson), *One Woman's War*, London: Allan Wingate, 1958.
Merchant Shipping, UK., lost by enemy action, London: H.M.S.O., 1947.
Merseyside, Bombers Over, Liverpool: Daily Post & Echo Ltd., 1943.
Metternich, Princess Tatiana, *Tatiana*, London: Heinemann, 1976.
Michel, Henri, *The Shadow War* (trans. Richard Barry), London: André Deutsch, 1972.
Michie, Allan, *Ernie Bevin, Britain's Labour Boss*, in *Life*, New York, 11 November, 1940.
Minart, Colonel Jacques P. C., *Vincennes Secteur 4* (2 Vols.), Éditions Berger-Leyrault, 1945.
Minney, R. J. (ed.), *The Private Papers of Hore-Belisha*, London: William Collins, 1960.
Moen, Lars, *Under the Iron Heel*, London: Robert Hale, 1941.
Mollett, Ralph, *Jersey under the Swastika*, London: The Hyperion Press, 1945.
Mosley, Leonard, *Backs to the Wall*, London: Weidenfeld & Nicolson, 1971; *Lindbergh*, London: Hodder & Stoughton, 1976; *The Reich Marshal*, London: Weidenfeld & Nicolson, 1974.

Mouchotte, René, *The Mouchotte Diaries* (trans. Philip John Stead), London: Staples Press, 1956.

Muggeridge, Malcolm, *Chronicles of Wasted Time, Vol. II: The Infernal Grove*, London: Collins, 1973.

Muir, Peter, *War Without Music*, New York: Charles Scribner's, 1940.

Murphy, Robert, *Diplomat among Warriors*, London: Collins, 1964.

Murrow, Edward R., *This is London*, London: Cassell, 1961.

Myklebost, Tor, *They came as Friends* (trans. Trygve M. Ager), London: Victor Gollancz, 1943.

Nicolson, Sir Harold, *Diaries and Letters, 1939–45*, London: William Collins, 1967.

Nixon, Barbara, *Raiders Overhead*, London: Lindsay Drummond, 1943.

Nixon, St John C., *Daimler, 1896–1946*, London: Foulis, 1946.

Norris, Frank, *Free France, Poor and Paralysed, waits for Germany to Finish War*, in *Life*, New York, 16 September, 1940.

O'Brien, T. H., *Civil Defence*, London: H.M.S.O./Longmans, 1955.

Oliphant, Sir Lancelot, *An Ambassador in Bonds*, London: Putnam, 1946.

Olsen, Olaf, *Two Eggs on my Plate*, London: George Allen & Unwin, 1952.

Orlow, Dietrich, *The History of the Nazi Party*, Vol. II, Newton Abbot: David & Charles, 1973.

Overstraeten, General Raoul Van, *A La Service de Belgique*, Vol. I, Paris: Plon, 1960.

Paasikivi, Juho, *Toimintani Moskovassa ja Suomessa, 1939–41*, Porvoo: Werner Söderstrom, 1959.

Paine, Jr, Ralph Delaye, *France Collapsed from Internal Decay*, in *Life*, New York, 8 July, 1940.

Palmer, Paul, *Denmark in Nazi Chains*, London: Lindsay Drummond, 1942.

Panter-Downes, Molly, *London War Notes*, London: Longman, 1972.

Parker, Robert, *HQ Budapest*, New York: Farrar & Rinehart, 1944.

Parkinson, Roger, *Peace for our Time*, London: Rupert Hart-Davis, 1971; *Blood, Toil, Tears and Sweat*, London: Rupert Hart-Davis, Macgibbon, 1973.

Parrott, Sir Cecil, *The Tightrope*, London: Faber & Faber, 1975.

Passy, Colonel, *10, Duke Street, Londres*, Monte Carlo: Raoul Solar, 1947.

Paul, Oscar D., *Farewell France!* London: Victor Gollancz, 1941.

Pawle, Gerald, *The Secret War*, London: George Harrap, 1956; *The War and Colonel Warden*, London: George Harrap, 1963.

Paxton, Robert, *Vichy France*, London: Barrie & Jenkins, 1972.

Payne, Robert, *The Life and Death of Adolf Hitler*, London: Jonathan Cape, 1973.

Peabody, Polly, *Occupied Territory*, London: Cresset Press, 1941.

Pelz, Stephen E., *Race to Pearl Harbour*, Cambridge, Mass.: Harvard University Press, 1974.

Perau, J., *Priester im Heere Hitlers*, Essen: Ludgerus, 1952.

Perry, Colin, *Boy in the Blitz*, London: Leo Cooper, 1972.

Petrow, Richard, *The Bitter Years*, London: Hodder & Stoughton, 1974.

Picht, Werner, *The Campaign in Norway*, Prague: Orbis, 1940.

Porter, Roy P., *Uncensored France*, New York: Dial Press, 1942.

Pratt, John (ed.), *The War at Sea, 1939–45*, London: Hutchinson, 1967.

Price, Alfred, *Instruments of Darkness*, London: William Kimber, 1967.

Prüller, Wilhelm, *Diary of a German Soldier* (ed. H. C. Robbins Landon & Sebastian Leitner), London: Faber & Faber, 1963.

Pruszynski, Ksawery, *Poland Fights Back*, London: Hodder & Stoughton, 1941.

Puttkamer, Karl Jesko von, *Die Unheimliche See*, Munich: Kuehne, 1952.

Raczynski, Count Edward, *In Allied London*, London: Weidenfeld & Nicolson, 1962.

Reith, Lord, *Diaries*, London: Collins, 1975.

Reitlinger, Gerald, *The Final Solution*, London: Vallentine Mitchell, edn. of 1968.

Reynaud, Paul, *In the Thick of the Fight* (trans. James D. Lambert), London: Cassell, 1955.

Richards, Denis, *The Royal Air Force, Vol. I, The Fight at Odds*, London: H.M.S.O., 1953.

Rieckhoff, H. J., *Trumpf oder Bluff*, Genf: Interavia, 1945.

Riess, Curt, *Underground Europe*, London: John Long, 1943.
Rigby, Françoise, *In Defiance*, London: Elek Books, 1960.
Ritchie, Charles, *The Siren Years*, London: Macmillan, 1974.
Robb, Nesca, *An Ulsterwoman in England*, Cambridge: The University Press, 1942.
Robertson, Terence, *The Golden Horseshoe*, London: Evans Bros., 1955.
Rohwer, Jürgen (and Hümmelchen, G.), *Chronik des Seekrieges, 1939–45*, Oldenburg: Stalling, 1968.
Rommel Papers, The, (ed. B. H. Liddell Hart, trans. Paul Findlay), London: William Collins, 1953.
Roon, Ger Van, *German Resistance to Hitler* (trans. Peter Ludlow), New York: Van Nostrand Reinhold, 1971.
Roosevelt, Franklin D., *Wartime Correspondence with Pope Pius XII*, New York: Macmillan, 1947.
Roskill, Stephen, *Churchill and the Admirals*, London: William Collins, 1977; *British Naval Policy between the Wars*, London: William Heinemann, 1976.
Ross, Alan, *The Forties*, London: Weidenfeld & Nicolson, 1950.
Rothberg, Abraham, *Eyewitness History of World War II*, New York: Bantam Books, 1966.
Rothenstein, Sir John, *Brave Day, Hideous Night*, London: Hamish Hamilton, 1966.
Rouchaud, Martine, *Journal d'une Petite Fille*, Paris: Gallimard, 1945.
Rowe, Vivian, *The Great Wall of France*, London: Putnam, 1959.
Roy, Dilip Kumar, *Netaji—The Man*, Bombay: Chaupatti, 1966.
Roy, Jules, *The Trial of Marshal Pétain* (trans. Robert Baldick), London: Faber & Faber, 1968.
Roy, Pravash Chandra, *Subhas Chandra*, Rajshahi: Mitra Bros., 1929.
Royde-Smith, Naomi, *Outside Information*, London: Macmillan, 1941.
Ruby, General Edmond, *Sedan, Terre d'Epreuve*, Paris: Flammarion, 1948.
Ruge, Vice-Admiral Friedrich, *Sea Warfare* (trans. Cmdr. M. G. Saunders, R.N.), London: Cassell, 1957.
Russell, William, *Berlin Embassy*, London: Michael Joseph, 1942.
Saint-Exupéry, Antoine de, *Flight to Arms* (trans. Lewis Galantière), London: William Heinemann, edn. of 1955.
Salesse, Simone, *I Was a Refugee in France*, Cape Town: Galvin & Sales Ltd., 1942.
Sansom, William, *Westminster in War*, London: Faber & Faber, 1947.
Sarkar, Sudhira, *Subhas Chandra*, Calcutta: J. C. Bannerjee, 1939.
Saunders, Hilary St George, *Left Handshake*, London: William Collins, 1949.
Schellenberg, Walter, *The Schellenberg Memoirs* (ed. and trans. Louis Hagen), London: André Deutsch, 1956.
Schirach, Henriette von, *The Price of Glory* (trans. Willi Frischauer), London: Frederick Muller, 1960.
Schlabrendorff, Fabian von, *The Secret War against Hitler* (trans. Hilda Simon), London: Hodder & Stoughton, 1966.
Schmidt, Paul, *Hitler's Interpreter* (ed. R. H. C. Steel), London: William Heinemann, 1951.
Scobbie, Irene, *Sweden*, London: Ernest Benn, 1972.
Scott, Sir Harold, *Your Obedient Servant*, London: André Deutsch, 1959.
Shakespeare, Sir Geoffrey, *Let Candles Be Brought In*, London: Macdonald, 1949.
Shelton, John, *A Night in Little Park Street*, London: Britannicus Liber, 1950.
Sherwood, Robert, *The White House Papers of Harry Hopkins, Vol. I*, London: Eyre & Spottiswoode, 1948.
Shipley, Rev. S. Paul, *Bristol Siren Nights*, Bristol: Rankin Bros. Ltd., 1943.
Shirer, William, *Berlin Diary*, London: Hamish Hamilton, 1941; *The Rise and Fall of the Third Reich*, New York: Simon & Schuster, 1959; *The Collapse of the Third Republic*, London: William Heinemann, Secker & Warburg, 1970.
Sicard, Etienne, *The Battle of Mers-el-Kebir*, in *Life*, New York, 4 November, 1940.
Simon, Paul, *One Enemy Only* (trans. W. G. Corp), London: Hodder & Stoughton, 1943.
Simoni, Leonardo, *Berlino, Ambasciata d'Italia*, Rome: Migliaresi, 1946.

Singh, Durlab, *The Rebel President*, Lahore: Hero Publications, 1941.

Smuts, Field-Marshal Jan C., *Selections from the Smuts Papers, Vol. VI* (ed. Jean Van Der Poel), London: Cambridge University Press, 1973.

Smyth, Brigadier, The Rt. Hon. Sir John, *Leadership in War*, Newton Abbot: David & Charles, 1974.

Soloviev, Mikhail, *My Nine Lives in the Red Army* (trans. Henry C. Stevens), New York: David McKay, 1955.

Snoep, J., *Nederland in de Branding*, Dordrecht: De Longte, 1945.

Someren, Liesje Van, *Escape from Holland*, London: Herbert Jenkins, 1942.

Soubiran, André, *J'étais Médecin, avec les Chars*, Paris: Didier, 1943.

Soustelle, Jacques, *Envers et Contre Tout* (2 Vols.), Paris: Robert Laffont, 1950.

Spanier, Ginette, *The Long Road to Freedom*, London: Robert Hale, 1976.

Spears, Major-General Sir Edward, *Assignment to Catastrophe* (2 Vols.), London: William Heinemann, 1954.

Speer, Albert, *Inside the Third Reich* (trans. Richard & Clara Winston), London: Weidenfeld & Nicolson, 1976.

Stam, Wim., *Kruit en Bloesem*, Amsterdam: Bigot & Van Rossum, no date.

Stein, George, *The Waffen S.S., 1939–45*, Ithaca, N.Y.: Cornell University Press, 1966.

Stephan, Enno, *Spies in Ireland* (trans. Arthur Davidson), London: Macdonald, 1963.

Stimson, Henry C. and Bundy, McGeorge, *On Active Service in Peace and War*, New York: Harper, 1948.

St-John, Robert, *Foreign Correspondent*, London: Hutchinson, 1960.

Stout, Rex, *The Illustrious Dunderheads*, New York: Alfred Knopf, 1942.

Stowe, Leland, *A Few Thousand Nazis Seized Norway*, in *Life*, New York, 10 May, 1940; *No Other Road to Freedom*, London: Faber & Faber, 1942.

Strijbos, Jan Pieter, *De Noordvaarders*, Amsterdam: L. J. Veen, 1946.

Tanner, Väinö, *The Winter War*, Stanford, Cal.: Stanford University Press, 1957.

Taylor, A. J. P., *The Second World War*, London: Hamish Hamilton, 1975; (ed.), *Churchill —Four Faces and the Man*, London: Pelican Books, 1973; *The Origins of The Second World War*, London: Hamish Hamilton, 1961; *Beaverbrook*, London: Hamish Hamilton, 1972; *English History, 1914–45*, London: Oxford University Press, 1965.

Taylor, Telford, *The March of Conquest*, London: Edward Hulton, 1959; *The Breaking Wave*, London: Weidenfeld & Nicolson, 1967.

Teissier Du Cros, Janet, *Divided Loyalties*, London: Hamish Hamilton, 1962.

Ter Weele, Carl Frits, *Inside Holland*, in *Life*, New York, 14 October, 1940.

Thiry, N., *La Belgique pendant la guerre*, Paris: Hachette, 1947.

Thomas, John Oram, *The Giant Killers*, London: Michael Joseph, 1975.

Thompson, Rear-Admiral George, *Blue Pencil Admiral*, London: Sampson Low, Marston, 1947.

Thompson, Laurence, *1940: Year of Legend, Year of History*, London: William Collins, 1966.

Tissier, Lt.-Col. Pierre, *I Worked with Laval*, London: George Harrap, 1942.

Toland, John, *Adolf Hitler*, New York: Doubleday, 1976.

Tony-Revillon, M., *Mes Carnets*, Paris: Lieutier, 1945.

Torris, J. M., *Narvik*, New York: Brentanos, 1943.

Toye, Hugh, *The Springing Tiger*, London: Cassell, 1959.

Tree, Ronald, *When the Moon was High*, London: Macmillan, 1975.

Trial of the major war criminals before the International Military Tribunal, Nuremberg, 1947–49, (42 Vols.), Washington, D.C.: U.S. Government Printing Office, 1949/51.

True Story of Pearl Harbor, The, in *U.S. News and World Report*, Washington, D.C.: 11 December, 1961.

True to Type: A Selection of Letters and Diaries from German Soldiers and Civilians, London: Hutchinson, 1945.

Turner, E. S., *The Phoney War on the Home Front*, London: Michael Joseph, 1961.

Tute, Warren, *The Deadly Stroke*, London: William Collins, 1973.

Twyford, Henry, *It Came to our Door*, Plymouth: Underhill, 1946.

Undset, Sigrid, *Return to the Future* (trans. Henriette C. K. Naeseth), New York: Alfred Knopf, 1942; *My Escape from Norway*, in *Life*, New York, 10 June, 1940.

245

Upton, Anthony F., *Finland in Crisis, 1940–41*, London: Faber & Faber, 1964: *Finland, 1939–40*, London: Davis-Poynter, 1976.

Van Creveld, Martin, *Hitler's Strategy, 1940–41: The Balkan Clue*, London: Cambridge University Press, 1973.

Van Duren, Theo, *Orange Above*, London: Staples Press, 1956.

Van Heerde, H., *Tusschen Vuur en Ijzer*, Meppel: Boom & Zoon, no date.

Van Kempen, Bep, *Te Mogen Helpen*, Assen: Born, no date.

Van Paassen, Pierre, *That Day Alone*, London: Michael Joseph, 1943.

Vian, Admiral of the Fleet Sir Philip, *Action This Day*, London: Frederick Muller, 1960

Vidalenc, Jean, *L'Exode de mai-juin, 1940*, Paris: Presses Universitaires de France, 1957.

Vogt, Benjamin, *Mennesket Vidkun och Forraederen Quisling*, Oslo: Aschehoug, 1965

Vomécourt, Phillippe de, *Who Lived to See the Day*, London: Hutchinson, 1961.

Waldeck, Countess Rosa Von, *Athenée Palace, Bucharest*, London: Constable, 1943.

Walker, David, *Death at my Heels*, London: Chapman & Hall, 1942.

Warlimont, General Walter, *Inside Hitler's Headquarters* (trans. R. H. Barry), London: Weidenfeld & Nicolson, 1964.

Warmbrunn, Werner, *The Dutch under German Occupation*, Stanford, Cal.: Stanford University Press, 1963.

Warner, Geoffrey, *Pierre Laval and the Eclipse of France*, London: Eyre & Spottiswoode, 1968.

Wassey, Michael, *Ordeal by Fire*, London: Secker & Warburg, 1941.

Waterfield, Gordon, *What Happened to France*, London: John Murray, 1940.

Watney, John, *He Also Served*, London: Hamish Hamilton, 1971.

Watson-Watt, Sir Robert, *Three Steps to Victory*, London: Odhams Press, 1958.

Watt, Donald Cameron, *Too Serious a Business*, London: Temple Smith, 1975.

Welles, Sumner, *A Time for Decision*, New York: Harpers, 1944.

Werth, Alexander, *The Last Days of Paris*, London: Hamish Hamilton, 1940.

Westphal, General Siegfried, *The German Army in the West*, London: Cassell, 1951.

Weygand, General Maxime, *Recalled To Service* (trans. E. W. Dickes), London: William Heinemann, 1952.

Wheatley, Ronald, *Operation Sealion*, Oxford: The Clarendon Press, 1958.

Wheeler-Bennett, Sir John, *Special Relationships: America in Peace and War*, London: Macmillan, 1975; *John Anderson, Viscount Waverley*, London: Macmillan, 1962; (ed.), *Action This Day*, London: Macmillan, 1968; *The Nemesis of Power*, London: Macmillan, 1953; *King George VI*, London: Macmillan, 1958.

While, Jack, *Fire! Fire!* London: Frederick Muller, 1944.

White, Theodore H. (with Annalee Jacoby), *Thunder Out of China*, London: Victor Gollancz, 1947.

White, William L., *Atlantic Crossing on U.S. Destroyer*, in *Life*, New York, 2 December, 1940.

Whittington-Egan, Richard, *Liverpool Roundabout*, Liverpool. Philip, Son & Nephew, 1957.

Wilhelmina, H.R.H., Princess of the Netherlands, *Lonely but not Alone* (trans. John Peereboon), London: Hutchinson, 1964.

Williams, Francis, *A Prime Minister Remembers*, London: Heinemann, 1961.

Williams, John, *The Ides of May*, London: Constable, 1968; *The Guns of Dakar*, London: William Heinemann, 1976.

Wilson, Louis Abbott, *London Firefighter*, in *Life*, New York, 21 October, 1940.

Winter, Dr Harry, *Coventry*, in *Life*, New York, 20 January, 1941.

Winterbotham, Group Captain F. W., *The Ultra Secret*, London: Weidenfeld & Nicolson, 1974.

Wolfit, Sir Donald, *First Interval*, London,: Odhams Press, 1954.

Woodman, Dorothy, *Europe Rises*, London: Victor Gollancz, 1943.

Woodward, David, *Front Line and Front Page*, London: Eyre & Spottiswoode. 1943.

Wrench, John Evelyn, *Immortal Years*, London: Hutchinson, 1945.

Wright, Myrtle, *Norwegian Diary*, London: Friendspeace International Relations Committee, 1974.

Wright, Robert, *Dowding and the Battle of Britain*, London: Macdonald, 1969.
Wuorinen, John, *Finland and World War II*, New York: The Ronald Press, 1948.
Young, A. P., *The "X" Documents*, London: André Deutsch, 1974.
Young, Brigadier Desmond, *Rommel*, London: Collins, 1950.
Young, Gordon, *Outposts of War*, London: Hodder & Stoughton, 1941.
Young, Kenneth, *Churchill and Beaverbrook*, London: Eyre & Spottiswoode, 1966.
Youth at War, London: Batsford, 1944.
Zbszewski, Karl, *The Fight for Narvik*, London: Lindsay Drummond, 1940.
Zimmerman-Wolf, R. S., *Het woord als wapen*, Gravenhage: Martinus-Nijhoff, 1945.
Zoller, Albert, *Hitler Privat*, Dusseldorf: Droste, 1949.
Zuckermann, Professor Solly, *From Apes to Warlords*, London: Hamish Hamilton, 1978.

MANUSCRIPT SOURCES

Aitken, Sir William Maxwell, 1st Bt., 1st Baron Beaverbrook, Ministry of Aircraft Production Papers, May–Dec., 1940. (*House of Lords Record Office, London*).

Alexander, Albert Victor, Earl Alexander of Hillsborough, 1st Lord of the Admiralty, Memos and Correspondence, Feb.–Dec., 1940. (*Churchill College, Cambridge*).

Bliss, Don C., Groth, Edward M., White, J. C. & Wilson, Thomas M., Reports from the American Consulate-General, Calcutta, India, Feb.–Nov., 1940. (*U.S. National Archives, Washington, D.C.*).

Blumentritt, General Günther, Dunkirk, 1940: an unpublished study. (*Author's Collection*).

Bullitt, William C., U.S. Ambassdor to France, Telegrams to State Department. (*U.S. National Archives, Washington, D.C.*).

Caffery, Jefferson, U.S. Ambassador to Brazil, Telegrams to State Department. (*U.S. National Archives*).

Chamberlain, (Arthur) Neville, Prime Minister, 1937–May, 1940, Lord President of the Council, May–Nov., 1940; Diary and Correspondence. (*University of Birmingham, Warwickshire, Special Collections, and University College Library, Cambridge*).

Chatfield, Sir (Alfred) Ernle Montacute, 1st Baron Chatfield, Minister for the Co-Ordination of Defence, January 1939–April, 1940: Miscellaneous correspondence. (*National Maritime Museum, Greenwich, South London*).

Crookshank, Captain Harry Frederick Comfort, Financial Secretary to the Treasury, May–Dec., 1940: Miscellaneous Papers. (*Bodleian Library, Oxford*).

Dalton, (Edward) Hugh (John Neale), Baron Dalton, Minister of Economic Warfare, May, 1940–1942: Diary. (*British Library of Political and Economic Science, London*).

Deichmann, General Paul. *Actions of No II Flying Corps in the Battle of Britain. German Attacks on R.A.F. Ground Targets, 13-8-40 – 6-9-40: a study. Mass Day attacks on London: a monograph. Some Reasons for the Switch to Night Bombing: an appreciation. The Struggle for Air Superiority During Phase I of the Battle of Britain.*

First Flying Corps, Luftwaffe, Operational Orders for Attacks 'Sea of Light' and 'Loge'.

Gefechtskalendar, Air Fleets Two and Three, 1-8-40–15-9-40. (*All studies from the Luftwaffe Karlsruhe Collection, Freiburg, Germany, translated for the author by Nadia Radowitz*).

Goering, Reichmarschall Hermann, Conference Decisions of July 21, August 1, 3, 15 and 19. (*Luftwaffe Karlsruhe Collection, Freiburg*).

Gordon, George A., U.S. Envoy-Extraordinary and Minister Plenipotentiary to The Netherlands, Telegrams to State Department. (*U.S. National Archives*).

Gort, General The Viscount. *War Diary and Official Correspondence.* (*Courtesy the late Earl of Munster*).

Grabmann, General Walter. The Fighter's Role in The Battle of Britain: a study. (*Luftwaffe Karlsruhe Collection, Freiburg*).

Gray, David S., U.S. Envoy-Extraordinary and Minister Plenipotentiary to Eire, Telegrams to State Department. (*U.S. National Archives*).

Greiner, Helmuth. The Battle of Britain, 4-9-40 – 7-9-40. (*Luftwaffe Karlsruhe Collection, Freiburg*).

Grew, Joseph C., U.S. Ambassador to Japan. Telegrams to State Department. (*U.S. National Archives*).

Hoare, Sir Samuel John Gurney, 2nd Bt. Viscount Templewood, Lord Privy Seal and Member of the War Cabinet, Sept. 1939–April, 1940; Ambassador to Spain from June, 1940: Diary and Correspondence. (*University Library, Cambridge*).

248

Hudson, Brigadier Charles, Diary. (*Courtesy Mrs Gladys Hudson*).

Ibel, General Max. The 27th Fighter Group, Luftwaffe: a private diary. (*Courtesy General Ibel*).

Kennedy, Joseph P., U.S. Ambassador to Great Britain. Telegrams to State Department. (*U.S. National Archives*).

Kirk, Alexander C., U.S. Chargé d'Affaires in Germany. Telegrams to State Department. (*U.S. National Archives*).

Lindemann, Professor Frederick (Lord Cherwell). The Cherwell Papers. (*Nuffield College, Oxford*).

McVeagh, Lincoln., U.S. Envoy-Extraordinary and Minister Plenipotentiary to Greece. Telegrams to State Department. (*U.S. National Archives*).

Margesson, (Henry) David (Reginald) Margesson, 1st Viscount Margesson, Secretary of State for War, 1940–42: Miscellaneous Papers. (*Churchill College. Cambridge*).

Marquis, Sir Frederick James, 1st Earl of Woolton, Minister of Food, 1940–43: Diary and Memoranda. (*Bodleian Library, Oxford*).

Mass-Observation Archive, The. File Reports, 1940. (*University of Sussex*).

Milch, Generalfeldmarschall Erhard. Report of the Inspector-General of the Luftwaffe, 25-8-40. (*Luftwaffe Karlsruhe Collection, Freiburg*).

Monckton, Sir Walter Turner, Deputy Director General, Ministry of Information. Memoranda and Reports on Internees. (*Bodleian Library, Oxford*).

Morrison, Herbert Stanley, Baron Morrison of Lambeth, Minister of Supply, May–Oct., 1940; Secretary of State for Home Affairs and Home Security, 1940–45. Miscellaneous Memoranda. (*Nuffield College. Oxford*).

Osterkamp, General Theo. Experiences as Fighter Leader 2 on The Channel. (*Luftwaffe Karlsruhe Collection, Freiburg*).

Page, Wing-Cdr. Geoffrey. Autobiography: unpublished MSS. (*Courtesy W/Cdr. Page*).

Phillips, William, U.S. Ambassador Extraordinary and Plenipotentiary to Italy. Telegrams to State Department. (*U.S. National Archives*).

Public Record Office, Kew, Surrey – Series CAB: Cabinet Papers – F.O.: Foreign Office Papers – H.O.: Home Office Papers – PREM: Prime Minister's Papers.

Richtofen, General The Baron von, Private Diary, (*Luftwaffe Karlsruhe Collection. Freiburg*).

Salmuth, General Hans von. Private Diary. (*Courtesy General von Salmuth*).

Seidemann, General Hans. Actions of No VIII Flying Corps on the Channel Coast. (*Luftwaffe Karlsruhe Collection, Freiburg*).

Sinclair, Sir Archibald Henry Macdonald, 4th Bt., 1st Viscount Thurso, Secretary of State for Air, 1940–45; Air Ministry Papers. (*Public Record Office, Kew, Surrey*).

Speidel, General Wilhelm. The Western Campaign: a study. (*U.S. Historical Division, Karlsruhe, Germany*).

Stanhope, James Richard, 7th Earl Stanhope, 13th Earl of Chesterfield, Lord President of the Council, 1939–May, 1940: Miscellaneous Correspondence. (*Kent County Archives, Maidstone, Kent*).

Steinhardt, Laurence A., U.S. Ambassador in the Soviet Union, Telegrams to State Department. (*U.S. National Archives*).

United States Strategic Bombing Survey Records: including Record Group 243: interrogations of General Karl Koller, Professor Messerschmitt, Dr Albert Speer, General Werner Junck, Dr Kurt Tank, Generalfeldmarschall Hugo Sperrle, General Werner Kreipe, General Halder, Generalfeldmarschall Albert Kesselring, Feldmarschall Wilhelm Keitel, General Adolf Galland. (*U.S. National Archives*).

Wallace, Captain (David) Euan, Ministry of Transport, 1939–May, 1940: Private Diary. (*Bodleian Library, Oxford*).

Weddell, Alexander W., U.S. Ambassador in Spain. Telegrams to State Department. (*U.S. National Archives*).

Weir, Sir William Douglas, 1st Viscount Weir, Director-General of Explosives, Ministry of Supply, 1939–41: Official Correspondence. (*Churchill College, Cambridge*).

Wood, Sir (Howard) Kingsley, Secretary of State for Air, 1938–April, 1940: private correspondence with Winston Churchill. (*Public Record Office, Kew, Surrey*).

INDEX

Names, titles and posts are those held at the time during the events described

251

252

253

informs Churchill of his research, 121; 171; and Coventry air-raid, 208
Jong, Louis de, 56
Joubert, Air Marshal Sir Philip, 94, 95
Junck, *Oberst* Werner, 161

Kai-Shek, Generalissimo Chiang, on Japanese threat, 138; on Communists, 139
Karl Peters, German depot-ship, 34
Kaupisch, General Leonhard, 37
Keitel, *Generaloberst* Wilhelm, 55, 116
Kelly, Sir David, 135
Kennedy, Brigadier John, 52
Kennedy, Joseph P., 27, 64, 92
Kennedy, Paddy, 81
Kesselring, General Albert, 75
King, George, 22
King, Mackenzie, on possible refuge for the King, 92
King's Own Yorkshire Infantry, in Norway, 46
Kirkpatrick, Ivone, 7
Kleffens, Eelco van, 56, 59
Kleist, General Ewald von, 88
Kluge, *Generaloberst* Gunther Hans von, 73–4
Knickebein, German detector beam discovered, 93–5, 120–1.
Knox, Frank L., 115, 202
Koeltz, General, 77
Koestler, Arthur, 102
Koht, Halvdan, 22, 37
Konoye, Prince Fumimaro, 195
Kretschmer, *Kapitänleutnant* Otto, sinks merchant ships, 147–50; 163, 197–8; taken prisoner, 220
Kurusu, Saburo, 194

Lackner, *Oberst*, 60
Lancashire Fusiliers, 81
Laski, Harold, 51, 52
Latin America, reaction to German influences, 143–4; Act of Havana, 145
Latvia, occupied by Red Army, 140
Laval, Pierre, appointed Pétain's Vice-President, 129; meets Polly Peabody, 132; meets Hitler, 206
Le Luc, Rear Admiral, sends French ships to support Gensoul, 127, 128
Lend-Lease, 217–18
Lewis, Leslie, 183
Lindbergh, Colonel Charles A., 2, 63
Lindemann, Prof. Frederick, 121, 150, 151
Lindsay, Captain Martin, 49
Linlithgow, Lord, 33
Lithuania, occupied by Red Army, 140

Ljungberg, Colonel Birger, 37
Lloyd George, David, 49
Local Defence Volunteers *see* Home Guard
Lockey, Captain Bernard, 82
London, blitz, 171, 176–8; shelters, 191–2; survival during, 203–4; Christmas raid, 222; shortage of water, 223; Wren churches destroyed, 224
London Fire Brigade, 169, 190, 191
Lossberg, *Oberst* Bernhard von, 153
Lothian, Lord, 2, 107, 130, 217
Lovell, Malcolm R., 135
Low Countries, attacked, 54–61
Luftwaffe, and Battle of Britain, 159–62
Luukkanen, Captain Eino, 13, 23–5
Lupescu, Magda, 142, 169
Lutzow, 30
Luxembourg, hostile vote against Germany, 189

MacDonald, Malcolm, discussions with de Valera, 119
Mackesy, General Pierse, 28–9, 45
Mackie, Corporal, finds Knickebein beam in Anson, 120–1
Macmillan, Harold, 50
Maginot Line, 5, 65
Magog, sunk by U-Boats 99, 148
Mandel, Georges, 67
Mannerheim, Field Marshal Carl Gustav, his defence line, 13; determination to fight on, 16; opts for peace, 26
Manstein, *Generalleutnant* Fritz von, 55
Mao Tse-Tung, 139
Marchant, Hilde, 214
Margerie, Roland de, 95
Margesson, Captain David, 50
Marina, S.S., 183
Mass Observation Organisation, 92–3
Massey Shaw, 87
Matsuoka, Yosuke, 194
Matthews, Very Rev. William, 172
Maugham, Somerset, 152
Mauny, Lt. Victor de, 72–3
Mekhlis, Leo Zakharovich, 14, 15
Mers-el-Kebir, French Fleet sunk, 128
Milch, General Erhard, 10
Mölders, *Hauptmann* Werner, 96–8, 116; misgivings on war, 146; shot down, 147; 170, 171, 179, 195–6, 220
Monckton, Sir Walter, 123
Morgan, J. P., 2
Morgenthau, Henry, 17, 130
Morrison, Herbert, demands resignation of Chamberlain, 49; 52; compels fire-watching, 224

255

130; Burma Road closure, 138; on Chinese Communism, 139; reviews troops, 166; renounces food aid to France, 187; third term, 199–200; rumours on his private life, 201; letter from Churchill on outlook for 1941, 216; Lend-Lease, 218; Christmas 'Fireside Chat', 221

Rotterdam, attack on, 60

Royal Air Force, air mines, 150; pilot shortage, 151; Battle of Britain, 155–62, 176–9

Royal Family, German plans to seize as hostages, 165–6; and the blitz, 203

Ruby, General Edouard, 57, 58

Ruge, General Otto, 46, 98

Rumania, 11; Hitler's demands on, 141; Bessarabia annexed by Russia, 142; and 'Vienna Award', 168

Rundstedt, *Generaloberst* Gerd von, 55, 73–4

Russia, demands on Finland, 13; army's weakness in Finland, 14–15; takes Viipuri, 23; Finnish defeat, 25–6; occupies Baltic States, 140; annexes Bessarabia, 142; Hitler's decision to attack, 153

St Vincent Millay, Edna, 107

Salmuth, *Generalleutnant* Hans von, 88

San, Aung, 136

Sandler, Rickard, 11

Sargent, Orme, 125

Sas, Major J. G., 56

Savarkar, Vinayak Damodar, 136

Scharnhorst, 30, 36

Scharroo, Colonel, 60

Schlieffen plan, 55

Schmid, *Generalleutnant* Josef, 75

'Sea Lion', code name for invasion of Britain, 153; alert issued in England, 173–5; postponed, 179

Searle, Sapper Bill, 85

Seidenfaden, Erik, scoop on Finnish armistice, 25; learns of invasion of Denmark, 35–6; sees effect of invasion of Norway, 43; hears Italy's declaration of war, 105

Sellers, Sergeant (R.A.F.) Raymond, 158

Seydlitz, 30

Shearburn, Mary, Churchill's secretary, 89–90

Sherwood, Robert E., 200

Sicard, *Lieutenant de Vaisseau* Etienne, 128

Sikorski, General Wladyslaw, 66

Simon, Sir John, 50

Sinclair, Sir Archibald, 50, 151, 193

Six, Dr Franz, 165

Smith, Captain Harry, 71

Smuts, Jan, 49, 152

Soddu, General Ubaldo, 105

Soloviev, Troop Commander Mikhail, disillusioned with Red Army in Finland, 14–15; on bravery of Finns, 26

Somerville, Vice-Admiral Sir James, 126; opens fire on French Fleet, 128; ashamed at the action, 129

South Africa, raises troops, 92

Spain, policy, 11; Hitler's unsuccessful attempt in reaching agreement with, 205–6

Spears, Major-General Edward, 48; appointed Liaison Officer to Reynaud, 66; 67

Speedwell, H.M.S., 88

Speer, Albert, charged to reconstruct Berlin and other cities, 116; 154

Stalin, Joseph, accepts Mannerheim's peace offer, 26

Stanley, Oliver, 51

Starkey, Captain Stanton, 80

Stassen, Harold, 63

Stauning, Thorvald, on a Nordic alliance, 11; rejects mobilisation for Denmark, 35

Steinhardt, Lawrence A., 26

Stephenson, Pilot Officer Paddy, 178

Stevens, Edmund, 48

Stimson, Henry G., 115

Strasbourg, 126, 128

Stuart, Prof. Francis, 120

submarine warfare, 147–50, 197–8

Sun IV, 84

Sweden, on neutrality, 11; feeling on defeat of Finland, 27; British plan to seize oil-fields, 29

Switzerland, 11; forms National Redoubt, 140

Taft, Robert, 130

Taranto, Italian ships sunk there by British, 201–2

Taylor, Myron Charles, appointed U.S. representative to Vatican, 1

Teleki, Count Paul, 140

Temple, Lt.-Com. John, 81

Tennant, Captain William, 72, 75, 76, 77, 87

Terboven, Josef, 41, 134

Thompson, Dorothy, on Finland's defeat, 27

Thompson, Squadron Leader John, 158

Thompson, Det.-Ins. Walter, 51, 202

1941

ARMAGEDDON

CONTENTS

ILLUSTRATIONS

Between pages 118 *and* 119

10 (a) General Guderian on the Russian Front
   (b) Marshal Timoshenko
   (c) General Zhukov

11 (a) Russian peasants fleeing before the German advance on Moscow
   (b) General Dovator's cavalry units on their way to defend Moscow

12 (a) Russian Front: a German tank rumbles over a slit trench with Russians cowering underneath
   (b) Red Army men dislodging Germans from a village

13 (a) General Douglas MacArthur
   (b) American and Philippine troops surrender to the Japanese at Bataan

14 (a) The crematoria at Buchenwald concentration camp
   (b) Lager Nordhausen camp

15 (a) U.S.S. *California* sinking after the Japanese attack on Pearl Harbor
   (b) The wreckage at the Naval Air Station, Pearl Harbor

16   British troops marching along the road to Cyrene with the ancient town behind them

1

"Thy People Shall Be My People"

1 January–12 March, 1941

IN GLASGOW, SCOTLAND, a bitter wind was driving across the River Clyde. By 9 p.m. on Friday, 17 January, snow was drifting from the mountains by Ben Lomond, a white noiseless cloud blanketing tenements and shipyards, but it brought no added warmth. At nightfall the thermometer had showed 24 degrees Fahrenheit and still falling. On Sauchiehall Street, the city's main artery, a few latecomers huddled in the tram shelters, stamping their feet, small foggy haloes of breath trapped by the nipping air.

In Room 21, on the first floor of the four-star North British Hotel, a select private dinner party was drawing to a close. It was now that the host, the Secretary of State designate for Scotland, Tom Johnston, turned to his guest of honour, Prime Minister Winston Churchill. Would President Franklin D. Roosevelt's emissary, who had just returned with the Premier from inspecting the Home Fleet at Scapa Flow, the naval base in the Orkney Islands used by the Fleet in both world wars, care to address the company? All eyes now focused on Harry Lloyd Hopkins, Roosevelt's lanky unkempt personal adviser, as he rose to his feet.

It was an historic moment. His voice barely pitched above a whisper, Hopkins seemed to direct his words to Churchill alone. "I suppose you want to know," he began, "what I am going to say to President Roosevelt on my return. Well, I'm going to quote you one verse from that Book of Books in the truth of which Mr Johnston's mother and my own Scottish mother was brought up. 'Whither thou goest, I will go; and where thou lodgest I will lodge; thy people shall be my people, and thy God my God'." Then, his voice cracking, Hopkins added three words that formed no part of the Book of Ruth: "Even to the end."

"The words seemed like a rope thrown to a drowning man," Churchill's personal physician, Sir Charles Wilson (later Lord Moran) always remembered, but they seemed even more to Churchill. There, in the warm cathedral silence of Room 21, the Premier had broken down and was weeping unashamedly.

*

1

On this 502nd day of World War Two, Churchill had cause for emotion. Only the frail presence of Harry Hopkins, symbolising Roosevelt's determination to provide Britain and her allies with "all aid short of war", stood between the nation and defeat by Hitler's Germany. The beleaguered defiance of the British following the Dunkirk evacuation of 1940 now seemed an echo from the past. Ahead loomed a grimmer reality: the months when Adolf Hitler's Directive No 23 – "to concentrate every means of waging war by sea and air on enemy supplies" – began to bite deep.

Within six weeks, 104 ships – 400,000 tons of merchant shipping – would be lost, a rate of attrition totalling seven million tons a year, more than three times the building capacity of the shipyards. The sole solution was one of make-do-and-mend: 40,000 men were to be released from the armed forces to clear a huge backlog of 800,000 tons of shipping awaiting repair. The Luftwaffe response was a blitz on ports like Plymouth and Liverpool, destroying thousands more tons of supplies.

By now Hitler seemed omnipotent. For six months his troops had manned the ramparts unchallenged from the North Cape to the Pyrenees, and his recent message to the *Wehrmacht* only underlined their invincibility: "Armed as never before we stand at the door of the New Year." Already it seemed an old war: since June, 1940, London had been playing host to six governments in exile.* The Maginot Line, that 1940 symbol of France's play-safe strategy was fast being dismantled: 8,000 of its stoves had gone to heat Berlin's air-raid shelters, its 50,000 tons of steel plate were bound for the smelting furnaces of the Ruhr. Many of its heavy guns now faced the English Channel coastline.

But the threat of a German landing – Hitler's much-vaunted "Operation Sea Lion" – which had haunted the British for seven months was fast receding. "Invasion has, for the present, been given a back seat," the Minister of Aircraft Production, Lord Beaverbrook, wrote to his old friend, Sir Samuel Hoare, the British Ambassador in Spain, "The possibility of strangulation by blockade holds the stage." Thus for 48 million Britons, the buff-coloured ration book had become a way of life, and a symbol of the poorest diet the nation had ever known. "The danger is worse than in the last war," the Minister of Food, Lord Woolton, had asserted as early as New Year's Day, which at once prompted a measured rebuke from Churchill – "I am afraid that your statement will be much used by enemy propaganda and it might even encourage the Germans. . . ."

Every housewife, reduced to four ounces of bacon a week, two ounces of butter and two ounces of tea was now a combatant on what Woolton had dubbed "The Kitchen Front", concocting such strange stomach-stretchers as Woolton Pie (mainly vegetables and potatoes), Lentil Roast

* France, Holland, Belgium, Norway, Poland and Czechoslovakia.

2

and Carrot Tart, glazed with lemon jelly. The meat ration, 1s 2d worth a week, bought only three quarters of a pound of stewing beef or two small chops; one egg per fortnight was the most that one could hope for. Onions had become as rare as oranges, lemons and bananas; even before Hopkins returned to Washington, a one and a half pound onion fetched £4 3s 4d in a raffle. In one London suburb, a rumour of apples saw a mile-long queue forming at 6 a.m.

In an era when bureaucracy seemed rampant, Britain had become a land of slogans; not for twenty-three years had its people been so exhorted and cajoled. The streets were loud with hoardings and posters: "Don't Be A Food Hog" – "Careless Talk Costs Lives" – "Make Do and Mend". "Dig for Victory" was in itself an illustration of the change the land had undergone; seventeen million acres were now under cultivation and even the Tower of London's famous moat was given over to cabbages.

It all added up to a slow battle of attrition, a drab progression of milkless, eggless, and meatless days, a far cry from the heady euphoria of the Battle of Britain and the London blitz. Waning British morale was now of such concern to the War Cabinet that 10,000 bureaucrats were compiling reports based on surveys of 200,000 letters that were intercepted each month. Any man in the street would have confirmed their findings free of charge: few saw the war ending in a year, fewer still saw how it could end at all.

No comfort could be derived from occupied Europe; under Hitler's hegemony, the people had retreated into themselves. Food was a mild obsession with almost every nation, and not surprisingly; in Paris, a turnip was a meal for a gourmet and many Belgians and Dutchmen had lost up to fifteen pounds in weight. Gold was still jealously hoarded, as a hedge against harder times yet; the value of a *napoléon d'or* had now increased seven-fold. Day and night, the streets were shrouded in brooding silence; ninety percent of private cars were off the road and a secondhand bicycle, priced at 2,500 francs, was precious enough to be kept under lock and key. Among the young, Nazis and anti-Nazis alike found common ground: a bitter contempt for the bourgeois past.

Cut off in their island fortress, the British, by degrees, were succumbing to an insidious apathy. The 300 scrutators of the Mass Observation Organisation, who reported on current topics to the Ministry of Information, noted that four people out of ten no longer followed the war news at all. Absenteeism had doubled in many war factories, while in others a three-hour stint was an average working day. Although legend would hail this as a halcyon period of industrial relations, 1,077,000 working days would be lost through stoppages before the year was out.

Factory workers were failing to clock on, many busmen refused to drive in air raids, dockers were staging a go-slow and coalmen were

3

reluctant to deliver coal. The reasons were not hard to find; in their innermost hearts the British sensed that this was a war they might survive but could never win, without the aid of the world's two most unlikely participants: the United States and Soviet Russia.

"All I can say," summed up one xenophobic Briton, "is the world would be all right with no foreigners."

Thus in the weeks to come Harry Hopkins was to become both the staunch friend and the inspirational driving force of which the war-weary British so sorely stood in need.

*

At first glance, Hopkins was an unlikely ally for the robust Churchill. At 51, he was a man living on borrowed time, a gaunt lean mid-Westerner, his face haggard and sallow, in rumpled loosely hanging clothes. "His lips," noted Sir Charles Wilson clinically, "were blanched, as if he had been bleeding internally" – as in the past he had. Only narrowly had Hopkins survived an operation for stomach cancer, and even now, plagued by a chronic liver deficiency and pernicious anaemia, he was kept alive by a twice-monthly blood transfusion.

A harness-maker's son from Sioux City, Iowa, and a one-time social worker, Hopkins had first won Roosevelt's trust as an energetic Secretary of Commerce. Later, on a symbolic date – 10 May, 1940, when Hitler struck at Belgium and Holland – he had moved into the White House as a guest and stayed thereafter. Working mostly in a disreputable old bathrobe from a bedroom that had once been Abraham Lincoln's study, his aura, as one man recalled it, was one of "quick cigarettes, thinning hair, brief sarcasms, fraying suits of clothes."

His mission, coinciding with Roosevelt's unprecedented election to a third term of office, was to interpret Churchill's thinking to the President. As what one diplomat termed "the fairy godfather of Lend-Lease" – Roosevelt's December, 1940 decision to supply Britain with munitions for free, to be paid for in kind when the war was over – Hopkins himself saw his role as "a catalyst between two prima-donnas", the emotional rhetorical Churchill and the often devious, frequently ruthless, Roosevelt, who nevertheless had one bond in common: a hatred of Nazi-ism.

It was a hatred that Hopkins shared to the hilt, above all other pre-occupations. Often tactless and irreverent, he had scant patience with Churchill's flights of oratory, as the Premier was to discover during the first week-end they spent together. "After the war, we must make a good life for the cottagers," Churchill promised Hopkins, the onetime social worker, over brandy and cigars, and was startled when Hopkins responded violently, "I dont give a damn about your cottagers – we're only

4

interested in seeing that goddam sonofabitch gets licked." But Churchill took it in good part; from that time on, impressed by Hopkins' incisive brain, he dubbed him "Lord Root-of-the-Matter".

From the day of his arrival, 9 January, Hopkins' purpose was to find out what made the British tick, and he set to work with a will. "They must prove that they are doing their best before we go all out for them," he told the American Military Attaché, General Raymond E. Lee, and to this end, in thirty-one days, he talked to 300 men and women. "Am seeing everything from bombs to President's cousins," he cabled Roosevelt on 14 January. Among his witnesses was King George VI who showed a properly regal disdain for almost all his Cabinet save Churchill. "Beaverbrook . . . clearly he does not trust . . . Bevin* among the Labour crowd, talks too much . . . Attlee and Greenwood* have no real power in the Labour movement . . ."

Yet despite his admiration for the British, Hopkins knew deep misgivings. Impressed as he was by Churchill's determination to resist, he was still appalled by the lack of means to do so. Already, he felt, the British were expecting too much – Lend-Lease on an unprecedented scale, a declaration of war by Roosevelt before the summer was out. In vain Hopkins pointed out that only Congress could declare war, and many representatives were implacably hostile to this concept.

His warnings were timely. On Wednesday 15 January, two days before he dined with Churchill in Glasgow, hearings had begun in a bitter no-holds-barred debate in which a powerful caucus of men sought to avert all United States involvement in Adolf Hitler's war.

*

Long before 10 a.m., the big Ways and Means Committee Room in the new House Office building on Washington's Capitol Hill had been crowded out. Behind the horseshoe desk, puffing pipes, cigars and cigarettes, sat 23 members of the House Foreign Affairs Committee; in the centre of the curve, the chairman, little Congressman Sol Bloom, faced a semi-circle of witness chairs.

There was tension in the air and everybody felt it. The President's Lend-Lease plan, appropriately numbered House Bill No 1776, was majestically vague in its language – "A Bill to Further Promote the Defense of the U.S. and For Other Purposes" – but its purport was clear. Under this bill powers would go to Franklin Roosevelt such as no American had ever before sought.

The power to order any arsenal, shipyard or factory to manufacture

---

* Minister of Labour Ernest Bevin, Deputy Premier Clement Attlee and Minister without portfolio Arthur Greenwood were Labour MPs who had joined Churchill's coalition government in May 1940.

any defense articles the President might name, for one. The power to communicate defense information to any Government he chose, for another. Above all, a third power that might prove a political hot potato: the right to allow the British Fleet to use the harbours of New York and Norfolk, Virginia, to carry out repairs at American expense. If the Bill became law it would be a tacit non-shooting alliance with Britain and all other nations who helped to keep the war away from American shores.

In a sense the weeks of debate that would follow were a mirror image of the United States, its polarised fears and aspirations – a debate which as Roosevelt said was to rage "in every newspaper, on every wavelength – over every cracker barrel in the land". As the Committee's first witness, the Secretary of State, 69-year-old Cordell Hull, clad in a shiny blue serge suit, his face as pale as candle-wax under silver-white hair, read his prepared statement, his long slender hands seemed to tremble slightly. His voice deep with conviction as he charted the aggressions of Germany, Italy and Japan since 1931, he told the Committee flatly: "The most serious question today for this country is whether the control of the high seas shall pass into the hands of powers bent on a programme of unlimited conquest."

The early afternoon saw Treasury Secretary Henry Morgenthau Jr, flanked by seven aides, succeed to the stand. A humourless intense anti-Nazi – whose criterion for hiring a staffer was "Does he hate Hitler's guts?" – it was Morgenthau's lot to reveal for the first time in history the confidential balance sheet of another nation's finances. While the war was costing Britain $500,000,000 a day, the Secretary stressed, all British assets quickly convertible into dollars had been spent or obligated before 1 January. "Slow assets", nominally valued at £3,868,000 could not be liquidated in time to obviate the need for United States aid.

The British held virtually no gold – while dollar exchange assets available were only $1,775,000 against the annual requirement of $3,019,000,000.

This was startling news to many like the outgoing Vice President, John Nance Garner, who in a noisy whisky-flushed Cabinet oration was to charge that the British had billions to spend and were short-changing the United States. Morgenthau replied obliquely that "the British financial cow was just about dry", but the assertion was made in no mood of blind trust. As the Treasury Secretary explained to Roosevelt, secret reports from the Federal Reserve Bank of New York had monitored every financial move the British had made since Lend-Lease was mooted.

Other voices from the President's Cabinet took up the tocsin. On 16 January, Secretary of War Henry Stimson, 73, "Light Horse Harry", warned that a failure to pass the Bill would not only bring about a British defeat but plunge America into the war in 90 days. Following him on the stand, the tough ruddy-cheeked Navy Secretary, Frank Knox, produced telling statistics. America was building a two ocean Navy in 72 private yards and 11 Navy yards – but completion lay six years away. If the Royal Navy gave up the United States' strength would fall steadily behind the combined Axis fleets.

These were the authentic voices of American interventionism – whose ranks would soon include such diverse warriors as Mrs Calvin Coolidge, widow of the thirtieth U.S. President, Allen Dulles, lawyer and future head of the Office of Strategic Services in Switzerland, the department store owner Marshall Field, film magnates Darryl F. Zanuck and Spyros Skouras and Dan Tobin of the Teamsters Union.

But contrary voices were heard, not only from the witness chairs but across the length and breadth of America and through all their speeches the horror of war ran like a scarlet thread. These were the isolationists, perhaps 800,000 strong, spread among 700 separate organisations, and their sincere belief was that America could best serve the cause of civilisation by staying aloof from this war. This quarrel was not of America's making, nor did it infringe on America's security – yet Roosevelt, like Woodrow Wilson 23 years earlier, resolutely sought an international role for the United States.

Above all, the isolationists were united by a profound distrust of Roosevelt's motivation: as the first President in American history ever to serve a third term, the first to guide the nation's destiny from a wheel chair following a polio attack, would he also be the first to wage war without declaring it? On 6 January, leafing through a big black leather binder to deliver his State of the Union message to the 77th Congress he had spoken for the first time of a post-war world cleansed of Nazi-ism that would embody the Four Freedoms: freedom of speech, freedom from want, freedom to worship God in one's own way, freedom from fear. But although devotees like his Secretary of Agriculture Claude Wickard saw him as "like Atlas, in that the whole world rested on his shoulders", no Republican applause greeted his peroration.

Two weeks later, on 20 January, his 10.30 a.m. inauguration at St John's Church – a reinauguration as portentous as Caesar's – had likewise struck a chilling note. Following his speech, no high school bands or festive floats with pretty girls had taken the stage, as in happier years. Instead only U.S. Army riflemen wearing drab khaki, marched with bayonets fixed, eyes staring intently ahead under steel helmets. The rumbling of tanks, heavy military trucks and heavier guns was heard along Constitution Avenue. Then as the cold blue sky darkened, almost 300 military aircraft, silver red-tipped bodies glistening, ripped the sky above the White House and the roof tops of the quiet city.

These were more planes than most American citizens had ever seen or would ever wish to see.

Thus the isolationists before the House Affairs Committee were swift to disclaim that the war was America's business. The distinguished aviator Colonel Charles Lindbergh, darling of the American First Committee, in flatly opposing the Bill, called for 20,000 planes to defend the United States and a negotiated Anglo-German peace. General Hugh Johnson, sometime columnist and former Chief of the National Recovery Administration, claimed the bill gave Roosevelt totalitarian powers and lashed out against "humanitarian lollypopping".

Some were more forthright still. One kingpin isolationist, Senator Burton Wheeler of Montana, claimed that the President's bill would "plough under every fourth American boy" – "the rottenest statement I ever heard in public life," raged Roosevelt. Senator Bulow saw Hitler as no menace at all. "If I were as certain of a place in Heaven as I am that Herr Hitler will never invade . . . I would feel just as if I were already in God's pocket."

In contrast to the studied courtesy of the public forums, spontaneous anti-Roosevelt propaganda struck a jarring and spiteful note. Outside the British Embassy on Massachussetts Avenue, paraded lady members of the Paul Revere Sentinels and the Women's Neutrality League, brandishing placards reading: "Benedict Arnold Helped England, Too". A cartoon in Captain Joseph Patterson's isolationist *New York Daily News*, set the sour keynote: outside a walk-up apartment house, a raddled harlot labelled War accosted a doughboy: "Come on in, I'll treat you right. I used to know your Daddy."

The former Ambassador to France, William Bullitt, saw Americans as indulging in a fatal fallacy: they looked to the Atlantic Ocean as the French had looked to the Maginot Line. In Chicago, John Wheeler Bennett, head of the Research Department of the British Information Service in New York, had oral proof of this. Following a courteous reception by the American First Executive Committee, he felt emboldened to ask: "When would you find it necessary to resist a German invasion?" One man replied in all seriousness: "When they cross the Rio Grande."

The same voices rehearsing the same arguments were to drone on for many weeks to come. Although the House Foreign Affairs Committee, concluding its public hearings on 29 January, threw the House open to a formal five-day debate on 3 February, the Senate's Foreign Relations Committee began its own hearings on 27 January. Thus, on 8 February, when the House passed the Bill by a vote of 260 to 165, Hull, Stimson, Knox and others were manfully repeating their testimony in the Senate's stifling Caucus Room, packed out with 1800 citizens who had shouldered their way into a room designed to hold 500.

The surprise witness arrived on the afternoon of Tuesday 11 February. Steered by a phalanx of policemen, a rumpled bear-like figure, a lock of hair drooping over one eye, shambled through the throng from a rear door to an excited buzz of comment. Heralded by a staccato popping of photographers' flash-bulbs, the least-likely deponent for the interventionist cause had arrived to take the stand on behalf of Lend-Lease: 48-year-old Wendell Willkie, the Wall Street lawyer and Republican candidate, whom Roosevelt had soundly defeated in November, 1940.

It was an eleventh-hour appearance; only at 12.30 that afternoon had Willkie's plane touched down at Washington's National Airport. But as one whose 18-day visit to England, as a private citizen travelling at his own expense, had been publicly blessed by the President, Willkie spoke as a man fresh from the front line. "I feel that I am walking through history," he had told newsmen after talking with Cabinet Ministers, policemen, air raid wardens and Tommies, but one simple incident had impressed him above all.

Driving through London's Trafalgar Square one noonday, the air-raid sirens had sounded and Willkie learned that German daylight raiders were approaching the capital. Yet incredibly, as ack-ack guns boomed overhead, the traffic rumbled on, and in the shadow of Nelson's Column, a group of old ladies, unperturbed, had continued to feed the pigeons.

It was known, too, that Willkie had had three long private talks with Churchill – talks which had left him impressed with the Premier's implacable determination. On a visit to Dublin, Willkie told Churchill, the Prime Minister Eamon de Valera had voiced a bitter complaint: since Eire was still neutral and refused to cede the former British treaty ports of Queenstown (now Cobh), Berehaven and Lough-Swilly, Churchill had clamped down a stringent economic blockade, denying Eire not only charter shipping, food, iron and steel but even guns to ward off a possible German invasion.

Churchill had only shrugged, unconcerned. "Any nation that is used for the battlefield in a dog-fight will cease to exist," he opined. "Perhaps it will be Irish soil."

Above all, Willkie had swallowed whole the bait that Churchill, in an effort to counteract Lindbergh's propaganda, had dangled before the American people. In a transatlantic broadcast on Sunday 9 February – for which Hopkins had stood in as co-author – Churchill had assured the nation that Britain required nothing of them beyond war material. "We shall not fail or falter," he promised. "We shall not weaken or tire. Give us the tools and we shall finish the job."

Thus Wilkie, speaking fast and urgently, now told the Senate Committee in all sincerity what they most wanted to hear: that the last thing the British contemplated was an American Expeditionary Force, "this year, nor next year".

Advocating that every American bomber save training planes should be sent to Britain post-haste, along with five or ten destroyers a month, he summed up: at the worst, it was a matter of self-preservation. Should

9

Britain fall, "we would be at war in a month" or at most "sixty days". But with American aid, Britain would not fall.

Others would speak up as trenchantly – notably Senator Alben Barkley, who opened the ensuing debate with the immortal words of Patrick Henry: "Is life so dear or peace so sweet as to be purchased at the price of chains or slavery? Forbid it, Almighty God." But it was Willkie's appeal to the national self-interest that ultimately turned the tide.

Meanwhile the British, anxious to prove their worth, were embarking on as dubious a military venture as even 1941 would witness.

*

Both the venture – and the decision – were rooted in history. As far back as April, 1939, following Mussolini's Good Friday invasion of Albania, Churchill's predecessor, Neville Chamberlain, had guaranteed Greece British support in the event of Axis aggression, extending the pledge to Turkey and Rumania. The question had remained hypothetical – until 28 October, 1940, when Benito Mussolini, *Il Duce* of Fascism, bent on scoring off Hitler for seizing oil-rich areas of Rumania, had sent four ill-equipped Italian divisions storming into Greece.

The chivalrous Churchill's immediate reaction – "We will give you all the help in our power" – proved premature. As the Greeks fought back like tigers, the Italians, within weeks, were in headlong retreat, surrounded at the ports of Durazzo and Valona, their backs to the sea. Moreover, the Greek Premier, Ioannis "Little John" Metaxas, known as the "carpet slippers dictator", had declined Churchill's offer, fearing German intervention.

Midway through January, Churchill was still insisting and Metaxas still demurring, although perhaps to discourage further importuning he put the price sky-high: he would accept a force of 200,000 well-equipped British troops. But the British, in any case, could send no reinforcements that would decisively affect the outcome. On 2 November, Secretary of State for War, Anthony Eden, had dismissed it in a two-word diary entry: "Strategic folly".

Two events now conspired to change the course of history. On 29 January Metaxas died of blood poisoning and his successor, an immaculate banker named Alexander Koryzis, promptly agreed to accept the British offer.

This was a bitter blow, for the only troops available would be stripped from the one theatre of war where the British were conducting a triumphant campaign: Libya. In the past two months, the Western Desert Force, under Lieutenant General Richard O'Connor, had advanced 500 miles, taken 130,000 Italian prisoners, 400 tanks, more than 1,000 guns and the major fortresses of Bardia and Tobruk.

It was now that Eden – who had become Foreign Secretary* on 23 December, 1940 – made a fatal error. "A vain feminine creature," as one Cabinet colleague had dubbed him, Eden had long seen himself as an elder statesman; now his aspiration was the creation of a Balkan bloc to thwart any German move southward – "The only chance to prevent the Balkans being devoured piecemeal". Hungary and Rumania had made common cause with the Axis, Bulgaria was wavering – but might not British intervention in Greece stiffen the resolve of Turkey and Yugoslavia?

It was a fond illusion. Although the Balkans loomed as the 1941 surrogate for Belgium and the Netherlands – "all little people waiting to be eaten one by one", noted the Minister for Economic Warfare, Hugh Dalton – what they sought above all was to wall themselves into fortresses of individual privacy. In Sofia, King Boris III of Bulgaria, an amiable lepidopterist who also collected mountain flower petals, fretted that Roosevelt's provocative broadcasts might involve the whole world in war: "national socialism may be good for Germany, fascism for Italy, and bolshevism for Russia but . . . none of these is wanted by Bulgaria".

King Boris, in any case, was hedging his bets: to circumvent what the U.S. Minister in Rumania termed "a period of peaceful bullying", fourteen Bulgarian airfields were already playing host to 280 Luftwaffe aircraft, their war material ferried thence by 40 special Luftwaffe trains.

It was the same in every capital. Turkey, despite an Anglo-Turkish pact of 1939 pleaded weakness of both arms and air-power; offered 10 R.A.F. squadrons they still proved what Sir Alexander Cadogan, Permanent Under Secretary to the Foreign Office called "timorous and sticky". At Beli Dvor, The White Palace, Belgrade, Prince Paul, the Regent of Yugoslavia, although a resolute Anglophile, saw the Allied cause as already doomed; his sole ambition was to pull out in September, when his nephew, 17-year-old King Peter II ascended the throne – "he would not go on with his duties for another day", reported the British Minister, Ronald Campbell. Faced with a Foreign Office proposition for a United Balkan Front, Prince Paul, shaking with rage, berated Campbell: "This stinks of Anthony!"

But one factor could hardly be denied: a British expedition to Greece, however foolhardy, might do much to convince the United States that Britain was still a contender worth backing.

Major-General Francis Davidson never forgot his first assignment as newly appointed Director of British Military Intelligence. On the hectic afternoon of 11 February following an urgent summons from the Chiefs of Staff, Davidson and a team of experts were given exactly four hours to draw up an appreciation (with maps) of German troop strengths in

---

* A post he had previously held from December 1935 to February, 1938.

Rumania and Bulgaria. On their report would hinge a crucial decision: whether to divert troops to Greece from Egypt and Libya.

At 5.30 p.m. Davidson was given three minutes by the Chiefs of Staff – General Sir John Dill, Admiral Sir Dudley Pound, Air Marshal Sir Charles Portal – to present a digest of his information. His conclusion: on their present track record, the Germans, if they invaded Greece, would reach Athens by 21 April.

One day later, as if Davidson had never uttered, Eden and Dill departed for Cairo to sell their plan willy-nilly to the trio charged with protecting Britain's Middle East dominion by land, sea and air: General Sir Archibald Wavell, Admiral Sir Andrew Cunningham and Air Chief Marshal Sir Arthur Longmore. Later the disgusted Davidson found that Churchill had even doodled in blue pencil all over his best strategic map, rendering it illegible.

Such was the British desperation to win American approval in the dawn of 1941.

*

Both at home and abroad many men entertained grave doubts. In Whitehall, two of the first to voice them, on 19 February, were Hugh Dalton and Sir Alexander Cadogan.

Might it not be better, both men pondered, "to allow the Greeks, under pressure, to make a separate peace . . . better than having the country devastated to the last and better than putting in some of our own troops and having them not even evacuated but trapped and destroyed?".

It was a thought that Churchill, too, explored, next day with the War Cabinet – "in that case we could not very well blame them . . . we should have done our duty." Later that day he cabled Eden: "Do not feel yourselves obligated to a Greek enterprise if in your hearts you feel it will only be another Norwegian fiasco." This counsel profoundly shocked Sir Michael Palairet, the Grecophile British Minister in Athens. "I felt quite sick with horror when I read the Prime Minister's telegram," he confessed to Eden later. "I don't think I *could* have gone to the King with a message on those lines; *hara-kiri* on the Palace threshold seemed the only way out."

But Sir Michael's fears were groundless. Shuttling from Cairo to Athens and on to Ankara, Eden was bent on having his way. On 22 February, in a series of meetings with King George of the Hellenes that dragged on for forty-eight hours, Eden, backed by the Middle Eastern Commander-in-Chief, galvanised the Greeks like a high pressure armaments salesman – promising them 100,000 men, 240 field guns, 202 anti-tank guns, plus vastly inflated totals of medium guns, ack-ack

12

guns and tanks. Not surprisingly, King George and his cabinet assented readily.

Even Wavell, who had earlier feared the Greeks might crack, stressing that Crete spelt greater security for Egypt and Malta, was at last won over. "I can't help thinking," commented General Sir Hastings (later Lord) Ismay, Assistant Secretary to the War Cabinet, "that (Wavell) allowed political considerations to influence his military judgement."

All hopes of a Balkan bloc had already gone by the board. In Ankara the Turkish Cabinet proved ambivalent, despite Eden's attempts to rally them by reciting reams of Persian poetry at a ceremonial banquet. By 1 March, Bogdan Filov, the sad sick Premier of Bulgaria, racked by stomach ulcers, was to sign the Axis pact in Vienna in Hitler's presence. Prince Paul of Yugoslavia now so feared involvement that he refused even to slip away from Beli Dvor Palace to meet Eden in southern Serbia. "I can hardly grasp how I've been given the strength – so far – to stand all the strain," he excused himself, "but I can assure you that it's no easy task."

Another gravely worried man was Robert Menzies, the Australian Premier, then on a visit to London. Menzies had reason: of the 58,000 troops who were ultimately sent – barely half the number that Eden had promised – more than 17,000 would be Australians, a further 16,000 New Zealanders. Could he say to his colleagues, Menzies asked the War Cabinet, "that the venture had a substantial chance of success?"

Churchill, though equivocal, still struck at the heart of the matter. "If we forsook Greece it would have a bad effect in the United States."

Three days later, the Australians reluctantly agreed – on condition that contingency planning ensured that "evacuation (if it became necessary) could be successfully undertaken".

On 7 March, with the die finally cast, Churchill's planners felt nothing but consternation. His Director of Military Operations, Major-General Sir John Kennedy saw it as "a major error". Captain Ralph Edwards, Royal Navy, Director of Operations (Home) thought it "a very wrong policy . . . another Winston lunacy". As Minister of Aircraft Production Lord Beaverbrook set off for the Cabinet meeting that set Greece in motion, his parliamentary private secretary gave a soothsayer's warning: "Remember three words – Gallipoli – Narvik – Dunkirk."

Even Churchill felt it necessary to warn Eden: to mollify Australia and New Zealand, whose troops would bear the brunt of any fighting, the decision should be presented as one taken by Wavell and his fellow-commanders, not by the Foreign Secretary – "you have given us few facts or reasons . . . which can be presented to these Dominions as justifying the operation on any grounds but *noblesse oblige*".

In Washington, D.C., the reactions were all that Churchill might have hoped. Under Secretary of State Sumner Welles thought it "one of the wisest (decisions) taken during the war". Peppery little Harold Ickes, Roosevelt's Secretary of the Interior, noted: "Certainly the British have to stick to the end . . . They cannot afford to subject themselves to the charge of deserting their allies, as happened when the British were evacuated from Belgium." Rear Admiral Richmond Kelly Turner, Chief of the Navy's War Plans Division, agreed. "Sending British troops to Greece," he minuted the Chief of Naval Operations, Admiral Harold R. Stark, "has so weakened the British Army in Egypt that the Germans will have little difficulty in regaining all of Libya."

Yet Turner saw the entire venture as a moral necessity. "Abandoning Greece to its fate could have been an action so base and immoral that reinforcing them was necessary regardless of its influence on the future of Britain . . ."

*

In Athens, one American on the spot was less certain: Lincoln MacVeagh, the U.S. Minister and a longtime observer of the Grecian scene. If war comes to Greece, he predicted to Roosevelt, "the best that the Allies can look forward to is a succession of Thermopylaes". The Luftwaffe, he thought, would "take the place of the Persian arrows, darkening the sun, and British tenacity and Greek devotion would fight in the shades".

MacVeagh had been in no way reassured by a talk he had had with Anthony Eden during his time in Athens. "I think eventually the Yugo-slavs, Turks and Greeks will all be in the fighting," he had told MacVeagh airily, "but there will be a lot of slipping and sliding before that happens."

MacVeagh was politely sceptical. Weren't the British still living mainly on efforts and hope?

Eden, he recalled, was "singularly sanguine". "Even if Germany suc-ceeds in over-running Greece," he prophesied, "I don't see how this will help her. By that time we shall have cleaned up in the Middle East and be sitting pretty in Africa. In making war in the Balkans, Germany is only playing football in her own cabbage patch."

It was a strangely ill-timed assessment. Thirteen days earlier, General Enno von Rintelen, the German military attaché in Rome, had brought news to Benito Mussolini in his 40-roomed mansion, Villa Torlonia, that left the Duce beaming. Alarmed by Italian reverses in Libya, Hitler was coming to his Axis partner's rescue: a hastily-assembled 5th Light Motor-ised Division was to be despatched from Germany to serve as a "blocking detachment" in Tripolitania, Libya's northernmost province.

On 12 February, its new commander *Generalleutnant* Erwin Rommel, arrived in Tripoli.

*

Across the worn paving of Tripoli's main *piazza*, rumbled file upon file of 17-ton Mark IV Panzers, camouflaged in the newly-fashionable desert shade of sand-yellow. Motionless in their turrets, the commanders of the 5th Light Division, arrayed in olive-green tropical uniforms and peaked forage caps stared ahead of them, as impassive as the death's head badges adorning their lapels. At the saluting base, the commander of the newly-formed German Afrika Korps the stocky blue-eyed Rommel stood braced rigidly to attention beside the Italian commander in North Africa, the stooping 62-year-old General Italo Gariboldi.

Yet to Rommel's aide, *Leutnant* Heinz Werner Schmidt, the truly impressive realisation on this crisp spring morning was that his chief was as astute a propagandist as tactician. No sooner had the Panzers passed the saluting base than the column veered into a side street – and after fifteen minutes Schmidt was conscious that at least one Mark IV, with a faulty chain, had passed this way before. For the benefit of the cheering crowds – and any British agents who might be on hand – Rommel was stretching a meagre force of 50 tanks to the proportions of an armoured corps.

Deception – allied with audacity – was to play as great a part as armoured strength in the next phase of the desert battle and for this very reason, Rommel, former commander of the 7th Panzer, "the Ghost Division", who in May 1940 had time and again out-manoeuvred the British columns retreating to Dunkirk was destined to call almost every shot in the months ahead.

Three days after settling into his headquarters in Tripoli's opulent Hotel Uaddan, Rommel was fast formulating plans – plans which in no way coincided with the briefing he had received from the Army's Commander-in-Chief, *Generalfeldmarschall* Walther von Brauchitsch. The Afrika Korps' role, the Commander-in-Chief had stressed, was to be both limited and defensive. Führer Order No 22 of 11 January had made the situation plain: "The position in the Mediterranean, on strategical, political and psychological grounds, demands German aid. Tripolitania must be saved."

The German High Command, Von Brauchitsch warned, planned no decisive strike against the British in North Africa. By the end of May when the Afrika Korps was strengthened by the arrival of the 15th Panzer Division – Rommel might launch limited attacks against Agedabia, south of Beda Fomm, the site of Lieutenant-General O'Connor's last decisive victory. Later he might retake Benghazi, the seaport capital of Cyrenaica. In vain Rommel was to argue: "The Benghazi area can't be held by itself. We shall have to retake the whole of Cyrenaica." His instructions remained finite: to submit operational plans for this move to bolster sagging Italian morale not later than 20 April.

At 49, Rommel was in stark contrast to the top brass of the Army High

15

Command. Von Brauchitsch Rommel knew as a sensitive withdrawn patrician, who often retired to vomit after a tongue-lashing from Hitler. At times, too, Rommel had clashed with the Chief of Staff, the acerbic ambitious *Generaloberst* Franz Halder – "What did you ever do in war apart from sit on your backside in an office?", Rommel had once challenged him rashly. A schoolmaster's son lacking both money and influence, Rommel was a fighting general with an intuitive sixth sense of his enemy's weakness, dedicated to the twin concepts of speed and surprise – *Sturm, Swung, Wucht*, (Attack, Impetus, Weight) was his most quoted maxim. A virtual teetotaller and non-smoker, fascinated by military minutiae and devoted to just one woman, his wife, Lucie, he now lost no time in adapting to unfamiliar desert conditions. Would heavy tanks bog down in the sand, as Italian generals asserted? Would wheeled trucks do the same? Promptly, Rommel consulted *Leutnant* Hans-Otto Behrendt, an Egyptologist assigned to him as an Arabic interpreter and learned a desert warrior's first lesson: the secret was to drive on slightly soft tyres.

All through February, Rommel was exultant, for unknown to Von Brauchitsch, and in direct defiance of his orders, the first units of the 5th Light Division were already by 15 February, moving in convoy to the coastal village of Sirte, 300 miles from Tripoli – poised to strike, on 24 March, at the rose-red fort of El Agheila, 140 miles south of Benghazi. "we're going to advance to the Nile," Rommel boasted proudly to his staff officers.

The reasons for the High Command's caution were quite unknown to him, though to an outsider they made sound strategic sense. By slow degrees, throughout eastern Europe, three million German soldiers were massing to attack Soviet Russia.

*

Spring came early that year to the *Berghof*, Hitler's white-painted chalet-style retreat perched on the Obersalzberg, high in the Bavarian Alps. From the wide picture-windows of his pine-panelled workroom, the Führer and Chancellor of the Third Reich could see the first tender green breaking through white along the snowy slopes of the Untersberg, the sheltered sunstruck places where blue gentians and Alpine violets pierced the soil. He felt it more strongly still in his blood and bones: spring was the time when armies marched.

Now, as March dawned, Hitler was facing the most crucial decision of his life: the massive May land assault against Russia – Operation Barbarossa – that he had ordered as far back as December, 1940. Day and night now, the obsession rarely left him: the great drive to the east, embracing all the territories between the Vistula and the Ural Mountains, with a southward thrust towards the vast granaries of the Ukraine. It was

16

the *Drang nach Osten* of which Kaiser Wilhelm II had dreamed, which Hitler himself had charted in *Mein Kampf.*

At his broad desk, or relaxed in his green-tinted bath tub, or at the breakfast table sipping China tea, spreading his toast with mountains of jam, Hitler pondered each aspect of his strategy anew. Later it would be time to set down fresh thoughts on paper: one of his confidential secretaries Fräulein Johanna Wolf or Fräulein Christa Schröder would type the draft in huge letters designed to save his eyes before Hitler slashed revisions in green, blue and red pencil.

His motives for the drive were part economic, part idealistic. To harness the vast resources of slave labour, to seize the coal-rich Donets Basin as well as the oil-rich Caucasus, to provide *Lebensraum* for Germany's millions – these made sound economic sense. But to eliminate Russia – with whom he had concluded a mutual non-aggression pact in 1939 – was in the nature of a crusade; not only would he destroy the hated cradle of Bolshevism but "England's last hope", wiping out two enemies at one stroke. In Hitler's complex global reasoning, to turn east was also to turn west.

Three unknowns bedevilled his planning: the ultimate extent of American intervention; the true intentions of his third partner Japan; the Russian capacity for resistance. But like a busy area manager, he was laying plans to convert the Balkan states into compliant satellites; small wonder that on the Balkan bourse of rumour, business had never been more brisk. Hungary, Rumania, and now Bulgaria had fallen into line – and Prince Paul was under mounting pressure to adhere to the Tripartite Pact.

Marshal Henri Philippe Pétain, the octogenarian ruler of Vichy France, was under pressure too; in due time Hitler would seek to occupy Mediterranean ports in France, as well as North Africa, as well as passage for German troops through Tunisia for an attack on the British in Libya. The one man who had tacitly refused any transit for German troops scheduled to attack Gibraltar, General Francisco Franco, *Caudillo* of Spain, had now been crossed off the Führer's list. "The man has missed a historic chance," declared Hitler loftily, but Franco was shrewder. "The Germans are trying to deal in the skin before the lion has been killed," was his assessment of Hitler's plans for Britain.

Greece was an unlooked for factor in Hitler's time-table. Angered by Mussolini's ill-timed invasion, he had formulated no plans to rescue his Axis partner, as in Africa – but now the imminent British presence brought Greece into the spotlight. From Salonika, in northern Greece, the British had launched their drive on Austria–Hungary in World War One. That must not happen again.

Thus overnight, thanks to Eden's machinations, Greece was now of paramount importance to the success of Barbarossa. To seize Greece was

17

to seal off the Balkans, especially Rumania's Ploesti oilfields – both from Russia and from the British in the Eastern Mediterranean. It would provide a staging point for German troops massing for the Russian offensive – and prevent Britain and Russia joining forces when Germany turned east.

Hitler saw one thing plainly: time was of the essence. From Finland to the Balkan passes, the Red Army was a potential threat to every economic link: Balkan grain, Rumanian oil, even the timber, phosphates, chrome ore and platinum that Russia still scrupulously transshipped to Germany under the 1939 agreement. Would Barbarossa kill not only the goose but all its golden eggs? Perhaps – but the wary Hitler knew that Russia could renege on the agreement at any time it suited her.

"What one does not have but needs, one most conquer," Hitler summed up.

Not for one moment did he dream that it would all blow up in his face like a firecracker at a party. In the end, Barbarossa would bring about the entire chain of circumstance that Hitler had sought to forestall – forcing Russia and Britain into an uneasy alliance, engaging Russia and freeing Japan, in the Far East, for a titanic onslaught on the United States. But Hitler had no inkling. In this same month, during a brief reunion with his younger sister, Paula, he told her: "Do you know it is my absolute conviction that the Lord is holding His protecting hand above me?"

Henceforth, the clocks must tick against him, but now the days and nights fled towards spring, and, for the moment, spring spelt destiny.

*

All over Europe, men and women now made unobtrusive preparations for the holocaust ahead. It was as if, sensing Hitler's brooding presence, they sought to put their houses in order, as a sudden spasm of pain might impel a man to draft a will. "Impossible to think," noted a London-based Canadian diplomat, Charles Ritchie, "without his shadow falling across our thoughts."

In Stockholm, Sweden, Harold Elvin, a 32-year-old Englishman and son of a prominent trade unionist, wrote on impulse to an old friend of his father, Sir Stafford Cripps, the British Ambassador in Russia. A rolling stone who had once worked as an art director for film producer Alexander Korda, Elvin had later opted out to spend five years cycling as far east as Leningrad, as far south as Barcelona, living as the peasants did, honing his expenses to £1 a week. Now he begged Cripps: could the Ambassador find him some niche in the Moscow Embassy?

Though Sir Stafford's reply was discouraging – the only vacancy was as an assistant night watchman, without even Foreign Office grading, paying only £4 a week – Elvin agreed readily, booking an air passage to Moscow with a stopover at Riga. He had no real premonition: it was just that Moscow seemed the place to be.

*

In Brussels, Andrée de Jongh, a 24-year-old headmaster's daughter, came to a sudden decision. All through her youth at 73, Avenue Emile Verhaeren, in the middle-class suburb of Schaerbeck, she and her sister Suzanne had been taught by their father to revere the memory of Edith Cavell, the English nurse executed by the Germans in 1915 for helping Allied soldiers to escape. Now, with two medical diplomas to her own credit – both as nurse and ambulance attendant – Andrée thought back to the six months she had worked in the Hôpital St Jean, Bruges, tending both German and British soldiers as they lay side by side on straw pallets. Often until Christmas, 1940, when German military personnel took over the hospital, the idea had crossed her mind, "How stupid to cure these British soldiers if they're going to be taken prisoner by the Germans! Why not help them escape?"

Now, having returned to Brussels, Andrée de Jongh was determined to find the answer to that question. Petite, fair-haired, galvanised by such energy that Frédéric, her father, had christened her "Little Cyclone", she and a young radio repair mechanic Arnold de Pé, hit upon a solution. Their escape line should be routed where the Germans least expected it: not through Vichy France, where loyalties to Pétain might betray them but through the northern zone of Occupied France and thence to the Low Pyrenees. It would be a conspiracy of youth, with few organisers under 25 – and ultimately the most successful of all the escape lines.

*

At Ismailia, on the Suez Canal, 64 miles from Cairo, A.C.1 (Aircraftman First Class) Marcel Gerard Comeau, a 19-year-old aerial rigger with No 33 (Hurricane) Squadron, talked things over with his mate, Ken Eaton. Three years an R.A.F. regular, the lanky irrepressible Comeau was an expert at interpreting latrine rumours – and now orders had arrived that the squadron's 21 planes were to be sprayed with dark green and brown camouflage paint. To the "erks" (other ranks) of 33 Squadron this meant one thing: they were all "for Greece".

Comeau – whose Gallic name was derived from forebears in Nova Scotia – was in no way perturbed by the fact that the R.A.F. had just posted him to Kenya; he had no intention of "missing the fun". Around 1 March – coining a brand new motto, "Put a hundred miles between yourself and the parent unit" – he stowed away aboard the troopship *Dumana*, agog for his first view of Athens. Always searching for where

19

the action was hottest, he was to "desert" twice more before the year was out.

*

In Belgrade, the Yugoslav capital, 51-year-old Ruth Mitchell, a spirited redhead from Milwaukee, Wisconsin, was already at the scene of the action, but one question remained: How to become part of it? Twice married, with a grown-up son and daughter, Ruth and her family had long seen action as their birthright. Her father, John Lendrum Mitchell, Civil War veteran, United States Senator and banker, had built the 5,000 mile long Chicago, Milwaukee and St Paul railroad; the Mitchell family home, with its private race track, had covered the area of a full city block. Her brother Brigadier-General "Billy" Mitchell, United States Air Force, had been court-martialled in 1925, found guilty and resigned from the service after charging the War and Navy Departments with "incompetency and criminal negligence". His theory had been one that 1941 would amply validate: the aeroplane had rendered the battleship obsolete.

Following one's own bent regardless was thus the Mitchell way of life. Three years resident in Yugoslavia, as a student of Serbian folk-lore, Ruth's one-storey house in the Slavija Hill district of Belgrade had long been a cultural outpost, famed for poetry readings and spirited philosophical discussions.

A hundred-carat romantic, Ruth Mitchell looked back four months to one of the most stirring demonstrations she had ever witnessed: a column of marching men pouring down Slavija Hill to the nearby Orthodox Church. All of them wore the handsome brown black-embroidered costume of the Shumadiya peasant; their feet were shod in soundless upturned rawhide sandals and black astrakhan caps adorned their heads. Before them swayed black silver-fringed banners with a skull-and-crossbones emblem and this same device was repeated in metal on every man's breast.

These were the *Četniks*, Serbian freedom fighters loyal to King Peter, whose mystic order, formed to resist the Turkish invader, dated back centuries before the Treaty of Versailles, dismembering the old Habsburg Empire, carved a new country, Yugoslavia, from the kingdom of the Serbs, Croats and Slovenes.

Ruth had sounded out contacts. Never before had a foreigner, let alone a woman, been accepted by the *Četnik* movement, but her accomplishments – a skilled horse-woman, capable of foot-slogging thirty miles a day, with a private pilot's licence – swayed the balance. But before she could be enrolled as a despatch rider, a probationary period followed. She practised for hours with a dagger on a dangling bag of sawdust, quick thrusts upwards to reach the heart. Into her coat collar she sewed a cyanide capsule, sited so that it could be chewed despite bound hands. Her name was formally inscribed in an old well-worn book.

On 3 March came the day of her initiation. Accompanied by a sponsor, she once more crossed a snowy courtyard on the outskirts of Belgrade, mounting rickety wooden stairs to a two-room office. Behind a desk sat 70-year-old Voivoda Kosta Pechanats, the *Četnik* leader, whose guerilla bands, on the Salonika front, had tied down three German Army divisions in World War One. The dimly-lit room was thronged with portraits of Serbian fighters, past and present, offset by a glittering arsenal of daggers and swords.

Now, facing an icon of Sava, her right hand firm on a crossed dagger and revolver, Ruth Mitchell looked Pechanats firmly in the eye and repeated after him: *"Do smrti za Srbiju, tako mi Bog pomogao"* (Till death for Serbia, by the help of God).

Pechanats took the old worn book then and firmly drew a line through the name "Ruth Mitchell". His explanation would have daunted a woman less determined: "When you become one of us, we consider you as good as dead."

*

For House Bill 1776, the end came almost as an anti-climax. At 3.50 p.m. on Tuesday, 11 March, flanked only by a few staffers and White House photographers, Franklin Roosevelt solemnly and silently inscribed his name on a bill that became law by a final tally of 317 to 71. In recognition of the Bill's six sponsors – among them Senator Barkley, Congressman Bloom, Speaker Sam Rayburn – the President signed his name with six pens, a few letters at a time, cleansing them with six blotters before passing them over in tribute.

News from Washington was now news for the whole world. American flags flew in the streets of London. In Sydney, crowds sang *The Star Spangled Banner*. Canada's Premier, William Lyon Mackenzie King, called the law "one of the milestones of freedom". Prime Minister Jan Smuts of South Africa exulted: "Hitler has at last brought America into the war."

Only Hitler remained unimpressed. The message from the Berghof ran: "No power and no support coming from any part of the world can change the outcome of this battle . . . England will fall."

Behind the jubilant facade, the bonds of Anglo–American amity were albeit strained almost to snapping point. In Washington, D.C., Sir Edward Peacock, King George's personal financial adviser, who feared a buyer's market, was stalling determinedly on the liquidation of British investments – notably the American Viscose Corporation, the country's largest rayon producer. When Treasury Secretary Morgenthau complained, "They don't make a god damn move on this thing," the newly-appointed Ambassador, Lord Halifax, made a childish attempt to over-awe him. "Sir Edward Peacock has very powerful friends in England," he warned, "and he is very close to the Governor of the Bank of England."

Even so Halifax, on 20 February, had cabled a warning to Churchill: Britain "should without delay hand over to America our remaining financial resource in that country". But a month later, the Premier was still temporising – "it was impossible for us to continue to make concessions at short notice to meet the exigencies of United States politics". The business "should be allowed to simmer".

In truth, it was Morgenthau who was simmering, and finally under pressure, Halifax backed down; by the end of May the American Viscose Corporation came under the hammer. "In the end," noted Harold Ickes, "the British got about $87 million for a property reasonably worth $125 million."

It was in keeping with Roosevelt's grim determination that the British must pay their way; all along he had stressed to his Cabinet his insistence on hard cash. "What mattered was dollars, not properties," noted Agriculture Secretary Claude Wickard. "Holdings of railroads in South America and elsewhere were not wanted by us."

What one commentator called "'The White Cliffs of Dover'* stage of Anglo-American friendship" was almost a thing of the past: never far from the surface now was America's deeprooted suspicion of Britain as a rapacious colonial power looking first to her own ends. "The British are always foxy," Roosevelt had cautioned Willkie on his return from London, "and you have to be the same with them." Thus Churchill's suggestion that the United States should send a show-the-flag cruiser mission to the naval base at Singapore was rejected out of hand by Admiral Harold Stark: "Never absent from British minds are their post-war interests, commercial and military."

Churchill was profoundly shocked. Although in public he lauded Lend-Lease as "a new Magna Carta" and "the most unsordid act in history", the private realisation that the Commonwealth would pay the United States £1 million in 1941 for only seven per cent of its munitions cut him to the quick. All along he told the Ministry of Information's Harold Nicolson, he had believed "that we were exchanging a bunch of flowers for a sugar cake. But not at all, the Americans have done a hard business deal." In a mood of extreme rancour he told the Chancellor of the Exchequer, Sir Kingsley Wood: "We are not only to be skinned but flayed to the bone."

* A best-selling poem of 1940 by the American author Alice Duer Miller, celebrating the British way of life. It gave its name to a top-of-the-charts ballad (featured by Hildegarde) and later to a film (starring Irene Dunn).

In fact, both sides had little cause for complaint. Churchill's driving obsession was to bring about active American involvement; given all the "tools" in the world Britain could never have "finished the job" without American manpower and he knew it. Roosevelt saw Britain as the sole bulwark in a Nazi sea – but his avowed wish "to get rid of that silly foolish old dollar sign" was little more than a fantasy spun to divert the White House Press Corps.

Even the course of nature, it seemed, must be diverted in British interests. When Minister of Food Lord Woolton noted peremptorily that he would need fully 27,000 tons of canned salmon to titillate jaded British palates, Secretary of the Interior Ickes did the one thing possible. He extended the salmon run for five days to stock up the British larder.

What a later generation of politicians was to call the "special relationship" was at last under way – but a long and thorny road lay ahead for both nations.

2

"Convoys Mean Shooting and Shooting Means War"

13 March–14 April 1941

All through March Roosevelt rarely left the confines of the White House. In the shabby comfort of the Oval Office, with its soft green walls, he worked behind a desk wildly cluttered with miscellanea – gold oblong matchbook folders labelled, "Stolen from Franklin D. Roosevelt", a toy Missouri mule kicking Ol' Man Depression up the rear, cigarette lighters, a china pig, a cloth elephant. Yet there was no confusion in his thinking. Even 3,500 miles from Europe, his finger was on the pulse of history.

To London, on 10 March – one day before Lend-Lease became law – went 43-year-old William Averell Harriman, millionaire's son, merchant banker and croquet champion, now Roosevelt's newly-created "Defense Expediter" with instructions to "keep the British Isles afloat". Ahead of him, on 1 March, as the new Ambassador to the Court of St James's, had journeyed John Gilbert Winant, former head of the International Labour Organisation – charged with the task of wooing Britain's left wing, particularly Minister of Labour Ernest Bevin, should Churchill's government fall.

A slow-spoken Lincolnesque figure, described in a Foreign Office memorandum as "very earnest and very shy . . . a poor mixer and not blessed with small talk", Winant was to find his assignment taxing almost beyond endurance. During frequent weekends at Chequers, the Premier's country residence, Churchill would "have a go" at Winant, over Saturday luncheon, urging more and more Lend-Lease supplies, until 3 p.m. when he retired for a catnap. At this point an aide took up the cudgels – until Churchill refreshed from sleep, returned to badger the weary Winant into the small hours.

Already Roosevelt was striding rapidly away from the neutrality to which he publicly paid lip-service. Always he had been at pains to present Lend-Lease not as a step towards war but as a step away from it: this was a pious fiction. British ships would now be repaired in American docks; 8,000 young British pilots were to be trained on American airfields. Ten coastguard cutters were transferred to the Royal Navy. Next Roosevelt extended the American neutrality patrol zone to longitude 26 degrees west – bringing the United States' outermost line of potential defences to Greenland, 900 miles nearer to Europe, only three miles from the German war zone. Other strictly unneutral moves were in the pipeline: the Red Sea was declared open to U.S. shipping, so that arms could be taken to technically-neutral Egypt. Mindful of a probable British loss of 3,500,000 to 5,500,000 tons of merchant shipping – of which no more than 2,100,000 would be replaced by British and U.S. yards in 1941 – the President asked Congress for authority to seize all foreign shipping in U.S. harbours, including Vichy France's famous liner, *Normandie*, now quietly rusting at Manhattan's 48th Street pier.

For the time being, though, he stopped resolutely short of using American warships to convoy Lend-Lease goods. As Roosevelt had recently remarked to one visitor: "Convoys mean shooting and shooting means war."

Such moves were public knowledge – but unknown to Congress as Lend-Lease was under fire, Roosevelt had virtually smuggled a Trojan Horse into official Washington. As early as 29 January, six high-ranking British officers, all clad in mufti, had arrived unobtrusively for top-secret talks with their U.S. counterparts. Known as the A.B.C. meetings (American–British Conversations), the delegates were to huddle together on fourteen occasions between then and 29 March. Their terms of reference were an ultimate war between the United States and all the Axis powers, including Japan. The final A.B.C.–1 agreement, drawn up on 27 March, stressed one basic concept: Hitler's Germany loomed as the real enemy.

But Roosevelt was probing farther afield than England; his eyes and ears were everywhere. As his listening post inside Vichy France he had appointed as Ambassador Admiral William D. Leahy, whose official brief was to maintain cordial relations with Marshal Pétain – or, as Leahy himself put it, "to stiffen wavering Gallic vertebrae". In the third week of March, another observer, Colonel William J. ("Wild Bill") Donovan, one-time soldier and lawyer, reported back to the President, after a three-and-a-half month 30,000 mile trip through Europe, the Near East and Africa. Donovan, too, had stopped off in London – to lunch with Churchill and discuss "a relationship of mutual selfishness" – but he had ranged much farther afield: to Egypt to talk with Wavell, to Sofia, to chat with King Boris (six weeks before he joined the Axis), to Athens, Belgrade, Turkey, Palestine and Baghdad.

The drums were beating faster in the un-declared war and the mood that Donovan reported from the Balkans was one of fear – fear in Greece that too much British aid would provoke the Germans, fear in Belgrade that Prince Paul, following a mid-February parley with Hitler by his Prime Minister and Foreign Minister, would soon capitulate.

Now, not for the first time, Roosevelt was to make public promises that he was powerless to keep. On Saturday, 15 March, at a crowded dinner of the White House Press Correspondents Association, he came out with a trenchant speech that was beamed to Europe in fourteen languages: "The British people and their Grecian allies need ships. From America they will get ships. They need planes. From America they will get planes. Yes, from America they need food . . . They will get food."

This was fighting talk but specious fighting talk, falling far short of reality. One month earlier, on 14 February, Cordell Hull had told the Yugoslav Minister, Constantin Fotitć: "We can supply the materials of war to victims of aggression." In practice, Fotitć reported wanly to Prince Paul, he had looked to America for positive aid in vain. Only one armaments manufacturer had even agreed to consider an order for 96 anti-aircraft batteries – stressing that there would be an eighteen-month delay in delivery and that the prohibitive price would include the entire cost of the machines and tools.

It was as bad for the Greeks. Although Roosevelt's declaration was to be learned by rote in Athenian schools, along with the orations of Pericles, in practice no aid was forthcoming. Back in November, 1940, the Greek Minister, Constantin Diamantopoulos, had been promised 30 P-40 planes – but as 1941 dawned, the P-40s available, 300 in all, were found to have been allotted to Britain and China, now in the fourth year of her war with Japan. In January, the State Department resorted to dishonesty – denying that the November offer had ever specified P-40s. Instead, they would allot the Greeks 30 obsolete U.S. naval planes. When Diamantopoulos protested that Greece needed fighters, and 60 at least, Treasury Secretary Morgenthau told him boorishly: "Take the planes and shut up."

In February, when three-and-a-half months had passed, Assistant Secretary of State Adolf A. Berle – fearing that "to have the President's word discredited would run through the Balkans like a germ" – soothed the Minister that delivery might be expected in four weeks. On 26 March, Sumner Welles was still hoping that "a solution satisfactory to Greece will be found in the near future". Five days later, Hull cabled the Legation in Athens that planes were on their way: eight Grumman F3F-1 Navy fighters built in 1936, would proceed by slow boat to Suez. "We appear," noted one diplomat smugly, "to be well out of the woods in this matter."

Thus by degrees the suspicion was growing in Europe that Roosevelt's promises were designed to provoke token resistance by unarmed nations, in the hope of those nations finding favour with the American public. "Any nation which tamely submits on the grounds of being overrun," the President noted to Cordell Hull, "will receive less sympathy from the world than a nation which resists, even if this can be continued for only a few weeks." Obscurely he saw Abyssinia* as a case in point: "Abyssinia won world sympathy by a brief though useless resistance – and Abyssinia will be restored in some way not now foreseeable."

On 18 March, in one of his last talks with the U.S. Minister in Yugoslavia, Arthur Bliss Lane, Prince Paul was once more urged to stand firm – although with what Lane did not specify. Why not, the Minister urged, refuse to sign any pact with Hitler, keep diplomatic integrity intact and maintain Yugoslavia's reputation abroad?

Paul's reply sadly summed up the viewpoint of all the small and threatened nations. "You big nations are hard," he told Lane. "You talk of our honour but you are far away."

*

The British were now committed to a decision that had found favour with Roosevelt but would prolong the war in North Africa for two more years. The Greek expedition, finally launched on 4 March, had stripped General Sir Archibald Wavell to the bone. Cyrenaica, so recently a scene of triumph, was now "a passive battle zone", policed by a "minimum possible force" of half a division, ill-trained and ill-equipped, hovered over by one fighter squadron.

Moreover, the one Briton with a genuine intuition for desert warfare, the recently-knighted Lieutenant-General Sir Richard O'Connor, had been transferred from Cyrenaica to command rear echelon troops in Egypt. Into his shoes, as March dawned, as G.O.C., Western Desert Force, stepped Lieutenant-General Philip Neame, V.C., famous for lobbing improvised jam-pot bombs at the German trenches in 1914 – but a sapper, unversed in desert warfare. "Delay enemy's advance over the 150 miles from Agheila to Benghazi for two months," were his sole instructions from Wavell.

As Wavell was later to admit, he had mis-calculated fatally. Not until mid-March – "when it was rather too late" – visiting Benghazi, did he realise that the escarpment running south of the port, far from being defensible by a light mobile force, could be ascended almost everywhere. Nor had Wavell ever visited the salt marshes near El Agheila – which stretched twenty clear miles from the coast towards Libya's Great Sand Sea. Near-impassable to vehicles save at a few easily mined points, these could have formed "a formidable defensive barrier".

But Wavell, in any case, thought the Germans would launch no effective counter-attack earlier than May – echoing the very beliefs of the High Command in Berlin. Knowing Rommel's instructions to the letter

* Abyssinia (later Ethiopia) had been overrun by Mussolini's troops in a seven-month campaign from October 1935. The British restored Emperor Haile Selassie to his throne on 5 May, 1941.

27

through the daily intercepts of the Enigma machine,* Wavell had automatically assumed that an order to stand fast would be implicitly obeyed.

Both camps had reckoned without *General leutnant* Erwin Rommel – who knew nothing of Hitler's decision to invade Greece nor of his long term plan to launch Operation Barbarossa.

At dawn on 24 March, with the suddenness of a coronary attack, Rommel struck.

Deploying on a 1,000-yard front, scores of tanks and armoured cars of Major Imfried von Wechmar's 3rd Reconnaissance Group bored for the fort of El Agheila. Behind them groaned trucks whose drivers were obeying to the letter Rommel's canny precept: "Panzers to the head of all formations! Rear vehicles to raise dust – nothing but dust." For the first time, Rommel's desert tactics were put to a decisive test, for much of Von Wechmar's "armour" was incapable of firing a shot. Known as "The Cardboard Division" because of its Volkswagens mounted with wooden chassis, canvas coverings and dummy guns – "I won't hold it against you if you lose one or two", Rommel joked to Wechmar – their outlines in the swirling dust yet suggested a formidable fighting force. Promptly the British garrison of El Agheila fell back on Mersa el Brega, 30 miles east.

For the first, but not the last time in the desert, the British were to mistake Axis shadow for substance. At Mersa el Brega, on 31 March, the desert gate to Cyrenaica was breached by Rommel's 50 tanks – moving on a wide front to create maximum confusion, striking in concentration as battle was joined. Through the curtain of shattered white houses that the British had abandoned charged the men of the Afrika Korps chanting their newly-minted battlecry, "*Heia Safari!*" – a Bantu phrase meaning "Drive onward".

Now, as blindly as the Italians before O'Connor the British fell back without a fight – packed ignominiously 30 to a truck, nerves at breaking point from lack of sleep, faces masked with thick yellow dust like jaundice patients. Everywhere there was dire confusion. At Beda Fomm, Second-Lieutenant Roy Farran's first intimation of trouble was a convoy of British Service Corps trucks zizagging frantically along the coast towards Benghazi. Flagging them down, the astonished Farran heard from a near-speechless driver that the Germans had broken through on a wide front: the prelude to "seven of the most inglorious days in the

---

* The much discussed "Enigma" dated from 1938, when M.I.6, the British secret intelligence service, bought the secret of a German cipher machine (code-named "Enigma") from a Polish mathematician, who had worked in the Berlin factory where it was produced. His price was £10,000, a British passport and a French residential permit for himself and his wife. From an apartment on the Left Bank in Paris he created a replica of "Enigma" and a working model, codenamed "Ultra", was completed and sited at Bletchley Park, a Victorian mansion forty miles north of London. The value of the information was, of course, dependent on the British understanding the objective of any one battle.

history of the British Army". At Antelat, a panic-stricken corporal's scream "Mass retreat – the Jerries are coming", so outraged Lieutenant-Colonel Crichton Mitchell, a sapper, that he threatened to shoot the man on the spot.

In vain, Churchill had cabled Wavell: "I presume you are only waiting for the tortoise to stick his head out far enough before chopping it off." All initiative had been lost. Following Wavell's instructions to the letter – not to "hesitate to give up ground if necessary as far as Benghazi and even evacuate Benghazi if the situation demanded" – Neame made no attempt to visit the front but strove vainly to restore order from chaos with a series of desultory telegrams.

In this pell-mell 800-mile eight-day retreat, which the British with wry self-deprecation, were to christen "The Tobruk Derby" or "The Benghazi Handicap", orders and counter-orders multiplied. At Bardia, one company of Lieutenant Colonel Eustace Arderne's Durham Light Infantry were first instructed "Hold the fort" – a task once entrusted to 45,000 Italians – then, within hours, advised: "Believe you are surrounded. Blow everything." At Msus, Captain the Honourable Anthony Hore-Ruthven, told that an enemy column was approaching, blew up an entire divisional petrol dump – then, too late, recognised the "enemy" as a British patrol of the Long Range Desert Group.

At Rommel's Advanced H.Q. near the Agedabia landing ground, the air was alive with tension as runners scurried in and out with messages, and Major Georg Ehlert, the Ops officer, scrawled incisive red and blue marks on the talc of his operations map. "They're mad and now I've got them", Rommel crowed, as news of the headlong rout reached him for now, driven on by the demon of pursuit and in defiance of the High Command, he had resolved to take all Cyrenaica at one stroke. But unit after unit told the same bleak story: no more petrol.

Rommel would not be gainsaid. Promptly he ordered all the 5th Division's light trucks to be unloaded of supplies and formed into columns. Each driver was given 24 hours to return to the divisional depot and collect enough petrol, food and ammunition to see the campaign through. It was a dangerous gamble, a day and night when the division was powerless to move, becalmed in 110 degrees of desert heat – and one more chance that Neame failed to exploit.

Rommel's concept was now one of the boldest: to stage in reverse a 150-mile drive that O'Connor had launched in February across the wasteland of Cyrenaica to the tiny desert fort of Mechili. Simultaneously striking en route at Benghazi, Msus and Derna, three other columns would converge on Mechili. Later Rommel was to claim – and the Afrika Korps War Diary was to support him – that a go-ahead for this risky manoeuvre arrived at the eleventh hour from the Army High Command, thus nullifying the angry protests of General Gariboldi (nominally

Rommel's superior in this Italian theatre of war) that prior authority had not been obtained from Rome.

Yet all evidence suggests that this so-called 3 April directive was rigged. One day earlier, on 2 April, the High Command had ruled: "Even after the arrival of the 15th Panzer Division, an extensive operation with Tobruk as the objective cannot be undertaken for the time being." On that same evening Rommel confessed in a letter to his wife: "The brass at Tripoli, Rome and possibly Berlin will gasp. I took the risk against all orders and instructions because I saw an opportunity."

From Athens, Anthony Eden, disturbed by "more and more alarming telegrams . . . from Archie" had set off post-haste for Cairo – to find that Wavell, belatedly, had lost all faith in Neame's judgement and was set to replace him with O'Connor. O'Connor, though, diffident to a fault, felt that "changing horses in midstream would not really help matters". Instead, O'Connor gained Wavell's assent to a compromise. Might not he stand in as Neame's adviser until the battle front had stabilised?

As the British debated these military niceties Rommel's columns forged on for Mechili. But already despite his present successes some critical observers saw signs of a growing impetuousness which would ultimately undo Rommel. One commander, whose column was temporarily halted, was startled when a message fluttered from the cockpit of Rommel's Fieseler Storch spotter plane: "Unless you get going at once I shall come down, Rommel." To *Generalmajor* Heinrich Kirchheim, liaison officer with the Italian Brescia Division, Rommel's frenetic haste was self-defeating. Unwilling to allow his vehicles the needful two-hourly halt period to clean motors of sand, Rommel had tank after tank, truck after truck, drop by the wayside. Always insistent on keeping up with his lead tanks, he was often poorly oriented on the overall battle situation.

Even so, by 9 April, Rommel's whirlwind tactics had netted him a rich harvest of V.I.P. prisoners. At 3 a.m. on the pitch-dark night of 7 April, the big blue sedan carrying O'Connor, Neame and Colonel John Combe, of the 11th Hussars, was bogged down in a traffic jam on the outskirts of Derna. From the darkness sounded harsh voices, shouting instructions, and Neame's chauffeur volunteered: "I expect it's some of them Cypriot drivers, sir." Seconds later, the hapless brass were staring impotently into the levelled barrels of German sub-machine guns. Trapped one day later, after an encircling attack on Mechili that resembled a Sioux swoop on a stockade, was Major-General Michael Gambier-Parry, commander of the 2nd Armoured Division.

In high good humour, Rommel watched Gambier-Parry's command truck unloaded of its gear, then reached forward to annex an oversize pair of sun-and-sand goggles. "Booty – permissible I take it, even for a general," he grinned, adjusting them over the gold-braided rim of his peaked cap. The legend of the Desert Fox was born.

On this very day, a historic conference was taking place, 75 miles to the west, around a glass-topped table in the loggia of the waterfront Albergo Tobruch. Present were Wavell, Major-General J. D. Lavarack, commander of the 7th Australian Division, Major-General Leslie Morshead, commanding the Australian 9th, and his Chief of Staff, Colonel "Gaffer" Lloyd. One day earlier, on 7 April, Churchill had urged: "Tobruk . . . seems to be a place to be held to the death without thought of retirement." Now the commanders had met to decide how this might best be achieved, for so long as Tobruk held out as a bridgehead and sallyport on Rommel's flank, he could make no major advance into Egypt. His Afrika Korps would be denied the use of water supplies – and of the only suitable port east of Benghazi through which he could be supported.

Were they then, one man asked, to hold Tobruk whatever the cost?

Laconic as always, Wavell took his time replying. He took out his eye-glass, polished it, then called for a map. For a few minutes he studied it in silence, noting the thinly-garrisoned villages scattered across 450 miles of desert: Bardia, Sidi Barrani, Mersa Matruh. Then he told Lavarack drily, "There is nothing between you and Cairo."

*

It was an unlikely time and place for diplomats to gather: a dingy freight yard, hemmed in by tenement buildings, on the outskirts of Budapest. At this hour, 10 p.m. on Tuesday, 25 March, the sidings were almost deserted under sheeting rain; from across the tracks a steady shuffle of engines sounded and whistles cried in the night, a sound of horns and of hunting. On the makeshift platform, the Yugoslav Minister to Hungary, Svetozar Rašić, fidgeted uneasily flanked by his Legation staff and three men not normally welcome in Serbian company: the German, Japanese and Italian Ministers.

Minutes later, a special blue-and-gold passenger train slid into the yard, and at once Rašić boarded it, hastening through the slow-moving cars in search of his quarry, the Yugoslav Premier Dragiša Cvetković, a sallow gypsy-featured one-time financier, plagued by a liver ailment, and his Foreign Minister, the bald rotund Aleksander Cincar-Marković, known to Balkan foreign correspondents as "Stinker".

A shock awaited Rašić. Suddenly, as the train halted, Cvetković blundered from his compartment, seized Rašić by the arm and descended abruptly to the platform. "Mr President," Rašić chided, "Mr President, you must greet the Ministers."

Cvetković barely spared the diplomats a glance. "Never mind," he answered curtly, then lapsed into brooding silence. Suddenly he asked Rašić distractedly, "What could I do?"

There was no need for Cvetković to amplify. Almost seven hours

31

earlier, in the green-and-gold splendour of Vienna's Belvedere Palace, Premier and Foreign Minister had undergone their final humiliation. In the presence of the German and Italian Foreign Ministers, Joachim von Ribbentrop and the smooth amoral Count Galeazzo Ciano, Mussolini's son-in-law, both men had appended their signatures to the protocol of adherence to the Tripartite Pact.

Abruptly, still without deigning to acknowledge the diplomats, Cvetković returned to his compartment. Rašić followed behind. There he found his old chief, Cincar-Marković, fully as despondent as the Premier. For some time, the two men sat slumped at the window table, silent, apathetic. Still unregarded, the three Axis ministers waited patiently outside the Premier's saloon, ready to formally welcome the newest recruit to Adolf Hitler's sphere of influence.

"Please," Rašić urged, "at least when the train starts, look out of the window and wave your hand."

Cincar-Marković was bitter. "I would as soon wave my foot at them as my hand."

Sadly, Rašić returned to the platform: for all the good it had achieved, this meeting, scheduled for security reasons in the freight yard rather than the main railway station, might never have taken place. Then the train jerked forward, speeding for Belgrade across the rain-drenched Pannonian plain.

The signing of the Pact had been inevitable for weeks – ever since Prince Paul had returned on 5 March from a meeting with Hitler at the Berghof. All through the five-hour talk the Führer had stressed one point repeatedly: he could not protect Yugoslavia from a possible Italian invasion unless they signed the Pact. But Paul had jibbed; his people would never accept clauses permitting the Axis to use their territory to wage war. Hitler saw this as a trifle. He would not request passage for German troops through Yugoslavia.

On 6 March, Paul called a nine-man crown council meeting at the White Palace, in Dedinje, on the outskirts of Belgrade. But in truth there was little to discuss. The Allies had been forthcoming with nothing but calls to resist. The Yugoslav Army could hold out for little more than six weeks; after this food and ammunition would be exhausted. For two years Germany had controlled Czechoslovakia's Skoda Works, once Yugoslavia's prime source of arms.

When one man insisted that Yugoslavia should enter the war, "if only symbolically", the Minister of War, General Petar Pešić scoffed: "I'm an old soldier, but I've never heard of a symbolic war. What is it?"

Prince Paul was now a man tugged by many winds. A former graduate of Christ Church, Oxford, who held the Order of the Garter, Britain's oldest order of knighthood, he felt an instinctive kinship with the Allies; his wife, Princess Olga, was a member of the Greek Royal family, while his sister-in-law was the Duchess of Kent. "But," he told the Vice-Premier, Vladko Maček, "I cannot lead (our people) to slaughter, and that is what we must expect if we precipitate a war with Germany."

On 20 March, when the full cabinet convened, only three out of seventeen ministers declared against the Pact. Rumours of a coup to be carried out by the Air Force commander, the aged General Dušan Simović, were dismissed out of hand; who had ever heard of a *coup d'état* being broadcast in advance? Ahead, for Cvetković and his Foreign Minister, lay only their humiliating 25 March rendezvous in Vienna. "Bad news from Juggery," commented Hugh Dalton ruefully.

"This," the Yugoslav Minister in London, Ivan Subotić, told the unamused R. A. Butler of the Foreign Office, 'rather archly', "can be compared to the Munich period of your policy."

That night, an almost unearthly silence descended on Belgrade. In the city's *kafanas*, the coffee houses, where Serbian patriots foregathered, men and women wept quietly and unashamedly at the shame that had enveloped their country.

One woman was not weeping; instead she was suffused by a quiet sense of triumph. Two days earlier, on 23 March, Ruth Mitchell, the newly-enrolled American *Četnik*, had watched hordes of teenage schoolchildren stampeding through the streets, pressing leaflets on bystanders, as they chorused, *"Bolje rat, nego Pakt* – Better war than the Pact." Where children led, Ruth believed, adults would follow.

At 8 p.m. on 25 March, Ruth was dining with a group of British foreign correspondents at Belgrade's Hotel Bristol. All through the evening, knowing from her *Četnik* contacts that trouble was in the making, she had the curious feeling of "watching a play . . . calmly, politely eating while world-shattering events were brewing."

At 10 p.m., well aware that no one would believe her, Ruth yielded to temptation. "Let me tell you something," she said gently. "Within twenty-nine hours Prince Paul, Cvetković, Cincar-Marković and the whole Cabinet will be either prisoners or dead."

"They'll have to take peace even at the German price," one newsman countered. "They have no choice."

Ruth Mitchell leaned forward. "Telegraph your paper," she said, "that the Serbian peasants don't want peace at any price the Germans could ever offer. Tell England that the Serbs choose war."

The picture was to remain in her mind for years: the polite indulgent smiles of the men in the know, but still chivalrously content to humour the dinner-table caprices of a charming woman.

*

The first intimation of the coup came as casually as an invitation to take pot luck. On the afternoon of 26 March, Brigadier-General Bora Mirković, of the Yugoslav Air Force, paid a visit to the Zemun Airport headquarters of his Commander-in-Chief, General Dušan Simović. Mirković found that the old General was at home enjoying a siesta, though Mrs Simović, who answered his telephone call, at once volunteered to waken her husband. Mirković demurred: he had nothing urgent to say. But when the General did awake, would he drop by his own office?

Simović, a slim grey-haired man, took his time; it was 5 p.m. before he strolled in. Mirković's abrupt greeting rocked him on his heels: "I have decided to remove the traitors tonight."

Simović begged for a postponement – but in vain. As the field organiser of the coup, in which Simović was little more than a figurehead, Mirković was adamant that the hour had come. The entire Air Force, totally loyal to King Peter, already held the trump card of Zemun Airport. And other conspirators were spoiling for action: a division of the Royal Guards, including an infantry regiment, two cavalry regiments, and an artillery regiment, plus a battalion of tanks, a company of engineers, and other miscellaneous groups.

That night the streets of Belgrade were almost empty, silent and deserted under the lamplight. Only at midnight, was a steady rumbling heard along all the streets radiating off Kralja Alexandra, the city's main boulevard; grey-green Army tanks were moving into blockade positions, bulking squarely across the tram tracks, ugly 47-mm cannons restlessly traversing the darkness. On the Kralja Milana, an anti-aircraft gun, its muzzle lowered, commanded the whole street, even beyond the White Palace, to the Terazia, Belgrade's main square. Flitting shapes in Air Force blue advanced stealthily through the shadows.

At 2 a.m., a black Cadillac limousine screeched to a halt outside the home of Premier Dragiša Cvetković on fashionable Dedinje Hill. An Air Force officer, descending with a patrol of soldiers, found a guard barring his way: "The Premier cannot be disturbed."

The officer's drawn revolver was a proof of his earnest: "Nevertheless, disturb him!"

At dawn on 27 March – Belgrade – and all Yugoslavia – awoke to a sense of honour redeemed. Aboard the tramcars on Kralja Milana, early-rising commuters thronged the windows staring wide-eyed at the tanks and guns now looming everywhere. American flags and Union Jacks fluttered triumphantly from the balconies and shop fronts. On the broad boulevard of Mihilova, a voice took up the stirring national anthem, *Oi Serbia!* and thousands of lungs filled with air and took up the chant. Other voices were raised in counterpoint: *Zivala Engleska* (Long Live England) and *Petra Drugy* (Peter Our Friend).

In his bedroom in the White Palace, the 17-year-old King – whom the British Minister, Ronald Campbell, deemed "a pleasant boy, still rather young for his age, and immensely keen on anything mechanical" – was as much in the dark as any of his subjects. His first knowledge of the *coup* had come at 6 a.m., when his valet had shaken him violently awake to announce an urgent visit from the Commander of the Belgrade Garrison, General Kosić. Only then did the young King learn that troops had taken over General Staff Headquarters, the Ministry of War, and the General Post Office, and that all telephone cables had been cut.

At 9 a.m., as he switched on his radio, the King's confusion multiplied; what sounded like his own voice was announcing to the people that he had taken the royal power into his own hands, Prince Paul having resigned, and charged General Simović with the formation of a government.

Although these events came to pass before the day was out, the conspirators, unable to gain access to the Palace, had taken the bizarre step of calling on a young officer to impersonate his own monarch.

For thousands of citizens, the sound of freedom was the sound of breaking glass. The plate-glass windows of the German Travel Agency, with its big cotton swastikas mounted on flagpoles, were suddenly too tempting a target; rocks flew, and the wide windows collapsed in a pile of glittering shards. Across the street, the tramway workers were burning Hitler in effigy, and the innocent suffered along with the guilty. The Swedish envoy, mistaken for a German, was dragged from his car and beaten senseless.

Now the crowd advancing on the Terazia had become a broad human river, swelling to 40,000 strong, and the massed voices acquired a conscious powerful rhythm, like a Hawaiian war chant:

Bolje rat, nego Pakt!
Petra Drugy! Petra Drugy!
Bolje rat, nego Pakt!
Petra Drugy! Petra Drugy!

Inevitably that afternoon Ruth Mitchell was marching too – not with the crowds but with a 2,000-strong *Četnik* column, heading for the residence of Patriarch Gavrilo, of the Serb Orthodox Church. Standing under a heavy Byzantine arch, the old priest raised his hand in blessing, then suddenly, to Ruth's surprise, she was surrounded by other women from the column, hugging and kissing her, shedding their iron self-control to weep tears of joy that an American was marching with them. "England and America will stand by Serbia," Ruth promised them gravely, and years afterward she was to recall with bitterness, "My God, I still believed it. I believed I spoke the truth."

Common to all the crowd was the belief expressed by one Serbian officer: "Tomorrow we shall gladly die for having lived yesterday."

In London, the jubilation was intense, for the newly-created Special Operations Executive, administered by Hugh Dalton's Ministry of Economic Warfare, had for months been working towards this end, against stubborn Foreign Office opposition, funding the Serb Peasant's Party and other opposition groups to the tune of £5,000 a month – cash which was made available to them by the Legation's Air Attachés, Group Captain Hugh MacDonald and Wing Commander Tom Mapplebeck.

Dalton's one fear was that now the crunch had come the Serbs and Croats, notoriously hostile, would fall upon one another in preference to the Germans.

"Prince Paul would be so vexed if he ever found out," the Foreign Office had argued, but Dalton embodied the then fashionable British view, "Our friend has been a complete skunk. He has deceived our diplomats, as such gentlemanly skunks always do." Churchill was in complete accord. "Prince Palsy", as the Premier dubbed him, was "fit only for a life of luxurious seclusion." When Paul abdicated in favour of his nephew at 11.50 p.m. that day, departing with his wife for Greece, Churchill's conviction was only strengthened.

At the Foreign Office, the Yugoslav Minister Ivan Subotić, once more called on R. A. Butler to recall that a pledge had been kept; as First Lord of the Admiralty, Churchill had once expressed the hope that Yugoslavia would never forget her traditions. Now, his voice shaken by emotion, Subotić told Butler: *"Yugoslavie n'a pas démentie ses traditions."*

But in Berlin the storm cones were already hoisted. Hastening to the Reich Chancellery in response to an urgent summons at 11.55 a.m. on 27 March, *Generalfeldmarschall* Wilhelm Keitel, Chief of the Armed Forces, and *General Der Artillerie* Alfred Jodl, Chief of the Operations Staff, at first found the Führer making no sense. Shaking with rage, brandishing a telegram from Belgrade, his words were an incoherent torrent. He had no intention of standing for it. Now he would smash them once for all. It was time people got to know him better. He would clean up the Balkans "good and proper".

Within the hour, the storm had abated. To subdue Yugoslavia would mean a re-allocation of troops previously slated for Russia – 27 divisions in all, seven of them armoured – to strike simultaneously from Austria, Hungary, Rumania and Bulgaria under *Feldmarschall* Siegmund List, a tough brooding Swabian who had commanded the victorious Twelfth Army in the French campaign.

At 1 a.m., *Feldmarschall* von Brauchitsh and *Generaloberst* Halder arrived in the conference room, to be joined by Joachim von Ribbentrop. On fire with excitement, Hitler led them to the map table. His greeting was a challenge: "I have decided to destroy Yugoslavia. How much military force do you need? How much time?"

At Washington's old Willard Hotel, on Fourteenth and E Streets, where John Wilkes Booth had lodged on the day he shot Abraham Lincoln, the mood was festive. At 7 p.m. on Saturday, 5 April, the semi-annual white-tie dinner of the Gridiron Club had got under way in the long ballroom; all Washington officialdom, including the President, had gathered for a merry evening of speeches and lampoons.

The first news of import came when the hour was late. At the ballroom door, a *New York Times* office-boy handed a torn-off news-ticker scrap to a Secret Service guard, who passed it on to the *Times*'s bureau chief, Arthur Krock. Krock, in turn, handed it to Cordell Hull. Adjusting his pince-nez, the Secretary of State read impassively that Russia and Yugoslavia had signed a non-agression pact.

The dinner went on. Roosevelt made a fifteen-minute off-the-record speech. As he spoke another message arrived: when Roosevelt sat down, Krock passed it over. Soon after the President departed for the White House.

The time was a little past midnight on Palm Sunday, 6 April. A young moon had gone down, and Hitler had invaded Greece and Yugoslavia.

Five thousand miles away, the white city of Belgrade slept peacefully under the stars. Incredibly, there was no anticipation that Yugoslavia was doomed; with strange naiveté, General Simović was hoping for the best of both worlds. His new government wanted "to avoid discussion" of the Tripartite Pact; they would not denounce it, nor would they ratify it, for they did not wish to provoke Axis forces. The thought that Hitler was bent on revenge never once occurred to them.

A precise warning from the Yugoslav Military Attaché in Berlin, Colonel Vladmir Vauhnik, that an attack was imminent went unregarded. Was not 6 April a Sunday, the day that Simović had selected to marry off his daughter?

Ruth Mitchell's first intimation came around 7 a.m. In the sitting room of her house on Slaviǰa Hill, Michael, her Cossack houseman, had just laid her breakfast tray, and Ruth was fiddling with the knob of her short-wave radio. Suddenly the raucous voice of Joachim von Ribbentrop seemed to fill the room with hate: "*Die bomben fallen und jetzt in diesem Augenblick steht schon ganz Belgrad in Flammen.*" (The bombs fall and already now this instant all Belgrade is in flames.)

The usual lies, thought Ruth contemptuously. Although she listened intently, a Sunday silence enveloped the streets, broken only by the soft jingle of milk carts, the shuffle of peasant feet.

The lull was illusory. From his bedroom balcony in the Hotel Srpski Kralj, foreign correspondent Ray Brock, of the *New York Times*, was conscious that a mounting uneven drone had filled the air. Seconds

37

earlier he had checked his watch: 7.06 a.m. Now his breakfast coffee forgotten, Brock focused his binoculars and suddenly in the glinting sunlight, he saw them: sixty bombers, Heinkels, Dorniers and Stuka JU87s, sliding above the naked city. As he watched, thirty Stukas peeled from the formation, falling like falcons towards Zemun Airport. Then the bombs struck home.

A whistling ear-splitting inferno engulfed the streets of Belgrade. More than 1500 tons of bombs rained down on the city. With "a crack like a 100-yard whip", whole buildings disintegrated. Blinding flashes of flame ripped outwards, blotting out the streets in black and billowing smoke. Sticks of incendiaries clattered like tin trays, to burn with a blue-white light along the tram trucks. A torrent of bricks, glittering glass, and twisted sheet metal piled head-high along the pavements, coated with molten tar; on the Terazia, teak paving blocks torn loose by the bombs loomed like a surreal mountain.

All sound was mingled into an indescribable devil's chorus: the scream of diving Stukas, the slow, majestic cadence of church bells, the wailing of ambulance sirens, the insistent honking of car horns. Thick walls were toppling, and what seemed like waggonloads of tiles, but in the lobby of the Srpski Kralj nobody screamed and nobody spoke. On Slavija Hill, Ruth Mitchell was conscious of a terrifying wind that "drove like something solid through the house", then "a weird smooth sound like the tearing of heavy silk" as the neighbouring houses collapsed.

All over the city there were scenes of apocalyptic horror. Thus one man would recall a grocer's delivery van, impressed as an ambulance, piled high with bodies, among them a young girl wearing one silver slipper on her right foot. Her left leg had vanished altogether – "just like a fox would chew the leg of a bird".

Bombs had hit the zoo and wild animals stampeded panic-stricken through the burning streets; a polar bear, moaning piteously, hobbled towards the Sava River. Other bombs had struck the Terazia; in its centre yawned a crater thirty feet across, strewn with 300 torn and mutilated bodies. And no man who saw it ever forgot the spectacle of the Kralja Milana, the main shopping centre. As a landmine struck, more than 100 merchants had been raising their shop shutters; now outside almost every shop, as if arranged by a macabre stage director, a body lay inertly, face down in the rubble.

The horrors were not fleeting. Although the first raid lasted barely an hour, a second attack, more punitive still, began at 11 a.m. For almost seventy-two hours, waves of bombers moved back and forth across the city, like tractors ploughing a field, until 10,000 buildings had toppled and 17,000 civilians lay dead among their ruins.

Ruth Mitchell did not linger as a witness. Even as the first bombs fell she was struggling into her uniform: blue serge tunic with skull-and-crossbones insignia, a dagger and loaded automatic, black socks embroidered with roses. Soon after 11 a.m., in any case, she was forced to abandon her house forever; the building next door was in imminent danger of collapse. Already she had taken the wise precaution of sending Michael, her houseman, on ahead, with his wife, Sultana, to their little cottage on the outskirts of the city. This would be the first staging-post on her journey south.

By now, Ruth knew her instructions almost by heart. Somehow, by bus, by refugee train, even on foot, she must reach Montenegro, the smallest of Yugoslavia's constituted republics bounded by Albania and the Adriatic Sea. It would be a 160-mile journey, but all Četnik calculations were based on the belief that Podgoritsa airfield, on the Albanian border, would be the last stronghold to fall.

Here Ruth was to attach herself to the local Četnik formation, prepared for one of two roles. If the British landed in force on the Grecian coast and pushed north for Macedonia, Ruth was to act as liaison officer between the Četniks and the advancing British.

If they did not land, the alternative was bleaker: to discard her uniform and then, under the shield of an American passport, to begin a new life as a spy.

*

The British would not be advancing. Barely six days after Ruth Mitchell began her southern journey, two naval officers in impeccable white met over mid-morning sherry in an office on the dockside at Alexandria, overlooking the quarterdeck of the flagship H.M.S. *Warspite*. Rear-Admiral Harold Baillie-Grohman, Flag Officer Attached Middle East, had been summoned in a hurry from Cairo by the Commander-in-Chief of the Mediterranean Fleet, the pugnacious sandy-haired Admiral Sir Andrew Browne Cunningham.

The two men were old friends, and Cunningham lost no time in coming to the point. A signal from Rear-Admiral Charles Turle, the British Naval Attaché in Athens, gave only cause for alarm; the situation in Greece was deteriorating rapidly. Baillie-Grohman was to fly to Athens with all possible speed to sum up the situation for himself.

Cunningham could offer only one crumb of comfort: if an evacuation took place, offshore operations were unlikely to be hampered by the Italian Fleet. In a bloody three-minute battle on the night of 28 March, Cunningham had decisively savaged the Italians off the Mediterranean cape of Matapan – damaging their flagship, the 35,000 ton *Vittorio Veneto*, sinking three cruisers and four destroyers. From that day on, the Italian Navy would play no further decisive role in safeguarding Rommel's supply lines. For a moment Baillie-Groham stared out across

39

the sunlit harbour, where a fresh nor'easter bellied the sails of the *feluccas*, throwing a fine spray over the bows of picket-boats plying between ships and shore.

How long, he wondered, could the British hold out?

Cunningham, as always, was succinct: "Turle thinks we shall probably have to pull out within six weeks."

*

Adolf Hitler was angry, and with reason. The Yugoslav coup, coming as unexpectedly as a thunderclap, had seen his priorities go awry. On the morning of 27 March, the Führer had been preparing to grapple with an enigma that was also exercising diplomatic minds in Whitehall and Washington: the precise intentions of Japan in 1941.

On 26 March, the Japanese Foreign Minister, Yosuke Matsuoka, had arrived at Berlin's Anhalter Bahnhof to a red-carpet reception more suited to a film-star; as he descended shyly from the train, advancing with solemn timidity on Von Ribbentrop, interpreter Paul Schmidt thought compassionately of "a child who has lost his parents at a fair".

The appearance was deceptive. Although the pipe-smoking Matsuoka, with his dapper black moustache and gold-rimmed spectacles, radiated an air of gentle bonhomie – "an English country gentleman painted yellow", one news agency summed him up – he was a formidable in-fighter for Japanese interests. In 1933, he had been the first delegate to quit the League of Nations following Japan's invasion of Manchuria – a precedent later followed by Hitler and Mussolini. Now he saw the European war as a prime opportunity for Japan to pursue expansionist policies in South-East Asia and the Pacific. Not for nothing did one wall of his Tokyo home bear the motto: "When the west wind blows, fallen leaves are piled up in the east."

Moreover, Matsuoka had journeyed by way of Moscow, for three days of talks with Josef Stalin and Foreign Secretary Vyacheslav Molotov, and was slated to return for further talks – while in Washington, D.C., a new Japanese ambassador, the one-eyed Admiral Kichisaburo Nomura, a six-footer turning the scales at 200 pounds, had arrived with five spare glass-eyes for talks with Cordell Hull.

Hitler was uneasy. What about the Tripartite Pact, whereby Japan had allied herself with the Axis as far back as September, 1940? Why had Matsuoka found it necessary to visit Stalin – and was Nomura giving the Americans verbal guarantees?

From January onwards, Ribbentrop had been pestering the head of his Political Department, Ernst Woermann, for an analysis of the "true intentions" of the enigmatic Matsuoka. A month later he was urging the new ambassador, General Hiroshi Oshima, to attack the British naval base at Singapore – although the Philippines, which enjoyed common-wealth status under the United States, should be left alone. To attack them might be the very provocation Roosevelt sought.

Preoccupied with the destruction of Yugoslavia, only on the afternoon of 27 March could Hitler turn his attention to Japan. No sooner was Matsuoka seated than the Führer launched into a long diatribe on German invincibility like a boy boasting of his toy soldiers; in eighteen months he had crushed 60 Polish divisions, 6 Norwegian, 18 Dutch, 22 Belgian and 138 French.

For once the garrulous Matsuoka, known to his friends as "Mr 50,000 Words", had met his match. As Hitler ranted on, urging the importance of a Japanese attack in the Far East, the Foreign Minister sat speechless.

His first response struck Hitler like a bodyblow: "I can give no firm promise on behalf of Japan at this moment."

With scant conviction, he sought to justify himself. Japan was cor-rupted by weakling intellectuals, both in court circles and commercial life, all people who contrived to hamstring Matsuoka – "the sort of person who would like to capture the tiger cub but was not prepared to go into the den and take it away from its mother".

For the rest of his visit, Matsuoka remained politely non-committal. All Hitler's attempts to wrench the Tripartite Pact into an offensive against the British met with failure, for Japan had signed the Pact pri-marily as an act of retaliation against the United States; in 1940, angry that Japan's war with China still dragged on, Congress had ended trade agreements that went as far back as 1911. At times the Foreign Minister fell back on a scapegoat. Nodding towards Colonel Yatsugi Nagai, who was holding a watching brief for the Japanese Army, Matsuoka replied: "You'll have to ask him."

Ribbentrop's parting shot was patronising to a degree. After suggest-ing that Matsuoka send for maps of Singapore, he added pompously: "The Führer, who must certainly be considered the greatest expert of modern times on military matters could advise Japan as to the best methods for the attack on Singapore." But Matsuoka only smiled politely.

To Mussolini, Hitler later confided that Matsuoka had combined "the hypocrisy of an American Bible missionary with the craftiness of a Japanese Asiatic". It was a verdict that Cordell Hull, with his habitual log-cabin language, had long ago endorsed. "Matsuoka," snorted the Secretary of State, was "as crooked as a basket of fish-hooks."

*

According to perspective, the threat posed by Japan loomed large or small, as in a fairground's distorting mirror.

In London, a momentary alarm had flared briefly on 5 February: secret intelligence alerted the Foreign Office that "Japan had warned her Embassy staff . . . to reduce their contacts with the British authorities to a minimum, and to be prepared to leave the country at short notice." Promptly, Eden had summoned the Ambassador, Mamoru Shigemitsu, for "a full and outspoken discussion"; if Japan was planning aggression in the Far East, to synchronise with a German offensive, Britain would react with vigour.

Although Australia's Robert Menzies warned the Foreign Office: "One thing the Jap won't do is lose face. He'd rather fight," his caution fell on deaf ears – "what irresponsible rubbish these Antipodeans talk!" scoffed Sir Alexander Cadogan. But by mid-February, Churchill, a committed colonialist who saw the Japanese as an inferior race, was reassuring Roosevelt: "I am not myself convinced that this not a war of nerves." Although some believed that Japan was ready to wage war on Britain and the United States, "personally, I think the odds are definitely against that."

From Washington, the view was more ominous. Since her 1937 invasion of China, Japan and the United States had been embarked on a collision course; America had for years sustained Generalissimo Chiang Kai-shek's Chinese Nationalist regime in the profound belief that China was only the first stage in a Japanese drive to over-run all South-East Asia and the Pacific.

This basic concept lay behind Hull's weekly talks with Admiral Nomura, talks which were kept strictly secret from the British. What one Washington newspaper column was to term "a long-range exercise in diplomatic futility" was to drag on over nine months, always in the Secretary's private apartment at the Carlton Hotel, later at the Wardman Park, often from 8.30 p.m. to 10 p.m., while the long-suffering Frances Hull brewed endless pots of China tea.

"There is plenty of room in the Pacific for everybody," Roosevelt had emphasised at his first meeting with Nomura on 14 February, and this was the point on which Hull laid stress, but often he wondered how much the Admiral took in. Partially deaf, with uncertain English, he was given to sudden disconcerting guffaws out of context.

Even so, Hull, who saw diplomacy as preaching morality rather than negotiation, persevered. On 9 April, he laid down four basic if long-winded principles for transmission to Tokyo: respect for the territorial integrity and sovereignty of each and all nations, support of the principle of non-interference in the internal affairs of other countries, support of the principle of equality, including equality of commercial opportunity, non-disturbance of the status quo in the Pacific.

Meanwhile, Japan kept the world guessing. Four days later, a bombshell came from Moscow: on Easter Sunday, 13 April, Matsuoka, in a creditable impersonation of Bunyan's Mr Facing-Both-Ways, had signed a five-year neutrality pact with the Soviet Union. Stranger still, Josef Stalin, known widely as a recluse, arrived unescorted at the Moscow Station to bid the Foreign Minister farewell. Clad in a khaki képi and greatcoat over black boots, he bear-hugged Matsuoka three times, promising "We shall remain friends."

Then, as if amity was the keynote of this day, the dictator's glance lighted on the German military attaché, Colonel Hans Krebs. His head cocked, black eyes twinkling from a sallow face, Stalin enquired sharply, "German? German?" When Krebs assented, Stalin pumped his hand, assuring him, "We, too, shall remain friends – whatever happens."

In his fine walled villa, "The Eagle's Nest", at Hoanshan, across the Yangtse from Chungking, General Chiang Kai-shek heard of the pact with horror: would Russia now abandon the aid that they afforded him in turn for his tacit recognition of the 400,000-strong Eighth Route Army of Communists under General Chu Teh? But the word from Moscow was reassuring; if Chiang continued to resist the invaders, Soviet aid would still flow unchecked. Pact or no, Stalin would not risk a Japanese infiltration of Siberia.

But in Washington, too, the pact had struck a jarring note – and Chiang was swift to capitalise on the discord. More than once, in the past, a covert threat that he might be forced to come to terms with Japan had loosened American purse-strings. For Roosevelt, who looked to a postwar Asia dominated by a China inspired by the Four Freedoms, with America shaping the future in the Pacific, no prospect could be more alarming.

As early as February, he had sent Dr Lauchlin Currie, an ambitious economist, on a mission to patch up Chiang's fissure with the Communists, and Currie was swift to recommend a back-up team of American advisers who would iron out China's corrupt bureaucracy and implement liberal reforms. In truth, Currie had missed the point; while the Communists leaned on peasant support, the Nationalist regime depended largely on corrupt landlords. What Chiang wanted was not reforms but guns, planes and money.

Such was Roosevelt's determination to thwart Japan that these, too, would be forthcoming. In mid-April, the President signed a covert executive order authorising American airmen to resign from their services to form a volunteer group in China: the inception of the famous "Flying Tigers" under Colonel Claire Chennault, Chiang's American air adviser. China too, had qualified for Lend-Lease, and there was no lack of Washington wheeler-dealers on Chiang's payroll to lobby on his behalf. Among them were his brother-in-law, T. V. Soong, abetted by so many relatives that Treasury officials coined an acid jingle, "Sing a Song of Six Soongs", as well as Currie himself and former White House aide Thomas Corcoran, who had allegedly netted a down payment of $30,000.

Treasury Secretary Henry Morgenthau always recalled with disgust a luncheon with Roosevelt at about this time. Until now, Morgenthau had always insisted that aid be given in small, regulated amounts, to discourage currency speculation; if Chungking did not like it, they could "go jump in the Yangtse". But on this day Roosevelt had insisted: "We have to do something for the Chinese in order to save their face. I want you to make that $50 million loan right away."*

Morgenthau was aghast. "Well, Mr President, that is just like throwing it away."

Roosevelt was unyielding: "I know, but it is a question of face-saving." Reluctantly, Morgenthau gave in: the China lobbyists had beaten him to the draw.

The metaphor-of-the-month, embodying all Japan's fear of encirclement, was coined in Tokyo by an Army spokesman, Major Kunio Akiyama. "Japan," he proclaimed, "has the heart of a dove of peace, but a snake – the United States and Great Britain – has placed its egg in the dove's nest."

Urged to clarify, Akiyama was obliging: he had in mind the fortification of Singapore, the arrival of Australian troops in Malaya, the impending fortification of the Pacific islands of Samoa and Guam.

"What would hatch from the egg?" a correspondent asked curiously.

"God knows," the Major replied, "but the dove will protest vigorously."

*

In one war zone, the Germans faced a sudden setback. By mid-April, the fortress of Tobruk had become a thorn in Rommel's flesh, an obsession that was to dog him for seven months. The potential conqueror of Egypt and Suez stood halted on the threshhold of triumph by an impudent garrison. In time, looming disproportionately larger, the obsession would become fatal. Now he was in the front line day and night, flat on his belly, his mouth tight-lipped, cap perched on the back of his head as he studied the Australian lines through Zeiss binoculars: dug-outs like enormous yellow ant-hills festooned with barbed wire, silent as tombs under the burning sun.

To the 4th's Divisional Commander, *Generalmajor* Johannes Streich, Rommel insisted: "We must attack Tobruk with everything we have – before Tommy has time to dig in." So confident was he of success, he assured *Oberst* Herbert Olbrich of the 5th Armoured Regiment, "The enemy will retire immediately when your Panzers approach." Heartened by Rommel's belief in a speedy victory, one battalion even tagged its administration truck on to the rear of the assault column.

* The loan had been requested by Chiang on 17 April.

Nor did this confidence seem misplaced. At 5.20 a.m. on Easter Sunday, 14 April – an attack delayed by eight hours because the promised Italian guides failed to show up – the first wave of Streich's tanks bulled unmolested through a gap blasted in the wire. As Rommel had predicted, the Australians manning the perimeter posts made no attempt to engage them – but as the German infantry followed up, a murderous fire hit them from the rear and from this moment on men began to die. Oblivious to this, Streich's Panzers ground on. Soon they were two miles inside the perimeter – moving deeper by the minute into a deadly and elaborate trap.

Suddenly, a corridor of fire engulged the Panzers. Mobile anti-tank guns, rushed from nearby sectors and mounted on 1½ ton trucks by gunners of the Royal Horse Artillery, were firing from both flanks at a point-blank range of 600 yards. The massive turret of one 22-ton Mark IV tank was torn clean from its mountings. *Oberstleutnant* Gustav Ponath, commanding the 8th Machine Gun Battalion, who had driven brashly through the wire in his staff car, was blown to pieces by an anti-tank shell. In the terrible confusion that saw the loss of 17 tanks – at least one immobilised by an Australian ramming a crowbar into the tread sprocket – Streich's men fell back. "It was a witch's cauldron," one tank commander wrote later. "We were lucky to escape alive."

In the command truck that was his Advance Headquarters, Rommel was beside himself. "Your Panzers did not give of their best and left the infantry in the lurch," he blazed at Streich. Vainly Streich defended himself: his tanks would have reached their objectives, despite the searing fire, but deep well-camouflaged tank traps had checked them. Impatiently Rommel brushed his excuses aside. Both Streich and Olbrich, he charged, had "lacked resolution".

The entire course of the desert war was now to hinge on the struggle for Tobruk, for the fortress, Rommel well knew, was the one remaining bridgehead that could repel a mass advance on Egypt. Still he told *Generalmajor* Kirchheim, his liaison officer with the Italian Brescia Division, resolutely: "We'll be in Tobruk the day after tomorrow – and then our next goal is the Suez Canal."

But Rommel was tempting the fates. The 220 square miles that was Fortress Tobruk was now a hive of grim activity garrisoned by 23,000 determined men – Anzacs, Britons, Indians, even a Jewish transport unit with the Star of David on their trucks – commanded by an Australian fully as tenacious as Rommel himself.

Known to his troops as "Ming the Merciless", after the villain of the *Flash Gordon* comic strip, dark diminutive Major-General Leslie Morshead, 51, had been pictured by a World War One historian as "the nearest approach to a martinet among all the young Australian colonels". A onetime schoolmaster, the prickly Morshead's aim was nothing less than to convert Tobruk into a near-impregnable fortress. "There'll be no Dunkirk here," he told his brigadiers curtly. "If we have to get out we shall fight our way out. There is to be no surrender and no retreat."

Within days, the clog-shaped port, surrounded by high artillery look-out posts, was divided, like Caesar's Gaul, into three parts: the harbour zone, the inner and outer defence lines. Carved into 16 sectors – 140 strongpoints in all – the outer perimeter defences centred on the Red Line, a series of concrete dug-outs holding up to 15 men apiece. Two miles inland from the Red Line lay the Blue Line, a continuous mine-field so thickly sown that the sappers themselves lost track of them, zigzagged with barbed wire and strongpoints sited 500 yards apart. By Morshead's command, no man was excused strong-point duty unless too sick to fight.

And Morshead went further. Nothing so enraged him as the cock-a-hoop headline in one Australian daily: "Tobruk Can Take It". "We're not here to take it," he stormed. "We're here to give it." His accent was on the defensive-offensive: 20-man patrols, armed with bayonets and hand grenades, shod with sandals fashioned from old motor tyres, who nightly launched surprise attacks on the enemy lines. Soon even Rommel was aware of their deadly efficacy: approaching one Italian sector at dawn he stopped short in amazement at the sight of hundreds of discarded sun helmets decorated with the cock's feather plumes of the Bersaglieri Rifle Regiment. An entire battalion had been seized overnight. Not all en-joyed P.O.W. status. One patrol of Rajputs, warrior-caste Hindus from Jodphur, was rebuked for over-estimating their enemy dead. Nights later they returned with two small sacks – filled with 16 right ears and 16 left ears, still oozing blood.

For 242 days and nights, the eyes of the world were focused on the men whom the Axis propagandists had dubbed "The Rats of Tobruk". More than 50,000 letters from families, even unknown admirers, poured into the port's Post Office each week. Canny Army technicians aug-mented their pay packets churning out Tobruk souvenirs made from the grenades and shell-cases on the workshops' lathes. In the Red and Blue Lines, one scene was common to every strongpoint; men lying doggo for 13 daylight hours on end under corrugated-iron lean-tos, fighting bore-dom, weak from the sun, plagued by lice and sand flies and dysentery. To stir above ground by day was to court a sniper's bullet, and mealtimes were thus turned upside down. Men breakfasted at 9.30 p.m., took a hot lunch at midnight and dined before dawn.

Camouflage became the daily key to life or death. Helmets, even windshields, were daubed with anti-glare paint: the tracks of walking men, as visible from the air as chalk lines on a blackboard, were smoothed clear with camel thorn switches. Yet normal life of a sort went on among the dug-outs. Six mimeographed newspapers flourished, from "Tobruk Truth" to "Mud and Blood", the Catholic Church held services daily, and every few weeks Morshead rotated men from the defence lines to the coastal area, to enjoy cricket matches, sea bathing and amateur talent nights.

Motionless in their dug-outs, men dreamed impossible dreams. Imaginary pails of iced beer replaced the vile brackish water, and corned beef and tinned herring vanished before T-bone steaks. Pets, if they chanced upon them, were cherished like pedigree prize-winners. One Anzac dug-out acquired Myrtle, a tame magpie. A British flak battery adopted Larry the Lamb, an ancient sheep who relished corned beef and posted a sentry each night to guard him from would-be butchers.

In truth, Tobruk was never completely blockaded, since the harbour afforded a seaward access to Alexandria, 394 miles to the east. But air cover was almost non-existent, for Tobruk lay beyond the range of Egypt-based fighters and the harbour was littered with rusting wrecks, bulging from the water like dying sea-monsters, the harvest of 437 high-level Stuka raids. It was with good reason that the W.D.L.F. (Western Desert Lighter Flotilla), who brought supplies on "The Spud Run" from an Alexandria jetty called "The Condemned Cell" was rechristened "We Die Like Flies".

On the perimeter, a consciousness of hardships shared bred a wry camaraderie between besiegers and besieged. Both sides saw as fitting a war that spared women and children and cities, and both endured the same desert privations – water which "looked like coffee and tasted like sulphur", as one of Rommel's officers noted, which rusted a blade after three shaves, and canned meat the Italians called "potted old man". There were many fleeting relaxations of tension. Private Noel Sankey, in one dug-out always recalled how the Germans listened in attentive silence to his rendering of "Silent Night, Holy Night", then responded with "*Horst Wessel Lied*". Sergeant Walter Tuit, an Anzac stretcher-bearer, seeking casualties under a Red Cross flag in no-man's-land, was impressed when a lieutenant gave him a *Reichswehr* not the Hitler-salute, and another brought him fresh lemon squash. And each night, prompt on 9.57 p.m., Britons no less than Germans tuned into Radio Belgrade, to hear Lale Andersen sing the sad and sleepy tune that was to become the anthem of all the desert warriors:

> Underneath the lantern
> By the barrack gate
> Darling, I remember
> The way you used to wait.
>
> 'Twas there that you whispered tenderly
> That you loved me, you'd always be
> My Lili of the lamplight
> My own Lili Marlene . . .

47

3

"Do Not Succumb to Provocation"

15 April–18 May, 1941

EVERYONE WAS AGREED on one thing: whatever the reverses, Winston Churchill remained in good heart. As early as the end of March, he had told the Polish Ambassador, Count Edward Raczynski: "There might have been moments when I doubted our victory; there was never a moment when I expected our defeat." Midway through April, he expressed similar confidence to the Swedish Ambassador, Bjorn Prytz. He was, the Premier said, "an optimistic frog".

Seeing Prytz' bewilderment, Churchill expounded a parable: two frogs entered a dairy window to taste the milk. But both miscalculated; leaping straight into a bowl, they found the sides too high and slippery to escape. The pessimistic frog, losing heart, at once threw up its fore limbs and sank to the bottom. But the optimistic frog, hoping somehow to survive, floundered on all night, beating at the milk, and by morning was floating safely on a thick slab of butter.

"Now," Churchill summed up to the delighted Prytz, "I am an optimistic frog, too."

It was a heartening tale – but Churchill and his people had need for optimism. News came daily from the Balkan fronts, and all of it was bad. Yugoslavia was falling fast. For long hard months, the British had nursed their hopes – making much of the repulse of the Luftwaffe, the Greeks' brave stand, triumphs in Libya – and watched them grow. Now the gains of months were incredibly threatened.

As always, the key to Hitler's *blitzkrieg* was unremitting speed. Impelled by his Directive 25, on which *General der Artillerie* Alfred Jodl had laboured unceasingly until 4 a.m. on 28 March, that speed, day and night, never dropped below fifty miles an hour. As the dust-choked Panzer columns churned on, the priorities were ruthless; ten minutes after a breakdown, any Panzer with a complex mechanical fault was nosed off the road for salvage. Traffic control was streamlined; a full Panzer division stretched for more than sixty miles of highway, and from each tank turret a black-clad crewman, signalling with a red-and-white circular disc, controlled the speed of those who followed.

In two days, the tank tracks had straddled the entire Vardar River valley, dividing northern Greece from south-east Yugoslavia; in three days, Salonika; in six, the Serbian hills and Albania.

In the thermal spa of Vranjska Banya, 200 miles south of Belgrade, the plight of General Simović was typical of the whole muddled counter-offensive; with one small portable radio set, on loan from the British, he strove to maintain contact with six separate Yugoslav armies. But the Yugoslavs, although one million strong were fatally uncoordinated; attempting to defend the entire frontier, 1,860 miles long, Simović lost everything. Time was of the essence, yet whole units were creaking into battle in ox-carts that moved at three miles an hour.

Chaos reigned on every front. As fast as Simović mobilised troops, the new Foreign Minister, Momćilo Nincić, hoping for peace with Hitler, demobilised them. In the north-western region of Croatia, it was as Hugh Dalton had feared; thousands of soldiers saw the conflict as strictly a Serbian quarrel. Many units mutinied or went home. One entire brigade, including its commanding officer, surrendered to a German bicycle company. Another unit, throwing an officers' party, halted long enough to surrender, then settled down to serious drinking.

By 5 p.m. on 12 April, the swastika flew once more over the German legation in rubble-strewn Belgrade. Five days later, finding that King Peter, Simović and Nincić, had all left for Greece, the disgraced Aleksander Cincar-Marković was the only man left to return to the capital and sign the surrender.

Now, as a nation, Yugoslavia ceased to exist. Her place on the map of Europe was succeeded by a nominally independent Croatia, under Dr Ante Pavelić, a Mussolini protégé. Serbia was to become a German fiefdom; Montenegro an Italian puppet state.

This sense of a nation divided came home poignantly to Ruth Mitchell on a refugee train going south. At first the implications escaped her: a troop train going north had drawn level, its windows packed with drunken, dishevelled soldiers, taunting and gesticulating. Suddenly Ruth understood: the soldiers had tacked blue, white and red ribbons, the emblem of Croatia, onto their peaked caps.

Ruth sat quite still, not speaking, painfully conscious of the bulky automatic in her handbag. She was bewildered too. For months she had cherished the concept of belonging, of the brotherhood of *Četnik* freedom-fighters symbolised by the uniform she wore. Now she was cut off, without finite orders, uncertain as to whether the *Četniks* of Montenegro still held out.

Suddenly she felt helpless and alone.

*

In the gardens of the Tatoi Palace, fourteen miles from Athens, the long

49

shadows of cypress trees, striped the grass, jet-black against the setting sun. It was very close to dusk on Saturday, 19 April.

The men grouped round the long table in the Palace conference room contemplated nothing but disaster. At its head, King George II of the Hellenes, sat stiffly upright, his face drawn and haggard. By contrast, his Commander-in-Chief, General Alexandros Papagos, was slumped apathetically in his chair. The British contingent were solemn to a man: Wavell, his Chief of Staff, Lieutenant-General Sir Arthur Smith, the commander of the British Expeditionary Force in Greece, Lieutenant-General Sir Henry Maitland Wilson, and Rear-Admiral Harold Baillie-Grohman.

"We must know," Wavell said, and his voice was sharply edged, "whether the Greek Army can give effective support to General Wilson's left flank on the Thermopylae Line."

Papagos was morose. Less than twelve hours ago he had given orders for a division to proceed to Epirus, in north-western Greece, but whether they could stop the German advance, even if they arrived in time, he did not know. "What he did know," said Papagos vehemently, "was that the longer his armies continued to resist, the more defenceless Greek civilians would suffer."

Foremost in every man's mind were the tragic blunders of the last fifteen days. Eden's early discussions with the Greeks had always stressed one thing: both British and Greek troops would stand fast on the 70-mile long Aliakhmon Line, stretching from the Aliakhmon River to the Yugoslav frontier, and the Greeks would field thirty-five battalions. But all along Eden had failed to understand one crucial point: Papagos would make this stand only if Yugoslavia declared war.

Once Germany entered Bulgaria, Papagos had changed his stance; he could not risk shifting troops from Macedonia, for strafing Stukas might catch them on the move. All he could now offer for the Aliakhmon Line was three divisions – between sixteen to twenty-three battalions, as against the thirty-five promised.

In truth, Eden, who had promised 100,000 men and furnished only 58,000, had little cause for complaint; that privilege was reserved for the front-line troops. From 8 April onwards, the story of the Greek campaign became a story of punishing withdrawals, of long hard marches through mountain passes, where many men, clad only in desert shorts and pith helmets faced temperatures ten degrees below freezing, their hands and faces blue with cold.

A sense of let-down was everywhere apparent. It was small comfort to the men of the 3rd Battalion, Royal Tank Regiment, that Eden, on a visit, promised them new tank tracks before the battle began. By the time the spares did arrive the tanks had been abandoned, the links and pins of their tracks snapped like pipeclay by the harsh and rocky roads.

Supplies were a problem from the first. Incredibly, no Naval Officer-in-Charge had been appointed for the port of Piraeus; fire-fighting drill was thus non-existent. On the night of Sunday, 6 April, disaster struck. At 9 p.m., a low-level raid by German bombers blew 11 ammunition ships sky-high, shattering windows seven miles away, closing down the entire port for ten days. With this one raid, the Greek campaign was virtually lost before it had even started.

Air cover was almost non-existent. "More aeroplanes should be sent as quickly as possible," South Africa's Premier, Jan Smuts, counselled Churchill, "I am expediting another bomber squadron . . . and Beaverbrook should surely also disgorge from his hoard." But although Churchill had promised fifteen, perhaps up to twenty-two fighter squadrons, only eighty aircraft were sent, of which thirty were destroyed at a stroke in one ground attack. Thus the Luftwaffe held the sky; as King George and the British debated, the total R.A.F. fighter strength in Greece was one serviceable aircraft.

Now time was running out. On 18 April, Premier Alexander Koryzis, tormented by the fate that was overtaking his country, went quietly home and ended his life with two bullets. One day later, the swastika was hoisted on the summit of Mount Olympus. Now the Olympus Line, along with the Metaxas Line, the Aliakhmon Line, the Thermopylae Line, took its place in the rank of sad futile names that had stretched from Mannerheim to Maginot.

At Tatoi Palace, the conference room was dark now with the sombre shadows of evening; the King's master of ceremonies, Colonel Levidis, called the guards to draw the heavy window curtains. Then, as the lights were switched on and the double-doors closed, Wavell once again assured King George: as long as the Greeks fought on, the British would stand by them.

Then he added quietly, "But, your Majesty, if you and your Government wish us to leave, we will do so. The decision rests with you, sir."

Silence fell. The King held a brief whispered consultation with his Vice-Premier, Tsuderos. Then, gripping the arms of his chair, he looked slowly round the long table. "Gentlemen," he said, "we do not think there is time to reorganise our army in Epirus to give support to your left flank before the enemy attacks. Therefore it is our opinion that the British force should be withdrawn."

*

Aircraftman Marcel Gerard Comeau, who had "deserted" to Greece to get his fill of the action, was a sorely bewildered young man. Ever since his arrival in Athens at the beginning of March, Comeau had felt assured that victory was in the air. The welcome accorded to 33 Squadron's trucks

51

as they drove through the streets of Athens had been unforgettable: waving girls packing the wrought iron balconies, excited children running to keep pace, greybeards chorusing "Bravo!", while a rain of myrtle leaves and flower petals cascaded down on the Chevrolets.

Ahead of them the morning sun shone high and bright above the Acropolis, painting the Parthenon's pentelicon marble with breathtaking light and shade. And all the way to Eleusis airfield, twenty miles from Athens, the rapturous welcome had continued.

Nor was the action that Comeau had sought lacking for long. Posted with a squadron detachment to Paramythia, a muddy Albanian landing-ground in an icy valley, he and the others had grown daily more jubilant as the small band of fighters, almost unopposed, knocked down 28 Italian planes. Soon the squadron had moved nearer still to the fighting – to Larissa, 78 miles north of Athens.

Here, too, as the pilots' successes mounted, Comeau and the squadron's "erks" found the simple friendly villagers could never do enough for them. Night after night they feasted for a few coppers a head on whole sheep, spit-roasted in the main street, linking arms with the Greeks, drinking toast after toast to "Victory" and "Long life" in the pungent resin-tasting *retsina* wine.

By 6 April, when Hitler at last struck, Comeau had been posted yet again – this time to No 11 (Blenheim) Squadron at Almyros landing ground, on the eastern edge of the Thessalian plain. Put in charge of 100 women from the village of Exinopolis, who were constructing a dispersal road for the bombers, the young airman had a sneaking feeling that the war was being run for his benefit – "the happiest weeks of my life . . . eggs by the bucket-load and stewed octopus with beans."

All too soon this idyll ended. By 13 April, news came that the Greeks were crumbling. At Almyros, Comeau and the others listened uneasily to distant gunfire, eyes probing the skies for a Luftwaffe that had so far left them in peace. But on 15 April, they watched a tall black corona of smoke pulsing from Niamata airfield, over the hill. A Luftwaffe attack had destroyed every single Blenheim of the newly-arrived 113 Squadron.

On the evening of 16 April, Air Vice Marshal John D'Albiac, R.A.F. theatre commander, had ordered most squadrons to fall back on Athens.

From that moment on, the retreat was a spectacle familiar to any Dunkirk veteran. Along the rocky roads leading from Stylos to Lamia, from Lamia through Daphne, five-gallon petrol tins piled thirty feet high flared like beacons in the night as the British set fire to them. At least 8,000 vehicles – along with 209 aircraft – would be wrecked and left behind; the air was loud with the roar of engines racing at top speed, heavy with the smell of overheated cylinder blocks.

In little ports like Nauplia Bay and Myloi, the scene was familiar too: the long patient line of troops silhouetted at the shore line, motor barges, black and low-slung, chugging from the water's edge towards waiting corvettes and destroyers, the muttered interchanges between captains and beachmasters: "*Hyacinth* – I can take a hundred – tell them to get a move on."

As the ill-starred British Expeditionary Force pulled out, a wry jest passed through the ranks: the initials B.E.F. really stood for "Back Every Fortnight".

For Aircraftman Comeau, scrambling aboard the infantry assault ship *Glenearn*, the lump in his throat came close to choking him. Even at Nauplia, his last glimpse of Athens was still fresh in his mind; in the chilly evening, the streets had been deserted but the few old men loitering outside the taverns had still clapped their hands with great dignity, calling out "Bravo!" as the trucks groaned past. On 22 April, Greece had surrendered; five days later, the swastika flew from the west wall of the Acropolis. Where had it all gone wrong? Comeau wondered. Now he was bound for the island of Crete – but when the time came could the B.E.F. put up any better showing there?

*

It was perhaps no more than coincidence – yet in Churchill's darkest hour something impelled his long-standing pen-friend, Franklin Roosevelt, to seek more than a meeting of minds across the Atlantic Ocean. Quite suddenly the idea came to him: he wanted to trade ideas and aspirations face to face.

On the stifling hot Sunday of 20 April, with the thermometer trembling in the eighties, the President was entertaining an old friend at Hyde Park, his house on the Hudson River, 60 miles upstate from New York city. William Lyon Mackenzie King, the Canadian Prime Minister, was responding to a pressing invitation to discuss the war situation in Europe.

Coatless and tieless, in a white linen shirt, the President lounged comfortably on the verandah of the small cottage he had built facing the river. To Mackenzie King he seemed in thoughtful mood; he spoke of the "pretty tough time" he was having, of the "defeatist attitude" so widespread in America. Reverses in North Africa, the Yugoslav capitulation, the situation in Greece had "made everything look very dark for the present". There was only one thing to do, the President thought – "to let the people realise that it was only part of a larger plan".

That "larger plan" Roosevelt confided, now seemed to call for an urgent meeting with Churchill, with whom he was already in constant touch. ("We have been writing each other love letters for some time," was the way Churchill later put it to King.) It was now that Roosevelt began a measured review of likely meeting places.

Bermuda? That seemed too far away, and dangerous besides. Iceland was likewise too distant for a man confined to a wheelchair and so was Greenland. Then how about Newfoundland? "That," said the President thoughtfully, "seems to me to be the best place."

The Atlantic Charter – which history would record as the world's first summit meeting – was now in the making.

*

The British had need of such friends. As May dawned, their grasp on the world's trouble spots grew ever more tenuous.

In late March, Rashid Ali el-Gailani, a small, swarthy pro-Axis former premier of Iraq, where the British maintained two air bases, staged a coup with four colonels known as "The Golden Square", wresting power from the pro-British Regent, Amir Abdul Illah. On 3 April, hearing that four doctors, armed with a death certificate from heart failure, were prowling round his Baghdad palace, the Regent fled, huddled under rugs in the car of the U.S. Minister, Paul Knabenshue, and was flown to Basra, on the Persian Gulf.

For the British, the situation was alarming. Not only were their two air bases, at Habbaniya and Shaiba, vital staging posts for India and for Egypt; much of the allied war effort relied on the oil-rich areas around Mosul and Kirkul. If the Axis gained control of the pipe-line running from Haditha on the Euphrates River, south through Transjordan and Palestine to Haifa, their plight would be desperate.

Early in April, an intelligence source, code-named "MICE", reported to the War Office: "Rashid is being driven hard by the Axis and seems determined to go ahead. Is using Axis gold to bribe officials and is rapidly reorganising administration in external districts to eliminate Regent's supporters . . . Basra reports indicate conviction is growing there that British intend to take no action . . ."

Nor did they, for at this stage of the desert war Wavell was like a juggler balancing too many coloured balls: Greece, the Nile Valley, an imminent attack on Crete all loomed larger in his thoughts. To the horror of the British Ambassador in Egypt, Sir Miles Lampson (later Lord Killearn), the Commander-in-Chief had even contemplated asking Rashid Ali for "his terms". "I am aghast at the probable results of this climb-down," Lampson cabled Eden and three days later stressed again, "A crawl to Iraquis would be political disaster."

No man was more in agreement than Lieutenant-General Sir Claude Auchinleck, then Commander-in-Chief, India; he too, had warned Sir John Dill of the perils of ignoring Iraq. "Turkey, Iraq, Iran, Afghanistan and even Saudi Arabia will be involved in a general rot. If, on the other hand, we can hang on to this bastion we will always have a good chance of retrieving the situation."

As it was, Auchinleck's urgency saved the day. Towards the end of March he flew to Basra for a personal meeting with Wavell, to convince him that "bold action" was essential. Wearily, Wavell assented – though until then he had seen Iraq as no more than "a nuisance area on (his) eastern flank". "His credit is fast falling," noted Deputy Premier Clement Attlee. "He still thinks in terms of defending a line or a perimeter."

In truth, the Axis involvement in Iraq was half-hearted. Although Rashid Ali had long been a hat-in-hand supplicant of Hitler's, he was "driven hard" only by Ribbentrop, hopeful of fomenting an anti-British rising; the Führer was too deeply preoccupied with Greece, Yugoslavia and Barbarossa. The Chief of Staff to the Luftwaffe, General Hans Jeschonnek, was notably unresponsive; the Luftwaffe could spare few planes to transport arms to Iraq. Later Rashid Ali complained that such Axis arms as he did receive were so sub-standard as to be useless. Once Ribbentrop had talked grandly of a one million Reichsmark subsidy, but two instalments of £10,000 in gold were all Rashid received.

Nonetheless, Auchinleck's troops – one infantry brigade of the 10th Indian Division – were en route from Bombay to Basra and more were to follow. Ostensibly they were in transit to Palestine, and at first, in accordance with an existing treaty of alliance, Rashid Ali agreed to their landing. But soon, under pressure from the Iraqui Army, he modified his stance. No further troops must land until the first contingent had crossed the Palestine frontier.

When the Ambassador, Sir Kinahan Cornwallis, made it plain that more troops would arrive notwithstanding, the Iraquis, on 30 April, laid siege to the British Embassy and to Habbaniya airfield.

Although Rashid Ali grandiloquently proclaimed the thirty-day confict that ensued as "a Holy War", it was at best a holy skirmish. There were many ludicrous undertones. Habbaniya might boast its own polo ground and swimming pool, but most of its 80 aircraft – which included 32 Audaxes and 29 Oxfords – were better suited to an R.A.F. museum. When the few capable of take-off flew low over the city, dropping placatory leaflets in Arabic, they were greeted by a spatter of machine-gun fire. Promptly the airmen retaliated by showering down the leaflets parcel by parcel – still wrapped.

Inside the Embassy, where some 350 Britons had taken refuge, life under siege was a far cry from beleaguered Tobruk. Persian gardeners still tended the green lawns, and the Oriental Counsellor sent a daily list of supplies to the Iraqui Foreign Office. Each morning such creature-comforts as fresh lettuce, ice and apricots – along with face powder for the ladies – were delivered through the postern of the main gateway. The bar opened daily at 6 p.m., and Sir Kinahan Cornwallis settled to a few rounds of clock golf.

55

In the best Victorian tradition, help was on the way: a motley Palestine-based relief column, 2,000 strong, known as "Habforce", equipped with 500 vehicles and twelve days rations to cross 300 miles of desert. For one unit of the column, the 1st Cavalry Division, it was demeaning, to say the least; every officer had brought his own hunter from the English shires, yet now they were reduced to a role of truck-borne infantry. Along with them marched men of the 1,000 strong Arab Legion, under John Bagot Glubb, "Glubb Pasha", long-robed Bedus with ringleted hair and kohl-rimmed eyes, known as "Glubb's Girls" although their cross-belts of pointed bullets and silver-handled daggers showed that they meant business.

The need for "Habforce" had passed before the column ever assembled – the Habbaniya garrison having dispersed the besiegers with one sortie – but true to tradition they marched anyway, though it was 1 June before they reached Baghdad. Their commander, Major-General George Clark, visiting the Embassy, felt that it all smacked of another century, as indeed it did – "the scene there reminded me so much of what might have happened at Lucknow . . . the same Union Jack, the same garden and compound filled with British refugees, the same indomitable spirit".

But by then Rashid Ali had also conformed to tradition and escaped to Iran; his flash-in-the-pan rebellion was over, and the threat to British interests eliminated.

Even here, the British had profited from American friendship; not only had the U.S. Minister, Paul Knabenshue, helped the Regent escape, he had sheltered more than 130 Britons inside his Legation. Now the problem arose of how to reward him, a diplomatic headache that finally filled an entire Foreign Office file.

Could he be awarded a K.C.M.G? (Knight Commander of the Order of St Michael and St George). It seemed the State Department frowned on their diplomats accepting knighthoods. A gift of silver plate? This, too, was contrary to American protocol.

It was midway through July before an acceptable solution was found, and Knabenshue at last received his richly-earned gift: a signed photo of King George VI.

*

By 15 April, the imminent loss of Greece, with all its fighter fields had prompted Wavell to brood once more over the "Worst Possible Case" file he had opened in June, 1940. Now, fearing that Egypt would become untenable under air attack from Greek bases, allowing Rommel to advance unchecked, Wavell pondered the fall of Alexandria and Cairo, the ultimate abandonment of Egypt and Libya. It was a concept that angered Churchill more than any that his generals had yet propounded. In a towering rage, the Premier shouted at his Director of Military Operations, Major-General John Kennedy: "Wavell has 400,000 men. If they lose Egypt, blood will flow. I will have firing parties to shoot the generals."

But on 30 April, as Wavell had all along feared, Rommel, repulsed once but still undaunted, struck again at Tobruk.

It was an attack more lethal than any the Germans had yet launched – or, ultimately, encountered. In seventy-two hours of thrust and counter-thrust, Stukas, artillery and machine-gun fire flayed the battlefield – a barrage so intense that one Anzac signalman, crawling on his belly and mending severed barbed wire as he went, took $4\frac{1}{2}$ hours to cover the one-and-a-quarter miles between his company's post and Battalion H.Q. Red tracer criss-crossed the defence lines like Morse code come alive, and Rommel moved tirelessly everywhere, cursing, exhorting, even snaking on his belly like any front-line infantryman into the first trenches captured. "What the British risk in broad daylight," he tongue-lashed his engineers, "you can't even manage in the dark!" Angered that the Italians had not pressed home their attack, Rommel coldly warned their liaison officer, General Count Giorgio Calvi di Bergolo, the tall aquiline son-in-law of King Vittorio Emmanuele: "In future I shall expect the immediate execution of officers who show cowardice in the face of the enemy."

There was little doubt that Rommel was in earnest. His troops might adore him; his officers found his relentless goading a sore trial. One general, caught breakfasting as late as 6.30 a.m., was at once returned to Germany. On 1 May, a tank battalion commander who burst into tears of frustration in the last vain attack on Tobruk, was summarily court-martialled. Soon after Rommel dismissed *Generalmajor* Johannes Streich, with the curt comment: "You were far too concerned with the wellbeing of your troops."

"I can imagine no greater words of praise for a division commander," was Streich's rejoinder.

In the frenzied chaos of this battle, few men grasped with certainty who was winning – or for how long. One German doctor, approaching the wire in an ambulance furiously berated the Anzac who drew a bead on him; convinced that Rommel had taken Tobruk, he had arrived to treat the German wounded. (Seized as a P.O.W., he treated both sides impartially.) Corporal Bob McLeish and a team of Australian Bren gunners found themselves marooned in a trench under heavy fire, along with some German infantrymen. Their sergeant told McLeish reasonably "I don't know who'll be the prisoners – you or us. We'd better wait awhile until the shelling stops." At length, as the guns grew silent, more Germans entered the trench. "You're the prisoners," beamed the sergeant.

57

Few Germans fought the battle under such adverse conditions as *Leutnant* Bucher of the 104th Field Artillery Regiment and his runner, *Gemeine* Wievelhofe – in civilian life, both school-teachers. Racked with dysentery, they had removed their trousers to sponge their soiled seats with a mugful of coffee. A mortar shell blasted the garments to rags; until 4 May, when Rommel withdrew, both men were forced to fight a war in their underpants.

On hand to witness this systematic slaughter was *Generalleutnant* Friedrich Paulus, acting chief of the Army High Command, the curt icy disciplinarian who two years later was to surrender at Stalingrad. Three days earlier, Paulus, who dismissed Rommel as no more than "a thick-headed Swabian", had arrived on an urgent mission from *Generaloberst* Halder: somehow to hold "The Desert Fox" whom Halder stigmatised as "this soldier gone stark mad", in check. Now Paulus was appalled by what he saw. "The troops around Tobruk are fighting in conditions that are inhuman and intolerable," he told his conducting officer, *Leutnant* Heinz Werner Schmidt. "I am going to recommend to Berlin that we withdraw to a strong position at Gazala" – a fort 30 miles to the west.

Paulus saw one thing as plain: Rommel's brilliant but disobedient advance to Tobruk had not only failed to bring about a decisive victory, it had added another 700 miles to his already extended supply lines. All told, his Afrika Korps, the Luftwaffe, Italian troops and civilians in Libya needed a mind-boggling total of 116,000 tons of supplies a month – yet the port of Tripoli could handle 45,000 tons a month at most.

As Rommel hesitated, too stubborn to admit the truth of his defeat, a furious once-for-all halt order, transmitted on 3 May, arrived from von Brauchitsch, berating Rommel for his reckless disregard for life – in two days he had suffered over 1,900 casualties. Von Brauchitsch categorically forbade him to attack Tobruk again, or even advance into Egypt. Rommel was to hold his position, conserve his forces, and launch no further attacks. Sourly Rommel conceded to *Oberst* Hanshenning von Holtzendorff, commanding the 104th Field Artillery Regiment, "For the moment the siege of Tobruk will have to be abandoned." To Lucie, his wife, he confided his future pattern for disobedience: "The reports I send back, stating the conditions as they exist, don't suit their book. The result will be that we'll keep our mouths shut and report in the briefest form."

For the first time in the desert – or in any World War Two theatre – the Germans had been forced on the defensive, and with Rommel this realisation rankled bitterly. Other Afrika Korps reactions were more philosophic. One officer confessed in his diary: "What we experienced in Poland and on the Western Front was only a promenade compared with this." Another took the longest of long term views. "Ah well," he noted, "the Greeks also spent ten years before Troy."

Josef Stalin knew him as "Valter" but that was only one of his many aliases. In the Zagreb suburb where he lived with his common-law wife, Herta Has, and their baby son, Aleksander, they called him Engineer Slavko Babić; on the other side of the town he was Engineer Tomanek. Friends nicknamed him *Stari* (The Old Man), although in 1941 Josip Broz was only entering his forty-ninth year. Sometime in the 1930s, he had begun using another alias, common in his native Croatia, which the world would come to know: Tito.

Tito had been an organiser for the illegal Yugoslav Communist Party for seventeen years now. In Zagreb's Corso Kavana, his favourite café, he had long been a familiar sight to the waiters: a well-dressed stockily-built man with blue-grey eyes and a strongly-marked jaw, always in the same window seat, sipping strong coffee. As he studied his regular newspaper, *The Croat People*, he chain-smoked cigarettes in a strange holder shaped like a miniature pipe.

On 7 May, the ex-locksmith Tito had bade a long farewell both to Herta Has and the Corso Kavana. The time for action had come, though first certain precautions must be taken. Croatia was now a Fascist protectorate, and all private cars were being requisitioned; to hand in his Ford, Tito thought, might draw undue attention to himself. He called in some friendly masons; within hours, the car had been bricked up in his garage.

That evening, armed with a forged identity card and forged permits, Tito boarded the night train for Belgrade, 240 miles away. Travelling in another compartment was a girl communist; her task, when they reached Belgrade's Zemun Station, was to walk ahead through the police controls, ensuring that no special checks or changes in papers were required that day. Tito left nothing to chance.

Once past the controls, Tito knew he was safe. In Belgrade, he had almost as many accommodation addresses as aliases: a flat at 16A, Rumunska Street, another at 5, Doticeva Street, rooms in the Gladstone Street house of a wealthy party sympathiser, Vladislav Ribnikar, proprietor of the liberal newspaper, *Politika*. In Ribnikar's bathroom, a secret door in a cupboard behind the wash-basin led to a hiding place below the roof, housing a cache of sixteen hand grenades and two revolvers. Tito would never yield without a fight.

Once there, his first task would be to reactivate his secret radio link with Georgi Dimitrov, Secretary General of the Comintern in Moscow, whose code name was Deda (Grandfather). There was no time to lose. Tito had news for Deda that Josef Stalin at present refused to credit: all units scheduled for the invasion of Soviet Russia must be fully operational by 15 May.

All that year, the messages had flooded in, small alarming clues and pointers, as mosquito-shrill as static in the ether. It took a stubborn man, with a deeply-ingrained suspicion of Western motivation to ignore them. But Josef Stalin, it seemed, was such a man.

The first warning had come as early as January, when Sam E. Woods, the genial American commercial attaché in Berlin, received a tip-off from a German anti-Nazi with connections in high places. Plans for an attack on Russia, he told Woods, had been in the making since August 1940, and Hitler had boasted that he would have "only my soldiers from Vladivostok to Gibraltar". As details of the plan were firmed up, Woods and his contact were soon meeting regularly in the darkness of Berlin cinemas, where scribbled notes of the latest developments were slipped into the attaché's pocket.

Cordell Hull, fearing a "plant" passed this news to J. Edgar Hoover's Federal Bureau of Investigation, but Hoover thought the material authentic. Thus, on 20 March, Sumner Welles took the precaution of warning the Soviet Ambassador, Constantin Oumansky. Oumansky "turned very white", but promised to forward the information to the Kremlin.

Almost simultaneously, the American military attachés in Berlin were reporting that 15 million German soldiers were under arms, posing the question: Who were they going to fight?

Midway through February, Berlin buzzed with rumours. A conscience-stricken printer called at the Russian Consulate with one sample of a large newly-placed contract: a German–Russian conversation manual. There was little doubt as to its purpose. Printed in the Russian language were such disquieting gambits as "Where is the *kolkhoz* (collective farm) chairman?" "Are you a Communist?" "Hands up! I'll shoot!" "Surrender!"

April brought a fresh alarm from Berlin, this time from the Embassy's First Secretary, Valentin Berezhkov. During a cocktail party at the American Embassy, a Luftwaffe Major had told him frankly: "My squadron was recalled from North Africa yesterday and has received orders to transfer to the East – to Lodz." Many other detachments, he told Berezkhov, had made a similar move. "I do not know what it means, but I personally would not like anything to happen between our two countries."

Berezhkov lost no time in transmitting this information to Moscow.

It was not only rumours gleaned by diplomats that Stalin spurned; carefully-documented reports sent in by the Soviet Union's most brilliant spies received equally short shrift. From Tokyo, 45-year-old Doctor Richard Sorge, a hard-drinking womaniser who for eight years had functioned as a Moscow agent, was amassing a formidable dossier of German intentions. Ostensibly a representative of the German daily *Frankfurter Zeitung*, the Russian-born Sorge had entirely won the trust of all the German Embassy officials who counted – notably the Military Attaché, *Oberst* Max Kretschmer. After skilfully pumping Kretschmer, Sorge had reaped yet more damning evidence from a special envoy of the German War Ministry, *Oberst* Ritter von Niedermayer.

By 15 May, Sorge had obtained the precise date of Barbarossa – 22 June – from an old friend, *Oberst* Scholl, en route to Bangkok as Military Attaché. All this – even down to a copy of Hitler's fateful Directive 21, which had set preparations in motion – had been transmitted to Moscow by W/T from the end of April onwards. Yet only silence followed, and Sorge was to lament despairingly: "Why has Stalin not reacted?"

Week by week, the warnings grew more clamant – from Rudolf Rössler, known as Lucy, an agent operating inside Switzerland, from Viktor Sukulov-Gurevich, alias Kent, in Brussels, above all from the doyen of Soviet agents, Leopold Trepper, otherwise known as "Monsieur Gilbert" or "Le Grand Chef".

Identified by the call-sign PTX Moscov, Trepper, a dapper fastidious gourmet, Polish-born and Moscow-trained, had by degrees evolved a spymaster's dream: a network known to all *Abwehr* (German military intelligence) agents as "The Red Orchestra" yet one with a perfectly legitimate front. Operating from two offices – Simexco on Brussels' Rue Royale and Simex on the Champs-Elysées, Paris – their cover was near impregnable. Both firms supplied cement and construction materials to the German Organisation Todt, responsible for *Wehrmacht* military construction.

All but four Trepper employees were frontmen, convinced they were working for a sound business concern; one with Nazi leanings, even lent credibility to the establishment by barking "*Heil Hitler!*" when he lifted the phone. Soon the Principals of Simexco and Simex were receiving *Ausweis* or passes which opened every door to them. Over Black Market meals at Paris restaurants like Chez Kornilov, Trepper saw to it that his German guests drank deeply – ensuring his own sobriety by swallowing olive oil, which checks alcohol from acting on the system – and listened hard. At one such meal, Ludwig Kainz, a Todt engineer recently returned from the east, told of working on fortifications on the German–Russian border in Poland.

After that, Trepper had worked fast. As professionals, he and his agents never traded reports in cafés or restaurants but only in public places: lavatories, the Metro, or the Tuileries Gardens. Soon their information was too convincing to be gainsaid. In February, Trepper sent Moscow a detailed dispatch of all the divisions being withdrawn from

France and Belgium and sent to the frontier. By May, he had confirmed both Tito's 15 May readiness date and Sorge's date of attack.

It was in vain. On 20 March, Marshal Filipp Ivanovich Golikov, Director of Red Army Intelligence, had minuted his subordinates: "All the documents claiming that war is imminent must be regarded as forgeries emanating from British or even German sources."

On all important dispatches, filed by Sorge, Trepper and others, Golikov sedulously noted in the margin: "Double agent" or "British source".

This scepticism was, on the surface, readily encouraged by Josef Stalin. In April, a Czech agent named Shkvor, operating from Berlin, confirmed German troop concentrations, reporting that the Skoda Works in Prague had been ordered to halve deliveries of military equipment to Russia. On the margin of this report, Stalin minuted in red ink: "This is merely an English provocation. The perpetrator should be sought out and punished."

Yet, the surface impression was misleading. Stalin accepted the physical evidence as valid enough – but fatally miscalculated Hitler's true intentions. The Führer, he thought – and his secret police the N.K.V.D., were in full accord – was indulging in a gigantic bluff of sabre-rattling. Germany's threatening military moves would soon be followed up by blunt demands for economic, even territorial, concessions.

As a result, Stalin switched overnight to a policy of blatant appeasement – what U.S. Secretary of the Interior, Harold Ickes, called "a series of cuddles in the direction of Germany". Though the prices of material delivered were upped by 40 percent, supplies crossed the border at a frenetic rate: manganese, grain, chrome, crude oil, even 4,000 tons of rubber. And Stalin made further propitiatory moves – severing diplomatic relations with such German adversaries as Belgium, Norway, even, only a bare month after signing a non-aggression pact, with Yugoslavia.

All these were one-sided concessions which Hitler had not even sought.

For those waiting impatiently on the side-lines, it seemed that fear was the keynote. From Russia's south-west frontier, one corps commander, Marshal Rodion Malinovsky, a Spanish civil war veteran, begged for clarification: "Can we open fire if the enemy invades our territory?" The reply seemed strangely supine: "Do not succumb to provocation and do not open fire."

From the British Embassy, Moscow, Sir Stafford Cripps voiced a bitter complaint: the Foreign Office had given him no cards whatsoever to play. But, as Hugh Dalton commented accurately, "Whatever cards he had, he could not play them to effect . . . when the Russians were terrified of Germany."

Like many another ruler, Stalin had read the danger signs correctly –

but he somehow sought to postpone history. On 5 May, at a Kremlin reception, the dictator spoke for forty minutes to hundreds of young officers, new graduates from the military academies. Nor did he mince his words. The situation was extremely serious: a German attack in the near future was not to be ruled out.

But at this moment the Red Army was not strong enough to smash the *Wehrmacht*. Modern tanks were lacking, and, so, too, were modern planes. Thus the government was doing all it could, by diplomatic means, to stave off an attack until the autumn.

His conclusion was unwarrantably optimistic. Almost inevitably a war with Germany would be fought – but in 1942, under conditions by then far more favourable for the Red Army.

*

Another man was striving to swim against the current of history. Night after night he had lain sleepless in the bedroom of his house on Harthauser Strasse, in the Munich suburb of Harlaching. On the wall at the foot of the bed was pinned a giant map of a momentous 850-mile journey. Hour after hour he had lain propped up by pillows, a single reading lamp directed like a spotlight on this map, the room cloaked in darkness as he absorbed the details: distance, points of orientation, the course of his journey.

Walter Richard Rudolf Hess, Deputy Führer of the Third Reich, the trusted friend who had worked with Hitler on Part One of *Mein Kampf* in a cell in Landsberg Gaol, had pondered this mission for almost a year now. Time had only strengthened his convictions: the Barbarossa attack which Hess had long urged, would at last involve Germany in a two-front war. But Hitler, he believed, was far from seeking this, merely an understanding with England. And surely the English would never tolerate a Soviet victory over Germany?

But for the English to comprehend Hitler's intentions, someone had to make the first overture. This was the scenario that Rudolf Hess had drafted for himself – "a Parsifal", as one man saw him, who dreamed of a "great mediating act to save the Reich for Germany . . . and . . . for Hitler, his idol".

If he reached England, Hess knew exactly whom to contact. His close friend, Dr Albrecht Haushofer, son of the famous geo-politician who had been Hess' mentor, had long sought to establish friendly contacts with a group of powerful Britons – among them R. A. Butler, Under Secretary of State to the Foreign Office, Lord Dunglass, Neville Chamberlain's Parliamentary Private Secretary (later Lord Home of the Hirsel), above all, with the Duke of Hamilton and Brandon, Scotland's Premier Duke, and Lord Steward of His Majesty's Household.

Haushofer, who had met the Duke briefly at the 1936 Olympic Games, had formed the intriguing notion that part of a Lord Steward's duties must be to wait on King George VI at dinner. In the autumn of 1940, he had even written the Duke a friendly letter, routing it via Lisbon, though no reply had been forthcoming. Haushofer could not know that his letter had been intercepted by the censor, and had not been shown to the Duke until March 1941.

If only he could reach the Duke's country estate at Dungavel House, Lanarkshire, Scotland, Hess reasoned, he had only to produce Haushofer's visiting card to gain an audience with King George VI.

On the morning of 10 May, Hess knew that weather conditions were as good as he could hope for. Twice before he had attempted this lone mission, and twice, he had been forced back – once by inclement weather, once by a jammed aileron. Now the subterfuges of months were to pay off: the ME 110, which he had tricked Professor Willy Messerschmitt into modifying, grumbling about its limited range until the engineer fitted two auxiliary tanks, holding 700 litres each, into the wings; the twenty trial flights he had made to point out alleged defects; the top secret maps of forbidden air zones he had bespoken from Hitler's personal pilot, Hans Baur.

Those closest to him were uneasy, not quite knowing why. Hess had not confided in Ilse, his wife, but his constant trips to the Messerschmitt airfield at Augsburg could not pass unnoticed. Nor could the mysterious telephone calls relaying weather reports at regular intervals to Hess' secretary, Hildegard Fath. His adjutant, *Hauptmann* Karlheinz Pintsch, more in the secret, was even less reassured. Forced to confess his purpose, after his second abortive flight, Hess had claimed the Führer knew everything – but in that case, why had Hess entrusted him with a letter to Hitler to be delivered if the flight succeeded?

At 2.30 p.m., Ilse Hess was more puzzled still: her husband had arrived in her bedroom to take tea, as was his custom, but wearing the uniform of a *Hauptmann* in the Luftwaffe: light blue shirt, dark blue tie, blue-grey breeches, and high airman's boots. He offered no explanation, mentioning only a sudden summons to Berlin, which entailed another side-trip to Augsburg.

Unknown to Ilse, the last message she would receive from him for eight months was tucked unobtrusively away among their four-year-old son, Wolf's toys.

Shortly before 6 p.m., the Deputy Führer's Mercedes arrived at Augsburg airfield. In an ante-room of the administration building, Hess changed into a jacket matching his Luftwaffe trousers and fur-lined flying overalls. A silver-grey ME 110 had been man-handled from a hangar and lined up on the tarmac.

Now, climbing briskly into the Messerschmitt's cockpit, Hess completed the take-off drill, grinning and giving the thumbs-up sign to the airfield's research manager, Herr Piehl. Hunched against the slipstream, Piehl slipped the wooden chocks from the wheels and the little plane headed into the wind.

"How long will he be gone?" he asked *Hauptmann* Pintsch. "I've got better things to do on a Saturday than hang around here."

Pintsch stared at him unseeing. In his pocket he fingered the letter he must deliver to Hitler if Hess had not returned in four hours. "I've no idea," he said.

*

At Bentley Priory, the headquarters of Fighter Command, Royal Air Force, twelve miles north of London, the mood was one of grim expectancy. By 6.15 p.m. on 10 May, the moon was at the full – and the cold spring nights had now assumed a sinister significance in the calendar of *Reichsmarschall* Herman Göring's Luftwaffe.

On the night of 16 April, almost 700 bombers had attacked London for close on eight hours; three nights later, 400 bombers had made the two-way trip. In truth, the raids were designed to foster the illusion of an impending invasion, a smokescreen to divert attention from Operation Barbarossa, but as yet the British could take no comfort from this fact.

At 10.45 p.m., as British radar stations showed the first blips dancing forty miles into France, Squadron Leader Cyril Leman, in Fighter Command's Ops Room, rang his Commander-in-Chief, Air Marshal Sholto Douglas: "There's something big on tonight, sir."

Next door, in the underground Filter Room, Squadron Leader "Dickie" Richardson, the Junior Controller, was struggling to sort order from chaos. Below Richardson, who was perched in the Controller's gallery, a tense team of plotters, tight-packed round a giant map of the coastline from Penzance to Aberdeen, kept in nightly contact, using head-and-breast sets, with radar stations girdling the coast.

In the Ops .Room, as hushed and subdued as a city counting house, Sholto Douglas and Cyril Leman were also watching from the circular gallery; across the map of England, the W.A.A.F. plotters with the long-handled plotting rods eased an urgent thicket of red metal arrows towards the capital. On the gallery's wall map, the suffused lighting round the London region changed from yellow to red: danger imminent.

More than 500 bombers were heading for the capital, and soon Canewdon on the Thames estuary and other radar stations en route could report only "mass plots" to the Filter Room – so many aircraft winging west that the dancing white scallops on the radar screens fused into one colossal "blip". Section Officer Sadie Younger, who covered the estuary corner,

65

was to recall: "We worked only four-hour shifts but that was enough . . . a night like that sent you cross-eyed."

But the Filter Room's knottiest problem had arisen as early as 10.23 p.m. The W.A.A.F. plotting the northern sector of coastline had a sudden call: one of the radar stations showed a single plane crossing the coastline north-east of Alnwick, Northumberland. "Hey," Sadie Younger heard an irate plotter call, "What's that type doing up there? They should have told us there were some more coming in."

But as the minutes ticked by it seemed there weren't: merely a lone aircraft crossing the North Sea coastline at 300 m.p.h. Two fighters, trying to intercept it, had as promptly lost it.

Squadron Leader Richardson rubbed his eyes. It made no sense. A quick glance at the Movement Control Sheet confirmed what he really knew; no friendly aircraft was scheduled within miles of the spot. Yet no German bomber could touch above 180 m.p.h. His chief, Air Commodore Tom Webb-Bowen, came to the only decision possible: "Stick an 'X' on it."

This stamped it as doubtful, to be watched but left alone; there was little else to do. To mark it "Hostile" automatically called the local guns and fighters into action – and just conceivably it could be a friendly fighter in trouble.

Next door, in the Ops Room, Air Marshal Sholto Douglas became curious. He told Squadron Leader Leman: "Find out what it is – what it's doing." On the Ops Room control table the plane was marked by a red metal arrow; as Douglas watched, the W.A.A.F. plotters, ear-phones attuned to each fresh course the Filter Room gave, were slowly easing the plane north towards Edinburgh.

But Leman had one ace up his sleeve that the Filter Room could not play: the dozen-odd Observer Corps posts scattered across the moorland between the Northumbrian coastline and Edinburgh. If someone could catch a glimpse of the plane the whole problem might be solved. At 10.30 p.m. came bewildering news from Post A 3 at Chatton: "We've got a visual at 100 feet – it came from behind cloud. It's a Messerschmitt 110."

Sholto Douglas shook his head: "Impossible. No Messerschmitt would have the fuel to get to Edinburgh and back. Get another fix on it." Again Leman uncradled the phone, convinced in his own mind that Hitler had developed a new bomber. Within minutes came confirmation from Jedburgh. It was indeed a Messerschmitt, now hedge-hopping as low as fifty feet.

Sholto-Douglas made a snap decision: "Get the fighters up after it." Then a strange thing happened. For a while the plane became confused with the track of an R.A.F. Defiant flying in the same area. At 11.09 p.m. before the fighters had had time to make any contact, the observer post from Eaglesham came on the line. The plane had been shot down at

Bonnyton Moor, a few miles south-west of Glasgow. But with more phone calls the mystery deepened. No. 14 Group, R.A.F., controlling all fighters in Scotland, knew nothing about it.

The minutes passed but no more news came of the Messerschmitt. Douglas felt a strange sense of disquiet. Why had it made that lonely northern run – and who had shot it down? At 11.20 p.m., a W.A.A.F. removed the red metal arrow from the board; the pawn was out of play. But at 11.30, everyone was more preoccupied by that one mystery plane than by the hundreds now milling over London.

*

As the anti-aircraft batteries hammered from London's Regents Park, a group of Cockneys bedded down in a shelter by King's Cross Station, chorused, "Good, we're giving it to 'em." District Warden Rob Connell paused in a count of heads to ask curiously: "But s'pose a Jerry baled out in your back garden – what then?" Again, the reaction was unanimous: "Oh, that's different – offer the poor lad a cuppa char."

Four hundred miles away, at Floors Farm, near Eaglesham, south-west of Glasgow, Mrs McLean, a 64-year-old crofter's widow, was doing precisely that. For all the family it had been a hard day and by 11 p.m. she and her daughter Sophia were already in bed; David, her ploughman son, was in the next room also preparing for sleep. Suddenly, as from a long way off, Mrs McLean heard a strange droning; it went on and on as if half a dozen planes were circling the house. By this time David McLean had snuffed out the oil-lamp and dashed to the window – too late to see the plane rip violently into the ground 200 yards away but in time to see a parachutist drifting gently down.
flames.

Grabbing a hay-fork McLean dashed to the scene, to find an aviator in full flying kit alternately nursing a hurt ankle and fumbling with his parachute harness. When Mrs McLean saw David struggling back to the cottage, supporting a handsome black-browed stranger who admitted he was a German she felt "none too friendly" – but Scottish hospitality won the day. The poor man looked pale and tired and his ankle was so swollen that she just had to get the kettle boiling and offer him a cup of tea.

"Thank you, I never drink tea as late as this. I'll only have a glass of water," was the stranger's courteous reply.

So the McLeans and their visitor settled down to chat – as strange a tea-party as existed anywhere that night. The stranger gave his name with disarming frankness – Horn, *Hauptmann* Alfred Horn of Munich. Almost diffidently, David McLean explained that he had asked a farm worker, William Craig, to call in the military. "Please," said the visitor, "I think that would be best." Later he pulled out a pocket-book to produce a snapshot: "That's my son. I saw him this morning. God knows when I shall see him again."

Still the visitor sat chatting, seeming grateful for the comfort of a peat fire. He was so obviously a gentleman that Mrs McLean was fascinated – by his fluent English, his gold watch and bracelet, his easy manners. His one apparent concern was his parachute: "I should like to keep a piece as a souvenir. I am very lucky to be alive."

Presently, in answer to David's summons the tiny kitchen was boiling with people – two signallers from the Royal Signal Corps, who had arrived unarmed, a special constable on part-time duty, a Home Guards-man brandishing a World War One revolver. Asked if he was armed, the stranger spread his hands in a gesture: "You see all I have. My plane was unarmed also."

As the soldiers searched him, the McLeans stood silent and embar-rassed; it was as if through no fault of their own the hospitality had gone sour. But there was little to find: a box of German matches, a thick wad of papers, capsules of homeopathic medicine. The one thing that struck them was the number of photographs of himself and his family that the visitor seemed to carry. To the end he remained calm and smiling; when the time came to go, he bowed stiffly to Mrs McLean, thanking her profusely. As if to atone for the formalities of the search, one of the young signallers presented him with a bottle of milk which he had brought for his guard duty.

By 12.30 the McLeans had washed the tea-mugs and retired to bed – a little dazed by the night's drama, unaware that they had done anything more unusual than entertain an unlucky German airman.

Others were swiftly embroiled in the bizarre scenario. In the small hours of Sunday, 11 May, Wing Commander the Duke of Hamilton, commanding the R.A.F. fighter sector at Turnhouse, East Scotland, was roused from sleep by his Sector Controller. The pilot of a German plane that had crashed near Eaglesham had asked for the Duke by name.

At 10 a.m. the Duke along with Flight Lieutenant Benson, the R.A.F. Interrogating Officer for South Scotland, looked in on the prisoner – now in a private room at the Maryhill Military Hospital, Glasgow. When the German asked if the junior officer could withdraw, the Duke gave consent.

Once alone, the German relaxed, remarking conversationally, "I am sorry to have missed you in Lisbon." Then, seeing the Duke's look of bafflement, "I do not know if you recognise me, but I am Rudolf Hess." Gathering confidence he explained that he was as close to Hitler as any man alive. He had plans for a negotiated peace with England which he knew Hitler would regard as a basis for discussion. The Duke decided to temporise. "If it's a question of peace plans," he replied, "I think I should return with an interpreter." His one idea was to get out of the hospital as fast as might be, saying nothing to anyone until he had made personal contact with Sir Alexander Cadogan.

It was now 11 a.m. At the Foreign Office building on London's Whitehall, the only man the Duke could contact was Nicholas Lawford, one of Eden's private secretaries. But his allusions were veiled, and as Lawford struggled to make sense of a story "like an E. Phillips Oppenheim thriller", Churchill's Private Secretary, John Colville, strolled in. Cupping his hand over the receiver, Lawford whispered: "This may be a lunatic. He says he is the Duke of Hamilton, that something extraordinary has happened . . . he won't say what it's all about . . . I think he's a lunatic."

Suddenly Colville recalled a waking day-dream of Göring descending by parachute over London. Taking the phone, he asked with emphasis: "Has somebody arrived." After a long pause, the Duke replied: "Yes."

Intrigued, Colville called the Premier at Ditchley Park, the eighteenth-century Oxfordshire mansion of his friend Ronald Tree, where security decreed that the Premier spent all weekends when the moon was high. Partly curious, partly irked, Churchill kept asking: "Well, *who* has arrived."

"I don't know," Colville repeated patiently for the fourth time. "He won't say."

"It can't be Hitler," Churchill ventured.

Since Colville didn't think so, there was only one way to settle the matter; the Duke was bidden to fly south and report to the Premier.

Worn-out after a gruelling day, the Duke did not reach Ditchley until late that evening: owls were dipping like moths in the moonlit park and the great stone hall was cloaked in darkness. Inside, Churchill and a mixed party of thirty guests were just finishing a leisurely dinner; the premier was in expansive mood. The previous night's punitive raid on London had cost the Luftwaffe thirty-three bombers;* moreover, as a fervent film fan, Churchill was about to enjoy a private screening of *The Marx Brothers Go West*.

Later the Duke would always recall his meeting in camera with Churchill and the Secretary of State for Air, Sir Archibald Sinclair – both men seemingly incredulous at the news. "Do you mean we have got the Deputy Führer of the Third Reich in our hands?" Churchill asked with sonorous relish.

That, Hamilton replied, was what the prisoner had claimed. Suddenly, seeming to lose interest, Churchill remarked: "Well, Hess or no Hess, I am going to see the Marx Brothers."

The truth was that Churchill and his Cabinet were profoundly embarrassed. Ever since 1941 dawned, they had striven to impress America with their resolution to beat Hitler; even their disastrous showings in

* A figure later amended to fourteen.

Greece and Libya had been all to that end. Now Hess' arrival – whether speaking for the Führer or himself alone – was bound to unleash a floodtide of speculation: were the British prepared to contemplate a peace offer?

For the secret could hardly be kept. By 13 May, Hess's gaunt beetle-browed face glowered out from every front page – and the rumours multiplied. Had he come via Spain after discussing a peace deal with the appeasement-prone British Ambassador, Sir Samuel Hoare? Had he arrived to assassinate Churchill – or to make love to Unity Mitford?* Meanwhile, those who cherished puns enjoyed a field-day. Was he a Trojan Hess – or suffering from Hessteria? The answer to both was inevitable: Your Hess is as good as mine.

Churchill was appalled by what he deemed the irresponsible press coverage. Feature writers vied with one another to stress Hess's good looks, his clean living, his devotion to his wife and son. "The general effect of what had been published," the War Cabinet noted, "had been almost laudatory, and there had been no reference to Hess's record, which was as bloody as that of any of the Nazi leaders." Some journalists shared this conviction. Mollie Panter-Downes, London Correspondent of *The New Yorker*, commented: "The public was justly a bit muzzy as to whether it was reading about Hitler's right-hand man or Gary Cooper."

Within the Cabinet, argument raged: how could this imbroglio be turned to sound British advantage? At first, Ivone Kirkpatrick, a former First Secretary in Berlin, who could positively identify Hess, was flown north, there to question him on four separate occasions. Then, Churchill, having digested the trend of Hess's thinking, proposed quoting some excerpts in a House of Commons statement. Eden objected; the Germans should be kept guessing. He himself drafted an alternative statement – one approved by Lord Beaverbrook but opposed by Minister of Information Alfred Duff Cooper. In the small hours of Thursday, 15 May, Churchill flew into a tantrum; he would make his own statement or not at all.

"Then," Eden replied firmly, "no statement." "All right," Churchill raged, slamming down the phone, "No statement."

But was Hess in a fit mental state to negotiate a peace offer? Relays of psychiatrists who examined him, in Scotland and elsewhere, seemed to doubt it; one man compared him to "a caged ape, oozing hostility". Angered at being treated as a prisoner-of-war rather than as an envoy to King George VI, Hess had grown sullen and rancorous. Now the psychiatrists adjudged the German was suffering from hysterical amnesia, claustrophobia, paranoid schizophrenia, psychogenic disturbances,

---

* Unity Mitford, one of the six daughters of Lord Redesdale, and a former close associate of Hitler's. She had been returned to Britain from Germany in January 1940, suffering from an undisclosed injury.

70

hypochondria and delusions of persecution. It was small wonder that one man added a rider: Hess also had an inferiority complex.

On 17 May – the day after Hess was moved from Scotland to the Tower of London – Churchill thought it apposite to send Roosevelt a note of reassurance. "This is the old invitation to us to desert all our friends in order to save temporarily the greater part of our skin," he wrote soothingly. "Here we think it best to let the Press have a good run for a bit and keep the Germans guessing."

Roosevelt was sceptical. "I wonder what is really behind this story," was his only laconic comment.

One Foreign Office specialist, T. W. Whitehead, adviser on American affairs, shared the President's misgivings. "Our failure to publish any news about Hess has been turned to our disadvantage," he wrote. "The Germans have spread the idea that Hess has come over to England with a peace offer, and that our continued silence is evidence that the Cabinet are seriously considering the offer."

Even so, the German policy was one of snatching at straws. On the Obersalzberg, Hitler's interpreter, Paul Schmidt always recalled, the news of Hess's defection came "as if a bomb had hit the Berghof". Hitler's architect, Albert Speer, who had called with some sketches, remembered too, "the inarticulate almost animal outcry", as the Führer opened the letter brought by *Hauptmann* Karlheinz Pintsch. "Oh, My God! My God!" he burst out to Göring's representative, General Karl Bodenschatz. "He has flown to Britain."

In this moment, Hitler's fears were manifold – the fear of a threat to troop morale on the impending Barbarossa front, the fear that Mussolini would desert the Axis alliance to make his own peace terms with Britain, the fear that Hess, under a truth serum, would reveal the plans for the Russian attack. And supposing the wily Churchill induced Hess to broadcast over the B.B.C.?

Expert advice had been sought – including that of General Ernst Udet, World War One fighter ace and now technical chief of the Luftwaffe. Could Hess have reached his goal? Udet thought not: given the prevailing side winds he would probably have flown past England. Momentarily Hitler's spirits rose: "If only he would drown in the North Sea!" Ribbentrop, who was also consulted, fell back on his British affairs adviser, Fritz Hesse. Supposing Udet was wrong, was there any chance of the British making peace? Hesse thought it out of the question. Ribbentrop's lament was heartfelt: "If only the Führer wouldn't always be taken in by fools who trick him into believing there can be an easy peace with England."

Scapegoats were singled out on all sides. Not only Adjutant Pintsch but many of the staff of Augsburg airfield were arrested and locked up and, for good measure, since Hess had long dabbled in the occult and fringe medicine, scores of astrologers and naturopaths. Meanwhile Hitler himself oversaw the wording of the press release which announced to the world that Hess was mad: "The National Socialist Party regrets that this idealist fell prey to tragic hallucinations."

Some Germans, though, found the news less than surprising. The alarums past, interpreter Paul Schmidt returned home to Berlin and found himself discussing the contretemps with his gardener. The old man seemed quite unperturbed. "Didn't you know," he asked innocently, "that we're already governed by madmen?"

4

"He'll Never Beat Men Like These"

19 May–28 May, 1941

THE QUAYSIDE WAS bathed in the golden light of evening. The little group of men strolled slowly, laughing and chatting, drinking in the last of the sun. Once their host, Viggo Axelssen, ship's chandler, bachelor and *bon-viveur* of Kristiansand, Norway, did pause, borrowing a friend's spy-glass to scan the horizon, but too briefly to cause comment.

Eight miles away, beyond the Oksøy lighthouse, a group of ships was steaming west at high speed. Two were quite obviously camouflaged German warships, aircraft circling above, destroyers ahead, as they headed for the Norwegian fjords.

After eighteen months of war, it was a common sight for the subjugated Norwegians; no one even gave it a thought. And when Axelssen mentioned dropping by his office to fetch something, only a burst of laughter followed. That night the ship's chandler was giving a dinner party at the Kristiansand Club to celebrate the launching of a new boat; the "something" could only be a bottle of schnapps.

But once in his office near Vestre Strand-gade, Kristiansand's town centre, Axelssen worked fast. Scribbling a twelve-word message he pocketed it, setting out for the club. Now as his way led him past the bus station, he stopped off to trade gossip with Arne Moen, a grave-faced man wearing a peaked cap and a shiny serge uniform. Within the hour, as Axelssen was calling for a third round of drinks in the club's Red Room, Moen's bus was already grinding up the narrow road towards the port of Flekkefjord, sixty miles north-west.

The message which Axelssen had written, and which Moen had not even scanned, was now secure in a pocket of the bus's engine casing.

In his roomy grocer's shop on Flekkefjord's main street, the proprietor, Tor Njaa was still open for business. When Moen walked in, Njaa raised a silent eyebrow; although the bus driver ostensibly called for a packet of ersatz coffee, his presence always spelt urgency. Not pausing to remove his white jacket, the grocer stuffed Axelssen's message into his pocket, crossing the street to the dairy where Sofie Rørvik worked.

Once Njaa had left, Sofie took the crumpled paper, carefully

73

smoothing out the wrinkles before easing it into the top of her stocking, flat against her thigh. It was now around 6 p.m. on 20 May. The long summer night stretched ahead; not until after midnight would darkness fall.

Sofie's way out of town lay uphill, through a steep valley fringed with yellow catkins and giant oaks, a 10-mile cycle ride to the farm of young Gunwald Tomstad at Helle. The farm, six acres of arable, more than eighty acres of moors and woods, would never make Tomstad rich, but it was still an ideal centre for a spy ring. All sea traffic rounded Lista lighthouse, at the mouth of Flekkefjord, coming close in to obtain the protection of the German coastal batteries, and could thus be easily monitored.

Axelssen, Moen, Njaa, Sofie Rørvik, Tomstad himself, had one thing in common: all of them were secret agents in a coastal network that stretched 360 miles from Oslo to Stavanger. Tonight they were about to achieve their biggest coup in the entire war. The quarry that Axelssen had sighted was Germany's mightiest warship, the *Bismarck*, outward bound, along with the cruiser *Prinz Eugen*, on a three-month cruise to ravage the Atlantic convoys.

At Helle Farm, just as she had expected, Sofie found Tomstad closeted with his chief, Odd Starheim, a curly-headed shipowner's son who had escaped to Britain in 1940 to become one of the first Scandinavian agents of the Special Operations Executive. Returning to Norway in a British submarine on New Year's Eve, 1940, armed with a radio transmitter, Starheim's brief had been to set up a network based on Kristiansand, Norway's third largest port and now a German naval base.

This evening Axelssen's message had reached its fifth and final link. As Sofie waited, the two men set to work coding it.

Although they had known for some hours that the valley was encircled by German listening posts, both were too engrossed to realise that troops armed with special equipment were at this moment crossing the open spaces between the farm buildings.

Starheim was aware only of the need for urgency. Conceivably this message was the most important that his mission – with the unromantic code-name "Operation Cheese" – might ever accomplish. The two men mounted to the musty attic of the farmhouse, and Tomstad, opening an old suitcase, removed a small compact transmitter. Crouched in a cubby-hole, Starheim began calling Home Station, London.

Methodically, his fingers stabbed at the keys: "A battleship . . . probably German . . . passed Kristiansand . . ."

Outside the attic, on a stairway smelling of old timber and dust, Tomstad was standing guard, the muzzle of his automatic pistol trained on the stairs that led to the first floor. Faint far-off shouts were reaching him from the farmyard; the direction finder signals were now recording at maximum strength. If they broke in he would shoot and keep shooting, to ensure that the message got through.

This was the time of year when Helle was at its loveliest, when patches of blue anemones and bog cotton splotched the heath surrounding the farm. Would it soon be the time when all three of them had recourse to their cyanide capsules, ensuring death in nine seconds at the most, three if lucky?

". . . passed Kristiansand . . . heading west . . ."

To Sofie Rørvik, waiting below, the coded dots and dashes seemed as loud as hammer blows, resounding all over the house. Suddenly they stopped – so abruptly that Sofie and Tomstad himself had to bite their lips to stop themselves from crying out loud.

Starheim had completed the last three words of the message: ". . . escorted by three destroyers".

Tomstad had just one hope that his farm would go unmolested. Early that year, for love of country, he had deliberately assumed a pariah's role. Summoning courage, he had walked into Flekkefjord town hall and asked to join the Norwegian Nazi Party, the *Nasjonal Samling* (N.S.). He wore the Party's black uniform at rallies, and hung a framed portrait of their leader, Vidkun Quisling, in his hall. Now every villager and neighbour looked through him as though he were dead – but the N.S. leaders had come to trust him.

Now all of them would have to bluff, because their lives depended on it. Starheim must depart in broad daylight, a man with nothing to hide, and Sofie must go with him to help him past the control posts – the two of them walking like lovers, arms entwined, oblivious to everyone.

Armed with paint brush and tin, Tomstad mounted a ladder to an outhouse roof and watched them go. Soon they were a long way down the valley. Though a few Germans stopped and stared, calling out lewd suggestions, nobody barred their passage. Tomstad kept on painting until they were out of sight. Some soldiers crossed his yard just then, along with a Gestapo man, but seeing him they only smiled broadly and waved; they had no time to stop and chat.

Still painting, Tomstad felt his legs trembling. His cover had held; it was going to be all right. No one would come to question him; that same evening the great hunt was joined. But it had been close – very close.

*

Unknown to Starheim and his agents, their signal had now placed the *Bismarck* in double jeopardy.

Soon after midnight on 21 May, Commander Norman Denning, of Royal Naval Intelligence, had been roused from sleep in The Citadel, the ugly concrete headquarters of the Operational Intelligence Centre in

Whitehall, hard by Nelson's column. The British Naval Attaché, Captain Henry Denham, was cabling from Stockholm: the Swedish cruiser *Gotland* had spotted the German squadron's course and a friendly source had at once tipped Denham off.

The report had been graded B3 – source good, information possibly, but by no means certainly, correct.

Starheim's report, coming hard on the heels of Denham's now lent a new aspect of urgency. At 3.30 a.m. R.A.F. Coastal Command were alerted to scour the Norwegian coast from first light until the ships were located and identified. By early afternoon, the risks run by Starheim's agents were vindicated. A Spitfire of the Photographic Reconnaissance Unit had pinpointed *Bismarck* and *Prinz Eugen* in Korsfjord, the entrance to Bergen Harbour.

Events now moved swiftly. Aboard the new flagship of the Home Fleet, *King George V*, moored in Scapa Flow, a green telephone linking Scapa with London rang insistently. The Admiralty were briefing the Commander-in-Chief, Sir John Tovey, a small compact sea-dog with blue twinkling eyes, that trouble was imminent. Promptly Tovey ordered the cruiser *Suffolk*, patrolling the Denmark Straits, to keep a sharp look-out; her sister ship, *Norfolk*, was despatched from Iceland to relieve her.

Now a subdued buzz of rumour ran through Scapa's ships – men guessing something was afoot, yet unable to pin down details. Aboard the E-Class destroyer, H.M.S. *Electra*, Lieutenant Frank McLeod, the Chief Engineer, received the order: "Raise Steam". In fact, this was a routine signal, allowing the ship four hours to prepare for sea, but McLeod did not waste a moment; the force of those rumours was too potent. Within minutes came an order more imperative still: "Raise Steam With Despatch!"

This cut the preparation time to two hours – a sure sign of impending trouble. But soon another order halved the time-span yet again: "Raise Steam With All Despatch!"

Admiral Tovey faced a dilemma. The weather was changing by the minute and mist and rain were drifting; now he was beset by the fear that the Germans were already en route for the Atlantic, where eleven allied convoys lay at their mercy. By 9 p.m., as darkness fell, he came to a decision. Vice-Admiral Lancelot Holland, in the battle-cruiser *Hood*, was to take the battleship *Prince of Wales*, with the destroyers *Electra*, *Anthony*, *Echo*, *Icarus*, *Achates* and *Antelope* and proceed to Iceland for refuelling. Then they must take up a watchful stance south-west of the island.

Aboard every ship that formed this vanguard there was a pleasant tingle of expectancy. In *Electra*, Lieutenant McLeod cast a sharp but confident look over the organ loft of pipes that made up his engine room then reported to the captain, Commander Cecil May: "Steam for twenty knots, sir . . . third boiler will be ready in the next half hour." Simultaneously, the First Lieutenant, Richard Jenner-Fust, also reached the bridge: "Ship secured for sea, sir . . . Slip Rope wove."

It was the same on every ship. Only forty minutes had elapsed since Tovey's signal, yet now only the Slip Ropes – slim wire hawsers – secured the destroyers to the buoys.

Towards midnight on 21 May they slipped their moorings, one by one, forming line ahead to pass through the Switha Gate, heading for the Pentland Firth and their rendezvous with *Hood* and *Prince of Wales*. Now all hands were furiously preoccupied with the preliminaries for action – priming depth charges, arming torpedoes, checking guns, manhandling "ready use" ammunition.

One mood was common to all: a calm and absolute confidence. Aboard *Electra*, when the Captain's steward asked Gunnery Officer Timothy Cain, "Think we'll have luck, sir?", Cain was buoyant. "We won't *need* luck, not with the *Hood* for company." In *Prince of Wales*, all ranks felt the same. With an audible click the loud-speakers switched on and Captain John Leach, a stocky much-loved West Countryman, hailed the ship's company: "The odds are that they are making for the Atlantic to prey on our convoys . . . What we have to hope now is that we intercept them and bring them to action."

As the tannoys clicked off, there was an audible sigh of relief. It was the real thing at last and nothing could stop them. Midshipman Kenneth Townsend-Green still recalls, "We enjoyed the invincibility of it all," a sentiment echoed by Petty Officer David Hunter. "She was a great ship – unsinkable."

These were comforting illusions – yet totally unwarranted. Although all naval men took a fierce and irrational pride in "the mighty *Hood*", she was now, after twenty-two years in service, an obsolescent hybrid. Despite her eight 15-inch guns she was a warhorse from another age, built for speed but not for slogging, her deck protection, at maximum, no more than three inches thick.

Ironically, the same truth held good both for the *Prince of Wales* and her German quarry. Laid down on New Year's Day 1937 as Job No 3968 at Cammell Laird's shipyard, Birkenhead, it was not until 4 May, 1939, that she had gone down the slipway, launched by the Princess Royal. With her 1,612 crew – 110 officers, 1,502 ratings – she was virtually a floating town; Ordinary Seaman Gerald Cooper still recalls, "It took you several weeks to find your way round." Although she displaced 35,000 tons, fully 15,000 was accounted for by armour plating, but this luxury was to be paid for in gun power and speed. At best the *Prince* could muster 28 knots against *Bismarck*'s 30.

Her special pride was her ten new-type 14-inch guns, designed for greater penetration and a higher rate of fire, but two of the new-type turrets were still giving trouble and tonight she was sailing with more than 100 civilian contractors still aboard her, desperately trying to locate the faults. Even so, Churchill, who had twice served as First Lord of the Admiralty, looked to her as "something that could catch and kill" for he believed as implicitly as Roosevelt, one time Secretary of the Navy, that in 1941 sea power would decide the world's fate.

Although Hitler had private misgivings, the *Kriegsmarine* took as fierce a pride in the *Bismarck* – not for nothing had the *Prinz Eugen* ungrudgingly dubbed her "Big Brother". One sixth of a mile long, 120 feet wide, displacing more than 50,000 tons fully laden, she was the mightiest warship afloat. Her armament – eight radar-controlled 15-inch guns, with landing space for six aircraft – was as formidable as the statistics that naval enthusiasts loved to quote: a crew 2,400 strong, a wiring system so complex it comprised 28,000 miles of electrical circuits, Krupp armour, thirteen inches thick, fashioned from specially hardened Wotan steel that protected her sides and turrets. Commissioned in February, 1941, and thus a novice alongside the newly-built *Prince*, who achieved it on 19 January, she had one factor in common with her British pursuer: both were deemed unsinkable.

At 11 p.m. on 22 May, on receipt of the code-word REBEL, Tovey, in *King George V*, along with four cruisers, six destroyers and the aircraft carrier *Victorious*, moved out of Scapa to join in the pursuit. Twenty ships now made part of the hunt that Odd Starheim had set in motion.

Yet the most formidable adversaries the *Bismarck* faced pointed a cogent moral for all naval powers in the months that lay ahead: the nine near-obsolete Swordfish torpedo-bombers of No 825 Fleet Air Arm Squadron, unwieldy single-engined biplanes fashioned from wood, fabric and metal struts, lashed down on the heaving flight-deck of H.M.S. *Victorious*.

*

One Allied spy was less lucky. For Ruth Mitchell, her *Četnik* crusade was over almost before it had begun.

In the weeks since leaving Belgrade, she had followed a tortuous 160-mile route – by refugee train to Chacak, thence to Ujiće, where King Peter and his ministers had briefly encamped, finally after sixteen hours in a cattle truck to Sarajevo, where the seeds of World War One had been sown. From Sarajevo she had boarded a baggage car to Mostar, then on to Herzegnovi beside the blue Adriatic. At long last she had reached Montenegro.

It was here that Ruth knew a brief temptation. A Serb she had known in Belgrade, on the staff of the British Legation, warned her there was no time to lose. Those British diplomats still left were making for Risan, 13 miles down the coast, in the hope of a last minute evacuation by seaplane and submarine. "Will you go now?" he urged. "Tomorrow may be too late."

Ruth Mitchell thought long and hard. Her ties with England were longstanding; once, in another life, as the wife of Stanley Knowles, a housemaster at Tonbridge School, she had become deeply attached to the English countryside and the English way of life. Her son by her first husband, John Lendrum van Breda, was at this moment a Pilot Officer in the Royal Air Force, serving in the Western Desert. It was three months – the time when Rommel arrived in North Africa – since she had heard from him.

Her other choice was a thornier road: on the run by day and night, the broiling sun of a Balkan summer giving place to the soaking rains of winter, cold rocks for a bed, hard black bread, cheese and an onion for food.

But finally she realised she had already chosen – on the day when Pechanats drew the line through her name in the old time-worn book. She was a *Četnik*. The question was: where should she go to best serve the *Četnik* cause?

Logic suggested the port of Dubrovnik. As the largest city on the Montenegrin coast, it would certainly house Italian military headquarters. A spy with an American passport might do useful work there – though the passport, Ruth realised with a sudden sinking of the heart, was no longer valid. She had been due to renew it at the American Legation on Monday 7 April – the day after the great bombardment of the city. All she could hope was that the Italians would find the bold American eagle, stamped in bright gold on the cover, too impressive to be looked at askance.

Luck was with her; two Yugoslav naval officers, heading down the coast, agreed to give her a lift. With her *Četnik* uniform now stowed inside her grip, Ruth, conventionally attired in dress and head scarf, reached Dubrovnik around 20 April.

Once there she lost no time in putting the past behind her. Her uniform and insignia she concealed under bomb rubble in the garden of her first staging post, the run-down Hotel Gradats. An old friend from America, Laura McCullaugh, who passed each spring at the Pension Ivy, hid Ruth's *Četnik* pass in a sponge bag and buried it in a flower bed.

By early May, when Dubrovnik, under Italian tutelage, had been rechristened Ragusa, Ruth had settled into a small hotel near the naval base at Gruzuh, two miles from the city. Armed with a large-scale map of the port, a capacious marketing basket and a pair of dark glasses, she set out each morning along the cliffs to "shop" for gun emplacements.

By degrees she was amassing a sizeable dossier of information – but how could she transmit it to those who most needed to know?

Again, luck seemed to be with her. On 17 May, in the dappled half-light of a grape trellis behind a provision store, she held a brief whispered rendezvous with a *Četnik* agent named Vaso, a Montenegrin frontier policeman she had met on her journey south. Vaso had electrifying news: A *Četnik* rising was planned for 28 June, the anniversary of a great Serbian battle, and Ruth was needed at headquarters. Vaso himself would meet her 31 miles inland, in the tiny town of Nikšić, and guide her to the new leader, Colonel Draža Mihailović.

Ruth was bewildered. Had Pechanats renounced the leadership? But Vaso just scowled and answered evasively; only later did Ruth learn with shame that Pechanats had sold out to the Germans.

But at last she had made the longed-for contact. At dawn on 23 May, she would leave to join Mihailović.

The afternoon of 22 May was warm and sunny. Towards 5 p.m. Ruth enjoyed a leisurely swim, then dried off on the beach. Then, donning a shirt and grey flannel slacks, she headed for the deserted hotel dining-room, a large glassed-in terrace overlooking the bay.

In cheerful mood, whistling softly, she noted the setting sun throwing a rose-gold glow on the white wall opposite the window. The glow had entrapped her shadow, and now, for the fun of it, still whistling, Ruth began to gyrate, a slow rhythmic waltz movement, intrigued by the shifting shadow patterns on the wall.

Abruptly Ruth stopped. Her shadow was now hemmed in by two other shadows, one long and thin, the other smaller. Turning, she faced two rubber-shod men in plain clothes.

She knew at once who they were. "Ruth Mitchell? We are the Gestapo. You will come with us at once."

*

Aircraftman Marcel Gerard Comeau had a strange sense of fore-boding. As early as 19 May – three days before Ruth Mitchell's arrest in Dubrovnik – Comeau had the uneasy sensation that the debâcle he had experienced in Greece had been only the dress-rehearsal for a greater disaster in Crete.

What Comeau had witnessed as the assault ship *Glenearn* limped into the main harbour at Suda Bay had scarcely suggested grim preparedness. He himself tramped down the gangplank to the jetty but on other ships men were less fortunate; as the Stukas screamed low over the water, some leapt overboard in mid-harbour, swimming for their lives to dry land. But once ashore, they found no permanent accommodation to house them and few tents; most slept in their clothes among the olive trees. Transport was non-existent. While Comeau foot-slogged the twenty miles to Maleme airfield, other landing grounds were further-flung – thirty miles to Retimo, sixty-five to Heraklion.

The troops that he passed along the way seemed in sorry shape – dishevelled, unshaven, their nerves at snapping point after the constant strafing. They were embittered, too, by the lack of air cover and Comeau's blue uniform brought a barrage of taunts and catcalls: "R – A – bloody F – Rare as Bloody Fairies." It was a bitter pill to swallow.

Of the 44,000 men – 29,000 British and Dominion troops, 15,000 Greeks – flung together as an improvised defence force, only 8,700 had come fresh from the Middle East; others demoralised or wounded in Greece, lacked even rifles. Typical of the square pegs plugging the round hole of Crete were the men of the 1005th Dock Operating Company. Impressed as stevedores because they hailed from British ports, all of them were in fact shipping clerks, fresh from office stools. Following one day's Stuka bombardment, almost 100 men reported sick, suffering from "nervous prostration". On 3 May they were replaced by Australian volunteers.

Although the newly-appointed Commander-in-Chief, Major General Bernard Freyberg, V.C., a battle-scarred New Zealander and a veteran of Gallipoli, had not seen fit to accept the offer, one stout-hearted body of men might have served him as well. As May dawned, they had petitioned him en masse:

> We wholeheartedly put ourselves under your service, dangerous or not, provided that the cause of our Allied effort is fulfilled . . .
> Respectfully yours,
> The convicts of the Island of Crete.

But so many supplies had been left behind in Greece, even seasoned troops would have found the going hard. One New Zealander, Second-Lieutenant Charles Upham, of the 20th (N.Z.) Battalion always recalled it as "a pauper's campaign" from first to last – no entrenching tools, "mortars without baseplates, Vickers guns without tripods". One unit even improvised artillery sights from slivers of wood and chewing gum. Most Australians used herring tins for dixies and whittled spoons from olive wood, but many men, like Comeau himself, never saw hot food during the entire campaign. One doctor, Lieutenant Theodore Stephanides, attached to the Cyprus Regiment, found drugs so short he fell back on a knowledge of botany – decocting herbal draughts from plantains, mallows and mulberry leaves.

Even so, Comeau knew contentment of a kind. Realising that No 11 (Blenheim) Squadron would make little headway against the Stukas, the youngster had "deserted" yet again – re-attaching himself to the Hurricane ground crews of No 33 Squadron of Maleme. Wedged between the sea and the coast road, the airfield lay at the base of the wooded 340-foot Kavkazia Hill; here, at least, Comeau enjoyed the shelter of a tent, though there were only duckboards to sleep on and a warm reunion with old friends like Ken Eaton, Tubby Dixon and Paddy Rennie.

Innocent of the battle plan, they wondered idly: How would Crete be defended when the time came?

Few men realised it, but Crete was virtually indefensible from the start. Although the island was 170 miles long, only one major narrow road followed the northern coastline. So limited were its port facilities that at Suda only two ships could berth at a time; at Canea, unloading was feasible only by lighter. Anti-aircraft, artillery and tanks were woefully short; of the twenty-one tanks that Wavell could spare, all proved defective, lacking cooling systems for the guns and even wireless communication. No air cover was possible from North Africa, 400 miles away; in theory, the island would be self-supporting.

But only in theory. On 19 May, no more than six aircraft – three Hurricanes, three obsolete Gladiators – were left on the entire island, too few to serve any useful purpose. On this same day they were flown back to Egypt.

For a long time Comeau and his mates wandered round the air strip, then drifted listlessly back to their tents. It seemed strange to be aircraftmen without any aircraft to repair – when the battle had not even started.

*

On the morning of this same day, in an ornate rococo suite on the second floor of the Hotel Grande Bretagne, Athens, a group of junior officers had gathered for an eleventh-hour briefing. For maximum security, the room had been hermetically sealed and shuttered against the sunlight, but the secret was not kept for long. Suspended from a gilded cornice, they espied a giant map of Crete.

For a moment there was a burst of excited comment and chatter, until General Kurt Student, the genial crop-headed commander of the Seventh Air Division, hushed them with a soft, *"Mein Herren, Ich bitte Sie."*

Then, in what Baron Friedrich von der Heydte, commanding the 1st Battalion, Third Parachute Regiment, recalled as "a quiet but clear, slightly vibrant voice", Student outlined his plan. The concept was both bold and unprecedented: to capture an entire island, 100 miles from the Greek mainland, by air attack and vertical assault. Although Hitler had finally assented – persuaded that seizing Crete would ensure his dominion in the Aegean, negate a threat to Rumania's Ploesti oil-fields and ensure Turkish neutrality – the project was originally the brainchild of

Hermann Göring, determined to revenge the reverses of the Battle of Britain.

But Student, a dedicated professional had worked for the plan until it had become part of his life. Now he shared his secret with the men who must make it a reality: the island was to be attacked by paratroops at four different points simultaneously. The target of the Assault Regiment, dropping to the west, was the airfield at Maleme. The Third Regiment was to seize Canea, Crete's capital. While the First Regiment struck at the town and airfield at Heraklion, the Second Regiment was allotted identical targets at Retimo.

The logistics were staggering. As 10,000 parachutists were drifting from the sky, a further 750 would be landing by gliders, both DFS 230s, carrying ten men, and Gotha 242s, holding up to twenty-five. A back-up force of 5,000 would travel by JU-52 transports, the old Luftwaffe workhorses known as "Auntie Ju". For mopping-up operations, a seaborne force of 7,000 men would land on Day Two.

Nothing had been left to chance. Each paratrooper would carry three days' emergency rations: specially prepared *Wittler* bread, sliced and wrapped in cellophane, processed chocolate, tartaric acid, sugar, biscuits, thirst-quenchers, cigarettes, phonetic phrasebooks, even contraceptives. Each man's wrists and ankles would be heavily padded, to lessen the risk of sprains.

Security was absolute. Paybooks were replaced by identity cards, giving no hint of the bearer's unit. Parachute sing-songs were to be strictly forbidden. Even the proud badge of the paratrooper – a plunging eagle in an oval garland of oak and laurel leaves – must be removed for the duration.

A colour code for parachutes would streamline the operation further still – black for other ranks' supplies, red for officers, white for ammunition, yellow for medical supplies. On landing, each section leader would fire a white Very light if all was well, a red Very light if trouble threatened, a cluster of three white lights to signal, Objective Gained.

As the conference broke up, each battalion commander was conscious of one vital factor: unless at least one airfield was seized, and seized early, enabling follow-up troops and supplies to be flown in, what the Luftwaffe had styled "Operation Mercury" would swiftly grind to an ignominious standstill.

*

"I cannot feel that there was any real grip shown by Middle East H.Q. upon this operation," Churchill was to comment irascibly. "They regarded it as a tiresome commitment . . . No one in high authority seems to have sat down for two or three mornings together and endeavoured to take a full forward view of what would happen . . ."

There is no doubt that Churchill was right. Since November, 1940, six different commanders had briefly held sway in Crete, but in six months no one had given them any positive directives as to what was expected of them. Freyberg, the seventh, had taken over on 30 April, but as First Secretary Harold Caccia reported from the British Legation in Athens: "As far as I could see no serious attempt to prepare defences had been made until a few weeks ago. Even barbed wire on the beaches was being improvised."

Yet on the morning of Tuesday, 20 May, as he breakfasted serenely in his dug-out headquarters near Canea, Freyberg's mood was one of buoyant optimism. "Am not the least anxious about an airborne attack," he cabled Churchill on 5 May, for in anticipation of a major assault from the sea he had positioned many of his troops at forward strongpoints along the coast.

Yet by strange irony, Freyberg this morning was better briefed than almost any World War Two commander to date. Precise details of Hitler's Directive No 28, including troop strengths, times and dispositions had long been available to him through the Ultra intercepts; to this end Hut No 6, which housed the duty cipher watch at Bletchley Park, had been working overtime for weeks. Although Freyberg was never privy to the existence of the "Enigma" machine – the information, he thought, came from a disgruntled stool-pigeon in Berlin – he knew exactly what the Germans planned for Crete.

Yet one simple truth eluded him: the airfields were the prime target. Unaware that German paratroop strength was limited – 10,000 men were the maximum available – and convinced that the JU-52s could crash-land on any stretch of beach they saw, it was a seaborne attack Freyberg feared above all.

To counter the attacks, he had thus split his command into four semi-independent bodies, functioning from Maleme, Retimo, Heraklion and Suda. Yet communications were so primitive each command was virtually on its own, operating in the dark. One hundred field wireless sets, one man argued later, might still have saved Crete. One runner, journeying the 45 miles from Retimo to Freyberg's H.Q. took six days to do it, memorising three separate passwords as he went.

Freyberg, though, was certain that a diversified command could cope with all eventualities. Towards 7 a.m., as the first gliders loomed silently overhead, the Commander-in-Chief, with the satisfied air of a man finding his dinner guests punctual, remarked, "They're dead on time."

All over the island, at this moment, men stood mesmerised by the most naked display of air power that they had ever seen. Rarely in a modern battle had such a host of visual impressions been registered: the JU-52s moving sluggishly over Heraklion, "huge black beasts with yellow noses", the silvery tapering wings of the gliders, passing "as silently as

84

ghosts with just a swishing sound", the puffs of french chalk drifting on a light breeze as the parachutes snapped open.

The similes that men conjured up bespoke the depths of their emotions. For Major Geoffrey Cox, a New Zealander, the sound of Bren gun bullets clipping rocks and branches as the Allies opened up was "like the clatter of a million lawn-mowers all at once". Strangely, the impressions were often festive. To one man, the drifting parachutes, billowing open as low as 300 feet recalled "the balloons coming down at the end of a party". To another the spilling hordes of troopers were "like handfuls of confetti in the bright sunlight".

Most men were stunned by the precision of the exercise. As the gliders ploughed relentlessly on, slicing through olive trees, bushes, shallow stone walls, bombers moved in their wake, softening up the opposition "with the methodical monotony of coolies planting rice". Everywhere the valleys were littered with discarded parachutes "like huge discarded mushrooms", though not all Germans made it to the target. One JU-52, caught by lethal Bofors fire, erupted in flames, its occupants scrambling for safety "like plums spilled from a burst bag".

Marcel Comeau, who had thirsted for action, suddenly had all he could handle. Busy searching for his pipe, which he had mislaid, he let the others go ahead of him to the mess tent; only in the moment of finding it was he aware of a throbbing crescendo of engines. Ducking through the tent flap he saw overhead a vast glinting armada of planes, JU-88s, Heinkels and Dorniers, showering bombs on the R.A.F. lines and the New Zealanders' camp at the base of Kavkazia Hill. For thirty minutes on end the bombs tore at the soft soil "until it hung in the air like a blanket, blotting out the sun".

Grabbing a rifle, Comeau had just dived headfirst for a foxhole when the sound of rushing air filled his ears. Open-mouthed he saw a glider, swooping low through the curtain of dust, disappearing towards the west. Then, with a snapping crack of olive branches, another glider appeared, careering straight towards him. Before Comeau had time to duck it had bulldozed into the tent he had just vacated, slewing half round, spraying him with loose dirt. Then it stopped dead in its dust cloud, one wing dug into the bank behind Comeau.

Doubling under its wing, "feeling pretty scared", Comeau scrambled up the bank, heading for higher ground. At that moment, the glider door opened to disgorge a dazed-looking German and Comeau, at almost point-blank range, shot him dead. The man spun backward onto a second paratrooper – a time-span long enough for Comeau to eject and re-load. The second man was holding his head in his hands as Comeau fired again, toppling him in a heap to block the darkness of the doorway.

Hastily the airman ejected the empty cartridge case but the next round jammed; sweating and cursing he wrestled with the bolt but could not budge it. Now, from the corner of his eye, he saw the remaining Germans piling from the glider, and more men racing through the trees from a second glider which had landed. With bursts of rapid fire tattooing the soft earth ahead of him Comeau raced for Kavkazia Hill, along with a motley group of New Zealanders who had survived the bombing.

The German plan seemed simple now: to take Kavkazia Hill, to silence the Bofors guns surrounding the landing field and thus secure Maleme. If Kavkazia was held, the allies stood a chance. Comeau and the others were determined that it should be held.

"The enemy entered Crete as a conquering power," the Chiefs of Staff were to assure Churchill later, but the Germans had no such impression. Some paratroopers, jumping too soon, landed in the sea off Maleme; others misled by green jump masters, hit drop zones far from their planned positions. Private Melville Hill-Rennie, of the 20th (N.Z.) Battalion, saw one German plane that had plainly misjudged its height. Although he counted thirty-five bodies tumble from the plane, not one parachute had opened before the men struck the ground.

In some gliders that remained on course, landing without damage, only silence prevailed; every man was dead in his seat, his neck snapped by the impact. Another, landing at 75 miles an hour, ripped itself apart against the ironwork of a bridge. The 3rd Battalion of the 1st Assault Regiment, landing east of Maleme, were mostly caught and killed within minutes of landing; by dusk only 200 out of 600 men remained alive. Asked if he needed help in mopping up, a New Zealand commander replied curtly: "They'll all be dead before you can get a man here."

Top commanders proved as vulnerable as privates. *Generalleutnant* Wilhelm Sussmann, commanding the Centre Group, was killed soon after take-off when his glider crashed on an island within sight of Athens. *Generalmajor* Eugen Meindl, who headed the Maleme operation, was seriously wounded soon after landing. Even men who landed securely felt cut off and at a loss for orders. Baron Friedrich von der Heydte found himself suspended from a fig tree like a latter-day Absalom, without one of his battalion in sight. Heydte finally caught up with his headquarters company at their rendezvous point, Galatas Jail, but although radio contact had been made with four companies, only one company had made fleeting contact with the British. "We felt we were all alone in this valley," Heydte recalled later.

Of the thousands who dropped this morning, the plight of 18-year-old *Fallschirmjäger* (Paratrooper) Walter Goltz, of the Assault Regiment's 3rd Battalion, somehow emerges as typical. Aboard his JU-52, Goltz was fourth in line to jump, but as he made to leave the plane, the transport's nose was peppered with bullets. Next a shell burst under the port wing; as Goltz jumped the plane was out of control and banking steeply.

As the full force of the wind hit him, Goltz's goggles were ripped from his face; the Junkers had been flying too high and he took a long time to land in a deep valley south-east of Kavkazia Hill. Tramping through an olive grove, he found no sign of life, either British or German; the dozen men who comprised his "stick" had all been killed.

Later that morning, he met four more survivors and all of them remained in hiding until late afternoon. Then, venturing forth along the dried-up irrigation canal encircling the hill, they chanced on another twenty Germans – half of them wounded. Using old ladders for stretchers they finally brought their wounded to a communal field hospital by the Tavronitis river, east of Maleme.

Only that evening – some twelve hours after landing – was Goltz given finite orders to take up a defensive position west of Maleme.

By dusk on 20 May, it was plain that Student had fatally miscalculated. By striking at too many airfields simultaneously – a move urged on him by Hitler – he had failed to secure any of his objectives at all. Although casualty figures have always been in dispute – 4,500 men by some counts, more than 6,000 by others – the effort had cost him dear. The loss of aircraft was phenomenal – although estimates again ranged from 271 to close on 400.

"The days of the parachute troops are over," Hitler told Student testily, following an exhaustive inquest on Crete; from this time on German paratroopers were deployed only as elite infantrymen.

Then, at 9 p.m., one commander took a decision which turned the whole campaign upside down. All that day, Lieutenant-Colonel Lionel Andrew, V.C. commanding the 22nd (N.Z.) Battalion, had been under withering mortar fire in his headquarters at Maleme. Wounded by a shell splinter, Andrew was at his wit's end; for hours now he had lost all signal and runner contact with three of his five companies, and the conviction grew on him that they had been overwhelmed. Knowing he could not hold the airfield and the slopes of Kavkazia, with only 200 men, Andrew decided he must withdraw.

Three miles east, in Platanias village, the Brigade Commander, Brigadier James Hargest, had heard nothing but success stories all day. When Andrew made radio contact at 9 p.m., seeking permission to withdraw, the wireless battery was fading fast; Hargest could barely hear him. In any case, he assumed that Andrew was merely adjusting his perimeter. As he replied, "If you must, you must," the wireless went dead.

By 2 a.m., Andrew had pulled out his remaining men away from Kavkazia Hill to a point nearly two miles east of Maleme – unaware that the three missing companies were still holding out, both on the airfield perimeter and on Kavkazia. And as the New Zealanders moved out, the Germans of the Assault Regiment began a slow wary night trek along the undefended slopes.

Student tried a bold gamble. By first light, the Assault Regiment had taken most of Maleme and the high ground to the south. Then, at 8 a.m., as three and a half companies of paratroopers landed in a drop zone out of British range, a JU-52 risked a perilous touchdown on the beach. By 8.10 a.m. another had landed – this time on Maleme. By 5 p.m., an air shuttle service from Greece was throwing in troops at a breathtaking rate; one day later, planes ferrying in forty men at a time were landing every three minutes.

Now it would be only a matter of days. With the loss of Maleme, Crete was lost.

Marcel Comeau didn't know what to make of it. In the small hours of 21 May, one of Andrew's missing companies – "D" Company under Captain T. C. Campbell – realising they had been abandoned, decided they too must pull out. By chance they awoke Comeau and a handful of "erks" on the summit of Kavkazia. Now, dazed with sleep, weighed down by a Lewis gun on his shoulder, Comeau made part of their retreat – a nightmare journey through rocky defiles and tall stands of Aleppo pines, over tumbled piles of German bodies, smelling of blood and *ersatz* coffee, past bloated shapes, still twisted in their harnesses, suspended from darkened trees.

It was some time before the full irony of the retreat came home to Comeau: victory had come to Student not by a stirring feat of arms but by the failure of a wireless battery.

*

In Europe, the British were daily losing ground. Soon, apart from the two and a half square miles of Gibraltar, not one inch of continental European soil would be under British military control. But in the North Atlantic, their luck was holding.

All through 23 May, two among the twenty ships dogging the battleship *Bismarck* kept in determined pursuit, closing the gap at a steady 60 miles an hour. Then at 7.22 p.m., the starboard after look-out on the bridge of the cruiser *Suffolk* achieved a first sighting: the black mass of the *Bismarck,* with *Prinz Eugen* in attendance, looming from mist on the starboard quarter. "Two ships bearing Green One Four Oh," came his excited shout.

Fifteen miles away, the cruiser *Norfolk* was steaming through drifting wraiths of fog; her captain, Alfred Phillips, was munching cheese-on-toast in his sea cabin when his Yeoman of Signals arrived in haste with news from the *Suffolk* – "One battleship one cruiser in sight bearing 020 degrees distant 7 miles. Course 240 degrees." At once Phillips increased speed, heading for open water but misjudging the direction. Emerging from fog, he saw *Bismarck* only six miles ahead, coming straight for him.

Five orange-brown salvoes had straddled the oily swell before *Norfolk* regained the safety of the fog.

It was not a combat that the Germans sought. This Atlantic sortie was, in fact, a piecemeal deployment of their forces: the *Tirpitz*, the second giant battleship in the *Bismarck* class still had four months crew-training ahead of her, the battleship *Scharnhorst* was undergoing repair to her boilers, the 30,000 ton *Gneisenau* was out of service for six months following damage by a British aerial torpedo. Although a bold attempt to shake the Royal Navy's control of the Atlantic had seemed necessary, the Fleet Commander, Admiral Günther Lütjens, had received due warning from the Commander-in-Chief, *Grossadmiral* Erich Raeder. "Needless to say," Raeder had stressed, "you will have to operate with prudence and care."

It was an admonition Lütjens would obey to the letter. A dour taciturn veteran, whose whole life was the Navy, Lütjens had seen too many Fleet Commanders dismissed after tangling with the *Kriegsmarine* – among them his old friend and predecessor, Admiral Wilhelm Marschall. "I know what they want," he had told Marschall just before sailing, "and shall carry out their orders."

"The primary objective is the destruction of the enemy's carrying capacity," ran his *Kriegsmarine* directive. "Enemy warships will be engaged only in furtherance of this objective, and provided such engagement can take place without excessive risk."

Raeder, too, had displayed a similar prudence. Mindful of Hitler's innate scepticism regarding the deployment of capital ships, it was not until 22 May, on a visit to Hitler's private apartment in Munich, that he broke the news that *Bismarck* had sailed.

Hitler was alarmed. He recalled that on 5 May, when he inspected *Bismarck* in Gotenhafen, Lütjens had expressed reservations about British torpedo-aircraft. Now he asked Raeder point-blank: "*Herr Grossadmiral*, can't we fetch the ships back?" But Raeder was adamant: any such move would have an adverse effect on naval morale.

Accordingly, Hitler backed down – but from 24 May on, his every fear was to be justified.

Late on 23 May, the sighting reports from *Norfolk* and *Suffolk* had reached *Hood* and *Prince of Wales*, 300 miles away. Thus all through the Arctic night the chase continued, through the snow squalls and ice floes of the Denmark Strait, then on through the white walls of Atlantic spindrift. "We had a 'white out' every two minutes," Sub-Lieutenant Michael Buxton remembers from *Prince of Wales*, "so hit with tremendous spray you couldn't see anything – the whole ship was just white."

At 5.35 a.m. on 24 May, Vice Admiral Lancelot Holland, in *Hood*, first sighted his quarry. At once, not waiting to gather cruisers or destroyers. Holland hoisted his flag signal, "Blue Pendant Four" to *Hood*'s yardarm, then turned towards *Bismarck*.

The Germans were ready. As early as 4.35 a.m., *Prinz Eugen*'s second gunnery officer *Korvettenkapitän* Paul Schmalenbach had ordered, "War-watch stand by!" The listening plot had reported the sound of ships' screws from two fast-moving turbine ships at 280 degrees. Simultaneously, aboard *Bismarck*, the officer of the watch, *Kapitänleutnant* Werner Nobis, ordered, "All hands to action stations! Clear the decks for action!" All over the German ships alarm bells rang stridently, and the iron deck plates vibrated to the rhythm of thousands of sea-boots as men doubled to take up battle positions.

Now, in these last moments, men focused their minds on anything rather than the battle that lay ahead. Sub-Lieutenant Michael Buxton swivelling his field-glasses aboard *Prince*, sighted one of the rarest of all migrant birds, the Great Northern Diver. Promptly he called up his friend, Sub-Lieutenant Esmond Knight, actor and ornithologist, sited in the Air Defence Position above the bridge: "There she is – you have a look at her." Knight was delighted – unaware that the bird was almost the last thing he would ever see.

On the bridge of *Prince of Wales* Captain John Leach had sent a last minute summons to the Chaplain, the Reverend W. G. Parker. A prayer he imperfectly remembered – that of Sir Jacob Astley before the battle of Edgehill in 1642 – might be apposite at this moment. It was a timely inspiration. Many men still recall that as the battleship closed in for action, Parker's voice was resounding in every corner of the ship from crow's nest to engine room: "O Lord, Thou knowest how busy we must be today, if we forget Thee do not Thou forget us; for Christ's sake. Amen."

Then, at 25,000 yards range, with a storm of sound that almost knocked her gunners senseless, *Hood* opened fire.

From this maelstrom of sound, few retained more than swift traumatic impressions. As *Hood*'s first four shells, weighing a ton apiece, screamed from the muzzles at 1,600 miles an hour, an agitated petty officer on *Prinz Eugen*'s bridge called out: "He's fired." *Kapitän* Hellmuth Brinkmann replied quietly, "Of course he's fired, man. Now let's see what comes of it."

What came of it was disaster for the British. *Hood* was still striving like *Prince of Wales*, to find the German range; in any case, half of *Prince*'s heavy armament, including her rear turret, was inoperative through jamming, but the German guns were dead on target from the first.

Hood was hit and tall leaping flames were seen to spread amidships; warned of a fire in the Ready Use lockers, Admiral Holland was heard to say, "Leave it till the ammunition is gone." But it was too late. Around 6 a.m. *Hood* was straddled again, and abruptly she blew up, vomiting

90

Carley floats and seamen, lockers and portholes, fuel tanks, guns and 42,000 tons of steel plating in a pillar of orange fire that rose 1,000 feet high.

"My God," Marine Peter Dunstan heard Captain Leach shout, "The *Hood*'s blown up!", but within three minutes she had wallowed from sight; most men's impressions were subliminal. Dunstan's C.O., Captain Derek Aylwin, saw only "an amazing orange glow and bits and pieces falling through the air". In *Bismarck*, the majority were below decks, and the news came only by intercom; one man always recalled the long drawn out shout of the gunnery officer, *Freggatenkapitän* Adalbert Schneider, "She's blowing *uuuuup!*" Aboard *Prinz Eugen*, it was the war artist, *Leutnant* J. C. Schmitz, a trained observer, who carefully noted an "ashen-grey cloud . . . glowing red at the rims," finally transmuted to a "sinister fir-tree shape".

"The mighty *Hood*" had gone – and with her 95 officers and 1,324 men, all save three of her company.

Few men aboard the *Prince of Wales* could really credit it. In the S 4 turret, Boy Seaman Edward Grindley heard someone ask incredulously, "Gone? Where to?" Petty Officer Frederick Kenshole, in the Y Engine Room, chided his informant: "Don't start rumours." Able Seaman Charles Wright believed it, but felt "as though Buckingham Palace had been laid flat". Leading Telegraphist Bernard Campion had to repeat the news twice to his mate, Leading Telegraphist Priddle. Following an ominous silence, Priddle remarked weakly, "I'm changing me knickers".

In England, the news was heard with consternation. Despite her age, *Hood* had been venerated like few others; a showpiece of naval reviews, the ship that always showed the flag when it was needed, her picture featured in school books and on the walls of private homes. In London, the First Lord of the Admiralty, A. V. Alexander, was so overcome he retired to his private sanctum to play "O God, Our Help in Ages Past" on his harmonium. Churchill seemed less perturbed. William Averell Harriman, weekending at Chequers, the Premier's country retreat, was awoken at 7 a.m. to find Churchill, wearing a yellow sweater over an abbreviated nightshirt, standing beside his bed. "Hell of a battle going on," he ground out. "The *Hood* is sunk. Hell of a battle."

Churchill, for his part, had high hopes that a U.S. navy ship might be in the offing, prompting *Bismarck* to open fire and bring America into the war.

It was now the *Prince of Wales*' turn; the range had closed to 18,000 yards and both Germans were out to cripple her. Twelve minutes after the battle commenced, they achieved their aim; she was straddled by four of *Bismarck*'s heavy shells, three from *Prinz Eugen* – one of which, failing to explode, lodged beside the oil tank. But others wrought appalling havoc, slicing clean through her bridge, wrecking her compass platform, the echo-sounding gear, the radar office, the aircraft recovery crane, all the boats and several cabins.

Below decks, few were conscious of the carnage. Stoker Norman Portlock, in X Engine Room, felt the battleship "keel hard to port, like a motor bike turning" but those aloft knew unimaginable horrors. Sub-Lieutenant Esmond Knight remembered the last salvo as "a great rushing cyclone" that doomed him, in the space of seconds to the ranks of the warblinded, never to perceive anything but dim shapes again. Leading Telegraphist Bernard Campion, in the Remote Control Office below the bridge, was appalled to see blood pouring down the voicepipe, saturating his signal pads. Sub-Lieutenant Michael Buxton hastened from the Main Armament Directory Control Tower to find "no bridge – nothing but hairs on it, like dog's hairs, and blood – all one's friends".

Holed below the waterline, shipping 400 tons of water, the *Prince of Wales* was in no shape to carry on the fight. Leach now reached a sensible decision: the moment had come to break off action, make smoke and join the shadowing cruisers until the damage was repaired and the guns overhauled. At 6.13 a.m. he disengaged to the south-east.

It was left to *Hood*'s destroyers, among them the *Electra*, to search for *Hood*'s survivors and for two hours, in line abreast, they steamed hard southwards. Yet search as they might the sea lay empty – nothing but patches of oil, tangled piles of wreckage, a lone marine's hat. Then they espied them – two men swimming, one on a raft, but no other sign of life.

Incredulously, the Chief Engineer, Lieutenant Frank McLeod voiced what all of them felt: "But there *must* be more of them – there can't be only *three* of them. Where are the others?"

But there were no others – only a remarkable trio of three survivors. The first man helped aboard, Able Seaman R. E. Tilburn, shook himself like an angry dog and cursed officers and ratings impartially: "And what's up with you – you poverty-stricken crowd? Ain't you got no bloody boats?"

The second, Ordinary Signalman A. E. Briggs, asked eagerly who his rescuers were then let out a disgusted groan: "Now isn't that just my rotten luck – to be picked up by a *Chatham ship*."

The third, Midshipman W. J. Dundas, confronted the First Lieutenant to apologise with a sunny smile, "So sorry I can't salute sir – I'm afraid I've lost my cap."

As the trio were led off to the Sick Bay, *Electra*'s captain, Commander Cecil May, smiled for the first time that day. "There's one thing the Hun forgets," was his patriotic prediction. "He'll never beat men like these."

*

Captain John Leach and his crew were barely aware of it but *Prince of*

Wales had done better than they knew. Of the eighteen salvoes she had loosed off before disengaging, three 14-inch projectiles had done irreparable damage – holing *Bismarck*'s fuel tanks, lowering her bow by one degree, slowing her to 28 knots.

Minutes later, *Kapitän zur Zee* Brinkmann, on the bridge of *Prinz Eugen*, received an urgent signal from *Bismarck*'s commander, Ernst Lindemann: "From the *Bismarck*, Captain to Captain. Please see if I am leaving a trail of oil." A rating on the cruiser's bridge soon confirmed that fear: "There is a dark patch below the starboard hawser! A hit!"

As the flagship turned to starboard, ahead of *Prinz Eugen*, the men lining the cruiser's decks fell silent: a broad snakelike irridescent band of oil, shimmering in rainbow colours, was travelling in her wake. Any contact unit, any cruiser, any aircraft needed only follow that to keep its quarry under constant surveillance.

Aboard *Bismarck*, both Lütjens and Lindemann saw only one course of action: the battleship's Atlantic foray was over almost before it had begun. *Prinz Eugen* could be detached for independent cruiser warfare – but with one boiler room out of action, serious flooding and a steady drain of fuel, *Bismarck* needed repairs. Her one hope now was to reach the Normandy dock at St Nazaire, almost 1,500 miles away on the coast of Brittany.

"Intend to shake off enemy as follows," Lütjens signalled Brinkmann at 2.20 p.m. "During rain showers, *Bismarck* will move off on westerly course." But the enemy would not be shaken, and as the day wore on Lütjens' signals to the *Kriegsmarine* grew increasingly despondent. At 7.14 p.m. he admitted: "Enemy maintains contact." At 8.56 p.m.: "Impossible to shake off enemy owing to radar. Proceeding directly to Brest owing to fuel situation."

For the hunt was now on with a vengeance, and to square accounts for *Hood* warships were being vectored towards intercept over thousands of square miles of ocean. Admiral Tovey, in *King George V*, was already en route from Scapa Flow, along with four cruisers, six destroyers and the aircraft carrier *Victorious*, but now others were swelling the pack: Force H from Gibraltar, under Admiral Sir James Somerville brought *Renown*, *Sheffield* and the carrier *Ark Royal* into the fray. The battleship *Rodney*, en route to Boston for a refit, was about-turned in mid-Atlantic, along with the destroyers *Somali*, *Tartar*, and *Mashona*. Soon the 4th Destroyer Flotilla, under Captain Philip Vian, whose rescue of the *Altmark* prisoners had made headlines in 1940, were hastening to the scene.

Soon after midnight, Lütjens' worst fears were realised; for the first time the British struck from the air. All that day the carrier *Victorious* had battled northwest at 30 knots. Now at 10.14 p.m., nine Swordfish biplanes of 825 Squadron, each with an 18-inch torpedo slung from its belly, took off from the rain-lashed flight deck, across a heaving 32-foot swell. Diving through a curtain of flak, they saw one torpedo strike home on *Bismarck*. The damage was minimal – but a precedent had been set.

Then, around 3 a.m. on 25 May, *Bismarck* contrived to evade her pursuers. Now, for fully thirty hours, she steamed hard, undetected, for the south-east. Following thirty-six hours at action stations, officers and men relaxed, thankful at last to wash and shave and relish hot food. For Lütjens, who was fifty-two this day, a brief telegram arrived from his Führer: "Best wishes on your birthday. Adolf Hitler."

But Lütjens was feeling far from festive. Almost a thousand miles of ocean lay ahead and the meteorologist, Dr Externbrink, held out no prospect of merciful fog on the voyage to France. At noon, when the admiral addressed *Bismarck*'s crew over the loud-speaker system, his mood was sombre. "The British are massing their forces to destroy us," he told them bluntly, "and we shall have another battle with them before we reach home."

Then he added: "It may well be a question of victory or death. If we have to die, let us take with us as many of the enemy as we can."

It was a blow to morale from which few men fully recovered. The third gunnery officer, Burkard, the Baron von Müllenheim-Rechberg, who had not heard the speech, was aghast when a petty officer offered him a free translation: "The admiral says we haven't a hope, sir, the whole British Fleet is after us and they are bound to find us." The engineer officer, *Korvettenkapitän* Gerhard Junack, going on watch below, found his men equally disheartened. Worse, some of Lütjens' staff officers had now taken, in defiance of regulations, to wearing their life-jackets under their uniforms.

But not until 10.30 a.m. on 26 May, was *Bismarck* sighted again – this time by a Catalina aircraft on loan from the U.S. Navy, with an American co-pilot, Ensign Leonard B. Smith. Her position lent new urgency to the quest. She was now 690 miles north and west of Brest, drawing hourly closer to the Luftwaffe's air umbrella.

Just as Hitler had feared, air power proved decisive. Towards 9 p.m. on 26 May, fifteen Swordfish from the carrier *Ark Royal* took off from a flight deck whose up-and-down movement was now 56 feet – the height of a four-storey house. Twisting and turning like snipe from port to starboard, they struck at *Bismarck* for fully thirty minutes, and this time their blows were decisive. One torpedo, striking under the turn of the bilge aft, jammed her port rudder in a hard-over position.

Now *Bismarck* was slowed to 8 knots, veering in sluggish circles, a sitting target for the British. At 9.40 p.m. Lütjens acknowledged this in a signal to Berlin: "Ship unmanoeuvrable. We fight to the last shell. Long live the Führer."

Dawn on 27 May brought only the inevitability of death. At 8.47 a.m.

94

Admiral Tovey at last arrived in *King George V*, *Rodney* in consort, their grey sides glinting in the morning sun. At 16,000 yards range both ships opened fire, brilliant orange flashes from the heavy guns followed by white fountains of spray. "Get closer, get closer," Tovey ordered repeatedly, "I can't see enough hits." But the shells were striking home on *Bismarck*'s foremast and fire control platform with deadly accuracy. In *Rodney*'s cordite-handling room, Petty Officer Glue, making chalk crosses on a hopper door to signify salvoes, notched up twenty almost before he had realised it.

In these last hours, men's feelings were inextricably mixed. Aboard *Tartar*, a young sub-lieutenant, Ludovic Kennedy, thought compassionately of wolves closing in on their prey. Sub-Lieutenant Eryk Sopocko, of the Polish Navy, serving in *Rodney*, thought of his ravaged homeland and felt no such pity. As he watched Rodney's gun crews, dripping with sweat, smeared black with cordite, he told himself: "Justice, you still exist."

To some it was the most stirring battle ever known; in the destroyer *Sikh*, one excited rating fired a third torpedo before the first and second had even hit the water. For many below decks, the issue was still in doubt. In *Rodney*'s "X" turret, a Marine captain, sighting *Bismarck* through his periscope, yelled excitedly, "She's on fire from stem to stern." Back came a query from the shell-handling room: "Who, sir, us or them?"

Bismarck was doomed and all aboard her knew it. *Ark Royal* was over the horizon, impatient for another strike, *Norfolk*, who had dogged her from the first, was standing by, and now Vian's destroyers and other ships ringed her on all sides. But there was no thought of surrender. For forty minutes her guns blazed back defiance, though Tovey found it incredible that any ship could stay afloat after such a beating. "Somebody get me my darts!" he barked, irascibly. "Let's see if we can't finish her off with those!"

But *Bismarck* would decide her own fate. At 10.15 a.m. *Korvettenkapitän* Gerhard Junack, in the mid-ships engine room, heard *Freggatenkapitän* Walter Lehmann on the telephone: "Prepare for Measure 5." That meant, place explosive charges with time fuses in the cooling water intakes and open the seacocks. As they evacuated the engine room, once this was done, Junack rallied his men, "We'll all meet again on the Reeperbahn" – the red light district of Hamburg.

They acted just in time. Three minutes later, the cruiser *Dorsetshire* ranging from port to starboard hit her with three Mark VII torpedoes from 2,600 yards range. By now, her entire hull was swarming with black ant-shapes, men scurrying in frantic haste to evade the icy sea. At 10.57 a.m., 400 miles off Brest, she heeled to port, sinking very fast by the stern.

Her survivors were tragically few. Of 2,400 men aboard *Bismarck*,

Dorsetshire picked up eighty men, *Maori* another twenty, but a sudden alarm that a U-Boat was hovering prompted both captains to ring down for full speed. Hundreds of men, clawing frantically at the paintwork as the sides slipped by, were cut to pieces by the churning screws.

Later the Ministry of Information was to roundly condemn a B.B.C. account of *Bismarck*'s last hours as "nauseating and sentimental", but the men who had brought her to bay felt differently.

"She had put up a most gallant fight against impossible odds," Tovey told the Admiralty unrepentantly, "worthy of the old days of the Imperial German Navy. It is unfortunate that 'for political reasons' this fact cannot be made public."

*

For one group of men, the news brought a sense of vindication. A thousand miles from the scene of action, in the Red Room of the Kristiansand Club, Norway, Viggo Axelssen, the ship's chandler, was drinking quietly with a group of friends. Word of the *Bismarck*'s fate had just reached them, and now Axelssen recalled vividly the message he had scribbled only seven evenings ago, the journey that had begun with Arne Moen's bus and ended in the farmhouse attic at Helle.

"Gentlemen!" he said, raising his glass, and all of them stood as one. "Thirty-five thousand tons."

They drained their glasses, repeating the figure solemnly. It signified the *Bismarck*'s "official" tonnage, given out to comply with the 1936 Anglo-German Naval Treaty, limiting the displacement of capital ships. Then Axelssen opened the connecting door to the dining room, where other members had already begun their evening meal. They, too, were asked to rise and drink the same toast.

Every man rose silently, raising his glass, but nobody said a word.

*

"She's sunk!"

In the Oval Office of the White House, Franklin D. Roosevelt had just had word from the Navy Department. Hanging up the phone he turned to his speech-writers, Samuel I, Rosenman and Robert E. Sherwood with as much satisfaction as if "he had himself fired the torpedo".

The news had come at a grimly appropriate time. That same evening, in a speech to the Governing Board of the Pan-American Union, to be broadcast to the world by international hook-up – what he liked to call a "Fireside Chat" – the President was moving another step forward in his undeclared war. He was about to proclaim a state of unlimited national emergency.

96

As always, there were factors that it would be impolitic to spell out. For the State Department, Cordell Hull had vetoed all mention of the fact that Admiral Harold R. Stark, Chief of Naval Operations, had with great misgivings transferred three battleships, one carrier, four cruisers, and two destroyer squadrons from the Pacific to the Atlantic – leaving the Pacific Fleet at Pearl Harbor, Hawaii, in every major respect inferior to the Japanese. To be both aggressive in the Atlantic and peaceful in the Pacific was, as Roosevelt saw it, no easy task.

Typically Roosevelt was keeping abreast – but never ahead – of American public opinion. "I am waiting to be pushed into the situation," he told Treasury Secretary Morgenthau in mid-May, but what the British Ambassador, Lord Halifax, called "his policy of gradualness" drove some of his colleagues to distraction. When Roosevelt maintained mildly that Atlantic Patrols were a step in the right direction, Secretary of War Stimson snorted: "Keep on walking, Mr President – keep on walking!" One week earlier, his former Ambassador to France, William C. Bullitt, told Roosevelt pointedly, "There is a desire (by the nation) to know the facts *from you.*"

From London's front line, the need seemed more urgent still. "When the Gallup poll shows 19% for war now," wrote Averell Harriman in a letter which found its way to Roosevelt, "and 68% for war if necessary to save the British, America must be a nation of ostriches. Don't they read the newspapers or listen to the radio? Are we to continue to hide behind the skirts of these poor British women who are holding up the civil defence here?"

Roosevelt was less certain. To be sure, two isolationist newspapers, the St Louis *Post-Dispatch* and the Detroit *Free Press*, had announced a change of heart – "the die is cast," said the *Free Press*, "we are in the war" – and defence was still a popular and non-controversial issue. The cost of defence had upped the income tax rate from 2.2 per cent to 6.6 per cent, and few had grumbled; federal excises for defence now accounted for eight cents on every pack of cigarettes, $4 per gallon of liquor, 25 cents on a gallon of gasoline. Yet war, by contrast, was still an emotive issue. Only recently, isolationists in Congress had protested bitterly when the Army bespoke "overseas caps" from the textile industry: the very word suggested another American Expeditionary Force.

Under the relentless goading of Harry Hopkins, whom one admirer christened "Generalissimo of the Needle Brigade", United States production was at last gathering momentum – for defence, if not for war. Steel was short, and so was aluminium, but from March onwards the target had been set: 2,400 planes, 951 tanks would reach Britain before the year was out. Letters routed to Government departments now took on the aspect of a litany – "My dear Mr Secretary, I find that the defence of the United Kingdom is vital to the defence of the United States" – and a floodtide of supplies followed: 100,000 cases of evaporated milk, 11,000 tons of eggs, 6,000 hogsheads of tobacco, 200,000 gas masks, service, 18,772 drawers, cotton, ankle-length, 43,002 jerkins, felt.

Fully $5 million had been earmarked for aviation bases, and three million new workers had swelled the ranks of heavy industry; red, white and blue banners, looming above the assembly lines, warned, TIME IS SHORT. But there was another side to the coin and Roosevelt knew it: other assembly lines were still producing five million private automobiles a year, the highest total in United States history.

Hence the President's declaration of a state of emergency – to instil a sense of urgency many citizens were far from feeling.

On the hot and stifling night of 27 May, his black-tie audience gathered in an incongruously genteel setting: the East Room of the White House, lavishly decorated with small silver bowls of pink roses. As the President faced a battery of microphones his audience waited apprehensively, perched on small gilded chairs once used for White House musicales. The French windows were flung wide to combat the heat, and the scent of honeysuckle drifted from the south portico.

But Roosevelt was not really addressing this audience – the Ambassadors and Ministers from the twenty Latin-American republics – at all. His words were aimed at the world – at the neutral, the enslaved, above all to the uninvolved, disinterested people of America, where a quarter of all homes still lacked running water, a third were without flush toilets, and the largest single cause of ill-health was malnutrition. Of what concern was Hitler's Europe to them?

"Some people seem to think," Roosevelt began, by way of explanation, "that we are not attacked until bombs actually drop in the streets of New York or San Francisco or New Orleans or Chicago. But they are simply shutting their eyes to the lesson that we must learn from the fate of every nation that the Nazis have conquered."

By now, he reasoned, Americans must realise that "it would be suicide to wait until they are in our front yard". Old-fashioned commonsense called for the use of a strategy that would prevent the enemy gaining any such foothold – which was why he proposed to add more ships, more planes, to the North and South Atlantic patrols.

"Our Bunker Hill of tomorrow," he warned farsightedly, "may be several thousand miles from Boston."

Just as he had anticipated, the speech drew only a polite spatter of applause. The guests drifted out on to the South Lawn, to sip fruit punch and lemonade by the light of Japanese lanterns. Roosevelt relaxed happily as Irving Berlin launched into a piano rendition of "Alexander's Ragtime Band", later retiring to bed. It was here that Sherwood found him in seventh heaven, the coverlet littered with more than a thousand telegrams that had poured in since the broadcast.

"They're 95 percent favourable!" Roosevelt exulted. "And I figured I'd be lucky to get an even break on this speech." The United States, it seemed, was at last coming alive to the peril.

Outsiders were less convinced. Soon after, Sir James Dunn, an astute Canadian banker, sent a measured assessment of the state of the nation to his old friend and fellow countryman, Lord Beaverbrook – a view which "The Beaver" hastened to pass on to Churchill.

"The states of Michigan, Wisconsin, Minnesota and the Dakotas form an isolationist bloc under Lindbergh and *The Chicago Tribune*", Dunn opined. "John L. Lewis* is a Communist bent on smashing the Capitalist system. Philip Murray† thinks that this is Labour's chance and does not feel that the Hitler menace is real."

"The U.S.A." Dunn concluded, "is not yet frightened enough to get the representatives behind Roosevelt."

* John L. Lewis, leader of the United Mine Workers' Union, had called out the soft coal miners for a month-long strike in April. He had already branded Roosevelt as a war-monger.
† Philip Murray of the Congress of Industrial Organisations (C.I.O.) had likewise opposed Lend-Lease.

"No Peace, No Rest, No Halting Place, No Parley"

29 May–21 June, 1941

THE LONG NIGHT marches had begun again, and the mountain passes echoed to the trudging feet of weary men. In places, the white rocky roadsides resembled an open-air quartermaster's stores; in the bitterness of defeat, men were abandoning rifles, bandoliers, packs, blankets, gas-masks, hand grenades, even empty water bottles. "The limit of endurance has been reached," Freyberg signalled Wavell on 26 May. "Our position is hopeless." The end in Crete was very near.

Wavell himself was close to despair. "I have never seen him so gloomy!" the British Ambassador in Cairo, Sir Miles Lampson, cabled Eden. "Archie was in the depths of depression – especially concerning equipment – 'All right,' he said against the ice-creamers, but useless against the 'Boche'." Even now, the lesson of Crete had escaped the Commander-in-Chief: whoever did not command the air above the sea faced annihilation or unacceptable loss. Faced with a 30 to 1 air superiority, the British had never stood a chance.

The R.A.F.'s new Commander-in-Chief, Middle East, Air Marshal Sir Arthur Tedder, saw this clearly. "Root of situation is secure air bases," he signalled the Chief of Air Staff on 30 May. "This campaign is primarily a battle for aerodromes."

At the last, Crete had become a series of small swirling actions – gallant in themselves, yet lacking all cohesion. One force dislodged Student's paratroopers from a village strongpoint by dropping a beehive down their chimney. Near Galatas, Captain Michael Forrester, attached to the Greek Military Mission, charged into battle wearing shorts and a long yellow jersey, leading a posse of 100 Cretans, many of them women armed with ancient fowling pieces, one man with a serrated breadknife fastened to the end of a shotgun.

A young New Zealander, 33-year-old Second Lieutenant Charles Upham, of the 20th (N.Z.) Battalion proved a one-man task force in himself. On 21 May, though racked by dysentery and subsisting on con-densed milk, Upham had led a counter-charge at Maleme airfield, des-troying a machine-gun nest of eight men. Wounded in the shoulder, he still led his platoon with his arm in a sling – striding up and down a ridge to draw German fire, picking off two more Germans by propping his rifle in a tree fork. Then, after leading a final rearguard action up a 600-foot ravine, Upham took time out to free some tethered mules – to be led, weeping tears of frustration, aboard a Navy destroyer. His was the sole Victoria Cross to be awarded in the Cretan campaign.

The true reality was now inglorious evacuation. On 28 May, the Navy prepared to live up to their Dunkirk tradition of one year back: regardless of loss, the troops must be moved out. "It takes the Navy three years to build a new ship," Admiral Sir Andrew Cunningham reasoned. "It will take three hundred years to build a new tradition."

Thus for three days the evacuation continued – under relentless low-level strafing that cost them three cruisers and six destroyers, badly damaging a further seventeen. Aircraftman Marcel Comeau saw it from the seaside village of Sfakia, almost too weary to walk another step. Yet somehow he forced himself to toil back up the ravine; the knowledge that rescue was conditional on bringing back all the walking-wounded and stretcher cases lent a magical power to his legs. At 3 a.m. on 29 May – the last day but one of the evacuation – Comeau scrambled aboard the destroyer *Killearn*, en route for Alexandria.

But many men, like Lieutenant Theodore Stephanides, a medical officer with the Cyprus Regiment, had cause to wonder. "I knew that I was taking part in a retreat," he recalled later, "in fact I wondered if it could not be called more correctly a rout." For the first time in his service career, Stephanides was conscious of seeing naked panic that came close to breaking point, and of small shabby subterfuges that shocked him deeply. More than one man, he knew, had thrown away his steel helmet, tied on a field dressing and claimed Red Cross evacuation as "walking wounded".

It was with some justice, the doctor reflected, that a bitter gibe had been coined on the sandy beaches: that every man taking part in the Cretan evacuation would soon receive a medal inscribed, EX CRETA.

*

In England, the angry inquests began within days. At Church House, Westminster, the temporary debating chamber for Members of Parliament following crippling bomb damage to the House of Commons, the Ministry of Information's Harold Nicolson noted that Churchill was unusually diffident as he entered the chamber on Tuesday 10 June. As he passed along the front bench, he stooped to ask a Cabinet colleague, "Where is the ladies' gallery?"

Nicolson knew why: in the flaring debate that followed, Churchill needed the solace of knowing that Clementine, his wife of more than thirty-two years, was seated comfortably and within his view.

There was much to debate – news, wrote the U.S. Military Attaché, General Raymond E. Lee, "of the sort that would have made Kipling wince". True, some 15,000 men had been ferried to safety, but the losses were staggering – 11,835 prisoners, 1,742 killed or missing, 1,737 wounded. The R.A.F. had lost 46 planes – while Cunningham's Mediterranean Fleet was reduced to two battleships, two cruisers and thirteen destroyers ready for service. Many citizens were fast accepting the view of the military historian Liddell Hart; British hearts of oak were being betrayed by their leaders' oaken heads. "Greece and Crete," noted Mass Observation's weekly report, "have put people back into a state of doubt worse than Dunkirk."

But more powerful voices than Britain's M.P.'s were airing trenchant criticisms. Of the troops left behind in Crete, 3,000 were Australians, more than 800 New Zealanders, and many Australian Labour Party supporters were clamantly accusing the United Kingdom of "cold blooded murder" in sending green ill-armed troops to be "butchered" in Crete. In one secret session of Parliament, the Minister of the Army, Percy Claude Spender, saw the country's morale as now so low that "one hostile armoured division would be sufficient to conquer Australia".

In Wellington, New Zealand, Prime Minister Peter Fraser felt the same sense of betrayal. "I would strongly urge in the name of the New Zealand Government," he had pressured Churchill on 24 May, "that all possible additional support by air and sea be immediately provided, especially additional air assistance that can be released from all other quarters including United Kingdom." To this broadest of hints, the Premier responded tartly: "Suggestion that we are holding back air assistance for the sake of the United Kingdom is really quite unfounded."

For a rift was opening that would never quite be healed. From Cairo Sir Miles Lampson reported: "It is being freely said . . . that at best there has been tragic mismanagement and at the worst criminal lack of care for men's lives." In Alexandria, Admiral Cunningham admitted to "considerable odium . . . and scraps ashore", for many airmen had been mercilessly worked over by the Anzacs in the bars of the port. The demand for air cover at all times was now a near-pathological obsession. As Chief of the Air Staff, Portal spoke out frankly to General Ralph Royce, the U.S. Air Attaché: "AOC-in-C, Middle East under intense pressure from both Army and Navy for air support and protection . . . getting standing patrols for the defence troops . . . which is an unusual and uneconomical practice."

The truth was that Churchill, anxious to impress America at all costs, was fast alienating his Dominion Allies. All along, policy in Greece and south-east Europe had been wholly decided in London, without reference to Wellington or Canberra. When Churchill's Secretary of State for Dominion Affairs, Lord Cranborne, pressed him to confide in them more freely, the Premier, paternalist to a fault, disagreed. "Frankly, I do not see the object of spouting all this stuff out – some of it injurious, if it leaked – unless it is thought that the Dominions require to be frightened into doing their duty."

"There was a curious element in the British make-up," complained Lieutenant-General Sir Thomas Blamey, the Australian Commander-in-Chief, "which led them to look on the Dominions as appendages of Great Britain." Many Australian Labourites were more forthright; the British were looking on the Dominions as a prime source of cannon fodder. Nor was Churchill the only Briton mortally to wound Australian susceptibilities. Premier Robert Menzies, meeting Lieutenant-General Sir Henry Maitland-Wilson, fully expected a tribute to the Anzac rearguard in Greece. Instead Wilson, with ill-concealed distaste, told him, "Your . . . soldiers are terribly badly disciplined and cause a great deal of trouble."

On 12 June, at St James's Palace, speaking to a massed audience of diplomats and Dominions High Commissioners, Churchill gave a rousing pledge that Britain would "fight on till life is gone or victory won", and that Hitler would find "no peace, no rest, no halting place, no parley". But from this time on, Churchill would find the Dominions resolved on one thing: the British must bear their share of the fighting or take the consequences.

This would prove a major setback in the months to come, for Britain sorely needed Commonwealth support. Canada was unavowedly staunch, with 65 percent of her national income earmarked to meet war obligations, but South Africa posed more of a questionmark. Despite Churchill's longstanding friendship with her Premier, Field Marshal Jan Smuts, the country had entered the war by the slim margin of 80 votes to 67. Many Afrikaaners, descendants of the stubborn Dutch farmers who had waged the Boer War, saw this as a British, not a South African quarrel – a sentiment fanned by Dr Josef Göbbels' nightly propaganda broadcasts from Zeesen. From among two million whites only a volunteer force of 150,000 had signed on for service "anywhere in Africa", adopting the orange-red shoulder flashes known as *rooi lusses*.*

The irony was that America was now as dissatisfied with the British war effort as the Dominions. Following a Middle East inspection, the air attaché, General Royce, summed up the attitude prevailing there: slovenly, shiftless, apathetic, and Luddite when faced with unfamiliar machinery. Although an old friend, Averell Harriman still had to be blunt with Churchill; the waste of equipment by British troops was "incredible". From his vantage point at the Ministry of Economic Warfare, Hugh Dalton saw the danger signs; disquieting stories were current in America concerning Churchill and his entourage.

* A figure later increased to 186,218.

Harriman was growing daily more disillusioned, and so, too, was Winant. "There is much comment on Crete and our failure to provide air cover," Dalton noted. "It is said that many important decisions are taken over here late at night in a state of sozzlement" – a reference to Churchill's interminable small-hours meetings with his Chiefs of Staff, liberally fortified by brandy and soda.

Despite their outward unity, rumour had it that Churchill and his ministers were now irrevocably at loggerheads. For once, rumour did not lie. At one luncheon for industrial correspondents, Beaverbrook, soon to become Minister of Supply, astounded the company by launching into a tirade against all his colleagues save Churchill, Eden and the First Lord, A. V. Alexander. Then weeping brokenly, he blundered from the room. It was no lone example. Minister of Information Alfred Duff Cooper, "a little flushed before (lunch) and more flushed afterwards," devoted one Press Conference to berating the entire Cabinet. "I don't know why you think *I* have any information for you," he sneered. "Nobody tells me anything."

Beaverbrook was a red rag to many colleagues; before War Cabinet meetings, Minister of Labour Ernest Bevin always slipped his false teeth into his pocket, lest he bite through his tongue in sheer annoyance. Others distrusted his influence on Churchill – in his presence, one man noted, "Winston is like a chicken in front of a cobra." Beaverbrook was likewise anathema to the Minister of Works, Lord Reith – "to no one is the vulgar designation shit more appropriately applied".

Beaverbrook, for his part, never ceased his efforts to discredit Bevin with Churchill: Bevin's threat, in 1940, to prosecute him for allegedly overworking juveniles in aircraft factories still rankled bitterly. It was a campaign that had the warm support of Brendan Bracken, Churchill's redhaired crony and later Minister of Information – though "not fit to be a Minister" in the view of Lord Privy Seal Clement Attlee.

Dalton's own guns were trained on Alfred Duff Cooper – "This little pig" – while reserving a spatter of grapeshot for Eden; the Foreign Secretary was "a nervy fusser", with the manner of "a peevish child seizing all the toys". For good measure, the Chancellor of the Duchy of Lancaster, Lord Hankey, denounced the entire War Cabinet: "They struck me as a set of 'yes-men', leaving the running of the war entirely to Churchill."

"All this ridiculous business of personal relations will be seen in retrospect as quite fantastic," Dalton was to record sadly. "We were supposed to be fighting the Germans, but a large number of the participants were really fighting each other, intriguing, back-biting and feeling injured and jealous."

*

104

In one respect, at least, Churchill's Cabinet were fully in accord: their profound distrust of the men who ruled unoccupied France from the little spa town of Vichy. "A Turkish bath planted with trees," as one man described it, Vichy with its rambling turn-of-the-century hotels, crammed with potted palms and rattan chairs, was somehow symbolic of the weary languor that had settled upon France.

Their distrust focused primarily on two men: 84-year-old Marshal Henri Phillipe Pétain, whose luncheon table at the Hôtel Parc et Majestic was hidden from the faithful by a wicker screen, and 59-year-old Admiral Jean François Darlan, an able ambitious schemer, who travelled everywhere in a personal train equipped with two bathrooms and a 24-piece naval orchestra.

While Pétain harboured no great love for the Germans – "I am a prisoner," he would quaveringly assure Roosevelt's ambassador, Admiral Leahy – Darlan unashamedly embraced the concept of Nietzschean superman. "British and American soldiers demand beefsteak," he told Leahy patronisingly. "The Germans can live on a few prepared pills." And anticipating a German victory Darlan was mindful that France should be on the winning side. With this end in view, on 10 February, he had annexed no less than four Ministerial portfolios – Vice President, Minister of Foreign Affairs, Minister of the Interior,* and Minister of Information.

Early in May, Darlan had found himself courted by Germany. Syria, over which Vichy France held a mandate, was needed as a staging post for German planes abetting the short-lived Rashid Ali rising in Iraq. In return, the Führer might make concessions on such factors as daily occupation charges and the return of German-held French prisoners.

Darlan now saw a chance for France to escape from armistice constraints and assume a voluntary neutral role in Hitler's New Order. Promptly he agreed. By 9 May, German planes and technicians were touching down at Aleppo airport.

This gesture of compliance was to cost him dear; at one and the same time Darlan was to destroy all world sympathy for Vichy France and ultimately to lose Syria.

In vain did Cordell Hull warn the French of the dangers of transit. "Vichy had gone straight into the arms of the German Government," he accused Pétain's ambassador, Gaston Henry-Haye. His condemnation of Pétain was more scathing still; the transit was "a gratuitous act of vast military aid to Hitler".

Unlike the British, who had no official diplomatic relations with Vichy, Roosevelt had always been careful to maintain a dialogue with Pétain and Darlan. The advantages seemed manifold: to ensure that Darlan maintained control of the French Fleet and kept the Germans from French

* A Ministry he later ceded to Pierre Pucheu.

North Africa, to block collaboration with her colonies and prevent economic collapse. For these reasons, Robert Murphy, a craggy affable diplomat in Algiers, had established a liaison with General Maxime Weygand, Pétain's Delegate General in French North Africa.

To Hull, British intransigence over France seemed counterproductive: lacking support from Britain, what incentive did the French have to resist Germany? Although he cautioned Henry-Haye to "play down his controversial utterances . . . both alike suffer from clashes that arouse feeling", Hull also took Lord Halifax to task. Unless the British showed flexibility, allowing American goods to reach France, Darlan might yield up the Fleet – "Lazarus, in a state of great hunger, felt extremely grateful to the rich man when he was permitted to pick up a few crumbs that fell from his table".

Unknown to Hull, though, Eden had his own private pipeline to Weygand: a Polish engineer, code-named "Lancelot", who shuttled between Cairo, Lisbon and Tangier. Weygand needed both wheat and petrol and a tacit "gentlemen's agreement" had thus been reached; both sides would proclaim overt hostility, to lull Hitler's suspicions, and supplies for North Africa would filter discreetly through the British blockade.

If the French were ever to fight again as Allies, Churchill believed, it would be on North African soil or not at all.

Originally the Premier and Wavell had hoped that General Henri-Fernand Dentz, who commanded 30,000 French troops in Syria, along with local levies, would resist the German incursion. But by mid-May, some 70 Axis bombers and fighters, and forty transports, had made use of Syrian landing fields. Plainly Dentz was obeying Pétain to the letter.

Now one man saw his chance. For almost a year General Charles André Marie de Gaulle, leader of the Free French forces, had been a man consigned to the wilderness. Although the British were backing him to the tune of £8 million a year, not more than 50,000 Frenchmen had flocked to his banner – some in England, more in French Equatorial Africa and the Cameroons. From the first, the British had treated him with cautious reserve; he was acknowledged as chief only of those "who rallied to him".

"Why have you brought this lanky gloomy Brigadier?" Churchill had asked Major-General Edward Spears, his personal liaison officer with the French, when the two returned to London in June, 1940, and Spears had to be honest. "No one else would come." But by December, 1940, after an Anglo-de Gaulle attempt to seize the port of Dakar, Senegal, had been ignominiously beaten off, Churchill was spoiling for a change.

Privately, Pétain told Leahy, Churchill had sent him word that "de Gaulle had been of no assistance to the British cause", which left the Marshal wondering "why the British do not eliminate him". The truth was Churchill had tried and failed. Since de Gaulle's attempt to rally all French possessions below the Sahara under his banner had fallen through, the Premier had tried to inveigle Weygand into supplanting him – and been tersely rebuffed.

To play second fiddle was intolerable to the larger-than-life de Gaulle. A 6 ft 4 in ramrod, ascetic and humourless – "a head like a banana and hips like a woman", commented Dalton unkindly – the General saw himself, like the Sun King, Louis XIV, as the embodiment of French honour. At one Savoy Hotel luncheon, he charged Harold Nicolson that the Ministry of Information was "Pétainist". When Nicolson protested that the Ministry was working "for all France", the outraged de Gaulle trumpeted, "*La France entière? C'est moi!*"

From Brazzaville, on the Congo, capital of the Free French colonial empire, the British Consul, Robert Parr, strove to clarify de Gaulle's viewpoint: "If Great Britain attaches so little value to the moral side of the movement . . . instead of fostering it by all possible means she weakens it by complaisance towards Vichy . . . he (de Gaulle) must decide what is his fundamental duty for France, for whom he is trustee."

But the British, for the most part, were more in accord with the advice Hoare offered from Madrid: "If our propaganda gives the impression that everybody left in France is a traitor and only the émigrés are patriots, we shall push France not only temporarily but permanently into the Axis."

De Gaulle, though, was not easily gainsaid, and this was his hour. Wavell, warned by Sir Miles Lampson that speed was essential, was "not particularly communicative or responsive", but found he had no choice. A German foothold in Syria would prove intolerable. With Churchill's blessing de Gaulle flew from London to Cairo with instructions to map out a Syrian campaign.

At one stroke de Gaulle had achieved all he had fought for: his own private war in which his Free French would face the Germans, at one and the same time avenging the shame of Vichy, ensuring his own position as leader and weakening Roosevelt's insidious link with Pétain.

Even this early, Churchill was finding de Gaulle a sore trial. A resolute trencherman, he bitterly resented the French leader's habit of interrupting his meal-times with long impassioned phone calls. On one such occasion, at Chequers, Churchill refused the call, but de Gaulle persisted so assiduously that Sawyers, the valet, begged the Premier to yield. Cheeks crimson, his napkin crumpled, Churchill strode from the dining room.

Ten minutes later, returning to rapidly cooling soup, Churchill, still crimson, was enveloped in mulish silence. Suddenly he burst out: "Bloody de Gaulle! He had the impertinence to tell me that the French regard him as the reincarnation of Joan of Arc."

As always, Churchill had had the last word. "I found it very necessary to remind him that we had to burn the first!"

*

Even by 1941 standards, it was a bizarre campaign. Security was totally lacking, and so, too, were shock tactics; at 2 a.m. on Sunday, 8 June, the forces that crossed the frontiers of Syria in a three-pronged drive from Palestine, Iraq and Trans-Jordan, advanced boldly in bright moonlight, to the resounding strains of Free French bands blasting out *La Marseillaise*. As if to emphasise the strange dichotomy, even their banners were at cross-purposes: before a shot was ever fired, a white flag of truce was hoisted alongside the *Tricouleur* as they marched.

Hasty improvisation was evident from the first. The Free French, 6,000 strong under their Field Commander, General Paul Louis Le Gentilhomme, had been augmented by the only forces the hard pressed Wavell could muster – two brigades of the Australian 7th Division, the 5th Indian Infantry Brigade, and those veterans of the relief column, "Habforce" – "almost as many sprigs of the nobility as Henry V had led to Agincourt", one man recalled, their ranks later swelled by Prince Aly Khan and 1,000 Ismaili horsemen raised from his father's followers.

Military hardware was conspicuously lacking. For their part, the Free French could muster exactly eight guns and ten light tanks; while some fought from astride camels, others were on horseback or in armoured cars. Some British troops – to the appropriate strains of "We are Fred Karno's Army" – moved up in old ramshackle omnibuses with patched roofs or in citrus trucks still slippery with orange peel. Air cover for the entire striking force was sixty aircraft, many of them manned by pilots straight from flying school.

Courtesy and conciliation were the keynotes from the first. The Australians were under orders to wear slouch hats, not steel helmets, until actually fired upon; at Tibnine, ten miles beyond the frontier, the mayor approached one column led by Lieutenant-Colonel A. B. MacDonald, with a novel request. Could he telephone to Tyre, their next objective, to enquire if the invaders would be welcome? Only when the answer was affirmative did the column press on.

The question was, welcomed by whom? For the one factor normally indispensable to a battle – a determined enemy – was missing from the first: within hours of the frontier crossing, the Germans had written Syria off. From all the airfields, the German ground staffs were hastily flown back to Europe or evacuated by train through Turkey. As the columns forged on in search of them, hundreds of Germans and Italians were passing peacefully through Ankara.

The way now lay open to a tragic situation: a civil war, in which

Frenchmen for the first time raised their hands against Frenchmen. It was a situation de Gaulle had never remotely foreseen; the advance of de Gaulle troops, he believed, would meet an onrush of Vichyites who had seen the light, eager to embrace his cause.

It was a fatal error. Only one prominent Frenchman, Colonel Philibert Collet, commanding a troop of fair-skinned Muslim Circassians, led his forces over the frontier – but of the ten squadrons that rode with him all but three changed their minds and rode back. It was Collet who broke the daunting news to General Georges Catroux, de Gaulle's Commander-in-Chief: even Vichyites feeling sympathy with the Free French would resist their invasion on principle.

"What fine fellows the Free French are," General Spears, now heading a Mission to de Gaulle, wrote to Brendan Bracken, "but alas! Dr Göbbels himself could not make them (the opposition) believe it." The Syrians were equally disenchanted. "All the inhabitants loathe French in any form," Lampson cabled Eden, "Free French just as much as Vichy."

Both Pétain and Darlan hoped for bitter resistance – "the demonstration of loyalty to Germany . . . can improve the position of metropolitan France" – but their hopes were barely realised. Many Vichyites did fight gamely, but as the war rumbled on for thirty-four days over dry chalky highways, through squalid stone villages, the tragedy of fratricide was more often averted. One Free French unit captured a hill by advancing with their rifles slung over their shoulders; the Vichyites who held it refused to open fire. In one battle, two men poised to lob grenades at one another, suddenly realised that they were brothers. Collet's Circassians, meeting up with their own kind, fell on their necks with tears of joy.

One unit of the 6th *Demi-Brigade*, Foreign Legion, ambushed a patrol of the 13th *Demi-Brigade*, and took them prisoner. Then their C.O., ordering the guard to present arms, made an oddly moving little speech: "You are firstly *légionnaires*, secondly you are prisoners of war, and only in the end are you my enemy."

War correspondents hastening to the front for a scoop found an almost pastoral peace. Cecil Brown, of C.B.S., heading for Beirut, pictured swarms of tanks and guns and thousands of men milling up the coastal road. Twelve miles from the city he caught up with the advance post: four near-naked Australians, splotched with purple antiseptic skin dye, lying behind a barbed wire barrier, fronted by a double row of land mines. To Brown's chagrin, not a tank or a gun was in sight.

All along the front, fighting instinct was fast waning. Lieutenant-General John Evetts, newly-appointed British commander, assessed the mood swiftly, then called the Australian divisional commander, Major-General J. D. Lavarack, at Advance Headquarters, Nazareth. "The Free French forces are extremely tired," he reported frankly, "and have little or no desire to go on killing their brother Frenchmen . . . it is doubtful whether they can be persuaded to advance even against feeble resistance."

Thus, by 20 June, the Vichy French were as anxious to evacuate the Syrian capital, Damascus, as Evetts was to seize it. One day later, at 1.30 p.m., watched by thousands of silent Moslems, Damascus "fell" before an onslaught of two Free French colonels, two Australians, a British major and two armoured cars. The allied army, following up later, had to by-pass the main street – not because of war or barricades but because the authorities were renewing the tram tracks. Their triumphal entry into the city wound, to spirited applause, through the heart of the brothel quarter.

There had been needless tragedies, even so. At Kisweh Fort, outside Damascus, British ack-ack hit a Vichy transport plane; of the three men aboard, only the sergeant-pilot lingered long enough to unburden himself to Major Bernard Fergusson, British liaison officer with the Free French. Squeezing Fergusson's arm, the dying man twice asked him plaintively: "*Pourquoi nous combattons? Pourquoi?*"

Fergusson did not think to answer that they were fighting because of one man's obsession that he alone was the soul of France – an obsession that by 12 July had caused more than a thousand deaths on either side.

For it was at 0.01 hours on that date, following the thrice-repeated code-word "Robert-Robert-Robert", that the cease-fire came into effect on all fronts – and for de Gaulle another bigger battle was then beginning.

*

They were days as terrible as a nightmare, yet as exciting as a dream. One unwary move, one rigid adherence to, or departure from, orders could bring the three great uncommitted powers – Japan, Russia, the United States – closer to war.

At 5 a.m. on 21 May – before the ships pursuing the *Bismarck* had even readied for action – one man made such a move. That morning the submarine U-69 was surfaced on the oily swell of the South Atlantic, 750 miles off Freetown, Sierra Leone, and the mood aboard her was sullen. "The Laughing Cow" which grinned from her conning tower, an emblem selected at random from a French cheese carton *La Vache qui Rit*, was belying her nickname. Despite sunny weather, it was weeks since the U-boat had sighted an enemy masthead. Worse, her commander, *Käpitänleutnant* Jost Metzler had just committed the unforgiveable crime of shaving at sea – a sure omen of bad luck.

It was not long in coming. Metzler, who had passed the warm tropical night on the bridge, had just retired below when the cry rang out, "Commander to the bridge." Grabbing his hat and scaling the steep iron companionway, Metzler soon saw why. Three miles away, the look-out had sighted the navigation lights of a 5,000 ton freighter.

Metzler was at once suspicious. The merchantman might be a neutral – but unusually she bore no illuminated flag aft and neither her national colours nor the name of her country were painted on her hull.

As U-69 turned towards the ship, closing to 1,000 yards, another strange factor became apparent. The freighter's cargo, stacked on her after-deck, consisted primarily of top-heavy crates. "Either she's got aeroplane parts on board," surmised *Leutnant zur Zee* Auermann, the First Lieutenant, "or else she's a Q-ship."

Every submariner was justly wary of Q-ships – armed merchantmen with concealed guns such as had been used to trap submarines in World War One. "Ask for her name," Metzler ordered, and Bade, the helmsman, bent to his Morse lamp. The answer blinked back through the grey dawn: "*S.S. Robin Moor.*"

Now Metzler grew more dubious. A quick check with *Lloyd's Register* and *Groener's Shipping List* revealed no such vessel. As was customary, Metzler ordered the freighter to stop and lower a small boat, bearing the captain and his papers.

But the rowboat that pulled towards them around 6.30 a.m., crewed by eight sailors, brought no captain and no papers – merely the Chief Officer standing nonchalantly in the bow, a cigarette gummed to his lower lip. By now it was light enough for Metzler to see the legend "S.S. Exmoor, New York" on the freighter's stern, and the Stars and Stripes, though unilluminated on her hull. The Chief Officer's explanation seemed perfunctory, to say the least. The freighter had been sold two weeks back to the Sea Shipping Company and renamed. There had been no time to repaint her.

Metzler was in a quandary. Time and again, *Konteradmiral* Karl Dönitz, the submarine chief, had reiterated Hitler's orders: incidents with United States vessels must at all costs be avoided. This cautious naval policy, spelt out on 25 April, was to be stressed again on 9 June and 7 July: Roosevelt must be given no cause for provocation. Acting on advice from Dr Hans Thomsen, the chargé in Washington, German newspapers were to refrain from attacking Roosevelt and from overtly endorsing isolationists like Lindbergh.

Fully as anxious to placate Roosevelt as Stalin was to placate Hitler, the Führer's view of the United States was a strange one, fostered by his genial incompetent Military Attaché, General Friedrich von Boetticher: the country was split between sober, moderate, patriotic and pro-German General Staff and a rabble of warmongering politicians and pressmen, dominated by international Jewry.

Apart from an abortive 1924 attempt to screw Nazi Party funds from the motor magnate, Henry Ford, Hitler had dismissed America from his thoughts. Convinced that the country harboured 13 million unemployed and that the wrong side had won the Civil War, he decried the American way of life "as a concept . . . inspired by the most vulgar commercialism". Unless sorely provoked, such "a mongrel society" could never threaten Germany.

Hence Jost Metzler's dilemma on the sultry morning of 21 May. He had erred in stopping an American ship – but plainly the *Robin Moor*, in contravention of the Neutrality Act, was carrying contraband. Although the Chief Officer would admit only to motor cycle parts and tractors, bound for Capetown, Helmsman Bade, a onetime Merchant Navy loading officer, was sceptical. "Aircraft, *Herr Käleunt*," was his estimate, "if they were really car parts, then they must be omnibuses."

Metzler came to a decision. The crew had twenty minutes to abandon ship and take to the lifeboats: after this *Robin Moor* would be sunk. Her captain must report to "The Laughing Cow" with all despatch, bringing his papers and bills of lading.

Still Metzler worried. He was acting contrary to orders – but just as surely *Robin Moor* was carrying contraband by which German lives would be forfeit. When Captain E. W. Meyers boarded U-69, saluting politely as he came, his papers were so obviously genuine that Metzler gave him one last chance. "Your ship is carrying contraband and I have to sink it," he explained. "Have you anything to say?"

Meyers made no attempt to deny it, merely spreading his hands. "I'm sorry, I can't help it," was all he said.

Soon after, Metzler felt a sense of vindication. One torpedo hit *Robin Moor* amidships: thirty three shells from U-69's 8.8 cm deck gun finished the job. But as she sank wearily by the stern, to the gunners' excited cries of "La Vache qui Rit", a tell-tale carpet of flotsam was bobbing on the oily water: the broken fragments of aircraft wings, huge aircraft tyres.

Now a complication arose. In their haste to abandon ship, *Robin Moor*'s 38-strong crew, along with eight civilian passengers, had neglected to stock up on food – and Metzler had been forced to deplete his own stores of bread, butter, brandy and medicine. To ensure their safety he took the ship's four lifeboats in tow for several hours, only casting off when a gentle current would steer them to the African shore. That evening, under cover of dusk, he radioed U-Boat Command headquarters, at Lorient, of the plight of the castaways. Neutral steamers would now be on the alert.

Although Metzler could not know it, lifeboats carrying eleven of the survivors were soon after caught in a contrary current and swept out into the Atlantic; it was not until 11 June that the Brazilian steamer *Ozorio* which had sighted them, landed them at Pernambuco. (The remaining 35 reached Capetown two days earlier.)

Aboard U-69 the hapless Metzler was now given no respite at all. From his Lorient headquarters, 'The Big Sea Lion,' as Dönitz was known, followed one furious and peremptory signal with another: "Report immediately why *Robin Moor* was sunk". Only by degrees did the U-Boat commander realise that he was at the storm centre of an international incident.

For Roosevelt's reaction had been violent and immediate, and his condemnation echoed round the world. In a ringing message to Congress he spoke of "the acts of an international outlaw", of "a policy of frightfulness and intimidation", of "conquest based on lawlessness and terror on land and piracy on the sea". It was a message Sumner Welles swiftly passed on to the Chargé, Hans Thomsen, though ending with due regard to protocol: "Accept, Sir, the renewed assurance of my high consideration".

And Roosevelt took other steps, much farther reaching. On 14 June, just as Treasury Secretary Morgenthau had urged for months, he froze Axis assets in the United States, along with those of other European countries not then frozen. He closed down all twenty-five German consulates. Following reports of German submarines in Iceland's coastal waters, he accepted Churchill's invitation to take over from the British garrison that had been holding Iceland ever since its mother country, Denmark, had been overrun in 1940.

Churchill was delighted, envisaging the liberation of another division for his beloved Middle East. Long before 7 July, when the 1st Brigade United States Marine Corps took over Camp Alafoss, 15 miles from Reykjavik – "Rinky Dink" to the Marines – the Premier was assuring Roosevelt: "I am much encouraged by . . . your Marines taking over that cold place."

Roosevelt, too, was in high good humour. "When I took Iceland the market went up two points," he reminded Morgenthau skittishly. "There are a lot of places I can take. I can take the Azores for you. Just let me know . . ."*

The one man who viewed the take-over with real trepidation was Admiral Harold R. Stark, Chief of Naval Operations. "There is so much potential dynamite in this order," he wrote to Hopkins, "that I feel it should have his (Roosevelt's) O.K. before I send it over to you . . . I will wait the final "execute" until I get word from the President."

The far-reaching implications of Metzler's action were chilling indeed, Stark felt – "I realise that this is practically an act of war."

*

* At the end of March, this had been Portugal's most earnest hope. Fearing a German invasion, 10,000 crack Portuguese troops had been transported from Lisbon to the Azores, where the destroyer, *Lina* was standing by to steam for Lisbon and rescue Dr Antonio Salazar, the dictator, and his government, if need be. Portugal, Hull was informed, would accept United States "protection".

113

In the silence of his study at No 10 Downing Street, Churchill was hunched in his favourite leather chair. With growing disquiet, he studied the cable before him, which Wavell had despatched from Cairo on 30 May. Due to the inferiority of tanks and armoured cars, the Commander-in-Chief hazarded, prospects in the Western Desert were in no way bright. Uncradling the phone, Churchill called Field Marshal Sir John Dill to outline the gist of the despatch. "That," Churchill contended, "is the message of a tired and beaten man."

Initially Wavell had opposed an intervention in Greece, and since then Churchill's dissatisfaction with him had grown. As early as 19 May, he had debated exchanging him with Lieutenant-General Sir Claude Auchinleck, India's commander. Following Crete, Attlee, too, had been sharply critical of Wavell – "I do not think he has really freed his mind from the Maginot Line complex. Everything outside the Egyptian perimeter he regards as commitments not opportunities." On 28 May, made fretful by Wavell's inaction, Churchill once more took him sharply to task: "Now . . . is the time to fight a decisive battle in Libya and go on day after day facing all necessary losses until you have beaten the life out of General Rommel's army."

But Wavell's pessimism did not abate. On 12 May, a convoy code-named "Tiger" had reached Suez with 238 tanks; by sailing the risky Mediterranean route forty days had been saved. But many of the "Tiger Cubs" as Churchill christened them, were in the sorriest shape – gear-boxes cracked, tracks unserviceable, all of them lacking sand filters. Action before mid-June, Wavell warned was out of the question – "even tigers have teething troubles." Churchill received the news without comment, but the calm was illusory. Wavell's days were numbered.

So were the days of many of his men, for the task allotted the "Tiger Cubs" was daunting: a three-pronged 150-mile attack launched from Mersa Matruh, designed to destroy all enemy forces east of Tobruk. Most vital target of all was the German-held Halfaya Pass, a 300-foot gash in the coastal escarpment running parallel with the Mediterranean shoreline, for through it must pass not only any advance into Egypt but any westward invasion. He who held Halfaya held the Tripoli-Alexandria road.

At 2.30 a.m. on 15 June, the move to the front began. Soon, on a scale never before witnessed, almost 500 tanks would clash. But as the red pinpoints of rear lights inched forward in the darkness, it was as if Wavell's sense of foreboding pressed in upon his troops. "There is battle in the air tonight," one man wrote in his diary. "It lies thick upon the tongue." Only Brigadier Ian Erskine looked further than the morrow: his under-strength 22nd Guards Brigade had been beefed up with a battalion of Durham Light Infantry to upset all his plans.

To Major-General Frank Messervy, the wiry irrepressible commander of the 4th Indian Division, Erskine complained: "Light Infantry march at a much faster pace than the Guards. What the hell am I going to do when the Brigade has to march on a ceremonial parade in Cairo?"

In his command post on the rim of Halfaya Pass, *Hauptmann* Wilhelm Bach, commanding the 1st Battalion, 104th Field Artillery Regiment, anxiously awaited news of the British. Clad in an open-necked shirt with pale blue braces supporting voluminous khaki shorts, puffing contentedly on a cigar, the portly 50-year-old Bach was a far cry from the Afrika Korps stereotype. Known to his troops as "The Pastor of Halfaya" – in civil life he had been pastor of the Evangelical Church at Mannheim – Bach, calm and paternal, still commanded the unswerving loyalty of the die-hards the British knew as "the seven-day men". These were the men who manned Halfaya's machine gun nests and gun emplacements, victualled with food and water for seven days at a time, knowing they must fight to the last bullet and the last drop of water.

On the night of 14 June, Bach's field telephone rang. He listened, then told his deputy *Leutnant* Friedl Schmidt, "Something's in the air. It's tonight or early tomorrow morning."

Towards 6 a.m. on 15 June, the faint throb of motors was borne towards the pass. Through powerful field glasses, Bach and the "seven day men" now saw on the horizon tiny black dots trailing a giant plume of dust. The British were perhaps two miles away. "Under no circumstances fire," Bach passed the word quietly. "Let them come on."

Slowly the tanks advanced. On paper, at least, this attack, codenamed "Operation Battleaxe", seemed feasible for Wavell had a four to one advantage in tanks, a two to one advantage in troops. By degrees the early morning silence was broken by the sharp crack of artillery as the British guns opened up. Shell craters pitted the biscuit-brown heights and columns of smoke arose. Still Bach's men, and the Italian battery under Major Leopoldo Pardo, held their fire.

At 9.15 a.m., Lieutenant-Colonel Walter O'Carroll, of the 4th Royal Tanks, heard with satisfaction the radio code-message, "Pink Spots": the action was under control and going well. Then the appalled last words of Major C. G. Miles, in the lead tank, burst in his eardrums: "Good God! They've got large calibre guns dug in and they're tearing my tanks to pieces."

It was true. From concealed emplacements all along the cliffside, Rommel's most deadly weapon had for the first time come into devastating play: Flak 88 anti-aircraft guns, used now in an anti-tank role, firing 22-lb shells that could tear holes as big as basket-balls in a Matilda a mile distant. As the whiplash crack of high-velocity shot sounded, three tanks stopped dead to burst asunder in billows of crimson flame and black oily smoke. In these moments, as eleven out of twelve tanks took fire like blowtorches, the fate of Halfaya was decided.

Due to lack of air cover – caused by wireless breakdowns and poor coordination between air and ground troops – the carnage was absolute. Stukas swooped unopposed from the sun, and General Messervy, sitting on the fender of a three-ton truck awaiting a mug of tea, saw a stick of bombs blast his Indian mess-waiter to fragments. British *sang-froid* to the fore, Messervy called, "Will someone be good enough to get me another cup? And I'm afraid you'll have to find another chap to bring it." Around now a dispatch rider arrived at Messervy's H.Q. with a strangely inappropriate message from Churchill to the troops: "The eyes of the world are on you, and Britain knows that her sons will conquer." On his own initiative, Captain Donald Bateman stuffed it unbroadcast into his pocket.

Five times the British sought to storm the pass, and five times Bach's men, swigging on water spiked with aniseed to slake their thirst, repulsed them. As supplies ran low, Major Pardo collected old Italian artillery shells, had them polished and greased, then fired them. Everywhere men clung like limpets to the dour slopes, and every ridge and bone-dry watercourse took its toll. But at last, at 11 a.m. on 17 June, Messervy, lacking word from the G.O.C. ordered Western Desert Force to withdraw on his own initiative to escape annihilation. Halfaya would be "Hell-Fire" Pass to the British from this time on.

Shortly, on the desert airstrip, Messervy confronted a grim-faced Wavell. "I thought he was going to sack me," Messervy recalled later, for Wavell stared at him for long minutes before breaking silence. "I think you were right to withdraw in the circumstances," was all Wavell said finally, "but orders should have come from H.Q. Western Desert Force."

*

In England, Wavell's terse admission of defeat – "Am very sorry for failure of 'Battleaxe'" brought only consternation. How many tanks "Battleaxe" had cost the British was always open to doubt – estimates ranged from 80 to 99 – but what hit hardest was the knowledge that in 12 days Rommel had achieved everything save Tobruk's fall, that had taken O'Connor 50. Sir Alexander Cadogan best summed up the mood of disillusion: "Wavells and suchlike are no good against (the Germans). It is like putting me up to play Bobby Jones over 36 holes."

The outcome was inevitable. Early on the morning of 21 June, Wavell's Chief of Staff, Lieutenant-General Sir Arthur Smith, arrived at his chief's house on Cairo's Gezira Island. Wavell was in the bathroom shaving, cheeks daubed with lather, razor poised. Quietly Smith read out a signal which had just arrived from Churchill: "I have come to the conclusion that public interest will best be served by appointment of General Auchinleck to relieve you in command of armies of Middle East . . ."

Wavell stared ahead. With no emotion, no regret, he said, "The Prime Minister's quite right. This job needs a new eye and a new hand." Then he went on shaving.

*

Harold Elvin, the footloose young Englishman who had felt that Moscow was the place to be, was having second thoughts. From all the war fronts the news flooded in daily – the sinking of the *Robin Moor*, the conflict in Syria, the debacle at Halfaya – but the British Embassy, a sprawling pile built by a sugar-beet baron on the Sofiiskaya Embankment, overlooking the Moscow River, was an enclave of funereal silence.

After three months Elvin's routine as assistant night watchman had become almost second nature. Every other night, at 9 p.m., he left his room in the West Wing to take up his post in the main hallway, a canopied seat lit by a single reading lamp. There, until 8 a.m. next day, he was almost a fixture – browsing through piles of *Punch* and *Country Life* borrowed from the English Church Library, breaking off to patrol his rounds, sometimes repairing to the kitchen to brew tea.

Sometimes, in the small hours, the chief watchman, Sergeant Bill Eldredge, a cheerful Cockney veteran of the Indian Army, would join him for a schoolboy feast of egg and onions on toast. But often, as on 9 June, there was only brooding silence as Elvin surveyed the familiar nightly scene: the life-size oil paintings of Edward VII and Queen Victoria, offset by linenfold panelling, the immense expanse of red carpeting that stretched beyond the hall to the giant oak staircase, on to the 15 foot landing window.

Mostly Elvin welcomed this solitude. With a staff of twenty sobersided bachelors, Embassy life by day was often oppressive. Though all were English, Elvin, as a lowly night watchman, was treated as beyond the pale; on duty journeys in an Embassy car, Elvin rode in front with Bumagin, the chauffeur, ignored by the career diplomats riding in the back. Following Embassy pressure, even his old schoolfellow from Southend Grammar School, the Reuter correspondent Maurice Lovell, told him shamefacedly, "I want to keep my job here, so I can't afford to mix with you".

As often in the past, Elvin fell back on the resources of the country. Time off meant hours spent at the Bolshoi Ballet, or watching the crowds in Gorki Park, eating ices served by waitresses in pretty blue embroidered blouses. At other times he strolled in Red Square, with its bowls of blood red carnations and neat blue balustrades, or among the pavilions and food stalls of the Ermitage Gardens. With a pang he felt closer to Savalief, the Ambassador's butler, or Fedor, the porter, than to his own class-ridden compatriots.

As an old friend of his father's, Sir Stafford Cripps proved a democratic exception – but in one respect he, too, had proved a sore disappointment. On the April day that Elvin first met him he had come up with a prophecy so hare-brained that even on this June night, three months later, the sense of disillusion still persisted.

Gesturing at the huge wall map in his book-lined study, Cripps had predicted suddenly, "Germany will flood through Europe this way – and they will next amass their forces here," pointing to the Russian border. "Of course," he went on, "they will send out a feeler towards Moscow and Leningrad but more serious will be hundreds-of-miles encircling movements, which will surround both in pincers".

Elvin remained silent. A trade unionist's son, he had admired the Socialist Cripps for more than a decade – yet now his idol was voicing "the biggest load of craziness I had heard from any worthy". Cripps, he had since heard, had laboured equally hard to convince the Kremlin – and been rejected out of hand.

Hadn't Germany enough enemies already? Elvin had asked himself ever since that day. Could they be so insane? Of course they could not. In a year's time Moscow would be as peaceful and inviolate as she was tonight, silent under a late pall of snow.

But in the small hours of 9 June, a small voice had begun gnawing like conscience in Elvin's mind: And yet . . . and yet . . .

*

Another man was similarly beset by doubts. Amid all the panoply of that summer afternoon, 21-year-old *Fähnrich* (Ensign-Cadet) Peter Neumann found his mind constantly straying from the goal he had so long awaited: his graduation from the S.S. *Junkerschule* (Officer Cadets Training Unit) at Bad Tölz, in the Bavarian Alps, south of Munich.

Neumann had been anticipating this day for three years now: the moment when he stood braced rigidly to attention, along with all the others on the parade ground, hearing the roll of thunder as the band crashed into *Deutschland über Alles*, absurdly proud that he now made one of the *Schutzstaffeln* (SS), the elite unit of Hitler's assault troops with their jet-black uniforms, silver death's heads adorning their caps, the twin lightning flashes on the right lapels of their tunics.

The setting was perfect for such a moment: the great black S.S. banners and swastikas flapping against the white walls of the school, the buzzards wheeling in a clear bright sky above the Karwendel Alps, the dark motionless columns of youngsters as far as the eye could see.

It was no day for doubts, Neumann recognised. And yet . . .

Like all young Germans who had embraced the Nazi Party, Neumann had been truly indoctrinated in his teens. He could recite all the injustices

118

that had brought "Adi", as the cadets called Hitler, to power: the monstrous inequity of the Treaty of Versailles, the six million unemployed queueing at the soup kitchens, the ten million Germans who had turned in despair to Communism. Above all, the lasting harm that the Jews had done to Germany and to all Europe.

The Jews were the subject of all Neumann's niggling doubts.

A ticket collector's son from Wittenberg, south of Berlin, he had first found the Nazi ideology heady stuff – a prospect of grandeur, an escape from his father's peevish whining, from the steamy kitchen at 37 Heiligengasse, where his mother, her arms always damp and red with scrubbing, seemed to toil from morning to night.

At first in the 27th Troop of the Wittenberg Hitler Youth, Neumann had seen only the glory: that great day of the oath-taking, in the forest of Havel, when Baldur von Schirach, their leader, had arrived to address them in the Opel Käpitan bearing his grey and gold flag. On that day, hundreds of them, clasping the daggers engraved in gothic lettering *Treue bis auf dem Tod* (Faithful unto death) had sworn that fidelity to their Chancellor, Adolf Hitler.

In pursuit of that ideal, Neumann had gone on to tread a rougher road. The Holstein *Reichsnational Politische Schule* (Reich National Political Training College), with its harping on racial purity – "the Führer has said that the mixing of races was unacceptable" – had been heavy going at times, but it was nothing to the endurance tests that followed. Posted to Vogelsang Castle, near Aachen, where all the Nazi elite were trained, Neumann had mastered strange skills for a nineteen-year-old. He learned to overpower half-starved Alsatian dogs that had been trained to go for the throat, to break in wild Arab colts without using a saddle.

Before he was twenty he had learned to run a mile and a half, then wash in an icy stream. "Iron discipline. Perpetual obedience" ran the Party slogan, and to this end Neumann and the other cadets were ordered to forfeit half their meals for an entire month. On one visit of inspection Reinhard Heydrich, chief assistant to the S.S. *Reichsführer*, Heinrich Himmler, promised them "a war of liberation", but not all of them lived to fight it. Now the training had grown tougher still; they doubled to overcome strongpoints under a barrage of live ammunition. No man lived if he failed to dig a foxhole and burrow for shelter within twenty minutes; a Benz armoured car, advancing relentlessly, ground him into the mud. In one month the rate of accidental deaths rose to thirty-two.

But Neumann had survived it all; he was now a fully-fledged S.S. officer. One by one now the cadets were moving forward, mounting the steps of the tribunal to receive their brevets from the Commandant, *Sturmbannführer* (S.S. Major) Richard Schultze. To each man he murmured a word of congratulation, but Neumann barely heard. In his ears once again, there echoed the voice of Professor von Arensdorf, his mentor at the Berlin War Academy.

"It is our national duty, it is a matter of life and death, to exterminate the Jew. We must either strike him down or he will murder us . . ."

There lay the core of his doubt: the verb "exterminate". Neumann believed implicitly that Jews must be eliminated from certain professions. And never again should Jews gain control in matters vital to Germany.

But exterminate? Eliminate? Perhaps it was just a question of semantics, after all.

*

On Sunday, 30 March, more than 200 senior German commanders and their staff officers had assembled in the small panelled chamber of the Reichchancellery's Cabinet Room, settling themselves in gilded chairs bespoken from the nearby Propaganda Ministry. Hitler had summoned them, but nobody knew why. Promptly at 11 a.m. the audience rose smartly to their feet; the Führer had entered by a rear-door, making his way to the speaker's lectern mounted on a small rostrum.

It was a wide-ranging speech, which followed, lasting almost three hours; as Hitler broached topic after topic – Mussolini's misfortune in Libya, the iniquities of the Churchill clique, the partitioning of Yugoslavia – many a man found his attention wandering.

But interest quickened immediately when he switched to Operation Barbarossa. It was now, he confirmed, set for 22 June. "We have the chance to smash Russia while our own back is free," he avowed. "That chance will not return so soon. I would be betraying the future of the German people if I did not seize it now!"

His next words struck a vague chord of alarm; in many minds a warning bell rang, presaging the monstrous genocide to come. It would be a very different war from that fought in the west, Hitler warned them. Now it would be a clash of ideologies, shorn of chivalry. "The war against Russia will be such that it cannot be fought in a knightly fashion! This struggle . . . will have to be conducted with unprecedented, merciless and unrelenting harshness." In the East, cruelty now would be "kindness for the future". All Russian commissars instantly recognised by the red stars enclosing a golden hammer and sickle on their sleeves, were criminals and must be liquidated – "it is not our job to see that these criminals survive".

Did Hitler sense the instinctive repulsion felt by almost every man present? At all events, he tacitly acknowledged it. "I know the necessity of making war in such a manner is beyond the comprehension of you generals," he told them loftily, "but I cannot and will not change my orders and I insist that they be carried out with unquestioning and unconditional obedience."

"They sat there before him in stubborn silence," *Oberst* Walter Warlimont, of the Führer's Operations Department, recalled the scene later. "Otherwise not a hand moved and not a word was spoken but by him."

But no sooner had Hitler departed than many words were spoken, angry and embittered words that crowded to every man's lips. The honour of the German Army was at stake, and all of them knew it. Hemming in the Commander-in-Chief, *Feldmarschall* von Brauchitsch, they gave vent to a storm of protest, led by the three Army Group commanders on whom the invasion devolved, Gerd von Rundstedt, Fedor von Bock and Ritter von Leeb. What each man had envisaged as a legitimate theatre of war was now to become a vast laboratory, transforming the master plan of the Third Reich into nightmare reality.

At the Posen headquarters of Bock's Army Group Centre, his Chief of Staff, *Generalleutnant* Hans von Salmuth and his Operations Officer, *Generalmajor* Henning von Tresckow, pronounced the order "a disaster"; both men sought ways and means to "persuade at least the divisional commanders by word of mouth to try to circumvent the order". As Tresckow put it, "If international law is to be broken, let the Russians break it first and not us." The commander of the Thirty-Ninth Corps, General Rudolf Schmidt, called for the order to be rescinded; it was important "to show the Russian people that they had some hope for the future". The Seventeenth Armoured Division's *Generalmajor* Ritter von Thoma later admitted that no commissar captured by his division had ever been shot.

Since only twelve copies of the "Commissar Order" were transmitted, many commanders, like *Generalleutnant* Fritz Erich von Manstein, commanding 56 Panzer Corps, took the easy way out; they failed to pass the message down the chain of command. *Generaloberst* Heinz Guderian, leading Panzer Group Two, was barely aware the order existed, since Bock had never told him. "The Army High Command wants to turn professional soldiers into clergymen," was Hitler's angry reaction later.

But one group of men would know no such luxury of choice, for the oath of loyalty they had sworn placed obedience to Hitler's commands above God, above mercy, above humanity. Wherever killers were needed, 3,000 black-clad S.S. men on Russian soil would always fulfil this role.

Neumann did not know this.

*

It was the shortest night of that year, the summer solstice. Yet to many men the twilight hours of Saturday 21 June seemed the longest night of all their lives. Under the pale floodlight of a hunter's moon they waited, as hour followed hour, in fear and expectation.

Adolf Hitler, the impresario who was mounting this extravaganza, had adjourned as always after dinner to the salon of the Berlin Reichchancellery. It was a haven of deep easy chairs and shaded lights, and outwardly Hitler seemed calm and confident. His architect, Albert Speer, found that the Führer had even taken care of the musical effects, playing a few bars of Liszt's *Les Préludes* on the gramophone. "You'll hear that often in the near future, because it is going to be our victory fanfare for the Russian campaign."

Inwardly, he veered between total self-assurance and gnawing doubt. In a moment of frankness, he admitted: "We know absolutely nothing about Russia. It might be one big soap bubble, but it might just as well turn out to be very different." "A door opened before us," was how he described the suspense later, "and we didn't know what was behind it". In a letter to Mussolini, dictated on this day, he revealed something of the strain he had undergone: ". . . months of continuous nerveracking waiting are ending in the hardest decision of my life . . . I have . . . finally reached the decision to cut the noose before it can be drawn tight."

Along the 3,000-mile border stretching from Petsamo to the Black Sea, few Russians realised that the hour was at hand. Seventeen years of Stalinist oppression had stifled almost all initiative; even the most senior commanders were wary of interpreting signs and portents. Although 170 divisions were distributed throughout five military districts – Leningrad, Baltic, Western, Kiev, and Odessa – no emergency mobilisation had been permitted even now, in the hope of placating Hitler. In Moscow, the Chief Marshal of Artillery, Nikolai Voronov, had plucked up courage to raise the build-up of German troops with the Deputy People's Commissar of Defence, Marshal G. I. Kulik. But Kulik refused to discuss it: "This is big politics. It's not our business."

Other men were noting small signs that suggested trouble. General Ivan Rediuninsky, commanding the 15th Rifle Corps in the Kiev Military District, heard of the strange conduct of many German border sentries; until a week ago they had saluted Russian officers on sight, but now they churlishly turned their backs. In Sevastopol, headquarters of the Black Sea Fleet, Captain N. G. Rybalko, the officer of the day, was conscious of another disturbing factor. The three German freighters that plied the Black Sea had all withdrawn to Rumanian and Bulgarian ports.

At Minsk, Colonel I. T. Starinov, a mining expert, sat in on a phone call between the district commander, General Dmitri Pavlov, and an unknown informant. In a palpable effort to keep his temper in check, Pavlov kept repeating "I know it has been reported. I know. Those at the top know better than we. That's all!" Then he slammed down the receiver.

Earlier that day Pavlov had received an urgent message from Major-General V. E. Klimovskikh, his Chief of Staff, reporting, "From the woods, sound of engines." This, too, he had shrugged off; Pavlov was to pass this Saturday evening in a box at the Minsk Officer's Club, watching a popular comedy, *The Wedding at Malinovka.*

In the thicket of yellow government buildings and frescoed palaces that made up the Kremlin compound, a strange ambivalence prevailed. Towards 2 p.m. this day, General I. V. Tuilinev, commanding Moscow Military District, received a call from Stalin himself. The dictator told him: "Note that the situation is uneasy, and you should bring the troops of Moscow's anti-aircraft defence to 75 per cent of combat readiness."

Yet on this same afternoon, responding to a Tass news agency flash of 14 June that the war scare was "clumsy cooked-up propaganda", thousands of Russian soldiers were proceeding on leave – many of them to the Black Sea resort of Sochi.

On the German side of the border, there was uncertainty, too. If every man knew his objective and what was expected of him, there were still small last-minute qualms: Shall I be afraid? Supposing I am wounded? This last thought was especially prevalent in the 4th Company, Panzer Lehr Regiment, encamped in a dense pine forest at Pratulin, on the Polish bank of the River Bug. Although extra comforts had been issued – including a bottle of brandy for every four men – scarcely anyone touched a drop. In spite of sulfonamide, the spectre of a stomach wound haunted them.

Among those curious as to how he would comport himself in battle was *Assistenzart* (Assistant Surgeon) Heinrich Haape, medical officer of the 800-strong 3rd Battalion, Infantry Regiment 18, attached to the 6th Division of Bock's Army Group Centre. At 31, Haape was in the unique position of being both the battalion's oldest officer and the most junior member of the mess. In twelve months of Army life, he had witnessed some strange anomalies. Although a fully-qualified doctor on the staff of The Kaiser-Wilhelm Hospital, Duisburg, it was weeks before the Army had handed back his stethoscope and scalpel. First he must learn to dig a field-latrine and administer a bed-pan.

Now, in a camp near the Lithuanian border, Haape thought back to a question posed by his medical non-com *Oberfeldwebel* Wegener, "Do we have to give the Russians first aid too?" Haape had replied firmly, "We're not the judges, Wegener – our job is to help the wounded, Russians and Germans alike." It was a conviction that he held profoundly – and one that would be put sternly to the test in the months that lay ahead.

All along the moonlit frontier, men lay in hiding. For six nights now they had trailed like a parade of ghosts through the pale light, digging narrow anti-tank slits within sight of the border, retreating to quarters before dawn. Now at last they were ready. Some whiled away the last hours with a game of Skat. Others settled to last-minute chores – writing letters home, washing up their mess-tins, polishing their boots or the brass belt buckles inscribed *Gott mit uns*.

Some had travelled a long road already. In units like the *Leibstandarte* Adolf Hitler, every truck bore the likeness of the Parthenon painted in white lead on its bonnet, a proud record of past campaigns like a luggage label tacked on a suitcase. Others were wondering just how far this journey would take them. In the 3rd Battalion of the 39th Panzer Regiment, a curious non-com asked *Oberleutnant* Weidner: "What's it all about, *Herr-Leutnant*? Are we having a go at Ivan? Or are we driving through Russia to get to the Tommies in Iran?"

Many still recall how the rivers stank. In the damp June evening, the smell of silt permeated men's tunics and the manes of the baggage horses; the smell of the Black Sea shores was the mingled odour of attar of roses and horses' urine. But more than anything it was the small sounds that men remembered from that night. War correspondent Gunther Heysing, covering the front at Biala Podlaska for the *Berliner Borsenzeitung*, treasured the tinny resonance of a mouth organ solo of *Antje the Blonde*. *Gemeiner Soldat* Reinhold Pabel, an infantryman with the 6th Division, marvelled at a woman's soft voice from a far-off field, singing an Ukrainian folk song. To thousands more, the overture to battle would always be the deep plaintive night-long croaking of the bull frogs along the banks of the Bug.

At 11 p.m. an urgent code message was routed from Berlin to all commanders waiting in the East: "Dortmund, Mohn, Kresse, Aster, Aster." The die was cast; and the attack was on. Slowly, inexorably, the minutes ticked away, leaving three million men poised on the edge of eternity.

6

"We Have Only To Kick In The Door"

22 June–30 July, 1941

SOON AFTER MIDNIGHT, a train whistled mournfully. On the Fourth Army front, between Brest-Litovsk and Lomza, the sound came unexpectedly, fretting nerves already tense. Then, in the pale light, the locomotive was suddenly visible, shuffling over the frontier bridge from Russian to German territory: the international Moscow–Berlin express, a long freight train filled with grain clanking behind it. Josef Stalin was making his last delivery to his erstwhile ally, Adolf Hitler.

At 1 a.m. the move to battle stations began. The forces were advancing to their start-lines: 186 divisions, including 154 German, 14 Russian and 18 Finnish. Now was the time for each separate Army command to transmit its call-sign indicating full and final readiness – *"Wotan"* from Von Rundstedt's Army Group South, near Jassy, *"Kyffhäuser"* from *Feldmarschall* Gunther von Kluge's Fourth Army on the Bug. In their tents and office buses, the staff officers, bent over maps and written orders, conversed only in undertones.

The luminous minute-hands of their synchronised watches crawled slowly towards zero hour: 3.15 a.m.

Suddenly it was as if a master electrician had thrown a switch. One minute there was only absolute silence, then, along 3,000 miles of frontier, the order passed from post to post, "Troop, open fire!" Then the guns of Barbarossa spoke.

With an ear-splitting earth-shaking roar the front erupted in flame. More than 7,000 guns poured a storm of fire onto the Russian positions. On the Ninth Army front, north of the Pripet Marshes, crouching German troops saw the high wooden Russian watch towers collapse in shaking yellow flames. Dimly audible through the inferno came the frantic baying of frontier guard dogs.

Caught up in a kind of frenzy, men surpassed their own expectations. As the first salvoes screamed into space, *Oberleutnant* Zumpe, of 3rd Company, 135th Infantry Regiment, leaped from the ditch by the Brest–Litovsk railway embankment, with a frantic yell of "Let's go!" Steel helmets mushroomed from the tall grass behind him, and men raced like torch-bearers for the bridge. As they doubled along the high parapet,

125

the guns drowned out the clatter of boots on planking; one burst of sub-machine gun fire and the Soviet sentry toppled. Then Zumpe, sliding a green shield over the lens of his flashlight, waved it like a berserk stationmaster towards the German side of the bridge.

The first armoured scout cars jolted forward. It was 3.17 a.m., and far overhead the tail lights of the German fighters were winking towards the east, the first of more than 2,000 planes that would strike this day.

Not all crossed so easily as Zumpe. *Gemeine* Reinhold Pabel of the 6th Army, was only one of many infantrymen paddling for dear life across the Bug in a rubber dinghy, weighed down by light anti-tank guns and heavy machine guns. Behind them sappers set to work erecting pontoon bridges.

On the face of it, the assault plan was working to perfection. Von Leeb's Army Group North was forging from East Prussia towards Leningrad; Von Rundstedt's Army Group South driving for Kiev from Lublin; Von Bock's Army Group Centre advancing on either side of the Minsk–Smolensk–Moscow line. Through the stands of waving grain, stitched with purple mallows, through a glowing Van Gogh landscape of sunflower fields the grey legions of *Wehrmacht* and *Waffen* S.S. swept on. On this first day, surprise was total: 10,000 prisoners were taken, 1,200 aircraft destroyed on 66 Belorussian airfields.

Like a vast travelling workshop, the columns rolled on, trailing a pungent blue vapour of Panzer exhausts in their wake; streaking ahead of the streams of horse-drawn wagons came a steady chain of trucks, their drivers bawling peremptorily, "*Weg! Weg!*" (Make way). On the horizon, the rhythmic boom of guns pulsed like a giant piston. By the wayside, white acacia-wood crosses marked the graves of those who had fallen to snipers' bullets.

By order of the fanatical *Feldmarschall* Walter von Reichenau, every junior commander in Sixth Army was forced to inscribe the legend, "Pursuit without rest" above his mapboard – but it was the same on every front. Despite the choking clouds of yellow dust, the speed was relentless: a steady unwavering 22 miles a day on roads that were little more than rutted cart-tracks.

"Keep going, keep going," *Generalleutnant* Erich von Manstein exhorted his panzers. "Never mind about your flanks. Never mind about cover." Like other commanders, Manstein sensed that Russia could never be conquered and occupied: only bold incisive forays might overthrow the regime and paralyse its potential. Four days and five hours after zero hour, Manstein had completed a non-stop 200-mile dash through Russian territory.

Guderian, too, lancing for Smolensk, the gateway to Moscow, with Panzer Group Two, knew the same urgency. To combat a log-jam of traffic threatened by 87,000 vehicles, he set up a three-category priority system – with fighting men taking precedence over all. When the commander of the Herman Göring Luftwaffe Communications Regiment complained bitterly about his No 3 priority, Guderian asked tersely, "Can telegraph posts shoot?" When the man shook his head, Guderian retorted, "And that's why you'll keep No 3 priority."

The speed brought hardships in its wake. Now the Panzers were moving so fast, the supply wagons could not keep pace; one unit survived for three days on tinned tomatoes and mineral water. Some took to living off the land like old-time mercenaries. Helmut Pabst, and his 9th Army signals unit, after breakfasting, lunching and dining off dry bread, fell back on onions and turnips plucked from the fields and milk from peasants' churns.

Even top commanders enjoyed no mess privileges. "Heat, gnats, dust," Guderian wrote to his wife, Gretel. "I am missing my bath." Manstein hailed a roast chicken dinner as manna from heaven; his usual evening fare was smoked sausage and rye bread smeared with margarine.

But the pace could not continue. Slowly, even now, the Russians like a patient awakening from an anaesthetic, were taking the decisions that had to be taken to turn the tide.

*

In the Russian lines, total confusion had reigned. Nobody knew what was happening or what to do. At 11 p.m. on the Saturday, the Naval Commander-in-Chief, Admiral of the Fleet Nikolai Kuznetsov, was working late at his Moscow headquarters when Marshal Semeon Timoshenko, People's Commissar of Defence, telephoned abruptly. "There is very important news," he said. "Come to my office."

Along with his deputy, Rear Admiral Vladmir Alafuzov, Kuznetsov set off down Frunze Street, for a small building located opposite the Defence Commissariat. Climbing to the second floor, they found Timoshenko, a bald hard-eyed man of 46, in conclave with his Chief of Staff, General Georgi Zhukov. Though a breeze stirred the heavy magenta curtains, the heat was stifling; Zhukov, working on a pile of telegraph blanks, had his tunic unbuttoned.

Naming no sources, Timoshenko told the naval officers that an attack by Germany was now considered possible. The fleets must be ordered to combat readiness.

"In the event of attack, are they allowed to open fire?" Kuznetsov asked promptly. The appeasement tactics of recent months were still fresh in his mind.

Timoshenko said yes. "Run to headquarters," he told Admiral Alafuzov, "and send a telegram to the fleets immediately." Then, as Alafuzov hesitated, "Run!"

127

It was no time to stand on dignity. At a brisk jog-trot, Alafuzov set off up the sultry canyon of Frunze Street. It was already past midnight on 22 June.

Back in his office, Kuznetsov came to a decision: telegrams could take time, and time was pressing. Uncradling the phone, he called the commanders of the Baltic, Northern and Black Sea Fleets to pass on Timoshenko's message. Every man's reaction, he noted, was the same as his own: But can we open fire?

His task discharged, Kuznetsov stretched out on a leather divan, courting sleep. But already at 3 a.m. the yellow light of dawn filled the sky and sleep would not come. Then the phone rang shrilly, and answering Kuznetsov heard the excited voice of Vice Admiral Filip Oktyabrsky, the Black Sea Fleet commander.

"An air raid has been carried out against Sevastopol," he stammered. "Anti-aircraft is fighting off the attack!"

Oktyabrsky did not add that the Chief of the Fleet Anti-Aircraft Defence I. S. Zhilin, had been bitterly reluctant to comply. "Keep in mind that you bear full responsibility," he cautioned the Duty Officer, Captain Rybalko. "I am entering it in the combat operations log." Incensed at the shilly-shallying, Rybalko shouted, "Write what you want, but open fire on those planes."

In Moscow, others were proving harder to convince. At Naval Headquarters, Kuznetsov received an irate call from the Secretary of the Party's Central Committee, Georgi Malenkov: "Do you understand what you are reporting?"

"I understand," Kuznetsov replied patiently. "War has started."

The trouble was Malenkov did not believe a word of it. He at once called Sevastopol to check, only to hear Oktyabrsky assure him sharply, "Yes, yes, we are being bombed." At that moment, the Commander-in-Chief could scarcely hear Moscow; mammoth explosions were shaking the walls and windows of his room.

But already a virus of indecision had fatally infected the men whose rapid decisions were needed. Moscow's Military District Commander, General Tiulinev, looked in on Zhukov soon after 3.15 a.m. to see the Chief of Staff replacing his phone. "German aircraft are bombing Kovno, Rovno, Sevastopol and Odessa." Zhukov announced. Then he added, "We reported that to Stalin but he continues to regard it as a provocation by German generals."

To the men on the spot, the strange lethargy of the High Command was almost too frustrating to bear. One border unit signalled frantically, "We are being fired on. What shall we do?" Back from headquarters came a chilly rebuke: "You must be insane. And why is your signal not in code?"

At Bialystok, General Ivan Boldin, deputy commander of the Special Western Military District had no less than four agitated telephone calls from Marshal Timoshenko. Despite his earlier alerting of the fleets Timoshenko was now stressing that "no actions are to be taken against the Germans without our consent". Beside himself, Boldin shouted back, "Cities are burning, people are dying . . . Comrade Marshal, we must act . . . this is no provocation . . . the Germans have started a war!"

But it was not a war which Moscow acknowledged. The mining expert, Colonel Starinov, reached the town of Kobrin in a lull between air raids, hoping desperately for some bulletins from the Defence Commissariat. Instead he found the main square black with refugees piling into trucks, heedless of the loudspeakers blasting out Radio Moscow's 6 a.m. Keep-fit class: "Stretch your arms out, bend! Livelier! Up down, up down . . ."

A few men strove to restore order from chaos, but finite instructions were few. At Minsk, General Dmitri Pavlov, convinced that trouble threatened, did transmit the code-word GROZA – signifying full combat readiness – but many units never received the signal. Major-General Potaturchev, commanding the Soviet 4th Armoured Division, seeking orders from his superiors, was told mysteriously, "We've got to wait."

At 5 a.m., two hours after zero hour, an order did come – "Occupy envisaged positions" – but no military manoeuvre was thus implied. Instead, the division was to melt into the vast forest east of Bialystok and go into hiding. Seven days later, there was no division to hide; shot up by Stukas, picked off piecemeal by Panzers, the proud 4th Armoured was a scrapheap of smoking wreckage.

Those who looked to the Kremlin for leadership looked in vain. Although Stalin, on 6 May, had assumed the Premiership – with Vyaches-lav Molotov doubling as Deputy Premier and Foreign Commissar – the new Premier remained obstinately mute. At noon, on 22 June, it was Molotov's voice that Muscovites heard from rooftop loudspeakers all over the city: "Brothers and sisters, our cause is just. The enemy will be beaten. We shall triumph." Later Nikita Kruschev was to charge that for four days Stalin had retreated to his second-floor office, locking himself in and refusing to see anyone. A despairing cry burst from him: "All that Lenin created we have lost forever."

The first heads were swift to roll. Both Lieutenant-General P. V. Rychagov, Air Commander of the Baltic District, and Major-General A. A. Korobkov, Fourth Army commander, were ordered to Moscow and shot. Lieutenant-General Kopets, chief of the Soviet Bomber Command, escaped this fate only narrowly; faced with a loss of 800 bombers, he committed suicide on 23 June.

But as the beaten armies fell back, it was plain that more positive measures were needed to stop the rot.

On the baking hot afternoon of 27 June, the trans-Siberian express came to an unscheduled stop in the little railway station of Novosibirsk, 900 miles east of the Ural Mountains. Hastening along the train, the stationmaster and a military official at length located the special compartment of Lieutenant-General Andrei Eremenko. A squarely-built former Red Army N.C.O., Eremenko heard their message impassively: "Comrade General, the Defence Minister requests you to leave the train and continue your journey by air."

One day later, on the evening of 28 June, Eremenko was reporting to a cold and angry Timoshenko at the War Ministry. Timoshenko was succinct; the new arrival was to replace General Pavlov, as Commander-in-Chief of the Western Front. "What is the task of that front?" Eremenko asked precisely.

Timoshenko answered him in five words: "To stop the enemy advance."

*

It was the mining expert, Colonel Starinov, who saw the shape of things to come. On the day that he arrived in Minsk, General Pavlov and his principal commanders were taken out and shot. Now Starinov had come to render a report to one of the few senior staff officers who had kept his job.

But as he entered the man's office an extraordinary transformation took place. The man turned deathly white. His hands were shaking, and a nervous tic convulsed his entire face.

Suddenly he began to stammer pitiably, "I was with the troops . . . and I did everything . . . I am not guilty of anything . . ."

Wonderingly, Starinov now realised that the man was staring not at him but beyond his shoulder – to the two green-capped N.V.K.D. (secret police) officers who travelled with him to ensure his safe conduct from zone to zone.

That fear would dominate the whole campaign from this time on, Starinov realised. Any failure, any breach of duty, however unintentional, would always trigger the nightmare vision of a call from the men with the green caps.

*

At Hitler's headquarters, the news of the Russian defeats was received – for more reasons than one – with unrelieved delight.

As often with a major campaign, Hitler had relocated his headquarters staff close to the battle zone. At 2.45 p.m. on 23 June, a special train had borne them away from Berlin-Grünewald to the area designated Security Zone One – which Hitler called the *Wolfsschanze* (Wolf's Lair) – in the Forest of Görlitz, a few miles from Rastenburg, East Prussia.

It was a setting to daunt the stoutest heart: a huddle of wooden blockhouses, humming day and night with the rattle of electric ventilation, its every window facing north to humour the sun-hating Hitler. Invisible from the air, through camouflage netting suspended at tree-top height, the site was dotted with marshy ponds and stagnant mosquito-infested lakes – "a cross between a cloister and a concentration camp", was Jodl's dour summary. Silence reigned eternally, save for the gunshot crack of a breaking branch or a sudden explosion as a fox touched off a mine.

Every man thus had high hopes that his sojourn here would be brief. At first, such hopes seemed feasible. "We have only to kick in the door," Hitler had summed up the Russian enterprise to Jodl, "and the whole rotten structure will come crushing down!" His generals, so dubious regarding the 1940 campaign in the west, now saw the Führer as near-infallible. On Sunday, 29 June, they had ample proof; twelve Special Announcements, or victory bulletins, were broadcast every fifteen minutes of the day, preceded by a blast of trumpets and Hitler's chosen Liszt prelude – "Like a county fair side-show", one listener commented in disgust.

It was Hitler who had insisted on a whole week of waiting to maximise the impact, despite Göbbels' sarcastic comment, "If the announcements are held up much longer the public will think the troops have reached the Indian frontier."

But such was Hitler's initial euphoria that his staff was carried on the floodtide. Certainly the Führer could have no doubts as to the outcome, for he had despatched a special engineer team to blow up the Kremlin. Then, too, there was his forward-looking approach in allotting "Oil Brigades" to each army group, special detachments to exploit the first oil-rich territory captured – even though the units would have to cover the 1,400 miles between the frontier and Baku on the Caspian Sea before winter approached. "It would probably be no exaggeration," Halder noted in his diary, "to say that the campaign against Russia has been won in the first fortnight."

To Hitler's architect, Albert Speer, this seemed no less than the truth. Already, in anticipation of victory Hitler had extended his list of German cities slated for reconstruction to twenty-seven – and contracts to the value of thirty million Reichsmarks had been awarded to granite companies in six different countries. Barely three weeks before Barbarossa was launched, Hitler had founded his own transport fleet and set up shipyards in Berlin and Wismar – with plans to build 1,000 cargo boats to transport the granite on order.

And didn't it seem likely, the generals reasoned, that the British would at last see sense? Hitler, at any rate, had made it plain that all western Europe could be theirs in return for a free hand in the east. On 22 June, the German Ambassador in Ankara, the canny Franz von Papen, had put this proposition through a novel intermediary, the Turkish Foreign Minister, Sükrü Saracoglu – who passed it on, as intended, to the British Ambassador, Sir Hughe Knatchbull-Hugessen.

But there was one essential proviso: neither Great Britain nor the United States should associate themselves with Russia in the war that had now begun.

"Do you mean that they should not contract a marriage?" Saracoglu asked.

"That is my meaning," von Papen replied, primly.

*

"When Barbarossa begins," Hitler had predicted as far back as February, "the world will hold its breath and make no comment." It was strangely wishful thinking. Before 22 June had run its course, the world was commenting as never before since World War Two began.

Anthony Eden, weekending at Chequers, always associated Barbarossa with the most unpalatable before-breakfast gift he had ever received: a mammoth Cuban cigar on a silver salver presented at 7.30 a.m. by Churchill's valet, Sawyers. "The Prime Minister's compliments and the German armies have invaded Russia." ("We savoured the relief," Eden related, "but not for me at that hour the cigar.") Within the day, Churchill was broadcasting to the nation a statement in part reprinted by *Pravda*: "No one has been a more consistent opponent of communism than I . . . I will unsay no word that I have spoken about it. But all this fades away before the spectacle which is now unfolding . . . Any man or state which fights on against Nazidom will have our aid . . . we shall give whatever help we can to Russia and the Russian people."

Even in the Axis camp, many were aghast at the news. Benito Mussolini, awoken at 3 a.m. in his bedroom at Villa Mussolini, on the Adriatic Coast at Riccione, had the word from his son-in-law, Count Ciano, calling from Rome: Hitler's letter had yet to reach him. His black eyes squinting against the harsh light of the bed lamp, the Duce told his wife matter-of-factly: "My dear Rachele, that means we've lost the war."

An implacable anti-Communist like Pope Pius XII, in Vatican City, might hail the war as a crusade, "high-minded gallantry in defence of the foundations of Christian culture," but most Italians shared the Duce's view, notably his Minister of Currency and Exchange, Raffaele Riccardi. "At this stage of affairs," Riccardi recorded sourly, "the one thing that might yet surprise me would be finding a pregnant man."

Some saw the widening of the combat, like Churchill himself, in terms of sorely-needed reinforcements. In Algiers, General Maxime Weygand, the Commander-in-Chief, French North Africa, had long looked askance at the faith of the State Department's Robert Murphy: if Britain would win in the end, as Murphy believed, who would furnish the extra divisions? On that day, summoning Murphy to his villa, the excited Weygand told him: "Now I know where they will come from – Russia!"

Others, long opposed to the conflict, knew a change of heart. Along with Herbert Agar and Dorothy Parker, fellow interventionists, the playwright Robert Sherwood arrived to address a Fight for Freedom Rally at the Golden Gate Ballroom on Lenox Avenue, Harlem. Outside the usual pickets jeered and taunted them, brandishing Communist-inspired banners that proclaimed them "tools of British and Wall Street Imperialism". Ninety minutes later, they had vanished; word had reached the picket line that it was now a workers' war, too.

A few were openly sceptical. At a party given by his Ministry of Propaganda that Sunday afternoon, Dr Josef Göbbels reiterated his prophecy that it would be an eight-week campaign at most. Turning to the film star, Olga Tschechowa, Chekhov's niece, he said, "We have a Russian expert here. Will we be in Moscow by Christmas?" Irked by his manner, the actress replied, "You know Russia, the endless land. Even Napoleon had to retreat." Ten minutes later, an adjutant approached her. "I imagine, madame, you are ready to leave. The car is outside."

At the British Embassy, Moscow, it was close to midnight on 22 June. Harold Elvin had just set off on the first of his nightly patrols when Fedor, the porter, came hastening after him. An anonymous Russian was on the phone with a strange request; he wanted to speak to an Englishman – any Englishman. As the only staff member on duty, Elvin accepted the call.

"We fight together, I think?" were the unknown's first anxious words, and in this moment Elvin felt curiously moved: a man whose face he would never see was seeking reassurance, a sense of comradeship, in a world that was disintegrating before his eyes.

"Yes, I think so," he replied, trying to infuse his voice with confidence, but the Russian was too disturbed, or knew too little English, to carry the conversation further. "I shake your hand," was all he said before ringing off.

*

But across the world many men and women had grave misgivings. A compact with Russia seemed as incompatible as a working agreement with Hitler: could the free world consciously opt for a choice of tyrannies? A London businesswoman, Hilda Neal, summed up in her diary what thousands, perhaps millions, felt: "I want no alliance with a nation steeped in blood."

Those like her were thunderstruck by Churchill's emotional impulsive pledge. Franco's ambassador in London, the Duke of Alba, reported to Madrid a rumour that *The Times*, at the eleventh hour, had had to scrap a leader attacking a Russian alliance after hearing the Premier's broadcast. There was not, and never could be, an alliance, Eden took pains to reassure Alba, but ordinary citizens were sceptical. When the Reverend Philip Russell, vicar of Lythe, near Whitby, Yorkshire, called for prayers for Russia from the pulpit, his cousin, Nurse Kathleen Phipps, mused, "Philip is nothing if not up-to-date." But back at her hospital, the matron set her firmly to rights: "Stalin is not a nice person, Nurse – one has to be very careful these days."

Many shared these sentiments. Sir Stafford Cripps might urge from Moscow, "We must not try and play too safe on information if we want the Russians to fight our battles all out," but others saw the connection as anathema. On 8 July, when the first Russian trade mission arrived at London's Euston Station, the Vice Chief of the Imperial General Staff, Lieutenant-General Sir Henry Pownall, warned his adjutant: "Don't let any of those photographers take me shaking hands with the Russian general." At a private dinner party, the new Minister of Aircraft Production, Lieutenant Colonel John Moore-Brabazon, expressed a hope trade unionists were swift to condemn once the news leaked out: let the Russians and Germans destroy one another while the British Commonwealth built up her forces. In the United States, Senator Harry Truman of Missouri struck a similar note: "If we see that Germany is winning we ought to help Russia and if Russia is winning we ought to help Germany and that way let them kill as many as possible . . ."

Roosevelt, as so often happened, was content to let Churchill take the lead. Cautious and oblique as always, he went no farther than to unfreeze Soviet dollar funds, thus enabling them to buy weapons, at the same time declaring that the Neutrality Act would not be invoked against Russia, thus permitting American shipping to enter ports like Vladivostok. For the rest he was content to await the Russians' shopping list and on 8 July he got it: a staggering two billion dollars worth of requirements, including 3,000 pursuit planes and 3,000 bombers.

The concept outraged as many Americans as it pleased. Ex-President Herbert Hoover proclaimed: "It makes the whole argument of joining the war to bring the Four Freedoms a gargantuan jest." The *New Republic* columnist John T. Flynn, demanded: "Are we fighting to make Europe safe for Communism?" Others scoffed at "Packages for Petrograd" or what wits called "Lenin-Lease"; the *Wall Street Journal* stated frankly: "The principal difference between Mr Hitler and Mr Stalin is the size of their respective moustaches." The isolationist Congressman Hamilton Fish proposed – not entirely in jest – that Roosevelt should invite Stalin to Washington, to have him baptised in the White House pool.

Then, as later, Roosevelt was curiously impervious to Russia's potential for evil. "Dear Bill," he wrote to Leahy in Vichy on 26 June,

134

". . . Now comes the Russian diversion. If it is more than just that it will mean the liberation of Europe from Nazi domination . . . I do not think we need worry about any possibility of Russian domination." As a former Ambassador to the Soviet Union, William C. Bullitt did give the President clear warning of Soviet imperialism, but Roosevelt would have none of it. "I think if I give him (Stalin) everything I possibly can and ask nothing from him in return, *noblesse oblige*, he won't try to annex anything." In vain Bullitt pointed out that "when he talked of *noblesse oblige* he was not speaking of the Duke of Norfolk but of a Caucasian bandit whose only thought when he got something for nothing was that the other fellow was an ass".

Hopkins, who flew to Moscow on 30 July for two meetings with Stalin, backed the President's judgement. "Give us anti-aircraft guns and the aluminium and we can fight for three or four years," the dictator told him confidently, giving the impression of "talking to a perfectly co-ordinated machine, an intelligent machine". "I would hardly call Uncle Joe a pleasant man, although he was interesting enough," he wrote to Ismay later, "and I think I got what I wanted but you never can be sure about that. . . ."

In the end the priorities of *realpolitik* prevailed. If the first job was the extirpation of Hitler, then Russia must be aided, and few interventionists then saw Soviet power as a threat to the Western democracies. Even hitherto isolationist journals were united on that score. "The two English-speaking nations," prophesied the St Louis *Post-Dispatch*, "will exercise the decisive voices at the peace table." "An awakened democracy," thought the Dallas *Morning News*, "will now take steps after Hitler is beaten to make sure that the Russian brand of political communism stays home."

As Oscar Cox, of the Office of Emergency Management's Division of Defence Aid, summed up in a memo to Hopkins: "Our main objective in spending billions on defence is to see to it that Hitler does not rule the world – including us." It was left to Assistant Secretary of State Adolf A. Berle, on the eve of Hopkins' departure for Moscow, to view this new and uneasy alliance clear-sightedly.

"The Russian hatred of Britain," he minuted Hopkins, "is if possible more deeply implanted than the Russian hatred of Germany, though Fate puts them on the same side for the moment.

"Eastern Europe is looking out for itself: not for the British or for us. We can be of help to one another now . . . but we cannot bet our whole shirt on the continuance of the relationship."

He ended on a bleak note of caution: "Therefore, for God's sake, tell the sentimentalists to watch themselves."

*

135

Benito Mussolini summed it up as aptly as any man: "This war has now assumed the character of a war between two worlds."

The Duce spoke the truth. On 22 June, the one military enigma remaining was Japan. Thousands who had stood on the sidelines until this moment were now rallying to Hitler as the great anti-Bolshevik crusader. "The destruction of Russian communism is now inevitable," General Francisco Franco, who had wanted no part of the war, told the American Ambassador, Alexander Weddell, and to hasten its end he offered a volunteer force of 18,000 strong to fight on the Russian front, the famous Blue Division under General Múñoz Grandes. On 27 June, after planes with Russian markings had bombed the frontier town of Kassa – allegedly a plot cooked up between the German Air Attaché in Budapest and the Hungarian General Staff – the Regent, Admiral Nicholas Horthy, weighed in with ten divisions.

General Ion Antonescu, chief of Rumania's fascist "Iron Guard" had been delighted to enter the fray. "Of course, I'll be there from the start," he told Hitler, after promises of Bessarabia and other territory, "When it's a question of action against the Slavs you can always count on Rumania."

Although Europe's two staunchest neutrals – Switzerland and Turkey – stayed staunchly neutral, others felt too keenly to remain uninvolved. Denmark severed relations with Moscow, like Vichy France, closed down its one communist newspaper and rounded up all known Reds: soon the Regiment Nordland, made up of Danish, Dutch and Norwegian Nazis, took their place on the Finnish front, along with Regiment Westland, sympathisers from Belgium and Holland, augmenting eighteen Finnish divisions. Sweden, while walking a tightrope of neutrality, still yielded to pressure; on 25 June, the *Riksdag* in Stockholm sanctioned the passage of the *Wehrmacht*'s Engelbrecht Division from Norway across Swedish soil to the front in Finland.

The strangest participant was Italy. Despite his instinctive reaction that the war was lost, Mussolini never ceased in his attempts to transform the volatile Italians into a nation of scowling humourless warriors. Although Hitler had not asked for troops, Italian honour – which Mussolini equated with his own – demanded that they should be made available. Promptly he offered four divisions three of infantry, one of cavalry – plus ninety planes lacking an anti-freeze system.

Outfitted with the same summer uniforms and cardboard shoes that had served them in the French campaign of 1940, these troops were to die cursing their Duce in temperatures 36° below zero. But Mussolini's ego was mortally wounded that Rommel's men had redressed the balance in Libya, so go they must.

To flaunt his unity with the *Wehrmacht*, Mussolini reviewed his Russian Expeditionary Force at Verona accompanied by only one man –

General Enno von Rintelen, the tall aquiline Military Attaché in Rome. As the Duce took the salute, bolt upright in his car, the German in the back seat struggled with conflicting emotions – pity for the marching men in their threadbare uniforms, the slap of their broken shoes on the stone flags drowned only by the drum-beat, and amazement that any man as intelligent as Mussolini could so delude himself.

As the last contingent, to a fanfare of brass, wheeled towards the waiting troop trains in Verona Station, the Duce turned to von Rintelen, his eyes misty. "There," he told the speechless General, "go the finest troops in the world."

*

Whatever their nationality, these men had one factor in common: a determination that Communism must be destroyed root and branch. *Fähnrich* Peter Neumann, by contrast, a youngster trained to kill, was still beset by fear and indecision.

After the passing-out parade at Bad Tölz, Neumann had been posted overnight – to the headquarters staff of the *Standartenführer* (S.S. Colonel) of the Nordland Regiment, attached to the 5th Waffen S.S. (Viking) Division. At Lublin, he found the regiment already on the move; tank engines were revving up, whistle blasts and orders echoed all over the courtyard of the old Polish barracks. All night the sky throbbed with the droning of Dorniers, Focke-Wulfs and Stukas, wave after wave of them flying eastward.

A little before noon on 28 June, *Standartenführer* Willi Schleyer called his officers together in a large draughty hangar for a final briefing. "Gentlemen," he told them, his voice low-pitched and serious, "we advance on Kremenetz. We move off at dawn tomorrow." From the large plan spread on the floor before him he made the position plain: attached to *Generaloberst* Ewald von Kleist's right wing they would advance east-south-east as a unit of Rundstedt's Army Group South.

Schleyer paused then, as if to gauge their reactions. Then, eyeing them fixedly, he announced, "We have also received special instructions concerning the Russian People's Commissars, captured in action or arrested in the occupied territory. In no case are we authorised to take them prisoner. The order is explicit! They must be killed at once. . . ."

Attempting a smile, he made a vague gesture with his hand. "That's all, gentlemen."

It came home to Neumann that all the derring-do manoeuvres of the past years were over. He was in the S.S. and the S.S. was at war.

Yet on the following days, as the division swept forward towards the vast Ukrainian granary, Neumann knew no fear – only a strange exhilaration. Through Wisnia, its blackened buildings "hollow and empty as stage

137

sets", they passed on to open country, through charred wheatfields and abandoned farms, suffocated by the smell of hot oil and petrol, the dust forming a hard thick mask on their hands and faces.

Suddenly the leading tank formations ground to a halt, their guns belching fire. The cry rang out *"Kampf Verband! Los, Los!"* ("Battle formation, at the double!") Almost before he realised it, Neumann had jumped from his armoured T.C.V. (troop-carrying vehicle) and was racing into action behind a group of anti-tank gunners.

Ahead of them, Russians were doubling in short sudden spurts, trying not to be seen in the forest glades, and Neumann, his finger on the trigger of his machine-pistol, emptied a whole magazine in their wake. The manoeuvres at Vogelsang came vividly back to him, and he, too, ran in short bursts, dropping flat every few yards. Dimly he glimpsed a group of panzer grenadiers staring at him dumbfounded: an ensign racing into battle, yelling like a simple private.

Now the Russians were giving up: fifteen of them had risen from the ground, casting their rifles far from them, raising their hands in surrender. A hail of bullets cut them down like saplings.

Neumann stood rooted to the spot. Something had now gone very much awry. They were prisoners, weren't they, prisoners who had surrendered?

But he had not been afraid. He had seen a man take aim at him, fired first, and seen his adversary's head burst open. It was him or me, Neumann thought, the first man I ever killed, but I was not afraid.

Standartenführer Schleyer was fatherly: "Seems you got on all right in your first skirmish . . . carry on the good work and we may make something of you yet." His best friend, *Fähnrich* Franz Hättenschwiller, ribbed him mercilessly, but there was no mistaking the pride in his voice: "Running hell-for-leather to get his head shot off at the first sound of gunfire! For God's sake, man, you should have kept down. It wasn't your job to run after the Russkis like a greyhound!"

Secretly pleased, Neumann mumbled: "I saw everybody jumping out from the trucks . . . I thought the Reds were making a mass attack."

Next day, 30 June, in a small village outside Lwow, he was more frightened than he had ever been.

On this Monday morning, Neumann was attached to *Untersturmführer* (S.S. Second-Lieutenant) Scholtzberg, commanding the light corps of panzer grenadiers; as a new boy, he must become familiar with different forms of combat. But a determined Russian resistance, backed by a heavy Voroshilov 12 mm machine gun aimed from a second-storey window, stalled their advance. Calling a halt, Scholtzberg had just sent for two tanks to winkle the Russians out when an S.S. man doubled up.

"Sir, we've caught about ten Bolsheviks and two of them are civilians. What'll we do with them, sir?" Scholtzberg ordered, "Bring them here."

1a Harold Elvin in Moscow

1b Major James Devereux, defender of Wake Island

1c Ruth Mitchell

1d Andrée de Jongh in 1941

2a Aircraftman Marcel-Gerard Comeau survivor of Greece and Crete

2b Dr Heinrich Haape on the Russian Front

Invasion of Crete. The second wave of German parachutists descending and grouping on the ground

3b Evacuation of Greece. Weary Tommies asleep on board a troopship

3c Bombing of allied shipping in Suda Bay, Crete

4a President Roosevelt and Churchill (seated left) at a service on board
HMS *Prince of Wales* in August

4b Harry Hopkins and Sir Alexander Cadogan on board HMS *Prince of Wales*

5a General Catroux, General Le Gentilhomme and their Staff entering Damascus through deserted streets on 26 June

5b General de Gaulle inspecting a Guard of Honour of Free French at Beirut on 29 July

6a As the *Prince of Wales* sinks the crew scramble aboard HMS *Express*

6b The wreckage of the Messersch 110 fighter plane in which Ru Hess flew to Scot

6c Lord Beaverbrook

7a Field-Marshal Rommel

7b Australians in the caves where they lived in Tobruk

8a HMS *Hood* blown up off Greenland, as seen from the *Prinz Eugen*

8b Yosuke Matsuoka, Japanese Foreign Minister, returning from his visit to Europe

8c Marshal Tito

9a The siege of Leningrad. Nevsky Prospekt during shelling

9b Lake Ladoga road of life

10a General Guderian at an airfield on the Russian Front briefing his staff

10b Marshal Timoshenko

10c General Zhukov

11a Russian peasants fleeing before the German advance on Moscow

11b General Dovator's cavalry units on their way to defend Moscow

12a Russian Front: a German tank rumbles over a slit trench with Russians cowering underneath

12b Red Army men dislodging Germans from a village

13a General Douglas MacArthur

13b American and Philippine troops surrender to the Japanese at Bataan

14a The crematoria at Buchenwald concentration camp in which the corpses of those gassed, at the rate of 2,000 an hour, were burned

14b Lager Nordhausen camp where the bodies of hundreds of former slave workers were discovered by the U.S. army in 1945

15a USS *California* sinking after the Japanese attack on Pearl Harbor

15b The wreckage at the Naval Air Station, Pearl Harbor

16 British troops marching along the road to Cyrene with the ancient town behind them

They were the first Russians Neumann had ever seen at close quarters, all of them bearded, with shaven heads and waxy skins. The two civilians wore gold stars on their sleeves: Commissars. Then Scholtzberg caught his eye and nodded. "They're all yours, Neumann! You deal with them."

Sweat was suddenly coursing down his body, as if he stood naked in a shower bath. They had to be shot, *Standartenführer* Schleyer had said so, but not by him, please God not by him.

Scholtzberg was understanding. "You'd rather not? Relax, Neumann. Libesis will handle this little formality!" He signed to *Rottenführer* (S.S. Lance-Corporal) Libesis, a cheerful Tyrolean peasant who had twice won the Iron Cross in battle, and Libesis quietly, casually, as if he had all the time in the world, approached the Commissars.

"*Narodnii Komissar li voui?*" ("You are a People's Commissar?"), he asked each man.

"*Da. Potchemo?*" ("Yes. Why?") they replied, surprised.

With agonising slowness, Neumann saw Libesis take his Mauser from his holster, loading it before the Russians' eyes. Then he aimed at each shaven head in turn, squeezing the trigger.

Suddenly there were no more People's Commissars at all. Neumann stood quite still, not moving, not speaking. Later it struck him that he never again saw the eight Red Army prisoners.

At least, he thought dully, they had been spared the tortures of a long captivity.

*

On Army Group Centre's front, driving hard for the River Memel across the Lithuanian plains, *Assistenzart* Heinrich Haape had also discovered that it was a war which gave no quarter.

Haape would never forget the trauma of his first two days in the field. In a hollow near an old farmhouse he had found the still warm bodies of six men: a medical officer from another battalion, clutching a blood-stained Red Cross flag, his stretcher bearer and four patients. A horrified eye-witness filled in the details: the doctor had been treating the men when the Russians opened fire on the hollow, and at once he had leaped up, waving the flag frantically, but still the Russians had fired and kept on firing until nothing moved.

Haape was silent for a long time, then abruptly he tore off his Red Cross armband. "It means nothing to the Russians," he said bitterly. "There's no Geneva Convention here. I'm a soldier like the rest of you now."

It was all a far cry from the Kaiser-Wilhelm Hospital, Duisberg. In brief moments of respite, Haape tried to capture the flavour of his new life in letters to his fiancée, the opera singer, Martha Arazym. Jolting up and down the columns, sometimes in his Mercedes, sometimes on horse-back, a doctor ate on the march, as and when he could, mostly goulash and peas from the field kitchens – "Never pass up a goulash cannon," was the sage advice of the Regimental commander, *Oberst* Becker.

Each day brought problems that a civilian doctor never remotely encountered. The battalion crossed the Memel without a single casualty, but next day the march was slowed to a crawl. Eight hundred men who had bathed their burning feet in the river, were hobbling on cruelly blistered soles.

Haape's next battalion order had a novel ring: unless no marching was envisaged for twenty-four hours all soldiers were forbidden to wash or bathe their feet. "Instead . . . it is recommended that the feet be rubbed with dripping or deer fat." The battalion would stink to high heaven from this time on – but at least they would march unimpeded.

How did you stop soldiers drinking from peasants' wells, thus risking dysentery? It was Haape's orderly, *Gefreiter* Mühler, who solved this problem: a subtle rumour was passed through the ranks that the Russians were poisoning the water. The first two dozen men who fell in for "treatment" were promptly dosed with charcoal and castor oil. After that they gave the wells a wide berth.

Week by week, as the battalion moved on through stifling dust, Haape grappled with fresh problems. Bitter experience taught him to forbid a morsel of food for six hours before a major battle: even one slice of bread caused extra blood to flow to the intestines, increasing the risk of internal haemorrhage in the event of a stomach wound. He saw to it that every man had a green camouflaged mosquito net; no fighting soldier could give of his best after a night of torment from the vicious Pripet Marsh gnats they nicknamed "Stukas".

"Everyone has to be a soldier here," Haape argued, when his courage was praised, but the 3rd Battalion saw him as "a real fighting man's doctor". On 14 July, when the battle of Gomely loomed, Haape left his stationary casualty post in the rear, moving up with one orderly to set up a dressing station in a foxhole on the battlefield itself. There, in the nine hours that it took the battalion to pierce the 1,100-mile long Stalin Line, a ribbon of redoubts stretching east of the Pripet Marshes, Haape, armed with a small Braun-Melsungen blood transfusion apparatus, saved many lives.

That night, along with *Leutnant* Jakobi, of the battalion's 12th Company, Haape drank a solemn toast in captured vodka: "Here's to the liberation of Russia and Christmas in the Kremlin!"

"I don't want to be a soldier," Haape confided. "I'd go home and marry Martha tomorrow." For both men had the feeling that night that the war might soon be over. Moscow, they knew, was "just over the horizon" – some 300 miles north-west.

Then, on 30 July, a million men heard a near-incredible order: "Prepare for defensive positions." From Velikiye Luki southwards to Roslavi, 400 miles of line became static. Panzers, motorised units, pioneers, artillery, infantry – all were frozen in their tracks.

It was then that Haape took thought of Hitler's lowly combatant status in World War One – "The corporal's wand waved over Army Group Centre and turned it to stone".

*

In the barracks and blockhouses of the *Wolfsschanze*, there was consternation. Barbarossa was barely five weeks old, and Adolf Hitler had twice seen fit to meddle with his generals' strategy. The results were to prove catastrophic.

As early as 26 June, 56 Panzer Group's bold 200-mile dash to the town of Daugavapils had paid off; all Manstein's instinct now was to forge on towards Leningrad. Plainly, with the Russians hopelessly confused, the thrust cried out for exploitation. But Hitler, as so often in a campaign's early stages, felt his confidence ebbing. He ordered Manstein to stand fast until the infantry caught up with him.

"This was certainly the 'safe' staff college solution," Manstein acknowledged later, but equally it destroyed all element of surprise. In the six days that Manstein was halted, General Fedor Kuznetzov, commanding the Special Baltic Military District, was working day and night to plug the breach, hurling in reserves from Minsk, Moscow, Pskov. Unwittingly Hitler had helped Leningrad to buy time.

"Perpetual interference by the Führer . . . is becoming a scourge which will eventually be intolerable," Halder noted in his diary on 14 June; on 28 June, he wrote despairingly, "He's playing warlord again," and with reason. On 30 June, overruling Halder and Brauchitsch, Hitler switched priorities. Both men agreed with Bock and Guderian that Moscow was probably within their grasp, and with it decisive victory. Hitler disagreed: Moscow could wait. Instead Guderian was to be diverted south, to aid Rundstedt's Army Group secure the fertile land of the Ukraine, Panzer Group Three, under *Generaloberst* Hermann Hoth was moved up to help Leeb's Army Group North subdue Leningrad, the cradle of Bolshevism.

For Hitler, as his closest associates saw, was racked by doubts. On 27 June, he made a sober admission to Ribbentrop, who was paying a visit: "If I had had the slightest inkling of this gigantic Red Army assemblage I would never have taken the decision to attack."

What had gone wrong? As Hitler was to admit to Mussolini, "for the first time since the beginning of the conflict, the German military intelligence had failed". Overweening confidence that Russia would crumble – "this clay colossus with a head", Hitler had sneered – had resulted in a

141

woeful lack of planning and preparation. As a result, no winter clothing had been allotted for the troops, only three months supply of fuel was scheduled for the advancing armies, and fully a third of Germany's divisions remained in the west.

The reassuring reports of Hans Krebs, the Military Attaché in Moscow, that Russia was twenty years behind the times had helped foster this illusion, but Krebs was a young man on the make, adept at telling Hitler what he wanted to hear.

To be sure, the reconnaissance planes of *Oberst* Theodor Rowehl's Special Purposes Squadron had violated Russian air space scores of times, flying as low as 2,600 feet, their cameras turning over. But even diamond-clear prints could not reveal the existence of the Russians' T-34 tank, which was now taking the field, a 27 tonner whose armour plating was impervious to everything save the Flak 88s Rommel had employed at Halfaya. Nor could photographs reveal that the Soviet Air Force had in excess of 8,000 aircraft or the astonishing rate at which Soviet industry was churning out replacements.

Even in mid-July, when Germany had knocked out 8,000 Russian tanks, they still came on, a lumbering non-stop chain; by 30 July, this figure had been upped to 12,000 but still they came. As with the tanks, so with the men. "At the start of this war, we reckoned with about 200 enemy divisions," Halder noted. "So far we have already counted 360."

On 4 August, visiting Army Group Centre, Hitler was to let fall an admission that for the first time gave the men in the field a hint of things to come. "Had I known they had as many tanks as that," he told Bock and Guderian ruefully, "I'd have thought twice before invading."

*

In the Officers' Mess of No 82 (Blenheim) Squadron, R.A.F. Bomber Command, they remembered him as "Ten Minute" Jenkins. It was an obituary of a kind: he had been posted to the squadron and taken off from Bodney, in Norfolk, on his first operational flight. Ten minutes after crossing the Belgian coast he was dead.

It remained a record, even among the seventeen squadrons of Bomber Command, but only marginally. As the summer of 1941 wore on, no bomber crew, for the best of reasons, could precisely define a tour of operations: no one had ever completed one.

The losses were inextricably linked with Marshal Timoshenko's frantic efforts to turn the German floodtide in Russia. As early as 27 June, Ivan Maisky, the bearded irrepressible little Russian Ambassador, had urged the creation of a Second Front on a notably receptive Lord Beaverbrook – and been as coldly rebuked by Eden. The idea had been Maisky's own, but by 18 July Stalin had taken up the cudgels. What he sought from

Churchill was primarily an offensive in Northern France to divert Hitler's armies from the east – or, failing this, twenty-five to thirty British divisions to fight on the Russian front.

They were demands that Churchill was powerless to meet – yet it was vital to convince both Stalin and Roosevelt that Britain was still in earnest. In Washington, as Hopkins told Churchill frankly on 24 July, criticisms of Britain now had a cutting edge. To most Americans, the Premier's preoccupation with the Middle East smacked of "colonialism" – "The American public had never heard of Benghazi and were really not quite sure whether the Nile flows north or south." The British, many felt, were resting on their laurels; of the 43 per cent of Britons who welcomed the Russian attack, Mass Observation reported many as complacent – "It will keep Germany busy and give us a rest," or "A good thing somebody else is carrying the baby."

Such sentiments were reported from as far away as the Balkans; from Budapest, Roosevelt's Minister, Herbert Pell, relayed the belief that "they (the British) are seizing the opportunity of a temporarily distracted German attention to take tea and go on weekends while someone else fights for them".

To counter such rumours, Churchill and his Cabinet saw only one answer: a non-stop offensive by the 500 aircraft of Bomber Command, backstopped by Lend-Lease supplies. "Our entire hope of building up a decisive margin of hitting power . . . rests on the achievements of a great expansion of heavy bomber output in the United States," the Secretary of State for Air, Sinclair, wrote to Hopkins. ". . . anything that can be done to secure additional releases of B17s and B24s now would have a direct effect on our ability to hit German and Italian targets . . ."

But overnight the British found the honeymoon was over; from now on they must take their place in the queue. Priority on Lend-Lease goods, Averell Harriman explained firmly, was a thing of the past; as a frontline combatant, Russia would claim her fair share of what U.S. aid was available. In Washington, the Russian Ambassador, Constantin Oumansky, put it more bluntly: the Russians were doing "ninety per cent of the fighting and should get ninety per cent of the stuff".

Even so, a showing must be made, and the onus rested squarely on Bomber Command. "My bombing offensive is not a gamble," Portal declared, as Chief of Air Staff. "Its dividend is certain; it is a gilt-edged investment." But as the five-man crews of Bomber Command soon discovered, the most certain dividend was death.

Day after day, through June and July, the gallant suicidal sorties continued. On 4 July, Wing Commander Hughie Edwards, a 27-year-old Australian, led 15 Blenheims from 105 and 107 Squadrons in loose vics of three from the Norfolk coast, skimming low over the water towards the German port of Bremen. Three aircraft, unable to keep up the 200-knot pace, turned for home before Bremen was even sighted – a bowl of smoky haze, its harbour mouth criss-crossed by a lethal tangle of barrage balloons and deadly cables. Flying through a lethal rain of flak, they sowed an inferno of fire and hissing steam and paid the price. Although Edwards was to win the V.C. for his leadership, five out of twelve planes did not return – "equivalent to a serious reverse, which no amount of propaganda can turn into a success," Göbbels commented.

It was the third attempt to cripple Bremen in four days, an aim which had become an obsession with the ruthless Air Officer Commanding No 2 Group, Air Vice Marshal Donald Stevenson. Although such daylight strikes took a terrible toll – the Blenheims, with scant fire-power, were almost 200 m.p.h. slower than Luftwaffe fighters and were within their range for ninety minutes after crossing the coast – Stevenson would not let up. "Churchill wants it!" he stormed at one dissident, hurling his inkwell at the wall.

Most bomber-types available in 1941 were almost as vulnerable. The Wellington, its guns unable to traverse to a full right angle with the aircraft, was thus helpless against a beam attack; lacking self-sealing tanks, it needed only one unlucky hit to become a flying furnace. Its Mark 7 bombsight called for a rock-steady commercial airline approach to the target – certain suicide again. The Whitley's oxygen supply was always inadequate for long flights; its generators so uncertain that the wireless operators spent most of their trip dismantling and reassembling their sets.

On night flights, the ostensible targets were Germany's seventeen synthetic oil plants. But in reality this mattered little, for by August, a survey of 633 photographs taken by 500 bombers over a two-month period revealed a staggering deficiency. Only one-third of the bombers had got within five miles of the target; over the smoke-laden Ruhr, the total was one-tenth. At negligible cost to the German war effort or to civilian morale, 41,000 tons of bombs would claim 914 aircraft – one aircraft lost for every 45 tons of bombs dropped. But so long as the Red Army fought on, the bombing would continue.

So, too, would the daylight fighter sweeps pursue their policy of "leaning forward into France", until 426 pilots had been killed or taken prisoner, among the latter such Battle of Britain aces as Douglas Bader and Whitney Straight.

If the entire policy was in doubt, the airmen's courage never was. On the night of 7 July, 13,000 feet above the Zuider Zee, a Messerschmitt 110 rose from the darkness, to blast a Wellington bomber returning from a raid on Munster with cannon fire. The starboard engine took fire, fed by petrol from a split pipe; soon flames threatened to engulf the entire wing. Disaster was only averted by Sergeant James Allen Ward of No 75 (New Zealand) Squadron. Climbing out on to the fuselage, secured only by a rope round his waist, Ward descended three feet through howling darkness to the wing. Smothering the flames with a canvas engine cover, he somehow contrived a cautious return along the wing, back into the aircraft.

It was an exploit that merited not only Bomber Command's second V.C. of that summer, but an experience that Ward found infinitely more terrifying: a personal summons to No 10, Downing Street, to meet Winston Churchill. Ward was to die before the month was out, but the meeting was a trauma until the end: the long ticking moments of silence before Churchill finally entered his study, impeccably dressed as always in a short black coat and striped trousers, with a polka-dotted bow tie, as pink and groomed as if he had just stepped from a bath.

At first, Ward was struck dumb with stagefright, until Churchill asked him gently, "You feel very humble and awkward in my presence, don't you?" Even then Ward could venture nothing further than, "Yes, sir."

"Then," said Churchill, more gently still, "you can imagine how humble and awkward I feel in yours."

7

"At Last – We've Gotten Together"

D AY AND N I G H T, the knocking echoed insidiously. At times it was thin
and repetitive, as if a too-zealous carpenter was at work. At others it was
as loud as a creeping barrage, engulfing all Occupied Europe. Phoneti-
cally it was rendered as tat-tat-tat-too, three short bars and one long one,
the "fate-knocks-at-the-door" motif of Beethoven's Fifth Symphony.
Symbolically, to millions chafing under Hitler's yoke, it represented a
phrase that was to echo round the world: the Morse signal that spelt out V
for Victory.

Its conception had been inauspicious. In January, the head of the
B.B.C.'s Belgian Service in London, Victor de Laveleye, had urged his
countrymen to chalk V (for *victoire*) in all public places, a sign of their
confidence. Few had responded – until June, when a mystery voice on
B.B.C. short-wave radio, identified only as "Colonel Britton" broadcast
a Europe-wide call for daily harassment of the Germans.

"You are asked to join a disciplined army," the "Colonel" – in reality
Assistant European News Editor, Douglas Ritchie – told his listeners. "It
is a strange army, but one to which it is an honour to belong. It is an army
which the Germans fear . . . the night is your friend, the V is your sign
. . . splash the V from one end of Europe to the other."

It was as if a clarion call had sounded. All over Europe, as July ended,
the realisation had come that the German advance through Russia was
bogging down – hampered in part by torrential rains that slowed the pace
from 22 daily miles to eight, in part by stiffening resistance spearheaded
by a formidable trio of Marshals, Klimenti Voroshilov, defending
Leningrad, Semeon Timoshenko, before Moscow, and Semeon Bud-
yonny at Kiev. The message was not lost on Occupied Europe: resistance
could become a way of life.

From the North Cape to the Pyrenees, the V-sign resounded. It was a
tattoo beaten out on cafe tables to summon waiters, hammered on the
front door knockers of friends, blasted by impatient taxi horns, shrilled
by freight train whistles. Diners-out in restaurants set their knives and
forks in V-formation; householders set the hands of stopped clocks at five
minutes past eleven. In every language, the message was the same:

victory, *victoire, vryheid* (freedom in Dutch), *Vitezstvi* (victory, in Czech) *ve vil vinne* in Norwegian.

As a symbol the V crossed all frontiers – scrawled in lipstick on the backs of German officers' great-coats in Oslo, smeared in boot-blacking on the walls of German premises in Athens, etched on dustcoated German vehicles in Copenhagen. For every citizen who scrawled it had become aware of one truth: while they themselves could not win the war, they could help Adolf Hitler lose it.

Putting a brave face on things, Josef Göbbels claimed the V for his own countrymen. V did indeed stand for victory, a German victory – *Viktoria*, an obsolete word, unknown to most. A V flag was hung from the Eiffel Tower and painters were set to work stencilling Vs on German box-cars. It was a subtle mistake; if the V-sign was not *verboten*, the occupying troops must make the best of it.

Other tokens of liberty abounded – in the tricolor scarves and Cross of Lorraine handbag fastenings sported by Parisian *midinettes*, in the Statue of Liberty buttonhole favours worn by young Danes. A new readiness to provoke the German ire had become apparent. In Prague, lamp-posts in the square surrounding the Gestapo H.Q. were ominously placarded *zadano* (reserved). A cheeky Copenhagen newsdealer advertised a new textbook: LEARN ENGLISH BEFORE THE TOMMIES ARRIVE. Ordered to remove the placard, he replaced it with another: LEARN GERMAN BEFORE OUR FRIENDS THE GERMANS DEPART.

Going slow, to sabotage the German war machine, had become almost second nature. Belgian coal miners, idling down the pits, reduced productivity by 36 per cent; at Bergen, other miners took two entire months to complete six feet of a fortification tunnel. Norwegian workers constructing a strategic German military highway put in "two hours for Hitler and six hours for King Haakon."

To bored Britons, the conquered lands now existed as little more than eight national anthems* played in rotation after Sunday's 9 p.m. news bulletin but those who had stayed behind cherished the memory of their exiled royalty. In Amsterdam, traffic lights turning orange – signifying W A I T – were always cheered lustily, a reminder of their beloved Queen Wilhelmina and the House of Orange. Norwegian street car conductors approaching streets named after the King, loudly and formally intoned, "His Majesty King Haakon Street".

In the wake of defiance, violence was swift to follow. In Holland, students of the closed-down universities at Delft and Leiden resurrected *Les Gueux* (The Beggars), a secret society formed in the sixteenth century to harass the Spanish overlords. "*Moffen*" (slang for German)

* An exception – until January 1942 – was the *Internationale* which Churchill sternly forbade, forcing the B.B.C. to compromise with the Kutusov 1812 March. Eden finally persuaded him to change his mind.

147

cocktails doctored with sulphuric acid, were served up so freely that few German troops now drank in public bars. Other favourite devices were poisoned pencils jabbed into German thighs in crowds or in darkened cinemas, and strychnine crystals dropped into plates of food from under the fingernails.

The lethal precedent had been set, and soon others joined the battle lines. On 12 August, an alarmed Marshal Pétain took to the air to share his fears with the public: "Frenchmen! . . . from several regions of France I have sensed for some weeks the rising of an evil wind. Worry is winning minds and doubt is seizing souls. The authority of my government is being questioned." The Marshal's fears were justified, for from 18 July onward and far into November, twenty-two major incidents were reported from all over France. In Paris, Bordeaux and Nantes, German military personnel were gunned down, and even Frenchmen were not immune – among them former Vice-Premier Pierre Laval and the collaborationist editor, Marcel Déat, although both men survived.

Soon the volleys of firing squads were beating like doom in all the cities of Europe. Paris, Belgrade, Warsaw were all to know the same relentlessly accelerating tempo of stabbings, shootings and booby-trap bombs, followed by their inevitable corollary: the mass trials, the clamped-down curfews, the execution of hostages by the hundred.

But the insistent V for victory drumbeat would never diminish now. An idea was fighting an idea.

*

In Yugoslavia, V stood for *vitestvo* (heroism), and certainly Josip Broz Tito's guerillas battled against heroic odds. As early as 1 July, Georgi Dimitrov, Secretary-General of the Comintern in Moscow, had passed the word to Tito's hideout on Belgrade's Gladstone Street: "The hour has struck when Communists must launch an open fight against the invaders."

Though Tito himself stayed in the capital until mid-September he lost no time in despatching lieutenants to the field – there to organise what he called "partisans", the name for the irregulars who had operated behind Napoleon's lines in Spain and Russia. It was to be all-out war from the first. On 5 July, speeding Milovan Djilas, a heftily-built student, to his native Montenegro, Tito enjoined him, "Shoot anyone . . . if he wavers or shows any lack of courage or discipline!" Rodoljub Colaković, a staffer on the Communist journal *Bomba*, bound for western Serbia, had similar instructions: "Use all possible means to terrorise the enemy."

Their beginnings were impressive: by mid-July, when he blew the vital Ralja railway bridge south of Belgrade with thirty-five kilos of ecrasite, Colaković had fully eighty armed men and a stolen machine-gun. None wore Communist badges, for their aim was to draw the entire nation into the struggle, but each man took an oath of loyalty. Day after day as new recruits flooded in, the same scene was enacted: thick knots of men standing bareheaded in a woodland clearing, the cold summer rain soaking their breeches and jerkins as they recited in chorus: "I, a son of the Serbian nation, swear on my honour . . ."

No man who swore that oath had an easy war ahead. Discipline was rigid and unrelenting; strong drink, even *slivovitz*, was forbidden, while looting or desertion merited the death penalty. Their life-style was primitive: a fortunate few had blankets or ground sheets but most bedded down in the bracken each night, awaking drenched by the morning dew. If breakfast was often blackberries, supper might be a slice of maize bread and a handful of wild damsons.

They moved covertly, by night, their raids marked by angry red explosions as barracks and workshops took fire, then withdrew as stealthily; low-pitched whistles signalled their progress through the woods.

Couriers came at regular intervals with letters from Tito. Always his instructions were virtually the same: undertake actions every day, seize arms and munitions, keep recruiting volunteers. This last was easy – "not everyone agreed to Communist leadership," Djilas exulted in Montenegro, "but no one was strong enough to challenge it."

If life was hard, they envied those who had it harder yet. "Over there on the Eastern front, that's the real war," one man told Djilas enviously, "where whole divisions burn up like matches."

In Valjevo, western Serbia, Colaković had word of a *Četnik* force, reputedly 40,000 strong under Colonel Draža Mihailović, a mild-mannered staff officer, operating from Mount Ravna Gora. At first he debated joining forces, but the detachment commander, Sergeant Zdravko Jovanović, was scornful. Three days with Mihailović had been enough for him; his men were *gibanicari*, a pejorative phrase meaning guzzlers of creampudding, most of whom went home to sleep at nights, instead of bivouacking under the stars.

In truth, Mihailović, fearing reprisals against civilians, had confined his followers to military targets: *Četniks* must not wage war against German personnel. Although Tito later, offered to serve under his command, the royalist Mihailović, more fearful of Communists than Germans, demurred. Soon his *Četniks* were to engage in all-out civil war against the partisans.

They proved no match for Tito's ruthlessly streamlined organisation. Whole villages rallied to Tito, risking German patrols to bring apples and hard boiled eggs to their woodland camps. Peasant wives joined together to wash and patch their linen. Even the children stood watch as daytime lookouts – "only a wild bird could fly over our village," one commander boasted.

As autumn drew on, even shelter would be forthcoming; the partisans slept in farmhouses perfumed with apples and newly-baked bread, at worst in peasant hovels smelling of mutton-fat and mould. But they remained hard and merciless and they took pride in it, for pity could have no place in the war they were fighting now.

At Žagarac, in Montenegro, partisans once brought bitter news to Milovan Djilas; his brother Aleksa had been gunned down in ambush by militiamen the day before. In true partisan spirit, Djilas feigned total indifference. "You can't," was his callous comment, "have a wedding feast without meat!"

*

It was a life that Ruth Mitchell herself would have relished, within the *Četnik* ranks – but from the day that the Gestapo seized her in Dubrovnik, her sole problem had been to survive.

In one respect, she was lucky. The *Četnik* badge and cap insignia which would have been her passport to Mihailović had been hidden beneath the floor of her bedroom closet; the Gestapo never found them. She was lucky, too, in preserving her illusions; for thirteen months she remained in ignorance of the bloody civil war which rent Yugoslavia apart.

All her life now hinged on patience – that and the ability to think fast. After two nights in a hot stuffy gaol cell in Dubrovnik, with only crusts of dry bread to eat, there followed a strangely courteous interrogation by *Sturmbannführer* von Nassenstein, the district Gestapo chief. Ruth, whose German was fluent, used all her wiles to disarm him. She was an American, writing a travel book, her family credentials impeccable. Of what could they possibly suspect her?

Von Nassenstein was non-committal. Her main interrogation would take place in Belgrade; a Croat detective would escort her there by train, but funds would be provided for her to travel there in comfort, first-class.

Another gaol *en route*, this time in Sarajevo, a small barred window, high up under sloping boards that formed a communal bed, with a stinking brimming drain for a lavatory. There were no blankets; along with fifteen other women, mostly small-time prostitutes, Ruth squatted on the floor. After darkness fell she spent that whole first night frantically crushing bedbugs.

At Gestapo H.Q., on Belgrade's Terazia, *Sturmbannführer* Seidl, a tall sallow S.S. officer, proved omniscient. On his desk a dossier twelve inches high listed everything there was to be known about Ruth Mitchell – her family, her friends, her kindergarten, her schools, every Balkan journey she had made, her *Četnik* contacts – even her photograph, wearing a *Četnik* cap. Ruth made light of it. She had interviewed "that old dotard Pechanats" in his cups, such good copy for her book, and he had pressed the cap on her as a souvenir.

On the fourth day of interrogation, the three-man panel assembled in Seidl's office reached their verdict: "We have complete proof that you are an agent of the British Intelligence Service."

Ruth Mitchell saw the warning light. She must lie as if her life depended on it – as indeed it did.

"I will say this," she said slowly. "If I die – it is certain that many German women will weep."

Aware that she had all their attention, she went on: Admiral Richard Byrd, the Polar explorer, and United States senator Harry Flood Byrd were both her brothers-in-law. (In truth, they were distant connections by marriage and Ruth had never met either of them, but her life was at stake.)

"Germany is straining every nerve and pouring out millions upon millions of marks trying to keep America out of the war," she reminded them. "If you shoot me when I am not guilty you may be sure my relatives will throw themselves with energy into working against Germany . . . my death might even be the actual small first cause of America entering the war against you."

Each man exchanged silent glances; she knew that for the moment at least her fate was deferred. Such was Hitler's determination to avoid provoking Roosevelt, her case must be referred to Berlin.

"*Meine Herren*," she concluded, "*zu sterben ist manchmal eine Ehre*" (Gentlemen, it is sometimes an honour to die).

But Ruth Mitchell was not to be accorded that honour. For two months she was penned in a 15 by 20 foot cell in the Gestapo prison, along with fourteen Serbian women. Once, perhaps in an effort to shake her resolve, she was shifted to the condemned cell – then returned as if nothing had happened.

At 7.30 a.m. on 3 August, she was transferred first to Austrian then to German soil. Graz, Vienna, Munich, Salzburg, Ulm, Berlin-Spandau – she passed in turn through all these gaols before finally joining the British women internees at Liebenau Internment camp, Württemberg, near Lake Constance.

Not until 30 June, 1942, after top-level diplomatic pressure, did she arrive back along with 900 other American citizens, on the last exchange ship to steam into New York harbour. It was hard to focus the Statue of Liberty on that clear bright morning; the tears were flowing too fast.

By then she had recognised the bitter truth of a prophecy made by a gypsy fortune-teller, Maroosia, in the one night she had spent in the gaol cell at Sarajevo. In many ways it summed up her entire Serbian idyll and the way it had gone awry. "You are going on a long journey . . . you will be . . . neither quickly free nor quite dead . . . pain and sorrow, great sorrow, but at the end the sea. Wide is the sea, very wide, but it is far away – and bitter the road to the sea."

*

In 1941, the underground war knew no respite. Even as Ruth Mitchell was passing through Zagreb in a prison train, *en route* for Austria, another woman, twenty-seven years her junior, was completing the last lap of a 700-mile journey that made resistance history.

Ever since February, Andrée de Jongh, the young Belgian girl who had determined to found her own escape line for Allied Troops, had resolutely explored ways and means. Back in the spring, she had even sold her jewels and borrowed unrepentantly from friends so that her fellow-conspirator, Arnold de Pé, could make a reconnaissance journey back to Bayonne, 20 miles from the Spanish frontier. After working there as a radio repair mechanic, he had known smugglers from Spain, who would act as guides – at a steep price of £12 a head.

By June, Andrée – who had taken the code-name "Dédée" – had been ready to go. Already, de Pé had established the links in the long chain down which the fugitives must pass: a train journey to the Belgian frontier at Quievrain; a crossing of the Somme near Amiens, to by-pass German checkpoints; a train to Paris; the night train to Bayonne; then a bicycle ride to the "safe" house of Elvire de Greef, mother of a family of Belgian refugees at Anglet. But there was farther yet to go: a tramp to a farm in the frontier village of Urrugne, followed by an all-night forced march over the Pyrenees to the British Consulate at San Sebastian, in northern Spain.

There were many willing passengers. All over Belgium, Britons lay in hiding in attics and barns: airmen who had been shot down in recent raids, soldiers who had still contrived to evade the Germans almost a year after Dunkirk. But few of them could speak French and eternal vigilance was necessary: a safe passage could hinge on the faulty tilt of a beret or an unfamiliar way with clogs. Meanwhile, in Brussels, the organisation now some twenty strong, was taking shape, Andrée was using her former skill as a poster designer to forge French ID cards. A brave teenager, 16-year-old Elise Maréchal, vetted all potential evaders who were channelled their way by doctors and priests, checking out possible Gestapo stool-pigeons. With an uncanny ear for English regional accents, she met each man separately inside a Brussels church, confirming his knowledge of Mae Wests and ditching procedures in the Channel – even letting drop a four-letter word to see if the listener blushed.

The first batch of "parcels", as Andrée called them, had left Brussels in early June; she and de Pé travelled with them. All had gone well until the party, eleven Belgians and an elderly English spinster, reached the

Somme – to find campers had pitched a tent near the rowboat de Pé had arranged to have hidden. Yet the river must be crossed – and only four of the party could swim.

Andrée was not deterred. Waiting until nightfall, she obtained a long coil of wire and an inflated inner tube from a nearby farm. Then, stripping off her clothes, she swam the forty yards to the French bank, securing the wire to a tree. For the next two hours she swam eleven times in succession across the dark river, helping the fugitives cling to the tube, which was threaded to the wire by a running noose.

By the end of June, the party had reached Elvire de Greef's house at Anglet. Elated, Andrée and de Pé returned to Brussels.

Now, in the first half of August, Andrée de Jongh had grown ambitious. To set up a regular liaison with the British she had decided to accompany the "parcels" every step of the way.

At No 30, Gran Via, the British Consulate of the old seaport of Bilbaó, the Vice-Consul, Arthur Dean, was at a loss for words. His junior, Vyvyan Pedrick, had entered his office with a highly dubious story: a girl who claimed she was Belgian had come all the way from Brussels bringing two Belgian volunteers and a Scottish soldier. Pedrick himself had questioned the Scot, Private Jim Cromar, of the 1st Battalion, Gordon Highlanders, who had been on the run ever since the battle of St Valery in June, 1940, and his story seemed to stand up.

Dean, a taciturn pipe-puffing ex-naval officer, was far from reassured. Since December 1939, a special branch of military intelligence, M.I.9, had existed to handle the escape and evasion of Allied Troops in Europe; by August, 1940, their task had been eased by the offer of M.I.6, the secret intelligence service, to set up an escape line from Marseilles to Spain. What more likely than that this girl was a German agent briefed to infiltrate the network?

True, Andrée's first appearance in his office was disarming. Dressed in a plain white blouse and tartan skirt, and flat shoes with white ankle socks, she radiated nothing so much as ardent determination.

"How long did your journey take?" Dean asked her.

"I have told you. About a week."

Dean was incredulous. "How did you cross the Pyrenees?"

Andrée's blue eyes sparkled with the memory of it. Her friends near Bayonne had procured a guide, a smuggler named Tomas, and she had pestered him unmercifully until he agreed to take all four of them. They had marched all night, eight hours at a stretch, with only a hunk of bread apiece, resting briefly in an abandoned watch-tower beset by swarms of fleas.

Once in Spain, another contact of Elvire de Greef, Señor Aracama, a garage proprietor, had lent her money and sheltered her party in his house at San Sebastian. Now, to put her escape line on a business basis, she needed funds to reimburse him – and the friends who had lent money to pay the guide.

Dean was non-committal. Only the Consul, William Graham, could decide on that. Andrée must return tomorrow.

Five days passed. Each day Andrée trudged to the Consulate from the small pension where Aracama had found her a room; each day she met the same dusty answer, "Come back tomorrow". Andrée grew desperate. Aracama was paying her keep – but how could she find the pesetas to pay him back?

Unknown to her, Andrée was already at the heart of a top-level diplomatic wrangle. Cables winged from Bilbao to Madrid, and from Madrid to M.I.9 in London. The Deputy Director of M.I.6, Sir Claude Dansey, was highly suspicious, for one: the girl was an obvious plant. When Bilbao insisted stubbornly on her integrity, Dansey shifted his stance. Genuine or no, a woman had no business mixing herself up in resistance work.

It was M.I.9's front man, Michael Creswell, an urbane 31-year-old Second Secretary at the Madrid Embassy, who turned the tide. Creswell had already worked with other embryo escape lines, ferrying British evaders and escapers across Spain; once he had gathered enough of them together to hire a coach and send them all down to Gibraltar disguised as students. On her next visit to the Consulate, Graham told Andrée thankfully: "Mr Creswell will now take the matter in hand."

Their rapport was immediate, the first of many warm meetings over a late supper. Money Creswell could supply in plenty; at any one time M.I.9 had a float of up to £5,000 in foreign currency. Give priority to airmen, he instructed her, the men best able to resume the battle against Hitler on their return. Above all, a regular routine must be established. "Each time you get to San Sebastian", Creswell told her, "phone me. We shall send the diplomatic car to a place nearby and take your 'parcels' to Madrid."

But on one point Andrée was adamant: her organisation must remain entirely Belgian, completely independent from London, with no professional agents, no radio contact, and few helpers over twenty-five. It had begun as a young people's network, and thus it would continue.

"When do you think you can come back with another party?" Creswell asked her on the last day.

"In three or four weeks time!"

"Then bring three more men with you."

Andrée was delighted. The British had accepted her and her escape line, and on her own terms: the "Dédée (later the Comet) Line." And Creswell had christened her "The Postman", too. Now it was up to her to ensure him a regular supply of "parcels".

Aboard H.M.S. *Prince of Wales*, at Scapa Flow in the Orkneys, the rumours – "buzzes", the lower deck called them – had been rife for days. Following her brief but decisive encounter with the *Bismarck* in May, the battleship had returned to Rosyth for much-needed repairs; action had been sorely lacking. Now word was afoot of a new and secret assignment, and the quantities of hams, turkeys and chickens arriving aboard suggested a V.I.P. mission of some moment.

Tantalised, the wardroom had even organised a shilling sweepstake to determine their new role, but most were sorely wide of the mark. "Taking Hess back to Germany" and "Taking some chorus girls to North Africa" were two prime favourites; even Sub-Lieutenant Alan Franklin's guess, "Taking the Grand Duchess of Luxembourg to Canada" seemed more on the cards than the unknown officer who hazarded: "Taking Winston Churchill to see Roosevelt."

Towards 11 a.m. on Monday, 4 August, they knew. Steaming fast through a grey veil of mist between Hoy and South Ronaldshay came the destroyer *Oribi* and as the battleship's crew mustered on her decks, the bosuns ramrod-straight beside the gangway, a familiar figure was suddenly visible on the destroyer's bridge: a chunky blue-suited figure sporting a yachting cap, a cigar clenched truculently between his jaws. Not a word was spoken but lips moved, and a whisper seemed to travel the whole length of the ship: "*It's Winston!*"

At that moment Churchill himself had eyes only for a man who stood alone on the battleship's fore-deck, a brown tweed overcoat draped loosely about him, his face as pale as a man close to death. "Ah, my dear friend, how are you?" Churchill greeted him. "How did you find Stalin?" and Harry Hopkins, weary beyond belief, after a nightmare twenty-four hour air journey through gale-force winds, replied, "I must tell you all about it".

The meeting that Roosevelt had mooted to Mackenzie King as far back as April was at last to become a reality. Events in the Balkans and North Africa had long made such a meeting impracticable, but now Hitler's eastern offensive had given them a breathing space. In the sheltered harbour of Placentia Bay, off the coast of Newfoundland, along with their advisers and chiefs of staffs, President and Premier would hold their first summit meeting, quite unknown to the world's Press.

The agenda featured urgent business. Midway through July, Japan had entered the war game in earnest; purely for "defensive purposes", she had pressured Vichy France to accept land, sea and air forces 50,000 strong in southern Indo-China. Darlan had temporised, but not for long. By 21 July Japanese transports were already steaming into Saigon harbour, preparing to take over bases on a long strip of Annamese coastline fronting the South China Sea, and the fine naval base on Camranh Bay. Now the Japanese Navy were only 750 miles from the British naval base at Singapore – while their airfields near Cape Cambodia lay barely 250 miles from Kota Bharu, the railhead of the Federated Malay States.

As always Darlan had blamed not himself but the United States. "I hoped the news would send squadrons of United States ships steaming into Saigon Harbour from Manila," he told Admiral Leahy ungraciously. "It is always the same story; the United States is too late."

In other respects, though, Roosevelt had acted swiftly. On 26 July, he clamped down an order freezing all Japanese assets, estimated at $131 million, in the United States. On 1 August, his embargo went further: the President banned the export of all aviation and motor fuel and other petroleum products to Japan.

Although Churchill was bound for Newfoundland, to urge the use of "hard language", on Roosevelt, the President had already struck the Japanese a body-blow. Japan could supply only 10 per cent of her own oil, with a further 10 per cent from the Dutch East Indies; the remaining 80 per cent had always come from the United States. Her own resources would last her three years at most – and now the Dutch East Indies, emboldened by Roosevelt, had reneged on their contract.

But Churchill gave no sign of preoccupation as the *Prince of Wales* churned at a steady 30 knots for Placentia Bay. Ensconced in the Admiral's sea cabin on the bridge, he was revelling in the trip like a Caribbean tourist. He challenged Hopkins to backgammon – and lost seven guineas in four days. He buried himself in C. S. Forester's best-seller, *Captain Horatio Hornblower, R.N.* Midshipman Michael Pruett, assigned as his escort aboard, was fascinated by the Premier's life-style – everything from his lilac siren suit to the cases of brandy, champagne and vintage wine that had accompanied his party, £450 worth all told. Sub-Lieutenant Michael Buxton was intrigued by his direct approach. At any given moment, Churchill might appear, on the bridge of all places, to demand: "Is there no one on? I've rung my bell for the last ten minutes. Where's my brandy and soda?"

Surgeon Lieutenant-Commander Dick Caldwell, summoned to treat Churchill for a ricked back muscle, found him in a high good humour despite the discomfort. "Do you allow your patients to smoke cigars?" he enquired, puffing defiantly away, and Caldwell was tact itself: "I think it would probably depend on the cigar, sir."

"All this ozone is making me sleepy," Churchill complained to his personal aide, Commander C. R. Thompson. "I have difficulty in driving myself to two hours work a day." Hopkins, for one, was delighted. "The Prime Minister failed to work yesterday for the first time in his life," he wrote gleefully to Ismay on 7 August, and he marvelled at the harmony of the trip: "There is never a cross word between any of the services. They know better than to discuss Crete in mixed company."

Harmony or not, they were working apace – as if preparing themselves after twenty-three months of war for some exalted game of Consequences. Sir Alexander Cadogan debated how to present Britain's viewpoint to his opposite number, Sumner Welles. General Sir John Dill, Admiral Sir Dudley Pound and Air Vice Marshal Wilfred Freeman, standing in for Portal, laboured on Joint Chiefs of Staff papers in the hope of impressing General George C. Marshall, Chief of Staff, Admiral Harold R. Stark, and General Henry Harley "Hap" Arnold, Chief of the Army Air Corps.

But it was at night, after dinner at 9 p.m., that Churchill most came into his own. No sooner was dinner over and the tables cleared in the 60-foot long wardroom, dominated by an irreverent Gillray caricature of the Prince Regent, than Royal Marine servants in white mess-jackets began moving chairs and couches from anteroom to diningroom. Soon Churchill would enter with his advisers, wearing the mess dress of the Royal Yacht Squadron, a navy-blue jacket, with brass buttons and blue trousers, to beam a benediction on the company. Ranged in serried ranks on chairs they made a curiously impressive sight under the brilliant lighting – their stiff winged collars and black ties offset by the gold lace of their cuffs threaded with colours that bespoke their calling; the surgeon's red, the paymaster's white. Then as the lights dimmed Churchill settled in his armchair for his bedtime story – the nightly film show.

Whatever the choice, he entered into the spirit of it. He thrilled to Leslie Howard carrying off refugees from Nazi Germany in *Pimpernel Smith*. He chortled at Hedy Lamarr and Clark Gable in *Comrade X* and at Jean Arthur in *The Devil and Miss Jones*. Humphrey Bogart in *High Sierra*, hurtling to his death down a mountainside, produced a ribald, "And a good time was had by all!" Somehow he sandwiched in two showings of Laurence Olivier and Vivien Leigh in *Lady Hamilton* – which he was seeing for the fifth time – sobbing without constraint on each occasion.

Only one anxiety troubled him at times: would he and Roosevelt achieve a true meeting of minds? "I wonder if he will like me," he had asked Harriman in trepidation, when the trip was first mooted, and Hopkins, too, noted this constant preoccupation as the days wore on – "you'd have thought he was being carried up into the heavens to meet God".

The doubt was soon resolved. On the morning of Saturday, 9 August, the *Prince of Wales* slowed to come about at her berth in the dark waters of Placentia Bay. At that moment the early summer mists parted as if by magic, and the battleship, her White Ensign hoisted, was suddenly surrounded by a log-jam of American warships, the Stars and Stripes aloft, their decks lined with cheering crews. Beyond a wavering coastline of desolate beaches and coves the land rose by degrees to dark fir-clad hills.

High on the outside platform of the Admiral's bridge, his sandy hair still ruffled from sleep, Churchill watched and waited anxiously. It was 9 a.m. and all the sixty-seven years of his life had pointed to this moment: his first faraway glimpse of a man in a Palm Beach suit, sitting patiently in a wheel chair on the quarterdeck of the heavy cruiser *Augusta*.

*

"At last – we've gotten together."

"We have."

As Roosevelt's Secret Service bodyguard, Mike Reilly, recorded it, the greeting between the two leaders, after a bosun had piped the Premier aboard *Augusta* and the bands had crashed into the national anthems, was strangely banal – yet in the space of three days history would be made.

On the face of it, those days were one long orgy of hospitality. A buffet luncheon in the cabin of Vice-Admiral Ernest J. King, the Atlantic Fleet commander, was merely an appetiser for the dinner that Roosevelt staged that night for Churchill aboard *Augusta*. Heavy silver, wavering candles and the sheen of inlaid panelling provided a gracious setting for a hearty meal of vegetable puree, broiled spring chicken with buttered peas, candied sweet potatoes and mushroom gravy, followed by spinach omelette and chocolate ice cream. Since American warships were, by tradition, "dry", the guests made do with the heady wine of Churchill's oratory.

Nor were the lower decks forgotten. On the Saturday afternoon, a shining chain of U.S. motor boats brought a pyramid of 1,502 cartons to *Prince of Wales'* gangway; with Roosevelt's compliments and best wishes, each carton contained an orange, two apples, 200 Lucky Strike cigarettes and half a pound of cheese for every rating. Next day, Sunday, aboard *Prince of Wales*, Churchill hosted a luncheon worthy of a Lord Mayor's banquet in peacetime, although to stage it had been touch-and-go: caviar with vodka (which Hopkins had brought as a present from Stalin), turtle soup (which Commander Thompson had salvaged from the basement of a London grocer) and roast grouse (as the season had been advanced to 1 August, the Chief Steward had picked up a dozen brace in Inverness). A Royal Marine Band lilted through music ranging from *The Student Prince* to the *United States Marine Hymn*. That night, not to be outdone, Roosevelt feted Churchill all over again.

Beneath the convivial surface, the formal toasts, both leaders were cautiously feeling their way, hoping for common ground. After the Saturday night dinner, Churchill gave a bravura performance as he

158

reviewed the whole panorama of 1941 to date – now hunching forward, now braced against his chair back, slewing his cigar from cheek to cheek, stressing Britain's valour – and the need for American intervention – with all the force at his command. Roosevelt listened intently, fiddling with his pincenez, doodling with a burnt match, but plainly impressed for all that.

What, he asked Churchill at one point, did he think of Hitler's chances with Barbarossa? "I think," the Premier answered resonantly, "that he made a mistake, that his ego is about to strangle him."

It was plain, too, that Roosevelt was feeling his way not only with Churchill but with the American public. "I shall never declare war," he confided in a curiously revealing phrase. "I shall make war."

It was at Sunday's church service that Churchill saw his biggest chance for a break-through. "I have chosen some grand hymns," he confided to all within earshot, and like a busy stage-manager he worked in with the sailors helping to arrange the *Prince of Wales* quarterdeck – shifting chairs to right and left, fussing with the folds of the Union Jack. The true significance of this morning was not lost on him. As Roosevelt, in a blue doublebreasted suit, crossed a narrow gangway from *Augusta* to the destroyer, a cane held in his right hand, assisted by his son Elliott on his left, it was plain that he was attempting perhaps his longest walk since stricken with polio. Moving slowly, the full length of the ship, to his place of honour on the quarterdeck, flanked by a guard of 250 U.S. Marines and sailors, he stood rigidly at attention for both national anthems. Now Churchill was visibly moved. Fiddling with a handkerchief, he feigned a head cold, but the tears were not far away.

It was an unforgettable scene: the two leaders side by side, in the centre of a hollow square, the Union Jack and the Stars and Stripes draped together on the pulpit, the British and American sailors close together, white caps doffed, as they bent over their hymn sheets and the first of Churchill's hymns, *O God Our Help in Ages Past* soared out across the silent bay. Following Royal Naval custom, Captain Leach read the lesson, its text from Joshua hand-picked to suggest amity – "I will not fail thee nor forsake thee. Be strong and of good courage" – before the chaplains offered prayers for Roosevelt, for King George VI, for all those in invaded countries. Other hymns spoke of war and of a common plight and resolution: *Onward Christian Soldiers*, and *Eternal Father, strong to save*.

"The same language, the same hymns, and, more or less, the same ideals," Churchill mused later. "I have an idea that something really big may be happening – something really big."

But Churchill was in some measure doomed to disappointment. Already, on the Saturday afternoon, Welles and Cadogan had spent three hours thrashing out almost all the points the leaders would discuss aboard *Augusta* on Monday 12 August: the Azores, Vichy and French

North Africa, the Far East, the main points of the joint statement known to history as the Atlantic Charter. The divergency of opinion had been apparent even then: while Churchill had journeyed to Placentia Bay to wrest commitments from Roosevelt, the President had come determined to evade them.

There was still common ground for agreement. If Britain occupied the Canary Islands, pre-empting a German attack through Spain, she could not live up to her promise to defend the Azores. In this case – provided Portugal requested the move – Roosevelt agreed to do so in her stead. On Japan, despite the "hard language" Churchill urged, the President proved more wary. "Leave that to me," he told Churchill. "I think I can baby them along for three months." To save Japan's face, his instinct was to parley: to drag out the talks between Hull and Nomura, in the hope that Tokyo would see the light and pull out of Indo-China.

Foremost in Roosevelt's mind was the intention of delaying any showdown until his Army and Navy were stronger and public opinion more receptive. "Shooting?" he had echoed to his Cabinet, when the risk of convoys to Iceland was raised. "Well, a little shooting might arouse this country from its lethargy and help in passing the extension of the (Selective Service) Act." His instinct was sure: on 12 August, as the full-dress conferences were held, the Act, which on 16 October, 1940, had seen the registration of all American males between twenty-one and thirty-five for the first peacetime conscription, was renewed by just one vote.*

Roosevelt was not surprised; for months the graffiti "O.H.I.O." had been scrawled on the walls of training camp latrines all over America. It referred not to the Buckeye State but to "over the hill in October": if the draftees were not released and sent home they would desert.

In the teeth of such opposition, Roosevelt was profoundly disturbed when Churchill told Hopkins: "I would rather have an American declaration of war now and no supplies for six months than double the supplies and no declaration." "That is a hard saying," Roosevelt said, his face clouding over, when Hopkins passed this on.

All through that August Monday, the Americans were finding Britain's war priorities woefully unrealistic. In their main appreciation, the British Chiefs of Staff had stressed: "It is in bombing, on a scale undreamt of in the last war, that we find the new weapon on which we must principally depend for the destruction of German economic life and morale." Even before discussions opened, General "Hap" Arnold had scrawled a large and eloquent marginal query beside this item. On coming face to face

---

* A press conference at which Wavell's successor, General Sir Claude Auchinleck, had told U.S. correspondents, "We are certainly going to need American manpower, just as we did in the last war," had not helped the Bill's passage. On 11 July, Churchill had rebuked Auchinleck: "I fear your remarks will be exploited by the isolationists and will be an impediment to the end we all desire. Mr. Winant tells me . . . that your remarks will be unhelpful."

with Air Vice Marshal Freeman, Arnold was stunned: this mooted campaign was based on the assumption that America could furnish 6,000 more bombers than she was then producing.

Bitterly aggrieved, Freeman dashed off a memo to Hopkins: "I must let you know how depressed I am that it is impossible for me to state our case for increased production of the heavy bomber . . . it was made clear to me at my first meeting with Arnold that, far from getting more, we were going to get considerably less."

There were other trenchant criticisms. General George Marshall, normally temperate, saw British preoccupations with the Middle East – to which the Americans assigned No 4 priority, well below the United Kingdom, Singapore and the ocean trade routes – as making little sense. Now the Russian front was paramount, the British should abandon the theatre or downgrade their effort. Admiral Harold Stark agreed; the British should re-evaluate all their priorities.

Yet progress of a kind had been made. Churchill had seen how hamstrung Roosevelt was by American memories of World War One and the League of Nations, the ever-present thundercloud of isolationism – "the mid-West is our problem", the President told one of Leach's officers, "They have never seen a ship and they know nothing about war." Roosevelt had glimpsed the Premier's deep attachment to Dominions and Empire; to Welles' chagrin, Churchill had roundly refused to amend the Ottawa Agreements of 1932, when Britain and her Dominions had met the threat of Depression by building a closed economic unit, shutting out many items of American trade.

It remained only to draft a Joint Declaration: a commitment isolationists were swift to condemn as ranging a technically neutral country alongside a belligerent power. So hastily did Churchill act to clear it with his War Cabinet that Clement Attlee roused from his bed after midnight, called a Cabinet meeting for 1.45 a.m. and was cabling back suggested amendments to Churchill by 4 a.m.

In truth, the declaration was little more than a patched-up press release, replete with high minded phrases. Britain and America sought "no aggrandisement" and "no territorial changes" that did not accord "with the freely expressed wishes of the people concerned": they respected the right of all peoples to choose their own form of government; they sought to secure for all "improved labour standards, economic advancement, and social security". After "the final destruction of Nazi tyranny", they hoped to "see established a peace which will afford to all nations the means of dwelling in safety".

World reactions, for the most part were disillusioned; the abiding hope of the Allied nations, that America would now enter the war, had not been fulfilled. Oliver Harvey, Eden's Private Secretary, thought it "a terribly woolly document, full of all the old clichés of the League of

Nations period". In Moscow, Sir Stafford Cripps dismissed it as "no bloody good at all – it means nothing to the Balkans or the Baltic". At Buckingham Palace, a puzzled King George VI noted "It said all the right things but how are we going to carry them out? Most of the peoples of Europe will have forgotten that they ever had a government of their own when the war is over." In Washington, the German chargé, Dr Hans Thomsen, scoffed: "The fools have learned nothing in twenty years."

Late on 12 August, the time had come for Premier and President to part. As the *Prince of Wales* steamed out of Placentia Bay, Roosevelt was there to bid her farewell, standing bareheaded on *Augusta*'s quarterdeck: the wistful strains of *Auld Lang Syne* rolled out across the waters towards the fir-clad hills. Both men could at least take comfort in one truth: each had found a comrade and an ally in the struggle that lay ahead.

"I am not a religious man," Churchill blurted out in one of their moments together, "but I thank God that such a man as you is the head of your government at a time like this." It was his bodyguard, Detective-Inspector Walter Thompson, who broke it to him later that the President felt the same.

"How is he standing up to it, Thompson? How is he really?" Roosevelt had asked the detective, and Thompson could reassure him: the Premier had deep reserves of energy, replenished by constant catnaps. "Is he hard to handle?" Roosevelt asked curiously, and the Special Branch man had to admit it: "Yes, sir. He is reckless and self-willed. Restraint of any kind is unendurable."

"Well, take care of him," Roosevelt counselled, then pronounced the verdict that Churchill would always treasure, "He's about the greatest man in the world." "In fact," he added, after reflection, "he may very likely be *the* greatest."

8

"Shoot Everyone Who Shows A Wry Face"

13 August–30 September, 1941

WAS JOSEF STALIN'S staunchest ally Adolf Hitler himself? On Saturday 23 August, *Generaloberst* Heinz Guderian, commanding Panzer Group Two, had cause to wonder.

Before 10 a.m. that day, Guderian's Fieseler Storch touched down at Borisov airfield; minutes later, a car was bearing him to the headquarters of Bock's Army Group Centre. The commanders of the Fourth, Ninth and Second Armies – *Feldmarschall* Gunther von Kluge, *Generaloberst* Adolf Strauss and *Generaloberst Freiherr* von Weichs – had also just arrived. Each man was keenly awaiting a visitor from Hitler's headquarters: *Generaloberst* Franz Halder, Chief of the General Staff.

His arrival, at 11 a.m., came in the nature of a shock: Halder looked ill and depressed. In tired measured tones he came straight to the gist of Hitler's Directive No 34, dated 21 August: "The Führer has decided to conduct neither the operation against Leningrad, as previously envisaged by him, nor the offensive against Moscow, as proposed by the Army General Staff, but to take possession first of the Ukraine and the Crimea."

After a moment of stunned silence, Guderian burst out: "This can't be true."

Halder was fatalistic. "It is true. We spent five weeks wrangling for the drive on Moscow."

Now *Feldmarschall* von Bock broke in: "What can we do against this decision?" Halder shook his head resignedly. "It is immutable."

Guderian was persistent. In the warm discussion that followed he made his views plain: a drive for Kiev, the Ukrainian capital, would inevitably see the tanks bogged down in a winter campaign long before turning north and reaching Moscow. By then the roads and supply conditions would be appalling. His own Panzer group had not known one day's respite since Barbarossa was launched.

Von Bock came to a decision. Since Guderian argued so persuasively, he should accompany Halder back to the *Wolfsschanze*, request an interview with the Führer and try to win him over. But late that afternoon, before Halder's JU-88 took off over the endless fields of white

163

shocked corn, von Bock recalled to Guderian the apocryphal words of an officer of the guard at Worms when Martin Luther set off to justify his faith to the Emperor Charles V: "Little monk, little monk, yours is a difficult road".

It was dusk before the plane landed Halder and Guderian at Lötzen airfield, East Prussia. Their way to the *Wolfsschanze* led them through groves of tall oak trees, through clusters of low grey huts, their roofs camouflaged by shrubs that flanked the asphalted road, ending at the "Führer Hut" – surrounded by a double fence, bristling with sentries. Here only special yellow passes gained entry to the inner sanctum.

For two hours Guderian waited in suspense. The cool Baltic air drifted through the fine mosquito netting covering the open windows, and with it the stench of petrol; waging war on the midges that Hitler detested, the engineers were spraying every pond in the neighbourhood, but still the insects persisted. It was dark before the summons came to Hitler's map room.

Guderian began circumspectly, feeling his way. Hitler had no inkling of why he had sought this interview and Halder, moreover, had not been invited to sit in. Guderian was on his own, and he knew it; little support could be expected from Keitel, leaning negligently against the map table, or from Jodl, studiously taking notes. Overtly his intention must be to report on Panzer Group Two: engine breakdowns, supply problems, a balanced realistic view.

It was Hitler himself who supplied his cue: "Do you consider your troops are still capable of a major effort?"

Guderian sensed all of them watching him intently. "If the troops are set a great objective," he answered deliberately, "the kind that would inspire every man of them – yes."

"You are, of course, thinking of Moscow?" Hitler countered.

"Yes, my Führer. May I have permission to give my reasons?"

Hitler seemed open to conviction. "By all means, Guderian. Say whatever's on your mind."

Guderian seized his chance. "Moscow cannot be compared with Paris or Warsaw, my Führer. Moscow is not only the head and the heart of the Soviet Union – it is also its communications centre, its political brain, an important industrial area, above all the hub of the transport system. The fall of Moscow will decide the war."

Hitler said nothing. Guderian was warming to his subject. Stalin knew that the fall of Moscow would mean his final defeat, he insisted, and for this reason he would deploy his entire military strength before the capital. It was thus before Moscow, and only there, that the *Wehrmacht* could destroy the flower of the Red Army, and once Moscow was taken all else would follow.

Striding to a map, Guderian stabbed his forefinger at the Yelnya bridgehead, barely 250 miles from the city. That bridgehead, he explained, was still open at this moment; routeing instructions, transport schedules, even signposts denoting the mileage to Moscow were all in readiness. The panzers could move off that very night to smash Timoshenko before Yelnya. "Let us march towards Moscow," Guderian pleaded, "we shall take it."

It was now that Hitler joined him at the map table, but his finger hovered not over Yelnya but above a region more than 300 miles to the south: the Ukraine. "My generals have all read Clausewitz," he announced sharply, "but they understand nothing of wartime economics." One by one he ticked off the commodities he sought: "We need the grain of the Ukraine. The industrial area of the Donets must work for us, instead of for Stalin. The Russian oil supplies of the Caucasus must be cut off . . . above all we must gain control of the Crimea . . . this dangerous aircraft carrier operating against the Rumanian oilfields."

Guderian stood silent. Now the weeks of planning and scheming with his chief of operations, *Oberstleutnant* Fritz Bayerlein, had gone for nothing. What could he, a field commander, say to a politician who thought not like a Clausewitz but like a colonialist – in terms of coal and oil, wheat and eggs?

All soldiers could do now was obey orders – or perhaps die trying.

*

In a large ornately-furnished room on Tehran's Ferdowsi Avenue, overlooking a lush semi-tropical park, the Minister of the Third Reich, Dr Erwin Ettel, was drafting a cable. It would be bitter news for the Foreign Ministry in Berlin, but Ettel was duty bound to pass on the tip given to him by Zoulfikar Pasha, the pro-Axis Egyptian Ambassador: Iran was one oil-rich region Hitler would never occupy. The British and the Russians were planning to seize it first.

The source was King Farouk of Egypt himself, no friend of the British, who stressed that with Barbarossa a *fait accompli* Iran – most especially the British-subsidised Anglo-Iranian oilfield – was now vulnerable to an attack from Russian soil. Then, too, the 870-mile-long trans-Iranian railway was the one practicable land route to carry war supplies from the Persian Gulf to the Caspian Sea. These were prizes Russia and Britain could not afford to yield.

The ostensible bone of contention was the 2,500-strong workforce of German civilians employed by Iran's railway and telegraph systems, and in industrial plants. To the British, they were a latent fifth column, but since Churchill was cool on invasion what the War Cabinet called "firm but friendly demands" to deport them were pressed on the Iranian government. The result was a skilful exercise in diplomatic foot-dragging.

At first claiming that only 700 Germans were involved and that deportation would be "unneutral", the Prime Minister, Ali Mansur, next agreed to banish twenty-four forthwith, later upping the figure to thirty per month. On 8 August, the British were still patiently negotiating; they wanted "a drastic reduction" before the month ended, an eighty per cent reduction by mid-September.

The Russians were of sterner mettle. On 13 August, the Ambassador to Iran, A. S. Tehernikh, delivering his *aide-memoire*, followed up with a verbal message: the Soviets would require an answer within three days – "almost, but not quite, an ultimatum and . . . rather disquieting," to the British Foreign Office. It was now on the cards that Russia, contrary to her undertaking, would beat the British to the start-line.

It was a risk the British could not afford to take. At dawn on 25 August, the first khaki-clad columns were rolling across the border from Iraq; Indian troops, landing at the port of Bandar Shahpur, secured the world's largest oil-cracking plant at Abadan. Simultaneously, down the shores of the Caspian Sea, came the mechanised Cossacks of General Max Sinenko, their western column closing on Tabriz, their eastern on the port of Bandar Shah.

On 30 August, after eighty hours of combat – and one day after the Iranians sought an armistice – a yellow cyclone of dust extending for hundreds of miles through the horse-shoe bends and passes signalled that the British and Russian columns were converging. At Kazvin, 90 miles north-west of Tehran, they joined up to pump hands in the main square, the British to marvel at the loose grey smocks, blue breeches and old-style needle-type bayonets of the Russians, the Russians to goggle at the Gurkhas' khaki shorts.

One man had been outraged by the proceedings from the first: 65-year-old Reza Pahlavi, His Imperial Majesty, Shah in Shah (King of Kings), Shadow of the Almighty, Vice-Regent of God and Centre of the Universe. A one-time Colonel of the Persian Cossack Brigade, who had seized power from the effete Quajar dynasty in 1921, Reza was a despot of the Haroun-al-Raschid school, who detested both British and Russians alike. On learning of the invasion, his first step was a frantic cable in French to Roosevelt: in a manner "brusque et sans préavis", his frontiers had been violated. After a full week's pause for reflection, Roosevelt replied blandly: "I hope Your Majesty will concur with me in believing that we must view the situation in its full perspective of present world events. . . ." He had, he added, asked both countries to state publicly that they had no designs on Iran's independence.

This was cold comfort for the Shah, a fanatic nationalist who in 1935 had re-christened "Persia" "Iran" after the nation which dated back before Cyrus, Darius and Xerxes. Since then he had waxed rich both on British royalties and German technological skills, and until now his rule

166

had been absolute. His moody rages were notorious; for "tiresome gabbling" he once booted 21-year-old Crown Prince Muhammad Reza into a fountain but a jockey who lost a race merited a kick in the groin, a train driver arriving late was dragged from the footplate and trampled senseless. Now, incensed by the ineptitude of his armed forces in halting the Anglo-Russian tide, he sought out scapegoats. Summoning his War Minister, General Ahmed Nakhchevan, to the Palace, he slashed him about the head and face with a sabre, screaming "Throw that carrion into prison!" The General survived the ordeal, unlike the Chief of the Air Force, who was shot out of hand.

The Shah's one thought now was to keep his seat on the Peacock Throne, and to safeguard his position he dispatched twenty-seven truck-loads of gold and jewels to Isfahan, 150 miles south.

But Axis puppets would merit only ruthless treatment from this time on, as the British were making plain. To Sir Reader Bullard, the mild-mannered old Ambassador, who liked to read Dickens aloud to his guests, Churchill cabled harshly: "Dismiss from your mind any idea of a generous policy towards the Germans to please the Persians or anyone else." Next day, 4 September, he told the War Cabinet unequivocally: "It is important that we should have complete control over Persia during the war." The British G.O.C., Lieutenant-General E. P. Quinan, was left in no doubt as to his role: if the Shah tried to leave for Isfahan to set up an independent government, he "should be seized and held".

Unknown to the Shah, a bizarre attempt at king-making was soon to take place at the Boulestin Restaurant, a haven for gourmets off the Strand in London. Trifling with the idea of restoring the Quajar dynasty to the Peacock Throne, Harold Nicolson, of the Ministry of Information, and Horace Seymour of the Foreign Office, had invited Prince Hassan Quajar to lunch.

A devoted Anglophile, who was studying the English classics at Rhyll University, the Prince proved a disappointment from the first. Perhaps his son, Drummond Quajar – "c'est un nom écossais" – might prove eligible; after graduating from Worcester College, Oxford, the lad was at a loose end. "Does he speak Persian?" asked Nicolson hopefully. "Pas un mot," the Prince replied delightedly, "Pas un seul mot."

It was with some relief that Nicolson, on 16 September, heard that the Shah had abdicated and that the *Majlis*, Iran's 136-man National Assembly, had approved the Crown Prince, Muhammad Reza Pahlavi, as his successor.*

Three weeks later, the U.S. Minister in Tehran, Louis G. Dreyfus, passed two pleasant hours beneath the cool white pillars of the Shah's

* Who, on 16 January, 1979, was driven from his country by the elderly fanatic Ayatollah Khomeini to seek refuge successively in Egypt, Morocco, Mexico, the United States and Panama. He died in exile in Cairo on 27 July, 1980.

167

summer palace, conversing on world affairs in French. In the light of later events, his report to the State Department had a certain irony: "Shah . . . voluntarily espouses democratic cause because he is strongly against totalitarian doctrines . . . after remarking that his father had been unfortunate in being surrounded by bad advisers, he said he would govern constitutionally and look after the welfare of his people.

"He closed the conversation by referring warmly to the United States, which he thought would play an important role in the peace. He said he would be very happy to be an ally of America."

*

It was the first notable instance of whole-hearted Anglo-Soviet cooperation – and Rudolf Hess was baffled.

On 22 June, Hess, who weeks earlier had been moved to Mytchett Place, a secluded manor house near Aldershot, Hampshire, had heard the news of Barbarossa with a strangely wry smile. "So they have started after all," was his only comment, and it was plain that he saw a German victory as only weeks away. Yet as the months dragged by and the Russians held out, Hess grew increasingly more puzzled. What could imperialist Britain hope to gain by alignment with Communist barbarians?

By degrees he had set down his thoughts in a 12-page memorandum, a strange mixture of threats and cajolery, which he hoped would find favour with the British government. In part it read:

> Germany, for her part, wishes a reasonable peace. She is ready to conclude this without victory over England. . . . The question then, is whether the difference in aims is so great that all the sacrifices involved in a continuation of the war *must* be made – that is, all sacrifices of human beings, buildings, of irreplaceable works of art, destroyed factories, wharves, port installations, ships, of national wealth. . . .
>
> I can give an assurance that Germany has not in mind the capitulation of the British Isles. . . . An occupation of the whole island – for any length of time – be it either before or after its capitulation, does not come into the question – for Germany would be burdened with the feeding of the population.
>
> It must not be forgotten that the longer the war lasts, the more will the balance of power between England and America move in favour of the latter. . . .
>
> In conclusion: England might ask herself whether it pays her, at great sacrifice, to make the most precarious effort to conquer the Axis, and into the bargain, to strengthen with certainty Bolshevik Russia as an immensely more dangerous opponent to her Empire.

168

At 7.30 p.m. on Tuesday, 9 September, in the seclusion of his bed-room, the Deputy Führer spent an inconclusive hour talking over the memorandum with an old acquaintance from pre-war days, Lord Beaver-brook; the Iranian coup seemed to lend new urgency to his appeal. As the new Minister of Supply, Beaverbrook was shortly to depart on a trade mission to Stalin but whether Hess knew this – or that in talks with the Russians Beaverbrook would disclaim all notions of a peace treaty – is unclear. For security reasons, the Special Branch men who bugged their conversation gave Hess his usual code-name, "Jonathan" while Beaver-brook was "Dr Livingstone".

When Beaverbrook referred bitterly to the war – "the whole thing is bloody" – Hess was swift to respond. "Yes, the whole thing is bloody, but we can use our blood for better things. You can use your blood in your colonies and for your Empire, and we can use our blood for the East. We need ground for our population."

To the end he was bitter that his peace mission had been slighted: "I thought I can come here and find a certain commonsense."

Beaverbrook's reply summed up the whole embittered paradox of which 1941 was fast becoming the embodiment: a world in which men killed and must go on killing as if by reflex action. "Very difficult, you know, to find commonsense when a war is on," he told the German. He added ruefully: "Once you get into the blood and the guns and the sacrifices, then reason goes."

*

Nearer to the battlefront, the perspectives were different. At the British Embassy in Moscow, Harold Elvin felt closer to the Russian people with every day that passed.

As early as 27 June, Sir Stafford Cripps had returned from London, with a full-scale Military Mission, under Lieutenant-General Noel Mason-MacFarlane, in tow, but the attitude of some of its members had shocked Elvin profoundly. One army Captain had remarked cynically: "Of course we have to keep most of our arms back to fight this country when Germany is finished."

Yet Elvin could only marvel at the spirit of the people. Like the Londoners of 1940, the Muscovites had been swift to adapt. Now, at dusk, Red Square was almost deserted; only black flocks of rooks cawed over the Kremlin walls, circling the square red block that was Lenin's mausoleum like scraps of charred paper. But behind closed doors and darkened windows, a fierce activity prevailed. At the factory benches, couples were working side by side; husbands were teaching their jobs to their wives before departing for the front. Teenagers patrolled at twilight, warning householders of faulty black-outs, checking sandbags and water

169

pails in case of incendiary raids. All younger children had been evacuated from the city – placed in the care of Moscow's manicurists, who now had sterner tasks to perform. At the National Hotel – where portraits of Hitler and Mussolini had only lately replaced those of Neville Chamberlain and the Archbishop of Canterbury as the architects of World War Two – women workers had now replaced the men as waiters and dishwashers.

Camouflage loomed everywhere. The gold onion domes of the Kremlin vanished beneath a coating of battleship-grey. The façade of the Great Palace was screened by a net festooned with green branches. The Bolshoi Theatre was hung with canvas, painted with false entrance doorways. Anti-aircraft batteries, screened by leaves, lay secreted in the clusters of pine and birch dotting the city. Each night, 750,000 people bedded down beneath the blue-and-gold mosaic ceilings of the Moscow subway stations – "exactly what Metro-Goldwyn-Mayer would think an air-raid shelter should look like", sniffed the noted film director Sergei Eisenstein.

Moscow's first air-raid warning came to a shrilling of whistles and a wailing of sirens on the night of 21 July, followed by the mighty roll of the ack-ack barrage, the crump of explosions. Soon the raids had become a siege, and Elvin was fire-watching at the Embassy every fourth night in addition to his other duties. At dawn he retired to his bedroom in the West Wing groggy with lack of sleep.

It was at 2 a.m. on 11 August when his deeper involvement began; the cheerful cockney, Sergeant Bill Eldredge, called him to the switchboard. He explained that a girl had rung the Embassy, wanting to "gab Russki." But it turned out that Eldredge was wrong: a Russian girl was feeling a desperate need to talk English.

To Elvin it would always be the strangest of all his Moscow encounters, symbolic of the lonely immensity of the land, her people's infinite capacity for suffering. He heard the girl's first words with a chill of foreboding.

"I've lost both mother and father at Minsk in the war. I heard tonight. I'm alone. My name is Tamara. I was mad to know what to do. I can't sleep . . . I'm absolutely alone. I thought I'll ring up the British Embassy, maybe I could speak with an Englishman for an hour . . . will you speak to me for one hour?"

That night it was Bill Eldredge who made the tea and brought it to the switchboard. Hardly realising what he said, Elvin talked on for fully two hours, striving to understand, to bring comfort. The next night, she called again at 2 a.m. Another two hours went by. Soon it had become second nature, talking for hours night after night to a girl whose face he had never seen, a fixture at the switchboard in the main hallway, only the harsh light of the single reading lamp probing the shadows.

They met only twice: once in the Tretiakov Art Gallery, timorously at

170

first, each wondering what the other would be like. The second time was on 11 September, at an all-night dance at Moscow University, where Tamara was a student. Later, in a darkened classroom, they made love until dawn.

After that everything went wrong. In the small hours of each night, the telephone link was maintained, but Elvin, laid up with synovitis in his left knee, was confined to his bedroom, watching the barges slide down the Moscow River, past the high red crenellated walls of the Kremlin. On 23 September, she phoned for the last time.

For weeks now she had been a volunteer, digging trenches outside Moscow, but at last, after repeatedly nagging the authorities, her wish had been granted: she was heading for the front line. Elvin was appalled. "To do what?" he asked her.

Tamara was vague. "Red Cross, digging trenches – do you think they might let me fight?" Her voice was tender and puzzled by turns. "My English friend . . . Room 10, Tretiakov Art Gallery, I will always remember." Suddenly she asked, "Tell me something, I keep asking myself . . ."

"Yes, Tamara?"

"You know my mother and father were killed by the Germans?"

"Yes, Tamara," Elvin said again.

"*Why?*"

Long after, Elvin would remember with pain that he had found no answer to that question.

*

Churchill was disgruntled as September dawned. Despite his new-found rapport with Roosevelt – and a timely success in Iran – the war for the first time in months had reached stalemate. Moreover, a groundswell of enthusiasm for all things Russian – and thus a tacit acceptance of Communism – was sweeping Britain.

Already intellectual left-wingers had created a thousand committees and societies to promote the Soviet cause, blithely brushing aside long-held reservations about Stalinist oppression – "why worry about the colour of the fireman's socks during a fire?" was one Briton's pithy appraisal. Mass Observers reported the widespread "feeling, again obscure and often incoherent, that Russia was a working man's country" – and that 60 per cent of people, nagged by a vague guilt that Britain's role was now secondary, felt that more help should be given her. They noted, too, "a kind of secure cheerfulness . . . unknown since the fall of Greece" – and that Stalin's appearance on a newsreel was a signal for prolonged applause.

To Churchill it seemed that the Russian cause now loomed larger than that of the Empire. In September, a "Tanks for Russia Week", launched by the canny Beaverbrook as Minister of Supply, saw an unprecedented response; in one Kent railway works, 1,000 freight waggons for Russia were completed within ten weeks, despite seventy-six air-raid warnings. At Birmingham, where workers daubed "Marx" "Lenin" and "Another for Joe" on their finished products, the Ambassador, Ivan Maisky, was hoisted high on to a tank while workers sang the *Internationale*.

That winter the august Athenaeum Club on London's Pall Mall elected Maisky to its membership.

As sales of the *Soviet War News* climbed to 50,000 weekly, and British Communist Party membership neared an all-time level of 65,000, a subtle propaganda campaign to heighten British workers' guilt-feelings was early apparent. Until now, men and women had felt themselves hard done by, given their daily short commons, a clothes rationing system of 66 coupons a year, with even jam and honey restricted by a points system. Now they were assailed by posters plastered on doors and hoardings that proclaimed: RUSSIAN WORKERS FIGHT FOR US! RUSSIAN WORKERS BURN THEIR HOMES FOR US!! DO WE REALISE? DO WE CARE? That early graffiti on railway arches, STOP THIS IMPERIALIST WAR, had soon given way to SECOND FRONT NOW. In one instance, a Party poster's blatant politicisation prompted the censor to step in: below the slogan THE RED ARMY'S FIGHT IS YOUR FIGHT loomed the parrot-cries, Remove pro-Fascists from high places – End Employers' mis-management and waste – Restore T.U. (Trade Union) Rights and *Daily Worker*.*

This was not Churchill's only cause for disquiet. If he grieved that the spirit of Empire was waning much of his Empire, even this early in the war, was already bent on secession.

From 16 August on, Article III of the Atlantic Charter had caused a ferment that would not be stilled. In final form, it read: ". . . they respect the right of all peoples to choose the form of government under which they will live; and they wish to see sovereign rights and self-government restored to those who have been forcibly deprived of them."

At once the able and progressive Governor of Burma, Sir Reginald Dorman-Smith, warned that the Burmese, under their ambitious Premier, U Saw, would use this lever to push for full post-war self-government; many nations under British rule felt as enslaved as Norway or Belgium. This in turn alarmed the Colonial Secretary, Lord Moyne; how could he countenance self-government for Gibraltar, Aden, The Gambia, Hong Kong, to name but a few? On 4 September, the War Cabinet decided firmly that the Charter was concerned solely with Nazi-dominated European nations. It had no connection with the British

* The *Daily Worker* had been banned by the Minister of Home Security, Herbert Morrison, from 21 January, 1941. It was not re-licensed until 26 August, 1942.

Empire's internal affairs – or with relations between the United States and the Philippines.

Nonetheless, facing the House of Commons on 9 September, Churchill phrased things more subtly. The Charter had no connection with people who owed "allegiance to the British Crown" – since Britain was already pledged to help India, Burma and other countries obtain equal partnership in the Commonwealth once the war was ended.

This promise of jam in a far-off tomorrow incensed many nationalists – among them Mahatma Gandhi, one of the few leaders of the Indian National Congress who remained at liberty, for in eleven months 5,000 Indians had been clapped into jail for civil disobedience, among them the former President Jawaharlal Nehru. Their argument had some cogency: if Britain was really fighting for democracy, she should prove it by granting India Dominion status.

America should not aid Britain without guarantee, Gandhi maintained now. "She should ask what will happen to India, Asia and African possessions. She should withdraw any help unless there are guarantees of human liberties. . . ." U Saw, who had convinced Dorman-Smith of this – but not Churchill – was rash enough to appeal to Roosevelt over the Premier's head. Urging him not to "regard the case of Burma as a domestic issue for the British Empire", U Saw warned "The world's faith in the genuineness of the war aims enunciated by you and Mr Churchill will depend on the view you take on this point."

It was in vain. "The Prime Minister of Burma lacks authority to treat with foreign governments upon his own initiative," Hull advised the President, who did not even bother to acknowledge the letter. On the strength of a brief parley he held with the Japanese, Churchill was to jail U Saw too.

Visitors to the Far East were well aware of the danger signs. The Commander-in-Chief, Air Chief Marshal Sir Robert Brooke-Popham, after passing through Calcutta, reported to Ismay of "a difference between the bazaars and the business quarter" too marked "to please a defender of democracy"; he found the Europeans "too plutocratic, too well-dressed, and seemed very far-removed from the war". Profits took priority over all; since one practice air-raid warning had cost the jute manufacturers 40,000 rupees (about £2,500) in lost man-hours it had not been repeated. In Dutch East Indian cities like Batavia, the ace Filipino reporter Carlos Romulo found the Javanese leaders ready and waiting to collaborate with any Japanese invasion. Had not Queen Wilhelmina also denied that the Atlantic Charter applied to them?

Such aspirations Churchill would never fully grasp. "As regards India," the Secretary of State, Leopold Amery lamented, "(he) has never got beyond the early Kipling stage." At times brutally dismissive – "what those people need is the *sjambok*", he once told Dorman-Smith

– at others he saw the Empire through a rose-tinted haze recalling a Victorian Durbar. "If the Japs were to invade," he confidently predicted, "it would make the Indians loyal to the King Emperor for a hundred years."

It was already much too late. Throughout almost all of Asia now, the white man was truly hated; the sky was black with chickens coming home to roost.

*

Roosevelt apart, Churchill was increasingly at odds with all his erstwhile allies. The reason was not hard to find: neither British factory workers, Asian nationalist leaders or Dominions generals saw the prime objective of the war as the preservation of the British Empire.

"The P.M. is interested only in victory and not in the purposes of victory," the Labour pundit Harold Laski wrote to Justice Felix Frankfurter of the Supreme Court, an intimate of Roosevelt's, "He will seek to preserve 'traditional Britain' at all costs . . . he has set his face backwards and not forward in the concepts of the post-war world."

Another man galled beyond endurance by Churchill's imperialist stance was General Charles de Gaulle. As the Syrian campaign had ended de Gaulle had been enraged to find that his doughty Free French, having served their purpose, had been coolly set aside; in the twenty-two clauses of the armistice treaty signed between Britain and Vichy France no mention had even been made of them. His private war had been fought in vain – for while the British guaranteed Syria ultimate independence, they were keeping a tight hold on the terrain for the duration.

"White with suppressed passion," de Gaulle invaded the Cairo office of the Minister of State Oliver Lyttelton both denouncing the treaty and refusing to accept it. When he thrust forward a document withdrawing all Free French Forces from the Middle East Command, Lyttelton promptly tore it up.

In the end though, Lyttelton saw the justice of de Gaulle's complaints; he reversed many Armistice clauses in favour of the Free French, who now took over all war material and both Syrian and Lebanese levies, as well as recruiting 6,000 Vichyites to their own ranks. But between Cairo and London de Gaulle left what Churchill was to call "a trail of Anglophobia" behind him; the gulf between the two men was widening daily.

In Churchill's eyes, de Gaulle's cardinal sin was an interview he granted the *Chicago Daily News* on 27 August in Brazzaville. Hinting that Britain's tenuous relationship with Vichy was a means of maintaining contact with Hitler, the General next broached the idea of offering West African naval bases to the United States. Nor would he seek destroyers in

174

return – a sneering reference to Britain's ceding of eight crucial Atlantic bases in 1940 in return for fifty over-age U.S. destroyers. Churchill's explosion of rage when he heard resembled an old-time vaudeville comedian; tearing his cigar from his mouth he first hurled it on the floor then jumped on it. He had been waiting for three months for an excuse to get rid of the General, he trumpeted – "de Gaulle was to feel the draught the minute he arrived".

And that he did. Four days later, when he reached London, even the Spears Mission was forbidden to contact him; any request for a meeting was to be summarily refused. Broadcast facilities, if sought, must be withheld by the B.B.C. Nor was de Gaulle free to leave the country again; M.I.5, the British counter-intelligence agency, was to dog his footsteps night and day.

De Gaulle promptly saw the red light. In a noonday meeting with Churchill on 12 September, he proved the soul of conciliation. "While he, de Gaulle, was yet an infant in politics," he told the Premier, and "that what he said had sometimes been directed to individuals who deserved it," fundamentally he had always been, and always would be, loyal to Churchill. Without demur, he agreed to the formation of an eight-man Free French National Committee which, on paper at least, diluted his dictatorial powers.

Only much later did Churchill realise that de Gaulle's apparent readiness to comply had been prompted as always by the same unswerving ambition: the official recognition by Russia and all the refugee governments in London that he alone was the true leader of the Free French.

Churchill's other problems were less easily resolved. The rift with the Dominions, so noticeable after the fall of Greece and Crete, was now an outright impasse. On 28 August, faced with a vote of no-confidence by his Labour opposition, the Australian Prime Minister, Robert Menzies, resigned; his successor, Arthur Fadden, took office with a bare majority of one. At this point, the demands of Lieutenant-General Sir Thomas Blamey, the Australian C-in-C in the Middle East, became insistent. By 29 August, the 18th Australian Brigade had been withdrawn from Tobruk. Now Blamey sought to strip Tobruk of all the Anzacs remaining – and the reassembly of all Australian forces under his sole command.

It was a move Churchill mightily opposed – but in view of mounting Australian pressure he had little choice. On 11 September, he had reluctantly agreed – "irrespective of the cost entailed and the injury to future prospects" – if the Australians insisted. Three days later, Fadden did insist. The Australians had held Tobruk against Rommel since April, in the most gruelling climate that Allied troops had yet endured.

On 18 September, Churchill's Most Secret cipher telegram to Auchinleck made his own feelings plain: "Great allowances must be made for a Government with a majority of one playing politics with a bitter

Opposition, part of whom at least are isolationist in sentiment. Whatever your and our personal feelings may be, it is our duty at all costs to prevent an open dispute with the Australian Government. Any public controversy would injure foundations of Empire and be disastrous to our general position in the war."

"I would feel inclined to suggest informal message should be made to Australian Government suggesting the replacement of Blamey whose conduct I regard as weak and disingenuous," Lyttelton counselled from Cairo, advice which the Premier felt it prudent to ignore. On 30 September, he once more appealed to Fadden to modify his decision, leaving two Australian brigades still in Tobruk – a request Fadden refused on the day that his Government, too, was overthrown.

The new Australian Premier, Labour's bespectacled John Curtin, gave Churchill more cause for hope. On assuming office he had made two top-level requests: an increase in Australia's petrol supplies and the dispatch of a first-class battleship to the Pacific.

Although Churchill bore more than his fair share of the blame for the decision that followed, this request for a battleship did originate with Curtin – who might still be prevailed on to retain those brigades in Tobruk. Accordingly – "in spite of protests from the Commander-in-Chief, Home Fleet" – Churchill reluctantly agreed to humour the Australians – "we are sending forthwith our newest battleship, *Prince of Wales*, to join *Repulse* in Indian Ocean."

If he had hoped for a benign turn-about in Canberra as a result, he had hoped in vain. On 15 October, Curtin proved as adamant as his predecessor: the brigades were to be withdrawn from Tobruk. Now Churchill's sense of black frustration was complete. "We are at war with almost every country," he was to rage bitterly to Beaverbrook, "including Australia!"

*

On the eastern front, *Fähnrich* Peter Neumann knew a constant turmoil of emotions. One day he would be fully convinced that the S.S. mission was just. On the next, agonising doubts would assail him all over again.

At Lvov, in the Ukraine, on 3 July, despite the pall of filth and decay hanging over the city, Neumann felt better. In their pell-mell retreat, the Red Army had spared nothing and nobody. Bodies of Russian and Polish "political" prisoners – often men and women jailed for being late for work – lay where they had been gunned down all over the courtyard of the N.K.V.D. prison. Fleeing in trucks and carts, the soldiers had opened fire on every building indiscriminately. In the silent streets, relatives were rummaging among the dead, and blue-black clouds of flies rose from the piled corpses.

No longer would he feel such remorse in liquidating Russians, Neumann told himself confidently.

But at Zhitomir, on 28 July, he again had cause to wonder. By degrees, as the Viking Division adapted to its executioner's role, the screw was tightening: now not only Commissars but all Jewish functionaries, civil or military, were to be shot without trial. Shocked, Neumann watched his fellow ensign Karl von Reckner, empty his Mauser without compunction into a group of labour camp officials. Was this the same Karl he had once watched as a schoolboy, playing softball on the sands by the *Aussen-Alster*, Hamburg? His finger had not even wavered on the trigger.

As the division forged deeper into the Ukraine the war of nerves was stepped up. In some ruined villages, every object remaining was a potential booby-trap – the interior of a samovar, a vodka bottle, a bucket suspended in a well. Neumann and the others learned to toss a handful of grenades into any building before entering it, triggering off the explosions.

Always they were conscious of the partisan presence, whole battalions of eyes noting their passage, yet always they were invisible. In the forest of Krasnaja, their TCVs, jolting over ruts and potholes, covered every road for a radius of twenty miles and found no one. But the partisans were there. On 23 September, the bodies of three S.S. sentries were recovered from the woods. One man's face was no more than an obscene wound; after beating him to death and bayoneting him the partisans had rammed a tree branch into his mouth.

In the hamlet of Krasnaja, *Untersturmführer* (Second-Lieutenant) van Kolden, a thick-set Dutchman of the Nordland Regiment, had assembled the entire population in the market square. In front of them, screened by grey blankets, lay the German dead. One of the S.S. men was sobbing quietly.

Van Kolden was holding himself in check, but not for long. "Walk them past it," he ordered two of his men, "let them taste and smell it, so that they can see what might happen to them." Then anger, like a haemorrhage, flooded his mind, and he seized a machine pistol from a non-com. "What *is* going to happen to them," he screamed, opening fire.

Chaos descended. The Russians in the front rank slumped and fell like straw men. The dusty expanse of the market square was suddenly a sea of shabbily-clad peasants, fighting to get away. Almost every S.S. man present had lost control. The hammering of machine-pistols was unbearably loud, drowning out the terrified screams of women and children. Great splashes of blood stained the ochre-coloured ground; a suffocating cloud of black smoke was rising from the thatched roofs.

Neumann realised that all semblance of discipline had gone: they were beasts and nothing could check them. Nonetheless he must try. He saw *Rottenführer* Libesis, propped stupefied against a wall, swaying from side

177

to side as if he was drunk, and he shouted urgently into the corporal's ear: "Libesis, you must help me to stop this horror" But above the shattering barrage of sound Libesis could barely hear him. "Nothing to be done," he mumbled stupidly.

Neumann expostulated, "But these people didn't kill the men on guard duty."

"Doesn't matter," Libesis answered, like a man in a trance, "They could have saved themselves by giving us information. They must pay."

Neumann could bear it no longer; the screams seemed to be exploding inside his head. Grabbing his Mauser, he hastened on to *Unterscharführer* Diekener of his own platoon. The Sergeant's whole face was scored with blood-red streaks: the scars left by women's fingernails.

"Diekener," he shouted, "call your men to order. This frightful butchery is unworthy of the uniform we wear!" Diekener's response was no more than an ugly grin. "You're an S.S. man now, *Fähnrich*. It's your pals that have been butchered."

Neumann was beside himself: "I shall have you sent to punishment camp for refusing to obey an order." The threat was like a cold douche, bringing Diekener to his senses. "*Entschuldigen, Herr Fähnrich, zu Befehl*" (I'm sorry, sir. As you say, sir!), he answered, with a sharp click of the heels. But no one heeded the long blast that Diekener blew on his whistle.

In a black rage, *Untersturmführer* von Kolden came striding up. For a moment he listened incredulously to Neumann's stammered protests then cut him brutally short: "Massacre? You haven't seen anything yet, you poor bloody little *Fähnrich*. If we don't teach these damned moujiks a few sharp lessons . . . listen, Neumann . . . in war a soldier kills and enjoys killing."

A sudden hush had fallen on the market square. All firing now ceased. Dazedly, like men deep in shock, the S.S. soldiers were staring at the piles of black-clad bodies, at the blood staining their hands, as if somehow striving to establish a connection. A woman kneeled beside a corpse, her arms raised to heaven, howling terribly like a dog.

Truck horns were sounding urgently and whistles shrilled: it was time to be gone.

Neumann slumped at the wayside, his head in his hands. Kill or be killed, he thought desperately, but where did the true justice lie? Assuming, of course, that such a thing even existed.

*

Not all were so squeamish. In the wake of the advancing armies, 3,000 black-clad S.S. men, travelling in trucks that bore the sign of the swastika, were embarking on a holocaust. For the first time in history murder

178

was being planned on an assembly line basis: they were hunting five million Jews spread over a million square kilometres of territory, a sword of genocide sweeping from east to west.

As far back as January, twelve top S.S. leaders had answered a summons from *Reichsführer* Heinrich Himmler, the mild-mannered ex-chicken farmer heading the Gestapo and S.S., to convene at Wewelsburg, an unique replica of a medieval castle near Paderborn, Westphalia. Among those present were Reinhard Heydrich, chief of the Reich Security Main Office (R.S.H.A.), S.S. General Karl Wolff, and *Obergruppenführer* (Lieutenant-General) Erich von dem Bach-Zelewski, an expert on partisan warfare.

As yet there had been no official announcement regarding Barbarossa, until Himmler revealed bluntly that the Führer had decided to strike a mortal blow against Russia. "The purpose of the campaign", he told them, as Zelewski was to recall it, "is to reduce the Slav populations by thirty millions." His precedent, according to Wolff, was the Spanish Inquisition – "what the Jesuits did for Rome, the S.S. must do for the Nazi Party!"

In the weeks that followed, Heydrich and Zelewski were busy men, but in the meantime Himmler had succeeded in his quest for someone who, in his own words, was "superhuman-inhuman" – a man devoid of every humane reflex. Located at 116, Kurfürstenstrasse, Berlin, as head of Department B4, the Section for Jewish Affairs, this was Adolf Eichmann, a man who so hated Jews that as a teenager he had learned Yiddish and Hebrew, the better to wage war against them. It was Eichmann who now took charge of Aktion 14 F 13, the "final solution" of the Jewish question.

This most secret objective of Hitler's career was never committed to paper by the Führer himself. Only on 3 March, weeks before his notorious "Commissar" directive to his generals, did he dictate to Jodl: "The Bolshevist-Jewish intelligentsia must be eliminated, as having been the 'oppressor' up to now." No hint was given that the life of every Jew would be forfeit – although by 16 July, conferring with Göring and others, Hitler was plainly aware that mass executions were under way. These were necessary, he maintained, to pacify the vast terrain – "shoot everyone who shows a wry face".

By April, the leaders of the four *Einsatzgruppe* (Action Groups) had been briefed as to the targets they sought: all male Jews, Communist functionaries, "second-class Asiatics" and "gypsies". No group must operate within 200 kilometres of an Army headquarters, in case the fighting men got wind of it, but their territories were clearly defined. On 15 July, when they went into action, Group A, under *Brigadeführer* (Brigadier) Walter Stahlecker spread a reign of terror through Latvia, Lithuania and Estonia, Group B, under Arthur Nebe, operated between the Baltic states and the Ukraine: Dr Otto Rasch's Group C had the Ukraine as their killing-ground, while Otto Ohlendorf's Group D worked between Bessarabia and the Crimea.

The tally of their dead beggared description. By April, 1942, Stahlecker's group had eliminated 249,420 victims, three-quarters of them by gassing. In this grisly numbers game, the other groups, by comparison, lagged far behind – 95,000 destroyed by Rasch's men, 90,000 by Ohlendorf's, some 45,000 by Nebe's – but of six million Jews for whom a "final solution" was found, two million were to meet their fate at the hands of the *Einsatzgruppen*.

They did not die in dignity. "S.S. drove the people along the road at a running pace," testified one eye-witness to the massacre of 5,000 Jews at Rovno, Poland, "hitting them until they reached the waiting freight train. Coach after coach was filled as the screaming of women and children and the cracking of whips and rifle shots resounded unceasingly. Since families or groups had barricaded themselves in strong buildings, where the doors could not be forced, they were blown open with handgrenades. . . . Younger people tried to get across the railway tracks and over a small river to get away. Part of the area was illuminated by rockets. . . . All through the night these beaten, hounded and wounded people moved along. . . . Women carried their dead children in their arms, children pulled and dragged their dead parents by their arms and legs down the road towards the train. . . . Again and again the cries 'Open the door, open the door' echoed through the ghetto."

No one was immune. "I saw dozens of corpses of all ages and both sexes," the same witness recalled. "Pieces of clothing, shoes, stockings, jackets, hats, coats, were lying in the streets. At the corner of a house lay a baby less than a year old with its skull crushed. Blood and brains were scattered over the house wall. The child was dressed only in a little shirt. The S.S. commander, Pütz, was walking up and down a row of about eighty to a hundred male Jews, who were crouching on the ground. He had a heavy dog-whip in his hand."

All over Russia, as September wore on, the same nightmare was re-enacted. Now 1941 saw the true nadir of World War Two, a world unknown to Afrika Korps men and Luftwaffe fighter pilots, a world in which ideological aims constituted an absolute. One unwilling witness, Major Rösler, commanding the 528th Infantry Regiment, always recalled how a fierce fusillade of rifle fire aroused him in his billet at Zhitomir. Hastening to investigate, he chanced on a pit brimming with Jewish bodies of all ages and both sexes – among them an old white-bearded man clutching a cane in his left hand. Horrified to see he was still breathing, Rösler ordered a policeman to shoot him. Smiling, the man shook his head: "I have already shot him seven times in the stomach. He can die on his own now".

180

It was no lone example. In their fearful zeal, the *Einsatzgruppen* seemed to vie with one another for mindless bestiality. Russian Jews were tortured with red-hot iron bars; eyes were gouged out, stomachs ripped open, feet, hands, fingers, ears and noses hacked off. One Russian battalion commander and his Commissar were nailed to stakes by the arms and legs before five-point stars were carved in their bodies with knives.

In this catalogue of horrors, one of the worst of all the massacres was perpetrated by *Standartenführer* Paul Blobel, a tall bearded one-time architect attached to Action Group C. On 29 September, after Kiev, the beautiful capital of the Ukraine had fallen, almost 34,000 Jews were herded into a sandy gorge called Babyi-Yar, the Ravine of the Women, on the outskirts of the city. An old woman guarding a cemetery, M. S. Loutsenko, remembered that day: "Right there they were laying them down . . . and they were screaming . . . Mother of God, how they were screaming . . . and they were smashing their skulls with shovels".

Unknown to most Germans, mass genocide was already a fact of life inside the Third Reich. Every householder knew – many of them with shame – that the Jews had long been targets for discrimination: special ration cards, freckled with tiny "Js" denied them the purchase of fresh vegetables, meat and chocolate. From September on, they were further distinguished by a yellow Star of David, the size of a side-plate, sewn on their clothing; from October, all family allowances and sickness benefits were revoked. The first stage had been deprivation; the next was deportation.

It began, on a gigantic scale, in mid-October. From all the main-line city stations, Berlin and Hamburg, Munich and Frankfurt-am-Main, goods trains loaded with human freight, 1,000 strong, began heading north; 20,000 souls were to leave on 15 October alone. Their destination was the ghetto at Lodz, but soon more trains still were leaving for other ghettos: Warsaw, Kovno, Minsk and Riga. Two years earlier, Eichmann had even toyed with the concept of a mighty ghetto for 4 million Jews under an S.S. police government on the island of Madagascar, but that time was long past. The ghettos had replaced that fancy, but these, too, were no more than a transitional phase before the real slaughter began. "The faster we get rid of them the better," exulted Eichmann's aid, Rolf Günther.

In the contemporary documentation, euphemisms abounded, a strange example of high-level military schizophrenia. On 31 July, Göring, as chairman of the Ministerial Defence Council, sent a jargon-clogged memo to Heydrich, ordering him to "prepare a master plan for the measures – organisational, concrete and material – preparatory to the implementation of the sought-for final solution". "Special treatment" or "emigration" stood in for evacuation and deportation; "disposition" was, in truth, "extermination". And the means for this had long been at hand.

All through 1940 and 1941, the concentration camps had been growing in number, replacing the onetime labour and detention camps until they were thirty in all: names that would live in infamy, like Auschwitz, housing up to 100,000 victims over fifteen square miles, Bergen-Belsen, Chelmno, Neuengamme, Birkenau and Treblinka. The pattern for all of them had been set in the summer of 1941, when Eichmann called on Auschwitz' commandant, Rudolf Höss, to discuss practicable ways and means of eliminating not only every German Jew but suspect Poles, "idlers", gypsies, psychopaths with criminal records and many dissident clergymen. That could only be achieved by gassing, Höss ventured. Given suitable gas-proofed premises, he thought it possible to dispose of 800 people at a time.

The gas in question was Cyclon B, a prussic acid preparation used to destroy vermin, and, mercifully, few of those who succumbed to its fumes had any inkling as to their fate. At Auschwitz and other camps, a polite fiction was maintained; all new arrivals must shower and undergo a delousing process. Even close at hand, the gas chambers, labelled BATHS, looked altogether innocuous; the manicured lawns and trim flower-borders that masked their roofs also hid the mushroom vents which housed the gas crystals. Only sprightly music, selections from *The Merry Widow* and *The Tales of Hoffmann*, soothed them on their way, played by an orchestra of pretty young girls in white blouses and navy-blue skirts.

Only when they had undressed and the massive doors of the bath chamber slid shut did the more perceptive note that the floor had no drains, that no water spouted from the overhead showers. Then, as the gas came hissing from the vents, mass panic set in, but by now it was too late. Thirty minutes later it was all over. The bodies had ceased to writhe, the gold teeth and the women's hair, which Himmler had specified as "strategic material", had been removed by special commando teams, the last journey to the crematoria had begun.

"I began to hate the Jews," one Hebrew teenager wrote feelingly about this time, "Not only the Orthodox, but all of them. I hated their names, their faces, their manner of speech, their humour and their nervous diligence . . .

"I hated the Jews because I hated the sight of death."

*

A golden opportunity had been lost, and every soldier serving on the eastern front knew it. The chance of dealing Russian Communism a mortal blow and toppling Josef Stalin's regime had gone irretrievably.

From the first, Hitler's fatal error had been to look on Russia as one nation – a homogeneous race of despised *untermenschen*. The truth was that 187 million Russians were made up of 170 different races speaking 140 different tongues – among them embittered ethnic minorities like the Balts, the Ukrainians and the Cossacks, who remembered that 20 million had died in the purges since the October Revolution.

The first German troops to cross the border were overwhelmed by their reception. In Kiev, which fell on 19 September – ten days before the enormity of Babyi-Yar – Reinhold Pabel, who entered with the 6th Division, watched with astonishment as an old white-bearded patriarch draped a huge roll of unused street-car tickets round a sergeant's neck, in the style of a Hawaiian garland. Another approached the first car-load of German officers bearing a tray with a loaf of bread and a salt-shaker – the traditional Slavic symbol of welcome. Families vied with one another to bear the conquering soldiers home for a bath and a meal; huge posters proclaiming HITLER THE LIBERATOR loomed everywhere.

"The people look on us as liberators," Guderian wrote home to his wife, Gretel. "It is to be hoped they will not be disappointed."

Many top commanders shared this hope. Von Rundstedt's first action in the Ukraine was to restore the churches to the people; soon ikons and chalices which had been hidden from the Commissars gleamed once again on the altars, and in the eighteenth-century church at Poltava, when von Rundstedt attended Divine Service, *Te Deums* resounded again from the old walls. At Borisov, north-east of Minsk, when the *Wehrmacht* refurbished the Orthodox Church, until then a Bolshevik store, thousands crowded the square and streets for the opening service; von Bock, arriving from Army Group Centre, passed over a carpet of clean white sand into a nave decked out with green branches.

On his own initiative, von Bock had already taken steps to harness this chain of good-will. Attached to his headquarters with the rank of Captain was a 45-year-old Riga businessman, Wilfred Strik-Strikfeldt who had served in the Tsarist Army. What Bock proposed, using Strikfeldt as his liaison officer, was a scheme that had the full approval of Göbbels, for one: the creation of a Russian Liberation Army aligned with a puppet government modelled on Vichy lines.

Plainly, when 11,000 Red Army men deserted overnight from one assault group alone, this was fertile ground. In the space of months, Strikfeldt had enlisted 800,000 Red Army personnel – "our Ivans" – in a war against Josef Stalin.

Another visionary with high hopes for the future was Alfred Rosenberg, a leading Nazi thinker, who had been appointed Commissioner for the East European Region; he was looking, he told his staff on 20 June, to the "voluntary co-operation" of 40 million men. But this dream, like von Bock's, was to remain an illusion. On 4 August, visiting Bock's headquarters, Hitler significantly refused to receive Stikfeldt and hear his report on progress to date.

No reply was later forthcoming from the *Wolfsschanze* when von Bock passed on an offer from the city fathers of Smolensk to raise a liberation army of one million men – but a curt order was passed to the Ministry of Propaganda, forbidding Göbbels to visit the front for discussions with von Bock.

In a Russia dominated by the Third Reich such citizens as survived would serve no other function than as slave-labour for the conquerors. To elevate them to combatant status, even to educate them, would be fatal, in Hitler's view – "the people should know just enough to recognise the signs on the roads".

Thus, by perverse irony, Nazi ideology ultimately brought about the very results that it was pledged to destroy. In time the ravages of the *Einsatzgruppen* would unite the Russian people against the invader as never before. Within four years the Communist floodtide would engulf all Eastern Europe – the Baltic States, Poland, Hungary, Rumania, Bulgaria, East Germany, Czechoslovakia were all to become Soviet vassals.

A victory over Bolshevism had been thrown away.

*

It was not the only mistake to cost Hitler dear that autumn. Already, despite the doubts of many advisers, he had insisted that Russia must be invaded. He had delayed stubbornly in ordering an advance on Moscow. Now, with the collapse of the Ukraine to the south and Leningrad invested to the north, he once more switched priorities. On 26 September, he ordered a vast new offensive – Operation Typhoon, timed for 2 October – to concentrate on Moscow itself.

Only the sixty divisions required for the army of occupation in a defeated Russia had thus far been issued with winter clothing – but the new edict decreed that the *Wehrmacht* must "break the enemy on the threshold of winter".

Hitler had no plans for a winter campaign at all.

184

9

"Let No One Forget, Let Nothing Be Forgotten"

1 October–5 November, 1941

THE HUSHED ENCLAVE of the British Embassy in Moscow was suddenly alive with bustling urgency and rumours. Harold Elvin, now back on night duty, should long ago have retired to bed. But somehow he could not resist inventing minor chores as an excuse for lingering on all morning in the main hallway – "the world buzzed so; and was so alive".

On 28 September, a full-scale Anglo-American mission, more than forty strong, led by Lord Beaverbrook and Averell Harriman, had arrived in Moscow for talks with Stalin and Molotov. In the next three days of conferences, much that was crucial to the outcome of World War Two would be decided – and Elvin had the heady sense of living through history.

It was a delegation which the Military Mission, after kicking its heels with black frustration since 26 June, viewed with mixed feelings. From the first the Russian attitude had been one of surly suspicion – coupled with a greedy readiness to take while yielding nothing in return. "The Russian motto", Lieutenant General Mason-MacFarlane reported angrily to the War Office, "is 'give nothing at all – as slowly as possible' "; his Mission had degenerated into "an inglorious battle of wits between two powers supposedly in the position of allies". His colleagues fared no better. Laurence Cadbury, heading the Economic Mission with two oil experts to advise him, was told bluntly: "What is there to confer about? All we need from you is a supply of arms and a Second Front." Air Vice Marshal Conrad Collier, of the Air Supply Committee, had to do all his business with the Foreign Affairs Liaison Department; no one would even tell him where the Air Ministry building was located.

What were the medium frequency bands used by Russian fighters? The Russians refused to say. How did they set about tackling tanks from the air? The answer was a sullen silence. How many anti-tank guns were allotted to a division? That would depend on the type of division. For example an infantry division? That would depend on where it had to fight.

When Sir Stafford Cripps protested spiritedly to Stalin, the dictator replied sarcastically, "Is it proposed to exchange all State secrets in future?"

The Americans on the spot knew an identical problem. Ambassador Laurence Steinhardt reported to the State Department that in the course of 1940 fully 300 letters had gone unanswered by Molotov and things were little better now. American military observers had been forbidden all access to the war zone – yet a blatant request had been routed to the War Department for Soviet engineers to tour U.S. military plants. "The list of the military secrets requested itself shows very efficient espionage," commented Assistant Secretary of State Adolf A. Berle.

Into this bleak climate of mutual distrust, Beaverbrook, the go-getting Canadian newspaper proprietor, arrived like a buoyant wind from the steppes. The new Minister of Supply saw it as a hurry-up operation from the first. "If one goes to do a job like this and stays in a place more than six days you lose your authority," he told Under Secretary of State for Air Harold Balfour. To this end Beaverbrook had long decided that his mission was to be "a Christmas tree party . . . there must be no excuse for the Russians thinking they were not getting a fair share of the gifts on the tree".

"They want the moon and we haven't got it," Ismay, who made one of the party, wrote to Brooke-Popham, but all along Beaverbrook acted as if the British had. Harriman, for one, saw danger in this: "Beaverbrook was disposed to hand over every conceivable American weapon or material to the Russians without counting the cost to Britain". But Beaverbrook, far-sightedly, sensed that for the foreseeable future Britain's war-role would be mainly peripheral. In the months to come the entire war would hinge on the success or failure of Russian resistance.

If the first meeting with Stalin – at 9 p.m. on 28 September, in a second-floor office littered with brimming ashtrays, overlooking the Moscow River – was cordial enough, the second, at 7 p.m. on 29 May, reduced Beaverbrook and Harriman to "an indigo blue mood". "Unmannerly and disinterested," the dictator tossed aside letters of introduction from Roosevelt and Churchill without even glancing at them. "The paucity of your offers clearly shows that you want to see the Soviet Union defeated," he told Harriman rudely.

Not until a third meeting, on the evening of 30 September, did Stalin's mood change mercurially. "It is up to the three of us to prove Göbbels a liar," he remarked expansively, doodling red wolves on the scratch-pad before him, and it was now with some dismay that Harriman time and again heard Beaverbrook yield to the Russian front Great Britain's share of American supplies: 25,000 tons of electrolytic copper, 1,800 fighter aircraft, 2,250 tanks, 500 anti-tank guns, 23,000 tommy-guns, 27,000 tons of rubber, 250,000 greatcoats. It was small wonder that their interpreter, the former diplomat Maxim Litvinov, forgetting his humble role, bounded from his chair, crying, "Now we have won the war!"

At 6 p.m. on 1 October, the bulk of the Beaverbrook-Harriman entourage glimpsed Stalin for the first time in a strangely sybaritic setting: a pillared French-style dining room in the Kremlin, lined with banked arum lilies, its sixteen-foot high double doors inlaid with gold-leaf carving and the arms of Catherine the Great surmounted by golden cherubs. As the dictator entered, clad in a pepper-and-salt gabardine tunic buttoned to the neck, an eerie hush descended on the room. "He moved stealthily like a wild animal in search of prey," Ismay noted, but Harold Balfour was less impressed. "At first glance he looks like a typical jobbing gardener, until you look at his eyes . . . (they) bear out his name – The Man of Steel – although they twinkle kindly."

In the three and a half hour banquet which followed, a Tsarist feast in which caviar gave place to sucking pig, soup, fish and two varieties of game, those eyes rarely ceased their twinkling: Stalin was geniality itself. In the course of drinking thirty-two toasts he downed an entire bottle of champagne – an evening only marred, in Cripps' view, by Stalin's sneering reference to Roosevelt's policy of keeping out of the war "in order to be able to impose peace terms when the right moment arrived". Balfour preserved a warmer memory: at the moment he proposed a toast to the Soviet Air Force, the dictator, whose son Vasily was a pilot at Stalingrad, rose from his seat and walked heavily down the table to clink glasses with Balfour.

On the final day, 2 October, Beaverbrook, too, was in euphoric mood as the leaders gathered to sign a trade agreement in Molotov's office. Here, he wisecracked, were the seeds of a profitable business: to buy hundreds of ordinary two shilling pens and sell them at vast profit as "the genuine pen that signed the Moscow Conference Agreement". Although Litvinov achieved a passable translation, Molotov's face remained frozen: such capitalist levity was lost on him.

"Everything now depends on getting the pig to market," Beaverbrook wrote to Hopkins next day, and he was as good as his word. Back in London, where the Cabinet was dismayed to realise that Britain had been stripped to the bone, Beaverbrook now engulfed his colleagues with a flood-tide of pro-Soviet memoranda. "Surely Americans will be willing to go a bit short for Russians who are actually fighting," ran one of the more scathing, urging U.S. planes for Archangel. "We must give the Russians their daily bread," ran another, "we must take a pull at own own belts so that our friends may sit at our dinner table". He urged the Colonial Office – vainly – to strip Malaya of locomotives, the better to ship Russian supplies along the trans-Iranian railway. "You are expected to respect the production lines always and treat them as the Ark of the Covenant," he berated the Secretary of State for War, David Margesson, when delivery of 500 trucks to Russia fell behind schedule.

"The public are at last unanimous in accepting the wicked ogre of last year as the loyal friend of today," he enthused to his old friend Sir Samuel Hoare.

British manufacturers, too, were taken severely to task. Enraged to learn that a U.S. Office of Production Management team had found British machine tool factories so inefficient they were cancelling all Lend-Lease supplies until further notice, Beaverbrook summoned 200 factory chiefs to a secret session in Essex Hall, off the Strand. "This is not the easy war we had last time," he tongue-lashed them. "It is harsh and cruel and everyone of us is bound to be hurt, you, me and everybody." The time had come, he told them flatly, for British industry to put its house in order, so that America might once again ship them machine tools – for the benefit of Russia.

It was none too soon. At this same moment, on a 150-mile front defended only by 15 half-trained Soviet "armies", the Germans,, like Napoleon before them, were lancing towards Moscow.

*

In those first golden days of autumn, success seemed assured. In one short day, Guderian's Panzer Group Two forged 85 miles towards Moscow; on the fourth day, Orel, 256 miles south of the capital, crumbled before the *Wehrmacht*. From 8 October, in one of the most perfect battles of encirclement in military history, the double battle of Vyazma and Bryansk, the Russians were to lose 663,000 prisoners, 12,412 tanks, and 5,412 guns. The road to Moscow had been cleared.

The advance would be a near-run thing, even so. On 6 October, as *Feldmarschall* Fedor von Bock left his command train at Smolensk, he noted that the Russian sky was now leaden grey; a chill and ominous wind was blowing from the north. By afternoon, a cold rain was falling on the northern sectors of Army Group Centre's front. Towards evening, the temperature dropped still further; the rain was turning to snow.

Following an agitated telephone call from Guderian, Bock teletyped the Army High Command: where were his long-promised winter supplies? The reply was ambivalent at best: if Bock attended to his responsibilities, the supply officers would attend to theirs.

In the lower echelons, a certain unease prevailed. In the 3rd Battalion of Infantry Regiment 18, *Assistenzart* Henrich Haape noted with dismay the absence of winter clothing – and that as his unit thrust on for Sychevka, the trucks were churning the snow ever deeper into the moist rich earth. Soon men were struggling in black mud up to their knees.

"The mud seemed bottomless," Haape noted; there was good reason for the soldiers to christen it "buna" – synthetic rubber – for often it sucked the calf boots from their legs. Now the pace was slowed again, from eight miles a day to three. Supply columns could no longer reach the front; petrol for the stranded panzers was brought by huge cargo-carrying gliders towed by Heinkels, crash-landing near the lines. The thirty daily train loads of supplies on which Bock depended were no longer forthcoming; hot food was now the exception, not the rule. Awarded the Iron Cross First Class for devotion to duty, Haape celebrated with a hot meal he would long remember: potatoes French-fried in castor oil.

Despite this snail's pace, the mood in Moscow was now frantic. On 7 October, Marshal Semeon Timoshenko and his deputy, General Eremenko, were relieved of their commands; with the realisation that the road to Moscow was virtually undefended, Stalin flung the bitingly-sarcastic General Georgi Zhukov into the breach as commander of Western Army Group.

All through the night of 7 October, Zhukov toured the Western Army front – intently studying a map with the aid of a flashlight, fighting off fatigue by stopping the car for 300-yard jogging sessions. The situation was desperate; to cover the 135-mile Moscow front Zhukov had a total of 45 battalions against the 150 he needed. But Zhukov would contenance no strategic withdrawal. "He ordered us to stand to the death," General Konstantin Rokossovsky, commanding the 16th Army, recalled, "without retreating a step."

A thousand miles away, in Tokyo, one man now contrived to swing the balance: the master-spy Richard Sorge, whose earlier warnings concerning Barbarossa had gone for nothing. Now, as if by way of atonement, Stalin belatedly gave credence to the tenor of Sorge's recent reports: Japan had no plans to attack Siberia, as Hitler had urged, but instead was contemplating an attack on Britain and the United States. Thus near Borodino, 62 miles from Moscow, where Napoleon had fought another battle as bloody, the *Wehrmacht*, on 14 October, met the first of 30 Siberian divisions – the 32nd Rifle – that Stalin was transferring from the Far East. They died where they stood, but they, and the vast sea of black mud, bought time for Moscow.

It was as well, for a wave of defeatism had swept the city – heightened by the funeral pyre of black smoke from the Kremlin's chimneys as secret papers were burned, the news that Lenin's coffin had been removed to safety from the mausoleum in Red Square. "The maddened Fascist beast is threatening Moscow", *Pravda* trumpeted, on 16 October, but three days later the Stavka, the State Defence Committee, in declaring a state of siege, nipped the panic in the bud. More than 200,000 Muscovites were called to the colours, given twenty days field training, then shipped to the front. More than half a million old men, women and teenagers were mobilised to build a second line of defence: 1,400 pill-boxes, 60 miles of anti-tank ditches, more than 5,000 miles of infantry trenches.

By mid-October, Moscow was a city on the move: almost 500 factory complexes and their 200,000 workers were moving house in 71,000 freight cars, to the safety of the Urals and Siberia. Mile after mile of boxcars with little smokestacks, housing the workers, and flat cars transporting lathes, generators and stamping mills were hammering east over the trans-Siberian railway, to the floodlit factory towns beyond the range of the German bombers: Chelyabinsk, in the southern Urals, Sverdlovsk, where Tsar Nicholas and his family had met their death. Almost two million people were leaving the capital – among them Harold Elvin.

It was on 15 October that the young night watchman got his marching orders: all foreign embassies were to transfer to Kuibyshev, once Samara, the terminus of the ancient caravan route from India and China, 525 miles to the east. It was one of the most hectic days that Elvin could ever remember; before even packing his bags he had to cart sack after sack of documents to the Embassy's incinerator, working against time.

At 9 p.m., picking his way through the teeming chaos of Moscow's Kazan Railway Station, Elvin was thoughtful. Under the soaring arches of the waiting hall, every inch of floor space was choked with women, children, soldiers and militia. The air was thick with mingled odours: woollen shawls and poverty, damp sheepskin, human breath rank with herring and chopped onion. But it was the contrast between the refugees' lot and his own that came home to him now.

At his feet were three suitcases crammed with clothes and books, but Elvin had left much more behind: two armchairs, a second-hand piano. But the armchairs and pianos of these people were already piled in the streets as barricades. The shabby kaftans and the rag coats were all the clothes they had. Back in London, Elvin had a home to call his own, but this station floor was their only home, the bundles they carried the sole furnishings: the woman with her one electric kettle, the old man with his iron bedstead.

Tonight, he would be out of it, Elvin thought, moving 500 miles nearer to safety, but where would these people be? Perhaps crammed with dozens of others into an open truck meant for two horses, blanketed by drifting snow, with no lavatories, only the loaves they had brought for sustenance. So did they resent him, warm in his eight-guinea overcoat, favoured as less than 500 people in this territory of 187 millions were favoured?

They would be justified, surely, in tearing him asunder – and didn't he, in his heart of hearts, know that they would?

Of course, once in Kuibyshev he would feel differently, Elvin knew. In Kuibyshev, the painful multitude would have faded from his vision. There would come a way – given time – to square it all with his conscience.

*

By October, four Russian cities – all of them under siege – loomed large in the world's headlines. How steadfastly they held out was a yardstick for the future, a token of the collective will to resist.

Inevitably, most attention focussed on Moscow, where Stalin and the Politburo were staying put, but other cities knew greater hardship. Sevastopol, on the Black Sea, early adapted to siege conditions: from 30 October onwards, thousands moved underground, to the onetime champagne cellars of Tsarist days, to set up munitions workshops and tailors' co-operatives off the narrow warren of passages christened "Trade Union Lane" and "Internationale Street". Here they held out for eight months, sustained by a communal kitchen, a first-aid post, a crèche, a nursery, a school, a cinema and a lecture and games room.

Two hundred and fifty miles north, in the port of Odessa, the citizens displayed an almost Anglo-Saxon phlegm; already 86,000 troops had left the city but despite a nightly bombardment of 2,000-lb parachute mines life by day went on much as usual. Housewives in summer dresses, armed with string bags, still went shopping for cabbages in the open air market; later, sitting comfortably on their porches, they converted old caviar tins into land-mines before strolling with their husbands to the defence posts at the city limits. Outside the telegraph office a placard set the placid keynote: "We deliver cables to all parts of the Soviet Union but for the moment we cannot absolutely guarantee punctual delivery". The stoicism was in vain; by 16 October, in a daring Dunkirk-style operation executed by night, the last 35,000 troops were shipped out to reinforce Sevastopol.

No Russian city faced a greater endurance test than Leningrad. The white city of Peter the Great – once known as Petrograd, once as St Petersburg – had always been an unique metropolis: the city of Pavlov and Njinsky, Dostoevsky and Pushkin. Here in the network of canals and castles – "a stone labyrinth", Trotsky had called it – offset by the glory of the Winter Palace and the Hermitage Museum, great art and architecture had flowered but so, too, nourished by poverty and oppression, had the Russian Revolution.

For this reason alone, Hitler had decreed that the "Venice of the North", which was equally the cradle of Bolshevism, must be obliterated from the earth.

From 8 September on, Leningrad had effectively been isolated from the world behind 5,000 pill boxes, 480 miles of anti-tank batteries, 17,874 miles of trenches, besieged by Von Leeb's 700,000-strong Army Group North. As early as 21 August, the alarm had been sounded, "The enemy is at the gates!"; the defensive Luga Line, which followed the Luga River, as close as forty miles southwest of the city was crumbling. Now the biggest guns in all Europe were trained on the city from six great artillery investments: cannon from Skoda, Krupp and Schneider, railway guns of calibres as high as 420 mm, firing 900-kilo shells over distances of up to 31,000 yards. At least 100,000 of these shells were to destroy 3,174 buildings.

Ahead of the citizens stretched 900 days of a like ordeal.

On 9 September, when Dmitri Pavlov, a dark vigorous 36-year-old supply official despatched by Moscow, reached Leningrad airport in his DC-3, he found the city's reserves in sorry shape. To support more than three million inhabitants and 200,000 Red Army defenders, Leningrad had just 33 days supply of meat, 35 days of grain and flour, 30 days of cereals. The only supply route open lay across Lake Ladoga, the huge body of water to the north-east – but there were no boats, piers, road and rail facilities or warehouses to accumulate substantial supplies.

Worse, on the very day that Pavlov arrived, German incendiaries fired the vast Badaev warehouse, Leningrad's four-acre larder, which had housed almost all of the city's flour, butter and sugar. The time was not far distant when men and women would unashamedly grub at the charred earth to salvage grains of melted sugar and chocolate.

But there was no thought of surrender. For almost two and a half centuries Leningrad had been a proud city, its cultural heritage derived from Paris and Rome, disdainful of uncouth, provincial Moscow. Time and again in the months that followed Pavlov was forced to reduce the rations, until by 20 November no heavy worker could expect more than five ounces of bread a day. But they would not yield. Rather than surrender their city to Hitler, Admiral Vladimir Tributs, commander of the Baltic Fleet, had orders to blow it up – with thousands of buildings mined to explode at the touch of a plunger.

Hunger became a preoccupation ousting all others. Dogs and cats went early to the pot; by November, pet-owners were as extinct a species as their pets. The guinea pigs and rabbits vanished from their cages at the Erisman Hospital. Some scavenged in the Botanical Gardens, rooting up valuable flower bulbs to eat. Others were reduced to eating leather, tree-bark, carpenter's glue, even lipstick and face powder. Hunger allowed no choice.

To appease their craving, Pavlov showed rare ingenuity. To combat scurvy, fruiterers were instructed to extract Vitamin C from pine needles, thirty tons of infusion per day. A nauseating if nutritious jelly was compounded from 2,000 tons of sheep guts, spiked with cloves to disguise the smell. Edible cellulose and chaff helped stretch the bread ration still further.

In November, the deaths began: 11,085 deaths from dystrophy were recorded for this month alone. Of Leningrad's three million inhabitants, at least a million would die before this siege had ended. "Today it is so simple to die", a housewife, Yelena Skryabina, recorded in her diary, "you just begin to lose interest, then you lie on the bed and you never again get up."

Whatever the cost to their souls, some were determined to survive. In the Sennaya (Haymarket), the infamous slum haunted by pimps and peddlers, where Dostoevsky had written *Crime and Punishment*, men and women with fine rosy faces were known to feast covertly on meat patties made from human flesh.

Soon the bright red and yellow sleds of the children began to appear, narrow sleds, their runners squeaking everywhere on the broad boulevards. There were no more automobiles in the city; the sleds had been brought into use to transport the dead.

The bodies lay everywhere – not only in their beds but in the streets and the yards, inside trolley buses that had frozen in their tracks in the heart of the city. Often they lay there for days at a time. When the snow came to carpet the streets many disappeared altogether – only to re-emerge from their shrouds of ice when the sun brought a sharp spring thaw.

It was the coldest winter that Leningrad had ever known. Even in the hospital wards, which lacked both electricity and heating, the temperature never rose above 35 degrees Fahrenheit. In apartment houses, where bombardment had broken eighty per cent of all windows, it was worse. Water pipes froze, then burst. At least 10,000 wooden houses were torn down for firewood. Most citizens went to bed wearing both topcoats and gloves. "Even the tears froze within the people of Leningrad," one survivor recalled.

Yet life of a sort went on among the ruins. On the night of 19 September, the composer Dmitri Shostakovich, invited three friends to his fifth-floor apartment on Skorokhod Ulitsa to hear the opening movements of his uncompleted Seventh Symphony, the "Leningrad" Symphony. As he launched into the Second Movement, the air-raid siren sounded, but defiantly, to the crashing counterpoint of bombs and anti-aircraft fire, Shostakovich played on.

Only years later did he reveal that the anger and anguish exploding from every chord was prompted as much by his revulsion against the Kremlin's reign of terror as by Hitler's onslaught – "it's not about Leningrad under siege, it's about the Leningrad that Stalin destroyed and Hitler merely·finished off".

Most theatres were still packed out, though to beat the nightly air-raid siren all performances were timed for 4 p.m.: *La Dame Aux Camellias* enjoyed as long a run as Tchaikovsky's *Eugene Onegin*. At one theatre, where the last act of Shakespeare's *Othello* was cut short by the siren, first-timers crowded backstage after the all-clear to ask the cast: "Did Desdemona get killed – and was Iago found out?"

On 18 November, a frail hope dawned for the first time since the blockade began. A small reconnaissance party organised by Andrei Zhdanov, the Leningrad party chief, set off on foot across ice-bound Lake Ladoga, followed cautiously by a man on horseback. What they

193

found excited them profoundly: the ice was now five inches thick, strong enough to bear horse-drawn sleds with light loads. But four days later, a truck column was to make it, returning with 33 tons of supplies. What all Leningrad came to know as "The Road of Life" was achieving a tenuous reality.

It was 237 miles long and in places 80 miles wide and it terminated at the railheads of Podborove and Zabore. Only much later, in January, did the ice freeze to a depth of three feet, enough to bear the weight of fully-loaded trucks. For the most part, until the city was relieved in January, 1944, it was a team of 350 horsemen who made the trip, sharing their bread with their horses as they rode. At best they could bring in 361 tons a day against the 2,000 needed, but what mattered to Leningrad was that they tried.

Long after, the courage of those who held out was to be enshrined in a tribute from the poet, Olga Berggolts, etched on a wall in the city's Piskarevsky Cemetery:

> *We cannot number the noble*
> *Ones who lie beneath the eternal granite,*
> *But of those honoured by this stone*
> *Let no one forget, let nothing be*
> *forgotten*

*

The stubbornness of the Russian resistance was not lost on the world – particularly on the German home front.

Ironically, it was Hitler himself who drew attention to their valour – by a stunt which Göbbels was to describe as "the worst mistake he had ever come across in propaganda". On 9 October, the Reich Press Chief, Dr Otto Dietrich, called a special noonday Press conference in the red plush theatre hall of the Ministry of Propaganda. To the baffled foreign correspondents who attended, Dietrich announced that as of this moment the Russians were finished, locked in two German steel pockets before Moscow – "on that, gentlemen, I stake my whole journalistic experience!"

A tidal wave of euphoria followed. All over Germany the huge red headlines of the Nazi party's official newspaper *Der Völkischer Beobachter* proclaimed: THE GREAT HOUR HAS COME! THE EASTERN CAMPAIGN HAS ENDED! In Berlin, an excited butcher hailed every bystander into his shop to dole out free gifts of sausages. In Baarz's beer-hall, behind Unter den Linden, weeping customers rose to sing *Deutschland über Alles*. Wreaths of roses were hung on every tank in sight. Bookshops broke out with a rash of Russian grammars.

In fact, Hitler's sole purpose in ordering the announcement had been

194

to apply pressure on an indecisive Japan: if they wanted to acquire Siberian territory, now was the time to join in the war. Hence Dietrich's briefing: to signal a victory-that-never-was in the east.

The result was a bitter backlash of disillusion. A cynical public noted that the *Sondermeldung* special High Command victory broadcasts – were now invoked even for one-horse Russian villages absent from any map. Newspaper sales slumped by 40 per cent; now the people listened more attentively to the ticking clock featured by the B.B.C.'s Foreign Service, the German voice that murmured after every seventh tick, "Every seven seconds a German dies in Russia. Is it your husband? Is it your son? Is it your brother?". For Leningrad and Sebastopol were still holding out, and each week the letters returned from the front stamped in red ink GEFALLEN were increasing.

The lesson was being taken boldly to heart: Hitler was no longer the invincible force of 1940. Even Turkey, which in June had signed a treaty with Germany, despite an already existing Anglo-Turkish alliance, was drawing apart. Although under relentless pressure from Hitler's economic negotiator in the Balkans, Dr Karl Clodius, to ship valuable chrome to Germany, Numan Menemencioglu, of the Turkish Foreign Office, was stalling adeptly. The previous trade agreement with Britain, he explained blandly, was the stumbling block; it was valid until 1943.

Thus the final German-Turkish dinner, at Karpiç's restaurant in Ankara, where champagne was priced at £35 a bottle, was a glum affair. Ambassador Franz von Papen and Clodius were visibly smarting at that day's final rebuff. Plainly German stock was reaching a low ebb; the stalemate on the eastern front was making its mark.

The evening came to an end finally, and now Karpiç's dance musicians seized their cue. As the German delegation, headed by von Papen, filed dourly from the restaurant, the orchestra swung of one accord into a time-honoured favourite, "I Can't Give You Anything But Love, Baby".

*

In the North Atlantic, the long cold war was suddenly hotting up. The camouflage of U.S. neutrality was wearing paper-thin; "all measures short of war" had become a shooting war.

Thursday 4 September marked a turning-point in U.S. naval history. At 8.40 a.m. on that day, the warship U.S.S. *Greer* was proceeding at a steady $17\frac{1}{2}$ knots on the Iceland mail run, when a British naval plane, patrolling overhead, signalled the captain, Lieutenant-Commander Laurence H. Frost, that a U-Boat was lurking in her vicinity. Promptly *Greer* began an erratic zig-zag, increased speed and went to general quarters, maintaining sound contact with the submarine for three hours. The pilot asked whether *Greer* planned to attack, but Frost's reply was negative. After dropping depth charges at random the British plane retired.

The "incident" the U.S. Navy had so long awaited was suddenly established fact. Stung, the U-Boat lashed out indiscriminately; the white wake of a torpedo streaked towards the little destroyer. Miraculously dodging first one, then two torpedoes, the *Greer* let fly with depth charges. At latitude 62° 45'N, longitude 27° 37'W, the sea was suddenly boiling like a vortex as America entered World War Two.

Five days later, after *Greer* had safely reached Iceland, Roosevelt gave Hitler due warning. In a Fireside Chat that became known as the "shoot-on-sight" speech, he declared resolutely, "We have sought no shooting war with Hitler. We do not seek it now. But . . . when you see a rattlesnake poised to strike, you do not wait until he has struck before you crush him. . . . From now on, if German or Italian vessels enter the waters, the protection of which is necessary for American defence, they do so at their own peril."

It was a speech which bitterly disappointed both allies and interventionists alike. From Pretoria, Field Marshal Jan Smuts demanded of Eden: "One wonders what stronger situation he is looking forward to. If he is determined to leave the initiative of entering the war to Germany, he may be disappointed". Roosevelt was unperturbed. "He said that if he asked for a declaration of war, he wouldn't get it and opinion would swing against him," Halifax reported to Churchill, "declarations of war were . . . out of fashion." But "provided he put the right label on the bottle, it might not be too difficult to get acceptance of anything he wanted".

When David (later Lord) Eccles, of the Ministry of Economic Warfare, urged a more belligerent course on the President, Roosevelt was less circumspect: "You might as well ask me to piss into the wind".

For Roosevelt saw the dichotomy clearly: while 70 per cent of Americans wished to break Hitler, 70 per cent equally wanted to stay clear of war at all costs. Theirs was still a land of peace and plenty: an August move by Secretary of the Interior Harold Ickes to conserve gasoline by locking all filling-station pumps twelve hours a day provoked savage hostility. Returning from vacation, Ickes found his entire backyard piled with spoiled cabbages and dead cats.

"If Hitler makes a peace offer," Ickes noted in his diary, "it is going to make a very difficult domestic situation. Americans want war so little . . . we are in an age when we are more interested in movies and the radio and baseball and automobiles than in the fundamental verities of life."

Even so, some of Roosevelt's Cabinet were standing up to be counted and voice the President's unspoken thoughts – none more stridently than his doughty Republican Secretary of the Navy, Frank Knox. "The time to use our Navy to clear the Atlantic of the German menace is at hand," he told one Boston audience, prompting a delighted reaction from Supreme

Court Justice Felix Frankfurter: "When you're impeached, can I leave the Bench and become one of your Counsel?" In October, Knox was to tell the American Bar Association at Indianapolis, "When we have defeated Hitler and destroyed this Nazi bid for world dominion, we must set up conditions which will prevent the rise of new Hitlers." It brought a spontaneous tribute from the columnist Walter Lippmann: "It is the speech that Woodrow Wilson should have delivered in 1917 . . . you said it magnificently, as men do when they speak the whole truth."

Other incidents, following hard on the *Greer*, helped temper public opinion. 17 October saw the first U.S. casualty list of World War Two: on this dark and icy night a torpedo striking on the starboard side of U.S.S. *Kearny*, one of a division of five destroyers escorting a convoy of fifty merchantmen, took the lives of eleven men, the first of 292,000 Americans to die in the battles of World War Two. On 31 October, 600 miles west of Ireland, the destroyer *Reuben James* took a torpedo in her port side; of that ship's company of 160 men, only 45 – no officers among them – were saved.

But by then America had taken one more step – this time a giant one – towards total war. On 27 October, in a properly apposite setting – the annual Navy League dinner in the vast Gold Ballroom of Washington's Mayflower Hotel – Roosevelt came out with a fighting speech reporting his readiness to the American people: "We have wished to avoid shooting. But the shooting has started. And history has recorded who fired the first shot."

On 13 November, though by the chillingly narrow margin of 212 to 194, Congress duly amended the Neutrality Act – thus permitting the future arming of all U.S. merchantmen and granting them free passage to the war zones.

It seemed a qualified endorsement of Roosevelt's own words: "In the long run, however, all that matters is who will fire the last shot."

*

Roosevelt was sighting on the wrong target; as yet all Hitler's preoccupations were centred on the east. One group of men, by contrast, were already on the brink of an all-out war against the United States.

The story went back at least as far as 31 July – five days after Roosevelt had frozen all Japanese assets and cut off her oil supplies. Then Admiral Osami Nagano, the Naval Chief of Staff, sought an audience at the Imperial Palace with the Emperor Hirohito. Warning of an imminent oil famine, he suggested a desperate attack.

"Will you win a great victory?" asked the 40-year-old Emperor directly, "Like the battle of Tsushima?" – the occasion when Japan had worsted the Russian Fleet in May, 1905.

"I am sorry but that will not be possible," Nagano answered ruefully.

"Then," the Emperor predicted, "this war will be a desperate one."

By the morning of 6 September, Hirohito had reached a decision. Summoning the Marquis Koichi Kido, the Lord Keeper of the Privy Seal, to his presence, the Emperor announced a break with precedent. When the Imperial Conference began at 10 a.m. that day, he would make his own views known. Both his ministers and service chiefs would receive due warning that so long as prospects for peace remained he would not sanction war.

This decision was in keeping with the sentiments of his Prime Minister, Prince Fumimaro Konoye, an effete hypochondriac who likewise opposed war but lacked both drive and resolution. To date Konoye's most telling blow for peace had been struck in July when he submitted the resignation of himself and his Cabinet. Promptly the Emperor had invited him to head up a new one, and Konoye complied – but this time the pro-Axis Yosuke Matsuoka, who had conferred with Hitler in March, was dropped as Foreign Minister.

As always, according to precedent, the conference of 6 September was held in Room One, East, of the Imperial Palace, the Emperor seated before a golden screen, the delegates, in their stockinged feet, sitting at attention on hard chairs, their fingers, in deference to the imperial power, rigid along the seams of their trousers. But as the conference got under way, Hirohito saw plainly that all talk of further negotiations with the United States was so much verbiage. Bereft of the strategic materials they needed to support a population increasing by millions annually, the delegates' minds were already geared to war.

Abruptly, "very flushed in the face", Hirohito rose. The delegates were nonplussed; except to formally open and close a conference, the Emperor never spoke.

Had not the chiefs of his armed forces, he asked, no opinion as to which should prevail – war or diplomacy? If so, why had they not stated it? "As for myself," Hirohito ventured, "I have no doubt of the answer. I would like to read you a poem which was written by my grandfather, the great Emperor Meiji." Then, drawing a piece of paper from the pocket of his formal suit, he recited in a plaintive high-pitched voice:

> The seas surround all quarters of the globe,
> And my heart cries out to the nations of the world
> Why then do the winds and waves of strife
> Disrupt the peace between us?

The Emperor sat down and the company bowed their obeisance. No man present had any doubt as to his meaning. It was a tacit invitation, in Kido's phrase, to "wipe the slate clean", to "go back to blank paper".

But when the discussions began, on 23 October, a new factor had emerged: one week earlier, Prince Konoye had resigned and the former Minister for War, 57-year-old Hideki Tojo, took his place. An incisive quick-thinking *samurai*, whose Army nickname was "The Razor", Tojo, who fretted his way through fifty cigarettes and twelve cups of coffee a day, was not irrevocably war-oriented. Still, he was determined to break the deadlock of indecision.

Ten days of deliberations followed – at times desultory, at others tense and ill-humoured. But over every meeting one spectre hovered like a thunderhead: the oil of which Roosevelt had deprived them. If Japan went to war, she had one year's oil supply at best – and the Navy alone used 400 tons per hour. To switch to synthetic oil would involve a three-year conversion programme costing two billion yen.

By 30 October, the delegates saw just three alternatives. A policy of caution would mean at least ten years of hardship, or *gashin-shotan* – literally "to sleep on kindling and lick gall" – for the people. Or Japan could declare war now, with all the risk that this entailed. Thirdly, she could pursue the policy favoured by Foreign Minister Shigenori Togo – "to undertake both diplomacy and military operations simultaneously".

On 1 November, a decision on deadlines dragged on into an angry seventeen-hour meeting. General Ko Tsukada, the Army Vice Chief of Staff, saw a deadline no later than 13 November as imperative – a proposal denounced by Togo as "outrageous". The Navy were prepared to defer their deadline until 20 November – although Admiral Nagano warned with great emphasis: "The time for war will not come later". In the end, Prime Minister Tojo himself swung the balance: midnight on 30 November.

At the fourteen-man Imperial Conference of 5 November, these decisions were finalised. Preparations for war would go ahead, while striving to settle matters by diplomacy. In silence, the Emperor heard that an experienced career diplomat, Saburo Kurusu, who one year earlier had signed the Tripartite Pact with Germany and Italy, was en route to Washington to bolster the flagging morale of old Admiral Nomura.

Their task would be no easy one. Under Plan "B", which the diplomats were authorised to discuss with Cordell Hull, Japan would agree to move her troops from southern to northern Indo-China – but in return the United States must supply her with one million tons of aviation fuel a year, help ensure a supply of raw materials from the Dutch East Indies, and cease all aid to Chiang Kai-shek's China.

No man doubted that the gulf could be bridged. But it was up to the United States to do the bridging.

199

10

"Just Read This – And The War Is Won"

6 November–6 December, 1941

THE BRITISH SAW the Japanese threat as still little more than hypothetical. As far back as 12 August, aboard H.M.S. *Prince of Wales*, Churchill had told his ministers that he did not think the Japanese would go to war with Britain. As late as 1 December, his attitude before the Cabinet was unwontedly passive – "we should not resist or attempt to forestall a Japanese attack on the Kra Isthmus (in the Gulf of Siam) unless we had satisfactory assurance from the United States that they would join us."

Thailand (formerly Siam) would, like every Balkan State before her, be urged to resist aggression, although no arms or aircraft could be spared to help out – prompting a spirited protest from the Minister in Bangkok, Sir Josiah Crosby. "The men now in power in Thailand (Siam) are nearly all of them little more than children. This is especially true of the Prime Minister . . . would it not be franker for us to advise Thailand to put up no physical resistance . . . to play the role of Denmark and content herself with a verbal protest against invasion? . . . I find our attitude towards Thailand disconcertingly ambiguous."

It was the Middle East, not the Far East, that was still absorbing Britain – a preoccupation wholeheartedly shared by their old adversary Rommel.

In Rome on 15 November, "The Desert Fox" was celebrating his fiftieth birthday along with General Hans von Ravenstein, commanding 21st Panzer Division, and their respective wives. But over lunch at the smart Hotel Eden, Ravenstein sensed that despite his chief's presence in the Eternal City, his heart and mind were rooted in the desert. For a time Rommel listened abstractedly as Lucie Rommel and Frau von Ravenstein extolled the wonders of St Peter's. Suddenly he broke in: "You know, von Ravenstein, I've been thinking again about what we ought to do with those infantry battalions . . ."

Rommel had cause for preoccupation; once again he had won a victory over his own top brass. Told off by the High Command to concentrate on an imminent British attack and leave Tobruk alone, Rommel was beside himself. With von Ravenstein he flew to Rome for a bitter wrangle with the Military Attaché, General Enno von Rintelen, whose advice, Rommel suspected, had prompted the ukase. Reviling von Rintelen as "a coward and a friend of the Italians", Rommel promptly seized the phone and called Jodl, in Berlin.

"I hear that you wish me to give up the attack on Tobruk," Rommel stormed. "I am completely disgusted." The 21st Panzer Division, he insisted, whose commander was there beside him, could counter any British advance whilst Tobruk was invested. "Can you guarantee," Jodl asked cautiously "that there is no danger?" When Rommel shouted that they had his personal guarantee, Jodl gave in. The attack was timed for 23 November.

For two months now, Rommel had postponed this offensive – bedevilled by a system of priorities which had sped 154 divisions to the Russian front yet grudged more than two for North Africa, hampered by non-stop British harassment of his Mediterranean supply convoys. From Naples, *Oberst* Gerhart Müller, of the 5th Panzer Regiment, reported more than 1,000 Afrika Korps men bogged down in the port, vainly awaiting transportation – while on the African shores, a shortage of trucks decreed that only three-quarters of the stores arriving ever reached the front. For the first time Rommel was forced to acknowledge the truth of von Ravenstein's sour dictum; "The desert is a tactician's paradise and a quartermaster's hell."

As yet, Rommel had no suspicion of the magnitude of a British thrust, code-named Crusader, nor of its grandiloquent objective: to engage and destroy all Axis armour at one stroke and reoccupy Cyrenaica. Simultaneously, on the code-word "Pop", the besieged garrison of Tobruk – 32,000 men, including those of Major-General Stanislaw Kopanski's Polish Brigade, who had been shipped in on moonless autumn nights following Curtin's ultimatum to replace the original Anzac defenders – would stage a breakout. Their target was the tiny fort of El Duda, 8 miles south; here they would link up with the forces advancing to relieve Tobruk.

This was Britain's threefold chance to redeem the shame of Operation Battleaxe: a second front to help the Russians, with the hope of knocking Mussolini's troops out of the war for good and all and of convincing Washington's sceptics that the Middle East campaign rated more than a number four priority.

But as Wavell's successor, General Sir Claude Auchinleck had two serious failings: a poor judgement of the man for the job, a bigoted loyalty to the man thus picked. Moreover – like Wavell but unlike Rommel – Auchinleck had opted to conduct his war from G.H.Q., almost 600 miles from the front line. Standing in for him at Advanced H.Q., Fort Maddalena, as Commander of the newly-formed Eighth Imperial Army was his personal choice for the post, General Sir Alan Gordon Cunningham, 54, the younger brother of the Admiral. Cunningham, who had never commanded armour nor seen service in the desert, had been given just two months to form and train the major fighting arm that replaced Western Desert Force.

At 9 p.m. on 16 November, deep in his underground dugout, Cunningham, flanked by war correspondents sipping whisky-and-sodas round a plain trestle table, had appeared confident enough. "A hoarse-voiced cherub of a man", as one recalled him, he promised them: "I am going to seek old Rommel out and destroy him and his armour."

Unknown to the war correspondents was the uncompromising verdict which Major-General Bernard Freyberg had delivered to Cunningham two days back. In one sentence Freyberg had charted the woeful misfortunes of Eighth Army for the next seven months.

"You are attacking five Italian divisions and more than a German division with two brigades of South Africans," he warned Cunningham. "You will fail and we shall be ordered in the end to march upon Tobruk."

Along with Major-General William "Strafer" Gott, of the 7th Armoured Division, and Lieutenant-General Sir Willoughby Norrie, commanding 30 Corps, Freyberg had urged a powerful force of three armoured brigades striking as one. Now, to his dismay, Cunningham planned not only to split armour from armour but tanks from infantry – leaving every unit wide open to be engulfed by Rommel.

Even so, hopes were high. At first light on 18 November, under a sullen downpour split by forked white lightning, the men of the Eighth Army heard the burst of machine-gun fire that signalled the "off" as the force moved out across the desert – "like a regiment of monstrous snails", as one man saw them, heading for The Wire, the rust-corroded barrier, 6 feet high and 9 feet wide, that Mussolini had erected in 1932 to stop the Bedouins leaving Libya.

For the first time since Beda Fomm, most men felt a warm glow of confidence. At last there was an abundance of everything – more than 375,000 fighting men, 700-plus gun-armed tanks, among them 200 Chrysler M-3s, known as Honeys, the first U.S. Tanks ever to taste war. Unit after unit thrilled to the thunder of 700 R.A.F. planes criss-crossing the lowering skies – snub-nosed Hurricanes, big twin-engined Beaufighters, even high Flying Fortresses. The Chief Engineer of 30 Corps, Brigadier George Clifton, was so sure of victory he had taken along 24 cans of Rheingold beer to celebrate. Even the dubious Freyberg had at last overcome his reservations. He assured Brigadier John Harding of 13 Corps: "Good God! We are frothing to go. We are not frightened of a few tanks."

Auchinleck was less confident. Goaded to action by Churchill's constant nagging – "there are always excellent reasons in favour of retreats. Victory rewards those whose willpower overcomes these reasons" – he confided his doubts in letters to Ismay. "This is not really a very flexible army," he wrote. "One can not just pick up a division and hurl it across the map as one did at staff college," and later, "All these months of labour and thought can be set at nought in one afternoon."

At Ain El Gazala Rommel was taken entirely by surprise. *Leutnant* Heinz Werner Schmidt was always to recall that when he handed Rommel the first report of the frontier crossing from Reconnaissance Unit 33, "The Desert Fox" commented only, "Unbelievable!" Still obsessed with the capture of Tobruk, he had always been unwilling to accept Crusader as more than a cautious British probe. When von Ravenstein sought permission to move an armoured troop towards the frontier, Rommel cautioned: "We mustn't lose our nerve."

Now, Cunningham, too, erred fatally. Puzzled by Rommel's failure to react to his first thrust, he spread his armour on a seek-and-find mission across the face of the desert. One brigade, the 22nd Armoured, was sped to Bir El Gubi, south of Tobruk, to tangle with the Italian Ariete Division. The 7th Armoured made for Sidi Rezegh, a key airfield off the main Axis highway. The 4th stayed put at Gabrh Saleh, 50 miles inside the wire.

Already those close to Cunningham felt he was fast losing his grip. To ten weeks of overwork and emotional strain was added now the uncertainty of a battle he was ill-equipped to control. Moreover, a heavy pipe-smoker, he had been forced, on the eve of battle, to quit smoking by his oculist on account of eye-strain. Haggard with nervous fatigue, he confided in Air Marshal Sir Arthur Tedder, Air Commander of the Middle East: "I wish I knew what Rommel meant to do."

What Rommel, now alerted, meant to do was what he had done so often before: to profit by the British misuse of their own armour. From the first luck was with him. On the night of Saturday, 22 November, *Oberstleutnant* Hans Cramer's 8th Panzer Division by chance overran the H.Q. of Brigadier Alec Gatehouse's 4th Armoured Brigade – capturing 35 tanks and all their guns and armoured cars. The most substantial armoured force in 8th Army had ceased to be a fighting entity.

On 23 November, the aptly named *Totensonntag* (The Sunday of the Dead), the date marked in the Lutheran calendar for the Germans to recall the fallen of World War One, Rommel closed in for the kill at Sidi Rezegh.

What followed was stark slaughter – a battle as pitifully uncoordinated as any that Eighth Army was to wage. Achieving little more than "a cavalry charge on tracks", the remnants of 4th Armoured Brigade and the 22nd Brigade hit the battlefield 75 minutes apart – with no more coherent purpose than to shoot it out with any German tank in sight. Swinging away and back across five miles of desert, in whirlwinds of yellow dust, "tanks duelled with tanks", as one man pictured it, "in running almost hand-to-hand fights, firing nearly point-blank, twisting, dodging, sprinting, with screaming tracks and whining engines that rose to a shriek as they changed gear".

For every man who fought at Sidi Rezegh there were painful often indelible memories. For Private Reginald Crimp, an infantryman, it was the crash of mortar bombs "like train doors slamming at Clapham Junction, South London, in the rush hour". For Reuter correspondent Alaric Jacob it was a knocked out tank burning with a red lambent flame "like a roasted chestnut". Few men bore from this battlefield as strange a souvenir as Gunner Andy Graham, from Christchurch, New Zealand: the armour-piercing shell that had torn off his left foot.

No man more exemplified this suicidal derring-do than Brigadier "Jock" Campbell, of Cunningham's Command Support Group. Determined that his tanks should carry out a cavalry charge against an enemy now outnumbering them by two to one, the stalwart 48-year-old Campbell, attired in a brown leather golf jacket and corduroy trousers, wheeled among the tanks standing bolt upright in an open staff car, waving alternate red and blue flags for Stop and Go. At times manning a machine-gun on a disabled Stuka, at others, a 25-pounder, Campbell harried the British tanks as relentlessly as he did the Germans – hurling both rocks and abuse at any commander who dared reverse from the action.

When one officer protested that a frontal charge was plain suicide, Campbell – awarded the Victoria Cross for this day's action – blazed at him: "That's what you're soldiers for – to die". If any tank withdrew one yard, Campbell threatened, his artillery would open fire on it.

It was small wonder that Rommel, meeting up with a captured brigadier, harangued him like a war college lecturer: "What difference does it make if you have two tanks to my one when you spread them out and let me smash them in detail? You presented me with three armoured brigades in succession."

Twenty miles due north of Sidi Rezegh, at Tobruk, the break-out was under way but with fearsome losses. Shuffling through darkness along a corridor of white marker tape, the 2nd Battalion of The Black Watch, the kilted Highland regiment, moved out into no-man's-land to "press against a solid wall of lead" – rallied by Pipe-Major Roy's bagpipes skirling the regimental march *Highland Laddie*. Soon a forest of rifles embedded in the sand by their bayonets – the signal for stretcher-bearers – told of the break-out's grim toll. Hit three times, Pipe-Major Roy was carried to the Regimental Aid Post – playing on, swathed in bandages, to the astonishment of wounded German P.O.W.s, who tried to peer beneath his kilt.

But almost three-quarters of the Highlanders had fallen before they had won a sally-port 400 yards broad and deep – and four more blood-stained days would elapse before a British Tommy and a New Zealand infantryman clasped hands at El Duda.

Incredibly, Cunningham as yet had no inkling that the battle was almost lost; due to delays and inaccurate situation reports, no up-to-date intelligence had reached Fort Maddalena. Not until the evening of *Totensonntag* was the paralysing truth revealed to him: 7th Armoured Brigade, which had joined battle with 129 tanks, had lost every one. The 22nd Armoured, starting with 158, had lost all but 30. Of the 4th Armoured Brigade, nothing was known.

Then, at 10.30 a.m. on 24 November, Rommel embarked on the one manoeuvre Cunningham had dreaded. Leaving *Oberst* Siegfried Westphal, his Chief of Intelligence, in charge of H.Q., Rommel and the Afrika Korps set off on a wild dash for The Wire, a 40-mile-long column bent on spreading chaos among the British rear echelons like wolves stampeding a flock of sheep.

Over 1,000 square miles of desert, confusion spread like fire under a leaning wind. At H.Q. Corps, Cunningham was mulling over his course of action with General Sir Willoughby Norrie when the first dull *crump* of shells was heard from the west. Hard on their heels came Rommel himself, upright in his staff car, sunglasses pushed up on his forehead, urging his escort of twenty despatch riders "General Cunningham! Go and take him!" Barely in time, Cunningham was bundled into a staff car, driven, accelerator to floorboards, to the nearest desert strip and hustled aboard a departing Blenheim. As it took off it cleared a three-ton truck by inches.

Now the retreat became total. Columns of inky smoke pockmarked the desert as clerks fired secret records. Signallers fumbled frantically to coil up the miles of wire which made up the telephone networks. But not only the British were confused. So headlong was Rommel's dash for The Wire that he entirely overlooked the two crucial storage dumps, each 6 miles square, on which Cunningham's forces were depending: Field Supply Dump 63, 15 miles south-east of Bir El Gubi and Dump 65, 15 miles south-east of Gabrh Saleh. "If we had known about those dumps," von Ravenstein was later to mourn, "we could have won the battle."

The omission was not surprising. Entire units – British, German and Italian – were now hopelessly intertwined. "Libya was a madhouse," one man recorded. "Operational maps now looked like surrealistic masterpieces." One British military policeman spent several hours on point duty patiently directing German transport and everywhere there were strange encounters. One officer, seeking refuge in an apparently deserted truck, found its Italian driver fast asleep in the cabin. Calling on his faulty Italian, he jammed a pistol in the man's stomach, whispering "*Alto in mano*". Swift to comply, the Italian corrected him politely, "*Mani in alto*" (Hands up). Few men were more off course than the truck driver whom Captain the Earl of Onslow met heading for Msus – once more in Rommel's hands. Doggedly insistent that a rest and recreation area had

205

been set up there, the driver was carrying a grand piano to deliver to its canteen.

Above all, on the night of 24 November, Rommel himself was lost. Shortly after storming through the gap in The Wire that Eighth Army had breached, along with his Chief of Staff, *Generalmajor* Alfred Gause, Rommel's staff car broke down. By chance, General Ludwig Crüwell, Afrika Corps Commander, with his Chief of Staff, *Oberst* Fritz Bayerlein, hove in sight driving a captured British vehicle – to offer the lonely shivering figures a ride.

Impatient as ever, once the driver could not locate the gap, Rommel grabbed the wheel himself – "barging fruitlessly up and down The Wire like a bewildered bee on a window-pane." Finally even Rommel gave up. Only when dawn broke did they realise they had passed a restless night among the scattered positions of the 4th Indian Division. Unchallenged they slipped away.

With the realisation that in four days Crusader had cost Eighth Army 530 tanks, disillusion stretched to the topmost levels. Among those most embittered was Freyberg, now convinced like many Commonwealth commanders that British tactics, profligate of lives, would see the end of his Kiwis. Standing on his right he demanded – and got – his forces transferred to Syria.

Auchinleck was swift to act. Arriving from Cairo, following a secret summons from Cunningham's Chief Staff Officer, Brigadier Sandy Galloway, he told Cunningham curtly, "It is not your business to consider Egypt's safety but to get on with the battle". But by 25 November, Tedder, the R.A.F. commander, had gone further still. Returning to Cairo from the front, Tedder reported to Captain Oliver Lyttelton, Churchill's Minister of State for the Middle East.

"You mean that Cunningham is not confident of winning the battle?" Lyttelton asked. When Tedder assented, Lyttelton decided, "Then he must be relieved tonight. I shall urge this course on Auchinleck." On 26 November, a new commander took over: Lieutenant-General Neil Ritchie.

*

More than 2,000 miles west of Hawaii, on Wake Island, in the North Pacific, one man had an unique opportunity to ponder Japan's intentions at first hand: Major James Patrick Sinnott Devereux, commander of the 378-strong Detachment of the 1st U.S. Marine Battalion on Wake Island. As the island's senior officer, Devereux's duties included the welcoming of all dignitaries passing through on the Pan-American Clipper – and thus, on 12 November, he found himself in the lobby of Wake's Pan-American Hotel, sipping highballs with Saburo Kurusu, Japan's newest envoy to Washington.

Plump and suave, in a pin-striped business suit, Kurusu seemed cordial enough, although confessing to one anxiety. "Please", he begged, "I don't want to be bothered by the Press." Devereux was reassuring. Few pressmen had ever set foot on Wake Island, a desolate two-square mile atoll of sand and coral discovered by the British in 1796 and claimed as a U.S. possession in 1899. Until Pan-American had set up a Clipper refuelling station in 1935, Wake had been notable only as a designated bird sanctuary. Even now Devereux's Marines and 1,200 civilian contractors engaged in converting the island base into a $20 million naval air station made up the sole population.

Twice, in their hour-long talk, Devereux noted, Kurusu mentioned his American wife, the former Alice Little of Chicago, as if to establish kinship. "If people could travel more," he said, "and come to know each other in their home countries perhaps these things would not come up."

Devereux was genuinely puzzled. What was the real purpose behind this man's mission? Was it a smokescreen, with Japan already bent on war? Or was Kurusu in earnest when he said, "I am just going to Washington to see what I can do. I hope I can straighten out affairs and avoid trouble?"

In his heart, Devereux believed that Kurusu meant it – but when the time came for the envoy to board the Clipper for San Francisco the Major could still not be sure.

Kurusu's intentions were not the only problem to confront Devereux since assuming command of Wake's Marines on 15 October. A dapper wiry 38-year-old with a pencil-line moustache, 5 feet 5 inches in height, Devereux in no way resembled the archetypal U.S. Marine but in eighteen years service he had known his share of trouble-spots: China, Nicaragua, Cuba. But now, in mid-November, the biggest problem was posed by Wake itself.

In the event of war, Wake Island would form a vital link in the chain of widely separated American islands stretching from Dutch Harbor in the Aleutians almost to the Equator. These outposts would become the U.S. first line of defence, of which the core was the Hawaiian island of Oahu, the base of the U.S. Pacific Fleet at Pearl Harbor. The nearest American bases were Midway, 1,000 miles east, and Guam, 1,000 miles west – but of all these island outposts it was Wake, with its trim white buildings and green woods, where the ocean swell on the reef boomed incessantly night and day, that lay nearest to Japan.

Yet if war threatened, the U.S. had thus far taken few precautions. Even now, Devereux was woefully understrength; his establishment was set at 43 officers, 939 men, but when the 6th Marine Battalion would arrive to backstop him, and bring him up to strength, nobody knew. No briefing had been given him on taking up command – and until an emergency arose, he lacked authority to set the contractor's men to work on gun emplacements. Much of the time his Marines had to suspend their training to act as refuelling crews for the new B-17s bound for the Philippines – leaving too little time to work up their skills as artillerymen.

Sometime in November, a message arrived from Naval Headquarters at Pearl Harbor to give Devereux further food for thought. It read:

INTERNATIONAL SITUATION INDICATES
YOU SHOULD BE ON THE ALERT

Promptly Devereux queried:

DOES INTERNATIONAL SITUATION INDICATE
EMPLOYMENT OF THE CONTRACTOR'S MEN ON
DEFENSE INSTALLATIONS WHICH ARE FAR
FROM COMPLETE?

It was two days before the reply arrived: negative. But Devereux at once felt easier. The situation must be less explosive than he had thought.

Even so, he worried: Wake Island's radar equipment had gone missing. Searching enquiries established that it had long been crated but was still sitting on the dockside at Pearl Harbor awaiting shipment – a long way down the list of assigned priorities. Understandably, Devereux chafed, for at the moment he was totally dependent on the look-outs atop Wake's two 50-ft steel water towers. Their eyes and ears were the sole detection devices he had.

Devereux looked back wryly to January, 1941, when he had arrived in Washington on leave to see his family. No sooner had he reached the capital than he was under orders to depart: a posting to Pearl Harbor had come up. His brother Ashton, driving him to the railroad station, had wondered what the sudden orders signified.

Devereux laughed. "Oh," he hazarded, "I'll probably wind up on some little spit-kit of an island."

And if war came?, his brother wondered.

Devereux was to prove all too accurate a prophet. "Your guess is as good as mine – but I'll probably end up eating fish and rice."

*

In Washington, D.C., Cordell Hull was angry. In the last week of November, he saw the British and the Chinese as greater threats to the fragile balance of peace than Japan itself.

On 20 November, Thanksgiving Day, Nomura and the newly-arrived Kurusu had handed the Secretary of State the current set of proposals which the Imperial Conference had finalised on 5 November in Tokyo. "It was an ultimatum," Hull was to recall, ". . . the commitments we should have to make were virtually a surrender."

Even so, Hull persevered. For two days he and his staff worked hard on a counter-proposal, a three-month *modus vivendi* which would tide both parties over while future talks continued. Japan, Hull posited, should withdraw from southern Indo-China – and reduce her forces in northern Indo-China to 25,000. In return, the U.S. would agree to a limited resumption of trade: petroleum, though for civilian use only, food and medical supplies, raw cotton. Meanwhile all U.S. restrictions on Japanese imports would be lifted.

At the same time, the State Department would urge Britain, Australia and the Dutch East Indies to take similar measures.

Whether Japan would have entertained any such proposition is open to doubt – but in the event they had no chance. In Chungking, Chiang Kai-shek, outraged by the proposal, fired off a cable to Churchill, who, in turn cautioned Roosevelt, "Of course it is for you to handle this business, and we certainly do not want an additional war. There is only one point that disquiets us. What about Chiang Kai-shek? Is he not having a very thin diet?" The Cabinet, too, were uneasy: "a Munich in the Far East?", queried Dalton in his diary. In Washington, Chiang's brother-in-law, T.V. Soong, along with the Chinese Ambassador, Professor Hu Shih, reacted so violently in a meeting with Roosevelt that the President, alarmed, soothed Soong: "Don't take your shirt off."

Simultaneously, on the morning of 26 November, came an intelligence report of Japanese troop movements heading south of Formosa. The truce formula was dead from that moment on. Hull was instructed on 26 November to draw up a ten-point proposal reiterating all Washington's most imperative demands.

Roosevelt was not, perhaps, displeased. At a Cabinet meeting on 7 November, as Attorney General Francis Biddle noted, the President was hopeful that an "incident" in the Pacific – not the Atlantic – would force the issue of war – "everyone would think of this as naval warfare, excluding the possibility of an (American) expeditionary force". The dark shadow of "foreign wars" was never far from the conference table.

Hull, though, was incensed beyond measure: because of Churchill and Chiang, his efforts for a Far Eastern concordat had gone for nothing. "It would have been better," he wrote Halifax angrily, "if Churchill had sent a strong cable back to Chiang Kai-shek telling him to brace up and fight with the same zeal as the Germans and Japanese are displaying."

For the weary old Secretary of State, it was the end of the line. "I have washed my hands of it," he told Secretary for War Stimson, "and now it is in the hands of you and Knox – the Army and the Navy."

*

Hull's faith, if touching, was unfounded. From the South China Sea to the Pacific, America's outposts lay naked to attack.

Of all these bases, none was more vulnerable than Pearl Harbor itself. Sited eight miles from the Hawaiian capital of Honolulu and the bars and clip-joints of downtown Waikiki, Pearl had long spelt home to the officers and ratings manning the 96 ships which made up the U.S. Pacific Fleet.

Yet for ten years its nakedness had been a byword. From 1931 on, every member of each graduating class in Japan's naval academy had faced one $64,000 question: How would you launch a surprise assault on Pearl Harbor? Back in 1936, the U.S. war games and drills in the Hawaiian Islands had all been planned on the basis of a surprise attack on Pearl – in which Japan had been code-named "Orange". In 1938, the defenses had cropped up again in a War Department survey – "there can be little doubt the Hawaiian Islands will be the initial scene of action".

The problem was that the Islands lacked any unified command. On paper, the Army, under Lieutenant-General Walter C. Short, commanding general of the Hawaiian Department, was responsible for defence, including the naval base and its military installations. In practice, though, Short kept a respectful distance from Admiral Husband E. Kimmel, the caustic Kentuckian C-in-C of the Pacific Fleet, and Kimmel maintained the same distance from Short. Cordial companions on the golf course, they were still chary of trading inter-service intelligence.

Not that there was much to trade. Neither Kimmel nor Short – any more than Vice-Admiral William F. Halsey, commanding the carriers of Task Force 8 from his flagship *Enterprise* – were aware that back in August 1940, Colonel William Friedman, the chief cryptoanalyst of the War Department, had cracked the Japanese diplomatic cipher system, code-named "Purple". The next step, emulating the British success with "Enigma", had been to build a replica of the "Purple" Machine. Between 1 July, 1941, and 7 December, 294 Japanese messages were to be intercepted, deciphered, translated into English and given the code-name "Magic".

But the men in command at Pearl Harbor – "America's billion-dollar fist in the Pacific", to the propagandists – were never privy to these messages. So tight was naval security that no "Purple" Machine even existed at Pearl; while four were retained in Washington, a fifth was held by the naval base at Cavite, in the Philippines. Even in Washington, the distribution methods had a cloak-and-dagger ring. Digests – but never verbatim transcripts – of up to 130 intercepts a day were rushed in locked brief-cases by special messengers to Roosevelt and his chief advisers who scanned them without taking notes while the messenger stood by. All copies but one were then burned.

Not until around 1 December did Kimmel, for the first time, light on a chance reference to "Purple" in a dispatch from the Chief of Naval Operations, Admiral Harold Stark. "What," he asked his Fleet Intelligence Officer, Lieutenant-Commander Edwin T. Layton, in bafflement, "is a purple machine?" Layton, equally in the dark, promised to try and find out.

Kimmel, who had been promoted over thirty-two Admirals to his present post, was far from complacent. To counter a surprise attack by fast carrier based aircraft he had time and again pressed for a pool of 250 reconnaissance planes – but the Navy Department, seeing a more pressing need elsewhere, refused to supply them. Thus, when Halsey's carriers were absent on a mission, Kimmel was forced to keep his battleships anchored in Pearl for lack of air cover.

Back in January, 1941, his predecessor, Admiral James O. Richardson had pressed both Roosevelt and Knox to recall the Fleet to the West Coast; Pearl Harbor was accessible only through a single entrance channel which all ships, coming and going, had to use. The interview concluded, Roosevelt asked Knox in disgust. "What's the matter with Jo? Has he become yellow?" Shortly after, Richardson was relegated to the General Board – "the boneyard".

Six months later, in June, Kimmel, who saw Pearl Harbor as "a damned mouse trap", told Roosevelt the same unpalatable truth. "If they sink one ship in the entrance of the harbor they have the whole Fleet bottled up and it can't get out," he emphasised, "The only place for the Fleet to be if the Japanese should attack is at sea, and not in port."

This simple equation had even been perceived by 22-year-old Margaret Spruance, daughter of the newly-appointed commander of Cruiser Division 5. On a sightseeing tour around Honolulu, the ships lined up on "Battleship Row", alongside the palm-fringed naval air station at Ford Island, struck her as appallingly at risk. "Dad," she asked, "what is there to stop the Japs from bombing our ships in the harbor?" His voice pregnant with sarcasm, Admiral Raymond A. Spruance replied, "They are not supposed to do it that way."

In justice to the service chiefs, the very volume of "Magic" intercepts was self-defeating. As often as danger threatened Hawaii, alarums were reported from the Panama Canal, from San Diego, Vladivostok, the Philippines, the Caribbean. Thus, on 27 November, when Stark routed a signal to Kimmel which began, "This is to be considered a war warning", the C-in-C's first reaction was, Where? The Kra Peninsula? Borneo? Siberia?

Lacking salient facts, men now jumped to false conclusions. Kimmel, fearing a submarine attack, warned the Fleet accordingly. General Short, similarly alerted by Army intelligence, saw danger from one source only: sabotage by Hawaii's 157,905 Japanese civilians. As a precaution he ordered that all planes at Hickam and Wheeler Fields should line up on their ramps wingtip to wingtip, as neatly as at an air review. Then he reported on his action – but no adverse comment was forthcoming from the War Department.

211

Nor was Short ever warned that a vital code-phrase, *Higashi No Kaze Ame* (East Wind Rain) was on the point of being transmitted. Its purport was "Please destroy all code papers": relations between Japan and the United States were about to be severed.

At this time another factor was troubling Kimmel – though he did not see fit to confide his worry to Short. On 1 December, his combat intelligence Division, under Lieutenant-Commander Joseph J. Rochefort, had reported that the Japanese Navy had changed its call signs; since 16 November they had had no contact with the carriers of the First and Second Japanese Fleets, still believed to be in their home waters in the Kure-Sasebo area.

On 1 December, Kimmel asked Commander Layton to check with Cavite as to the carriers' whereabouts – but next day Layton reported that he had drawn a blank.

"What, you don't know where the carriers are?" Kimmel said incredulously, "Do you mean they could be rounding Diamond Head (the extinct volcanic crater dominating Waikiki) and you wouldn't know it?"

Layton was optimistic. He hoped the carriers would be sighted long before that.

*

In a six-roomed air-conditioned penthouse on the fifth floor of the Manila Hotel, a man was pacing. At this time of day, the "blue hour", as the cocktail hour was known, it had become his evening routine, pacing as the setting sun dipped in splendour behind the Bataan Peninsula, pacing as the clangour of bells drove swooping battalions of bats from belfries all over the city; as rhythmically as a metronome, back and forth without cessation, while a cooling breeze from the balcony brought the scent of the white ginger flowers that he loved. At 60, Lieutenant-General Douglas MacArthur, recently-appointed chief of the U.S. Army Forces in the Far East, had good reason to pace and much to ponder.

"By God, it was Destiny that brought me here! It was Destiny," was MacArthur's reaction to his appointment, and the hyperbole was typical of the man. In fact, MacArthur had been a fixture in the Manila Hotel on Dewey Boulevard since 1936, serving as Military Adviser to the new Commonwealth Government of the Philippines under President Manuel Quezon. But when Roosevelt imposed his Japanese oil embargo on 26 July and created a new Army command in the Philippines – calling the forces of the Philippine Department and the Philippine Army into U.S. service for the duration of the emergency – MacArthur, five years on the spot, had seemed the logical choice for C-in-C.

Flamboyant, mercurial, a showman to his fingertips, MacArthur had no doubt he would succeed. Success was as much a part of him as his public persona: the long ebony cigarette holder, the crisply starched

212

uniforms he changed three times daily, his habit of punctuating every monologue with, "Get me? Understand? Follow me?" Some people found his presence overwhelming – "a tendency to deliver a speech to a hundred instead of answering a simple question in a few words", noted his counterpart in Singapore, Brooke-Popham – yet his staff gave him the same devoted loyalty as his wife of four years, Jean, to whom the General, after a character in Mark Twain's *A Connecticut Yankee at the Court of King Arthur*, was always "Sir Boss".

"I don't *think* that the Philippines can defend themselves," MacArthur had told Quezon, as long ago as 1934, "I *know* they can," and this unswerving optimism was to bring about a drastic last-minute policy reversal in the Far East. Fired by MacArthur's belief that enemy troops could be met at the waterline and driven back into the sea – and the promise of 100 B-17 heavy bombers, the Flying Fortress, by December – the idea had gained currency in Washington that the main island, Luzon, perhaps other islands as well, could be held against a Japanese attack.

This was in marked contrast to the earlier view that while Hawaii must be held at all costs, the Philippines, when it came to the crunch, were virtually indefensible. But just as Stalin had looked to the postponement of war until the Red Army called the shots, Roosevelt, too, was anticipating a war which, conveniently for America, would not erupt until 1 April, 1942.

"Dick", MacArthur hailed his Chief of Staff, Major-General Richard K. Sutherland, on 4 November, when an "Eyes Only" letter from General George Marshall arrived from Washington, "They are going to give us everything we have asked for." But again his infectious enthusiasm was outpacing events. Although the letter approved his fight-them-on-the-beaches strategy, promising tanks, guns and infantrymen, these promises, too, were predicated on an April, 1942 completion date.

At best, by mid-December, MacArthur would have 137,000 men under arms against the 200,000 he had anticipated – at least 80,000 of them Filipino trainees outfitted with cheap pith helmets, rubber tennis shoes and ancient Lee-Enfield rifles. The planes, too, would be forthcoming – but work on the airfields to house them had only now begun.

In the final outcome the Philippines were as helpless against attack as Pearl Harbor, but to the end, even if he suspected this, nothing of it showed in MacArthur's mien.

Clark Lee, Manila's Associated Press correspondent, who glimpsed him about this time, could only marvel at the confidence of the man as he strode towards his office at No 1, Calle Victoria: the rigidly-braced shoulders, the jaunty tilt of his gold-braided cap, the cigarette smouldering in the long holder.

"He looked completely sure of himself," Lee recalled, "He looked like a man who couldn't lose."

Fifteen hundred miles south-west of Manila, in a one-story wooden frame building inside the Singapore Naval Base, Air Chief Marshal Sir Robert Brooke-Popham, the British C-in-C, Far East, faced problems of a different order. Unlike MacArthur he knew the terrible vulnerability of his command structure. His difficulty was to drive this home to Churchill and the Chiefs of Staff.

For sixteen years, the "impregnable fortress" of Singapore had been a myth in the making. Only a select few on the spot knew the painful reality: Singapore was a £60 million floating dockyard whose sole defence was six 15-inch naval guns pointing mutely out to sea. From the landward side, "Singraltar", as the embittered Secretary of Defence for Malaya, C. A. Vlieland, dubbed it, was guarded only by a skein of barbed wire.

As far back as 1923, the Chief of Air Staff, Air Chief Marshal Sir Hugh Trenchard, had protested vigorously at this antediluvian system of defence, urging that air power must play its part – a theory totally rejected by the First Sea Lord, Admiral of the Fleet Earl Beatty. At that time Trenchard had pressed for three squadrons of torpedo bombers, a squadron of fighters, two of bombers and a reconnaissance flight. But the Navy had won the day. In 1926 – in what he later acknowledged as "the worst blunder of my career" – Trenchard had backed down.

The basic concept was that a frontal assault on the naval base by a hostile fleet could be held off for ninety days – after which the Eastern Fleet would arrive. But in November, 1941, the Eastern Fleet was a reality only on paper. Just as with MacArthur's Philippine task force, the Admiralty was looking to March, 1942, as the earliest possible assembly date.

A year earlier, on assuming command, Brooke-Popham had been fatally acquiescent. "Our job in the Far East is not to press for facilities that cannot be given," he wrote virtuously to Ismay, "but to utilise every resource that we have got or can acquire locally." Too late he was to realise that only a tactic of unrelenting pressure could ever galvanise the Chiefs of Staff. While agreeing in principle that "582 aircraft is an ideal" they felt that "336 should give very fair degree of security" – but even these were never to arrive.

Unlike the Philippines, which had planes in plenty but few airfields to accommodate them, Brooke-Popham had fully thirty airfields, all of them garrisoned by combat troops, but only 141 operational planes. Of these most were obsolescent Lockheed-Hudsons, Brewster Buffalo fighters and Wildebeeste torpedo-bombers – for the Chiefs of Staff held that "the Buffalo appears to be eminently satisfactory and would probably prove more than a match for any Japanese aircraft".

Behind this myopia lay a crucial fallacy: that Singapore Island and its naval base could be held without defending the three million acres of rubber plantations that made up the Malayan Peninsula. In 1937, the Chief of Staff to the G.O.C., Malaya Command, Colonel Arthur Percival – who by 1941 was himself G.O.C. – had pointed out that an attack from Thailand or Northern Malaya was both feasible and probable, but the War Office had turned down all requests for tanks. The north-east monsoon would make an east coast landing impossible; the jungle, in any case was "impenetrable" to troops. It was a belief that died hard. The one man who disagreed, Lieutenant Colonel Ian Stewart, commanding the 2nd Battalion, Argyll and Sutherland Highlanders, who led his troops on a 90-mile jungle route march, found no favour with Percival's staff officers – "Stewart's ideas on jungle training are those of a crank".

A disturbing lack of urgency was everywhere apparent. Brigadier Ivan Simson, Malaya's Chief Engineer, was shocked to find up-country troops totally ignorant of neutralising enemy tanks – yet he knew that official War Office pamphlets on the subject had arrived from London months ago. Investigating, he found them still lying, neatly tied in bundles, in a cupboard at Military Headquarters in Fort Canning. No one had ever seen fit to distribute them.

The R.A.F. were as bad. At Seletar airfield, on Malaya's east coast, Pilot Officer Roy Bulcock, an Australian, was staggered to see the Transit Store piled almost to the roof with 3,000 cases of material. All of them were destined for up-country airfields – but had lain there undistributed for more than eighteen months.

All over the Far East, the "fortress" mentality prevailed with British and Americans alike. "No place is indefensible . . .," MacArthur was to assert. "To say the Philippines are indefensible is merely to say that they are inadequately defended." A similar myth was then current regarding Pearl Harbor; "the island of Oahu, due to its fortifications, its garrison, and its physical characteristics is believed to be the strongest fortress in the world", General Marshall maintained in a minute to Roosevelt, and later he added, "Presence of Fleet reduces threat of major attack". "Singapore was not a fortress, though this was a thing few were allowed to know," one of Percival's staff officers revealed, "or, if they knew, to admit, for this would have been imperial heresy."

Though separated by thousands of miles of ocean, life in Manila and Honolulu still had much in common with life in Singapore and in the British Crown Colony of Hong Kong. All were polyglot commercial entrepôts, where money talked loudest, and in a babel of tongues; in Malaya, the nine largest tin mining companies had shown an average profit increase of 321 percent in 1940. In a climate as warm and steamy as a Turkish bath, the siesta was everywhere a way of life; rarely did the temperature drop below 80 degrees Fahrenheit. All were communities where, even in 1941, with half the world in arms, life for the expatriates was still ordered and secure, soothed by a minimum of three Chinese or Filipino servants.

There were still certain niceties and social gradations observed; in Hong Kong status was determined by how far up the Peak, 1,823 feet above sea level, a householder lived. At the Peninsula Hotel, just as at Honolulu's Royal Hawaiian, white dinner jackets were *de rigueur* and ten-page menus commonplace; the "in" drink was the gimlet, gin, lime juice and ice, the only hard liquor that General MacArthur touched. There was still time for pleasures that much of the world had forgotten; the weekly racing at Hong Kong's Happy Valley and tournaments on Honolulu's Mainalua Golf Course, sea-bathing parties, midnight movie matinees and charity balls. At Singapore's Seaview Hotel, one Sunday ritual had lately been established: before luncheon was served, the drinkers on the pillared terrace seized up the small rectangular song-sheets placed on each table and launched into a lusty chorus of *There'll Always Be An England*.

Whether American or British, these communities had another factor in comi ion: an abiding contempt for the Japanese. They saw them, without exception, as a race of comical little men with thick spectacles, bow legs and buck teeth. Because they rode on their mothers' backs as babies they were known to suffer from vertigo; they were so near-sighted that only one in 5,000 of their rifle shots would ever register. They read and wrote backwards, and turned a key to the left to open a door. Their assembly lines could turn out 200 planes a month at most. (The true figure was 426.) Their pilots were a byword for ineptitude. (In fact, cadets had a minimum 300 flying hours against a U.S. cadet's 200; carrier pilots averaged 800 hours). Above all, the notion that they could worst red-blooded Americans or true-blue Britons in battle was farcical, so say the least.

It was an attitude perfectly summed up by the distasteful query of an Australian battalion commander when Brooke-Popham inspected his troops. "Don't you think, sir," he asked, "that they are worthy of some better enemy than the Japanese?"

*

On Monday, 1 December, Hull made one last attempt to stem the Japanese tide. In his large gloomy State Department Office, which most closely resembled a railway station waiting room, dominated by an 11-ft high rubber plant, Kurusu and Nomura sat as they had done so many times before, slumped awkwardly in deep black leather armchairs. "Japan does not have to use a sword to gain for herself a seat at the head of the table," Hull emphasised yet again, unimpressed by Kurusu's assertions that Japan's purposes were different from Hitler's and that Premier Tojo could keep the military in check. "I put them wholly on the defensive," Hull later reported by phone to Halifax, ". . . I let them understand that I couldn't take care of things any longer as long as they kept inching on and on . . . I made it just as clear as I could."

No doubt he succeeded – but both Nomura and Kurusu were well aware that in Tokyo a different clock was ticking. Since the fateful Imperial Conference of 5 November, Japan had been pressing urgently for guarantees that in event of war Germany would honour the Tripartite Pact – even should Japan prove the aggressor. That would be automatic, Ribbentrop had assured them. On 30 November, the Japanese Ambassador in Berlin, General Hiroshi Oshima, warned both Hitler and Ribbentrop: "This war may come quicker than anyone dreams".

None knew this better than Kurusu. Soon after the meeting with Hull, he had discussed the darkening diplomatic horizon with Hidenari Terasaki, a young Foreign Service official. "Mr Ambassador," Terasaki asked him boldly, "why don't you become a national traitor? Why don't you go ahead and say to the Americans: 'We *will* get out of China?' . . . The war party knows . . . they will have to leave China, but they all prefer war with the United States . . . to admitting they have made such a mistake."

But time was running out, and both men knew it. On 3 December, in the Embassy's backyard on Massachusetts Avenue, clerks were already at work burning bales of secret papers.

Events now moved swiftly. On this same day, using Raoul Desvernine, a Washington attorney for the Japanese Mitsui interests as an intermediary, Kurusu met up at the Mayflower Hotel with a man who had once enjoyed a close relationship with Roosevelt: the 71-year-old financier and economist, Bernard Baruch. Urgently, Kurusu hammered home his message: the Japanese people and the Emperor wanted peace, but the war lords "were sitting with a loaded gun in each hand". The one solution, as Kurusu saw it, was to immobilise the military – with the President making a direct personal appeal to the Emperor.

Baruch was non-committal. The proposal, he wrote in a memo, "did not seem to be anything into which anybody could put their teeth". But at this eleventh hour anything was worth a try. He would, he promised Kurusu, convey his message to the White House.

*

It was already too late. On Thursday, 4 December, a squat (5ft 3in) muscular man awkwardly clad in a blue civilian suit was shouldering his way through the rush hour crowds at Yokohama Central Station. Like almost all his fellow passengers, he carried a large *furoshiki* – a square of coloured cloth tied at the corners – the accepted Japanese way of carrying parcels. But this was a parcel with a difference. Inside it, glinting with

217

gold braid, was the uniform of a full admiral of the Imperial Japanese Navy.

Admiral Isoroku Yamamoto, C-in-C of the Japanese Combined Fleet, was en route to Hiroshima, where his flagship *Nagato* lay at anchor, surrounded by seven of the world's largest battleships.

It was to be his last day ashore for some time; the Admiral had been making his farewells. He took time out to visit his geisha, Kikuji, whom he had loved for six years, and sprawl on the straw-matting floor to play a game of *hana fuda* – flower cards – for a small wager. Then, having won seven yen, he dropped in on a small private party at Naval Headquarters. Many toasts were drunk to the success of Yamamoto's mission, though the Admiral, a teetotaller, took only token sips of *sake*.

As his train steamed southwards from Yokohama, through the frost-speckled rice fields, Yamamoto's mind went back over the angry arguments of the last months – arguments which had only been clinched, on 20 October, by his threat to resign his commission and retire to civil life. Only then had Admiral Nagano, as Chief of Naval Staff, given Yamamoto his reluctant blessing: "If he has that much confidence he must be allowed to carry on".

A onetime Naval Attaché in Washington, Yamamoto was bitterly opposed to war; he had seen the nation's industrial might from close quarters. Yet if war was inevitable, he remained convinced, the one way to remove a danger to Japan's southern flank was to wipe out the U.S. Pacific Fleet at Pearl Harbor, Hawaii – much as Hermann Göring had sought to knock out the R.A.F. as a prelude to the invasion of Britain.

His fellow admirals, seeing too many risks attached, had tried to argue him out of it. It was in vain. No sooner were objections raised than Yamamoto and his staff came up with solutions that worked. His plan for aerial torpedo attacks faced two prime obstacles: Pearl Harbor was both narrow (only 500 yards at some points) and shallow (thirty-eight feet) and was probably equipped with torpedo nets. To solve this problem, Yamamoto ordered the naval ordnance factories to supply him with 1,000-lb torpedos on the British model – but to equip them with special wooden stabiliser fins, ensuring they ran straight when hitting the water.

Such an operation called for well-trained pilots, daring enough to launch their torpedos from as low as 25 feet, but Yamamoto had these, too. At Kagoshima Bay, south of Kyushu, he had found a harbour that was a replica of Pearl, accessible only through a single entrance channel – and from then on the three-man crews had the time of their lives. In line of duty, their instructions were to buzz civilians and buildings impartially – dodging between telephone posts and chimneys, terrifying every fishing boat skipper across the bay. After fifty practice runs, low-altitude flights became second nature; bombing results showed an eighty per cent success rate.

Nothing was left to chance. Aboard *Akagi*, the flagship of Vice-Admiral Chuichi Nagumo commanding the six carrier task force, Commander Minoru Genda, in charge of planning, and Commander Mitsuo Fuchida, commanding all groups of the First Air Fleet, worked for days on a seven-foot square mock-up of the island of Oahu. At length they had memorised every hangar and drydock, the lay-out of the Navy Yard, the alignment of the battleships along the two-mile stretch of Ford Island.

Yet Yamamoto still remembered it as all too close for comfort. Had it not been for his threat of resignation – staking everything on his belief – "Operation Z", as it was code-named, would already be no more than a bulky folder gathering dust in a drawer at Naval Headquarters.

In Hiroshima, the wide waters of the bay seemed curiously empty when he arrived to board his flagship, Yamamoto knew why. At 5.30 p.m. on 2 December, with the diplomatic deadline long past, a coded signal had gone from Naval Headquarters in Tokyo to the powerful Pearl Harbor Striking Force, thirty-two ships strong. Already they were far away, pitching in the sullen waters of the North Pacific, bound for Pearl Harbor.

The message was one they had long awaited: CLIMB MOUNT NIITAKA. It meant: Begin The War.

*

At 7 a.m. on 4 December, before Yamamoto had even boarded his train in Yokohama, a convoy of twenty troop transports, all of them under 10,000 tons, had steamed at a laborious nine knots out of Samah Harbour, on Hainan Island, in the South China Sea. In a tiny airless cabin aboard the armoured headquarter's ship, *Ryujo Maru,* General Tomoyuki Yamashita, newly-appointed commander of the 25th Japanese Army, was in reflective mood.

His briefing was to invade north-eastern Malaya without warning and ultimately to capture the naval base at Singapore – tasks which seemed to call for tactics well-known to Hitler's *Wehrmacht* but alien to the Japanese until now.

It was an undertaking that the stocky imperturbable Yamashita had viewed soberly from the first. Following a brief parting from his wife, Hisako, in a cold bare room in the Japanese Officer's Club, Tokyo, he had flown to Hainan via Formosa and Saigon, making only one modest purchase along the way: a straw mat to sleep on in the tropical heat. At Samah, where the hotel proprietress had offered him her own daughter as a compliment, Yamashita had ordered a staff officer: "Take this girl away. She is a victim. When I am going to fight the enemy so soon how can I take a virgin tonight?"

Just as at Pearl Harbor, the Malayan attack called for speed and surprise, and Yamashita's formations had been pared down accordingly.

219

Streamlined for speedy landings and for moving fast through jungle, each division numbered only 12,000 men. Thus he would hit the Malayan coastline with barely 24,000 men – reinforced by 12,000 more from Indo-China and a submissive Thailand when the time came for the assault on Singapore.

The plan had called for much re-thinking. The men of the 5th and 18th Cavalry Divisions, mostly tough ex-coal miners from northern Kyushu, had been forced to undergo remount training, abandoning their horses in favour of bicycles; more than 6,000 cheap Japanese bicycles were now packed into the holds of the troop transports. As Yamashita envisaged it, the bicycle brigades would streak ahead of tanks and infantry as Hitler's Panzers had carved through France in 1940: 6,000 cyclists armed with rifles and grenades, pedalling as one, often for twenty hours a day, carrying only two days supply of rice, with the supply trucks often 100 miles behind. Two mechanics, attached to each battalion, would service up to twenty bicycles a day.

Since most had only seen service in Manchuria, Colonel Masanobu Tsuji, the Director of Military Operations, had come up with an ingenious concept: 40,000 copies of a pamphlet crammed with all the tropical expertise that a staff of thirty had gleaned from talks with sea captains, merchants and University professors. Covering everything from weapon care – "Make sure damp weapons do not rust" – to bivouacs – "the wood of mangrove trees burns well in its native state" – its title was buoyantly optimistic: "JUST READ THIS – AND THE WAR IS WON".

And Tsuji had made another decisive contribution to the campaign. On 22 October, after a five-hour reconnaissance flight in an unarmed plane, he noted that the airfields of Kota Bharu and Alor Star must be the prime objectives of the invasion. Failing this, British torpedo-bombers would certainly wreak havoc with the convoy's escort – two cruisers, ten destroyers and five submarines, which, for security reasons, were travelling 200 miles distant until the appointed Malayan rendezvous.

Yamashita, in approving these targets, still had minor reservations. Headquarters had been able to provide only small-scale maps of Malaya, and none of Singapore at all; thus far the man slated to topple the Singapore bastion had done all his planning from a high school atlas. And there was one other drawback, though doubtless he would overcome it: all his Army service had been in Europe or Manchuria.

Until the week he had paused in Saigon. the occasion of his fifty-sixth birthday, Yamashita had never seen a jungle in his life.

*

Saturday, 6 December, dawned crisp and cloudless in Washington, D.C. In Rock Creek Park, at the northern end of Connecticut Avenue, early morning horseback riders noted a hint of frost in the air, but a high bright sun was rising to the east, gilding the dome of the Capitol Building.

At 9.30 a.m., Stephen T. Early, the Presidential Press Secretary, was holding his usual morning conference with Washington's newsmen in the White House's west wing – but, he stressed, he could not "see any need for pads and pencils or even minds" that morning. The President had given them a day off to do their Christmas shopping.

"I suppose he is over at the White House writing a declaration of war personally," one reporter hazarded, but Early had to disappoint him. "He is over at the White House but he is not writing at the present time. He is shaving . . . no appointments for today and none for tomorrow and I don't assume there will be."

In the low rambling Navy Department building on Constitution Avenue, Secretary Frank Knox was winding up his daily top-level naval meeting. "Gentlemen," he asked, as if seeking reassurance, "Are they going to hit us?"

Rear Admiral Richmond Kelly Turner, Chief of the Naval Operations War Plans Division, spoke for all those present. "No, Mr Secretary. They are going to hit the British. They are not ready for us yet."

All over the capital there was the same relaxed air, as if war and declarations of war were the last things on the public mind; this was a week-end for picnics in the Blue Ridge Mountains or the Sunday afternoon football game at Griffith Stadium. Only a few men, in a position to know or suspect, sensed that every tick of the clock was bringing the United States closer to war.

At 11 a.m. Saburo Kurusu was receiving a courtesy call from an old friend, Ferdinand L. Mayer, a 54-year-old retired career diplomat whom he had known when both had been assigned to Lima, Peru. "Fred," he had confided, after making sure that none of the Embassy Staff was within earshot, "we are in an awful mess."

Mayer was puzzled. All through their hour-long talk, he had an intuition that Kurusu was trying to convey "something of the most shocking import" – words that he could not bring himself to utter. More than once he reaffirmed that "the show was up" in China, that Tojo was only trying to save face; the stumbling block, as Kurusu saw it, was Hull and the State Department, who distrusted him profoundly. "We believe that President Roosevelt as arbiter between ourselves and the Chinese is the best move from our point of view," he told Mayer seriously.

As a longstanding friend, Mayer placed more faith in Kurusu's intentions than Baruch had done. He begged the Ambassador to dine at 8 p.m. at the Georgetown mansion of his friend, Ferdinand Lamot Belin, multi-millionaire industrialist and former Ambassador to Poland. There they might discuss some way of establishing a more personal link with the President.

But Roosevelt, after three leisurely days digesting Baruch's report, had at last decided to act. For much of this Saturday afternoon he was labouring on an appeal to Emperor Hirohito, to be conveyed by the Ambassador, Joseph C. Grew, urging a Japanese withdrawal from Indo-China. The people of the Philippines, the East Indies, Malaya and Thailand, he stressed "were sitting on a keg of dynamite – it is clear that a continuance of such a situation is unthinkable".

"I address myself to Your Majesty at this moment in the fervent hope that Your Majesty may, as I am doing, give thought in this definite emergency to ways of dispelling the dark clouds. . . ."

As his secretary, Grace Tully, withdrew to type it up, the President's wife, Eleanor, looked in with an old friend, Justine Polier, a children's court judge from New York. "Well, Justine", Roosevelt greeted her, "this son of man has just sent his final message to the Son of God".

It was again too late. A bureaucratic bottleneck in the Tokyo military censorship department was to hold up the coded cable for ten and a half hours – too late for the Emperor to even consider intercession.

Meanwhile, in the Navy's Cryptographic Department, where most of the staff were preparing to leave at noon, one translator, Mrs Dorothy Edgers, had grown curious. With time to kill, she had begun leafing through low-priority "Magic" intercepts: those dealing with Hawaii had been piling up for days. Now she was electrified by a message from Tokyo to Consul-General Kita in Honolulu, dated 2 December. From this time on he was to report daily concerning all movements of ships, berthing positions and torpedo netting at Pearl Harbor. There were other later messages in the same vein.

Intrigued, Mrs Edgers elected to stay on duty and work overtime. By 3 p.m. she had brought the intercepts up to date – in time to present her evidence to Lieutenant Commander Alvin Kramer, Chief of the Translation Department, who had just checked in for duty. Incredibly, Kramer was more intent on criticising her translation – until finally he laid the intercepts aside. "We'll get back to this on Monday," he dismissed the indignant Mrs Edgers.

All over Washington on this day there was the same resolute refusal to believe the worst – as if the one thing to be feared was the over-dramatic gesture or reaction. In the Navy Department building, by 4.30 p.m., thirteen parts of a wordy Fourteen-Part "Magic" message from Tokyo to the Washington Embassy had now reached the decoders' desks – but Commander Laurence E. Safford, Chief of Security Intelligence Communications, saw no reason to set aside his evening engagement. He left his best man, Lieutenant George W. Lynn, to sort out the tangle.

Elsewhere in the building, the same unbelief prevailed. In his office, Rear Admiral Richmond Kelly Turner was about to switch off his desk lamp when he looked up. The Chief of the Intelligence Division, Rear

Admiral Theodore Stark Wilkinson, was standing before his desk. "You are mistaken, Kelly," he said quietly.

Turner was nonplussed. "Mistaken in what?"

"Mistaken that Japan would attack the United States."

Turner only shrugged. Back in July he had named Pearl Harbor as a "probable" target – but not, as he had told Knox that morning, in the forseeable future. In silence, the two men walked side by side down the long corridor.

Even at the Japanese Embassy there was no overriding sense of urgency. Just as on Constitution Avenue, the first thirteen parts of the message had arrived and been sent to the decoding room, but after deciphering the first nine parts, the staff adjourned. Since a colleague was being posted to a new station, a farewell party was in order.

It was 10 p.m. before they returned to the job – by now muzzy with *sake* and with less heart for the task ahead. Nonetheless, by midnight, four more parts had been completed. But the vital fourteenth part had still not arrived.

On Constitution Avenue, the Navy Department had worked faster; the first thirteen parts of the message had been decoded by 8.30 p.m. It was now that Commander Kramer saw a probability that Japan was breaking off negotiations. He began placing a series of urgent calls.

Soon after 9 p.m. Kramer drove to the White House, handing a sealed pouch to the officer on duty, Lieutenant Lester Schulz. In the second-floor Oval Office, Schulz found Roosevelt working on his stamp collection, chatting with Hopkins, who was reclining on the sofa.

It took Roosevelt a good ten minutes to digest Japan's explanation of why they could not accept Hull's peremptory note of 26 November as a basis for negotiations. Then, passing the sheaf of papers to Hopkins, he said tersely, "This means war". Hopkins was disgruntled. "Since war is undoubtedly going to come at the convenience of the Japanese, it's too bad we can't strike the first blow."

"No, we can't do that," Roosevelt argued, "We are a democracy and a peaceful people." Then, raising his voice a trifle, "But we have a good record". Abruptly, he lifted the phone; he wanted an immediate connection with the Chief of Naval Operations. But the operator explained that Admiral Stark was not in his quarters; he was with a party at the National Theatre, watching *The Student Prince*.

Roosevelt hung up; he would call later. "I don't want to cause public alarm by having him paged in a theatre," he told Hopkins. He, too, was wary of the dramatic gesture.

On Massachusetts Avenue, the hour was late; midnight had come and gone, but the Embassy was still awaiting the fourteenth part from Tokyo.

Finally, the staff gave up and went home; war or no war, a man needed his sleep. And Sunday might be quite a long day.

11

"What Was That Place? Could You Spell It?"

7–13 December, 1941

NEVER HAD HAWAII seen a dawn like this. In the early morning light, the Pacific Ocean, 230 miles north of Oahu, teemed with shipping, their battle ensigns snapping in the wind: the giant aircraft carriers *Akagi*, *Kaga* and *Soryu*, the vast new flattop *Zuikaku*, the light carriers *Hiryu* and *Shokaku*, two brand-new cruisers, the *Tone* and the *Chikuma*, nine destroyers and two old battleships, all of them pitching in heavy grey swells that rolled them from 12 to 15 degrees. Normally, when a swell exceeded 5 degrees, all manoeuvres were cancelled. But today there could be no turning back.

Aboard the command ship, *Akagi*, Admiral Chuichi Nagumo, knew exactly what his planes had to do. At 5.30 a.m. this morning, Sunday, 7 December, two Zero float-planes from *Chikuma* and *Tone* would carry out a last pre-attack reconnaissance – checking that the U.S. Pacific Fleet, following long-standing custom, had returned to Oahu for the week-end. Then, if all was reported in order, two mighty waves, 353 planes in all, would hit Pearl Harbor: the first wave to be launched at 6 a.m., the second at 7.15 a.m. Mitsubishi high-level medium bombers, Aichi Type 99 dive bombers, Nakajima Type 97 torpedo bombers – all had their roles to play.

Below decks, pilots and crews had been chafing for hours; by 3.30 a.m., Hawaiian Time, all of them had been rousted from their bunks. Each man had pulled on clean *mawashi* (loincloths), good-luck bellybands and freshly-pressed red shirts – to indicate a warrior's disdain for blood. Breakfast brought an extra treat – *sekihan*, rice with red beans, and tai, a red snapper fish, both of them dishes reserved for ceremonial occasions. To mark the solemnity of this day, many men now donned traditional *hashamaki* headbands. Then it was time for final instructions; in the dimly-lit briefing room of the *Akagi*, Commander Mitsuo Fuchida noted, it was so crowded that many pilots were huddled in the passageway. As Fuchida left to board the commander's plane, singled out by its red and yellow striped tail, Commander Minoru Genda, who had planned this entire attack, quietly placed a hand on his shoulder. No words passed between them; there was no need.

Now, slowly, the six carriers swung into the east wind. Already, the planes were lined up on the flight decks, ready for take off, engines roaring and sputtering in the final warmup. Green lamps waved in a slow solemn arc, and one by one the fighters, led by Lieutenant Yoshio Shiga, raced down the runways, the torpedo planes and the dive bombers following, 183 planes streaking for Pearl Harbor.

On Oahu, at 6.30 a.m., one man had already written a small and intriguing footnote to history: Lieutenant William Woodward Outerbridge, U.S. Navy, who two days earlier had taken over his first command, the obsolescent destroyer U.S.S. *Ward*. At this hour, the harbour's torpedo net had been raised for an approaching vessel, the target ship *Antares*, and Outerbridge, roused from his bunk in the charthouse, was peering off the port bow at what he took to be a submarine's conning tower. Although Outerbridge could not know it, twenty Japanese submarines – including five midgets – were scheduled to wreak such havoc as they could once the main attack had started.

As Outerbridge shouted, "Go to general quarters", *Ward*, churning at 25 knots, closed to 100 yards; as her No 3 gun blasted the conning tower, the midget began to sink. "Drop depth charges," Outerbridge yelled, and four times the destroyer's whistle blasted, and four charges rolled from her stern.

But if Outerbridge was alerted to wage war, most men clung doggedly to peacetime. Because of a delay in decoding, *Ward*'s notification of the attack did not reach Captain John B. Earle, Admiral Kimmel's Chief of Staff, until 7.12 a.m. and even then Earle was doubtful. "We get so many of these false sightings," he told Admiral Claude C. Bloch, commander of the Fourteenth Naval District, and the Admiral agreed. "Ask for this to be verified," was his first reaction.

Forty miles north of Pearl Harbor, at Kahuku Point, Oahu's northernmost tip, two men briefly scented danger. Private George Elliott, Jnr., of the 515th Aircraft Signal Warning Service, had just spotted a large blip on his radar unit and called on his senior, Private Joseph Lockard, for clarification. Lockard was first convinced that the machine was acting up; no group so large had ever been registered on the oscilloscope. By now Elliott had traced the blip on the plotting board: 137 miles to the north and three degrees east. Excitedly, he urged the reluctant Lockard to call Fort Shafter, the Army's administrative headquarters.

Finally Elliott himself made the call – only to draw a blank. On this sleepy sun-drenched Sunday, the Information Centre could trace no one in authority save for Lieutenant Kermit Tyler, who was just finishing a four-hour shift at the Army's new interceptor centre. Though Tyler took the call and spoke to Lockard, he saw no occasion for urgency: planes were due in from the carrier *Enterprise* and Flying Fortresses were constantly passing through. But the blips were getting bigger by the

225

minute, Lockard told him, now only 90 miles from Oahu. "Well," Tyler reassured him, before hanging up, "don't worry about it."

Aboard the 96 vessels – including eight battleships, eight cruisers and twenty-nine destroyers – in harbour this morning, many men faced pressing problems – or so it seemed to them at this moment. Yeoman Durrell Conner had chosen the seclusion of the flag communications office in the battleship *California* to finish wrapping his Christmas presents on time. In the galley of the aircraft tender *Curtiss*, the cooks were praying that the turkey they had just committed to the oven would be done in time for lunch. Perhaps the most worried man in the U.S. Pacific Fleet this morning was Ensign Joe Taussig, aboard the battleship *Nevada*. He had never stood watch for morning colours before – so what size American flag should he order to be flown?

On this bright Sunday morning, with a light north east trade wind caressing the green cane fields, the white puffs of cumulus cloaking the peaks of the Koolau Range, it seemed the least probable place on earth for an all-out war to begin. This thought came vividly home to Fleet Chaplain William A. Maguire, aboard *Arizona*, as he marvelled at the dazzle of the sun on the blue-grey water. "Joe," he told his assistant, Seaman Joseph Workman, "this is one for the tourist!"

High above Kahuku, Commander Fuchida, now circling the west coast of Oahu, had much the same feeling: fringed by blue-green cane fields, the waters of Pearl glimmered blue and brilliant in the sun, recalling the huge mock-up he had studied for so long. At exactly 7.49 a.m., he radioed the code-phrase, "To . . . to . . . to", back to *Akagi*; it meant, "First wave attacking", and that at any moment the Americans would be fighting back. Yet now, as he neared the target, Fuchida was riveted with surprise. Of the 231 Army planes on Oahu, all were lined up wingtip to wingtip on Hickam, Bellows and Wheeler Fields, like the Marine planes at Ewa – secure against the sabotage that General Short had feared. Not even a puff of ack-ack stained the crystal sky.

It was now 7.53 a.m. and Fuchida radioed Nagumo again, "Tora, Tora, Tora!", firing a blue flare to alert the nearest fighter squadron as he did so. Translated, this meant "Tiger, tiger, tiger", or "Surprise Attack Achieved"; without a hint of opposition, the torpedo planes could head straight for "Battleship Row".

Now confusion arose. When the fighter leader failed to waggle his wings in acknowledgement, Fuchida fired a second blue flare; promptly Lieutenant Shiga took this as a warning that surprise had not been achieved. Then, following the pre-arranged plan, he headed for Hickam Field to clear the sky of U.S. fighters. Lieutenant Commander Kakuichi Takahashi, leading fifty-one dive bombers, misread the signal, too; he veered off to knock out Pearl Harbor's ack-ack. Only the forty torpedo planes under Lieutenant Commander Shigeharu Murata read the signals correctly, streaking for the forest of masts that was "Battleship Row". On the southern side of Ford Island they let fall the first torpedoes "like dragonflies dropping their eggs".

At 7.55 a.m., in the signal tower atop the Navy Yard water tank, seamen were just then hoisting the flag known as Prep, a white square in a solid field of blue, indicating that morning colours would rise in five minutes. It was at this moment that Pharmacist's Mate William Lynch, aboard *California*, heard a shipmate call: "The Russians must have a carrier visiting us. Here come some planes with the red balls showing clearly".

Within seconds he knew his error. As the first planes hurtled for Ford Island, the urgent voice of Commander Logan Ramsey, the Navy patrol plane operations officer, crackled from loudspeakers all over the harbour complex: "Air Raid Pearl Harbor! This is no Drill!"

The enormity of the attack was hard for any man to grasp. Few had even remotely suspected that hostilities were at hand. In the destroyer *Monaghan*, a seaman complained to Boatswain's Mate Thomas Donahue, "Hell, I didn't even know they were sore at us". Amid the shattering roar of the explosions, the geysering columns of water, the instinct of most was still to do what they had always done at this time. Aboard *Nevada*, Leader Oden McMillan and his 23-man band were already in position to play morning colours when Fuchida's 49 Kate bombers began their run-in. As the flight leader lay prone on his belly, watching through a peephole until his hurtling bombs "became small as poppy-seeds", McMillan's musicians crashed into "The Star-Spangled Banner" – and kept playing. Once they had started the National Anthem it never once occurred to them that they could stop – though they broke frantically for cover once the final note died.

Now, just after 8 a.m., the attack had barely started. Aboard *California*, the First Lieutenant, Lieutenant Commander M. N. Little, saw a high-flying plane bank steeply, followed by the bubble track of a torpedo; as it exploded a vast column of water mushroomed to port. Seaman W. W. Parker, on *Arizona*'s blister top, thought he was watching a dive-bombing practice; next instant a bomb had hit the forward turret, knifing downwards into the bowels of the ship. Then the battleship's boilers and forward magazines blew up, and with a violence few men have witnessed a column of blood-red smoke spewed thousands of feet skywards.

In one searing flash, 1,000 men had been wiped out. Even far above the target, Commander Fuchida felt his plane bouncing in the shock-wave like a ping-pong ball on a jet of water.

Radioman Glenn Lane, blown clean off the quarterdeck, was only one of many; from the cruiser *New Orleans*, 500 yards distant, Chaplain Howell Forgy saw the waters round *Arizona* as one vast "mass of bobbing oil-covered heads". And soon the fires were spreading; eighty feet to windward, *Arizona's* flames caught the stern and port quarter of the battleship *Tennessee*. Seaman S. F. Bowen, seeing a melting ball of fire shaped like a basketball descending, ran for dear life, noting that even his shoe laces were burning.

Now a wall of oily flame was advancing on the *West Virginia*; bomb splinters ripped at her bridge, cutting down Captain Mervyn Bennion with a fatal stomach wound. Soon she was listing so heavily that men crawled like flies along her decks; at once Lieutenant Claude Ricketts made for the counterflood valves, a brave but vain attempt. Although the after magazine was successfully flooded, to flood the forward magazine proved impossible; the water was now almost up to the main deck.

By 8.40 a.m., the second Japanese wave reached the target, 170 aircraft under Lieutenant Commander Shigekazu Shimazaki, but now the skies were so crowded they had to circle for fifteen minutes, like jet liners stacked by an airport. Chief Flight Petty Officer Juzo Mori's ambition – to die for a battleship rather than a cruiser – now seemed a vain one. Almost every battleship was already in mortal distress.

Midway along "Battleship Row", five torpedoes had struck the *Oklahoma* in as many minutes, cutting out her power, gouging open all that was left of her port side. As she wallowed into a 90-degree list, Commander Jesse Kenworthy ordered; "Abandon ship!"; *Oklahoma* was fast capsizing. Eight minutes later, she was bottom-up in the harbour mud, men scrambling as if on a giant treadmill along her rolling sides.

Aboard her, fully 125 men were still trapped, fighting for breath in a topsy-turvy world of random air-pockets, often no more than six inches square. Some never realised this until time had elapsed; Seaman George Murphy, splashing through the operating room of the ship's dispensary, wondered what section of *Oklahoma* could have rated a tiled ceiling. It never occurred to him that he was looking at the floor.

It would be thirty-six hours before rescue crews, working all night with oxy-acetylene torches, cut the surviving 32 men free from her hull.

Away from the harbour area, few citizens even realised a war had started; the tendency was to seek for natural causes. Nurse Freda Conine, awoken from off-duty sleep in the Navy Yard Hospital, imagined that technicians were blasting in the yard nearby. In the hillside suburb of Makalapa, Mrs Hall Mayfield, wife of Admiral Bloch's intelligence officer, also dismissed the explosions; she thought workmen were dynamiting a hole for her new mail-box post. Lieutenant Clarence Dickinson, heading inland from the carrier *Enterprise* with a squadron of Dauntless dive bombers, put the black drifting smoke down to farmers burning their cane fields – until swooping Zeros holed his gasoline tank and killed his radioman. Numb with shock, Dickinson bailed out.

Some found the news impossible to take in. Soon after landing on a dirt road west of Ewa Field, Dickinson hitched a lift from an elderly couple driving a blue sedan. The back seat was piled with a wicker basket and a Thermos bottle; the couple were bound for a picnic with friends at Fort Weaver. But although Dickinson begged them, "I must have a lift to Pearl Harbor. I've just been shot down!" his urgency escaped them. Time and again, as if explaining to a moron, the woman repeated, "But our friends are waiting for us. We are bringing the potato salad and they have the chicken".

It took a long time before it sank in: as of this moment the United States was at war.

Some were phlegmatic. Tai Sing Loe, the Navy's unofficial photographer, who specialised in souvenir portraits, stood amid all the holocaust, calmly snapping pictures of the burning fleet to adorn that year's Christmas card. Hubert Coryell, a senior citizen, watched the attack judicially from his hillside home, then, remarking, "Well, that was quite a show", drove off with his bow and arrows for archery practice at Kapiolani Park.

One man was consumed by bitter self-disgust. In his office at the submarine base, Admiral Husband E. Kimmel was standing with a group of officers, watching in ominous silence as the raid fanned across the harbor. Suddenly, with a slight "ping", a spent 50-calibre bullet broke through the window glass, striking Kimmel on the left breast before dropping to the floor. For a moment Kimmel just looked at it, then said quietly, "To bad it didn't kill me".

Most, once the realisation struck home, took thought mainly for others. In the Navy Yard Hospital, a shattered plaster cast beside a vacant bed was mute testimony that an officer with an injured leg had somehow contrived to hobble back to his ship. Lieutenant Harry Walker, junior medical officer of the *New Orleans*, who had undergone an appendectomy four days earlier, taped himself up and was on his feet for six hours at the Navy Hospital – operating, amputating, ingeniously using sterilised Flit guns to spray first-degree burns.

Inevitably, a few hewed resolutely to the rule book. At Wheeler Field, Second Lieutenant Robert Overstreet, of the 69th Aviation Ordnance Company, was arguing with a stubborn ordnance sergeant: Overstreet wanted both rifles and pistols, but the sergeant, shouting above the noise of the bombs, doubted he could supply them without written authorisation. When Overstreet exploded, "Hell, man, this is war", the non-com reluctantly gave in.

Even Ed Sheehan, a young shipyard worker employed at Drydock One, felt the need to go through the motions: arriving at the Shipfitter's Shop, in response to an urgent radio summons, his first instinct was to punch the time clock. But Foreman Dave Melville cut him short: "Never mind that, Eddie, for Christ's sake. Get on to Ten-Ten Dock and do what you can to help".

Obediently, Sheehan hastened on to Ten-Ten, the long quay facing Ford Island, on the harbour's eastern side, then he stopped dead. What he saw in that moment would live with him for ever.

The battleships were broken, crippled wrecks, seeming to writhe in an inferno of "orange flame and obscene black smoke". Only the cage-like top sections of the *West Virginia* and the *Tennessee* emerged dimly across the roiling waters. The *California* was listing heavily, licked by snapping fires. The *Arizona* was now almost completely hidden, her superstructure tilting crazily, among oily clouds rolling skywards in black cauliflower shapes.

Heads were bobbing in the black water; small white figures spilled from the sides of ships. Muffled explosions rumbled. Sudden gouts of flame stabbed the smoke, as fires ignited fuel or ammunition stores, illuminating the mass grave where 2,113 had died.

Rarely had men or ships taken such a beating – yet perversely they refused to acknowledge defeat. Once the first trauma of the attack had passed, seamen on ship after ship began fighting back with everything they had.

In the cruiser *New Orleans*, the lights had gone out and the ammunition hoists were out of action, but in the darkness men now formed human chains to move shells and powder from the magazines to the guns. All the time Chaplain Howell Forgy – himself forbidden to take any material part in this battle – slapped their grimy sweating backs, exhorting them, "Praise the Lord and pass the ammunition". It was no lone example. In *California*, before the order to abandon ship came at 10.20 a.m., Chief Radioman Thomas Reeves hung on alone in a burning passageway, manhandling ammunition until at last he fell unconscious and died. Water was surging into her forward air compressor station, but Machinist's Mate Robert Scott was still labouring to feed air to the five-inch guns. Though others, evacuating the station, begged Scott to follow them, he refused – "I'll stay here and give them air as long as the guns are going." The watertight doors closed behind him for the last time.

All rank and precedence were forgotten today. On the Flag Bridge of *Maryland*, Captain W. R. Carter, the Chief of Staff, told Commander W. F. Fitzgerald, the Staff Duty Officer, "We can't do much good up here. Let's go down to the guns and give them a hand". Promptly each man weighed in among the gun crews of the five-inch ack-ack batteries. Ensign Bill Ingram, who had swum from *Oklahoma* to man one of them, did receive a rebuke from the bridge – "on *Maryland* an officer is expected to wear his cap when he fights" – but others fought their first World War Two battle in less formal dress: *aloha* shirts, even bathing trunks. In the old cruiser *Raleigh*, Captain Bentham Simons directed the gun crews still dressed in the blue pyjamas he had worn when the attack began. Ensign Thomas Lombardi, helping the wounded on *West*

Virginia, cut a more bizarre figure still; arriving back from shore leave, he was still wearing a tropical dinner jacket and black tie.

Not only the warships were in fighting mood. Henry R. Danner, a Navy Yard machinist, noticed that gunners were needed on the battleship *Pennsylvania,* at present immobilised in Drydock One; without hesitation he doubled up the gangplank to become perhaps the first civilian in Navy history to form part of a combat gun crew. Aboard the YG-17, a 110-foot yard garbage scow, Chief Boatswain's Mate L. M. Jansen paused from collecting refuse to fight his old "honey barge" like a flagship, ordering his men to train their single fire hose on the burning *West Virginia* as strafing planes screamed low across the water.

Some ships tried to make a run for it – with only partial success. At 8.30 a.m. *Monaghan* was the first destroyer under way; en route down the channel she rammed the second midget sub to fall foul of the U.S. Navy, drove ashore, then righted herself, steaming out to sea while all the ships nearby rang with cheers. At 8.50 a.m., it was *Nevada*'s turn; already, for forty-five minutes, her guns had blazed defiance, downing at least one torpedo plane. Now she, too, made a break for it, steaming south-west down the channel – to many men the most inspiring sight they saw that day. But soon urgent signals were fluttering from the Naval District water tower: Stay clear of the channel. Reluctantly, the senior officer aboard, Lieutenant Commander Francis Thomas, saw the logic of it: if the Japanese sank *Nevada* in the entrance channel, the entire Pacific Fleet would be bottled up. Cutting his engines, Thomas nosed the battleship into Hospital Point, on the harbour's south shore. Again the dive bombers found her, wiping out the boat deck and most of its personnel.

At 1 p.m. back on *Akagi,* a heated discussion was at its height. Commander Fuchida felt he had arrived back just in time; refuelled and rearmed planes were being lined up on the flight deck, in readiness for a third attack, but Commander Genda, for one, was bitterly opposed to it. Hoping to sway the balance, Fuchida hastened to the bridge to report to Admiral Nagumo and his chief of staff, Rear Admiral Ryunosuke Kusaka.

"Four battleships definitely sunk," Fuchida reported succinctly, "One sank instantly, another capsized, two settled to the bottom of the bay and may have capsized."

Nagumo, he noted, looked pleased. "We may then conclude," he observed weightily, "that anticipated results have been achieved."

Fuchida was less certain. How much damage, he wondered, had been inflicted at Hickam and Wheeler Fields? (In fact, 188 planes had been destroyed and 159 damaged.) "We have achieved a great amount of destruction", he argued, "but it would be unwise to assume that we have destroyed everything. There are still many targets remaining that should be hit." In conclusion he stressed, "Therefore I recommend that another attack should be launched."

Genda disagreed. He was not in favour of risking planes and carriers any further. They had achieved all they could hope to do. By now the surprise factor had been lost. Fuchida saw it differently: a third attack might be vital to the outcome of the war. There were virtually no defences left – and a third raid might draw in carriers like the *Enterprise*.

Back in the home port of Kure, Admiral Yamamoto had already anticipated the final decision. Nagumo, like the Chief of Naval Staff, Nagano, and the other admirals had all fought bitterly against the attack on Pearl. Overruled, Nagumo, in the best traditions of the Imperial Japanese Navy, had given of his best to the operation and achieved everything that had been asked of him. But he was not a man to press his luck further.

Almost to himself, in the operations room of his flagship, *Nagato*, Yamamoto whispered: "Admiral Nagumo is going to withdraw".

Minutes later, just as he had anticipated, the news came through. On *Akagi*'s bridge, Admiral Kusaka had advised, "We should withdraw", and Nagumo had nodded his assent. "Please do."

The signal flags ran up on the yardarm then, ordering the change of course. By 1.30 p.m., the great fleet had swung about, heading for home across the Pacific.

*

All that Sunday morning, official Washington had been on edge. Everybody was expecting something big to break – not knowing what. As early as 7.30 a.m. Colonel Rufus S. Bratton, heading the Far Eastern Section of the Army's Intelligence Branch (G2) was relieved to find that a "Magic" intercept of the long-awaited fourteenth part of the Tokyo-Washington telegram had at length reached his desk.

Just as he had surmised, its conclusion was quite final: "The Japanese government regrets to have to notify hereby the American government that in view of the attitude of the American government it cannot but consider that it is impossible to reach an agreement through further negotiations".

Before 9 a.m., yet another intercept reached Bratton: "Will the ambassador please submit to the United States government (if possible to the Secretary of State) our reply to the United States at 1 p.m. on the 7th, your time".

By 11.30 a.m., men were sure of at least one thing: Something significant was timed for 1 p.m. this day. To Rear Admiral Theodore Stark Wilkinson, at the Navy Department, the fourteenth part constituted "fighting words". General George C. Marshall, as Chief of Staff, felt that a warning to Hawaii, Panama and the Philippines was called for – yet he hesitated to use the "scrambler" on his telephone in case of a wiretap.

In the end he decided to send a coded telegram through commercial channels, Western Union and R.C.A. Assigned no priority, it finally reached General Short via a messenger boy on a bicycle just as the attack was ending.

Admiral Stark had also noted the 1 p.m. deadline, but was fearful that a further alert, following his 27 November "war warning", might be crying wolf. Accordingly he made no further attempt to contact Kimmel.

At the State Department, Cordell Hull, who had also studied Togo's telegram, heard towards noon that Nomura and Kurusu had sought an appointment at 1 p.m. But at 1 p.m., Nomura phoned again: could Hull defer the meeting until 1.45?

Although Hull ascribed these delaying tactics to Japanese duplicity, the reverse was the case: the Embassy on Massachusetts Avenue was hopelessly ill-organised. Not until 10 a.m. this Sunday was the decoding office fully staffed – yet no regular secretary could be entrusted with typing up a top-secret message. The one man with security clearance, Katsuzo Okumura, a junior diplomat, was a two-finger typist at best. By 11 a.m., when he completed the first thirteen parts, Nomura was still unaware of what message he was to deliver at 1 p.m.

At this point, Okumura compounded confusion. Convinced that his amateurish typing would lose him face, he began typing the thirteen parts all over again.

In the large Oval Office at the White House, it was just another peaceful Sunday afternoon. Roosevelt, after finishing a leisurely tray lunch, was paring an apple; Hopkins, in a V-necked sweater and slacks, was lounging on the sofa, while Fala, Roosevelt's Scottie, begged for scraps. The brass ship's clock on the President's desk showed 1.47 p.m.

At that moment, the phone jangled, and Roosevelt, answering, heard the curiously calm voice of Frank Knox, calling from the Navy Department: "Mr President, it looks like the Japanese have attacked Pearl Harbor . . ."

"NO!" was Roosevelt's first shocked reaction, before calling Hull to break the news, though he added a caution, "We haven't confirmed it yet."

It was already 1.50 p.m., but Nomura and Kurusu had not yet reached the State Department; both men were still fretting in the Embassy foyer, waiting for the laggard Okumura to peck his way through the fourteenth part. It was 2.05 p.m. before an usher finally showed them into the State Department's waiting room.

Had the note been delivered at 1 p.m., Japan would have abided – albeit strictly – by the rules of war: at 7.50 a.m., Hawaiian Time, the time of the attack, it was 1.20 p.m. in Washington. The delivery of the note would have preceded the strike by perhaps twenty minutes – twenty-five at most. At 2.20 p.m., when Hull, having given the envoys fifteen minutes to cool their heels, agreed to receive them, Pearl Harbor had been under attack for more than an hour.

When Nomura apologised for the delay in decoding, Hull asked pointedly, "Why one o'clock?". But the Ambassador genuinely did not know. His black-ribboned prince-nez adjusted, Hull began to read the message all over again. Kurusu and Nomura remained awkwardly, standing; no one had invited them to sit down.

At last, with cold measured anger, Hull let fly. "In all my fifty years of public service," he told them, "I have never seen a document that was more crowded with infamous falsehoods and distortions; infamous falsehoods and distortions on a scale so huge that I never imagined until today that any government on this planet was capable of uttering them."

Nomura made to speak, then, but Hull, his right arm raised, cut him short. "Good day," he said with icy finality, but as the envoys departed, he reverted to the log-cabin language of his native Tennessee; an angry explosion of "scoundrels and piss-ants" burst from him.

At 5 p.m. secretary Grace Tully was called to Roosevelt's study. "I'm going before Congress tomorrow," the President told her, "I'd like to dictate my message. It will be short."

Then, inhaling deeply, he began – the same calm tone in which he always dictated his mail, Grace Tully noted, only today there was one difference. As he spoke each word, slowly and incisively, the President was specifying every punctuation mark and paragraph.

"Yesterday comma December 7 comma 1941 dash a date which will live in infamy dash . . ."

*

It was equally a date which would live in history. At long last, and irrevocably, the two-ocean war had come to America. A nation which had awoken dubious and divided on the morning of 7 December was now, by early afternoon, united by a common enemy, a common hurt.

For many, the news came with bewildering suddenness. In Washington, listeners to a sponsored radio programme heard an abrupt: "Flash! The Japanese have attacked the United States Fleet in Pearl Harbor! End of Flash – use Sweetheart Soap!" In New York, a disgruntled taxi-driver told Lieutenant-Commander Ewan Montagu, on a mission from the Admiralty in London, "They're putting out some radio programme like that one about the Martians invading the earth . . . something about the little yellow-bellies bombing Pearl Harbor." Only as he entered the Oyster Bar at Grand Central Station did the truth dawn on Montagu: a blind drunk naval rating, jamming a cigar into the officer's mouth,

234

sobbed, "Thank God we're buddies again!" Thus Montagu learned that England had a new ally.

There were early flashes of panic. Henry Morgenthau, who as Secretary of the Treasury controlled White House security, called for the entire guard to be quadrupled and issued with machine-guns – until Roosevelt, with his habitual calm, defused the tension. One helmeted bayoneted sentry for every 100 feet of fencing was all he would permit – nor would he shelter in the Treasury vault, he said, unless he could play poker with Morgenthau's hoard of gold.

All over the United States, the mood in these first hours, was uneasy. An incensed patriot chopped down four Japanese cherry trees in Washington's Tidal Basin. Soldiers at Santa Cruz, Monterey and Carmel evacuated 1,000 householders along a 40-mile stretch of coastline, speeding them inland for safety. Bellboys on the roof of Boston's Hotel Statler poured gallons of paint to mask the arrow indicating the airport. In Scarsale, New York, mothers began a vigil in parked cars outside the High School, ready to spirit their children home if bombers appeared.

In downtown Honolulu, nerves were at snapping point. Now, just as in London and Paris, in Berlin and Moscow, the street lamps had gone out. The few military cars in evidence crawled with blue-painted headlights. Silent frightened groups of people huddled in the lobbies of hotels and boarding-houses, listening for the first cry of the siren that would herald the Japanese return. "This town is sitting right on the edge of its chair," one observer noted, "all ready to get up and run somewhere."

Slowly the mood changed – to one of sober restraint and resolution. "Pull yourself together, young man," Hull told the lamenting Thai Minister, "we're going to lick the Hell out of them." Long lines piled up outside the recruiting offices; one New Yorker, finding the Army line too long, switched to the Navy line. The year's end would see 28,349 men newly enlisted. Tin Pan Alley weighed in with two eminently forgettable pop tunes, *Goodbye, Mama, I'm Off to Yokohama* and *I'm Gonna Slap a Dirty Little Jap*. In Honolulu, the sale of defense bonds increased tenfold. Under a misty ragged moon, crowds five deep pressed against the White House railings for hours on end. There was nothing they could usefully do there, but it seemed the place to be.

"That day ended isolation for any realist," that most xenophobic of Senators, Arthur Vandenberg, noted in his diary, and he spoke for hundreds of thousands like him. On 8 December – the day that Roosevelt, in a long blue Navy cloak, asked Congress for a declaration of war and got it within six-and-a-half minutes – the America First Committee disbanded, calling on all its members to support the war effort.

Now, like every American dwelling, the White House was dark at night; although the housekeeper, Mrs Henrietta Nesbitt had gone shopping for blackout material, she had secured only three bolts of cloth.

Black sateen shades and windows painted black proved the final solution. Under the portico of the driveway leading from the Pennsylvania Avenue entrance, the great white light that had burned for as long as anyone could remember was now dark.

Late on 8 December, it was Samuel I. Rosenman, Roosevelt's speech-writer, who pointed out this phenomenon to his collaborator, Robert E. Sherwood. "I wonder how long it will be before that light gets turned on again," he pondered.

Sherwood's reply voiced the sober truth. "I don't know – but until it does, the lights will stay turned off all over the world."

*

Elsewhere, reactions were mixed. Few were so uncompromising as Ramón Serrano Súner, Franco's pro-Axis brother-in-law and Minister of Foreign Affairs; on his instructions, his entire staff left their visiting cards at the Japanese Legation as a mark of esteem. More were fearful of what this portended, like old Marshal Pétain in Vichy. "Never before has the whole world been at war," he quavered to Admiral Leahy, ". . . I don't know what will come of it."

In the *Wolfsschanze*, East Prussia, Hitler's first reaction was to slap his thighs in delight, announcing "The turning point!" then he raced from his bunker through the icy darkness to break the news to Keitel and Jodl. Then a sobering thought struck him: "How strange that with Japan's aid we are destroying the positions of the white race in the Far East – and that Britain is fighting against Europe with those swine the Bolsheviks!" Nonetheless the Tripartite Pact must be honoured. On 11 December, Ribbentrop, summoning the hapless U.S. Chargé, Leland Morris, to the Foreign Office, screamed at him, "*Ihr Präsident hat diesen Krieg gewollt; jetzt hat er ihn.*" (Your President has wanted this war; now he has it.) On the same day Mussolini followed suit.

In England, the news was like a sudden reprieve. At 3 p.m. Washington time – 9 p.m. in London – the First Secretary, William Hayter, calling on behalf of Lord Halifax, broke the news of Pearl Harbor to a sleepy sounding Resident Clerk at the Foreign Office. The news, Hayter stressed, should be passed to the Prime Minister, but the clerk seemed doubtful of Churchill's interest. "What was that place?" he asked languidly, "could you spell it?"

In fact, Churchill's first intimation of the attack came, like most Britons, when the B.B.C.'s Alvar Lidell read the 9 p.m. news bulletin. Week-ending at Chequers, along with Ambassador Winant and Harriman, Churchill had spent much of dinner lost in thought, his head buried in his hands. Only when his butler-valet Sawyers carried in a small flip-top radio, a present from Hopkins, and the news came through, was

236

Churchill galvanised. Starting for the door, he announced resolutely, "We shall declare war on Japan." Winant, too, was swift to leave the table. "Good God," he expostulated, "you can't declare war on a radio announcement."

Not without difficulty, he coaxed the Premier into waiting until a call had been put through to the White House. "Mr President, what's this about Japan?" Churchill demanded peremptorily, once the connection was made, and Roosevelt told him, "It's quite true. . . . We are all in the same boat now."

"So we had won after all!" was the first thought that flashed through Churchill's mind.

Yet the mass of Britons knew no such euphoria. After twenty-seven weary months of war, the capacity to feel and react was almost dead. Not one American flag, Harold Nicolson noted, flew in the streets of London. In many regions Mass Observations reported "a feeling sometimes verging on sadistic pleasure that at last America is to know fully what war means". "All they have to do is send out . . . Errol Flynn and everything will be all right," was a typical sarcastic comment.

Even so, Britain now needed all the allies she could command. At 2 a.m. on 8 December, following three soaring red flares from the headquarters ship *Ryujo Maru*, 100 motor boats breasting nine-foot waves were bringing 24,000 men of the 25th Japanese Army ashore at Kota Bharu, Malaya. At 7 a.m. thirty-six Japanese fighters wiped out the entire island air force – seven planes – at Hong Kong's Kai Tak airport.

Now the battle was as wide as the world.

*

Port by port, fort by fort, the Far East was invested. Thailand capitulated without a shot after five-and-a-half hours. Guam Island, 1,000 miles west of Wake, fell on 10 December within the space of a morning, despite bitter resistance by blue-jackets and Marines; a Japanese naval captain, entering the nurses' quarters, told Ensign Leona Jackson: "So sorry to tell you – all your fleet sunk. All your ships on bottom. No more." Only one blue-jacket, Radioman 1st Class George Ray Tweed, relying on skills learned on hunting trips in Oregon, escaped the dragnet; taking to the underbrush armed only with a handsaw, a machete and a pocket-knife he survived for two-and-a-half years like a latter-day Robinson Crusoe, amassing $6,000 in back-pay.

It was not only at Pearl Harbor that the Americans were caught unawares. At noon on 10 December, eighty Japanese bombers winged their way unopposed to Cavite, eight miles south-west of Manila, the only American naval base in the Far East beyond Pearl Harbor, pounding it to rubble – a blow so crippling that Admiral Thomas C. Hart, commanding the United States Asiatic Fleet, reported Manila as no longer tenable. For three days earlier, in a disaster as great as Pearl Harbor itself, the Japanese had hit Clark Field, 65 miles north of Manila, destroying all but three out of 35 Flying Fortresses.

That it happened is undisputed; why will always be open to doubt. As Major-General Lewis Brereton, commanding the Far East Air Force, told it, five-and-a-half hours after the attack on Pearl – 7.30 a.m., 7 December, Manila time – he sought permission to bomb Formosa, known to be a Japanese stronghold, 600 miles north. But MacArthur's chief of staff, Major-General Richard K. Sutherland, after consulting with his chief, refused: "The General says . . . don't make the first overt act."

At 9.25 a.m., Brereton phoned Sutherland again – and again permission was refused. But some time after 10 a.m., Brereton was to claim, he discussed with MacArthur a photographic reconnaissance of Formosa by three Flying Fortresses, a prelude to a subsequent bombing attack. Later MacArthur hotly denied any knowledge of a Formosan sortie, although a radiogram bearing his name, perhaps sent by Sutherland, went to General Marshall on this day, mentioning a Formosa attack on 9 December. And at 11 a.m., following another call from Sutherland, Brereton was able to tell his staff that a bombing mission had been authorised – once photographs revealed the nature of the targets.

At this hour, the Fortresses were cruising over Mount Aryat, to avoid being caught on the ground; coded recall signals now instructed them to return to Clark. Three were equipped with cameras; 100-lb and 300-lb bombs were hoisted into the others. Now, inexplicably, Brereton called in all his fighters, fifty-plus P-40s, for refuelling. At noon, not one fighter was circling Clark Field.

Around this time, Luzon Island's one radar set, at Iba, on the west coast, picked up the first blips of a vast armada: 108 Mitsubishi bombers and 84 Zeros were heading for Clark. The warning never reached the field; the teletype operator, along with both pilots and crewmen, was then at lunch. All of them were off guard, since few of them even credited the news of Pearl Harbor; they dismissed it as a ruse by the top brass to keep them on their toes.

Some time after 12.10 and before 12.40 – such were the discrepancies in timing – pilots and crewmen, lolling on the parched grass, were smoking and passing the time of day, watching the three Fortresses of the reconnaissance unit taxi into position. Just then, a mile east of Clark, at Fort Stotensberg, taxi-driver George Setzer saw a great huddle of silver planes arriving from the northwest. "It's about time they came to help us," he said gleefully. At Clark Field the reaction was the same. As someone shouted, "Here comes the navy," a sergeant carefully focused his Kodak on the first V of planes – dropping now to 22,000 feet.

238

Lieutenant Edgar D. Whitcomb, a navigator with Colonel Eugene Eubank's 19th Bombardment Group, was heading for the colonel's headquarters seeking news of the mission. At the door he ran into his pilot, Lieutenant Ed Green. "Are we going to bomb?" he asked.

"Still no orders to bomb," Green replied, "but we may get some photos."

They never did. Abruptly Whitcomb heard "a loud crackling sound like that of dry boards being broken"; near at hand a pilot asked bemusedly, "Why are they dropping tinfoil?" In anguished reply, another man yelled, "That's not tinfoil, those are goddamned Japs." Already the P-40 pilots were racing for their cockpits – but only three of them even left the ground.

An inferno of flame swept the airfield. The reconnaissance Fortresses were the first to take fire, burning with a white lambent flame; flash fires sprang up in the long cogon grass, "roaring and crackling like an evil beast". Men ran frantically for slit trenches, finding all too few of them; in this sudden unforeseen attack, 55 were to die and more than 100 were wounded. Waves of planes – heavy bombers, dive bombers, fighters – swept the field for almost an hour until it was all but unrecognisable. A corona of dust and black oily smoke towered above the charred aircraft, visible as far as Manila, 65 miles away.

The sum total of American striking power in the western Pacific had been wiped out – and the war had barely started.

*

The British were faring as badly. Five days before Pearl Harbor, on 2 December, the battleship *Prince of Wales* – which ever since Placentia Bay had been known jovially as "Churchill's Yacht" – arrived in Singapore as an integral part of Force Z: the battleship herself, the old cruiser *Repulse* and the destroyers *Electra*, *Express*, *Vampire* and *Tenedos*. "A rumour was whispered," noted Gunner Russell Braddon, of the 2/15th Field Regiment, 8th Australian Division, "that they came to Malayan waters because the Australian Government had (using the possible withdrawal of its troops in the Middle East as a weapon) blackmailed the British Government into sending two capital ships out to Singapore."

Braddon and his mates had also noticed one strange omission: *Prince of Wales* and her sister ships had no air cover at all. The explanation was a last-minute mishap; the crack new aircraft carrier H.M.S. *Indomitable*, with a squadron of nine Hurricanes, which was to have watched over Force Z had run aground in the West Indies. Repairs would not be completed for twenty-five days – and with the situation in the Far East worsening daily, the two capital ships had been sent ahead in the hope of stabilising events.

Nor could the newly-appointed C-in-C of the British Eastern Fleet, Admiral Sir Tom Phillips, who had made *Prince of Wales* his flagship, rely on local reinforcements: Brooke-Popham's paucity of aircraft was now all too apparent. Following on his decision to sail north, intercept the Japanese convoys and sink their transports, Phillips thought he could wreak havoc among the invasion fleet given a modicum of fighter cover. Before sailing on 8 December, he made three requests of the air commander, Air Vice-Marshal Charles Pulford: reconnaissance 100 miles north of Force Z during daylight on 9 December, 100 miles reconnaissance, pivoting on Singora, 120 miles north of Kota Bharu, starting at first light on 10 December, and fighter protection in the area during this same day. Fulford's final reply, though unhelpful in tone – "Regret fighter protection impossible" – was nonetheless ambiguous.

Later, experts were to speculate that Phillips took this signal to mean that no fighter cover would be available anywhere in the Gulf of Siam – whereas the air chief was specifying the Singora area alone.

At mid-day on 8 December, Phillips had, in any case, made his decision plain at a meeting of his staff. There was the option, he said, of sailing "away to the East – Australia. Or we can go out and fight. Gentlemen, we sail at five o'clock."

At 53, Phillips, whose 5 ft 1 in. had earned him the nickname of "Tom Thumb" was not a man easily gainsaid. Moreover, like many naval officers, he had long believed that a properly-armed well-fought ship had nothing to fear from air power. This conviction had even led his old friend, Air Vice Marshal Arthur "Bomber" Harris, to tease him, "One day, Tom . . . your ship will be smashed to pieces by bombers and torpedo aircraft; as she sinks your last words will be, 'That was a ——————— great mine!' "

This light-hearted prophecy was unknown to the officers and ratings of *Prince of Wales*, but at twilight on Monday, 8 December, as the ships drew out into the Straits of Johore, the palm trees ashore etched against a blood-red sunset, some men had a curious intuition of disaster. Midshipman Kenneth Townsend-Green, transferred at the last minute to the Oerlikon guns, recalled telling the Gunnery Officer Lieutenant Commander Colin McMullen, that he felt he needed more practice – and how McMullen had replied, "Yes, well, I think you will tomorrow – and you'll be lucky if you live it out there." Back in Singapore, aboard H.M.S. *Mauritius*, Midshipman Henry Leach thought of his father's worried mien during their farewell dinner the night before. "Let 'em come," young Leach had said vaingloriously, "Let's have a go at them," and was startled when Captain Leach replied, "I don't think you have any idea of the enormity of the odds we are up against."

By 1.45 p.m. on 9 December, *Prince of Wales* and her escort were deep into the Gulf of Siam, steaming at 14 knots beneath lowering clouds, swept by dense squalls of tropical rain. Sighting nothing, they were unaware that they themselves had been sighted: on the Japanese submarine I–56 a radioman was at this moment tapping out an urgent message to the Navy's 22nd Air Flotilla in Saigon. But static made receipt of his message well-nigh impossible; not until 3 p.m. did Rear Admiral Sadaichi Matsunaga get word of the sighting. At once he ordered planes to prepare for an attack at sea.

Now a strange confusion arose. In *Prince of Wales'* "A" turret, soon after 9 p.m., a gunnery rating spotted a small flicker on his radar screen. Excitedly, he told Sub-Lieutenant Michael Buxton, "Do you know, sir, I think I saw something." For an instant Buxton saw it too – what appeared to be a small biplane 3,000 yards away – and rang the bridge. Phillips reached a logical conclusion: they had been spotted by Japanese planes and the surprise element was lost. Shortly, the disgruntled officers and men of Force Z heard a change of plan: they were returning to Singapore.

In fact, the planes which had forced Phillips to turn back had been Allied planes and had never even seen the British Fleet, but as the ships turned southward, Phillips received a sudden message from Singapore's Naval Base: ENEMY REPORTED LANDING AT KUANTAN – on Malaya's east coast, midway between Singapore and Kota Bharu. Soon after midnight, Phillips changed course, once more heading north for Kuantan.

Off Kuantan, fully an hour had passed before a heliograph from H.M.S. *Electra*, which had sped inshore to investigate, blinked across the water: PERFECT PEACE. Sub-Lieutenant Buxton was only one of many who cursed angrily: what on earth was the force doing, hanging about like this? By this time he and many like him had lost all confidence in Phillips.

As the morning wore on, it was the heat more than the Japanese that occupied men's minds. In the Cypher Office, five decks below, Paymaster Sub-Lieutenant Alec Compton noted a temperature of 110 degrees Fahrenheit; each man worked with a towel round his neck, to mop the perspiration, sipping constantly at fresh lime juice. In the boiler rooms, conditions were worse; the temperature by the gauge board showed 135 degrees Fahrenheit.

By 9 a.m. three Japanese groups – 96 high-level torpedo bombers, 10 search planes – had almost abandoned their quest for the British; banked clouds obscured their view. Then, at 10.15 a.m., as they turned for home, one plane sighted them; two battleships and three destroyers, 70 miles south-east of Kuantan. The fourth destroyer, *Tenedos*, was already returning to Singapore to refuel.

At 10.30 a.m. the search planes in turn made radio contact with the twenty-seven torpedo planes of Kanoya Air Group. The group's three squadrons now altered course.

In *Prince of Wales'* look-out station, Ordinary Seaman Daniel Stowell saw them first: a wave of high-level bombers glinting against the sun. Small black spheres were spilling from their hatches; to Sub-Lieutenant Alan Franklin they seemed to fall in diamond patterns. On all five ships bugles blared; from the loudspeakers came the urgent command, "Enemy aircraft approaching! Action Stations!" Within six minutes, battle was joined.

The noise was deafening. Aboard *Repulse*, C.B.S. correspondent Cecil Brown noted that even the chatter of the pom-poms, the "Chicago pianos" was obscured by the hard sharp crack of the 4-inch high altitude guns; red-blue flames burst from the muzzles, and empty cordite cases tumbled from their scuttles like a berserk jackpot machine. On the funnel-shaped muzzles the black paint began rising in blisters as big as a fist.

Yet few hits were scored. Once again, as in the *Bismarck* action, the pom-poms were jamming, one gun suffering twelve failures, another eight. Midshipman Townsend-Green noted disgustedly, "We might just as well have been firing blanks." At 11.41 a.m. the Japanese readied for the coup-de-grace: nine torpedo planes under Lieutenant Sadao Takai, dived for *Prince*'s port side. From her bridge, Midshipman Michael Pruett saw them clearly: pale blue torpedoes with silver fins.

On *Prince of Wales*' compass platform, Lieutenant Commander R. F. Harland, the torpedo specialist officer, had just remarked, "I think they're going to do a torpedo attack." But Phillips, he was almost certain, replied, "No they're not. There are no torpedo aircraft about."

At 11.44 a.m. they knew their error. At least one torpedo – possibly two – struck on the port side, aft of her bridge: in the Cypher Office Alec Compton was conscious of "a strange vibration like a boy running a stick along a stretch of corrugated iron". The projectile had found the 240-foot port after propellor shaft, but still it rotated like a giant flail, churning at 204 revolutions per minute, slicing through the water-tight comparments. In the S 4 turret, Boy Seaman Edward Grindley heard a vast booming sound as they burst one by one; more than twenty in the space of four minutes. The power supply had gone, and in the stifling darkness below decks the lights were going out.

At 12.10 p.m. the two black balls which told the other ships of Force Z that *Prince of Wales* was no longer under control were hoisted from her yardarm.

All over the doomed ship men had their private yardsticks of how serious things were. Leading Telegraphist Eric Shawyer, of Phillips' staff, was in the Wireless Office when he chanced to peer down the voice-pipe; in the Coding Office below he saw water racing and frothing, then blackness. The water had reached the top of the pipe. In the Bakery Flat, Petty Officer Charles Firbank was shaken to see a kettle of lime-juice tilt gently into a horizontal position. Leading Seaman Douglas

Spinks, in the Radar Office, realised that the ship had slowed to three knots.

At 12.33 p.m. *Repulse*, struck by five torpedoes, was seen capsizing two miles astern, along with 513 members of her crew still aboard. Still, some could barely take it in. Outside *Prince*'s Central Receiving Office, a stoker pelting down a ladder yelled, "The *Repulse* has gone!" prompting a vague query, "Where to? Singapore?" The reply was withering: "No, you bloody fool – to the bottom."

Within three days of Pearl Harbor, the myth of the impregnable battleship had ended for ever – but still the legend died hard. At 12.04 Captain William Tennant, aboard *Repulse*, had taken it on himself to signal Singapore: ENEMY AIRCRAFT BOMBING, and eleven old Brewster Buffalo fighters lumbered off to the rescue. Phillips, though, was stubborn to the last, seeking a naval solution. His one signal – at 12.50 p.m. – besought only destroyers and tugs.

There was little that either ships or aircraft could have done now. At 12.40 p.m. ten of Lieutenant Takeda's 2nd Squadron, Minoro Attack Group, flying wingtip to wingtip, loosed a salvo of seven bombs from directly overhead; one, bursting through an armoured deck, exploded in the Cinema Flat, where patients of an overflow casualty clearing station were clustered. In this narrow space, hundreds now died screaming, skinned alive by scalding steam.

From this nightmare of rushing water and red-hot steam, men bore brief indelible impressions. Leading Stoker Alfred Llewellyn saw a turret whip out of control to cut a boy seaman clean in half. Others recalled those who tried to fight their way through portholes but never made it. Marine Douglas Hall felt a depression so deep that even after swimming for safety he was swallowing great gulps of water and fumbling for the knot on his lifebelt, hoping to die.

Some were taking elaborate final precautions: Sub-Lieutenant Joseph Blackburn, scenting the pungent whiff of cordite, promptly put on his gas-mask. Sick Berth Attendant Walter Bridgewater safeguarded his stock of pound notes in the approved Navy way – inside a contraceptive. Others felt urgent last-minute regrets. Sub-Lieutenant Franklin recalls thinking, "I wish I'd studied harder at school". Midshipman Townsend-Green felt a sudden desperate need to live – "I can't die before I'm married".

Six minutes earlier Captain Leach, seeing the position as hopeless, had ordered all hands to abandon ship: *Express*, *Electra* and *Vampire* were already moving in to pick up survivors across a sea packed with bobbing heads "like a football field". Soon hundreds were lying prostrate on their red-hot decks, retching up black oil and sea-water. Even now, with the ship listing 40 degrees to port, there was no panic, only a strange decorum. Ordinary Seaman Douglas Marshall noted little groups carefully taking off their shoes, lining them up tidily by the taffrail as if outside a hotel bedroom door. Then men jumped, slid or dived into a black velvety carpet of oil two feet deep. At 1.20 p.m., with Admiral Phillips, Captain Leach and 327 officers and ratings still aboard, *Prince of Wales* wallowed from sight – creating a suction so great that Leading Telegraphist Bernard Campion, plunging far below the water, surfaced stripped of all his clothing save for one sock.

It was Lieutenant Haruki Iki, who had led the 3rd Squadron of the Kanoya Air Group, who paid a final tribute to the *bushido* with which the British had fought. Next day, at dawn, flying low over the sunken ships, he dropped bunches of wild flowers.

*

No Japanese bouquets were forthcoming for the defenders of Malaya, Hong Kong or the Philippines. In all three theatres, the Japanese re-action was unanimous: initial bewilderment gave place to scathing contempt.

As their troops thrust ever further from the Malayan frontier General Yamashita and his Director of Operations, Colonel Tsuji, at first were puzzled men. In thirty-six hours, they had met no enemy resistance worthy of the name. Abandoning the frontier the British had fallen back – blowing a trench 30 yards deep and 100 yards long across the road down which they retreated. "Is it the enemy we must fear?" one officer asked Tsuji. The Colonel was sceptical. "What we have to worry about is the quantity of gunpowder he has available for use."

On the rainy pitch-dark night of 11 December, Tsuji had proof of this. Thirty miles south of the frontier, the much-vaunted Jitra Line, six months under construction and intended as a divisional strongpoint for three months, was breached in fifteen hours by barely 500 men – at a cost of 27 killed, 83 wounded. More than 3,000 British and Indian troops surrendered. Behind them those who fled left 50 field-guns, 50 heavy machine guns, 300 trucks and armoured cars, plus three months provi-sions and ammunition.

Already fear was abroad – the fear expressed by one senior staff officer of 3 Indian Corps: "The little men will go through everything. Swamp, jungle, rivers, crocodiles – nothing seems to stop them." As early as 12 December, General Murray-Lyon, the commander of 11th Division, remarked uneasily of his troops, "I have not seen that look in men's eyes since March, 1918." Afterwards, Lieutenant-General Percival, as G.O.C., commented sourly that Lieutenant-General Sir Lewis Heath, 3 Corps Commander, had developed "a withdrawal complex", while Major-General Gordon Bennet, the Australian G.O.C., was jittery from the first – "the question of his own escape . . . I believe became an obsession with him". Yet Percival's own dispositions were equally to blame. Hewing strictly to the concept of "Fortress Singapore", he had retained five crack battalions to defend the island, leaving the rest of Malaya to his weakest divisions.

Air-cover was now non-existent – as the men of Force Z had discovered to their cost. At Kuantan, a new coastal airfield, the pilots of one Australian Hudson squadron had decamped for Singapore on the day of the invasion, leaving all their bombs and spare equipment on the field. "For the first and last time in my life I felt ashamed of being an Australian," confessed Pilot Officer Roy Bulcock, the transport officer, but many airfields witnessed the same scene. "There have been instances where aerodromes appear to have been abandoned in a state approaching panic," Brooke-Popham charged angrily. "Stores that will assist the enemy in his further advance have been left behind, material that is urgently required has been abandoned, and a general state of chaos has been evident."

To Alfred Duff Cooper, Churchill's resident Adviser for Far Eastern Affairs since September, that chaos had been evident for months. "Brooke-Popham", he wrote frankly to the Premier, "is a very much older man than his years warrant . . . sometimes seems on the verge of nervous collapse", nor was he much impressed by the Governor of the Straits Settlements, Sir Shenton Thomas – "the mouthpiece of the last person he speaks to". Percival came in for more damning comment still – "a nice, good man who began life as a schoolmaster. I am sometimes tempted to wish he had remained one . . . it is all a field-day at Aldershot to him. He . . . is always waiting for the umpire's whistle to signal cease fire and hopes that when that moment comes his military dispositions will be such as to receive approval."

For there was no brooking the facts: the commanders in Malaya were never remotely a match for the Japanese. "Carrying on even if reduced to a meagre diet of rice and rats and finally after firing one's last round dying sword in hand in the innermost keep may be romantic," Brooke-Popham had written truthfully, "but of little practical value." Yet in the long run his troops would have no other choice. Although he had been baffled, in December, 1940, to find that the War Committee had no agenda and kept no minutes, in one year as C-in-C he had wrought no change.

Percival, too, seemed unperturbed that there was barely enough artillery ammunition to fire twelve rounds a day and that all over Malaya 1918 Rolls Royce Armoured cars stood in for tanks. Cornered late in December by Brigadier Ivan Simson as to why he would permit no anti-tank defences, underwater obstacles, fire traps or mines to stall the Japanese advance, Percival, a tall negative man with buck teeth, gave the astonishing reply: "Defences are bad for morale – for both troops and civilians."

245

It was then that Simson realised that barring a miracle Singapore was as good as lost.

As the retreat continued the civil administration set no shining example. To the fury of Sir Shenton Thomas, all white civilians secretly evacuated Penang, the chief seaport of northern Malaya, abandoning their Asiatic servants in a town plastered with slogans, "Thanks to the Royal Air Force Your Homes Are Safe". Streaming in their wake, to the capital of Kuala Lumpur and beyond, came long lines of military lorries packed with carpets, rattan chairs, golf clubs, tennis rackets, even canaries in cages.

Thus abandoned, it was not surprising that many Asiatics, recalling their exclusion from the Atlantic Charter, made common cause with the invader. At Alor Star, on 13 December, Major Mohan Singh, a handsome Sikh prisoner from the 1/14 Punjab Regiment, met up for the first time with Major Iwaichi Fujiwara, of the 8th Section, 2nd Bureau, Imperial General Staff. Coining such slogans as "Asia for the Asiatics", it was the section's job to coax dissident Indians, Burmese and Thais to throw in their lot with Japan. Before the year was out, Mohan Singh had agreed to lead an Indian National Army, 10,000 strong, to fight against the British.

Behind the strangely craven conduct of troops and civilians lay a stark realisation: for the first they were facing up to Japan's true mettle. "Well," Sir Shenton had commented when Percival phoned him with news of the landings, "I suppose you'll shove the little men off." But by mid-December, he was writing ruefully to a friend: "The Jap is good. In the air and on land he has already done things which we didn't expect . . . we have underestimated (his) skill." Overnight, British and Americans alike were recognising the Japanese for what they were: hardy, fearless warriors, whose sharpshooting was accurate up to 1,000 yards, equipped with slit-toed rubber shoes that helped them climb swiftly and silently, men able to survive for five days on minimal rations of fish and rice, who were even equipped with medicine kits to treat themselves for malaria.

All over the Far East, it was the same melancholy story of too little and too late. In Hong Kong, the G.O.C., Major-General Christopher Maltby, had adopted the ambitious plan of defending the island from the mainland along an eleven-mile redoubt of pill-boxes called the Gin Drinker's Line – in happier days the scene of alcoholic picnics. Here two infantry brigades – six battalions – were to hold for at least a week while dockyards and oil installations were destroyed. Fate decreed otherwise. On the left of the line, covering the southern slopes of Tai Mo Shan mountain and the Shingmun Redoubt, was the 2nd Battalion, Royal Scots – now, racked with malaria, only 600 strong. On the night of 9 December, an all-out attack by Major-General Sano's crack 38th Division, took them by surprise. In disorder and confusion they fell back.

By mid-day on 11 December, a retreat across the harbour to the 32 square miles of Hong Kong island was the one way out.

That evening, the harbour in the dockside area of Kowloon was a scene of ugly chaos. All the time the little green Star ferries shuttled back and forth across the water, but hordes of angry cursing Chinese roamed the waterfront, looting and pillaging; swirling smoke from the dockyards, the mainland power station and the cement works, all destroyed on Maltby's orders, blanketed the wharves. To Ellen Field, wife of a ship's engineer, making the crossing with her three small daughters, "it was as though a great stone had been overturned and all sorts of creepy-crawly things were coming out".

There were flashes of initiative, even so. At G.H.Q., Admiral Chan Chak, a one-legged sea dog on loan from Chiang Kai-shek, no sooner heard the problem than he cried, "I fix. I go!" Stumping from the room to make his base on the waterfront he organised a fleet of motor sampans, the flat-bottomed riverboats used by all the Hong Kong Chinese. Soon they had joined the Star ferries, scurrying backwards and forwards with stores, ammunition and refugees.

As the troops fell blindly back, many were cut off from their units, but one man saw the need to regain his regiment without delay: 52-year-old Sweeper Bhokar, of the 2/14 Punjabis, who for thirty-three years had daily tended and scoured the "thunderboxes" – portable wooden commodes – of the Officer's Mess. Finding himself alone on the quayside, with the Japanese closing in, Sweeper Bhokar found an abandoned lifebelt and paddled his way across 500 yards of channel – once more attendant on the bowel movements of his *sahibs*.

The voyage across the harbour was to be the last journey for many. Gwen Dew, a free-lance American journalist, never forgot her ferry trip with a company of wounded men – watched over by a nurse who was herself bleeding profusely. "You are wounded, you must stop," one man espostulated. "I must go on," the nurse replied, "and I am dying." She was dead before the ferry reached the island's capital, Victoria.

That night, from balconies all over the city, the watchers saw no Christmas lights, only the rich red flames of the blazing oil-tanks, lapping the heavy skies above Kowloon. Zigzag flares of red and green leapt across the harbour. Smoke swirled in weird coils, forming fantastic designs of jet and sable. Outlandish rumours multiplied: incredibly, the Japanese had landed a cavalry troop on the island itself. From G.H.Q., Captain Freddie Guest, General Maltby's G 3 (Operations) investigated hastily – to find that racehorses had wormed loose from their stables and were cantering round Happy Valley Racecourse.

Manila, too, wore a cloak of darkness, a town beset by tensions. Trigger-happy sentries fired at any light that moved – often through open lounge windows. Offshore, the aircraft tender *Langley*, along with the light cruiser *Boise*, opened non-stop fire on a silver object someone had glimpsed through a telescope. Half an hour later they gave up sheepishly: they had opened fire on Venus.

On 10 December, at Aparri, 250 miles from Manila, on Luzon's north coast the Japanese had landed troops, and again at Vigon, on the northeast coast, 200 miles from the capital. Three days later, on 13 December, they struck in force at Legaspi, south-west of Manila. Each time, through no fault of their own, MacArthur's green troops suffered an ignominious mauling. Few men in his North Luzon Force, Major-General Jonathan M. Wainwright revealed, had steel helmets, entrenching tools, blankets, raincoats or even modern arms.

What little equipment they had reached them too late. If their mortars were twenty-five years old, 70 per cent of their shells were defective. And just as in Malaya what Lieutenant Colonel Ernest B. Miller, of the 194th Tank Battalion (National Guard) called "the poison of apathy" prevailed. Although Miller's M-3 tanks were equipped with 37-mm guns, oil, ammunition – and even permission to fire the guns – were withheld until the last. Only when the Japanese were looming in their sights did Miller's tanks first open fire.

All perspective vanished. From a nation of comic-strip warriors the Japanese had overnight become a race of supermen. At Aparri, an Air Force company under Lieutenant Alvin C. Hadley, was ordered to engage the enemy – but Hadley and his men, reporting 10,000 Japanese advancing, retreated without firing a shot. (The total Japanese involved: 400.) On this same day, Captain Colin P. Kelly, a B-17 pilot over Aparri, attacked what he thought was a battleship – then, winging back to his base, was fatally strafed by two Zeros. Soon the Press in Manila were exulting that Kelly had sunk the battleship *Haruna* – then 1,500 miles away in the Gulf of Siam. No battleship had been sunk at all – but Kelly, the war's first "hero", won a posthumous Congressional Medal of Honor.

But slowly, just as in the United States, the mood in the Far East was hardening. In the proud tradition of Leningrad and Tobruk, people were coming to terms with siege conditions, and a Hong Kong nurse, Day Sage, wrote for all the threatened strongholds: "Days were just people and their exposed nerves and their courage and sometimes their craven fear." Swiftly they learned to adapt. In Manila, the gleaming white Residence of the High Commissioner Francis B. Sayre, with its ground-floor fernery and semi-circular ballroom, now spelt home to 120 hard-pressed officials and their families – all of them sleeping in their clothes on mattresses, on floors buff-coloured from leaking sandbags, harassed by the constant wail of the air-raid siren.

In Hong Kong, the glossy Peninsula Hotel was equally stripped for action; a chequerboard of sticky paper festooned the plate-glass windows, as a precaution against blast; carpets and curtains had been piled at the ballroom's far end. At the Jockey Club Relief Hospital, the betting booths stood in as hospital cubicles, and Nurse Mabel Redwood found herself sharing, with four others, a huge blackwood bed once used by Chinese opium smokers. "Good job my husband shot himself," a room mate remarked conversationally. "He couldn't have stood this."

All were now aware of the new skills needed in a world engulfed by war: how to cook in brackish well water, how to sleep as and where they lay down each night. At Singapore General Hospital, Elfrieda (Freddy) Retz, a comely New York widow, signed on as an auxiliary nurse; each night she steeled herself to make her rounds among wounded men, armed with torch, forceps and kidney basin, extracting writhing maggots from their wounds – maggots laid by omnipresent tropical flies. In Manila, Father Forbes Monaghan, a Jesuit priest attached to the university, always remembered the student he found one night in the Ateneo de Manila's patio, catching sleep on a stone bench before sentry-go. When Monaghan suggested a cushion for his head and a mosquito net, the quiet reply came back: "No, Father. I don't want any of those things. I want to harden myself for the battlefield."

But wry humour, Monaghan noted, would be another potent weapon. American ineptitude had been so shocking that two Filipino Scholastics felt it was time to take precautionary measures, a large sign painted on the Ateneo roof: DON'T BOMB – WE ARE STUDYING JAPANESE.

*

On Wake Island, it was all as Major James Devereux had feared. No reinforcements would now be forthcoming from the 6th Marine Battalion, stranded in Honolulu. He and his 378 Marines must soldier on alone.

Although no longer the island's senior officer – a post which had been filled late in November by Commander Winfield Scott Cunningham, U.S. Navy – Devereux' Marines still constituted the island's fighting force; none of the 75 officers and blue-jackets who had arrived with Cunningham to man the naval air station was even armed. True, four days before war began, the twelve Grumman Wildcat fighters that made up Marine Fighter Squadron 211, under Major Paul Putnam, had flown into Wake – but on this new type of plane none of the pilots had more than 30 hours flying time.

By 11.30 a.m. on Monday, 8 December – still the morning of 7 December in Hawaii – the wiry little major had been working against the clock for four hours. He had still been shaving in his tent when news of Pearl Harbor reached him – so plainly it would soon be Wake's turn. Meanwhile there were endless details to finalise. What about bomb shelters and caches for supplies? How would he keep his strongpoints, thinly scattered across the four mile long island, supplied with food and water? As a priority, extra ammunition must be rushed to all positions.

Work was already proceeding apace on protective bunkers for the first six of Putnam's planes – and though none was available for immediate occupancy, all would be completed by 2 p.m. At seven strategic points, Devereux had 5-inch and 3-inch batteries in readiness – seventeen guns in all – but he was conscious of scraping the barrel. His "mobile reserve" would consist of four machine guns on a truck, manned by twelve Marines – ready to race to any point where the Japanese attempted a landing.

At 11.57 a.m., eight of Putnam's planes were parked on the strip, while four more patrolled uneasily – too high above the cloud ceiling to sight the bomber force skimming low above the water. At 11.58 a.m., it became an all too-familiar story.

In his office, sited at Camp One, Devereux was passing routine instructions by phone to Lieutenant Wally Lewis, commanding the guns at Peacock Point, the island's most easterly tip. Suddenly Lewis broke in urgently: "Major, there's a squadron of planes coming in from the south. Are they friendly?"

Next instant twenty-seven gently gliding bombers broke at barely 2,000 feet from a gusting squall of rain. Atop the 50-feet water towers the look-outs had seen and heard nothing; the booming surf on the reef blotted out all sound and for this last silent dive the Japanese had cut their motors. "Look! Their wheels are falling off!" a contractor's man shouted. Simultaneously, Devereux heard the first bombs exploding.

Just as at Pearl and at Clark Field, Putnam's planes were caught like sitting ducks. In one searing whoosh of flame, 25,000 gallons of aviation gasoline in the airfield's main tank soared upwards like a gusher, trembling above the coral like a heat-haze. Now the planes came lower still, making their bomb runs from 1,500 feet, too low for effective 3-inch fire to deter them. Four of Putnam's fliers fell, cut to pieces by bullets, in the act of racing for their planes. Unhampered, the bombers strafed Wake Island at will, plastering the Pan American station, riddling the Clipper at its dock like a colander.

The raid lasted only ten minutes – but thirty-four men lay dead or wounded, seven planes had been destroyed outright and the auxiliary engine of an eighth had been damaged beyond repair. Minutes later, as the four-plane patrol touched down, a ninth, bouncing over the pitted coral, broke its airscrew.

Three-quarters of Wake's air power had been knocked out with one punch – and hardly one blow that registered had been struck in return.

Calm and phlegmatic, Devereux did the best he could. If the Japanese were seeking a siege, Wake's Marines would do their best to oblige. The runway, mined with dynamite, was now connected with three generators, covered by machine-gun posts round the airfield. Beach patrols were organised to stand night watch along the shore. Devereux arranged with burly Dan Teters, the contractor's general superintendent, to take charge of all feeding arrangements – releasing more men for duty, though all would be restricted to two meals a day. It was now that Teters' men, though civilians, showed their fighting spirit – weighing in as look-outs and gun crews, hauling ammunition, repairing bomb damage.

Sixteen days of eternal vigilance was all that lay ahead of them now.

It was Private First Class Verne L. Wallace who unwittingly provided Wake's one diversion in that first twenty-four hours. At his look-out point on Peale Island, a coral spit to the west of Wake, he at last received a letter from his girl friend in Haverford, Pennsylvania. It had arrived with the Clipper that morning, but Wallace had been heeding the call to arms; by the time he received it from a friend that night, it was too dark to read. But just before manning his guns for the dawn alert he slit it open.

By mid-morning, his girl's words of comfort had passed all over the island, even reaching Devereux in the underground command post he had set up – "As long as you have to be away, darling, I'm so very, very happy you are in the Pacific where you won't be in any danger if war comes."

12

"Some Chicken! Some Neck!"

14 December, 1941–1 January, 1942

LATE ON THE afternoon of 5 December, St Nicholas' Eve, *Assistenzart* Heinrich Haape of Infantry Regiment 18, had stood with his friend *Oberleutnant* Graf von Kageneck in a whirling world of white, surveying the small and nondescript town of Klin. In the deathly silence the two men had eyes only for an unusual symbol: a small stone shed crammed with benches, an old wooden bin clamped to one wall. On the litter of tickets inside the bin, the two men could distinguish the cyrillic letters which by now they knew spelled MOSKVA.

This was the Klin tramway station, only ten miles from the capital's centre, and in this moment both men divined that no member of Hitler's *Wehrmacht* would ever advance farther than they towards the city.

For Haape and the men of the 3rd Battalion, these had been weeks of bitter frustration. As the cold tightened its grip, von Bock's Army Group Centre had ground to a halt almost within sight of Moscow. In this period of acute stalemate, Haape had battled against diseases unknown in Germany yet endemic all along the front: typhus and Kramer's hepatitis, Weil's disease, a spirochete caused by rat-polluted water, tularaemia, a sickness spread by the meat of infected animals.

"Moscow *must* fall," Kageneck had mused on that silent afternoon, "yet . . . I wonder."

But in the days that followed Haape had become ever more convinced that Moscow would remain inviolate. On 5 December, he had looked forward to nothing more than the seven weeks leave that was due to him; back in Duisburg, he and his fiancée Martha Arazym had planned to celebrate the New Year by formally announcing their engagement. Then, early on 17 December, an officer in an armoured car arrived with bleak news from 6th Divisional Headquarters: "A short directive has just been received from the Führer's headquarters cancelling all leave."

Haape soon knew why. In the small hours of 5 December, sensing that the Germans had reached the peak of their effort, Marshal Georgi Zhukov, combining three armies – the First Assault, the Tenth and the Twentieth – in one giant counter-offensive, struck back. Now, all along the front, 51 German divisions were in retreat.

For Haape each day became a nightmare. Swiftly the temperature was dropping – once to minus forty-eight degrees, four times colder than a deep-freezer. As the rough little pony ambulances struggled back towards Gorki, men's toes and feet froze into solid blocks inside their boots. All day his orderlies were at work, massaging the frozen limbs with snow or icy water until they became soft and pliable, before packing them in cotton wool and bandaging them heavily. Wounds froze as if in a tourniquet of ice. Even to urinate was agony.

By mid-December the Volga front seemed stunned into glacial silence. Often it took fifteen hours to start a vehicle, by dint of lighting small fires below the gear-box. Bread had to be hacked apart with an axe, then thawed out piece by piece. At night in the forests eerie cracks resounded as sharply as rifle shots: the sap was freezing in the trees.

In one division Guderian lost 1,200 men to frostbite in one day. On 9 December, one corps reported 1,500 cases – of which 350 warranted amputation. Eleven hundred army horses perished daily. The bitter blizzards were decimating Germans and Russians alike. Near Ozarovo, a rearguard of the 3rd Rifle Regiment chanced on a Russian cavalry troop motionless in the flickering light – the men huddled against horses which stood like equestrian statues, heads held high, eyes closed, tails caught by the wind. All of them were standing waist deep in snow and all of them were dead.

The German High Command's blind incomprehension of their needs enraged both generals and privates. In mid-November, Panzer Group Three had received their first sparse consignment of winter clothing – one greatcoat to each gun crew. At Fourth Army headquarters, the men received no warm clothing or ammunition at all: merely two goods trains of red wine frozen solid. On 30 November, von Bock had protested angrily to von Brauchitsch from a forward command post within sight of Moscow, emphasising that no winter supplies had arrived – "the army group no longer commands the strength to force a decision". Still von Brauchitsch repeated woodenly: "The Führer wants to know when Moscow will fall."

Too subservient to Hitler to speak his mind openly, von Brauchitsch now tossed and turned night after night, arguing with the Führer in his sleep.

Some were now openly in revolt. On 28 November, von Kleist's Panzer Group One had been driven from the great industrial city of Rostov, on the Don. Forbidden to dig in on the line of the Mius River, von Rundstedt resigned his command of Army Group South. Hitler was unrepentant. In a mood of black misanthropy, he told Erik Scavenius, the Danish Foreign Minister, who was visiting the *Wolfsschanze*, "If the German people are no longer so strong and ready for sacrifice that they will stake their own blood on their existence, they deserve to pass away and be annihilated by

253

another, stronger power." On the same day he told a Croatian diplomat, Mladen Lorković, "If that is the case I would not shed a tear for the German people."

In his own view, Hitler had valid reason for bitterness. Plainly victory in 1941 was now impossible – and with this realisation would come a reorientation of the entire German economy. Mindful always of the lessons of World War One, Hitler had long sought to avoid a repetition of 1918, with its collapse of home front morale. Until now his blitzkrieg economy, with its quick easy victories, had always cushioned the public from the impact of total war: more consumer goods had been produced in the Third Reich in 1941 than in all of 1940. By contrast, fighter production had only risen from 183 to 244 planes a month, bombers from 217 to 336. Machine guns came off the assembly line at half the 1918 level. But from now on, of necessity, the people must tighten their belts. They would come to know the years of pinching shortage long familiar to the British and the French.

But one commander as yet had no intention of resigning: *Generaloberst* Heinz Guderian. On 20 December, just as in August, he flew to East Prussia, intent on changing the Führer's mind by reasoned argument. Once again, it proved fruitless; indeed the gesture was to cost him his command. In his gloomy bunker at the *Wolfsschanze*, dominated by its oval portrait of Frederick the Great, Hitler argued passionately: "Once I've authorised a retreat there won't be any holding them. The troops will just run . . . (they) must dig their nails into the ground; they must dig in, and not yield an inch."

"My Führer," Guderian interposed, "the ground in Russia at present is frozen solid to a depth of four feet. No one can dig in there."

Hitler was patronising. "Then you must get the mortars to fire at the ground to make shell craters. That's what we did in Flanders in the first war."

"In Flanders," Guderian explained patiently, "the ground was soft. But in Russia the shells now produce holes no more than four inches deep and the size of a wash-basin – the soil is as hard as iron."

Five hours of inconclusive argument followed, before Guderian, leaving the situation room, heard Hitler remark to Keitel, "There goes a man I have not been able to convince."

But now all three German armies received a categorical order which revealed Hitler's ruthless aptitude to command: whatever the cost, they must stand fast. If overtly inhuman, it was still logical: though the toll was appalling and some positions were yielded, the Russians did not break through and there was no panic retreat. When the spring thaws came the *Wehrmacht* would still stand on a line deep inside "the endless land".

The cost was high. Reputations were tarnished; ranks were stripped away overnight. At least thirty-five divisional and corps commanders were relieved. Life was cheap; of the 800 men of the 3rd Battalion, Infantry Regiment 18, only twenty-eight came back, although one of them was Heinrich Haape. He was to soldier on for two more years on the Russian front, once tending 521 wounded in one day, before returning to marry his Martha, seeing out the rest of the war as Medical Officer for Strasbourg. But he long remembered how the news of impending change reached the battalion on the bitter Christmas Day of 1941.

It was in a small hamlet near Kosnarovo that his friend Kageneck broke the news to Haape and *Oberleutnant* Stolze, commanding the 10th Company. "Nearly all of our generals have been relieved of their posts," he told them, plainly shocked.

"Brauchitsch?" asked Stolze.

"Yes."

"Guderian?"

"Yes."

"Von Bock?"

"Yes."

"Kluge?"

It was the one count on which Kageneck could reassure them. Kluge was still in the field, having taken over Army Group Centre from von Bock. But *Generaloberst* Adolf Strauss had lost Ninth Army, *Generaloberst* Hermann Hoth had left Panzer Group Three, Leeb had been stripped of Army Group North. "We have a Christmas present, gentlemen," Kageneck told them, relishing their mystification, "a new commander."

Then, seeing the urgency in their faces, he broke it to them: "*Gefreiter* Adolf Hitler has assumed complete command of the entire German Wehrmacht.*"

*

As the armies reeled under the weight of Zhukov's counterthrust, Churchill was once again on the high seas.

Ever since the news of Pearl Harbor reached him, the Premier had nourished but one ambition: before the year was out, he and Roosevelt must renew the dialogue which had begun with such promise at Placentia Bay. Not a moment must be lost. By noon on Friday, 12 December, Churchill and his party, still stunned by the appalling news of *Prince of Wales*, had already reached Greenock and been piped aboard the battleship *Duke of York*.

Although Churchill was to describe the eight-day voyage as "like being in prison with the extra chance of being drowned", all who travelled with him – Harriman, Beaverbrook, Pound, Portal, Dill – observed something

255

more than a sea-change. His personal physician, Sir Charles Wilson, noted in wonder: "A younger man has taken his place . . . the tired dull look has gone from his eye; his face lights up as you enter his cabin". Yet Churchill, he knew, was not lacking in preoccupations. Foremost in his mind was the thought he expressed to Wilson: "They may concentrate upon Japan and leave us to deal with Germany. They have already stopped the stream of supplies that we were getting."

By 22 December, his impatience had reached fever-pitch; it was now as if every second counted. No sooner had the *Duke of York* berthed at Hampton Roads, Virginia, than Churchill, attired in the double-breasted knee-length coat and fore-and-aft cap of an Elder Brother of Trinity House, a British life-saving association, reached a snap decision: he must fly to meet the President. Harriman, Beaverbrook, Portal and Wilson should travel with him; the rest could follow by train. At precisely 6.58 p.m., following a forty-five minute flight, his Lockheed was screaming down the long necklace of light marking the runway at Washington's National Airport. A little way off, Roosevelt was already waiting, propped beside a black bulletproof limousine that had once belonged to Al Capone.

"I clasped his strong hand with comfort and pleasure," Churchill recalled later.

Already his arrival had caused a stir in the White House. Always as intent on impressing Churchill as the Premier was on impressing him, Roosevelt had insisted that a lion-skin rug presented to him years earlier by Emperor Haile Selassie of Abyssinia, must be unearthed at once and installed in the Oval Office. After hours of searching, housekeeper Henrietta Nesbitt ran it to earth in a nearby warehouse, but the White House guards set up for Churchill's visit refused her readmission; she had forgotten her pass. The lion – reeking strongly of mothballs – reached Roosevelt's study with only minutes to spare.

The President's chiefs of staff were equally concerned. Ensconced in the North-East Suite, with its tasteful Victorian prints, Churchill was located on the same corridor as Roosevelt and Hopkins – free to confer with them at hours when no service men were present. Though Roosevelt was wont to retire early, often the Premier's cavalier disregard of the clock prolonged the sessions until the small hours. Both leaders now slept late, with "Do Not Disturb" signs prominently displayed.

Refreshed by sleep, Churchill would then monopolise Roosevelt's every waking minute, bursting in at all hours in his dressing gown; when Senator Alben Barkley asked if he could "borrow" the Premier for a luncheon on Capitol Hill, Roosevelt whooped with joy. "For Heaven's sake, do! Give him a glass of Scotch and a good lunch and . . . I will get on with some desk work."

Thus Marshall, Stark and Arnold all had cause to wonder: how many commitments of American manpower to say nothing of hardware would Churchill cajole from the President?

On the surface, all was harmony. At twilight on Christmas Eve, a crowd 20,000 strong gathered outside the Executive Mansion, with Premier and President watching from a balcony, as the great Christmas tree was lighted in the White House grounds. Next day, falling in with the President's suggestion – "It is good for Winston to sing hymns with the Methodies" – he accompanied Roosevelt to the Foundry Methodist Church, standing side by side to sing "O Little Town of Bethlehem". Next day, facing Congress at his most eupeptic, Churchill confided, "I cannot help reflecting that if my father had been American and my mother British, instead of the other way round, I might have got here on my own." A shock wave of laughter rippled beneath the great dome, then as Churchill, in a slighting reference to the Japanese, demanded passionately, "What sort of people do they think we are?" they rose as one man, cheering him to the echo.

Behind the bonhomie, Churchill was urgently seeking the answers to three questions. Would Roosevelt stick to his former Atlantic First policy, with Germany as the Number One enemy? If so, how could Japan be slowed down in the Pacific during the interim? And how could an Allied command be coordinated through the vast theatres of the Atlantic and the Pacific?

On the first score, Roosevelt left him in no doubt. Germany was still the primary foe; the first objective must be victory in Europe. Meanwhile, the Western Hemisphere presented fewer problems than anticipated. The twenty-one republics of Latin America – which the State Department had warned could prove the springboard for any German attack on the United States – had shown a heartening degree of solidarity with their neighbour.

Cuba, Panama, the Dominican Republic, El Salvador, and Guatemala had all declared war on the Axis. Costa Rica, after discovering that she had already been at war with Germany for twenty-four years – a revolutionary government which took power in 1917 had not been recognised at Versailles – had affirmed her stance afresh. Nicaragua's General Anastasio Somoza, virtually a U.S. puppet, had promptly interned all aliens regardless of their sympathies. Brazil, Mexico and seven other republics, while neutral, were pro-U.S. Even Argentina, where pro-Axis newspapers like *El Pampero* employed five editors to serve jail sentences for subversion alternately, was standing by the Havana Convention of 1940.

Thus reassured, Churchill pressed ahead with his plans for Europe. If Germany was held in Russia, they might yet attack through Spain or Portugal into North Africa. To counter this he proposed a plan codenamed "Gymnast" – an American invasion of northwest Africa in the Casablanca area, to link up with an Eighth Army drive from the east into

Tunisia.* But to this suggestion Roosevelt and his chiefs of staff remained cool. An African adventure – drawing on United States manpower and weapons as from a common pool – smacked to them of the "peripheralism" for which Churchill had been criticised. Their thinking inclined to a long slow build-up, followed by a massive and lethal thrust into the heart of Germany

As the meetings wore on, tempers flared repeatedly – so hotly, Mrs Nesbitt noted in alarm, that during working repasts men angrily stubbed out their cigarette ends on the damask table cloths. Urged to remonstrate, Eleanor Roosevelt professed herself powerless – but later, one servant noted, the President was seen guiltily covering the latest burn under a salt cellar.

It was on Christmas Day, inappropriately, that the warmest dispute arose. On the previous evening, Marshall learned, Roosevelt and Churchill had discussed diverting to the British in Malaya reinforcements scheduled for the Philippines – should it prove impossible to get them to MacArthur. At once Marshall, Arnold, and a new War Department aide, Brigadier-General Dwight D. Eisenhower, called on Stimson to protest. Stimson, as angry as the chiefs, promptly rang Hopkins, threatening resignation if Roosevelt went ahead. Hopkins, equally concerned, taxed the two leaders with Stimson's bombshell – although both promptly denied the charge.

Yet the suggestion had been in the air. As early as 22 December, Portal and Air Vice Marshal Arthur "Bomber" Harris, heading the R.A.F. Mission in Washington, had met up for preliminary discussions with General "Hap" Arnold. Portal, Arnold noted at the time, was perfectly clear as to where the priorities lay. "The British," he stated complacently, "cannot afford to see Singapore pass by the board."

Unabashed, Arnold stared right back at him. "*We*," he said unequivocally, "cannot afford to see the Philippines pass by the board."

The argument was academic. Even as they spoke the Pacific and the entire Far East were already passing by the board.

*

Soon it would be dawn. In his command post, an underground ammunition magazine lying east of the airfield, Major James Devereux felt suddenly as helpless as "a blindfolded man in a prize fight". All communication with most of Wake Island's forward positions had been cut off.

At 1 a.m. on 23 December, Devereux had still had the situation in hand. At this hour a Japanese landing had been reported at Toki Point, the westernmost tip of the coral spit known as Peale. Twenty minutes later, machine-guns had opened fire on the southerly spit called Wilkes.

* As Operation Torch it was finally launched on 8 November, 1942.

Movements were reported off the southern beach of Wake; simultaneously, in four places, the Japanese were coming ashore. All along the reef red flares were bursting. Then the lines began to go dead, and the old "walkie-talkie" hand-sets proved useless as a stand-by.

Just as in Crete, the last hours on Wake were to become a series of small private battles, men feinting and lunging through darkness, uncertain as to who was friend or foe.

For Devereux it was a tragic outcome. Until this moment his Marines had inflicted on their aggressor what Commander Masatake Okuniya was later to call "one of the most humiliating defeats the Japanese Navy had ever suffered". Now the end was near.

After that first devastating air-raid on 8 December, the pattern of the assault had been clear. On 9 December and again next day, Japanese bombers had blasted the island until it was plain that the 24th Air Flotilla planned a piecemeal destruction of both ack-ack and seacoast batteries. Then, following the third strike, in the black pre-dawn silence of 11 December, a force 450 strong attempted a landing near Peacock Point.

Obstinately, Devereux had held his fire to the last: since the Japanese could outgun him, why reveal the strength and location of his sea-coast batteries before he needed to? "What does that little bastard want us to do?" one aggrieved gunner muttered, "Let 'em run over us without even spitting back?" But not until 6.10 a.m., when the eleven ships of the task force were within 4,500 yards of Peacock Point, did Devereux give the word.

His precaution paid off. On Wilkes, the two five-inch guns of Lieutenant John McAlister three times opened fire on the destroyer *Hayate*; enveloped in a black cloud of smoke the ship slid from sight. Now the gunners cheered so lustily that the outraged Sergeant Henry Bedell yelled at them, "Knock it off, you bastards. What d'ya think this is, a ball game?"

Other salvoes straddled the flagship, the light cruiser *Yubari*; the destroyer *Kisaragi* sank in a flaming orange ball. Then Major Paul Putnam's four remaining Wildcats swooped low over the task force, machine guns raking *Yubari*'s bridge. At once Rear Admiral Sadamichi Kajioka ordered the force to withdraw. Devereux's Marines had notched up their first victory.

It was the onset of a courageous stand which became a legend in its lifetime. In one day, Major Walter Bayler, a qualified recruiting officer, had to turn down 186 would-be Marines from Dan Teters' construction staff; without uniforms to distinguish them the Japanese might classify them as armed guerillas, fodder for a firing squad. A willingness of heart was everywhere apparent. As late as 17 December, a team under Lieutenant John Kinney was performing miracles keeping Putnam's planes aloft

– trading engines from plane to plane, even building new engines from spare parts and scrap.

"If they want this island," Corporal Hershal L. Miller avowed stubbornly, "they gotta pay for it."

The situation could hardly have been grimmer but men still found time to laugh – often, in classic banana-skin tradition, at the misfortunes of others. Food was short, but 17-year-old Private Roger Bamford, Wake's youngest Marine, who had lied about his age to enlist, foraged until he located a real meal: a can of chili con carne intended for thirteen men. Thereafter Bamford's frantic dives for the latrine produced howls of mirth. Sergeant Raymon Gragg, a Marine Corps veteran and a stickler for hygiene, found what he thought was a supply of foot powder and liberally doused his feet. He awoke to find his darkened foxhole alive with rats; by mistake he had used powdered cheese.

What little they heard of the outside world moved Wake's defenders to anger. One Stateside commentator's claim that Devereux had vaingloriously radioed, "SEND US MORE JAPS" provoked a bitter outcry. Devereux himself was irked by a non-stop barrage of banal instructions from Pearl Harbor: all personnel must keep their sleeves rolled down as a protection against bomb blast. Or, if they lacked glass to put in their barrack windows, use seismograph paper. For days now the men of Wake, grimy and sweating, reeking like polecats, had lived in foxholes, dizzy from lack of sleep, and the incessant pounding of the bombers – yet nobody at Pearl Harbor seemed to grasp the desperation of their plight.

Now, towards dawn on 23 December, Devereux knew that plight to be more desperate yet.

At least they would go down fighting. Lieutenant Robert Hanna, commanding the .50 machine guns at the airstrip, streaked for the beach to man the one gun that could immediately be brought to bear on the invaders: a three-inch ack-ack gun that lacked a crew. Blasting at the offshore destroyers he fired until the crowded decks were like a slaughter-pen; by the light of burning ships he could see Japanese soldiers tumbling from their sides, struggling to reach the shallows. All along the shoreline the Marines advanced to meet them, machine pistols chattering, grenades hurtling, until the inshore surf was churned to bloody froth.

At 5 a.m. Commander Winfield Cunningham, as the island's senior officer, sent a terse message to Pearl Harbor: "ENEMY ON ISLAND ISSUE IN DOUBT". But in truth there was little doubt left.

Though every step was contested, Devereux could spare only 85 Marines to guard the southern shoreline; there were all too many vulnerable landing places elsewhere. On the beach, Major Putnam's little band of aviators and crewmen fought their way back to Hanna's ack-ack gun then stopped dead – "This is as far as we go." Waves of Japanese burst against the tight little rock of twenty men, who could be killed or maimed but who would not retreat.

Devereux knew nothing of this. Was Putnam holding out? Were they ready to blow the airstrip as instructed? Again he had no means of knowing. Suddenly a wild-eyed civilian, near to collapse, clattered down the rocky steps into the dug-out. He had been cut off when the Japanese overran a strongpoint manned by Lieutenant Arthur Poindexter near Camp One. "They're killing 'em all," he mouthed, too overwrought to say more.

Suddenly Corporal Robert Brown, Devereux's linesman, stiffened. He was listening in on the warning network, and someone was whispering. The same words, repeated over and over like a litany: "There are Japanese in the bushes . . . there are definitely Japanese in the bushes. . . ."

"Who's there? Where are you?" Brown asked urgently, but the whispering just went on, carefully, monotonously, an unknown man, murmuring into a telephone, somewhere in the dark, trying to warn them before he died.

"There are Japanese in the bushes . . . there are definitely Japanese. . . ."

Then there was a burst of sound and what might have been a scream and no more whispering at all.

"I guess they got him," Brown said bleakly.

Dawn was breaking.

*

Crawling from his dug-out, Devereux could see the Japanese Fleet. The sight was breathtaking. The ships lay in a vast circle, girdling the entire island, far out of range of any gun he possessed. Their number seemed endless – some men counted twenty-seven of all types – although only thirteen were in sight of the island at this time.

It was 7 a.m., time to return to his command post and report to Commander Cunningham. But, Devereux stressed over the phone, any report must be based on guesswork and probabilities. No explosion had been heard from the airstrip, which suggested that the Japanese had now forged past that position. In which case, all forward positions had been overrun or were isolated in small "last stand" pockets. "That's the best I can judge the picture on the dope I've got," he concluded.

After a long pause, Cunningham replied, "Well, I guess we'd better give it to them."

Devereux could not believe his ears. Never in sixteen days had the thought of surrender occurred to him. All along he had thought only of

261

buying time until a task force came to their rescue.* A Marine never surrendered. Then, by degrees, he saw the logic of Cunningham's decision. The lives of 1,200 unarmed civilians were at stake. And the Japanese had the island surrounded. As Marine commander he could go on spending lives – but there was nothing he could now buy with them. "I'll pass the word," he said finally.

Hanging up, he ordered Sergeant John Hamas, a veteran of twenty years standing, "Fix up a white flag and pass the word to cease firing."

For a moment Hamas was thunderstruck. "Yes, sir," was all he said before leaving the dugout. Outside Devereux could hear him shouting; the sound was like a child, fighting back tears: "Major's orders! We're surrendering . . . Major's orders. . . ."

Close to tears himself, Devereux yelled from the dug-out entrance, "It's not my order, God damn it!"

These were memories he would carry with him through almost four years captivity in China and Japan: the tired dirt-streaked faces of the men as they threw away their machine pistols, Old Glory fluttering down from the flagpole, the last painful trek down the rocky road to meet the Japanese advance party, just a white rag tied to a swab handle hoisted above his head.

*

By Christmas Eve, the drums were sounding retreat. From Manila Bay to the South China Sea, men, dazed, dishevelled and uncomprehending, were falling back. It was a fitting climax to 1941, a year which had seen more ignominious withdrawals than any in history.

In blacked-out Manila, civilians behind closed shutters listened uneasily to the sound of mass withdrawal: the muffled drone of truck motors moving out of Fort McKinley's gates, tyres crunching over a brittle carpet of glass, the harsh cries of unseen sentries, pious Filipino troops responding with their password, *Adios Ko* (God be with you). As everywhere in 1941, their path was marked by destruction: the sickly-sweet stench of burning sugar cane on Highway 3, near San Fernando, a drizzling black rain of fuel showering down on the oil dumps at Pandacan. Enough petroleum to operate the Asiatic Fleet for two years was burning like a vision of hell.

Belatedly, MacArthur had shrugged off his first irresolution to attempt what the Japanese were to hail as "a great strategic move" – a sideslip into Bataan, twenty miles west, a rugged peninsula 25 miles long and 20 miles wide, its jungle-clad mountain spines rising to 4,700 feet. Here, if need

* The carrier *Saratoga*, with the men of Task Force 14, was 424 miles west of Wake on 23 December when Vice-Admiral William S. Pye, who had replaced Kimmel, recalled her to Pearl Harbor, two-and-a-half hours before the surrender. Pye was convinced that the timing was too fine, that the carrier would be lost along with Wake.

be, a last-ditch stand could be made for six months – provided the Navy could furnish supplies and reinforcements.

Yet until 23 December, MacArthur had stubbornly resisted any such move. Charging defeatism, he had refused all suggestions from his operations officers to stock Bataan with provisions as "a safety measure". Thus all supplies had been concentrated in the beach areas, where the Philippine Army of which he spoke so proudly would smash the Japanese at the waterline.

On 22 December, at Lingayen Gulf on Luzon's west coast, this proud vain dream fell apart.

Fighting with rifles and ancient water-cooled machine guns, the two green divisions of Philippine troops were in no shape to contest 43,000 men of General Masaharu Homma's 14th Army armed with tanks, pouring ashore from eighty-five transports. To MacArthur's chagrin they broke and ran.

Now a dearth of ships to run the Japanese blockade, a lack of planes to dominate the skies, made a retreat to Bataan inevitable.

It was no easy manoeuvre. To succeed, MacArthur had to coordinate two armies 160 miles apart, the North Luzon Force, 28,000 strong, under Major-General Jonathan "Skinny" Wainwright, and the 15,000 men of the South Luzon Force under Brigadier-General Albert M. Jones. In this masterpiece of split-second timing, MacArthur had to leapfrog his divisions as they fell back on a series of five delaying lines, holding, then blowing, 184 vital bridges in succession.

The retreat was a quartermaster's nightmare. Only 1,300 Q.M. troops existed to shift supplies for the 80,000 men who would ultimately reach Bataan, and everywhere the supply system broke down. Lieutenant-Colonel Ernest P. Miller, of the 194th Tank Battalion, never forgot the sight he and his men saw at Calumpit, twenty-five miles northwest of Manila, the penultimate bridge to be blown. As they watched a convoy of 150 supply trucks moved past them into the peninsula – and every one of them was empty.

It was the same story all over the island. At Cabanatuan, 50 million bushels of rice was left behind for the Japanese; almost all Fort Stotensberg's stores, near Clark Field, stayed on the warehouse shelves. In Manila's Port Area everything from sacks of wheat flour to canned cherries was abandoned to the mercy of looters. Nurse Juanita Redmond, arriving at Bataan with the staff of Base Hospital No 1, was horrified to see one soldier chewing on worm-infested wild rice. Still chewing calmly, the G.I. told her, "Listen, sister, you'll be eating worse than this . . . and be damn glad to get it." The soldier was right; by the first week of January, MacArthur was to place all personnel on half rations.

Yet despite the overtones of muddle, the retreat was a triumph of its kind. By 29 December, Wainwright had reached the last of the delaying lines, ten miles northeast of Calumpit. Here his three divisions and a cavalry regiment would have to stall the Japanese until field guns and the men of the South Luzon Force had passed into the peninsula. By a minor miracle they achieved it. For two days and nights, Calumpit became a ten-mile log-jam of naval guns, Long Toms (155-mm cannon), broken-down taxis, horse-drawn *calesas*, Packard limousines and ox-carts, shuttling back and forth with men and supplies. At first light on 31 December, the South Luzon Force began their crossing. At 6.15 a.m. on New Year's Day, following Wainwright's terse command, "Blow it", Calumpit Bridge disintegrated in a Niagara of molten fragments. Here, until 9 April, 1942, the defenders of Bataan held out.

MacArthur, too, was pulling out. At 9 a.m. on 24 December he knew it was time to bid farewell to his sumptuous penthouse on Dewey Boulevard. To save the civil population from the horrors of bombardment, Manila was to be declared an open city. Now MacArthur and his staff, along with the ailing President Manuel Quezon, Commissioner Francis B. Sayre, and a coterie of Philippine officials, would transfer their headquarters to the one installation that could truly be called a fortress: the island of Corregidor, three miles long and a third of a mile wide, called "the Gibraltar of the Pacific", thirty miles away across the bay, its mighty 100-foot long Malinta Tunnel protected by 300 feet of solid rock and soil.

It was a time for last-minute decisions: permitted only one suitcase, what did one pack when facing an uncertain future? As Christmas approached, MacArthur had sent his aide, Lieutenant-Colonel Sid Huff, to shop for lingerie and size-twelve dresses for Jean, his wife, but somehow Jean MacArthur didn't feel that such costly gifts would fit in with fortress life. "Sir Boss," she said, "they are beautiful," then tucked them away in a closet, as if knowing she would never see them again. Instead she packed her husband's gold field marshal's baton* and a white fuzzy stuffed rabbit called "Old Friend", the cherished toy of their three-year-old son Arthur.

Sid Huff, priding himself on his enterprise, found room in his suitcase for a fifth of whisky. He reached the island to find every man in the party had had the same idea. MacArthur himself packed a small pistol which had belonged to his father, himself a general, when serving in the Philippines. Typically, he went on record for history: "They'll never take *me* alive, Sid."

At dusk on Christmas Eve, MacArthur was the last man to step aboard the inter-island steamer *Don Esteban*. Soon they were gliding across the moonlit water towards the massive outline of the fortress, everyone lost in thought. "Mummy," young Arthur announced at frequent intervals, "I'm tired of Corregidor. Let's go home."

* MacArthur had been appointed a Field Marshal on becoming Quezon's Military Adviser in August 1936.

It was a sentiment that all would soon come to echo. For more than two months – when the island was abandoned and MacArthur ordered to Australia – 12,000 men and women were to live like moles in a temperature that rarely dropped below 95 degrees, in quarters so cramped that even bedside lockers were a physical impossibility. All night the tubercular Quezon's coughing fits racked the damp subterranean air. There was no laundry and no hot water; even cold water was limited and, at times, not to be had. "What shall I do with this?" one of Commissioner Sayre's aides asked him perplexedly one morning, holding out a half glass of water, "I drank a little of it, I shaved with some, I washed my face and brushed my teeth, and there's a whole half glass left over."

After midnight mass, Quezon noted, somehow nobody could find it in their hearts to wish each other "Merry Christmas".

*

Nurse Mabel Redwood was perplexed. It was the early afternoon of Christmas Day, and as she made her round of the wards in Hong Kong's Jockey Club Relief Hospital, thunder was rolling from the hills. Yet this was a day of crisp bright sunlight; not a thundercloud was in sight.

It was too early for her to realise that this was the ever-present sound of destruction. The guns of Hong Kong, which had fired almost non-stop for seventeen days, were being blown apart prior to surrender.

For hours the din of battle had been unremitting. In the sampan town of Aberdeen, Sub-Lieutenant Lewis Bush, R.N.V.R., of the 2nd Motor Torpedo Boat Flotilla, was deafened by the screech of mountain guns as the Japanese closed in from three directions, the rattle of machine gun fire, the steady crump of bombs. Incongruously, between lulls in the firing, a voice from a small cargo boat stranded in the harbour boomed over the water as a psychological warrior sought to soften up morale: "Go home, British soldiers, go home . . . think of the Cup Final and the Boat Race . . . Fish and chips. Roast beef and Yorkshire pudding. Piccadilly Circus. Leicester Square."

It had been a melancholy festival for all the island's defenders. Captain Charles Pope, of the Royal Engineers, toasted Captain Bill Price, of the Royal Rifles of Canada – one of two Canadian battalions sent to boost the morale of Chiang Kai-shek – in tinned beer, then settled to bully beef and biscuits. Bandsmen Johnny Hymus and Charlie Dickens dined in the open air on pickled onions and cognac. In his underground "battle box" headquarters, Major-General Christopher Maltby and his A.D.C., Second-Lieutenant Iain MacGregor sat on upturned ammunition boxes for a Christmas dinner of tinned asparagus and half a bottle of lukewarm Liebfraumilch.

Maltby knew full well that surrender was imminent. Seven days earlier, the Japanese had gained a foothold on the island; by noon on 20 December, half of Hong Kong was in their hands, and several strongpoints were already under siege. At the luxurious Repulse Bay Hotel, on the southern side, guests like the millionaire industrialist Jan Hendrik Marsman, who paid £10 a day for their suites, were queuing up for a drinking water ration surrounded by 500 Japanese; an attempt to seize the West Wing had only been foiled by a party of gunners and Canadians under Major Robert Templer, an artilleryman, hurtling grenades along a pile-carpeted corridor "for all the world as if we'd been in a bowling alley."

Yet only one days' water supply remained intact, fires were raging everywhere and ammunition was running low.

There had been many acts of spontaneous gallantry. At the Power Station of the Hong Kong Electric Company, *taipans* of the hitherto-derided Hong Kong Volunteer Defence Corps, most of them close to sixty, fought to the bitter end – men like the Hon. J. J. Paterson, chairman of Jardine, Matheson and Co, and Captain Jacques Egal, a Shanghai wine merchant, famed for his impeccable tussore suits and flowing cravats. Between them they held the station for a day and a night against a tidal wave of Japanese. That was on 19 December – the same day that Brigadier John Lawson, commanding the Canadian contingent, the Royal Rifles of Canada and the Winnipeg Grenadiers, had phoned Maltby from his Brigade Headquarters to announce matter-of-factly, "They're all round us. I'm going outside to shoot it out." On Christmas Day, when his body was found, eight Japanese lay dead in a semi-circle beside Lawson.

Twice – on 13 December and again on the 17th – the Japanese had sent a three-man peace mission to the Governor, Sir Mark Young, to be rebuffed on each occasion. "Cameraman?" one of them hailed the journalist, Gwen Dew, as they stepped from their launch, "Don't you want to take pictures?" As she snapped away Gwen Dew guessed that surrender was imminent; in the Hong Kong and Shanghai Bank building, American consular officials were burning bales of papers. But she could not then know that Sir Mark's hands were tied. On 21 December he was to beseech Whitehall: "Only remaining resistance open to us will be to hold for short time only a small pocket in centre of city, leaving bulk of mixed population to be over-run. I feel it will be my duty to ask terms before this position is reached. If H.M. Government feel able to give assent, please cable single word "Ability".

To this Churchill, in a spirit reminiscent of Omdurman but which took no account of the civil population, replied in part: "Every part of the island must be fought and the enemy resisted with the utmost stubbornness. . . . There must be vigorous fighting in the inner defences and, if the need be, from house to house. . . ."

At 3 p.m. on 25 December Maltby made a determined pilgrimage to Sir

266

Mark Young in Government House, emphasising that no further useful military resistance was possible. Fifteen minutes later, orders went out to all commanding officers to break off the fighting.

Now, fearing reprisals from drunken Japanese soldiers whose officers had lost all control of them, guests at the Repulse Bay and other hotels began dumping all available liquor down the bathroom drains. But soon these grew clogged, and a heady river of champagne, bourbon, Scotch and gin was coursing down the marble stairs.

It was just in time. At the St Stephen's College Emergency Hospital, on the narrow Stanley Peninsula, and at the Jockey Club Relief Hospital, fighting-drunk Japanese privates rampaged through the wards, bayoneting patients and raping nurses impartially; seventy were killed at St Stephen's alone. Soon the tiled floors were running red; mattresses and cushions saturated with blood lay everywhere. One by one the bodies, some with their ears cut off, were lugged to the courtyard, piled on top of mattresses and ignited, a pyre that was still blazing when darkness fell.

That was Christmas Day on Hong Kong Island in the year of Our Lord, 1941.

*

One woman was observing Christmas in the true spirit of the festival – risking her life that others might go free. In the frontier farmhouse at Urrugne, France, Andrée de Jongh, who on Christmas Eve was preparing to deliver four more "parcels" to the British, now loomed large on the Gestapo's "wanted" list.

The alarm had been sounded late in August, at the time when Andrée had impatiently awaited clearance by the Consulate in Bilbao. In that same period, a grey Opel car had drawn to a halt outside her parents' home at No 73, Avenue Emile Verhaeren, Brussels, and two tall blond civilians descended to ring the doorbell.

"Where is your daughter Andrée?" they asked Frédéric de Jongh without ceremony.

De Jongh shrugged resignedly, a father sadly disillusioned by the younger generation. "She left home months ago," he told them, "Young girls – you understand." Both his wife, Alice, and Andrée's married sister, Suzanne, lent credence to the charade. Who could have restrained a girl so headstrong? "Nowadays one cannot keep track of what young people will do," Frédéric de Jongh complained fretfully.

After an hour of inconclusive questioning, the Gestapo left. But it was plain that in some way they had obtained a complete description of Andrée.

Andrée's first intimation of this had come in the nick of time. On the way back to Brussels she had stopped off for the night at the house of

Elvire de Greef, near Anglet, the first place of refuge for the "parcels" after their journey from Bayonne. Here one of the network's couriers, a young ex-airman, Charles Morelle, had arrived with alarming news. Their colleague, Arnold de Pé, Andrée's earliest collaborator, had been arrested with all his party in the railway station at Lille – and under pressure someone had talked.

"Dédée, the Gestapo is looking for you," Morelle had warned, "You cannot go back to Belgium."

Andrée had accepted that truth stoically – but she was far from defeated. Now she would stay on in France and work from there. Her father would take over her role in Brussels and Morelle would act as go-between. She had made three trips over the Pyrenees since that time, delivering nine "parcels" in all. It was fitting that tonight, Christmas Eve, should mark the fifth.

In the farmhouse kitchen, a new guide, who had replaced Tomas, the smuggler, Florentino Goicoechea, a mighty Basque, sat in silence, swigging contentedly at his *bota*, a goatskin bottle of mountain wine, as Andrée outlined the route for the benefit of her "parcels". The four men – Tom Cox, Jack Hutton and Len Warburton, all R.A.F. aircrew noncoms, and Albert Daye, a Canadian – listened with frowning attention. Sometimes, Andrée warned them, a man could lose contact with his party in the darkness, risking internment in the Spanish concentration camp at Miranda del Ebro. Thus it was prudent to memorise landmarks from the map in advance: the wheeling beams of the lighthouse at Fuenterrabia and the lights of the frontier seaport of Irun; the foaming torrent of the Bidassoa River and the three peaks of the Trois Couronnes, marking the climax of the journey.

At 10 p.m. it was time to go. In the orange glow of the lamplight, Florentino now finished packing a bulky rucksack. Then, taking a giant draught of cognac, he inspected each man in turn, checking the fit of their rope-soled *espadrilles*. A man lagging behind with blistered feet could endanger the whole party. Finally he armed each with a stout stick.

The night was dry, yet the wind had a sickle-edge. With short quick steps like an Indian, Florentino took the lead; Andrée, following close behind, had perfected the same gait, to make the going easier. The airmen followed as best they could, toiling ever upward over rock and shale towards a sky hobnailed with stars. Halfway along the coast from St Jean de Luz, they glimpsed briefly, through howling blackness, the dark swooping shadows that the Fuenterrabia light cast across the valley. A long way off were pinpoints of light: the dockside and wharves of Irun.

Abruptly the weather changed. A stinging sleet swept the mountains and the path grew slippery. In this alien element, the airmen began to stumble and fall. But they scrambled on, bruised and breathless, clinging for dear life to shrubs and gnarled roots. Andrée, burdened only by a small pack, began to worry about Albert Daye. The Canadian had confided that his skull was fractured, held in place by gold clamps, a fact he had concealed from his Air Force medical board. "Don't worry if I black out," he had told her, "It often happens when I'm flying, but never for long."

But on a night like this, in mountain passes rising more than 4,000 feet? More than once Andrée cast an anxious glance to her rear.

Now began the tortuous descent to the Bidassoa valley. Mercifully the sleet died away. Tonight's escape would hinge on the weather, for a heavy snowfall or rain would render the Bidassoa impassable on foot. Then the only feasible crossing was inland, over a bridge which though floodlit was unguarded by sentries – but a further sixteen hours march for weary men.

Far away a roadway gleamed, leaden under the stars, marking the Spanish side of the river. Momentarily a car's headlights flickered, gilding a cascade of white water: the Bidassoa in spate. It was quiet there in the valley, on the eve of the nativity, with only the iron music of church bells borne on the cold air.

By degrees, a deep rhythmic pulsing became audible. Soon it filled the air until speech became impossible: the thunder of the Bidassoa tumbling towards the sea at Irun. "*Couchez-vous*", Florentino mouthed. Not far off, a brightly-lit frontier post glittered in the night, and armed men were patrolling. Squatting by the boiling water, the Basque stripped off his trousers, knotting them round his neck, before testing the water for depth. Andrée, who was wearing fisherman's trousers, did the same, bidding the airmen follow suit. Then one by one they stumbled out into the torrent until they were waist deep, the cold invading their loins like the chill of imminent death.

Once across the river came the riskiest part of all. With Florentino still in the lead, they scaled a rocky embankment to reach a railway line. In the distance they could see the red glow of an engine against the night. Scrabbling and cursing through a tangle of bushes, they reached the frontier road: the moment of truth.

Florentino had fallen flat, couched as still as a hare. From a thorn bush he saw the sentry at the frontier post, 100 yards away, wheel and turn. In a strange sprinting run the Basque flashed noiselessly across the roadway, then again fell flat. Doubling at intervals in his wake, came the airmen, now nearing the end of their tether; the last man across, Albert Daye, fell backwards with a clatter. It was Andrée, watchfully bringing up the rear, who hauled him to safety.

Now the way ahead, skirting the road which circled the Trois Couronnes, seemed endless. Still Florentino climbed, as effortlessly as a shepherd, rallying them at intervals with a cry of "*Dos cien metros*". Briefly, cresting the peak of a slope, they rested, wolfing bread and cheese. Generously Florentino passed round his *bota*, but Andrée, concerned, permitted them only one swig apiece. Already they were light-headed with fatigue, and several hours of marching lay ahead.

As the saffron dawn of Christmas Day suffused the sky, the four were lagging badly. Then, like a small determined terrier, Andrée brought up the rear, now cajoling, now rebuking. The heavy morning dew soaking their clothes, they moved blindly on. Now a sweet tintinnabulation of bells came through the morning mist; all at once they were blundering among a flock of sheep. They were nearing the village of Oyarzun.

Now Florentino moved ahead towards a small isolated farmhouse, eyes wary for the green uniforms and cocked hats of *carabineros*. Stooping to pick up a pebble, he tossed it at an upper window. Seconds later, a door swung open; a stout peasant woman, bustling them into her kitchen, set to work preparing *tortillas* and coffee.

But Andrée's Christmas Day was only now beginning. Even as the weary airmen were collapsing onto goosefeather beds, Andrée, after changing into the blouse and skirt she had brought in her pack, was setting off on a five-kilometre walk across the fields to Rentiera. From here, a tram ride took her to the flat of Señor Aracama, the garage proprietor, where she rested up for the day. That night, Aracama's car bore her back to the farmhouse to collect her "parcels" then on to a lonely rendezvous on the San Sebastian road. There a Sunbeam Talbot with CD plates, driven by Michael Creswell's chauffeur, Antonio, bore them on the next step of their journey to freedom.

She would make thirty-one more Pyreneean journeys, escorting 118 servicemen to the Allies, before the misty afternoon of 15 January, 1943, when Gestapo agents swooped on the farmhouse at Urrugne. Thereafter she fought her own private war: to survive the misery of two years in Ravensbrück and Mauthausen concentration camps.

But an ambition conceived as 1941 dawned – an escape line which brought 770 men to safety by June 1944 – had been realised. Andrée de Jongh had kept faith.

*

In his office in the West Wing of the White House, Press Secretary Stephen T. Early was belatedly catching up on his Christmas mail. It was with feeling that he wrote to his old friend Samuel I. Rosenman: "A week ago tonight a certain Naval person arrived. He left yesterday for Ottawa, I am sorry he has gone. Contrarily I am sorry that he is coming back. Pearl Harbor wasn't enough. We had to have Churchill too. Either one was enough. Both have been too much."

The man whose teams of secretaries and advisers had done so much to galvanise the staid small-town atmosphere of the White House was on this day, 29 December, engaged in goading and stimulating the Canadian Parliament – conjuring up a visionary future in which the separate elements of nation-states were annealed in the fires of war. He looked back to that time in 1940 when he had warned the French that whatever happened Britain would fight on alone – and how the generals had told Premier Reynaud and his Cabinet, "In three weeks England will have her neck wrung like a chicken."

Glowering across the lectern and the embattled months since he and Hopkins dined in Glasgow, Churchill's jaw was out-thrust, his voice a bulldog's growl. "Some chicken!" he rejoined defiantly, "Some neck!"

The cheering seemed to ring over the whole city of Ottawa.

It had been a year which marked the turning point of World War Two. Despite the bleak tenor of events, the seeds of victory had been sown in defeat; all that ensued in the next three years had already been foreshadowed. The era of battleship power had ended – as the Japanese would discover in June 1942 off Midway Island. The myth of the impregnable fortress had been severely dented, if not dispelled: Singapore would fall in February, yet Leningrad held out until January, 1944. Neutrality was now a luxury few could afford; in all Europe, only Sweden, Switzerland and Turkey remained uneasily on the sidelines until the end. Even the ultimate holocaust had been foreseen. On 17 December, at a top-secret meeting of twenty physicists in Tokyo's Naval Club, Captain Itoh of the Imperial Navy broached the possibility that some among them might develop an atomic weapon for Japan. But the doyen of the scientists, Dr Asada, was gloomy: "In my opinion only the United States has the potential to develop an atomic weapon."

The shadow of the Manhattan Project hung even then over the thirty-seven nations who were now at war. From a localised conflict which many had hoped to evade – or see ended by a fragile truce – the whole world had drifted towards Armageddon, "the battle of the great day of God Almighty".

The shifting of the war to the Far East was to end the white domination which had marked the last two hundred years. Britain, about to lose an empire, was to fight on for almost four years to regain it – "all, all shall be restored", Churchill said. America, by contrast, hoped to replace British dominion in the east with her own predominance. Both sides were doomed to disappointment, notably in Korea and Vietnam; already "Asia for the Asiatics" had won a moral victory, ending the age of imperialism.

So, too, with "Operation Barbarossa". The stubborn resistance of the Russian defensive, prompted in part by the *Einsatzgruppen*, would become a ferocious counteroffensive; the tidal wave of Russian "liberation", which few save Churchill would foresee, rang down an iron curtain "from Stettin, in the Baltic, to Trieste, in the Adriatic". This same

271

relentless repression prompted the vast exodus of Jews to the modern state of Israel – fomenting a Jewish–Arab conflict which has never been resolved.

Strangely, as 1941 ended, so many of the participants seemed like actors trapped in a gigantic frieze – condemned to mime the same gestures which had typified them all along. In Moscow, Stalin was still badgering Eden and Cadogan, who had arrived on a mission, for two prize concessions: a British Second Front and recognition of the new frontiers carved out by his 1940 annexation of the Baltic States. In Chungking, Chiang Kai-shek's demands for American money and supplies grew daily more clamant. Between Tito and Mihailović, in Yugoslavia, it was still war to the knife. De Gaulle, ever more intent on creating a rift between Roosevelt and Churchill, had on Christmas Eve enraged the State Department by seizing the Vichy-held island colony of St Pierre and Miquelon off the south coast of Newfoundland.

Only Rommel – for the time being at least – conceded that events had moved on and left him standing. By 9 December, having lost 33,000 killed, wounded and imprisoned and 300 tanks, he decided to temporarily abandon Tobruk – beating a fighting retreat through Gazala back to Agedabia. Six red flares arching into the winter sky marked the relief of Tobruk by its own garrison, and a corps commander despatched a signal that became a classic in Eighth Army circles: "Tobruk is relieved, but not as relieved as I am."

Thus, feinting and skirmishing like fighting cocks, the Germans fell back, with Eighth Army in spirited pursuit. "We chased them until 20 December," one tanker sergeant noted in his diary, "until they were right back behind the Agheila salt flats. We ran round them, over them and underneath them."

On New Year's Eve – when both sides saluted each other with a mammoth firework display of green, red, yellow and white flares – it was all as if it had never been. Once again Rommel's forces stood almost where they had when he assumed command eleven months back – in the great Sirte bend between Agedabia and Tripoli. And again Eighth Army held the airfields in the "bulge" of Cyrenaica.

Propped on the mantelpiece of a flat in the old port of Benghazi, the Germans had left the advancing British a point to ponder. Written in English, the message read: "We'll be back in three months, but in the meantime – A Merry Christmas!"

*

Early on New Year's Day, 1942, Roosevelt had a brainwave. For days, both during Churchill's visit and his sojourn in Ottawa, the two men had been pondering a fitting label for the league of twenty-six co-belligerents that now made common cause against the Axis. "Allied and Associated Powers" seemed a ponderous terminology, with a faint smack of Woodrow Wilson, though neither man could come up with anything better. But now time was pressing: Churchill had returned the previous night and the first signatures on the joint declaration were to be affixed that day.

Now Roosevelt saw the light. Pressing a bell he asked to be wheeled to the North-East Suite – to find Churchill still wallowing happily in his bath, at intervals ducking beneath the water, then surfacing again, blowing like a grampus. At first Roosevelt made to withdraw – until Sergeant Patrick Kinna, Churchill's shorthand writer, heard the Premier, naked and unashamed, extend a greeting often considered apocryphal: "Come in – I have nothing to conceal from the President of the United States!"

"How about United Nations?" Roosevelt called, as Churchill lifted a soapy head from the water.

Churchill paused to consider. Then, ducking again to rinse the last of the soap from his eyes, he re-surfaced, to turn a dripping gaze on the President.

"That," he said, "should do it."

There was a true climate of optimism then, four years before the Iron Curtain rang down. So perhaps their innocence could be forgiven.

ACKNOWLEDGEMENTS

This book, like its companion volume, *1940: The World in Flames*, derives in part from the recollections of several hundred eye-witnesses and in part from records and archive repositories in the United States and Great Britain. Those participants whose testimonies I have used are hereby gratefully acknowledged; the details of their individual contributions are listed in the appropriate section of the source apparatus.

I have to thank Dr Daniel J. Boorstin, Librarian of Congress, Washington, D.C., for the facilities he so kindly granted me during my visit, and especially Paul T. Heffron, Acting Chief of the Manuscript Division and his assistant, Marianne Roos. I am equally indebted to Dr William R. Emerson, Director, Franklin D. Roosevelt Memorial Library, Hyde Park, New York, for similar facilities, and to Mark Renovitch, Susan Bosanko, and John Ferris who generously directed my attention to a number of recent acquisitions. In Washington's National Archives, Edward J. Reese, Modern Military Branch, Military Archives Division, proved equally helpful.

British archives for this period have been growing apace annually, and for permission to study, and in many cases to quote from, the records in their keeping, I am grateful to the following: A. J. Nicholls, St Antony's College, Oxford; Corelli Barnett, Keeper of the Archives, Churchill College, Cambridge, and his most able assistants, Marion Stewart and Clare Stephens; Dr B. S. Benedikz, Head of Special Collections, University Library Birmingham; Dr Maurice Bond, Clerk of the Records, House of Lords and Dr A. J. P. Taylor; Patricia Methven, Military Archivist, and her assistant, Bridget Evans, of the Liddell Hart Centre for Military Archives, University of London, King's College; Catherine Pickett, of the India Office Library and Records (Foreign and Commonwealth Office); Professor David Pocock and Dorothy Wainwright, University of Sussex (The Mass-Observation Archive); Angela Raspin, British Library of Political and Economic Science (London School of Economics); Robert Shackleton, The Bodleian Library, Oxford, and Dr Peter Thwaites, Department of Documents, and his deputy, Philip Reed, at the Imperial War Museum, London.

As in the past I have been singularly lucky in the loyal band of researchers and translators who have continued to work at my side. Hildegard Anderson, as always, scrupulously covered many phases of my American research. Pamela Colman delved in many university libraries, and conducted a number of telling interviews. Joan St George Saunders solved many last-minute queries. Alexandra Lawrence pioneered the forbidding mass of documentation at the Public Record Office, later nobly reinforced by Margaret Duff, who also travelled hundreds of miles to interview scores of survivors. A special note of thanks, too, to Kim Marabella, who saw to all my travel arrangements from Pearl Harbor on.

My English and American publishers, Christopher Sinclair-Stevenson and Alfred A. Knopf Jr waited with exemplary patience for a manuscript long overdue, and I must acknowledge once again the matchless editorial counsel of Roger Machell. My agents in London and New York, Graham Watson and James Oliver Brown, offered the usual sterling moral support. Jill Beck oversaw a typescript which arrived at protracted intervals with her old aplomb. In addition I must thank the staffs of the Library of Congress, Printed Books Division, the New York Public Library, the Public Record Office, the British Library, the London Library and the Wiener Library for the help and courtesy that they at all times afforded.

My deepest debt, though, is to my wife, to whom this book is dedicated. Apart from typing the first draft she travelled with me many thousands of miles on our joint research project. The support she offered every inch of the way made all of it seem worthwhile.

274

SOURCE APPARATUS

Chapter One: "Thy People Shall Be My People"
The Hopkins' dinner is related by Moran. Hotel details of that time were kindly furnished by Judy Lask and Deborah Dudley, of British Transport Hotels Information Services, and P. K. Masser, General Manager, North British Hotel. For that day's weather I am grateful to J. G. Allardice, Senior Meteorological Officer, Glasgow Weather Centre.

For shipping losses and the Home Front, see Balfour, Calder, Costello and Hughes, Longmate, McLaine and Marwick. Woolton's statement is from the Woolton MSS., folio 12, Churchill to Woolton, January 2. Morale is dealt with by Mass Observation Files 568, *Morale in 1941.* and 925, *Absenteeism from Industrial Work.* Aspects of Hopkins are from Birkenhead, *Halifax*, Childs, William Crozier, Kenneth Davis and Harriman. Hopkins' own impression of his mission – including his talk with King George VI – are found in FDR, PSF, Safe File, Box 4, *Harry Hopkins* folder, and the Sherwood/Hopkins' papers, Box 304, Folder A, *Hopkins in London.*

General background to Lend-Lease is furnished by Acheson, Burns, Davis and Lindley, Kenneth Davis, Ickes, Jonas, Langer and Gleason, and Lash, *Roosevelt.* For isolationism and interventionism, see Chadwin, Dawson, Frye and Wheeler-Bennett, *Special.* Roosevelt's inauguration is based on items in Early's Papers, Scrapbook 1, Wickard's diary entry for 6 January, and Leonard Baker. Isolationist cartoons feature in *Time's* issue of 24 February. For Willkie in London, see Nicolson's MSS. diary entry for 1 February; for Dublin, see Beaverbrook Papers, File D 417, Beaverbrook to Churchill, 6 June. Barkley is in FDR, PPF, 5160, memo of 17 February.

General background on Greece (and in Chapters III and IV) is furnished by Buckley, *Greece*, Cadogan, Cervi, Eden and Parkinson. For the Balkans, especially Bulgaria, see PRO AIR 40/2023 and Foreign Relations of the United States (hereafter FRUS), Vol I, 273; also Dalton's diary entries of 3 February and 18 November. Prince Paul is from F.O. 954/33, fol. 241, Campbell to F.O., and Channon. For Greek intelligence, see Davidson Papers, File K, *Episodes Concerning Winston Churchill.*

Doubts on Greece are in Dalton's diary entry for 19 February, CAB 65 (WM) 19, and Edwards' diary for 7 March. Palairet's reaction is from F.O. 954/11, fol. 40, 7 March; Wavell's is fol. 26, 27 January. For Prince Paul to Eden, see F.O. 954/33, fol. 269, 19 March. Discussions with the Dominions are in CAB 65 (WM), 20, 21 and 26. Admiral Turner's views are in Hopkins' Papers, Box 154, Folder *Great Britain*, memo of 12 April. For MacVeagh to Roosevelt, see FDR, PSF, Box 54, *Greece* folder, letter of 8 March.

Material on Rommel (and in Chapters II, III, V, X and XIII) derives from the German monographs listed in the MSS bibliography, and from works by Carell, *Foxes*, Irving, *Fox*, Esebeck, Mellenthin, Heinz-Werner Schmidt and Desmond Young.

Hitler's strategy throughout is based on studies by Bullock, Friedlander, Hinsley, *Strategy*, Irving, *War*, and Rich. The story of Harold Elvin (and in Chapters V, VI, VIII and IX) is based on an interview he kindly granted the author to supplement his book. Mlle Andrée de Jongh, Sir Michael Creswell, and Lieutenant-Colonel J. M. Langley most helpfully furnished escape line material (and in Chapters VII and XII). Marcel-Gerard Comeau's story (continued in Chapters II, III and V) is adapted from his book, supplemented by an interview. Ruth Mitchell's story is as she told it, with supporting information from Mrs Ruth Van Breda Yahn, Mrs Lewis Pillsbury, and Robert G. Carroon, Curator of Research Collections, Milwaukee Country Historical Society. Anglo-American financial tensions are mirrored in CAB 65/(WM) 19 and 29, Wickard's diary entry for 16 January, and works by Blum, Ickes and Thorne. Churchill to Nicolson is the latter's MSS.

diary entry for 21 March. For the salmon run, see Hopkins' Papers, Box 155, Folder *Great Britain, Food*, Hopkins to Winant, 22 June.

Chapter Two: "Convoys Mean Shooting and Shooting Means War"
The American mission to London is derived from Bellush and Harriman; F.O. reactions to Winant are in F.O. 954/29, fol. 233, n.d. Roosevelt's unneutral neutrality is charted by Burns and by Matloff and Snell. U.S. – Yugoslav relations are in FRUS II, 944, 962 and Fotić; promises to Greece are in FRUS II, 670–712. For Roosevelt on Abyssinia, see FDR, PSF, Box 93, folder *Cordell Hull*, letter of 20 February. For the pact and subsequent coup in Yugoslavia, see Dalton's diary entries of 21, 27, 30 March and 17 April, and accounts by Elisabeth Barker, Brock, Hoptner, Kapetanović, King Peter II, Maitland, St John, Stowe and Leigh White. Subotić's encounters with Butler are found in F.O. 954/33, fols. 252 (21 March) and 273 (7 April). For Matsuoka, see Bullock, Davis and Lindley, Paul Schmidt, and Toland, *Sun*. Foreign Office apprehensions are in CAB 65 (WM), 14, plus Cadogan, Eden and Sir John Kennedy. For U.S. policy in China, see, principally Divine and Shaller; Morgenthau's argument with Roosevelt is his MSS diary entry for 21 April. Accounts of Tobruk from the Allied viewpoint are from Heckstall-Smith, Gavin Long, Wilmot and Yindrich.

Chapter Three: "Do Not Succumb to Provocation"
Churchill and the Poles is Nicolson's MSS diary entry for 26 March; the "frog" is from Maisky. The conference at Tatoi Palace is as described by Heckstall-Smith and Baillie-Grohman. Smuts' counsel on aircraft is from CAB 65 (WM), 27. The first concept of the Atlantic Charter is from Pickersgill.
Overall accounts of Iraq appear in Buckley, *Ventures*, Hirsowicz, Mockler and Stark. Secret intelligence on Rashid Ali is in F.O. 954/12, fol. 393 (7 April); Lampson's reactions are fols. 395 (3 May) and 396 (6 May). Auchinleck's warnings are from the Alanbrooke Papers, File 6/D/4bE, 12 April. For Attlee on Wavell, see Dalton's diary entry for 30 May. General Clark's report and the dilemma regarding the U.S. Minister are F.O. 954/12, fols. 401 (3 July) and 403 (17 July).
For Tito, see Auty, Clissold, *Whirlwind*, Dedijer and Djilas. Warnings to Stalin are featured by Bialer, Deakin, *Sorge*, Höhne, *Direktor*, Trepper and Weth, *War*; appeasement of Hitler is dealt with by Laqueur and Weinberg. For Cripps in Moscow, see Dalton's diary entry for 29 January. The American military attachés' reports are in the Hopkins' Papers, Box 188, *Military Intelligence Division Reports*, passim.
The best overall account of Hess' mission is in Douglas-Hamilton, supplemented by accounts from Colville, Ilse Hess, Kirkpatrick and Leasor. Fighter Command reactions were gleaned from the author's interviews with the late Duke of Hamilton, Marshal of the R.A.F. Lord Douglas of Kirtleside, C. H. Leman, "Dickie" Richardson and Sadie Younger. For Whitehead's view, see F.O. 954/29, fol. 209, 10 June.

Chapter Four: "He'll Never Beat Men Like These"
The exploits of Starheim's network are described in varying degrees by Cookridge, *SOE*, Hansson, and Kennedy, *Pursuit* – which also deals with initial preparations at Scapa Flow and the subsequent *Bismarck* battle. For my own account of the battle I have drawn on ADM 199/357, ADM 199/1187 (*Pursuit and Destruction of Bismarck*), ADM 1/11726 (*Loss of H.M.S. Hood*), supplemented by eye-witness accounts from the following: Derek Aylwin, Michael Buxton, Surgeon Vice-Admiral Sir Dick Caldwell, Bernard Campion, Peter Dunstan, Rear-Admiral John Dyer-Smith, Basil Elsmore, Charles Firbank, Lieutenant-Commander Alan Franklin, Edward Grindley, Douglas Hall, David Hunter, Leonard Jackson, Thomas Jenkins, William Johns, Frederick Kenshole, Jack Knight, Alfred Llewellyn, Herbert Minnett, Ronald Mullins, Norman Portlock, Michael Pruett, Commander Arthur Skipwith, Douglas Spinks, Lieutenant-Commander Richard Thomas-Ferrand, Kenneth Townsend-Green and Charles Wright. The majority of these also contributed material to Chapters VIII and XI. Published accounts of the battle are by Apps, Ash, Bekker, *Naval*, Broome, Busch, Cain, Franklin, Jameson, Sopocko and Thompson. For A. V. Alexander, see Dalton's diary entry for 26 May; the Ministry of Information reaction is from the Monckton Papers. File *B.B.C. Home News Criticism*, 31 May.

Operations in Crete are based on the file PREM 3/109, in particular fols. 31/34, Churchill's trenchant criticism of 14 June, and on published accounts by Bartz, Belchem, Buckley, *Greece*, Alan Clark, Davin, Heydte, Hill-Rennie, Jacobsen, Kippenberger, Lewin, Gavin Long, Mrazek, Sandford, Singleton-Gates, Spencer, Stephanides, Stewart and Whiting. Caccia's report, transmitted by Lampson to Eden, is F.O. 954/11, fol. 64, 27 May. Goltz' story is a typescript kindly loaned to the author by Marcel-Gerard Comeau.

Roosevelt's "State of Emergency" derives from published accounts by Davis and Lindley, Manchester, *Glory*, Rosenman and Sherwood. His "gradualness" is from Wood's papers (A 410.4), Halifax to Churchill, 13 June; his rebuke from Bullitt is from FDR, PPF, 1124, *William Bullitt*, 21 May; the floodtide of Lend-Lease is from FDR, PSF, Box 16, Folder *Lend-Lease*, items of 16 April, 7 May. Dunn's report is from Beaverbrook Papers, File D 417, Beaverbrook to Churchill, 5 June.

Chapter Five: "No Peace, No Rest, No Halting Place, No Parley"
Published sources on Crete are as listed for Chapter IV. For Wavell's despair, see F.O. 954/5, fol. 77, Lampson to Eden, 30 May; for Tedder to Portal, see PREM 3/109, fol. 73, 30 May. Churchill at Church House is Nicolson's MSS diary entry for 10 June. British morale is from Mass Observation Weekly Report No 1, dated 9 June.

The bitter Dominions reaction is denoted by F.O. 954/4, fol. 305 (New Zealand) and fols. 318–22 (Australia). Lampson's contribution is F.O. 954/11, fol. 65, Lampson to Eden, 28 May. Cunningham's report is from the Cunningham Papers, RKCN 1/9, Cunningham to Admiral Sir Algernon Willis, 12 June. For Portal to Royce, see Arnold's Papers, Box 39, 31 July. Churchill to Cranborne is from Garner; Blamey's comment from Thorne. For Menzies to Wilson, see Brooke-Popham Papers, V/1/13, Ismay to Brooke-Popham, 15 June. American disillusion is noted by Dalton in his diary entry for 2 June; his record of Cabinet dissensions is likewise from diary entries of 29 October, 1940, 26 February, 1941, 22 May, 11 and 27 June, 8 August, 17 September and 19 November, supplemented by Hollis and Leasor, Reith, and Roskill, *Hankey*.

Vichy material is based on studies by Cole, Crawley, Langer, *Gamble*, Lukacs, and Paxton. Darlan's "superman" concept is Leahy's MSS diary entry for 1 August. Hull to Henri-Haye is from Hull's Papers, Box 58, Folder 28, *Vichy France*, 18 January; to Halifax, from Folder 214, *Great Britain*, 7 March. Eden's pipeline to Weygand is in CAB 65 (WM) 8 and F.O. 954/8, fols. 141–44, 17 January. Aspects of de Gaulle are discussed by Elisabeth Barker, Boothby, Crawley and Schoenbrunn. For Pétain on de Gaulle, see FDR, PSF, Box 41, Folder *France*, Leahy to Roosevelt, 19 March. Dalton on de Gaulle is his diary entry for 7 October.

Parr's report is from F.O. 954/8, fol. 165, 14 May; Hoare's advice is from Beaverbrook's Papers, File C 308, *Sir Samuel Hoare*, 14 May. Wavell's reluctance is from F.O. 954/15, fol. 33, Lampson to F.O., 29 May. The Churchill – de Gaulle phone call was related to the author by Air Commodore James Coward, a luncheon guest.

The Syrian campaign is amply covered in works by Cecil Brown, Buckley, *Ventures*, Fergusson, *Trumpet*, Hirsowicz, and Mockler. For Spears to Bracken, see Churchill College Papers, ref. Sprs 1/50, 25 May; for Lampson's confirmation, see F.O. 954/5, fols. 130–33, Lampson to Eden, 25 October. The "Robin Moor" episode is from Metzler. Hitler's unique view of the U.S. is from Compton, Friedlander, and Weinberg, *Image*.

The Iceland take-over is in Hull's Papers, Box 49, Folder 145, Churchill to Roosevelt, 14 June, and Morgenthau's MSS. diary entry for 10 July. Stark's apprehension is from FDR, PSF, Box 55, *Iceland* Folder, Stark to Hopkins, 17 June. Portuguese aspirations feature in FDR, PSF, Box 93, Folder *Cordell Hull*, State Department report of 26 March. Neumann's story follows his own account. For the "Commissar Order", see Irving, *War*, Keitel, Krausnick, Macksey, *Guderian*, Manstein, Toland, *Hitler*, and Wheeler-Bennett, *Nemesis*.

Eve-of-Barbarossa Soviet impressions are from Bialer and Erickson; German reactions from Carell, *Hitler*, Malaparte, Pabel and Schutz.

Chapter Six: "We Have Only To Kick In The Door"
Barbarossa battle material is from Bialer, Blumentritt, Carell, *Hitler*, Erickson, Freiden, Macksey, *Guderian*, Malaparte, Manstein, Pabel, Pabst, Salisbury and Seaton. For Hitler's peace offer via Turkey, see F.O. 954/28, fol. 128, Knatchbull-Hugessen to F.O., 22 June,

and Nicolson's MSS diary entry for 23 June. World-wide Barbarossa reactions are from Chadwin, Ciano, Eden, Murphy, Sherwood, and Toland, *Hitler.*

Hilda Neal's reaction is from her diary entry of 23 June, likewise Kathleen Phipps' diary notations of 27 July and 7 August. Alba's dispatch is from Crozier, *Franco.* For Cripps, see F.O. 954/24, fol. 331, 2 July. Pownall is Nicolson's MSS. diary entry for 9 July. American reactions are noted by Burns, Davis and Lindley, Dawson and Fehrenbach. For Hopkins on Stalin, see Ismay Papers, ISMAY/IV/HOP, Hopkins to Ismay, 7 August. Cox and Berle are in the Sherwood/Hopkins' Papers, Box 305, Folder *Russia Attacked – Early Political Decisions,* Cox to Hopkins, 23 June, Berle to Hopkins, 30 July.

For Hungary, see Fenyo and Horthy. Mussolini at Verona was related to the author by General Enno von Rintelen. Bomber Command operations are covered by Barker, *Strike,* Frankland, Hastings, Richards and Wykeham. British complacency concerning the Russian campaign features in Mass Observation Weekly Report No 3, dated 23 June. For a Balkan report on the British attitude, see FDR, PSF, Box 54, Pell to Roosevelt, 21 October. For Sinclair to Hopkins, see the Arnold Papers, Box 38, Folder *Aircraft Allocations,* 27 July. Churchill's meeting with the airman is Dalton's diary entry for 12 December.

Chapter Seven: "At Last – We've Gotten Together"
Facets of European resistance and the V for Victory campaign are covered by Archer, Michael Balfour, Ehrlich, Kraus, Michel, Petrow, Viorst and *Time's* issues of 10 March, 17 March, 28 July, 4 August, 11 August and 29 September. For Tito's partisans see Auty, Clissold, *Whirlwind,* Colaković and Djilas. The principal sources for the Atlantic Charter are Franklin, H. V. Morton, Pawle, Reilly, Spring and Theodore Wilson. Darlan's reaction on Indo-China is from FDR, PSF, Box 4, Safe File *France,* Leahy to the State Department, 1 August. Churchill's estimation of Barbarossa is from the Sherwood/Hopkins Papers, Box 306, Folder *Atlantic Conference,* as is Freeman's letter to Hopkins of 11 August. For Roosevelt's determination not to declare war and Churchill's response, see F.O. 954/4, fol. 340, Churchill to Smuts, 9 November. For Arnold and Freeman, see the Arnold Papers, Box 39, *Strategy* Folder, memo of 10 August. Auchinleck's press conference crops up in F.O. 954/15, fol. 78, Churchill to Auchinleck, 11 July.

Chapter Eight: "Shoot Everyone Who Shows A Wry Face"
Guderian's journey to the *Wolfsschanze* is described by Carell, *Hitler.* For the German presence in Tehran, see *Documents on German Foreign Policy,* Vol XIII, P 103/4, and Kahn, *Spies.* War Cabinet pressure on Iran is from CAB 65 (WM) 79 and 82 and F.O. 954/19 fols. 129, 131, 8 and 11 August. Accounts of the campaign and the Shah's eccentricities are drawn from Brock, Buckley, *Ventures,* Dimbleby and Michie. The Shah's appeal to Roosevelt is from FDR, PSF, Box 55, *Iran* Folder, 26 August; Roosevelt replied on 2 September. Churchill's rebuke to Bullard and orders to seize the Shah are CAB 65 (WM) 89 and 93. Nicolson's flirtation with kingmaking form his MSS. diary entries for 13, 19 and 23 September. Dreyfus and the young Shah are in FRUS III, 470. For Beaverbrook's meeting with Hess, see Beaverbrook Papers, File D 443, *Rudolf Hess.* Moscow background is from Bourke-White, Caldwell, Cassidy and LeSueur.

British enthusiasm for Russia is explored in the following Mass Observation holdings: File No 848, *Public Opinion About Russia,* 27 August; File 915, *Second Front,* 16 October, and Weekly Reports No 12 of 11 August and No 21 of 22 September. The topic also features in the Sherwood/Hopkins' Papers, Box 397, Folder 1, *Postal Censorship Reports,* 25 July, and in works by Addison, Calder and Maisky. Pro-Communist posters are in the Bevin Papers, ref. BVN 2/2.

For the Atlantic Charter ferment see Collis, Louis and Thorne. U Saw's appeal to Roosevelt is FDR, PSF, Box 34, *Diplomatic, Burma,* letter of 26 November. For Calcutta, see Brooke-Popham Papers, BP V/1/2, Brooke-Popham to Ismay, 15 November, 1940.

Laski's letter, dated 13 August, is in the Frankfurter Papers, Container 75. For de Gaulle in Syria, see Elisabeth Barker, *Churchill,* Chandos and Mockler. Churchill's fury and M.I.5's surveillance of de Gaulle is from Spears Papers, St Antony's College, ref IIA/2, H. Somerville-Smith to Spears, 29 August and 6 September. For Dominions disputes see Channon, Hasluck, and CAB 65 (WM) 94 and 106, recording the demand for the *Prince of Wales.*

Genocide in Russia is fully dealt with by Bracher, Fest, Frischauer, Höhne, *Death's Head*, Musmanno, Reynolds, Russell and St George. The Jews are the subject of detailed studies by Davidowicz, Hilberg, Krausnick, Poliakov and Reitlinger, *Solution*. The teenager quoted is Lind. For the lost opportunity in Russia see Blumentritt, Cecil, Pabel, St George, Seaton and Strik-Strikfeldt.

Chapter Nine: "Let No One Forget, Let Nothing Be Forgotten"
Beaverbrook's Moscow mission is drawn principally from a typescript account by Harold Balfour and from the Beaverbrook files, D 90, *Cripps Controversy* and D 100, *Aid to Russia and the Russian Narrative*, plus published accounts by Harriman, Standley, A. J. P. Taylor, and Kenneth Young. Cadbury's dilemma is noted by Dalton on 19 September. Steinhardt to the State Department is FRUS I, 866. The Sherwood/Hopkins' Papers, Box 305, Folder *Russia Attacked*, contain Berle to Welles, 30 July and Beaverbrook to Hopkins, 4 October. Ismay to Brooke-Popham is BP V/1/17 of 16 September. Other Beaverbrook references are as follows: on the Americans, File D 71, *Balfour Visit to USA*, letter of 4 November; on inefficient British production, File D 78, *Meetings with Manufacturers*, conference transcripts of 28 October and 11 November; File D 359, Beaverbrook to Margesson, 1 September; File D 332, Beaverbrook to the Colonial Office, 3 September; File C 308, Beaverbrook to Hoare, 28 August.
For Leningrad I have drawn on works by Goure, Inber, Pavlov, Salisbury, Shostakovich, Skomorovsky, and Werth, *War*. Disillusion in Germany is noted by Michael Balfour, Fredborg, Howard Smith and Turney. The Ankara scene is reported by Brock.
The North Atlantic scene is covered by Morison. Smuts to Eden is F.O. 954/4, fol. 331, 13 September. For Halifax to Churchill, see Wood's Papers (A 410.4), letter of 11 October. Roosevelt to Eccles is Dalton's diary entry for 25 August. Knox's Papers, Container 4, *General Correspondence*, include Frankfurter's letter of 2 July and Lippmann's of 2 October. Events in Japan follow accounts by Butow, Ike, Mosley, *Hirohito*, Toland, *Shame* and Toland *Sun*.

Chapter Ten: "Just Read This – And The War Is Won"
Churchill's passivity is shown by CAB 65 (WM) 122. Thailand features in F.O. 954/6, fol. 485, Crosby to the F.O., 1 December. For British participation in the Middle East, see Agar-Hamilton, Barnett, Clifford, Connell, *Auchinleck*, Crimp, Fielding, Jacob, Maule, Onslow, and Tedder. Churchill's prodding of Auchinleck is from the Alanbrooke Papers, 6/d/4/C, 20 July. Auchinleck's letters are in Ismay/IV/CON/1A and IV/CON/1/IC, dated 29 September and 6 November.
Wake Island material (and in Chapters XI and XII) is based on an interview kindly granted by Brigadier-General James P. S. Devereux, as a supplement to his book, and on accounts by Bayler, Cunningham, Hough and Karig. Burns, Hull and Leith-Ross describe the attempted compromise with Japan; Dalton's diary entry is for 26 November. Roosevelt's hoped-for Pacific "incident" is from Biddle's Papers, Cabinet Meetings Folder, 7 November. Hull's anger with Halifax is shown by his letter of 29 November, Box 58, Folder 214, *Great Britain*.
Pearl Harbor's unpreparedness is based on the hearings of the Pearl Harbor Committee, and on analyses by Barnes, Brownlow, Buell, Burtness and Oder, Lombard, Lord, Pogue, Theobald, Trefousse, Waller and Wohlstetter. MacArthur material abounds in Brereton, Hersey, Huff, Clayton James, Kenney, Clark Lee, Manchester, *Caesar*, Matloff and Snell, Muggah and Charles Willoughby. Brooke-Popham's comment on MacArthur is from BP V/1/18, dated 10 October; his reluctance to press for equipment is BP V/11, dated 26 October, 1940. Malaya's ineffective defences follow Vlieland's MSS account; for Buffalo aircraft see F.O. 954/6, fols. 422–433, 11 April. The overplus of aerodromes is from Percival's Papers, File P 21, Item 49, *Personal Observations of Lt. Col. Ashmore*. Stewart's jungle training is from ADM 199/234, *Escapes from Hong Kong and Malaya*. General accounts appear in works by Louis Allen, Barber, Boyle, Bulcock and Simson; for Hong Kong social life see Carew and Lindsay. The Australian battalion commander is from BP V/1/8, letter to Ismay of 26 March.
Last-ditch negotiations in Washington are fully covered by Baruch, Butow, Davis and Lindley, Feis, Hoehling, Hull, Mosley, *Hirohito*, and Toland, *Sun*. Hull's telecon with

Halifax is in Hull's Papers, Box 66, Folder 289, *Great Britain, General,* memo of 1 January, 1942. Yamamoto and Yamashita derive from biographies by Potter. Malayan intelligence is from Tsuji. For Early's press conference, see the Early Scrapbook, Vol. II.

Chapter Eleven: "What Was That Place? Could You Spell It?"

The following accounts of Pearl Harbor, from the viewpoints of both participants, have been used for this reconstruction: Brownlow, Blake Clark, Page Cooper, Dickinson, Forgy, Barry Fox, Fuchida, Hough, Karig, Lord, Millis, *Pearl Harbor* (The Army Times) Sheehan, Toland and Wallin. Reactions in Washington and elsewhere are recorded by Acheson, Davis and Lindley, Fergusson, *Maze,* Hayter, Hoehling, Hull, Manchester, *Glory,* Montagu, Mosley, Reilly, Rosenman, Tully, Winant, and *Time's* issues of 15 and 22 December. For the White House blackout dilemma, see the Nesbitt Papers, Box 2, 7 December diary entry. The Honolulu mood is caught by Robert Casey.

For British apathy, see Mass Observation File No 1004, *Anti-American Sentiment,* report of 21 December, and Nicolson's MSS diary entry for 12 December.

The fall of Guam is described by Karig and Tweed; for Cavite, see Agoncillo, Toland, *Shame,* and William L. White. The riddle of Clark Field is treated at length by Brereton, Edmonds, Manchester, *Caesar,* Ernest P. Miller, Louis B. Morton, and Whitcomb. The loss of the *Prince of Wales* and *Repulse* is based primarily on the files ADM 199/1149, PREM 3/163/2, ADM 1/12181 (Reports of Survivors), ADM 1/11043 (Parliamentary Report) and ADM 116/4554 (Bucknill Committee Report), supplemented by reports by all those credited in Chapter IV, plus the following additional testimonials: Admiral Sir Henry Leach, the First Sea Lord; Joseph Blackburn, Alec Compton, Gerald Cooper, Anthony Gibbons, Graham Kipling, Geoffrey Marshall, Lieutenant-Commander Ronald Matheson, Eric Peal, Ronald Peal, J. E. Richardson; Eric Shawyer and Daniel Stowell. Published accounts from the British viewpoint are in Cecil Brown, Gallagher and Middlebrook and Mahoney; the Japanese viewpoint is given by Toland, *Sun.*

For the Japanese in Malaya, see Tsuji. The growing fear among the Allied contingent is from Percival's Papers, File P 24, item 75, typescript narrative by Lt. Col. F. R. N. Cobley. Percival's comments on Heath and Bennett are from File P 21, Percival's notes on the *Official History.* Brooke-Popham's anger is from BP V/5/49, dated 24 December. Duff-Cooper's verdict on the commanders is from PREM 3/161/2, dated 18 December. "Rats and rice" is from BP V/11 letter to Ismay, 26 October, 1940. The civilian retreat in Malaya is in PREM 3/168/7A, typescript account by G. Morgan of 23 July, 1942. Mohan Singh is based on Lebra, Sivaram and an interview granted to the author by Mohan Singh at Bidadari Camp, Singapore, in September, 1945.

Shenton Thomas' reassessment of the Japanese is from PREM 3/161/2, letter to Sir C. Parkinson, 17 December. For Hong Kong (and in Chapter XII) I have drawn on the files PREM 3/157/1 and 2, and CO 129/588/12, on diaries by Barbara Anslow, Day Sage Joyce, Dr Isaac Newton and Mabel Redwood, and on published works by Bertram, Wenzell Brown, Bush, Carew, Dew, Field, Guest, Harrop, Lindsay, Marsman and Priestwood. Events in Manila and the Philippines (and in chapter XII) derive from studies by Agoncillo, Coville, Friend, Hatchitt, Huff, James, Long, Manchester, *Caesar,* Monoghan, Claire Phillips, Prising, Quezon, Redmond, Sayre, Van Landingham and Amea Willoughby.

Chapter Twelve: "Some Chicken! Some Neck!"

December on the Volga front is taken from accounts by Carell, *Hitler,* Haape, Irving, *War,* Kern and Turney. Hitler's blitzkrieg economy is analysed by Cecil, Milward and Noakes.

Churchill's visit to Washington is noted in the Nesbitt Papers, Box 12, diary entry for 22 December. Strategic disagreements are recorded by Burns and Pogue. The situation in Latin America is from the Hopkins' Papers, Boxes 141, 142 and 143, FBI reports on "*The Fifth Column in Latin America*"; for Argentina in particular, see also Bradford. The Malaya-Philippines argument is from the Arnold Papers, Box 180, *Conference File,* notes for 22 December. For Early to Rosenman, see Early Papers, Box 26, letter of 29 December. Other aspects of Churchill's trip are noted by Barkley, Harriman and Moran.

The bathroom conference is from Davis and Lindley, and Pawle.

BIBLIOGRAPHY
PRINTED SOURCES

Acheson, Dean, *Present At The Creation*, London: Hamish Hamilton, 1970.
Addison, Paul, *The Road to 1945*, London: Jonathan Cape, 1975.
Agar-Hamilton, J. A., *The Sidi Rezegh Battles*, London: Oxford University Press, 1957.
Agoncillo, Teodoro, *The Fateful Years*, Vol. 1, Quezon City, Philippines: R. P. Garcia, 1945.
Allan, James, *No Citation*, London: Angus and Robertson, 1955.
Allen, Gwenfread, *Hawaii's War Years*, Honolulu: University of Hawaii Press, 1945.
Allen, Louis, *Singapore, 1941–42*, London: Davis-Poynter, 1977.
Andersson, Ingvar, *A History of Sweden* (trans. Carolyn Hannay), London: Weidenfeld & Nicolson, 1956.
Andreas-Friedrich, Ruth, *Berlin Underground* (trans. Barrows Mussey), London: Latimer House, 1948.
Apps, Lieut-Cdr. Michael, *Send Her Victorious*, London: William Kimber, 1971.
Archer, Laird, *Balkan Journal*, New York: W. W. Norton, 1944.
Armstrong, H. F., *Tito and Goliath*, London: Victor Gollancz, 1951.
Arnold, Gen. H. H., *Global Mission*, London: Hutchinson, 1951.
Ash, Bernard, *Someone Had Blundered*, London: Michael Joseph, 1960.
Attiwill, Kenneth, *The Singapore Story*, London: Frederick Muller, 1959.
Auty, Phyllis, *Tito*, London: Longman, 1970.
Auty, Phyllis & Clogg, Richard (eds), *British Policy Towards Wartime Resistance in Yugoslavia and Greece*, London: Macmillan, 1975.
Bahnemann, Gunther, *I Deserted Rommel*, London: Jarrolds, 1961.
Bailey, Douglas, *We Built and Destroyed*, London: Hurst & Blackett, 1944.
Baker, Leonard, *Roosevelt and Pearl Harbor*, New York: Macmillan, 1970.
Baldwin, Hanson W., *The Crucial Years*, London: Weidenfeld & Nicolson, 1976.
Balfour, Michael, *Propaganda in War, 1939–45*, London: Routledge & Kegan Paul, 1979.
Balfour, Neil and Mackay, Sally, *Paul of Yugoslavia*, London: Hamish Hamilton, 1980.
Barber, Noel, *Sinister Twilight: the Fall and Rise Again of Singapore*, London: William Collins, 1968.
Barker, Elisabeth, *Churchill and Eden at War*, London: Macmillan, 1978; *British Policy in South-East Europe in the Second World War*, London: Macmillan, 1976.
Barker, Ralph, *Strike Hard, Strike Sure*, London: Chatto & Windus, 1963.
Barkley, Alben W., *That Reminds Me*, Garden City, N.Y.: Doubleday, 1954.
Barnes, Harry Elmer, *Pearl Harbor After a Quarter of a Century*. New York: Arno Press and the New York Times, 1962.
Barnett, Corelli, *The Desert Generals*, London: William Kimber, 1960.
Bartz, Karl, *Swastika In The Air*, London: William Kimber, 1956.
Baruch, Bernard, *The Public Years*, London: Odhams Press, 1960.
Bayler, Lt.-Col. Walter L. J. (with Cecil Carnes), *Last Man Off Wake Island*, Indianapolis: Bobbs Merrill, 1943.
Beard, Charles A., *President Roosevelt and the Coming of War*, New Haven: Yale University Press, 1948.
Beesly, Patrick, *Very Special Admiral*, London: Hamish Hamilton, 1980; *Very Special Intelligence*, London: Hamish Hamilton, 1977.

Bekker, Cajus, *The Luftwaffe War Diaries* (trans. Frank Ziegler), London: Macdonald, 1966; *Hitler's Naval War* (trans. Frank Ziegler), London: Macdonald, 1974.

Belchem, Maj.-Gen. David, *All In the Day's March*, London: William Collins, 1978.

Bellush, Bernard, *He Walked Alone*, The Hague: Mouton, 1968.

Belote, James, *Corregidor*, New York: Harper & Row, 1967.

Bennett, Lt.-Gen. H. Gordon. *Why Singapore Fell*. Bombay: Thacker, 1945.

Bennett, Geoffrey. *The Loss of the Prince of Wales and the Repulse*, London: Ian Allen, 1973.

Bergot, Erwan, *The Afrika Korps* (trans. Richard Barry), London: Allan Wingate, 1976.

Berle, Adolf, *Navigating the Rapids* (ed. Beatrice Bishop Berle and Travis Beale Jacobs), New York: Harcourt Brace Jovanovich, 1973.

Berthold, Will, *The Sinking of the Bismarck* (trans. Michael Bullock), London: Longman Green, 1958.

Bertram, James M., *The Shadow of a War*, London: Victor Gollancz, 1947.

Bess, Demaree, *Our Frontier on the Danube*, in the Saturday Evening Post, Philadelphia, 24 May, 1941.

Bethell, Nicholas, *The Palestine Triangle*, London: André Deutsch, 1979.

Bialer, Seweryn (ed.), *Stalin and His Generals*, London: Souvenir Press, 1970.

Bird, Lt.-Col. Eugene, *The Loneliest Man In The World*, London: Secker & Warburg, 1974.

Birkenhead, Earl of, *Halifax: The Life of Lord Halifax*, London: Hamish Hamilton, 1965.

Bloom, Sol, *The Autobiography of Sol Bloom*, New York: Putnams, 1948.

Blum, John Morton, *From the Morgenthau Diaries: Years of Urgency, 1938–41*, Boston: Houghton Mifflin, 1965.

Blumentritt, General Gunther, *Rundstedt, The Soldier and the Man* (trans. Cuthbert Reaveley), London: Odhams Press, 1952.

Bohlen, Charles, *Witness to History*, London: Weidenfeld & Nicolson, 1973.

Bokun, Branko, *Spy in the Vatican*, London: Tom Stacey, 1973.

Bölcke, Willi A. (ed.), *The Secret Conferences of Dr Goebbels*, 1939–43 (trans. Ewald Osers), London: Weidenfeld & Nicolson, 1970.

Bolitho, Hector, *A Penguin in the Eyrie*, London: Hutchinson, 1955.

Bond, Brian (ed.), *Chief of Staff: The Diaries of Lieutenant-General Sir Henry Pownall*, Vol. II, London: Leo Cooper, 1974.

Boothby, Lord, *Recollections of a Rebel*, London: Hutchinson, 1978.

Borg, Dorothy & Okamoto, Shumpei (with Dale, K. A. Finlayson), *Pearl Harbor as History*, New York: Columbia University Press, 1973.

Borodin, George, *Red Surgeon*, London: Museum Press, 1944.

Borrie, John, *Despite Captivity*, London: William Kimber, 1975.

Bourke-White, Margaret, *Shooting the Russian War*, New York: Simon & Schuster, 1943.

Bourne, Geoffrey H., *Starvation in Europe*, London: George Allen & Unwin, 1943.

Boyle, Andrew, *Trenchard*, London: Collins, 1962.

Bracher, Karl Dietrich, *The German Dictatorship* (trans. Jean Steinberg), London: Weidenfeld & Nicolson, 1971.

Braddon, Russell, *The Naked Island*, London: Werner Laurie, 1951.

Bradford, Ernle, *The Mighty Hood*, London: Hodder & Stoughton, 1959.

Brereton, Lt.-Gen. Lewis H., *The Brereton Diaries:* New York: William Morrow, 1946.

Brock, Ray, *Nor Any Victory*, New York: Reynal & Hitchcock, 1942.

Broome, Capt Jack, R. N., *Make a Signal!* London: Putman, 1955.

Brown, Cecil B., *Suez to Singapore*, New York: Random House, 1942.

Brown, Wenzell, *Hong Kong Aftermath*, New York: Smith & Durrell, 1943.

Brownlow, Donald G., *The Accused: The Ordeal of Admiral Kimmel*, New York: Vantage Press, 1968.

Bryant, Sir Arthur, *The Turn of the Tide: The Alanbrooke Diaries*, London: William Collins, 1957.

Buchanan, A. Russell, *The United States and World War Two*, Vol. I, New York: Harper & Row, 1964.

Buckley, Christopher, *Five Ventures*, London: H.M.S.O., 1954; *Greece and Crete*, London: H.M.S.O., 1952.

Buell, Thomas, *The Quiet Warrior*, Boston: Little Brown, 1974.

Bulcock, Roy, *Of Death But Once*, Melbourne: F. W. Cheshire Pty Ltd., 1947.

Bullock, Alan, *The Life and Times of Ernest Bevin*, Vol. II, London: Heinemann, 1967; *Hitler*, London: Odhams Press, edn. of 1965.

Burns, Eugene, *Then There was One*, New York: Harcourt Brace, 1944.

Burns, James McGregor, *Roosevelt, The Soldier of Freedom*, London: Weidenfeld & Nicolson, 1971.

Burridge, Trevor, *British Labour and Hitler's war*, London: André Deutsch, 1976.

Burtness, Paoul S. (& Oder, Warren W.), *The Puzzle of Pearl Harbor*, Evanston, Ill.: Row, Peterson, 1962.

Busch, Fritz-Otto, *The Story of the Prinz Eugen* (trans. Eleanor Brockett), London: Robert Hale, 1960.

Bush, Lewis, *The Road to Inamura*, London: Robert Hale, 1961.

Butow, Robert J. C., *Tojo and the Coming of the War*, Princeton, N.J.: Princeton University Press, 1961.

Cadogan, Sir Alexander. *The Diaries* (ed. David Dilks), London: Cassell, 1971.

Caffrey, Kate, *Out in the Mid-Day Sun*, London: André Deutsch, 1974.

Cain, Lt.-Cdr. T. J. and Sellwood, A. V., *H.M.S. Electra*, London: Frederick Muller, 1959.

Calder, Angus, *The People's War*, London: Jonathan Cape, 1969.

Caldwell, Erskine, *Moscow Under Fire*, London: Hutchinson, 1942.

Cameron, Ian, *Red Duster, White Ensign*, London: Frederick Muller, 1959.

Carell, Paul, *Hitler's War on Russia* (trans. Ewald Osers), London: George Harrap, 1964; *The Foxes of the Desert* (trans. Mervyn Savill), New York: E. P. Dutton, 1961.

Carew, Tim, *The Fall of Hong Kong*, London: Anthony Blond, 1960.

Carlgren, W. M., *Swedish Foreign Policy During the Second World War* (trans. Arthur Spencer), London: Ernest Benn, 1977.

Carroll, Joseph T., *Ireland in the War Years*, New York: Crane Russak, 1975.

Casey, Lord, *Personal Experience*, London: Constable, 1962.

Casey, Robert J., *Torpedo Junction*, London: Jarrolds, 1944.

Cassidy, Henry C., *Moscow Dateline, 1941–3*, London: Cassell, 1943.

Cazalet, Victor, *With Sikorski to Russia*, London: The Curwen Press, 1942.

Cecil, Robert, *Hitler's Decision to Invade Russia*, London: Davis Poynter, 1975.

Cervi, Mario, *The Hollow Legions* (trans. Eric Mosbacher), London: Chatto & Windus, 1972.

Chadwin, Mark, *The Hawks of World War Two*, Chapel Hill, N.C.: University of North Carolina Press, 1968.

Chandos, Lord, *Memoirs*, London: The Bodley Head, 1962.

Channon, Sir Henry, *Chips, the Diaries of Sir Henry Channon* (ed. Robert Rhodes James), London: Weidenfeld & Nicolson, 1967.

Childs, Marquis W., *The President's Best Friend*, in The Saturday Evening Post, Philadelphia, April 19–26, 1941.

Churchill, Sir Winston S., *The Second World War*, Vol. III, *The Grand Alliance*, London: Cassell, 1950.

Ciano, Count Galeazzo, *The Ciano Diaries, 1939–43* (ed. Hugh Gibson), New York: Doubleday, 1946.

Ciano's Diplomatic Papers (ed. Malcolm Muggeridge, trans. Stuart Hood), London: Odham's Press, 1948.

Ciechanowski, Jan, *Defeat in Victory*, London: Victor Gollancz, 1947.

Clark, Alan, *The Fall of Crete*, London: Anthony Blond, 1962.

Clark, Blake, Remember Pearl Harbor, New York: Harper, 1942.

Clark, Ronald, *The Man Who Broke Purple*, London: Weidenfeld & Nicolson, 1977.

Clifford, Alexander, *Three Against Rommel*, London: George Harrap, 1943; *Crusader*, London: George Harrap, 1942.

Clissold, Stephen, *Whirlwind: An Account of Marshal Tito's Rise to Power*, London: The Cresset Press, 1949; (ed.), *Yugoslavia and the Soviet Union, 1939–73*, London: Oxford University Press, 1975.

Coffey, Thomas M., *Imperial Tragedy*, New York: Pinnacle Books, 1970.

Coit, Margaret L., *Mr. Baruch*, London: Victor Gollancz, 1958.

283

Colaković, Rodoljub, *Winning Freedom* (trans. Alec Brown), London: Lincolns-Prager, 1962
Collier, Richard, *The City That Wouldn't Die*, London: William Collins, 1960; *Duce!* London: William Collins, 1971; *The War in the Desert*, Alexandria, Va; Time-Life Books, 1977.
Collis, Maurice, *Last and First in Burma*, London: Faber & Faber, 1956.
Colville, Sir John, *Footprints in Time*, London: William Collins, 1976.
Comeau, Marcel, *Operation Mercury*, London: William Kimber, 1961.
Compton, James V., *The Swastika and the Eagle*, London: The Bodley Head, 1968.
Connell, John, *Wavell: Scholar and Soldier*, London: William Collins, 1964; (with Michael Roberts), *Wavell: Supreme Commander*: London: William Collins, 1969; *Auchinleck*, London: Cassell, 1959.
Cooke, Colin, *The Life of Richard Stafford Cripps*, London: Hodder & Stoughton, 1957.
Cookridge, E. H., *Gehlen, Spy of the Century*, London: Hodder & Stoughton, 1971; *Inside S.O.E.*, London: Arthur Barker, 1966.
Cooper, Diana, *Trumpets from The Steep*, London: Rupert Hart-Davis, 1969.
Cooper, Page, *Navy Nurse*, New York: McGraw-Hill, 1946.
Costello, John and Hughes, Terry, *The Battle of the Atlantic*, London: William Collins, 1977.
Craigie, Sir Robert, *Behind the Japanese Mask*, London: Hutchinson, 1946.
Crawley, Aidan, *De Gaulle*, London: William Collins, 1969.
Crimp, R. L., *The Diary of a Desert Rat* (ed. Alex Bowlby), London: Leo Cooper, 1971.
Crisp, Robert, *Brazen Chariots*, London: Frederick Muller, 1959; *The Gods were Neutral*, London: Frederick Muller, 1960.
Crozier, Brian, *Franco*, London: Eyre & Spottiswoode, 1967; *The Man Who Lost China*, London: Angus & Robertson, 1977.
Crozier, William, *Off the Record* (ed. A. J. P. Taylor), London: Hutchinson, 1973.
Cruikshank, Charles, *Deception in World War Two*, Oxford: Oxford University Press, 1979.
Cunningham of Hyndhope, Admiral of the Fleet, Lord, *A Sailor's Odyssey*, London: Hutchinson, 1951.
Cunningham, W. Scott (with Lydel Sims), *Wake Island Command*, Boston: Little Brown, 1961.
Current, Richard, *Secretary Stimson*, New Brunswick, N.J.: Rutgers University Press, 1954.
Czapski, Joseph, *The Inhuman Land* (trans. Gerard Hopkins), New York: Sheed & Ward, 1962.
D'Albas, Andrieu, *Death of a Navy* (trans. Anthony Rippon), London: Robert Hale, 1957.
Dallin, Alexander, *German Rule In Russia, 1941–4*, London: Macmillan, 1957.
Dallin, David J., *Soviet Russia's Foreign Policy, 1939–1942*, New Haven, Conn.: Yale University Press, 1943.
Dangerfield, Elma, *Beyond the Urals*, London: British League for European Freedom, 1946.
Darling, Donald, *Secret Sunday*, London: William Kimber, 1975.
Dawidowicz, Lucy S., *The War Against the Jews, 1939–45*, London: Weidenfeld & Nicolson, 1975.
Davies, Joseph E., *Mission to Moscow*, London: Victor Gollancz, 1942.
Davin, D. M., *Crete*, Wellington, N.Z.: Departmental of Internal Affairs, War History Branch, 1953.
Davis, Forrest and Lindley, Ernest K., *How War Came to America*, London: George Allen & Unwin, 1943.
Davis, Kenneth S., *The American Experience of War*, London: Secker & Warburg, 1967.
Dawson, Raymond H., *The Decision to aid Russia*, Chapel Hill, N.C., University of North Carolina Press, 1959.
Deakin, F. W. (with G. W. Storry), *The Case of Richard Sorge*, London: Chatto & Windus, 1966.
Dedijer, Vladimir, *With Tito Through the War*, London: Alexander Hamilton, 1951; *Tito Speaks*, London: Weidenfeld & Nicolson, 1953.

De Guingand, Maj.-Gen. Sir Francis, *Generals At War*, London: Hodder & Stoughton, 1964.
Demianova, Genia, *Comrade Genia*, London: Nicolson & Watson, 1941.
Devereux, Brig.-Gen. James P.S., *Wake Island* (revised edn), Canoga Park, Calif.: Major Books, 1978.
DeVilliers, Catherine, *Lieutenant Katia* (trans. Charlotte Haldane), London: Constable, 1964.
Devins, Joseph H. Jr., *The Vaagso Raid*, London: Robert Hale, 1967.
Dew, Gwen, *Prisoner of the Japs*, London: Hutchinson, 1944.
Dickinson, Clarence, *The Flying Guns*, New York: Charles Scribner, 1943.
Dimbleby, Richard, *The Frontiers are Green*, London: Hodder & Stoughton, 1943.
Divine, Robert A., *The Reluctant Belligerent: American Entry into World War Two*, New York: John Wiley, 1965.
Dixon, Cecil and Helibrunn, Otto, *Communist Guerilla Warfare*, London: George Allen & Unwin, 1954.
Dixon, Pierson J., *Double Diploma*, London: Hutchinson, 1968.
Djilas, Milovan, *Wartime* (trans. Michael B. Petrovich), London: Secker & Warburg, 1977.
Documents on British Foreign Policy, London: H.M.S.O., 1946 –
Documents on German Foreign Policy, London: H.M.S.O., 1948 –
I Documenti Diplomatici Italiani, Rome: Ministero degli Esteri, 1952.
Dönitz, Admiral Karl, *Memoirs: Ten Years and Twenty Days* (trans. R. H. Stevens and David Woodward), London: Weidenfeld & Nicolson, 1951.
Douglas-Hamilton, James, *Motive for a Mission*, Edinburgh: Mainstream Books, 1979.
Douglas of Kirtleside, Lord Marshal of the R.A.F. (with Robert Wright), *Combat and Command*, New York: Simon & Schuster, 1966.
Dulles, John W. F., *Vargas of Brazil*, Austin, Texas: University of Texas Press, 1967.
Durnford-Slater, Brigadier John, *Commando*, London: William Kimber, 1953.
Eden, Rt. Hon. Anthony (Lord Avon), *Memoirs, Vol II; The Reckoning*, London: Cassell, 1965.
Edmonds, Walter D., *What Happened at Clark Field*, in The Atlantic Monthly, Boston, July, 1951.
Ehrlich, Blake, *The French Resistance*, London: Chapman & Hall, 1966.
Elvin, Harold, *A Cockney in Moscow*, London: The Cresset Press, 1958.
Engel, Gerhard, *Heeresadjutant bei Hitler, 1938–43*, Stuttgart: Deutsche Verlags-Anstalt, 1974.
Ericson, John, *The Road to Stalingrad*, London: Weidenfeld & Nicolson, 1975.
Esebeck, Hans Gertt von, *Afrikanische Schicksaljahre, 1941–43*, Wiesbaden: Limes Verlag, 1949.
Falk, Stanley, *Seventy Days to Singapore*, London: Robert Hale, 1975.
Farago, Ladislas, *The Broken Seal*, London: Arthur Barker, 1967; *The Game of the Foxes*, London: Hodder & Stoughton, 1972.
Farran, Roy, *Winged Dagger*, London: William Collins, 1948.
Fearnside, G. H., *Sojourn in Tobruk*, Sydney: Rue Smith Pty Ltd., 1944.
Fehrenbach, T. R., *F.D.R.'s Undeclared War*, New York: David McKay, 1967.
Feis, Herbert, *The China Tangle*, Princeton, N.J.: Princeton University Press, 1953; *Churchill-Roosevelt-Stalin*, Princeton, N.J.: Princeton University Press, 1957; *The Road to Pearl Harbor*, Princeton, N.J.: Princeton University Press, 1950.
Fenyo, Mario D., *Hitler, Horthy and Hungary*, New Haven, Conn.: Yale University Press, 1972.
Fergusson, Bernard, *The Watery Maze*, London: William Collins, 1961; *The Black Watch and the King's Enemies*, London, William Collins, 1950; *The Trumpet in the Hall*, London: William Collins, 1970.
Fest, Joachim, *Hitler* (trans. Richard and Clara Winston), London: Weidenfeld & Nicolson, 1974.
Field, Ellen, *Twilight in Hong Kong*, London: Frederick Muller, 1960.
Fielding, Sean, *They Sought Rommel*, London: H.M.S.O., 1942.
Foot, M. R. D., *Resistance*, London: Eyre Methuen, 1976; and Langley, J. M. *M19*, London: The Bodley Head, 1979.

Ford, Corey, *Donovan of O.S.S.*, London: Robert Hale, 1971.

Foreign Relations of the United States (7 vols), Washington, D.C.: U.S. Government Printing Office, 1956–62.

Forgy, Howell, M., *And Pass the Ammunition*, New York: D. Appleton-Century Co., 1944.

Fotitch, Constantin, *The War We Lost*, New York: Viking Press, 1948.

Fox, Barry, *That Day of Pearl Harbor*, in Harper's Magazine, New York, January, 1943.

Frank, Wolfgang, *The Sea Wolves* (trans. Lt.-Cdr. R. O. B. Long, RNVR), London: Weidenfeld & Nicolson, 1958.

Frankland, Noble, *The Bombing Offensive Against Germany*, London: Faber & Faber, 1965.

Franklin, Alan and Gordon, *One Year of Life: The Story of H.M.S. Prince of Wales*, Edinburgh: William Blackwood, 1944.

Fredborg, Arvid, *Behind the Steel Wall*, London: George Harrap, 1944.

Freedman, Max (ed.), *Roosevelt and Frankfurter*, London: The Bodley Head, 1968.

Freiden, Seymour and Richardson, William (ed.), *The Fatal Decisions*, New York: William Sloane, 1956.

Friedlander, Saul, *Prelude to Downfall: Germany and the United States, 1939–41*, New York: Alfred Knopf, 1967.

Friend, Theodore, *Between Two Empires: Ordeal of the Philippines, 1929–46*, New Haven, Conn.: Yale University Press, 1965.

Frischauer, Willi, *Himmler*, London: Odhams Press, 1953.

Frye, Alton, *Nazi Germany and the American Hemisphere, 1933–41*, New Haven, Conn.: Yale University Press, 1967.

Fuchida Mitsuo, *I led the Air Attack on Pearl Harbor*, in United States Naval Institute Proceedings, Annapolis, Md., September, 1952.

Gafencu, Grigore, *Prelude to the Russian Campaign* (trans. E. Fletcher-Allen), London: Frederick Muller, 1945.

Gallagher, O. D., *Retreat in the East*, London: Harrap, 1942.

Garner, Joe, *The Commonwealth Office*, London: William Heinemann, 1978.

Gaulle, Gen. Charles de, *The Call to Honour, 1940–42* (trans. Jonathan Griffin), London: William Collins, 1955.

Gellhorn, Martha, *Travels with Myself and Another*, London: Allen Lane, 1978.

Geve, Thomas, *Youth in Chains*, Jerusalem: Rubin Mass., 1958.

Gilbert, Martin, *Final Journey*, London: Allen & Unwin, 1979.

Gilmour, O. W., *Singapore to Freedom*, London: E. J. Burrows, 1943.

Glover, Edwin, *In Seventy Days*, London: Frederick Muller, 1946.

Goldstein, Bernard, *The Stars Bear Witness* (trans. & ed. Leonard Shatzkin), London: Victor Gollancz, 1950.

Görlitz, Walter, *Paulus and Stalingrad* (trans. R. H. Stevens), London: Methuen, 1963.

Goure, Leon, *The Siege of Leningrad*, Stanford, Calif.: Stanford University Press, 1963.

Grenfell, Russell, *Main Fleet to Singapore*, London: Faber & Faber, 1951; *The Bismarck Episode*, London: Faber & Faber, 1948.

Grew, Joseph C., *Turbulent Era, Vol. II*, London: Hammond & Hammond, 1953.

Guderian, Gen. Heinz, *Panzer Leader* (trans. Constantine Fitzgibbon), London: Michael Joseph, 1952.

Guest, Freddie, *Escape From the Bloodied Sun*, London: Jarrolds, 1956.

Haape, Heinrich (with Dennis Hinshaw), *Moscow Tram Stop*, London: William Collins, 1957.

Hahn, Emily, *China To Me*, Garden City, N.Y. Doubleday, Doran, 1945.

Haldane, Charlotte, *Russian Newsreel*, London: Secker & Warburg, 1942.

Halder, Gen. Franz, *War Diaries*, Vols V–VII, Washington, D.C.: Infantry Journal Press, 1950.

Hamilton, Thomas, *Soldier Surgeon in Malaya*, Sydney: Angus & Robertson, 1958.

Hancock, Sir William K., *Smuts: The Fields of Force, 1919–50*, Cambridge: The University Press, 1968.

Hansson, Per., *The Greatest Gamble* (trans. Martin Michael), London: George Allen & Unwin, 1967.

286

Harriman, W., Averell and Abel, Elie, *Special Envoy to Churchill and Stalin, 1941–46*, London: Hutchinson, 1976.
Harrisson, Tom, *Living Through the Blitz*, London: William Collins, 1976.
Harrop, Phyllis, *Hong Kong Incident*, London: Eyre & Spottiswoode, 1943.
Hart, Capt. B. H. Liddell, *The Tanks*, Vol. II, London: Cassell, 1959.
Harvey, Oliver, *The War Diaries* (ed. John Harvey), London: William Collins, 1978.
Hasluck, Paul, *The Government and the People, Vol I*, Canberra: Australian War Memorial, 1952.
Hassell, Ulrich von, *The Von Hassell Diaries, 1938–44*, London: Hamish Hamilton, 1948.
Hastings, Max, *Bomber Command*, London: Michael Joseph, 1979.
Hatchitt, Eunice C., *Bataan Nurse*, in Collier's, New York, 1 August, 1942.
Heckstall-Smith, Anthony, *Tobruk*, London: Anthony Blond, 1957; (with Vice-Admiral H. T. Baillie-Grohman), *Greek Tragedy*, London: Anthony Blond, 1961.
Hemingway, Ernest, *By-line* (ed. William White), New York: Charles Scribner, 1967.
Hersey, John, *Men on Bataan*, New York: Alfred A. Knopf, 1943.
Hess, Rudolf and Ilse, *Prisoner of Peace* (trans. Meyrick Booth, ed. George Piti.), London: Britons Publishing Co., 1954.
Hesse, Fritz, *Hitler and the English* (ed. & trans. F. A. Voigt), London: Allan Wingate, 1954.
Heydte, Baron Friedrich von der, *Daedalus Returned* (trans. W. Stanley Moss), London: Hutchinson, 1958.
Higgins, Trumbull, *Hitler and Russia*, New York: The Macmillan Co., 1966.
Hilberg, Raul, *The Destruction of the European Jews*, London: W. H. Allen, 1961.
Hilger, Gustav and Meyer, Alfred G., *The Incompatible Allies*, New York: Macmillan, 1953.
Hill, Russell, *Desert War, 1941–42*, London: Jarrolds, 1943.
Hill-Rennie, Melville C (with Allan A. Michie), *Parachutes Coming Down*, in Harper's Magazine, New York, January, 1942.
Hillgruber, Andreas, *Staatsmänner und Diplomaten bei Hitler* (2 vols), Frankfurt-am-Main: Bernard & Graefe, 1967–70.
Hinshaw, David, *The Home Front*, New York: Putnam, 1943.
Hinsley, F. H. (with Thomas, E. E., Ransom, C. F. G. & Knight, R. C.), *British Intelligence in the Second World War*, Vol. I, London: H.M.S.O., 1979; *Hitler's Strategy*, Cambridge: Cambridge University Press, 1951.
Hirszowicz, Lukasz, *The Third Reich and the Arab East*, London: Routledge & Kegan Paul, 1966.
Hitler, Adolf, *The Testament of Adolf Hitler* (trans. R. H. Stevens, ed. Francois Genoud), London: Cassell, 1961; *Table Talk* (trans. Norman Cameron & R. H. Stevens), London: Weidenfeld & Nicolson, 1953.
Hoare, Sir Samuel, *Ambassador on Special Mission*, London: William Collins, 1946.
Hoehling, A. A., *The Week Before Pearl Harbor*, London: Robert Hale, 1964.
Hoess, Rudolf, *Commandant of Auschwitz* (trans. Constantine Fitzgibbon), London: Weidenfeld & Nicolson, 1951.
Hoffman, Peter, *The History of the German Resistance*, 1933–45 (trans. Richard Barry), London: Macdonald & Janes, 1977.
Höhne, Heinz, *Codeword: Direktor* (trans. Richard Barry), London: Secker & Warburg, 1971; *The Order of the Death's Head* (trans. Richard Barry), London: Secker & Warburg. 1969.
Hollingworth, Clare, *There's a German just behind me*, London: The Right Book Club, 1943.
Hollis, Lt.-Gen. Sir Leslie and Leasor, James, *War At The Top*, London: Michael Joseph, 1959.
Hoptner, J. R., *Yugoslavia in Crisis, 1934–41*, New York: Columbia University Press, 1962.
Horthy, Admiral Nicolas, *Memoirs*, London: Hutchinson, 1956.
Hotz, Robert B., *With General Chennault: The Story of the Flying Tigers*, New York: Coward-McCann, 1943.
Hough, Frank O., Verde E. Ludwig and Henry I. Shaw, Jr., *Pearl Harbor to Guadalcanal*, Washington, D.C.: U.S. Marine Corps Historical Branch, 1958.
Hourmouzios, S. L., *Starvation in Greece*, London: Harrison, 1943.

Huff, Sidney L. (with Joe Alex Morris), *My Fifteen Years with General MacArthur*, Philadelphia: Curtis Publishing Co., 1964.

Hull, Cordell, *Memoirs, Vol. II*, London: Hodder & Stoughton, 1948.

Hunt, Frazier, *The Untold Story of Douglas MacArthur*, London: Robert Hale, 1954.

Huss, Pierre, *Heil! And Farewell*, London: Herbert Jenkins, 1943.

Hutton, G. Bernard, *Hess: The Man and His Mission*, London: David Bruce & Watson, 1970.

Ickes, Harold, *The Secret Diary of Harold Ickes, Vol. III: The Lowering Clouds*, London: Weidenfeld & Nicolson, 1955.

Idriess, Ion L., *Horrie The Wog-Dog*, Sydney, N.S.W.: Angus & Robertson, 1945.

Ike, Nobutaka (ed.), *Japan's Decision for War*, Stanford, Cal.: Stanford University Press, 1967.

Inber, Vera, *Leningrad Diary* (trans. Serge M. Wolff and Rachel Grive), London: Hutchinson, 1971.

Ind, Lt.-Col. Allison, *Bataan: The Judgement Seat*, New York: Macmillan, 1944.

Irving, David, *The Trail of the Fox*, London: Weidenfeld & Nicolson, 1977; *The Rise and Fall of the Luftwaffe*, London: Weidenfeld & Nicolson, 1974; *Hitler's War*, London: Hodder & Stoughton, 1977.

Ismay, Lord, *Memoirs*, London: William Heinemann, 1961.

Jacob, Alaric, *A Traveller's War*, London: William Collins, 1944.

Jacobsen, Dr Hans-Adolf and Rohwer, Dr Jürgen, *Decisive Battles of World War Two: The German View* (trans. Edward Fitzgerald), London: André Deutsch, 1965.

James, D. Clayton, *The Years of MacArthur*, Vols I & II, London: Leo Cooper, 1970.

Jameson, William, *Ark Royal, 1939–41*, London: Rupert Hart-Davis, 1957.

Johnen, Wilhelm, *Duel Under the Stars* (trans. Mervyn Savill), London: William Kimber, 1957.

Jonas, Manfred, *Isolationism in America*, Ithaca, N.Y.: Cornell Press, 1966.

Jones, Prof. R. V., *Most Secret War*, London: Hamish Hamilton, 1978.

Jordan, Philip, *Russian Glory*, London: Cresset Press, 1942.

Jovićić, Lena, *Within Closed Frontiers*, London: W & R Chambers, 1956.

Kahn, David, *Hitler's Spies*, London: Hodder & Stoughton, 1978; *The Code Breakers*, London: Weidenfeld & Nicolson, 1966.

Kallay, Nicholas, *Hungarian Premier*, New York: Columbia University Press, 1954.

Kamenetsky, Ihor, *Hitler's Occupation of the Ukraine*, Milwaukee, Wis.: The Marquette University Press, 1960.

Kapetanović, Nicola, *Tito and his Partisans*, Belgrade: Jugosolvenska Knijiga, 1953.

Karig, Walter and Kelley, Wellbourne, *Battle Report: Pearl Harbor to Coral Sea*, New York: Farrar & Rinehart, 1944.

Kase, Toshikazu, *Eclipse of the Rising Sun* (ed. David Nelson Rowe), London: Jonathan Cape, 1951.

Kato, Masuo, *The Lost War*, New York: Alfred Knopf, 1946.

Kedward, H. R., *The Resistance in Vichy France*, London: Oxford University Press, 1978.

Keitel, Field Marshal Wilhelm, *Memoirs* (trans. David Irving), London: William Kimber, 1965.

Kennan, George, *Memoirs*, 1925–50, London: Hutchinson, 1968.

Kennedy, Major-Gen. Sir John, *The Business of War*, London: Hutchinson, 1951.

Kennedy, Ludovic, *Sub-Lieutenant*, London: Batsford, 1942; *Pursuit: The Chase and Sinking of the Bismarck*, London: William Collins, 1974.

Kenney, Gen. George C., *The MacArthur I Know*, New York: Duell, Sloane & Pearce, 1951.

Kern, Erich, *Dance of Death* (trans. Paul Findlay), London: William Collins, 1951.

Kesselring, Field-Marshal Albert, *Memoirs* (trans. Lynton Hudson), London: William Kimber, 1953.

Killearn Diaries, The (ed. Trefor E. Evans), London: Sidgwick & Jackson, 1972.

Kimche, Jon, *Spying for Peace*, London: Weidenfeld & Nicolson, 1961.

Kimmel, Admiral Husband E., *Admiral Kimmel's Story*, Chicago: Henry Regnery, 1955.

King, Cecil, *With Malice Toward None* (ed. William Armstrong), London: Sidgwick & Jackson, 1970.

King, Ernest J., and Whitehill, Walter M., *Fleet Admiral King*, London: Eyre & Spottiswoode, 1953.

Kingscote, Flavia, *Balkan Exit*, London: Geoffrey Bles, 1942.

Kippenberger, Gen. Sir Howard, *Infantry Brigadier*, London: Oxford University Press, 1949.

Kirby, Stanley W., *Singapore: The Chain of Disaster*, London: Cassell, 1971.

Kirkbride, Sir Alec Sleath, *A Crackle of Thorns*, London: John Murray, 1956.

Kirkpatrick, Sir Ivone, *The Inner Circle*, London: Macmillan, 1959.

Knatchbull-Hugessen, Sir Hughe, *Diplomat in Peace and War*, London: John Murray, 1949.

Knight, Frida, *The French Resistance, 1940–44*, London: Lawrence and Wishart, 1975.

Kot, Stanislaw, *Conversations with the Kremlin and Dispatches from Russia* (trans. & arranged by H. C. Stevens), London: Oxford University Press, 1963.

Kraus René, *Europe in Revolt*, London: Jarrolds, 1943.

Krausnick, Helmut; Buckheim, Hans; Broszat, Martin and Jacobsen, Hans-Adolf, *Anatomy of the S.S. State* (trans. Richard Barry, Marian Jackson and Dorothy Long), London: William Collins, 1968.

Krock, Arthur, *Memoirs*, London: Cassell, 1970.

Kuzin, Ilya, *Notes of a Guerilla Fighter*, London: Hutchinson, 1943.

Langer, Lawrence, *Our Vichy Gamble*, New York: Alfred Knopf, 1947.

Langer, William L. and Gleason, S. E., *The Undeclared War*, London: Royal Institute of International Affairs, 1953.

Langley, J. M., *Fight Another Day*, London: William Collins, 1974.

Laqueur, Walter, *Russia and Germany: A Century of Conflict*, Boston: Little Brown, 1965.

Lash, Joseph P., *Eleanor and Franklin*, London: André Deutsch, 1972; *Roosevelt and Churchill, 1939–41*, London: André Deutsch, 1977.

Leach, Barry, *German Strategy Against Russia, 1939–41*, Oxford: Clarendon Press, 1973.

Leahy, Adm. William, *I Was There*, London: Victor Gollancz, 1950.

Leasor, James, *Rudolf Hess, the Uninvited Envoy*, London: Allen & Unwin, 1962.

Lebra, Joyce, *Jungle Alliance*, Singapore: Asia Pacific Press, 1971.

Lee, Clark, *They Call it Pacific*, London: John Long, 1943.

Lee, Gen. Raymond E., *The London Observer* (ed. James Leutze), London: Hutchinson, 1972.

Legg, Frank, *The Gordon Bennett Story*, Sydney: Angus & Robertson, 1965.

Leith-Ross, Sir Frederick, *Money Talks*, London: Hutchinson, 1968.

Lenczowski, George, *Russia and the West in Iran, 1918–48*, Ithaca, N.Y.: Cornell University Press, 1949.

Lesueur, Larry, *Twelve Months that Changed the World*, London: George Harrap, 1944.

Lewin, Ronald, *The Life and Death of the Afrika Korps*, London: Batsford, 1977; *Ultra Goes to War*, London: Hutchinson, 1978.

Lindsay, Oliver, *The Lasting Honour*, London: Hamish Hamilton, 1978.

Loewenheim, Francis L., Langley, Harold D., and Jonas, Manfred, *Roosevelt and Churchill: Their Secret Wartime Correspondence*, London: Barrie & Jenkins, 1975.

Lombard, Helen, *While They Fought*, New York: Charles Scribner, 1947.

Long, Gavin, *MacArthur as Military Commander*, London: B. T. Batsford, 1969; *To Benghazi*, Canberra: Australian War Memorial, 1952; *Greece, Crete and Syria*, Canberra: Australian War Memorial, 1953.

Long, Breckinridge, *The War Diary* (ed. Fred L. Israel), Lincoln, Neb: University of Nebraska Press, 1966.

Longmate, Norman, *How We Lived Then*, London: Hutchinson, 1971.

Lord, Walter, *Day of Infamy*, London: Longmans, 1957.

Louis, William Roger, *Imperialism At Bay: the United States and the Decolonisation of the British Empire, 1941–1945*, London: Oxford University Press, 1978.

Lu, David J., *From the Marco Polo Bridge to Pearl Harbor*, Washington, D.C.: Public Affairs Press, 1961.

Lucas, James, *Panzer Army Africa*, London: Macdonald & Jane's, 1977.

Luff, John, *The Hidden Years*, Hong Kong: South China Morning Post, 1967.

Lukacs, John, *The Last European War, September, 1939 – December, 1941*, London: Routledge & Kegan Paul, 1976.

Macdonald, Alexander, *Revolt in Paradise*, New York: Stephen Daye, 1944.

Macksey, Kenneth, *Kesselring: The Making of the Luftwaffe*, London: Batsford, 1978; *Afrika Korps*, London: Macdonald, 1968; *Guderian*, London: Macdonald & Jane's, 1975; *The Partisans of Europe in World War Two*, London: Hart-Davis, Macgibbon, 1975.

Maclean, Fitzroy, *Disputed Barricade*, London: Jonathan Cape, 1957.

MacMillan, Richard, *Mediterranean Assignment*, New York: Doubleday Doran, 1943.

Macmurtrie, F. E., *The Cruise of the Bismarck*, London: Hutchinson, 1942.

Maisky, Ivan, *Memoirs of a Soviet Ambassador*, 1939–43, London: Hutchinson, 1967.

Maitland, Patrick, *European Dateline*, London: The Quality Press, 1946.

Malaparte, Curzio, *The Volga Rises in Europe* (trans. David Moore), London: Alvin Redman, 1957.

Malay, Armando J., *Occupied Philippines*, Manila: Filipiniana Book Guild, 1967.

Manchester, William, *The Glory and the Dream*, London: Michael Joseph, 1975; *American Caesar*, Boston: Little Brown, 1978.

Manstein, Field-Marshal Erich von, *Lost Victories* (ed. & trans. Anthony G. Powell), London: Methuen, 1958.

Marchal, Léon, *Vichy: Two Years of Deception*, New York: Macmillan, 1943.

Marsman, Jan Hendrik, *I escaped from Hong Kong*, Sydney, N.S.W., Angus & Robertson, 1943.

Martin, David, *Ally Betrayed: The Uncensored Story of Tito and Mihailović*, London: W. H. Allen, 1946.

Masters, Anthony, *The Summer That Bled*, London: Michael Joseph, 1972.

Matloff, Maurice & Snell Edwin M., *Strategic Planning for Coalition Warfare, 1941–1947*, Washington, D.C.: Office of the Chief of Military History, 1953.

Maugham, Robin, *Come to Dust*, London: Chapman & Hall, 1945.

Maule, Henry, *Spearhead General*, London: Odham's Press, 1961.

McLachlan, Donald, *Room 39*, London: Weidenfeld & Nicolson, 1968.

McLaine, Ian, *Ministry of Morale*, London: George Allen & Unwin, 1979.

McNeill, W. H., *America, Britain and Russia*, London: Oxford University Press (for the Royal Institute of International Affairs), 1953.

Meissner, Hans-Otto, *The Man with Three Faces*, London: Evans Bros., 1955.

Mellenthin, Maj.-Gen. F. W. von, *Panzer Battles* (trans. H. Betzler), London: Cassell, 1955.

Meskill, Johanna, *Hitler and Japan*, New York: Atherton, 1966.

Metzler, Jost, *The Laughing Cow* (trans. Mervyn Savill), London: William Kimber, 1955.

Michel, Henri, *The Shadow War* (trans. Richard Barry), London: André Deutsch, 1972.

Michie, Allan, *Retreat to Victory*, London: Allen & Unwin, 1942.

Middlebrook, Martin and Mahoney, Patrick, *Battleship: The Loss of the Prince of Wales and the Repulse*, London: Allen Lane, 1977.

Milazzo, Matteo, *The Chetnik Movement and the Yugoslav Resistance*, Baltimore, Md Johns Hopkins University Press, 1975.

Miller, Ernest, *Bataan Uncensored*, Long Prairie, Minn: The Hart Publications Inc., 1949.

Millis, Walter, *This is Pearl*, New York: William Morrow, 1947.

Milward, Alan S., *The Germany Economy at War*, London: Athlone Press, 1965.

Mitchell, Ruth, *The Serbs Choose War*, Garden City, N.Y.: Doubleday Doran, 1943.

Mockler, Anthony, *Our Enemies the French*, London: Leo Cooper, 1976.

Moffat, Jay Pierrepoint, *The Moffat Papers* (ed. Nancy Harvison Hooker), Cambridge, Mass: Harvard University Press, 1956.

Monaghan, Forbes, *Under the Red Sun*, New York: The Declan X, McMullen Co., 1946.

Montagu, Ewan, *Beyond Top Secret U*, London: Peter Davies, 1977.

Moorehead, Alan, *African Trilogy*, London: Hamish Hamilton, 1944.

Moran, Lord, *Winston Churchill: The Struggle for Survival*, 1940–65, London: Constable, 1966.

Morison, Elting E., *Turmoil and Tradition*, Boston: Houghton Mifflin, 1960.

Morison, Samuel Eliot, *The Rising Sun in the Pacific*, Boston: Little Brown, 1948; *The Battle of the Atlantic*, 1939–43, London: Oxford University Press, 1948.

Morrison, Ian, *Malayan Postscript*, London: Faber & Faber, 1942.

Morton, H. V., *Atlantic Meeting*, London: Methuen, 1943.

Morton, Louis, *The Fall of the Philippines*, Washington, D.C.: Office of the Chief of Military History, 1953.

Mosley, Leonard, *The Reich Marshal*, London: Weidenfeld & Nicolson, 1974; *Lindbergh*, London: Hodder & Stoughton, 1976; *Hirohito, Emperor of Japan*, Englewood Cliffs, N.J.: Prentice-Hall Inc., 1966.

Mrazek, James E., *The Glider War*, London: Robert Hale, 1975.

Muggah, Mary Gates and Railhiz, Paul H., *The MacArthur Story*, Chippewa Falls, Wis.: Chippewa Falls Book Agency, 1945.

Muir, Hugh, *European Junction*, London: Harrap, 1942.

Murphy, Robert, *Diplomat Among Warriors*, London: William Collins, 1964.

Musmanno, Michael, *The Eichmann Commandos*, London: Peter Davies, 1961.

Nazi-Soviet Relations (ed. Raymond James Sontag and James Stuart Beddie), Washington, D.C.: Department of State, 1948.

Neame, Lt.-Gen. Sir Philip, *Playing With Strife*, London: George Harrap, 1947.

Neave, Airey, *Little Cyclone*, London: Hodder & Stoughton, 1954.

Nepomuk, Jaroslav (with Owen John), *Hell's Mouth*, London: Peter Davies, 1974.

Neumann, Peter, *Other Men's Graves* (trans. Constantine Fitzgibbon), London: Weidenfeld & Nicolson, 1958.

Newlon, Clark, *The Fighting Douglas MacArthur*, New York: Dodd, Mead, 1965. ·

Nicolson, Harold, *Diaries and Letters, 1939–45* (ed. Nigel Nicolson), London: William Collins, 1967.

Nikitin, M. N. and Vagin, P. I., *The Crimes of the German Fascists in the Leningrad Region*, London: Hutchinson, 1946.

Noakes, Jeremy and Pridham, Geoffrey (ed.), *Documents on Nazism, 1941–45*, London: Jonathan Cape, 1974.

Okumiya, Masatake and Horikoshi, Jiro (with Martin Caidin), *Zero!*, New York: E. P. Dutton, 1956.

Onslow, The Earl of, *Men and Sand*, London: The Saint Catherine Press, 1961.

Orlow, Dietrich, *The History of the Nazi Party, Vol. II*, Newton Abbot: David & Charles, 1973.

Osgood, Robert E., *Ideals and Self-Interest in America's Foreign Relations*, Chicago: University of Chicago Press, 1953.

Pabel, Reinhold, *Enemies Are Human*, Philadelphia: John C. Winston Co., 1955.

Pabst, Helmut, *The Outermost Frontier* (trans. Andrew and Eva Wilson), London: William Kimber, 1957.

Padev, Michael, *Marshal Tito*, London: Frederick Muller, 1944.

Panter-Downes, Molly, *London War Notes*, London: Longman, 1972.

Parkinson, Roger, *Blood, Toil, Tears and Sweat*, London: Hart-Davis MacGibbon, 1973.

Pavillard, Stanley, *Bamboo Doctor*, London: Macmillan, 1960.

Pavlov, Dmitri, *Leningrad, 1941: The Blockade* (trans. John Clinton Adams), Chicago, Ill.: Chicago University Press, 1968.

Pavlović, K. St., *The Struggle of the Serbs*, London: Standard Art Book Co., 1943.

Pawle, Gerald, *The War and Colonel Warden*, London: George Harrap, 1963.

Paxton, Robert, *Vichy France*, London: Barrie & Jenkins, 1972.

Payne, Robert, *The Life and Death of Adolf Hitler*, London: Jonathan Cape, 1973.

Pearl Harbor and Hawaii: a Military History, by the Editors of The Army Times, New York: Walker & Co., 1971.

Pearl Harbor Attack: Hearing Before the Joint Committee on the Investigation of the Pearl Harbor Attack (39 vols). Washington, D.C.: Government Printing Office, 1946.

Pelz, Stephen E., *Race To Pearl Harbor*, Cambridge, Mass.: Harvard University Press, 1974.

Percival, Lt.-Gen. A. E., *The War in Malaya*, London: Eyre & Spottiswoode, 1949.

Perrault, Gilles, *The Red Orchestra* (trans. Peter Wiles and Len Ortzen), London: Arthur Barker, 1968.

Peter II, King of Yugoslavia, *A King's Heritage*, London: Cassell, 1955.

Petrow, Richard, *The Bitter Years*, London: Hodder & Stoughton, 1974.

Phillips, Claire (with Myron B. Goldsmith), *Manila Espionage*, Portland, Ore: Binfords & Mort, 1947.

Pickersgill, J. W., *The Mackenzie King Record*, Vol. I, Toronto: University of Toronto Press, 1960.

Pogue, Forrest, C., *George C Marshall*, Vol. II: Ordeal and Hope, 1939–42, New York: Viking, 1966.

Pokryshkin, Alexander, *Red Air Ace*, London: "Soviet War News", 1945.

Polevoi, Boris, *To the Last Breath*, London: Hutchinson, 1945.

Poliakov, Leon, *Harvest of Hate*, London: Elek Books, 1956.

Pollock, A. M., *Pienaar of Alamein*, Cape Town: Cape Times Ltd, 1943.

Poolman, Kenneth, *The Kelly*, London: William Kimber, 1954.

Popov, Dusko, *Spy/Counterspy*, London: Weidenfeld & Nicolson, 1974.

Posthumos, N. (ed.), *The Netherlands During German Occupation*, in the Annals of the American Academy of Political & Social Sciences, Vol. 245, Philadelphia, 1946.

Potter, John Deane, *Admiral of the Pacific*, London: Heinemann, 1965; *A Soldier Must Hang*, London: Frederick Muller, 1963.

Pratt, Julius W., *Cordell Hull* (2 vols), New York: Cooper Square, 1964.

Priestwood, Gwen, *Through Japanese Barbed Wire*, London: George Harrap, 1944.

Prising, Robin, *Manila, Goodbye*, London: William Heinemann, 1976.

Proudfoot, Malcolm, *European Refugees, 1939–52*, London: Faber & Faber, 1957.

Proulx, Benjamin A., *Underground from Hong Kong*, New York: E. P. Dutton, 1943.

Pyschoundakis, George, *The Cretan Runner* (trans. Patrick Leigh-Fermor), London: John Murray, 1955.

Quezon, Manuel, *The Good Fight*, New York: D. Appleton-Century, 1946.

Quirino, Eliseo, *A Day to Remember*, Manila: Benipayo Press, 1958.

Raczynski, Count Edward, *In Allied London*, London: Weidenfeld & Nicolson, 1962.

Raeder, Grand Admiral Erich, *Struggle for the Sea*, London: William Kimber, 1959.

Redmond, Juanita, *I Served on Bataan*, Philadelphia: J. B. Lippincott, 1943.

Reel, A. Frank, *The Case of General Yamashita*, Chicago: University of Chicago Press, 1949.

Rees, John (ed.), *The Case of Rudolf Hess*, London: William Heinemann, 1947.

Reilly, Michael F. (with William J. Slocum), *I Was Roosevelt's Shadow*, London: W. Foulsham, 1946.

Reiss, Johanna, *The Upstairs Room*, London: Oxford University Press, 1973.

Reith, Lord, *Diaries* (ed. Charles Stuart), London: Collins, 1975.

Reitlinger, Gerald, *The Final Solution*, London: Vallentine Mitchell, edn of 1968; *The House Built on Sand*, London: Weidenfeld & Nicolson, 1960; *The S.S.: Alibi of a Nation*, New York: Viking, 1957.

Reynolds, Quentin; Katz, Ephrain and Aldouby, Zwy., *Minister of Death*, London: Cassell, 1961.

Rich, Norman, *Hitler's War Aims* (2 vols), London: André Deutsch, 1973.

Richards, Denis, *Portal of Hungerford*, London: William Heinemann, 1978.

Ristić, D. N., *Yugoslavia's Revolution of 1941*, Stanford, Cal.: Hoover Institution Publication, 1966.

Ritchie, Charles, *The Siren Years*, London: Macmillan, 1974.

Roberts, Denis Russell, *Spotlight on Singapore*, London: Anthony Gibbs & Phillips, 1965.

Roberts, Michael and Trollip, A. E. G., *The South African Opposition*, London: Longman Green, 1947.

Rodger, George, *Desert Journey*, London: The Cresset Press, 1944.

The Rommel Papers (ed. B. H. Liddell Hart, trans. Paul Findlay), London: William Collins, 1953.

Romulo, Carlos P., *I Saw the Fall of the Philippines*, London: George Harrap, 1943.

Roosevelt, Elliott, *As He Saw It*, New York: Duell, Sloane & Pearce, 1946.

Roosevelt, James and Shalett, Sidney, *Affectionately F.D.R.*, New York: Harcourt Brace, 1959.

Rosenberg, Alfred, *Memoirs* (trans. Eric Posselt), Chicago: Ziff-Davis, 1949.

Rosenman, Samuel I., *Working with Roosevelt*, New York: Harper & Bos, 1952.

Roskill, Stephen, *Churchill and the Admirals*, London: William Collins, 1977; *Hankey, Man of Secrets*, Vol. III, London: William Collins, 1974.

Rossi, Angelo, *The Russo-German Alliance* (trans. John and Micheline Curren), London: Chapman & Hall, 1950.

Rozek, E. J., *Allied Wartime Diplomacy*, New York: John Wiley, 1958.

Rudel, Hans, *Stuka Pilot* (trans. Lynton Hudson), Dublin: Euphorion Books, 1952.

Ruge, Vice-Admiral Friedrich, *Sea Warfare* (trans. Cdr. M. G. Saunders, R.N.), London: Cassell, 1957.

Russell, Lord, *The Scourge of the Swastika*, London: Cassell, 1954.

Salisbury, Harrison, *The Siege of Leningrad*, London: Secker & Warburg, 1969.

Sandburg, Carl, *Home Front Memo*, New York: Harcourt Brace, 1943.

Sandford, Kenneth, *Mark of the Lion*, London: Hutchinson, 1962.

Sayre, Francis, *Glad Adventure*, New York: Macmillan, 1957.

Schellenberg, Walter, *The Schellenberg Memoirs* (ed. and trans. Louis Hagen), London: André Deutsch, 1956.

Schmidt, Heinz-Werner, *With Rommel In The Desert*, London: George Harrap, 1951.

Schmidt, Paul, *Hitler's Interpreter* (ed. R. H. C. Steed), London: William Heinemann, 1951.

Schoenbrun, David, *The Three Lives of Charles de Gaulle*, New York: Atheneum, 1966.

Schulze-Holthus, J. B., *Daybreak in Iran: A Story of the German Intelligence Service* (trans. Mervyn Savill), London: Staples Press, 1954.

Schütz, Dr W. W. and De Sevin, Dr B., *German Home Front*, London: Victor Gollancz, 1943.

Seaton, Albert, *The Russo-German War*, London: Arthur Barker, 1971.

Sevastopol, November 1941–July 1942, London: Hutchinson, 1943.

Shaller, Michael, *The U.S. Crusade in China, 1938–45*, New York: Columbia University Press, 1979.

Shaw, Stanford J. and Shaw, Ezal Kural, *History of the Ottoman Empire and Modern Turkey*, Vol. II. London: Cambridge University Press, 1971.

Sheehan, Ed., *One Sunday Morning*, Norfolk Island, Australia: Island Heritage Ltd., 1971.

Sherwood, Robert E., *The White House Papers of Harry Hopkins*, Vol. I, London: Eyre & Spottiswoode, 1948.

Shirer, William, *The Rise and Fall of the Third Reich*, New York: Simon & Schuster, 1959; *All About the Sinking of the Bismarck*, London: W. H. Allen, 1963.

Shostakovich, Dmitri, *Testimony* (as related to and edited by Solomon Volkov, trans. Antonina W. Bouis), London: Hamish Hamilton, 1979.

Simon, Rt Hon. Lord, *Retrospect*, London: Hutchinson, 1952.

Simons, Jessie, *While History Passed*, London: Heinemann, 1954.

Simson, Ivan, *Singapore: Too Little, Too Late*, London: Leo Cooper, 1970.

Sivaram, M., *The Road to Delhi*, Rutland, Vt: Charles E. Tuttle, 1966.

Skomorovsky, Boris and Morris, E. G., *The Siege of Leningrad*, New York: E. P. Dutton, 1944.

Smedley, Agnes, *The Battle Hymn of China*, New York: Knopf, 1943.

Smith, Gaddis, *American Diplomacy During World War Two, 1941–45*, New York: John Wiley, 1965.

Smith, Howard K., *Last Train from Berlin*, London: The Cresset Press, 1942.

Smuts, Field-Marshal Jan C., *Selections from the Smuts Papers*, Vol. VI (ed. Jean Van Der Poel), London: Cambridge University Press, 1973.

Smyth, Sir John, *Percival and the Tragedy of Singapore*, London: Macdonald, 1971.

Soames, Mary, *Clementine Churchill*, London: Cassell, 1979.

Sopocko, Eryk, *Gentlemen, the Bismarck Has Been Sunk*, London: Methuen, 1942.

Spears, Maj.-Gen. Sir Edward, *Fulfilment of a Mission*, London: Leo Cooper, 1977.

Speer, Albert, *Inside The Third Reich* (trans. Richard and Clara Winston), London: Weidenfeld & Nicolson, 1970.

Spencer, John Hall, *Battle for Crete*, London: Heinemann, 1962.

Spring, Howard, *In the Meantime*, London: Constable, 1942.

Stalin, Joseph, *Correspondence with Churchill, Attlee, Roosevelt and Truman*, Moscow: Foreign Languages Publishing House, 1957.

Standley, William H. and Ageton, Arthur A., *Admiral-Ambassador to Russia*, Chicago: Henry Regnery Co., 1955.

Stark, Freya, *East is West*, London: John Murray, 1945.

Stein, George H., *The Waffen S.S., 1939–45*, Ithaca, N.Y.: Cornell University Press, 1966.

Steinberg, Lucien, *Not as a Lamb: the Jews Against Hitler* (trans. Marion Hunter), Farnborough, Hants: Saxon House, 1974.

Stephanides, Theodore, *Climax in Crete*, London: Faber & Faber, 1956.

Stewart, I. McD. G., *The Struggle for Crete*, London: Oxford University Press, 1966.

St George, George, *The Road to Babyi-Yar*, London: Neville Spearman, 1967.

Stimson, Henry C. and Bundy, McGeorge, *On Active Service in Peace and War*, New York: Harper, 1948.

St-John, Robert, *Foreign Correspondent*, London: Hutchinson, 1960; *From the Land of Silent People*, London: George Harrap, 1942.

Stowe, Leland, *No Other Road To Freedom*, London: Faber & Faber, 1942.

Strik-Strikfeldt, Wilfred, *Against Stalin and Hitler: Memoir of the Liberation Movement, 1941–45* (trans. David Footman), London: Macmillan, 1970.

Sulzberger, C. L., *A Long Row of Candles*, London: Macdonald, 1969.

Syrkin, Marie, *Blessed is the Match*, London: Victor Gollancz, 1948.

Taylor, A. J. P., *Beaverbrook*, London: Hamish Hamilton, 1972; (ed.) *Churchill; Four Faces and the Man*, London: Allen Lane, 1969.

Tedder, Marshal of the R.A.F. Lord, *With Prejudice*, London: Cassell, 1966.

Theobald, Rear Admiral Robert A., *The Final Secret of Pearl Harbor*, New York: Devin-Adair, 1954.

Thomas, David, *Crete, 1941: the Battle At Sea*, London: André Deutsch, 1972.

Thompson, Kenneth, *H.M.S. Rodney At War*, London: Hollis & Carter, 1946.

Thompson, R. W., *Churchill and Morton*, London: Hodder & Stoughton, 1976.

Thomson, Richard Heywood, *Captive Kiwi*, Christchurch, N.Z.: Whitcombe & Tombs, 1964.

Thorne, Christopher, *Allies of a Kind: the United States, Britain, and the War Against Japan*, London: Hamish Hamilton, 1978.

Tiger Strikes, The, London: H.M.S.O., 1942.

Toland, John, *Adolf Hitler*, New York: Doubleday, 1976; *The Rising Sun*, London: Cassell, 1974; *But Not In Shame*, London: Anthony Gibbs & Phillips, 1961.

Trefousse, Hans L., *Failure of German Intelligence in the United States, in 1935–45*, in Mississippi Valley Historical Review, Nashville, Tenn., June 1955; *What Happened at Pearl Harbor*, New York: Twayne, 1958.

Trepper, Leopold, *The Great Game*, London: Michael Joseph, 1977.

Trial of the Major War Criminals before the International Military Tribunal, Nuremberg, 1947–49 (42 vols), Washington, D.C.: U.S. Government Printing Office, 1949/51.

Tsou, Tang, *America's Failure in China, 1941–50*, Chicago: The University of Chicago Press, 1963.

Tsuji, Col. Masanobu, *Singapore: the Japanese Version* (trans. Margaret E. Lake, ed. H. V. Howe), London: Constable, 1962.

Tuker, Lt-Gen. Sir Francis, *Approach to Battle*, London: Cassell, 1963.

Tully, Grace, *F.D.R. My Boss*, New York: Charles Scribner, 1949.

Turney, Alfred, *Disaster at Moscow*, London: Cassell, 1971.

Tweed, George R. (with Blake Clark), *Robinson Crusoe USN*, New York: McGraw Hill, 1945.

Umiatowski, Roman, *Poland, Russia and Great Britain, 1941–45*, London: Hollis & Carter, 1946.

Vali, Ferenc A., *Bridge Across the Bosphorous: the Foreign Policy of Turkey*, Baltimore, Md: Johns Hopkins University, 1971.

Van Creveld, Martin, *Hitler's Strategy, 1940–41: The Balkan Clue*, London: Cambridge University Press, 1973.

Vandenberg, A. H., *The Private Papers of Senator Vandenberg* (ed. Arthur H. Vandenberg, Jr, and Joe Alex Morris), London: Victor Gollancz, 1953.

Van Landingham, Charles, *I Saw Manila Die*, in The Saturday Evening Post, Philadelphia, 24 September, 1942.

Vian, Admiral of the Fleet Sir Philip, *Action This Day*, London: Frederick Muller, 1960.
Vintras, Roland, *The Portuguese Connection*, London: Bachman & Turner, 1974.
Viorst, Milton, *Hostile Allies: FDR and De Gaulle*, New York: Macmillan, 1965.
Virski, Fred, *My Life in the Red Army*, New York: Macmillan, 1949.
Vliensky, M., *War Behind Barbed Wire* (trans. O. Gorkachov), Moscow: Foreign Languages Publishing House, 1959.
Voyetekhov, Boris, *The Last Days of Sevastopol* (trans. Ralph Parker and V. M. Genne), London: Cassell, 1943.
Walker, David, *Death At My Heels*, London: Chapman & Hall, 1942.
Waller, George McGregor (ed.) *Pearl Harbor: FDR and the Coming of the War*, Boston: D. C. Heath, 1965.
Wallin, Vice-Admiral U.S.N., Homer, N., *Pearl Harbor: Why, How, Fleet Salvage and Final Appraisal*, Washington, D.C.: Office of Naval History, 1968.
Warlimont, Gen. Walter, *Inside Hitler's Headquarters* (trans. R. H. Barry), London: Weidenfeld & Nicolson, 1964.
Warmbrunn, Werner, *The Dutch Under German Occupation*, Stanford, Cal.: Stanford University Press, 1963.
Warner, Geoffrey, *Iraq and Syria, 1941*, London: Davis-Poynter, 1974.
Wason, Betty, *Miracle in Hellas*, London: Museum Press, 1943.
Wasserstein, Bernard, *Britain and the Jews of Europe, 1939–45*, Oxford: Clarendon Press, 1979.
Watson, Mark Skinner, *Chief of Staff: Pre-war Plans and Preparations*, Washington, D.C.: Office of the Chief of Military History, 1950.
Weinberg, Gerhard L., *Germany and the Soviet Union*, London: E. J. Brill, 1954; *Hitler's Image of the United States*, in The American Historical Review, Washington, D.C., July, 1964.
Weizsäcker, Ernst von, *Memoirs* (trans. John Andrews), London: Victor Gollancz, 1951.
Welles, Sumner, *The Time for Decision*, London: Hamish Hamilton, 1944.
Werth, Alexander, *Moscow '41*, London: Hamish Hamilton, 1942; *Russia at War, 1941–45*, London: Barrie & Rockcliff, 1964.
Westphal, Gen. Siegfried, *The German Army in the West*, London: Cassell, 1951.
Wettern, Desmond, *The Lonely Battle*, London: W. H. Allen, 1960.
Whaley, Barton, *Codeword Barbarossa*, Cambridge, Mass: M.I.T. Press, 1973.
Wheeler-Bennet, Sir John, *Special Relationships: America in Peace and War*, London: Macmillan, 1975; (ed.) *Action This Day*, London: Macmillan, 1968; *King George VI*, London: Macmillan, 1958; *The Nemesis of Power*, London: Macmillan, 1954.
Whelan, Russell, *The Flying Tigers*, London: MacDonald, 1943.
Whitcomb, Edgar, *Escape from Corregidor*, London: Allan Wingate, 1959.
White, Leigh, *The Long Balkan Night*, New York: Charles Scribner 1944.
White, Theodore, H. (with Annalee Jacoby), *Thunder Out of China*, London: Victor Gollancz, 1947.
White, W. L., *They Were Expendable*, London: Hamish Hamilton, 1942.
Whiting, Charles, *Hunters from the Sky*, London: Leo Cooper, 1975.
Wighton, Charles, *Eichmann: His Career and Crimes*, London: Odhams Press, 1951.
Wigmore, Lionel, *Australia in the War of 1939–45 (Army) The Japanese Thrust*, Adelaide: Griffin Press, 1957.
Williams, Francis, *A Prime Minister Remembers*, London: Heinemann, 1961.
Willoughby, Maj.-Gen. Charles A., *Sorge: Master Spy*, London: William Kimber, 1952; and Chamberlain, John, *MacArthur, 1941–51: Victory in the Pacific*, London: William Heinemann, 1956.
Wilmot, Chester, *Tobruk*, Sydney: Angus & Robertson, 1944.
Wiloughby, Amea, *I Was On Corregidor*, New York: Harper, 1943.
Wilson, Field Marshal Lord, *Eight Years Overseas*, London: Hutchinson, 1950.
Wilson, Theodore A., *The First Summit*, London: Macdonald, 1969.
Winant, John, *A Letter from Grosvenor Square*, London: Hodder & Stoughton, 1947.
Wingate, Sir Ronald, *Lord Ismay*, London: Hutchinson, 1970.
Wittner, Laurence (ed.), *MacArthur*, Englewood Cliffs, N.J.: Prentice-Hall, 1971.

Wohlstetter, Roberta, *Pearl Harbor: Warning and Decision*, Stanford, Cal.: Stanford University Press, 1962.

Wolff-Mönckeberg, Mathilde, *On The Other Side* (trans. and ed. Ruth Evans), London: Peter Owen, 1979.

Woodhouse, C. M., *The Struggle for Greece, 1941–9*, London: Hart-Davis, Macgibbon, 1976.

Woolton, Lord, *Memoirs*, London: Cassell, 1959.

Wright, Robert, *I Was a Hell Camp Prisoner*, London: Brown Watson, 1963.

Wykeham, Peter, *Fighter Command*, London, Putnam, 1960.

Young, Desmond, *Rommel,*, London: William Collins, 1950.

Young, Kenneth, *Churchill and Beaverbrook*, London: Eyre & Spottiswoode, 1966.

Young, Peter, *Storm from the Sea*, London: William Kimber.

Zhilin, Pavel, *They Sealed Their Own Doom*, Moscow: Progress Publishers, 1970.

Zieser, Benno, *In Their Shallow Graves* (trans. Alec Brown), London: Elek Books, 1956.

Zoller, Albert, *Douze ans auprès d'Hitler*, Paris: Juilliard, 1949.

MANUSCRIPT SOURCES

Aitken, Sir William Maxwell, 1st Bt., 1st Baron Beaverbrook, Ministry of Supply Papers and Personal Correspondence. (*House of Lords Record Office, London.*)

Alexander, Albert Victor, Earl Alexander of Hillsborough, First Lord of the Admiralty, Memos and Correspondence. (*Churchill College, Cambridge.*)

Anslow, Barbara Redwood, Hong Kong Diary, 1941–2. (*Imperial War Museum, Lambeth, South London.*)

Arnold, General Henry Harley, Chief of U.S. Army Air Force, Official Papers. (*Library of Congress MSS. Division, Washington, D.C.*)

Attlee, Clement Richard, 1st Earl Attlee, Lord Privy Seal, Miscellaneous Correspondence. (*Churchill College, Cambridge.*)

Balfour, Harold Harrington, 1st Baron Balfour of Inchrye, Under-Secretary of State for Air, Moscow Interlude: the Diary of a Mission. (*House of Lords Record Office, London.*)

Bevin, Ernest, Minister of Labour, 1940–5. Miscellaneous Correspondence. (*Churchill College, Cambridge.*)

Biddle, Francis B., U.S. Attorney-General, 1941–5. Records of Cabinet Meetings. (*Franklin D. Roosevelt Memorial Library, Hyde Park, New York.*)

Bötticher, Generalleutant Karl, The Occupation of Tobruk. (*MSS. D-062, Office of the Chief of Military History, National Archives. Washington D.C.*); The Role of Artillery in The Siege of Tobruk. (*MSS. D-045, repository as above.*)

Bollbrinker, Generalmajor Ernst. Surprise Attack on Tobruk. (*MSS. D-088, repository as above.*)

Brooke, Lieutenant-General Sir Alan Francis, 1st Baron Brookeborough, C-in-C, Home Forces, Chief of the Imperial General Staff, 1941–6. Diary and Miscellaneous Correspondence. (*Liddell Hart Centre for Military Archives, University of London, King's College.*)

Brooke-Popham, Air Chief Marshal Sir (Henry) Robert (Moore), C-in-C, Far East, 1940–1. Official Correspondence. (*Liddell Hart Centre for Military Archives, University of London, King's College.*)

Burgis, Lawrence Franklin. Assistant Secretary, War Cabinet, 1939–45. Memoirs. (*Churchill College, Cambridge.*)

Clapper, Raymond, author and political commentator. Miscellaneous Papers. (*Library of Congress MSS. Division, Washington, D.C.*)

Cox, Oscar D., legal adviser, U.S. Treasury; Division of Defense Aid, Office of Emergency Management. Diary, 1941. (*Franklin D. Roosevelt Memorial Library, Hyde Park, New York.*)

Coy, (Albert) Wayne, Special Assistant to the President; Office of Emergency Management. Official Correspondence. (*Franklin D. Roosevelt Memorial Library, Hyde Park, New York.*)

Cunningham, Admiral of the Fleet Andrew Browne, 2nd Viscount Cunningham of Hyndhope, C-in-C Mediterranean Fleet. Private Correspondence. (*Churchill College, Cambridge.*)

Dalton, (Edward) Hugh (John Neale), Minister of Economic Warfare, 1940–2. Diary, 1941. (*British Library of Political and Economic Science, London.*)

Davidson, Major-General Francis Henry Norman, Director of Military Intelligence, War Office, 1940–4. Miscellaneous Files. (*Liddell Hart Centre for Military Archives, University of London, King's College.*)

Dorman-Smith, Sir Reginald Hugh, Governor of Burma, 1941–6. Official Correspondence. (*India Office Library and Records, Foreign and Commonwealth Office, London.*)

Early, Stephen T., U.S. Presidential Press Secretary, 1933–45. Private correspondence and scrap-books. (*Franklin D. Roosevelt Memorial Library, Hyde Park, New York.*)

Eden, (Robert) Anthony, 1st Earl of Avon, Secretary of State for Foreign Affairs, 1940–5. Official correspondence and Memoranda. (*University of Birmingham, Warwickshire, Special Collections.*)

Edwards, Captain Ralph Alan Bevan, R.N., Director of Operations (Home). Private Diary. (*Churchill College, Cambridge.*)

Frankfurter, Justice Felix, Associate Justice of the U.S. Supreme Court, 1939–62. Private Correspondence. (*Library of Congress MSS. Division, Washington, D.C.*)

Hartmann, Oberst Hermann. Staff Libya, July–August, 1941. (*MSS. D-051, Office of the Chief of Military History, Washington, D.C.*)

Hodsoll, Wing-Commander Sir Eric John, Assistant Secretary. C.I.D. C.I.D. and Civil Defence Papers, 1941. (*Churchill College, Cambridge.*)

Hope, John Victor Alexander, 2nd Marquess of Linlithgow, Viceroy and Governor-General of India, 1936–43. Official Correspondence and Memoranda. (*India Office Library and Records, Foreign and Commonwealth Office, London.*)

Hopkins, Harry L. Special Adviser to the President, 1940–5. Official and Private Correspondence. (and Robert E. Sherwood). Official and Private Papers, Containers 304–8, forming the Robert E. Sherwood Collection). (*Franklin D. Roosevelt Memorial Library, Hyde Park, New York.*)

Holtzendorff, Generalmajor Hanshenning von. The Building of the Sidi Omar – Halfaya Pass Position. (*MSS. D-149, Office of the Chief of Military History, National Archives, Washington, D.C.*) The Build-up of the Gazala Position, May–June, 1941. (*MSS. D-212, repository as above.*) Reasons for Rommel's Successes. (*MSS. D-024, repository as above.*)

Hull, Cordell, U.S. Secretary of State, 1933–44. Official Correspondence and Memoranda. (*Library of Congress, MSS. Division, Washington, D.C.*)

Ismay, General Hastings Lionel, 1st Baron Ismay of Wormington, Deputy Secretary (Military) to War Cabinet, 1940–5. Private Correspondence and Memoranda. (*Liddell Hart Centre for Military Archives, University of London, King's College.*)

Joyce, Nurse Day Sage. Hong Kong Diary. (*Imperial War Museum, Lambeth, South London.*)

Kirchheim, Gen. Heinrich. Advance on Tobruk by the Italian Brescia Division, April, 1941. (*MSS. D-214.*) Withdrawal from Cyrenaica, April, 1941. (*MSS. D-349.*) Attack-Group Kirchheim, April–May, 1941. (*MSS. D-350, Office of the Chief of Military History, National Archives, Washington, D.C.*)

Knox, Franklin L. Secretary of the U.S. Navy, 1940–5. Diary; Official and Private Correspondence. (*Library of Congress, MSS. Division, Washington D.C.*)

Leahy, Admiral William D., Ambassador to Vichy France, 1941. Private Diary. (*Library of Congress, MSS. Division, Washington, D.C.*)

Marquis, Sir Frederick James, 1st Earl of Woolton, Minister of Food, 1940–3. Diary and Memoranda. (*Bodleian Library, Oxford.*)

Mass Observation Archive, The, Topic Files and Weekly Reports. (*University of Sussex.*)

Mellenthin, Generalmajor Friedrich Wilhelm. Supplement to Rommel's Successes in North Africa. (*MSS. D-084. Office of the Chief of Military History, National Archives, Washington, D.C.*)

Monckton, Sir Walter Turner, 1st Viscount Monckton of Brenchley, Director-General, Ministry of Information, 1940–1; Director-General of British Propaganda and Information Services, Cairo, 1941–2. Private Correspondence. (*Bodleian Library, Oxford.*)

Morgenthau, Henry, Jr, Secretary of the U.S. Treasury, 1934–45. Private Diary. (*Franklin D. Roosevelt Memorial Library, Hyde Park, New York.*)

Müller-Gebhard, Gen. Philip. Afrika Korps, 28–4–41–30–9–41). (*MSS. D-006, Office of the Chief of Military History, National Archives, Washington, D.C.*)

Neal, Hilda. London Diary. (*Imperial War Museum, Lambeth, South London.*)

Nehring, Gen. Walter et al. The African Campaign. (*Ref. T 3, Vols 1, 2, 3, 3a and 4, Office of the Chief of Military History, National Archives, Washington, D.C.*)

Nesbitt, Mrs Henrietta, housekeeper to the White House. Miscellaneous Papers. (*Library of Congress, MSS. Division, Washington, D.C.*)

298

Newton, Dr Isaac. Hong Kong Diary. (*Imperial War Museum, Lambeth, South London.*)

Nicolson, Harold George, Parliamentary Secretary to Ministry of Information, 1940–1. Private Diary. (*Balliol College, Oxford.*)

Penny, Henry. London Diary. (*Imperial War Museum, Lambeth, South London.*)

Percival, Lt.-Gen. Arthur, G.O.C. Malaya, Official and Private Papers. (*Imperial War Museum, Lambeth, South London.*)

Phipps, Nurse Kathleen, Private Diary. (*Imperial War Museum, Lambeth, South London.*)

Public Record Office, Kew, Surrey: Series ADM: Admiralty CAB: Cabinet Papers CO: Colonial Office Papers FO: Foreign Office Papers HO: Home Office Papers PREM: Prime Minister's Papers.

Rath, Generalmajor Hans-Joachim. 1st Stuka Wing, Feb.–May, 1941. (*MSS. D-004, Office of the Chief of Military History, National Archives, Washington, D.C.*)

Redwood, Mabel. Memoirs of World War Two. (*Imperial War Museum, Lambeth, South London.*)

Reissmann, Major Werner. Rommel's System of Fortifications in North Africa. (*MSS. D-082.*) Transportation of the 104th Armoured Infantry Regiment, April, 1941. (*MSS. D-047, Office of the Chief of Military History, National Archives, Washington, D.C.*)

Roosevelt, Franklin Delano. President of the United States, 1933–45. Papers As President, Official File (OF). Papers as President, President's Personal File. (PPF.) Papers As President, President's Secretary's File. (PSF.) (*Franklin D. Roosevelt Memorial Library, Hyde Park, New York.*)

Smith, Harold D., Director of the Budget, U.S. Treasury. Memoranda on Conferences with the President. (*Franklin D. Roosevelt Memorial Library, Hyde Park, New York.*)

Somerville, Admiral Sir James Fownes, R.N., C-in-C, Force "H". Personal and Naval Papers. (*Churchill College, Cambridge.*)

Spears, General Sir Edward Louis. Correspondence with Bracken, Churchill, Ismay etc. (*Ref Spears 1/50, Churchill College, Cambridge.*) Spears Mission Correspondence. (*Ref Spears 1/137. IIA 2–II/4, II/5, St Antony's College, Oxford.*)

Steinhardt, Laurence A., U.S. Ambassador in the Soviet Union. Private correspondence. (*Library of Congress, MSS. Division, Washington, D.C.*)

Strong, H. E., Miscellaneous Correspondence. (*Imperial War Museum, Lambeth, South London.*)

Vansittart, Sir Robert Gilbert, 1st Baron Vansittart, Chief Diplomatic Adviser to His Majesty's Government, 1938–41. Miscellaneous Cabinet Papers. (*Churchill College, Cambridge.*)

Vlieland, C. A., Secretary of Defence for Malaya, 1938–41. Disaster in the Far East, 1941–2: an unpublished monograph. (*Liddell Hart Centre for Military Archives, University of London, King's College.*)

Wickard, Claude, U.S. Secretary of Agriculture, 1940–5. Private Diary. (*Franklin D. Roosevelt Memorial Library, Hyde Park, New York.*)

Winant, John Gilbert, U.S. Ambassador to the Court of St James, 1941–6. Miscellaneous Papers. (*Franklin D. Roosevelt Memorial Library, Hyde Park, New York.*)

Wood, Edward Frederick Lindley, 1st Earl of Halifax. Selections from the Hickleton Papers. (*Ref.: A 410.4, 2 reels microfilm, Churchill College, Cambridge.*)

Wright, Leading Aircraftman Harry C., R.A.F.V.R. A Serviceman's Diary, 1941. (*Courtesy H. C. Wright, Whitehall, Hants.*)

Zeus, Major Franz. Defence of the Halfaya Pass, June 15–17, 1941. (*MSS. D 219, Office of the Chief of Military History, National Archives, Washington D.C.*)

Note: With the exception of the studies by Rath and Reissmann, listed above, all German monographs from the Office of the Chief of Military History were translated for the author by Hildegard Anderson.

INDEX

*Names, titles and posts are those held at the time
during the events described*

von, 15; forbids Rommel to attack Tobruk, 58; 121, 253; dismissed, 255
Brazil, 257
Brereton, Maj.-Gen. Lewis, permission to bomb Formosa rejected, 238
Bridgewater, Sick Berth Attendant Walter, 243
Briggs, Signalman A. E., survivor of *Hood*, 92
Brinkmann, *Kapitan zur Zee*, Hellmuth, commander of *Prinz Eugen*, 93
British Broadcasting Corporation, V call, 146–8
"Britton, Colonel" *see* Ritchie, Douglas
Brock, Ray, 37–8
Brooke-Popham, Air Chief Marshal Sir Robert, 173; on Macarthur, 213; vulnerability of his command, 214–15; anger at retreat, 245
Brown, Cecil, C.B.S. man in Syria, 109; on *Repulse*, 242
Brown, Corporal Robert, 261
Bucher, *Leutnant*, 58
Bulcock, Pilot Officer Roy, 215, 245
Bulgaria, German aircraft in, 11; pact with Axis, 13
Bullard, Sir Reader, 167
Bullitt, William C., 8, 97; warns Roosevelt about Russia, 135
Burma, 172
Bush, Lt Lewis, R.N.V.R., 265
Butler, R. A., 33; called on by Subotić, 36
Buxton, Lt Michael, R.N., in *Prince of Wales* action, 90–1; 156, 241

Caccia, Harold, comment on Crete, 84
Cadbury, Laurence, 185
Cain, Lt Timothy, R.N., 77
Cadogan, Sir Alexander, on Turkey, 11; doubts on support for Greece, 12; 42, 116
Caldwell, Surgeon Lt-Cdr Dick, 156
California, sunk at Pearl Harbor, 226, 227, 230
Campbell, Brigadier "Jock", awarded V.C. in Sidi Rezegh action, 204
Campbell, Ronald, 11
Campion, Leading Telegraphist Bernard, 244
Canada, war obligations, 103
Carter, Captain W. R., on *Maryland*, Pearl Harbor, 230
Catroux, General Georges, 109
Cavite, U.S. naval base, crippled, 237
Chak, Admiral Chan, 247
Chennault, Colonel Claire, 43
Chiang Kai-shek, General, America's policy towards, 43; protest at U.S.-Japanese talks, 209

China, American support, 42–3
Churchill, Winston, 1; relationship with Hopkins, 4–5; blockades Eire, 9; "give us the tools", 9; offer of aid to Greece, 10; warns Eden, 13; shocked by Lend-Lease terms, 22–3; cables Wavell in Libya, 29; Japanese threat, 42; anger at possible loss of Egypt, 57; news of Hess landing, 69; Cabinet arguments on Hess, 70–1; comments on Crete commitment, 83; news of *Hood* disaster, 91; Crete action criticism, 102; Dominion criticism, 102–3; pledge to "fight on", 103; on de Gaulle, 106–8; critical of Wavell, 114; promises help to Russia, 132; congratulates a V.C., 145; on board *Prince of Wales*, 155–60; meeting with Roosevelt, 158–62; on Atlantic Charter, 173; misconception of Empire, 173–4; Laski on, 174; quarrels with de Gaulle, 174–5; on Australian politics, 175–6; on Japanese threat, 200; cautions Roosevelt, 209; problems of intelligence services, 210–12; hears news of Pearl Harbor, 236–7; with Roosevelt in U.S., 255–8; on Hong Kong's fight, 266; Ottawa speech, 271; the name for U.N., 273
Cincar-Marković, Aleksander, Yugoslav Foreign Minister, signs Tripartite Pact, 31–2
Clark, Maj.-Gen. George, opinion on Embassy, Iraq, 56
Clifton, Brigadier George, 202
Clodius, Karl, 195
Colaković, Rudoljub, 148–9
Collet, Colonel Philibert, 109
Colville, John, contacts Churchill on Hess landing, 69
Combe, Colonel John, captured by Germans, 30
Comeau, Marcel Gerard, 19–20; arrival and evacuation from Greece, 51–3; in Crete, 80–2, 85–6, 88; evacuated, 101
Communist Party of G.B., 172
Compton, Lt Alec, R.N., 241, 242
Conine, Freda, 228
Connell, Warden Rob, 67
Coolidge, Mrs Calvin, 7
Cooper, Alfred Duff, 104; on the Malayan chaos, 245
Cornwallis, Sir Kinahan, his embassy in Iraq "besieged", 55–6
Corregidor, MacArthur retreats to, 264–265
Coryell, Hubert, 229
Costa Rica, 257
Cox, Oscar, 135
Cox, Tom, 268

301

303

Ravenstein, General Hans von, 200, 201, 205
Rediuninsky, General Ivan, 122
Redmond, Juanita, 263
Redwood, Mabel, 249, 265
Reichenau, *Feldmarschall*, Walter von, 126
Reith, Lord, comment on Beaverbrook, 104
Repulse, H.M.S., arrives Singapore, 239; sunk by Japanese aircraft, 242–3
Retz, Elfrieda (Freddy), 249
Reuben James, torpedo strikes, 197
Ribbentrop, Joachim von, at meeting with Japanese, 40–1; on peace with Britain, 71; reaction to U.S. war declaration, 236
Ribnikar, Vladislav, 59
Riccardi, Raffaele, 132
Richardson, Squadron Leader "Dickie", 65–6
Richardson, Admiral James O., 211
Rintelen, General Enno von, 14, 37
Ritchie, Charles, 18
Ritchie, Douglas ("Colonel Britton"), V call to Europe, 146
Ritchie, Lt-Gen. Neil, replaces Cunningham, 206
Robin Moor (*Exmoor*), S.S., sunk by U-boat 69, 111–13
Rochefort, Lt-Cdr Joseph J., 212
Rodney, H.M.S., *Bismarck* action, 95
Rommel, *Generalleutnant* Erwin, arrives in Libya, 14–16; begins his attack, 28–30; at Tobruk, 44–7; April 30 unsuccessful attack on Tobruk, 57–8; plan for further attack, 201; criticizes British tactics, 204; harasses British retreat, 205; overlooks British ammunition dumps, 205; abandons Tobruk, 272
Romulo, Carlos, 173
Roosevelt, Franklin D., third term inauguration, 7; opposition to his Lend-Lease, 7–8; signs Lend-Lease, 21–2; extends neutrality, 24–5; promise of aid to Greece, 26; aid to China, 43–4; plans to meet Churchill, 53–4; on Hess defection, 71; policy of "gradualness", 96–8; declaration of state of emergency, 98–9; relations with Vichy, 105; reaction to *Robin Moor* sinking, 113; aids Russia, 134–5; freezes Japanese assets, 156; meeting with Churchill, 158–62; on Iran, 166; warnings to Hitler, 196–7; reaction to Japanese movements, 209; personal appeal to Hirohito, 222; Japan rejects Hull's note, 223; hears news of Pearl Harbor, 233–4; meeting with Churchill, 255–8; suggests the name United Nations, 272–3

Rørvik, Sofie, 73–5
Rosenberg, Alfred, 183
Rosenman, Samuel I., 96, 236, 270
Rösler, Major, sees S.S. killings, 180
Rössler, Rudolf, 61
Rowehl, *Oberst* Theodor, 142
Roy, Pipe-Major, 204
Royal Air Force, bombing policy and losses, 143–5
Royce, General Ralph, 103
Rumania, support for Germany, 136
Rundstedt, General Gerd von, 121, 183; resigns, 253
Russell, Rev. Philip, 134
Russia, Hitler's plan to attack, 16–18, 60–3; war signs, 122–3; Germany invades, 125–31; Churchill's help promised, 132; help from U.S., 134–5; demands more aid from U.S., 143; invades Iran, 166; German troops in Ukraine, 183–4; Anglo-American mission in Moscow, 185–8; trade agreement signed, 187; German advance on Moscow, 188; Moscow siege, 189–90; German armies halted, 252–4
Russian Liberation Army, 183

Sage, Day, 248
Salmuth, *Generalleutnant* Hans von, 121
Sankey, Noel, 47
Sano, Maj.-Gen., 246
Saratoga, 262 n
Scavenius, Erik, 253
Schmidt, *Leutnant* Heinz Werner, 15
Schmidt, Paul, 71, 72
Schmidt, General Rudolf, 121
Schmitz, *Leutnant* J. C., 91
Scholtzberg, *Untersturmführer*, 138–9
Schutzstaffeln (S.S.), 118–20, 137–9; kills population of Krasnaja, 177–8; massacre of Jews, 178–82
Scott, Robert, 230
Sebastopol, under siege, 191
Setzer, George, 238
Shawyer, Leading Telegraphist Eric, 242
Sheehan, Ed., 229–30
Sherwood, Robert E., 96, 98, 133, 236
Shigemitsu, Mamoru, 42
Shimazaki, Lt-Cdr Shigekazu, commander of Japanese second wave at Pearl Harbor, 228
Shkvor, Czech agent, Stalin ignores his reports, 62
Short, Lt-Gen Walter C., 210–12
Shostakovich, Dmitri, composes "Leningrad" symphony, 193
Sidi Rezegh, 8th Army defeated, 203
Simons, Captain Bentham, 230
Simović, General Dušan, 33; charged to

308

373C